Lecture Notes in Computer Science   11359

Commenced Publication in 1973
Founding and Former Series Editors:
Gerhard Goos, Juris Hartmanis, and Jan van Leeuwen

More information about this series at http://www.springer.com/series/7410

Jean-Louis Lanet · Cristian Toma (Eds.)

Innovative Security Solutions for Information Technology and Communications

11th International Conference, SecITC 2018
Bucharest, Romania, November 8–9, 2018
Revised Selected Papers

 Springer

Editors
Jean-Louis Lanet 🆔
Inria-RBA
Rennes, France

Cristian Toma 🆔
Bucharest University of Economic Studies
Bucharest, Romania

ISSN 0302-9743 ISSN 1611-3349 (electronic)
Lecture Notes in Computer Science
ISBN 978-3-030-12941-5 ISBN 978-3-030-12942-2 (eBook)
https://doi.org/10.1007/978-3-030-12942-2

Library of Congress Control Number: 2019930852

LNCS Sublibrary: SL4 – Security and Cryptology

This Springer imprint is published by the registered company Springer Nature Switzerland AG
The registered company address is: Gewerbestrasse 11, 6330 Cham, Switzerland

Foreword

It is a privilege for me to write the foreword to the proceedings of this 11th anniversary of the conference. Indeed, SecITC 2018 was the 11th edition of the International Conference on Information Technology and Communication Security, which is held in Bucharest, Romania, every year. Throughout the years, SecITC has become a truly competitive publication venue with an acceptance rate between 33 and 50%, with a Program Committee of 50 experts from 20 countries, and with a long series of distinguished invited speakers. Starting four years ago, the conference proceedings are published in Springer's *Lecture Notes in Computer Science* series, and articles published in SecITC are indexed in most science databases.

The conference is unique in that it serves as an exchange forum between established researchers and students entering the field as well as industry players. I would like to particularly thank the Program Committee (PC) chairs, Jean-Louis Lanet and Cristian Toma, for an outstanding paper selection process conducted electronically. In response to the call for papers, the PC received 70 submissions of which 35 were chosen. To those the PC added seven invited keynote lectures by Paolo D'Arco, Jean-François Lalande and myself, and Denis Jean-Michel Baheux.

I also warmly thank the conference's Organizing Committee and Technical Support Team—Catalin Boja, Mihai Doinea, Cristian Ciurea, Bogdan Iancu, Diana Maimut, Luciana Morogan, Andrei-George Oprina, Marius Popa, Mihai Pura, Mihai Togan, George Teseleanu, and Marian Haiducu—for their precious contribution to the success of the event and for their dedication to the community.

I am certain that in the coming years SecITC will continue to grow and expand into a major cryptography and information security venue making Bucharest a traditional scientific meeting for the IT security research community.

December 2018

David Naccache

Foreword

Preface

This volume contains the papers presented at SecITC 2018, the 11th International Conference on Security for Information Technology and Communications (www. secitc.eu), held during November 8–9, 2018, in Bucharest. There were 70 submissions (three withdrawn by the authors) and each submitted paper was reviewed by at least two, and on average 2.7, Program Committee members. The committee decided to accept 35 papers and also three invited papers from the keynote talks. For 11 years, SecITC has been bringing together cybersecurity researchers, cryptographers, industry representatives, and graduate students. The conference focuses on research of any aspect of cyber security and cryptography. The papers present advances in the theory, design, implementation, analysis, verification, or evaluation of secure systems and algorithms.

The conference topics comprise all aspects of information security, including but not limited to the following areas: access control; cryptography, biometrics, and watermarking; application security; attacks and defenses; blockchain security and security aspects of alternative currencies; censorship and censorship-resistance; cloud and Web security; distributed systems security; embedded systems security; digital forensics; hardware security; information flow analysis; Internet of Things (IoT) security; intrusion detection and prevention system; language-based security; machine learning (artificial intelligence) used in security; malware and ransomware; mobile security; network security; new exploits; policy enforcements; privacy and anonymity; protocol security; reverse-engineering and code obfuscation; security architectures; side channel attacks; surveillance and anti-surveillance; system security; trust management.

One of SecITC's primary goals is to bring together researchers belonging to different communities and provide a forum that facilitates the informal exchanges necessary for new scientific collaborations.

We would like to acknowledge the work of the Program Committee, whose great efforts provided a proper framework for the selection of the papers. The conference was organized by the Bucharest University of Economic Studies, the Military Technical Academy, and the Advanced Technologies Institute.

December 2018

Jean-Louis Lanet
Cristian Toma

Organization

Program Committee

Elena Andreeva	Katholieke Universiteit Leuven, Belgium
Ludovic Apvrille	Telecom ParisTech, France
Lasse Berntzen	Buskerud and Vestfold University College, Norway
Ion Bica	Military Technical Academy, Romania
Catalin Boja	Bucharest Academy of Economic Studies, Romania
Guillaume Bouffard	ANSSI, France
Xiaofeng Chen	Xidian University, China
Cristian Ciurea	Academy of Economic Studies, Romania
Christophe Clavier	Université de Limoges, France
Paolo D'Arco	University of Salerno, Italy
Roberto De Prisco	University of Salerno, Italy
Eric Diehl	Sony Pictures, USA
Mihai Doinea	Bucharest University of Economic Studies, Romania
Eric Freyssinet	LORIA, France
Helena Handschuh	Rambus, USA
Shoichi Hirose	University of Fukui, Japan
Xinyi Huang	Fujian Normal University, China
Miroslaw Kutylowski	Wroclaw University of Technology, Poland
Jean-Louis Lanet	Inria-RBA, France
Giovanni Livraga	University of Milan, Italy
Florian Mendel	TU Graz, Austria
Kazuhiko Minematsu	NEC Corporation, Japan
David Naccache	ENS, France
Vincent Nicomette	LAAS/CNRS, France
Calinel Pasteanu	Oracle, Germany
Victor Patriciu	Military Technical Academy, Romania
Cezar Plesca	Military Technical Academy, Romania
Marius Popa	Bucharest University of Economic Studies, Romania
Reza Reyhanitabar	Katholieke Universiteit Leuven, Belgium
P. Y. A. Ryan	University of Luxembourg, Luxembourg
Emil Simion	University Politehnica of Bucharest, Romania
Agusti Solanas	Rovira i Virgili University, Spain
Rainer Steinwandt	Florida Atlantic University, USA
Ferucio Laurentiu Tiplea	Alexandru Ioan Cuza University of Iasi, Romania
Mihai Togan	Military Technical Academy, Romania
Cristian Toma	Bucharest University of Economic Studies, Romania
Tiberiu Vasilache	University Politehnica of Bucharest, Romania
Valérie Viet Triem Tong	CentraleSupelec, France

Guilin Wang	Huawei International Pte Ltd., Singapore
Qianhong Wu	Beihang University, China
Sule Yildirim-Yayilgan	Norwegian University of Science and Technology, Norway
Alin Zamfiroiu	Bucharest University of Economic Studies, Romania
Lei Zhang	East China Normal University, China

Additional Reviewers

Batista, Edgar
Casino, Fran
Catuogno, Luigi
Genc, Ziya A.
Kang, Burong
Lin, Chao
Ma, Xu
Maimut, Diana
Meng, Xinyu
Moussaileb, Routa
Pasteanu, Calinel
Pura, Mihai Lica

Reynaud, Léo
Roenne, Peter
Rozic, Vladimir
Symeonidis, Iraklis
Teseleanu, George
Trouchkine, Thomas
Velciu, Alexandru
Visoiu, Adrian
Wang, Jian
Zhang, Xiaoyu
Zhao, Hong
Zurini, Madalina

Contents

Ultralightweight Cryptography
Some Thoughts on Ten Years of Efforts

Paolo D'Arco[✉]

Dipartimento di Informatica, Università degli Studi di Salerno, Fisciano, Italy
pdarco@unisa.it

Abstract. The term *ultralightweight* refers to a special approach to cryptographic design, which uses just basic operations as *and, or, xor,* $+$ mod n and *cyclic shift*. It has been developed in the last years, in the context of authentication protocols, to provide very efficient and secure solutions. In this short note, we discuss the motivations behind its introduction, and outline its key ideas and features. By overviewing some previous works, and picking up from them some examples, we describe typical weaknesses which have been found in almost all the proposed protocols. We point out that, at the state of current knowledge, serious doubts about the soundness of the approach and, in general, about what can be obtained with it, are present. Nevertheless, since many questions are on the ground without answers, we argue that further investigations in the field are needed. To this aim, we throw a quick look at the close area of lightweight cryptography, briefly describing some successful design strategies and modeling techniques. We suggest that, instead of keeping pursuing ad-hoc solutions employing heuristic trials, working along these research directions could be beneficial also to the ultralightweight field.

1 Introduction

Authentication is a central issue in cryptographic research. Roughly speaking, it is the process through which a party can convince another party that it is, in fact, who or what it declares itself to be.

Along the years several techniques have been developed to solve the issue: currently, we have authentication protocols built on something *the party is*, e.g., the biometric solutions based on the iris or the fingerprint, or built on something *the party knows*, e.g., the solutions based on a password, a pin, a secret key, or based on something *the party holds*, e.g., the solutions based on a token, a smartcard, a physical device in general.

Authentication protocols enable organizations to keep their data and network infrastructures secure, by granting access to sensitive and valuable resources only

Based on the joint works of the last years with A. De Santis, R. De Prisco and X. Carpenter.

J.-L. Lanet and C. Toma (Eds.): SecITC 2018, LNCS 11359, pp. 1–16, 2019.
https://doi.org/10.1007/978-3-030-12942-2_1

to authenticated users, entities or processes. Authentication is a preliminary step in almost every secure application.

What makes authentication still subject of investigations is the *nature* of the computational environment surrounding us nowadays. The so called Internet of things (*IoT* for short) has extended the traditional communication network infrastructure to a pervasive system: a global heterogeneous environment, where a huge number of computational devices with very different capabilities collect, process and transmit information to the other devices present in the system.

If, from one side, the *IoT* opens plenty of new possibilities, e.g., environmental monitoring, risk control, dangerous situations management, sensitive areas surveillance, domotic, smart applications, on the other side, it introduces new challenges. Indeed, heavily-constrained devices, like cheap sensors or tiny RFID tags, cannot afford the computational burden required by protocols designed for traditional communication networks and devices. Tailored tools and strategies, less demanding in terms of computational power and storage requirements, are needed. And they have also to cope, in some settings, with unreliable media transmission.

2 A Look Back

In order to come up with efficient and secure solutions for heavily-constrained devices, around 2006 some authentication protocols using very simple operations, called M^2AP [19], LMAP [20] and EMAP [21], were presented. The hardware target they were addressing is represented by circuits with a few hundred gates, for example, the ones used in some applications of the radio frequency technology.

Radio Frequency Identification (RFID, for short) is a technology enabling automatic objects identification. Each object is labeled with a tiny integrated circuit equipped with a radio antenna, called *Tag*, whose *information content* can be received by another device, called *Reader*, without physical contact and at a distance of several meters. RFID Tags can perform computations. *Passive* Tags, the cheapest ones, do not have a power source: they receive energy for computation from the Readers and can perform very simple operations.

The M^2AP, LMAP and EMAP protocols were designed for passive Tags. However, all of them presented some weaknesses, which were used to set up efficient attacks.

SASI [5], introduced the next year, designed for providing Strong Authentication and Strong Integrity, received considerable attention both by cryptoanalysts and by designers. The paper which described the protocol, introduced some new ideas compared to the previous protocols, and provided a specification of the features of the ultralightweight approach. Indeed, Chien, in [5] offered a sort of categorization of protocols, according to the tools they need. He used: the term *full-fledged* to refer to the class of protocols requiring support for conventional cryptographic functions like symmetric encryption, hashing, or even public key cryptography; the term *simple* to refer to the class of protocols requiring random number generation and hashing; the term *lightweight* to refer to the class of protocols which require random number generation and simple checksum functions, and the term *ultralightweight* to refer to the class of protocols which only involve simple bitwise operations, like *and, or, xor,* $+ \bmod n$, and *cyclic shift.*

Let us look at it with some more details, and consider it in the context of RFID authentication. Two entities are involved: a Tag and a Reader[1]. The channel between the Reader and the Tag is susceptible to all the possible attacks. Each Tag has a *static identifier*, ID, a *pseudonym*, IDS, and *two keys*, K_1 and K_2. All of them are 96-bit strings. The pseudonym and the keys are shared with the Reader which, for each Tag with static identifier ID, stores in a table the tuple (IDS, K_1, K_2). After each successfull execution of the authentication protocol, the Tag and the Reader *update* such values. The authentication protocol is a four-round protocol and is depicted in Fig. 1.

Notice that the computations involve $\oplus$ (bitwise xor), $\vee$ (bitwise or), $+ \bmod 2^{96}$, and $Rot(x, y)$, where x and y are two 96-bit values, and the $Rot(\cdot, \cdot)$ operator shifts to the left in a cyclic way x by $z = f(y)$ positions, according to some f (e.g., Hamming weight $hw(y)$ or $y \bmod 2^{96}$).

The pseudonym and the keys are updated after each execution through certain updating functions. The Reader stores the new tuple (IDS', K_1', K_2'). The Tag stores two tuples, (IDS', K_1', K_2') and (IDS, K_1, K_2), because it might happen that the Tag updates the pseudonym and the keys, while the Server does not. Such an event for example might occur if a simple communication fault does not permit the Reader to get the value **D**, sent by the Tag during the 4-th round of the authentication protocol. Any time the Reader gets **IDS'** from the Tag, the Reader looks for a tuple (IDS', K_1', K_2'). If no entry is found, the Reader sends another **Hello** message to the Tag and the Tag replies with the old **IDS**. Hence, even if the Reader has not updated the tuple, the authentication protocol can be run by using the old one, i.e., (IDS, K_1, K_2). Of course, if no match is found also at the second interaction, the protocol fails.

However, as its predecessors, it was quickly broken in a few months, e.g., [6,13,22,23], and more refined attacks followed, e.g., [2,7].

In [7] the protocol was full broken. We described how the weaknesses, through a sequence of simple steps, could be used to compute in an efficient way *all* the secret data used for the authentication process.

To get an idea, let us give a quick look at the desynchronization attack provided in [7]. Let *Adv* be an adversary who controls the channel between the Reader and the Tag. *Adv*, in a first stage just looks at an execution of the authentication protocol and stores the messages **Hello**, **IDS**, **A||B||C** and **D** the parties send to each other.

Then, in a second stage, *Adv* interacts with the Tag. Roughly speaking, *Adv* resets the Tag to the state in which the Tag was at the time of the interaction with the Reader and, then, by using the transcript of the execution of the authentication protocol, induces the Tag to accept a new sequence **A'||B'||C'**.

---

[1] Actually, the entities are three: Tag, Reader, and a Backend Server. The channel between the Reader and the Backend Server is assumed to be secure. To simplify the description usually the Backend Server is not explicitly introduced and the Reader is assumed to perform directly the computations.

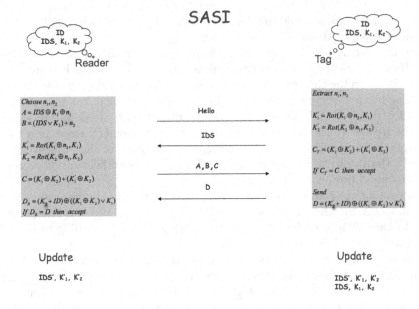

Fig. 1. SASI

Such a sequence drives the Tag to overwrite the new tuple ($\mathbf{IDS}'$, K_1', K_2'), computed at the end of the execution with the Reader. When Adv succeeds, Tag and Reader are de-synchonised. The new sequence $\mathbf{A}'||\mathbf{B}'||\mathbf{C}'$ is constructed by computing $\mathbf{C}'$ as a modification of $\mathbf{C}$ and by looking for a properly chosen $\mathbf{A}'$, obtained by flipping a single bit of $\mathbf{A}$. The value $\mathbf{B}$ stays the same.

Why does the attack work? Notice that, by definition

$$\mathbf{A} = \mathbf{IDS} \oplus K_1 \oplus n_1.$$

By flipping a bit in $\mathbf{A}$, Adv implicitly flips a bit of n_1. But n_1 is used to compute

$$K_2' = Rot(K_2 \oplus n_1, K_2).$$

Hence, by flipping a bit of n_1, Adv flips a bit of K_2', even if he *does not know* which one, since K_2 is unknown. Moreover, it is easy to check that, given two different positions, i and j, in n_1, by flipping the corresponding bits, the bits flipped in K_2' lie in two different positions i' and j'. Hence, any time Adv flips a bit in n_1, he flips a bit in a different position of K_2'. Since,

$$\mathbf{C} = (K_1 \oplus K_2') + (K_1' \oplus K_2),$$

and the values of K_1, K_1', and K_2 stay the same, Adv, by flipping a bit of n_1, changes the value of $(K_1 \oplus K_2')$. If this value is modified in the i-th position, which goes from 1 to 0, then $\mathbf{C}' = \mathbf{C} - 2^i$. Vice versa, if it changes from 0 to 1, then $\mathbf{C}' = \mathbf{C} + 2^i$.

Thus, Adv computes $\mathbf{C}' = \mathbf{C} \pm 2^0$ and tries all possible $\mathbf{A}'$ until he gets a triple accepted. Since Adv does not know a-priori whether, when he succeeds in changing $K'_2[0]$, he gets $\mathbf{C} + 2^0$ or $\mathbf{C} - 2^0$, the attack needs to be applied twice: once by setting $\mathbf{C}' = \mathbf{C} + 2^0$ and, if going through all possible $\mathbf{A}'$ no sequence is found, one more time by setting $\mathbf{C}' = \mathbf{C} - 2^0$ and trying again. Eventually, the procedure halts because at each iteration a different position of K'_2 is flipped, and going through all possible $\mathbf{A}'$ means trying all possible variations of K'_2, in which a single bit is flipped. Hence, there exists a certain iteraction, say the j-th one, which flips $K'_2[0]$ and produces either $\mathbf{C} + 2^0$ or $\mathbf{C} - 2^0$.

Notice that the attack leverages on the *malleability* of the values $\mathbf{A}, \mathbf{B}$ and $\mathbf{C}$. *Adv* can manipulate in a controlled way the transcript of a previous execution to impersonate the Reader. This is a common weakness in the design of many ultralightweight authentication protocol.

Moreover, in our case, once a sequence $\mathbf{A}'||\mathbf{B}||\mathbf{C}'$ which the Tag accepts is found, *Adv* discovers the value used in the rotation $Rot(K_2 \oplus n_1, K_2)$ to compute K'_2. Indeed, if the sequence $\mathbf{A}'||\mathbf{B}||\mathbf{C}'$ has been computed by flipping the bit $\mathbf{A}[j]$, then the value z of the rotation is exactly $95 - j$.

It seems a small information leakage, but as shown in [7], it opens the door to other leakages. Eventually, through more sofisticated analysis techniques, inspired by differential cryptanalysis, all the secret information stored in the Tag's memory, from the static ID to the secret keys, can be retrieved without accessing its memory but simply interactive with it a few hundred times.

Also this cascade-style leakage effect is a common trait in the design of many ultralightweight authentication protocol.

3   A General View

As pointed out in [4], almost all ultralightweight mutual authentication protocols proposed throughout the years can be seen as instances of one general framework, depicted in Fig. 2.

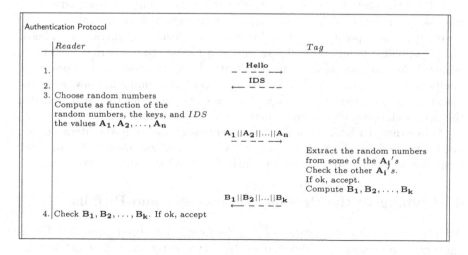

Fig. 2. General framework: steps of the authentication protocol

Each Tag has an ID, hardcoded into the circuit at production time and never revealed. Furthermore, the Tag has a pseudonym **IDS** and a few secret keys, which are stored in the Tag memory, and are usually updated after each successful execution of the protocol. All of these values are bit-strings. Readers are expected to be able to generate random or pseudo-random numbers. The Reader, for each Tag, stores in a table the pseudonym and the keys.

At the end of a successful execution, Reader and Tag update the pseudonym and all the secret keys. The updating functions use the IDS, the static ID and secret keys, as well as some of the random numbers, used in the last execution of the protocol. Moreover, many protocols require Reader and Tag to store both the new IDS and the new secret keys, as well as the old IDS and the old secret keys, to avoid desynchonization due to message lost.

The basic requirement for a protocol is correctness: if Reader and Tag start a protocol execution when they share at least one IDS and the corresponding secret keys, and no adversarial action or transmission error occur, then they should successfully complete the execution and authenticate each other.

The main security and privacy properties, which are usually goals in the design of ultralightweight authentication protocols, belong to the following list (they are not independent):

1. Resistance to impersonation attacks.
2. Anonymity and resistance to tracking.
3. Data confidentiality.
4. Forward security.
5. Explicit key confirmation and resistance to de-synchronization attack.
6. Resistance to replay attack.
7. Resistance to man-in-the-middle attack.
8. Resistance to disclosure attack.

Some of the above attacks can be launched by a *passive* adversary, who just eavesdrops the protocol executions, while the others require an *active* adversary, who can intercept, modify the messages and interact with the parties.

In [4] we have pointed out that in this area security and privacy are almost always espressed in an informal way, and as a *list of desiderata* that need to be achieved. No rigorous model is used to state clearly the goals and to prove the merits of a given protocol. The *proofs* are arguments aiming at convincing the reader of the goodness of the design. And, as shown in [7] for the SASI protocol, this approach opens the doors to unexpected consequences.

Notice that, RFID Tags are just an interesting case study the literature has mainly focused on. Neverthless, the following discussion applies also to other technologies, present and future, in which cheap and tiny devices are used.

4 Coming to the Present: Weaknesses and Pitfalls

Attacks on virtually all proposals in the literature have been published. Ultra-lightweight protocols are subverted easily, very shortly after their publication.

In an in-depth analysis [3] of 2015, the authors provided a description of the common weaknesses. Briefly, they belong to the following classes.

Poor Diffusion. Use of the so-called "T-functions". These are functions for which each bit in the output only depends on bits in the same or lower positions in the input. Binary operations (e.g. $\oplus, \wedge, \vee$) and modular addition are T-functions.

Linearity. It is the property that $f(a \oplus b) = f(a) \oplus f(b)$. In addition to $\oplus$, rotations and other permutations are linear. Linearity is a transitive relation and schemes entirely linear are easy to attacks.

Biased Output. Some operations have a biased output: OR ($\vee$) and AND ($\wedge$), for unbiased random bits x and y, have heavily (75%) biased outputs, respectively, towards 1 and 0. They leak information for both of their arguments. For example, if $x \vee y = 0$, then $x = y = 0$, which discloses both the inputs. With uniformly distributed input, this happens 25% of the time.

Rotations. Data-dependent rotations have only L possible outputs. Moreover, the distribution of these outputs is known a priori.

Poor Message Composition. Due to the constraints of ultralightweight protocols, messages are usually built using a handful of operations, and in many cases good confusion and diffusion levels are not satisfied.

Vulnerability to Knowledge Accumulation. If partial leakage of a static secret occurs in a round of a protocol, there is an obvious traceability issue. Moreover, as shown in the example before, the leakage amplifies in subsequent rounds.

Dubious Proofs of Security: Randomness Tests and Automated Provers. In many papers, security is proved by showing that the exchanged messages look random enough, using randomness test batteries. Unfortunately this does not prove any security level. Randomness may be simply the result of employing nonces in message mixing, and it is not a sufficient condition, neither is it a necessary one. Moreover, the use of logic modeling and formal protocol verification software, is another popular but flawed way of proving security of proposed ultralightweight protocols.

We kindly recommend the interested reader to have a look at [3] for a detailed discussion, and to [4] for further observations.

5   A Look to the Recent Past

In [8] we considered the design of several recently proposed ultralightweight authentication protocols. After [3], we expected to see a different development. Actually, our attention was caught because the new protocols appeared to be more structured, compared to other previous proposals. Indeed, all of these sort of generation 2.0 ultralightweight authentication protocols, base their security properties on some *transforms*. The transforms protect their input values by masking them via a processing stage, in which some secret values are involved and elementary operations, allowed by the low-power computational devices, are applied. We studied such transforms and pointed out that they achieve *poor confusion and diffusion* in the input-output mappings. Exploiting the weaknesses found, we constructed impersonation attacks against the protocols KMAP, RCIA, SASI+ and SLAP, which reduce from exponential to constant the number of trials needed to an adversary to impersonate the Reader to a Tag. We remarked that the results on the transforms can be used to attack *any* protocol based on them.

To get an idea, let us review just one of the protocols, RCIA. The interested reader is referred to [8] for the details and the analysis of the other protocols. The transform used in RCIA is called *recursive hash* and is defined as follows.

Recursive Hash. Let $x = b_1, b_2, \ldots, b_n$ be a string of n bits, and let ℓ and z be integers such that ℓ is a divisor of n and $z = n/\ell$. Moreover, let s be an integer value, called *seed*, such that $1 \leq s \leq z$. Then, dividing x into z chunks $x_1, \ldots, x_z$ of ℓ bits each, e.g., $x_i = b_{(i-1)\cdot\ell}, b_{(i-1)\cdot\ell+1}, \ldots, b_{i\cdot\ell-1}$, and denoting with $\text{Rot}(x, y)$ a right rotation of the string x by y positions, the recursive hash of x and s, denoted by $\text{Rh}(x, s)$ for short, is defined as:

$$x_1 \oplus x_s, \ldots, x_{s-1} \oplus x_s, \text{Rot}(x_s, \text{hw}(x_s)), x_{s+1} \oplus x_s, \ldots, x_{\frac{n}{\ell}} \oplus x_s.$$

Each chunk c_i of the recursive hash is the $\oplus$ of chunks x_i with x_s, except for chunk c_s, which is equal to x_s rotated by its Hamming weight $\text{hw}(x_s)$.

Let us look at an example: let $n = 24$ and $x = 100100101011110101111110$. Moreover, let $\ell = 6$ and, thus, $z = 4$. We get:

$x =$	x_1	x_2	x_3	x_4
	100100	101011	110101	111110

Let the seed s be equal to 3. The selected chunk is $x_3 = 110101$, whose Hamming weight is $\text{hw}(x_3) = 4$. Hence, the right rotation of x_3 is 010111. The recursive hash $\text{Rh}(x, s)$ is:

$x =$	x_1	x_2	x_3	x_4
	100100	101011	110101	111110
x_3 replicated	110101	110101		110101
$x_i \oplus x_3$	010001	011110		001011
x_3 rotated			010111	
$\text{Rh}(x, s)$	010001	011110	010111	001011
c_i	c_1	c_2	c_3	c_4

We have shown, in Lemmas 5 and 6 of [8], that if x is a string of n bits, chosen uniformly at random, and x' is a new string obtained from x by flipping two randomly selected bits, then, for any seed $s \in \{1, \ldots, z\}$, it holds that:

- $\text{Rh}(x, s)$ and $\text{Rh}(x', s)$ differ in two bits with probability at least $1/4$
- $\Pr[\text{hw}(\text{Rh}(x, s)) = \text{hw}(\text{Rh}(x', s))]$ is at least $1/2$.

Protocol description.

The Reader chooses n_1 and n_2 uniformly at random. Then, sets:

$P = n_1 \oplus n_2$

$s = hw(P) \bmod b$, for a certain fixed b

and computes:

$A = \text{Rot}(IDS, K_1) \oplus n_1$

$B = (\text{Rot}(IDS \wedge n_1, K_2) \wedge K_1) \oplus n_2$

$K_1^* = \text{Rot}(\text{Rh}(K_2, s), \text{Rh}(n_1, s)) \wedge K_1)$

$K_2^* = \text{Rot}(\text{Rh}(K_1, s), \text{Rh}(n_2, s)) \wedge K_2)$

$C = \text{Rot}(\text{Rh}(K_1^*, s), \text{Rh}(K_2^*, s)) \wedge \text{Rot}(\text{Rh}(n_1, s), \text{Rh}(n_2, s))$

The Tag checks C and computes:

$D = \text{Rot}(\text{Rh}(IDS, s), K_1^*)) \wedge (\text{Rot}(\text{Rh}(K_2^*, s), \text{Rh}(n_2, s)) \oplus IDS)$

Fig. 3. RCIA message computation

Such properties can be used to defy the authentication protocol through an impersonation attack. RCIA uses only the bitwise *and*, *or*, $Rot(\cdot, \cdot)$, and $\text{Rh}(\cdot, \cdot)$. Let us look at the exchanged messages (Fig. 3):

Impersonation Attack. Analyzing the equations used in the protocol, the following observations hold:

1. Flipping two bits of B is equivalent to flipping two bits of n_2 in the *same* positions.
2. Let $P' = n_1 \oplus n_2'$, where n_2' is equal to n_2 up to two flipped bits. Then, P' is equal to P up to two flipped bits. If the two flipped bits are the complement of each other, i.e., they are 01 or 10 respectively, we have that $hw(P') = hw(P)$. Since there are 2 good bit patterns out of 4 possible bit patterns, this event occurs with probability $1/2$.
3. If $hw(P') = hw(P)$, the structure of $\text{Rh}(\cdot, s)$ *does not change*, since the seed s is the same.
4. If $hw(\text{Rh}(n_2, s)) = hw(\text{Rh}(n_2', s))$, then the values K_2^*, $\text{Rh}(K_2^*, s)$ and C *do not change*.

Putting everything together, we proved that, if *Adv* eavesdrops an authentication session, stores $A||B||C$, and sets B' be equal to B up to two bits which are flipped, then, forcing the Tag to send the old IDS and replying with $A||B'||C$, *Adv* succeeds in impersonating the legal Reader with probability roughly equal to $\frac{1}{4}$. Thus, a few trials are sufficient to break the security of the authentication protocol.

In conclusion, the analysis of [8] shows that, more or less, nothing has changed compared to ten years ago.

6   A Look to the Future

Due to the above scenario, in [8] and [4], we pointed out that currently we have two choices: either we *give up* because it is difficult, or probably impossible, to achieve the security standard we get with other, much more powerful, digital devices, or we *try* to achieve a *reasonable* security level also in applications, using these cheap computing elements. We also noted that, unfortunately, the current state of knowledge is quite poor: we do not have a clear idea of what *reasonable* could mean, we do not have any impossibility result within a model for such ultralightweight protocols but, at the same time, all ultralightweight authentication protocols, designed according to ad hoc approaches, have been shown to suffer several weaknesses of different significance and impact. Anyway, despite the current situation, which may seem to indicate that ultralightweight protocols are bound to fail, there is no clear evidence that designing a secure protocol with such constraints is impossible.

To this aim, we have suggested to give a look at the close field of lightweight cryptography, as a source of inspiration for methodology, modeling, design strategies, and proof techniques. Let us elaborate a bit more on some of these points.

6.1   The HB-Like Protocol Family

A deeply studied approach to the design of lightweight authentication protocols is the one provided by the HB protocol [9], introduced to efficiently authenticate a human to a computer. The security of this family of protocols is based on the difficulty of solving the *learning parity with noise* (LPN) problem [9].

The protocol proposed by Hopper and Blum is simple and elegant. It requires n interactions. The two parties, V and P, share a binary secret vector $s \in \mathcal{Z}_2^\ell$. A single interaction consists of two rounds: in the first, V sends to P a challenge vector $r \in \mathcal{Z}_2^\ell$, chosen uniformly at random. In the second, P replies to V with a bit $z = r^T \cdot s + e$, where $e \in \{0,1\}$ is an error bit, chosen in such a way that $Prob[e = 1] = \tau$, for a certain $\tau < 1/2$. At the end of the second round, V accepts the interaction if $z = r^T \cdot s$; otherwise, it rejects. Eventually, V authenticates P if the execution of n interactions leads V to reject at most $\tau \cdot n$ times.

The protocol is secure against passive attacks but it fails against active attacks. The $HB+$ protocol [14] was introduced in order to achieve security against active attacks. The structure of the protocol stays the same, apart the following differences: the shared secret is a pair of binary vectors $(s_1, s_2) \in \mathcal{Z}_2^\ell$. A single interaction consists in three rounds: in the first, P sends a vector $r_P \in \mathcal{Z}_2^\ell$ to V, chosen uniformly at random. In the second, V sends to P a challenge vector $r_V \in \mathcal{Z}_2^\ell$, chosen uniformly at random. In the third, P replies to V with a bit $z = r_P^T \cdot s_1 + r_V^T \cdot s_2 + e$, where $e \in \{0,1\}$ is an error bit, chosen as before. At the end of the third round, V accepts the interaction if $z = r_P^T \cdot s_1 + r_V^T \cdot s_2$; otherwise, it rejects.

It was subsequently showed in [15] that the n interactions can be safely run in *parallel*, yielding to compact two-round and three-round protocols, respectively. Unfortunately, the authors of [12] showed that also $HB+$ is not resistant against

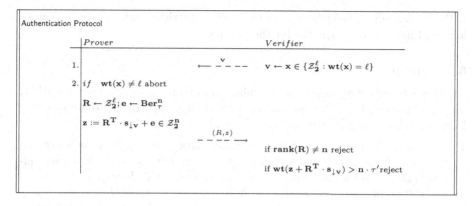

Fig. 4. Two-round authentication protocol

certain active attacks. Since then, several variants of $HB+$ have been proposed in the literature, but almost all of them present some problems [11]. An HB-like scheme, secure in an adversarial model comprising passive and certain active attacks, which has received considerable attention, was proposed in [10] and analysed in [17].

One of the lastest version, which departs from the original design of HB, can be found in [16]. The protocol is a two-round protocol, secure against certain active attacks.

The key idea in [16] is that the Verifier, instead of sending the random challenges to the Prover, chooses a random subsets of the bits of the secret s, which should be used as a sort of session key, in an interaction. In such a way, the Prover can generate the random challenges by himself.

Let us look at it in more details: let s be a shared secret of 2ℓ bits, let $s_{\downarrow v}$ be the subset of bits of s identified by the non-zero bits of v, let R be the matrix of the n challenges which are answered in parallel by the Prover, and let e be an n-bit vector chosen according to Ber_τ^n, a Bernoulli distribution with parameter τ, i.e., $Prob[e_i = 1] = \tau$, for $i = 1, \ldots, n$ and a certain $\tau < 1/2$. The protocol is given in Fig. 4:

The protocol is nice and very interesting because, after many years, it offers *a different way* of designing a two-round authentication protocol based on the LPN problem. Unfortunately, by looking at the suggested parameters for real implementation, also this version as the previous ones, do not fit the hardware constraints of very cheap passive Tags. See [1] for a detailed analysis of such a constraints.

Neverthless, on the positive side, it leaves open several questions: are there *other ways* to set up an authentication protocol based on the LPN problem, which enables the Prover (Tag) to store few hundred bits and moving the greatest part of the computation to the Verifier? Can the above protocols be simplified/approximated, in order to get a tradeoff between security and computation? Or do we need to rule out the possibility of achieving such a result by using the

LPN problem, given the efficiency of the known algorithms which solve the problem, and imply certain lengths for the parameters?

6.2 Squash

Another interesting approach to designing an authentication protocol for RFID Tags was proposed in [24]. The author noticed that the HB-like solutions suffer from several serious problems. Using his words:

1. *The tag needs an internal source of random bits. Real randomness is difficult to find and can be externally manipulated by the adversary, while pseudorandomness requires a large nonvolatile memory and lots of computations.*
2. *Since the proof of authenticity in these schemes is probabilistic, there is a small chance that a tag will fail to convince a Reader that it is valid even when both of them are honest and there are no adversaries.*
3. *There are several parameters involved (the length of the secret, the number of repetitions, the probability of the additive noise, etc.) and there is considerable debate about which values of these parameters will make the scheme sufficiently secure.*
4. *Over the last few years, a large number of attacks were developed against most of these schemes.*

The new approach was explicitly developed having as target tiny computing elements, equipped with few hundred bits of storage, e.g., 300 bits, and weak processing capabilities. Therein, a lightweight hash function, which can be used in RFID authentication, was described. Using the Rabin scheme as a secure starting point, the goal was to change it in multiple ways, which make it much more efficient but with provably equivalent security properties. The idea was to compute an excellent numerical approximation for a *short window of bits* in the middle of the ciphertext produced by the Rabin encryption function. The Rabin encryption function uses a modulus of a particular form, in such a way that computing these bits for an adversary is as hard as breaking the full Rabin scheme.

A basic version of the scheme was analysed in [18]. As far as we know, the approach of [24] has not been followed by other significant proposals. Hence, also here some natural questions are: can we lightening some other standard symmetric-key or public key primitives by means of approximation methods, which aim at reducing the computational burden on the parties, maintaining almost the same security of the original primitive? Or, at least, in a more realistic scenario, can we lightening with a graceful degradation of the security and privacy guarantees, compared to the original protocol? We believe that also this research line is worthy to keep pursuing in order to get an improvement in the field.

6.3 Lightweight Blockciphers, Stream Ciphers and Hash Functions

In [3] and, recently, in [4], it has been recalled that significant efforts have been made in the last years to develop ciphers and hash functions suitable for lightweight authentication and lightweight protocols in general. The PRESENT block cipher, the TRIVIUM and GRAIN stream ciphers, or the PHOTON and QUARK hash functions, are important examples of these efforts. And some others, like BLAKE or RC5, belonging to the so-called Add-Rotate-Xor algorithms, use the very same set of operations as ultralightweight protocols.

As stated in [4], while not quite fitting the same extreme constraints imposed on ultralightweight protocols, they are a step towards that direction. They also benefit from a much wider exposure and scrutiny. The design of ultralightweight authentication protocols starting from standard authentication protocols realized with these lightweight primitives is, therefore, another research line worthy to investigate.

6.4 Modeling

As we have pointed out before, a proper modeling and a rigorous analysis are usually missing. Building on previous works, from [25], many efforts within the lightweight community have been provided in order to set up suitable models. As standard in modern cryptography, the privacy and security definitions are based on *experiments*, run by a *challenger*, and played by a polynomially bounded *adversary*. The experiments are designed in such a way that, when the adversary wins, a property of the protocol is subverted. The adversary can interact with a *set of oracles* through *oracle queries*, reproducing real executions of the protocol. As an example, look at Fig. 5 for an overview of the oracles in Vaudenay's model.

The privacy property is espressed in the model in a very concise and powerful way: instead of listing resistance against specific attacks, it is required that,

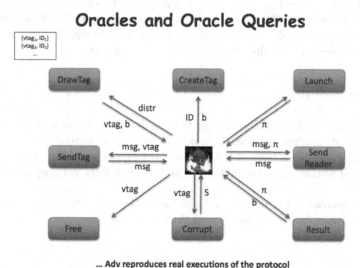

Fig. 5. Vaudenay's model

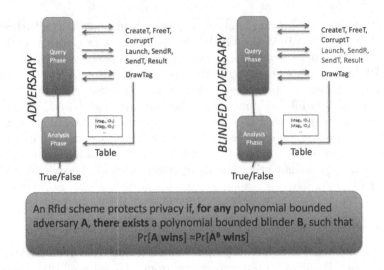

Fig. 6. Privacy notion in Vaudenay's model

whatever relation on the Tags the adversary tries to compute, taking advantage of the transcripts of protocol executions, he should be able to compute also without the transcripts, with essentially the same probability. Figure 6 graphically reproduce the formalization. The *blinder*, introduced in the second experiments, simulates the real transcript of the protocol, without access to the secret keys.

Apart its merits, Vaudenay's model, and the ones which followed, offer an important starting point for the modeling and the analysis also of ultra-lightweight authentication protocols. Some natural questions which perhaps deserve an answer: are these models appropriate as they are for ultralightweight authentication protocols? Do we need any relaxation? In which parts? It is clear that some efforts are worthy also along this research line.

7   Conclusions

Our knowledge in the ultralightweight field, as far as we know and have tried to briefly look at, is quite poor at the moment. Further investigations, in order to develop on a firm basis both the design and the analysis of new protocols, seem to be an interesting and challenging research topic for the coming up years.

Acknowledgement. I would like to thank Xavier Carpenter, Roberto De Prisco and Alfredo De Santis for helpful comments and suggestions.

References

1. Armknecht, F., Hamann, M., Mikhalev, V.: Lightweight authentication protocols on ultra-constrained RFIDs - myths and facts. In: Saxena, N., Sadeghi, A.-R. (eds.) RFIDSec 2014. LNCS, vol. 8651, pp. 1–18. Springer, Cham (2014). https://doi.org/10.1007/978-3-319-13066-8_1
2. Avoine, G., Carpent, X., Martin, B.: Strong authentication and strong integrity (SASI) is not that strong. In: Ors Yalcin, S.B. (ed.) RFIDSec 2010. LNCS, vol. 6370, pp. 50–64. Springer, Heidelberg (2010). https://doi.org/10.1007/978-3-642-16822-2_5
3. Avoine, G., Carpent, X., Hernandez-Castro, J.: Pitfalls in ultra-lightweight authentication protocol designs. IEEE Trans. Mob. Comput. **15**(9), 2317–2332 (2016)
4. Carpenter, X., D'Arco, P., De Prisco, R.: Ultralightweight authentication protocols. In: Hernandez-Castro, J., Avoine, G. (eds.) Selected Topics in Security of Ubiquitous Computing Systems (2019). ISBN 978-3-030-10591-4
5. Chien, H.: SASI: a new ultra-lightweight RFID authentication protocol providing strong authentication and strong integrity. IEEE Trans. Dependable Secure Comput. **4**(4), 337–340 (2007)
6. D'Arco, P., De Santis, A.: Weaknesses in a recent ultra-lightweight RFID authentication protocol. In: Vaudenay, S. (ed.) AFRICACRYPT 2008. LNCS, vol. 5023, pp. 27–39. Springer, Heidelberg (2008). https://doi.org/10.1007/978-3-540-68164-9_3
7. D'Arco, P., De Santis, A.: On ultra-lightweight RFID authentication protocols. IEEE Trans. Dependable Secure Comput. **8**(4), 548–563 (2011)
8. D'Arco, P., De Prisco, R.: Design weaknesses in recent ultra-lightweight RFID authentication protocols. In: Proceedings of the 33rd International Conference on Information Security and Privacy Protection (IFIP TC-11 SEC 2018), Pozna, Poland, pp. 18–20 (2018)
9. Hopper, N.J., Blum, M.: Secure human identification protocols. In: Boyd, C. (ed.) ASIACRYPT 2001. LNCS, vol. 2248, pp. 52–66. Springer, Heidelberg (2001). https://doi.org/10.1007/3-540-45682-1_4
10. Gilbert, H., Robshaw, M.J.B., Seurin, Y.: HB$^{\#}$: increasing the security and efficiency of HB^{+}. In: Smart, N. (ed.) EUROCRYPT 2008. LNCS, vol. 4965, pp. 361–378. Springer, Heidelberg (2008). https://doi.org/10.1007/978-3-540-78967-3_21
11. Gilbert, H., Robshaw, M.J.B., Seurin, Y.: Good variants of HB^{+} are hard to find. In: Tsudik, G. (ed.) FC 2008. LNCS, vol. 5143, pp. 156–170. Springer, Heidelberg (2008). https://doi.org/10.1007/978-3-540-85230-8_12
12. Gilbert, H., Robshaw, M.J.B., Sibert, H.: An active attack against HB^{+} a provably secure lightweight authentication protocol. Electron. Lett. **41**(21), 1169–1170 (2005)
13. Hernandez-Castro, J.C., Estevez-Tapiador, J.M., Peris-Lopez, P., Quisquater, J.-J.: Cryptanalysis of the SASI ultra-lightweight RFID authentication protocol with modular rotations. In: International Workshop on Coding and Cryptography - WCC 2009, Ullensvang, Norway, May 2009
14. Juels, A., Weis, S.A.: Authenticating pervasive devices with human protocols. In: Shoup, V. (ed.) CRYPTO 2005. LNCS, vol. 3621, pp. 293–308. Springer, Heidelberg (2005). https://doi.org/10.1007/11535218_18
15. Katz, J., Shin, J.S., Smith, A.: Parallel and concurrent security of the HB and HB^{+} protocols. J. Cryptology **23**(3), 402–421 (2010)

16. Kiltz, E., Pietrzak, K., Venturi, D., Cash, D., Jain, A.: Efficient authentication from hard learning problems. J. Cryptology **30**(4), 1238–1275 (2017)
17. Ouafi, K., Overbeck, R., Vaudenay, S.: On the security of HB$^{\#}$ against a man-in-the-middle attack. In: Pieprzyk, J. (ed.) ASIACRYPT 2008. LNCS, vol. 5350, pp. 108–124. Springer, Heidelberg (2008). https://doi.org/10.1007/978-3-540-89255-7_8
18. Ouafi, K., Vaudenay, S.: Smashing SQUASH-0. In: Joux, A. (ed.) EUROCRYPT 2009. LNCS, vol. 5479, pp. 300–312. Springer, Heidelberg (2009). https://doi.org/10.1007/978-3-642-01001-9_17
19. Peris-Lopez, P., Hernandez-Castro, J.C., Estevez-Tapiador, J.M., Ribagorda, A.: M^{2}AP: a minimalist mutual-authentication protocol for low-cost RFID tags. In: Ma, J., Jin, H., Yang, L.T., Tsai, J.J.-P. (eds.) UIC 2006. LNCS, vol. 4159, pp. 912–923. Springer, Heidelberg (2006). https://doi.org/10.1007/11833529_93
20. Peris-Lopez, P., Hernandez-Castro, J.C., Estevez-Tapiador, J.M., Ribagorda, A.: LMAP: a real lightweight mutual authentication protocol for low-cost RFID tags. In: Proceedings of the RFID Security Workshop, pp. 12–24 (2006)
21. Peris-Lopez, P., Hernandez-Castro, J.C., Estevez-Tapiador, J.M., Ribagorda, A.: EMAP: an efficient mutual-authentication protocol for low-cost RFID tags. In: Meersman, R., Tari, Z., Herrero, P. (eds.) OTM 2006. LNCS, vol. 4277, pp. 352–361. Springer, Heidelberg (2006). https://doi.org/10.1007/11915034_59
22. Phan, R.C.W.: Cryptanalysis of a new ultra-lightweight RFID authentication protocol - SASI. IEEE Trans. Dependable Secure Comput. **6**(4), 316–320 (2009)
23. Sun, H.-M., Ting, W.-C., Wang, K.-H.: On the Security of Chien's Ultralightweight RFID Authentication Protocol, eprint archive, no. 83, February 2008
24. Shamir, A.: SQUASH – a new MAC with provable security properties for highly constrained devices such as RFID tags. In: Nyberg, K. (ed.) FSE 2008. LNCS, vol. 5086, pp. 144–157. Springer, Heidelberg (2008). https://doi.org/10.1007/978-3-540-71039-4_9
25. Vaudenay, S.: On privacy models for RFID. In: Kurosawa, K. (ed.) ASIACRYPT 2007. LNCS, vol. 4833, pp. 68–87. Springer, Heidelberg (2007). https://doi.org/10.1007/978-3-540-76900-2_5

Android Malware Analysis: From Technical Difficulties to Scientific Challenges

Jean-François Lalande[(⊠)]

CentraleSupélec, Inria, Univ Rennes, CNRS, IRISA, 35065 Rennes, France
`jean-francois.lalande@inria.fr`

Abstract. Ten years ago, Google released the first version of its new operating system: Android. With an open market for third party applications, attackers started to develop malicious applications. Researchers started new works too. Inspired by previous techniques for Windows or GNU/Linux malware, a lot of papers introduced new ways of detecting, classifying, defeating Android malware. In this paper, we propose to explore the technical difficulties of experimenting with Android malware. These difficulties are encountered by researchers, each time they want to publish a solid experiment validating their approach. How to choose malware samples? How to process a large amount of malware? What happens if the experiment needs to execute dynamically a sample? The end of the paper presents the upcoming scientific challenges of the community interested in malware analysis.

Keywords: Malware analysis · Mobile phones

1 Introduction

Research about Android malware mainly addresses three types of problem: deciding if an application is a malware or not (detection), classifying a malware sample among families (classification) and explaining precisely what a sample is doing (characterization). These three types of contribution require a dataset of malware for performing experiments that support the proposed contribution. Nevertheless, performing reliable experiments is not as simple as expected. In addition with the difficulties to reproduce previous experiments, many technical difficulties can have an impact on the results.

This paper summarizes the encountered difficulties when experimenting with Android malware. In particular, we focus on the choice of the malware dataset, that can have a large influence on the outperformed results. Finally, we discuss the upcoming challenges when contributing to the field of malware analysis.

This work has received a French government support granted to the COMIN Labs excellence laboratory and managed by the National Research Agency in the "Investing for the Future" program under reference ANR-10-LABX-07-01.

J.-L. Lanet and C. Toma (Eds.): SecITC 2018, LNCS 11359, pp. 17–21, 2019.
https://doi.org/10.1007/978-3-030-12942-2_2

2   Designing Malware Analysis Experiments

2.1   Datasets

The choice of the dataset is of primary importance to discuss with accuracy the obtained results. As Android is quickly evolving, malware samples are quickly outdated and some of them cannot be installed on recent versions of the operating system. Thus, fundamental papers that have a lot of citations like Copper-Droid [13], IntelliDroid [15], TaintDroid [7], to name a few, suffer from outdated datasets or incompatibility problems. For example CopperDroid runs on several Android versions, which is fine, but uses three outdated datasets: Contagio mobile[1], the Genome Project [17] and samples provided by McAfee. Contagio mobile is a blog which contains few samples, posted by contributors. The Genome Project has now closed its service and the database cannot be accessed anymore. Finally, the samples obtained from a collaboration with McAfee is of course interesting but cannot be reproduced in other papers.

The size of the dataset makes experiments difficult to compare. For example, a recent paper about malicious libraries [5] provides results based on 1.3 millions of applications, whereas the experiments of TriggerScope for dealing with logic bombs evaluate the approach on 14 malware among 9,313 applications. Experiments are difficult to compare when there is so much difference between the processed number of applications. Additionally, most of the time, authors have to reimplement previous contributions, such as TriggerScope that reimplemented Kirin [8], DroidAPIMiner [1], and FlowDroid [4], which is obviously a lot of efforts.

New datasets recently appeared that try to address these problems. Andro-Zoo [3] is a large dataset of million of applications that is helpful for a having a large diversity of benign and malware applications. In particular, they provide pairs of applications that show that a lot malware applications are repackaged version of benign applications. The AMD dataset [14] is another contributions that provides 24,650 malware samples. Some contextual information (classes, actions,...) are provided that have been computed for a part by automatic tools and for the other part by a manual analysis. We believe that these two contributions for building reliable and documented datasets are an important step towards reproducible security experiments, but some questions remain, for example the lifespan of a dataset, used for training purpose [12].

2.2   Designing an Experiment

From our point of view, designing an experiment for malware analysis always follows the same steps. After selecting a sample to be analyzed from the dataset, authors process this sample by applying static or dynamic analysis techniques. Depending on there goals (detection, classification, characterization), they compare the obtained performances with the results obtained by other tools. Even if this process is simple to understand, several question arise:

---

[1] http://contagiominidump.blogspot.com.

Is the Sample Really a Malware? Picking up some sample from large unlabeled datasets or the play store gives a large variety of applications, representative of the reality. If this effort is continuous with time, authors are sure to capture new malware samples that appear on the play store before being removed. Then, samples should be analyzed to decide if they are malware or not, especially when evaluating a detection algorithm. For solving this issue, most of authors rely on VirusTotal to decide if a sample is malicious or not. We believe that it is not a good idea, because the analysis tools used by VirusTotal has no reason to decide accurately [10], especially for recent samples.

Where is the Payload? The answer should be provided by the dataset. Most of papers use heuristics for answering this question, for example the approach of Aafer et al. [1] that study the API used by each part of the code. The idea behind this heuristic is that the malicious parts of the code use specific APIs and can be exposed. Identifying the payload is especially important when studying multiple repackaged applications where the payload is hidden in the code of benign applications. Nevertheless, five years after Aafer et al.'s publication, the mentioned evasion techniques, reflection, native code, encryption, dynamic loading are widely used by malware. Even benign applications now use packers that use these techniques to protect their code [6].

Is the Static and Dynamic Analysis Possible? Most approaches analyze statically the sample before eventually executing it in a sandbox or a real smartphone. Few papers mention that a static and dynamic analysis can crash. As an example, Yang et al. [16] report in their paper that the executed sample crashes 76% of the time. The reasons behind these crashes remain unknown. It could be the setup of the experiment that is not reliable with the studied sample, for example a bad version of the operating systems, missing libraries such as the Google services, etc. For defeating the static analysis, malware can introduce some artifact for disturbing disassembly tools such as apktool [9].

Consequently, in the last years, we proposed several tools for automatizing the static and dynamic analysis of Android malware [2,11]. Our intention is to perform the classical steps of an analyzer: CFG extraction from a static analysis, payload identification using an heuristic similar to DroidAPIMiner, computation of execution paths, including the path that can use callbacks of the framework, and finally dynamic execution with an automatic exploration of the graphical interface. Additionally, we provide fallback methodologies when a difficulty is encountered. For example, if the Manifest file cannot be decoded, we provide a generated minimalistic one for our tools being able to run. Another example is the ability of GroddDroid to change a branching condition to force the execution flow towards a suspicious part of the code not analyzed yet.

Nevertheless, a lot of problems still exist when processing large amount of malware. The next section gives an overview of the remaining challenges.

3   Next Upcoming Challenges

As explained before, building reliable datasets remain a difficult challenge. Additionally, in some countries, sharing malicious codes is forbidden by the law. Some samples can also contain piggybacked code from copyrighted benign applications. These difficulties should be addressed by international consortiums that would provide a safe infrastructure for sharing resources. Such an effort could also help on the dataset labeling i.e. by determining the payload location, malware's actions, etc.

Experiments are also limited by the devices themselves. As it is hazardous to run a malware in an emulator, with anti analysis techniques, most of authors run their experiment on a real smartphone with an eventually modified operating system. In such conditions, running a clean execution of a malware, including a smartphone flashing step, requires several minutes. If several environments or parameters have to be tested the total running time becomes prohibitive.

Finally, these ten years of research efforts are intimately linked with Google's roadmap. In the near future, introducing a new operating system like Fuschia can lead to the restart of many results, at the price of few novelty. In the meantime, the ecosystems that Google try to promote has received few attention from the research community. For example, Android automotive, Wear OS has not being extensively studied and malware may exist on these platforms - if they don't already exist.

References

1. Aafer, Y., Du, W., Yin, H.: DroidAPIMiner: mining API-level features for robust malware detection in android. Secur. Privacy Commun. Netw. **127**, 86–103 (2013). https://doi.org/10.1007/978-3-319-04283-1_6
2. Abraham, A., Andriatsimandefitra, R., Brunelat, A., Lalande, J.F., Viet Triem Tong, V.: GroddDroid: a gorilla for triggering malicious behaviors. In: 2015 10th International Conference on Malicious and Unwanted Software, MALWARE 2015, Fajardo, Puerto Rico, pp. 119–127. IEEE Computer Society, October 2016. https://doi.org/10.1109/MALWARE.2015.7413692
3. Allix, K., Bissyandé, T.F., Klein, J., Le Traon, Y.: AndroZoo: collecting millions of Android apps for the research community. In: 13th International Workshop on Mining Software Repositories, Austin, USA, pp. 468–471. ACM Press, May 2016. https://doi.org/10.1145/2901739.2903508
4. Arzt, S., et al.: FlowDroid: precise context, flow, field, object-sensitive and lifecycle-aware taint analysis for android apps. In: ACM SIGPLAN Conference on Programming Language Design and Implementation, Edinburgh, UK, vol. 49, pp. 259–269. ACM Press, June 2014. https://doi.org/10.1145/2666356.2594299
5. Chen, K., et al.: Following devil's footprints: cross-platform analysis of potentially harmful libraries on Android and iOS. In: S&P (2016). https://doi.org/10.1109/SP.2016.29
6. Duan, Y., et al.: Things you may not know about android (un)packers: a systematic study based on whole-system emulation. In: 24th Annual Network and Distributed System Security Symposium, February 2018

7. Enck, W., et al.: TaintDroid: an information-flow tracking system for realtime privacy monitoring on smartphones. In: 9th USENIX Symposium on Operating Systems Design and Implementation, Vancouver, BC, Canada, pp. 393–407. USENIX Association, October 2010

8. Enck, W., Ongtang, M., Mcdaniel, P.: On Lightweight Mobile Phone Application Certification. Categories and Subject Descriptors (2009)

9. Kiss, N., Lalande, J.F., Leslous, M., Viet Triem Tong, V.: Kharon dataset: android malware under a microscope. In: The LASER Workshop: Learning from Authoritative Security Experiment Results, San Jose, United States, pp. 1–12. USENIX Association, May 2016

10. Lalande, J.F., Viêt Triem Tong, V., Leslous, M., Graux, P.: Challenges for reliable and large scale evaluation of android malware analysis. In: International Workshop on Security and High Performance Computing Systems, Orléans, France, pp. 1068–1070. IEEE Computer Society, July 2018. https://doi.org/10.1109/HPCS. 2018.00173

11. Leslous, M., Viet Triem Tong, V., Lalande, J.F., Genet, T.: GPFinder: tracking the invisible in android malware. In: 12th International Conference on Malicious and Unwanted Software, Fajardo, pp. 39–46. IEEE Conputer Society, October 2017. https://doi.org/10.1109/MALWARE.2017.8323955

12. Li, L., Meng, G., Klein, J., Malek, S. (eds.): 1st International Workshop on Advances in Mobile App Analysis, A-Mobile@ASE 2018, Montpellier, France, 4 September 2018. ACM Press (2018). https://doi.org/10.1145/3243218

13. Tam, K., Khan, S., Fattori, A., Cavallaro, L.: CopperDroid: automatic reconstruction of android malware behaviors. In: 22nd Annual Network and Distributed System Security Symposium, San Diego, California, USA. The Internet Society, February 2015

14. Wei, F., Li, Y., Roy, S., Ou, X., Zhou, W.: Deep ground truth analysis of current android malware. In: Polychronakis, M., Meier, M. (eds.) DIMVA 2017. LNCS, vol. 10327, pp. 252–276. Springer, Cham (2017). https://doi.org/10.1007/978-3-319-60876-1_12

15. Wong, M.Y., Lie, D.: IntelliDroid: a targeted input generator for the dynamic analysis of android malware. In: The Network and Distributed System Security Symposium, San Diego, USA, no. February, pp. 21–24. The Internet Society, February 2016. https://doi.org/10.14722/ndss.2016.23118

16. Yang, W., Kong, D., Xie, T., Gunter, C.A.: Malware detection in adversarial settings: exploiting feature evolutions and confusions in android apps. In: 33rd Annual Computer Security Applications Conference, Orlando, FL, USA, 4–8 December 2017, pp. 288–302 (2017). https://doi.org/10.1145/3134600.3134642

17. Zhou, Y., Jiang, X.: Dissecting android malware: characterization and evolution. In: IEEE Symposium on Security and Privacy, San Jose, USA, no. 4, pp. 95–109. IEEE Computer Society, May 2012. https://doi.org/10.1109/SP.2012.16

Post-quantum Cryptography and a (Qu)Bit More

Diana Maimuţ[1]([✉])[iD] and Emil Simion[1,2]

[1] Advanced Technologies Institute, Bucharest, Romania
`diana.maimut@dcti.ro`
[2] Politehnica University of Bucharest, Bucharest, Romania
`emil.simion@upb.ro`

Abstract. Probabilities govern our day to day lives. Undoubtedly, we construct many of our judgments based on assumptions. A scientific example is the case of public-key encryption, where hardness assumptions are the main ingredient of provable security. But, while such clever mathematical ideas mesmerized both researchers and users since the 1970's, a rather new assumption shakes the cryptographic world: the eventual construction of quantum computers. In this article, we provide the reader with a comprehensive overview regarding *post-quantum cryptography*. Compared to other well established surveys which underline the importance of designing post-quantum public-key cryptographic algorithms, we stress that symmetric key cryptography should receive the same amount of attention from the scientific community.

Keywords: Post-quantum cryptography · Quantum cryptography · Quantum computer · Quantum bit · Quantum cryptanalysis

1 Introduction

Probabilities govern our day to day lives. Undoubtedly, we construct many of our judgments based on assumptions. A scientific example is the case of public-key encryption, where hardness assumptions are the main ingredient of provable security. But, while such clever mathematical ideas mesmerized both researchers and users since the 1970's, a rather new assumption shakes the cryptographic world: the eventual construction of quantum computers.

Nonetheless, cryptography can be considered *antifragile*[1]: it usually benefits from cryptanalitic shocks [29]. A modern example may be considered *post-quantum cryptography* which started being established based on the fact that quantum computers will eventually become reality. *Post-quantum cryptography* or *quantum safe cryptography* represents a class of cryptographic algorithms which resists quantum attacks by design.

---

[1] For a detailed explanation of the concept the reader may refer to [33].

© Springer Nature Switzerland AG 2019
J.-L. Lanet and C. Toma (Eds.): SecITC 2018, LNCS 11359, pp. 22–28, 2019.
https://doi.org/10.1007/978-3-030-12942-2_3

1.1 The Current State of Quantum Computers

Classical computers operate on bits which are either 0 or 1. On the other side, quantum computers work with quantum bits (*qubits*) which can be both 0 and 1 at the same time[2] [11]. The construction of quantum computers currently faces two main issues: the lack of stability[3] and the small number of qubits[4]. Considering these problems solved, quantum computers could be widely adopted in 10 to 15 years from now. Security expert Baloo mentions that "some claim that a quantum computer with only 256 qubits could destroy the basis for all modern day encryption methods" [1]. Driving along the road to quantum supremacy, IBM launched its quantum cloud-based playground platform[5] *IBM Q Experience* [4] in 2016. Subsequently, IBM announced a 50-qubit quantum computer[6] in 2017, while Intel presented its 49-qubit chip (early 2018). In response to previous results, Google announced its 72-qubit processor (Bristlecone) at the beginning of 2018.

1.2 Quantum Computing and Cryptology

Quantum computing was proposed back in 1981 by Feynman [24]. He suggested the use of quantum mechanics for constructing an outstanding computer in terms of system architecture and performance. The importance of Feynman's exceptional idea for cryptography was perceived only twelve years later by Bernstein and Vazirani [17]. As a follow up of Simon's research presented in [40], Shor underlined in 1994 [39] that the emergence of quantum computers will threaten the very existence of public-key cryptography: currently hard instantiations of factoring and discrete logarithm problems would become efficient to solve. Another study was presented by Grover in 1996: the *quantum database search algorithm* [26].

As a direct consequence, post-quantum cryptography was suggested [16]. During the last few years, the National Institute for Standards and Technology (NIST) started showing interest in the standardization of quantum resistant cryptography and sponsored several related workshops. NSA's Information Assurance Directorate announced the beginning of the transition to quantum safe cryptography in 2015. In the same sense, the European Union funded two post-quantum cryptography projects: PQCrypto [5] and SAFEcrypto [6]. Furthermore, NIST started a competition for establishing quantum resistant cryptographic algorithms in 2016 [2].

1.2.1 Quantum Speed-Ups

Sometimes, a problem can be solved faster by a quantum computer than by a classical one. Such a process is denoted in the literature as *quantum speed-up*. The

---

[2] A state denoted as superposition.

[3] Quantum error correction and fault tolerant computations are targeted.

[4] For all practical purposes.

[5] 5 qubits.

[6] Which can maintain its quantum state for 90 μs.

most interesting class of speed-ups is represented by *exponential speed-ups* which happen when a problem taking an exponential amount of time on a classical computer can be performed with polynomial complexity on a quantum computer. In terms of speed-ups, the performance of Grover's algorithm is not as good as Shor's. However, being generic, Grover's method can be applied to a diversity of other problems (*e.g.* quantum attacks on symmetric key cryptosystems).

2   Post-quantum Cryptography

Besides proposing and analyzing new quantum resistant algorithms, researchers' goal was to increase the efficiency of already established schemes. We further discuss several public-key quantum resistant classes of algorithms (lattice-based, error correction code-based, multivariate quadratic equations-based, isogeny-based, keyless primitive-based[7]) as well as symmetric key primitives which are believed to be quantum safe.

2.1   Public-Key Cryptography

2.1.1   Lattice-Based Cryptography

Security assumptions of lattice-based cryptosystems are directly linked to the hardness of basis reduction and other related problems in random lattices [38]. Constructing on Ajtai's seminal work [7], Ajtai and Dwork [8] presented a provably secure cryptosystem under the assumption that a certain lattice problem is difficult in the worst-case. Nguyen and Stern have shown that the Ajtai-Dwork cryptosystem is only of theoretical interest [35]. Other public key lattice-based primitives that caught cryptographers' attention are the NTRU (Hoffstein–Pipher–Silverman) cryptosystem [27] and the signature scheme denoted as BLISS (Bimodal Lattice Signature Scheme) [3]. The attempts to solve lattice problems by quantum algorithms have had little success. The periodicity finding technique[8] [36] used by Shor's quantum factoring and other related algorithms may not be applicable to lattice problems. Nevertheless, lattice-based cryptography may still be prone to implementation attacks (*e.g.* side channel [19]).

2.1.2   Error Correction Code-Based Cryptography

McEliece described the first error-correction based cryptosystem in 1978 [31]. Its security is based on the hardness of decoding random linear error-correcting codes. Finding a codeword of given weight in a linear binary code is an $\mathcal{NP}$-complete problem [13]. As the initial parameters of the McEliece cryptosystem were broken by Bernstein et al., new secure parameters were proposed [15].

---

[7] *I.e.* hash-based.

[8] Periodicity finding is mainly based on quantum computers' capability of being in many states at the same time: to compute a function's period the device evaluates the function at all points simultaneously.

2.1.3   Multivariate Quadratic Equations (MQE)-Based Cryptography

MQE-based cryptosystems rely their security on the conjectured hardness of solving some polynomial equations systems[9]. Matsumoto and Imai proposed an inspiring construction called C* in 1988 [30]. Their results were preceded by other early studies, *e.g.* the one of [22]. A popular MQE cryptographic scheme entitled Hidden Fields Equations (HFE) was described by Patarin in 1996 [37]. Although the original HFE was broken, several of its variants are still standing.

2.1.4   Supersingular Elliptic Curve Isogeny-Based Cryptography

The security of isogeny-based cryptographic algorithms is related to the problem of constructing an isogeny between two supersingular curves with the same number of points [21]. Isogeny-based cryptographic schemes may be considered natural quantum safe replacements for the Diffie-Hellman and elliptic curve Diffie-Hellman key exchange protocols. An already well known isogeny-based protocol is the Supersingular Isogeny Diffie-Hellman (SIDH) [23].

2.2   Keyless Primitives: Hash-Based Cryptography

Merkle proposed a quantum-resistant hash-based signature scheme [32] in 1979. Unfortunately, the suggested scheme is stateful: the signer must keep a state (history record) that evolves as messages are being signed. Bernstein et al. presented stateless hash-based signatures in [14].

2.3   Symmetric Cryptography

Quantum Myths. The cryptographic community usually claims that the impact of quantum computing on symmetric key algorithms is way smaller than the consequences it brings to public key cryptographic schemes.

The typical example considered in this case by the crypto community is the block cipher AES [20]. If Grover's algorithm [26] can be used to speed up brute-force attacks against symmetric ciphers and collision-resistant hash functions, it was shown [12] that an ℓ-bit key provides $\frac{\ell}{2}$ bits of quantum security. Therefore, in a world equipped with stable quantum computers based on enough qubits, AES-256 would still offer 128 bits of security.

New Quantum Attacks. Other powerful quantum attack models which threaten the security of symmetric cryptography primitives started being studied[10] [25,28,34]: quantum generic meet-in-the-middle attacks on iterative block ciphers, quantum linear and differential attacks, improved algorithms for collisions or multicollisions. Various ways to overcome these difficulties in designing

---

[9] Put differently, the hard problem is to determine whether a system of MQEs has a solution over a field.

[10] Applications of Simon's and Kuperberg's algorithms.

post-quantum symmetric cryptography algorithms were described in [10]. The proposed changes were shown to be rather inefficient in terms of speed and data amount [18,34].

3   Conclusions and Research Directions

Much effort has to be spent by cryptographers for establishing realistic attack models in the modern quantum context. Adapting classical security definitions for encryption and authentication is one of the main goals of the (post-)quantum cryptography community. Progress has been made with respect to understanding the technical differences between security concepts in classical computational models and quantum computing models [9].

References

1. http://quantumbusiness.org/secure-communications-in-the-post-quantum-era-conversation-with-jaya-baloo-from-kpn
2. https://csrc.nist.gov/Projects/Post-Quantum-Cryptography
3. BLISS. http://bliss.di.ens.fr/
4. IBM Q Experience. https://quantumexperience.ng.bluemix.net/qx/experience
5. PQCrypto. https://cordis.europa.eu/project/rcn/194347_en.html
6. SAFEcrypto. www.safecrypto.eu
7. Ajtai, M.A.: Generating hard instances of lattice problems (extended abstract). In: Proceedings of the 28th Annual ACM Symposium on Theory of Computing. STOC 1996, pp. 99–108. ACM (1996)
8. Ajtai, M.A., Dwork, C.: A public-key cryptosystem with worst-case/average-case equivalence. In: Proceedings of the 29th Annual ACM Symposium on Theory of Computing. STOC 1997, pp. 284–293. ACM (1997)
9. Alagic, G., Gagliardoni, T., Majenz, C.: Unforgeable quantum encryption. In: Nielsen, J.B., Rijmen, V. (eds.) EUROCRYPT 2018. LNCS, vol. 10822, pp. 489–519. Springer, Cham (2018). https://doi.org/10.1007/978-3-319-78372-7_16
10. Alagic, G., Russell, A.: Quantum-secure symmetric-key cryptography based on hidden shifts. In: Coron, J.-S., Nielsen, J.B. (eds.) EUROCRYPT 2017. LNCS, vol. 10212, pp. 65–93. Springer, Cham (2017). https://doi.org/10.1007/978-3-319-56617-7_3
11. Aumasson, J.P.: Serious Cryptography: A Practical Introduction to Modern Encryption. No Starch Press, San Francisco (2017)
12. Bennett, C.H., Bernstein, E., Brassard, G., Vazirani, U.: Strengths and weaknesses of quantum computing. SIAM J. Comput. **26**(5), 1510–1523 (1997)
13. Berlekamp, E., McEliece, R., van Tilborg, H.: On the inherent intractability of certain coding problems (Corresp.). IEEE Trans. Inf. Theory **24**(3), 384–386 (2006)
14. Bernstein, D.J., et al.: SPHINCS: practical stateless hash-based signatures. In: Oswald, E., Fischlin, M. (eds.) EUROCRYPT 2015. LNCS, vol. 9056, pp. 368–397. Springer, Heidelberg (2015). https://doi.org/10.1007/978-3-662-46800-5_15
15. Bernstein, D.J., Lange, T., Peters, C.: Attacking and defending the McEliece cryptosystem. In: Buchmann, J., Ding, J. (eds.) PQCrypto 2008. LNCS, vol. 5299, pp. 31–46. Springer, Heidelberg (2008). https://doi.org/10.1007/978-3-540-88403-3_3

16. Bernstein, D.J.: Introduction to post-quantum Cryptography. In: Bernstein, D.J., Buchmann, J., Dahmen, E. (eds.) Post-Quantum Cryptography, pp. 1–14. Springer, Heidelberg (2009). https://doi.org/10.1007/978-3-540-88702-7_1

17. Bernstein, E., Vazirani, U.: Quantum complexity theory. In: Proceedings of the 25th Annual ACM Symposium on Theory of Computing, pp. 11–20. ACM (1993)

18. Bonnetain, X., Naya-Plasencia, M.: Hidden shift quantum cryptanalysis and implications. In: Peyrin, T., Galbraith, S. (eds.) ASIACRYPT 2018. LNCS, vol. 11272, pp. 560–592. Springer, Cham (2018). https://doi.org/10.1007/978-3-030-03326-2_19

19. Bruinderink, L.G., Hülsing, A., Lange, T., Yarom, Y.: Flush, gauss, and reload - a cache attack on the BLISS lattice-based signature scheme (2016). https://eprint.iacr.org/2016/300

20. Daemen, J., Rijmen, V.: The Design of Rijndael: AES - The Advanced Encryption Standard. Springer, Heidelberg (2002). https://doi.org/10.1007/978-3-662-04722-4

21. Delfs, C., Galbraith, S.D.: Computing isogenies between supersingular elliptic curves over $\mathbb{F}_p$. Des. Codes Crypt. **78**(2), 425–440 (2016)

22. Fell, H., Diffie, W.: Analysis of a public key approach based on polynomial substitution. In: Williams, H.C. (ed.) CRYPTO 1985. LNCS, vol. 218, pp. 340–349. Springer, Heidelberg (1986). https://doi.org/10.1007/3-540-39799-X_24

23. Feo, L.D., Jao, D., Plût, J.: Towards quantum-resistant cryptosystems from supersingular elliptic curve isogenies. https://eprint.iacr.org/2011/506

24. Feynman, R.P.: Simulating physics with computers. Int. J. Theor. Phys. **21**(6/7), 467–488 (1982)

25. Gagliardoni, T.: Quantum security of cryptographic primitives. Ph.D. thesis, Technische Universität Darmstadt (2017)

26. Grover, L.K.: A fast quantum mechanical algorithm for database search. In: Proceedings of the 28th Annual ACM Symposium on Theory of Computing - STOC 1996, pp. 212–219. ACM (1996)

27. Hoffstein, J., Pipher, J., Silverman, J.H.: NTRU: a ring-based public key cryptosystem. In: Buhler, J.P. (ed.) ANTS 1998. LNCS, vol. 1423, pp. 267–288. Springer, Heidelberg (1998). https://doi.org/10.1007/BFb0054868

28. Kaplan, M., Leurent, G., Leverrier, A., Naya-Plasencia, M.: Breaking symmetric cryptosystems using quantum period finding. In: Robshaw, M., Katz, J. (eds.) CRYPTO 2016. LNCS, vol. 9815, pp. 207–237. Springer, Heidelberg (2016). https://doi.org/10.1007/978-3-662-53008-5_8

29. Maimuţ, D.: Antifragilitatea: o nouă strategie în securitatea informaţiei. Ştiinţă & Tehnică **76**, 34–35 (2018)

30. Matsumoto, T., Imai, H.: Public quadratic polynomial-tuples for efficient signature-verification and message-encryption. In: Barstow, D., et al. (eds.) EUROCRYPT 1988. LNCS, vol. 330, pp. 419–453. Springer, Heidelberg (1988). https://doi.org/10.1007/3-540-45961-8_39

31. McEliece, R.J.: A public-key cryptosystem based on algebraic coding theory. DSN Prog. Rep. **42**(44), 114–116 (1978)

32. Merkle, R.C.: Secrecy, authentication, and public key systems. Ph.D. thesis (1979)

33. Nassim, N.T.: Antifragile: Things That Gain from Disorder. Random House, New York City (2012)

34. Naya-Plasencia, M.: Symmetric cryptography for long-term security. Habilitation thesis, Pierre et Marie Curie Université (2017)

35. Nguyen, P., Stern, J.: Cryptanalysis of the ajtai-dwork cryptosystem. In: Krawczyk, H. (ed.) CRYPTO 1998. LNCS, vol. 1462, pp. 223–242. Springer, Heidelberg (1998). https://doi.org/10.1007/BFb0055731

36. Nielsen, M.A., Chuang, I.L.: Quantum Computation and Quantum Information: 10th Anniversary Edition, 10th edn. Cambridge University Press, Cambridge (2011)

37. Patarin, J.: Hidden fields equations (HFE) and isomorphisms of polynomials (IP): two new families of asymmetric algorithms. In: Maurer, U. (ed.) EUROCRYPT 1996. LNCS, vol. 1070, pp. 33–48. Springer, Heidelberg (1996). https://doi.org/10.1007/3-540-68339-9_4

38. Regev, O.: Lattice-based cryptography. In: Dwork, C. (ed.) CRYPTO 2006. LNCS, vol. 4117, pp. 131–141. Springer, Heidelberg (2006). https://doi.org/10.1007/11818175_8

39. Shor, P.W.: Polynomial-time algorithms for prime factorization and discrete logarithms on a quantum computer. SIAM J. Comput. 26(5), 1484–1509 (1997)

40. Simon, D.R.: On the power of quantum computation. In: FOCS 1994, pp. 116–123. IEEE Computer Society (1994)

Normalization of *Java* Source Codes

Léopold Ouairy[1(✉)], Hélène Le-Bouder[2], and Jean-Louis Lanet[1]

[1] INRIA, Rennes, France
{leopold.ouairy,jean-louis.lanet}@inria.fr
[2] IMT-Atlantique, Rennes, France
helene.le-bouder@imt-atlantique.fr

Abstract. Security issues can be leveraged when input parameters are not checked. These missing checks can lead an application to an unexpected state where an attacker can get access to assets. The tool *Chucky-ng* aims at detecting such missing checks in source code. Such source codes are the only input required for *ChuckyJava*. Since it is sensible to the identifier names used in these source codes, we want to normalize them in order to improve its efficiency. To achieve this, we propose an algorithm which works in four steps. It renames constant, parameter, variable and method names. We evaluate the impact of this renaming on two different experiments. Since our results are concluding, we show the benefits of using our tool. Moreover, we suggest another new way to improve *Chucky-ng*.

Keywords: Applet security · Identifier renaming · Chucky-ng · Java Card

1 Introduction

An applet is a program embedded on *Java Cards*. Such applets contain secrets. Attackers can steal such secrets by exploiting wrong implementations of specifications. To do so, they try a fuzzing attack on the applet. This attack consists in sending many different messages to the card via the *Application Protocol Data Unit (APDU)* communication buffer. This *APDU* enables terminals to communicate with cards and vice versa. With this attack, attackers can detect and then exploit the wrong state machine of an applet. This exploit can lead the attackers to illegally obtain access to secret resources. This is possible if an applet omit to implement a check in a critical state, whereas the specification precises that such check shall be implemented. We want to protect applets by detecting those *missing-checks* in their source codes. Since applets are written in a subset of the *Java* language, we base our work on a version of *Chucky-ng* [3,8] adapted for *Java* source files. This version is entitled *ChuckyJava* and it directly works on source codes without the need to modify or annotate them. Such tool aims at detecting the *missing-checks* in applets by outputing an anomaly score between 1.00 and −1.00. If this anomaly score is 1.00, the applet forgets to perform a test. On the contrary, if the anomaly score is −1.00, then the applet is the only

© Springer Nature Switzerland AG 2019
J.-L. Lanet and C. Toma (Eds.): SecITC 2018, LNCS 11359, pp. 29–40, 2019.
https://doi.org/10.1007/978-3-030-12942-2_4

one to perform a test. Since there are false positives, an analyst is required in order to interpret *ChuckyJava*'s results.

We want to improve *ChuckyJava* by reducing the false positive rate and the entries of its report to analyze. Since it works with identifier names of constants, variables, parameters and methods, our idea is to normalize every identifier of an applet set. We suggest an algorithm to achieve this task and we need to develop the tool *IdentNormalize*. Such modifications can be adapted to other programming languages. However, our study focuses on *Java Card* applets. To benchmark our idea, we manually apply the modifications we recommend in the applet set. Then, we perform an analysis with *ChuckyJava* to verify if our idea improves the tool efficiency. Because our modifications are concluding, we suggest another idea to increase the *ChuckyJava* efficiency.

The context and state of the art are shown in Sect. 2. Our contribution is presented in Sect. 3. The results are explained in Sect. 4. Our future work is shown in Sect. 5. To finish, we conclude on our improvement in Sect. 6.

2   Context and State of the Art

2.1   How *Chucky-ng* Operates

Chucky-ng's objective is to detect wrong implementations of source codes. To do so, it first parses source code within a project. Then the analyst chooses a function to process. *Chucky-ng* groups similar functions to the one selected. Finally, it compares this group by giving an anomaly score for every expression existing in the function set. This anomaly score's range is $[-1.00, 1.00]$. An anomaly score of -1.00 informs the analyst that the function executes an expression where none of the other do. On the opposite, a function with an anomaly score of 1.00 does not execute an expression whereas the others do. These expression are sensible to the name of identifiers. Two expressions not using the same identifier are flagged as not similar, even if the functions are semantically identical. *ChuckyJava* [4] is based on *Chucky-ng* but parses *Java* files instead of *C/C++*. Moreover, we use a layer above *ChuckyJava*: *FetchVuln*. This last one automates *ChuckyJava* by requesting an analysis for every methods of the file. It reports the vulnerable methods, according to *ChuckyJava* in a single output file.

2.2   Tool Requirements

This section highlights the necessity for us to design a normalization tool. It has to normalize the variable, constant, parameter and methods names.

Identifier Names. A specification of a *Java Card* applet precises the commands to implement and the expected behavior of an applet once it receives the command. Since *ChuckyJava* works partly with identifiers, it would work optimized if every applet implementing a specification uses the exact same identifiers for constants, fields and parameter names. However, our work shows two applets which implement the *OpenPGP 2.0.1* specification can use really different identifiers. For example, the command *PUT- _DATA* is named *SET_DATA* in another applet. Even if both names have the same meaning, they are completely different for *ChuckyJava*. It would warn the user for an anomaly which is a false positive. Our tool has to rename such constants as either *PUT_DATA* or *SET_DATA*.

Method Names. Our tool has to normalize method names too. In *ChuckyJava*, there is a step where the tool gathers similar methods, using an unsupervised machine learning algorithm. The authors of *Chucky-ng*, the base of *ChuckyJava*, rely on a similarity of method names during its *neighborhood discovery* step. This step focuses on gathering the most similar methods (neighbors) within applet source codes, by using information retrieval techniques. Added to the *cosine distance* metric used, a distance reward bonus is added if the *Jaccard* distance between two method names are similar. The *Jaccard* distance measures the dissimilarity between two sets or two strings in our case. If the distance is closer to zero, then the strings are identical. On the opposite, if the distance is one, the strings have nothing in common. In our case, if they are not similar, a distance penalty is added to the method. As an example we have three methods *putData*. One of them forget to use a particular object of a meaningful type. *ChuckyJava* would not gather it as similar functions of *putData*, or even include a *getData* function. It would generate a lot of false positive. To prevent this, we want to force the gather of functions using the same names in order to compare methods implementing the same commands.

2.3 State of the Art

There are different techniques or tools that aims at normalizing methods names in source codes. *INFOX* [9] is a tool that aims at tracking forks for a project on *github*. It then extracts features and clusters code snippets in order to highlight similar code.

Another approach is based on word study within methods [6]. The authors have based their work on different methods to analyze the similarity of their semantics. It can be achieved by using a *WordNet* object structure to organize the words. This structure organizes the words in a hierarchical way. Based on this, one can use a similarity measure such as the *Lowest Common Subsumer* (*LCS*) to determine if two words are related. Another technique uses the definition of words to determine if a pair of word is similar. This last one is called glossed based technique. However, the authors conclude by precising that none of the tools seem to perform well and require improvements.

The paper [2] uses *Latent Semantic Indexing* (*LSI*). This technique groups term frequencies of documents in matrices. The tool works by gathering similar vocabulary words from comments and identifier names. The technique is to firstly retrieve information within source codes. Then, it is able to cluster the code snippets and label them. The analyst gets a comprehensive view of the code snippet topics, without needing to search in it a particular information.

This plugin for the *Microsoft's Phoenix* framework [7] enables an analyst to detect clone detection. It is based on techniques to detect biological identical *ADN* sequences to search for perfect matches. It works by using suffix trees (*AST*) and uses identifier names. It creates *AST* of functions and compares them. There are other plagiarism detection techniques available on the internet to discover clones of code.

The Requirements of Our Tool. The tool which clusters topics by extracting words from comments and identifier could fit to our prototype. In a future work, we have to adapt it for working with methods as the base unit. This could be possible since applets in general are production ones. In other words, their source code should be clean and commented in most of the cases. The *Phoenix*'s plugin could match our requirements. It works only with perfect matches. However, the authors claim that for near exact matches, we should use the *Smith-Waterman* [1] algorithm. It uses matrices to determine the similarity of code snippets.

3 Contribution

We have considered the *Latent Semantic Analysis* (*LSA*) approach for the method normalization step. However, such method is based on similarity and its results may not be always be true. For the rest, we have made the choice to rename identifiers by deducing the ones which fit almost every applet of the set. The tool works in four steps we develop:

1. remove of unused variables,
2. constant and field names normalization,
3. method names normalization,
4. parameter names normalization.

1. Remove Unused Variables. This step aims at removing unused variables. We work mainly on production applets. Some of them do not have any. However, it eliminates some useless output of *ChuckyJava*.

2. Constant and Field Names Normalization. IdentNormalizer tries to rename common constants within applet source codes. In most cases in specification implementation, the *short* constants defined at the beginning of the applets is the value of a specific command. This value may be unique. For example, the command *CHANGE_REFERENCE _DATA* has a value of *0x24* for its instruction byte. As it is declared once in an applet, we have a first step of comparison between constants of this value. We randomly choose the name for this constant by selecting a name in an applet and assigning it to the others. For constants using the same value at least twice in the source code should have different semantics, we prefer to not modify the names. We could replace all constants with their real values. However, *Chucky-ng* normalizes values as *$NUM*. For example, a *case 0x20* and a *case 0x30* would be transformed as *case $NUM*. By doing this, we would lose a lot of information. The tool normalizes the fields names too. For example, in the *OpenPGP* specification, there are three different *passwords* or *card holder verifications* which are *OwnerPin* objects. Some of them can be renamed as *ch1* or *pw1*. The trick here is to rename the identifiers by deducing their relations based on the object type *OwnerPin*. This technique renames identifiers regardless of any specification.

3. Method Names Normalization. It is not trivial to find which methods are similar. One way to gather similar methods is to analyze their name with the *Jaccard* distance. However, if two functions are semantically identical but use different names, they would not be flagged as similar. If two names are similar but semantically different such as *setData* and *getData*, then they could be flagged as similar, even if they do not have the same objective. We want to compare functions with the same objective together. One way to solve our problem is to use information retrieval techniques (*IR*). It is possible to rely on latent semantic indexing or analysis (*LSI, LSA*) on source code and comments to extract the main topic of methods. Kuhn *et al.* [2] propose a technique entitled *Semantic Clustering*. It is based on both *LSI* and clustering. The information retrieval step extracts identifier names and comments from the source code. Then, a clustering method gathers code snippets of similar topics. With this technique, it is possible to group similar functions together in sets of topics in order to rename those methods. However, since this technique is based on statistics, it could contain classification errors.

4. Parameter Names Normalization. At this point, the method names are normalized. This is an essential condition since we want to normalize parameter names. Even if function can use a different number of parameters, we rename the one that are used by every similar method names together. This is based on the type name. However, two functions can use twice the same type of object as parameter. In this case, within the function, it is possible to gather in a set the methods used by the first parameter and in another set the ones using the second parameter. By comparing those sets, it should be possible to determine if two are similar and should be renamed the same way. If the sets are identical, we suggest to leave the parameters names unchanged.

Summary of the Operation. Our tool *IdentNormalize* can be summed up as shown in Algorithm 1. It performs with a complexity of $O(2n)$ with n, the total number of files for all applets. However, the step of method names normalization may be more complex than $O(2n)$. The complexity of the tool depend on the *LSI* method's complexity.

Appendix A shows two different code snippets as S_1. Since they are semantically identical, our tool produces either two identical Appendix A.1 or two Appendix A.2 as S_1'. Only the class name remains unchanged.

Algorithm 1. How *IdentNormalizer* operates

Data: source codes of applets S_1
Result: The applet modified S_1'
forall the $s_1 \in S_1$ **do**
   | remove of unused variables;
   | constant and field names normalization;
end
$V_1 :=$ methods normalization names list;
forall the $s_1 \in S_1'$ **do**
   | method names normalization based on V_1;
   | parameter names normalization;
end

---

4 Results

4.1 Description of the Experiments

We have divided the experiments in two different sets. The first is experimented in a controlled environment. It contains one-file applets which perform a match-on-card algorithm. They have a similar structure and nearly the same number of methods. On the contrary, the second set is composed of four applets coming from different *github* sources. All of them implement the *OpenPGP v.2.0.1* specification [5]. However, their structure can be different and may interpret commands of the *APDU* in different ways. For each experiment, we present the result of *ChuckyJava* before and after the normalization method. Moreover, we compare only the results for the anomaly scores of -1.00 and 1.00. The reason behind this decision is because those numbers are the priority to focus on for an analyst.

4.2 Controlled Environment Experimentation

This set gathers eleven applets which were designed by students. Every applet is written within a single file. All of these applets are constructed with globally the same program structure. It focuses on the importance of the identifier normalization. From this set, we have divided the experiment in two experiments. We first perform a *ChuckyJava* analysis on the applets without any modification. Then, we apply our renaming algorithm on the set. We operate a second analysis

Table 1. Number of entries to analyse between the original set and the new one

	Number of entries for -1.00	Number of entries for 1.00
Original set	909	121
Improved set	726	151

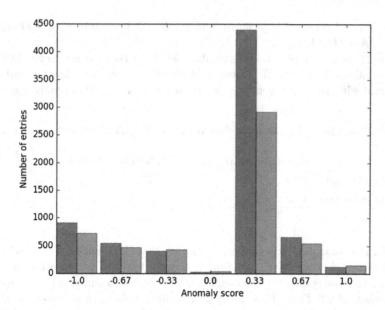

Fig. 1. The original set is on the left while the bar on the right represent the impact of *IdentNormalizer* in a controlled applet set

on this new set. We present the impact of such a renaming tool on *ChuckyJava* by comparing before and after our renaming step as shown in Table 1. This same table shows only the results we have obtained for the anomaly scores −1.00 and 1.00. However, Fig. 1. shows the values we get before and after renaming the identifiers for a few anomaly scores.

We can see that the number of entries for the anomaly score −1.00 decreases on our custom set. However, it increases for the 1.00 anomaly score. After analysing at the results, it is because we have now the entries as anomalies for the *tests/cases* of *switches*. Such entries are lines which *ChuckyJava* reports to the analyst. Each line precises the anomaly score, the expression associated to this score and the location of the expression in its *Java* file. It adds a benefit for using a normalization tool.

Conclusion. *IdentNormalizer* has reduced the entries to analyze manually of roughly 15%. It corresponds to a decrease of 153 entries. This score can be obtained as the top performance because this set only focuses on the importance of the identifiers since the applet's structures have minor differences.

4.3 Second Experimentation

We have gathered four applets implementing the *OpenPGP v2.0.1* specification. None of these applets come from the same author and have both different identifier names and program structures. Our applet set is composed of $MyPGPid^1$, $OpenPGPApplet^2$, $JCOpenPGP^3$, Gpg^4.

Figure 2 shows the result we have obtained from the first set to the last one which contains all the modifications. Table 2 summarizes the original number of results and with the improvements, for both −1.00 and 1.00 anomaly scores.

Table 2. Number of entries to analyse between the original set and the new one

	Number of entries for −1.00	Number of entries for 1.00
Original set	3769	255
Improved set	3443	351

As for the controlled experiment, we can see that the number of entries for the anomaly score *decreases* for the anomaly score −1.00 but increase for the 1.00. To summarize the result, we lose roughly 6% of entries to analyse. It corresponds to a decrease of 230 lines. This result may seem to be a bit low. However, this is mainly because *ChuckyJava* is really sensible to the program structure. Indeed,

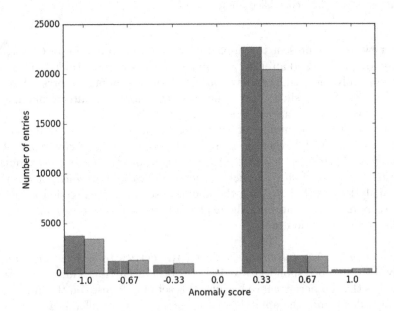

Fig. 2. The original set is on the left while the bar on the right represent the impact of *IdentNormalizer*, in a production applet set

---

[1] https://github.com/CSSHL/MyPGPid.

[2] https://github.com/Yubico/ykneo-openpgp.

[3] https://sourceforge.net/projects/jcopenpgp/.

[4] https://github.com/FluffyKaon/OpenPGP-Card.

it compares identifiers between applets to establish the anomaly score. However, since our applets are made from different authors and from different quality, we have concluded that the gain of 6% reflects the lower limit of this approach. For example, industrials may have structure pattern for the applets they implement, reducing the impact of such structure on the results of *ChuckyJava*.

5   Future Work

This section presents the future work which completes the identifier normalization problem. We have noticed three different structural problems. The first one concerns an assignation problem. The second one focuses on the order of instruction within the source code. The last one is about the optional functionalities which an implementation offers.

5.1   Assignation Type Problem

We are aware of several assignation type problem. For example, the vast majority of the applets creates three different variables *pw1*, *pw2* and *pw3* for the three different *OwnerPin(s)*. However, one applet has been designed to store them in an array of *OwnerPin*. When a method of *OwnerPin* is called, the identifier name of the array is used instead of one of the *pw*. Because of this, *ChuckyJava* generates false positives. It reports this applet with an anomaly score of 1.00 since it is the only one to use such an identifier. This creates one additional output every time the program uses this array.

5.2   Instructions Call Order

We are aware of a structural problem. Listing 1.1 shows a code snippet representing an applet using the *APDU* buffer as a field. Every time the applet receives a command, it first retrieves the *buffer* before calling the corresponding method. On the opposite, Listing 1.2 shows another applet retrieving the *APDU* buffer within each command method. However, even if those applets are semantically identical, they can be reported as anomaly. Because *ChuckyJava* analyzes methods as the base unit, it cannot see that the call to the *getBuffer* is made in another location in the source code. It adds additional false positive lines to the *ChuckyJava*'s report.

Listing 1.1. Snippet 1

```
byte[]  buffer = new byte[APDU_MAX_SIZE];
protected void process(APDU apdu) throws ISOException{
    buffer = apdu.getBuffer();
    switch(buffer[ISO7816.OFFSET_INS]){
        case VERIFY:
            verify(apdu);
            break;
        [...]
}
private void verify(APDU apdu){
    //Some code, using without calling the APDU
}
```

Listing 1.2. Snippet 2

```
protected void process(APDU apdu) throws ISOException{
    byte[] buffer = apdu.getBuffer();
    switch(buffer[ISO7816.OFFSET_INS]){
        case VERIFY:
            verify(apdu);
            break;
        [...]
}
private void verify(APDU apdu){
    byte[] buffer = apdu.getBuffer();
    //Some code, using the buffer
}
```

5.3   Optional Features

One last structure problem generating false positive is when a specification suggests optional features. As an example, the *OpenPGP v2.0.1* specification allows developers to use optional data objects (*DO*). If one applet decides to not implement them while the others do it, then the applet is flagged with many additional entries with an anomaly score of 1.00. On the opposite, if one option is implemented in only one applet, *ChuckyJava* generates entries with anomaly scores of −1.00. However, both the results are false positives since the implementation of the option is non mandatory.

6   Conclusion

We have developed *IdentNormalizer* which normalizes applet methods and identifiers names. It helps an analyst who uses *ChuckyJava* by reducing the number of entries between 6% to 15%. We have shown that the more the structure of an applet set is similar, the more *IdentNormalizer* is efficient. Our future work focuses mainly creating the tool that normalizes the identifiers. Moreover, we want to improve the efficiency of *ChuckyJava* by creating another tool which normalizes applet structures. As like *IdentNormalizer*, this new tool could be executed before performing an analysis with *ChuckyJava*.

A   Renaming example

A.1   Code snippet 1

```java
public static class Class01
{
        private final byte INS_VERIFY = (byte) 0x20;
        public void process(APDU apdu)
        {
                byte[] buffer = apdu.getBuffer();
                switch(buffer[ISO7816.OFFSET_INS])
                {
                        case INS_VERIFY:
                                verify(apdu);
                                break;
                        default:
                                ISOException.throwIt(ISO7816.SW_INS_NOT_SUPPORTED)
                                ↪ ;
                }
        }
}
```

A.2   Code snippet 2

```java
public static class Class02
{
        private final byte INSTRUCTION_VERIFIES = (byte) 0x20;
        public void process(APDU a)
        {
                byte[] apduBuffer = a.getBuffer();
                switch(buffer[ISO7816.OFFSET_INS])
                {
                        case INSTRUCTION_VERIFIES:
                                verify(a);
                                break;
                        default:
                                ISOException.throwIt(ISO7816.SW_INS_NOT_SUPPORTED)
                                ↪ ;
                }
        }
}
```

References

1. Greenan, K.: Method-level code clone detection on transformed abstract syntax trees using sequence matching algorithms (2005)
2. Kuhn, A., Ducasse, S., Girba, T.: Semantic clustering: Identifying topics in source code. Inf. Softw. Technol. **49**, 230–243 (2007)
3. Maier, A.: Assisted discovery of vulnerabilities in source code by analyzing program slices (2015)
4. Ouairy, L., Le-Bouder, H., Lanet, J.: Protection des systemes face aux attaques par fuzzing (2018)
5. Pietig, A.: Functional specification of the OpenPGP application on ISO smart card operating systems (2004)
6. Sridhara, G., Hill, E., Pollock, L., Vijay-Shanker, K.: Identifying word relations in software: a comparative study of semantic similarity tools (2008)
7. Tairas, R., Gray, J.: Phoenix-based clone detection using suffix trees (2006)

8. Yamaguchi, F., Wressnegger, C., Gascon, H., Rieck, K.: Chucky: exposing missing checks in source code for vulnerability discovery (2013)
9. Zhou, S., Stanciulescu, S., LeBenich, O., Xiong, Y., Wasowski, A., Kästner, C.: Identifying features in forks (2018)

HiddenApp - Securing Linux Applications Using ARM TrustZone

Veronica Velciu, Florin Stancu$^{(\boxtimes)}$, and Mihai Chiroiu

University POLITEHNICA of Bucharest, Bucharest, Romania
veronica.velciu@gmail.com, niflostancu@gmail.com, mihai.chiroiu@cs.pub.ro

Abstract. The security of an application depends not only on its design and programming, but also on the platform it runs on: the underlying Operating System and hardware. As today's systems get more and more complex, the probability of finding vulnerabilities increases and might compromise their security. In order to protect against this scenario, the idea of hardware-assisted trusted execution has appeared: technologies such as Intel SGX and ARM TrustZone promise to solve this by introducing additional checks inside the CPUs for specific resources to be accessible only by trusted programs running in isolated contexts. Our paper proposes a method to run unmodified GNU/Linux programs inside ARM TrustZone's secure domain, getting the trusted execution benefits while retaining accessibility of the OS's services (like file and network I/O) by using an automated system call proxying layer. We test that sample applications doing disk/network I/O can run unmodified, having only a small, constant latency overhead.

Keywords: Security · Trusted execution environment · ARM · TrustZone · SysCall · Proxying · Partitioning

1 Introduction

Technology has evolved at a fast pace lately: there is an increased interest in developing solutions to make our lives easier. This accelerated advancement also has some negative effects, as the data processed by these systems might be sensitive (e.g., the user's password). As the attack surface is getting larger, the number of potential attackers increases, so the security became of a greater concern.

The operating system (OS) is usually regarded as the reliable component of a software platform, charged with handling sensitive information: it provides mechanisms for protecting the data belonging to a program from the other processes running in the system. If an attacker finds an OS-level vulnerability, the security of all applications running on it is affected [11]. Because modern operating systems are often complex pieces of software, it is difficult to ensure their correctness and bugs are getting more and more common [12].

© Springer Nature Switzerland AG 2019
J.-L. Lanet and C. Toma (Eds.): SecITC 2018, LNCS 11359, pp. 41–52, 2019.
https://doi.org/10.1007/978-3-030-12942-2_5

To address this, hardware-based trusted execution technologies started to emerge [4], allowing programs to run in secure execution contexts, isolated even from the operating system, thus reducing the attack surface to just the platform and the application itself. Examples include Intel SGX Software Guard Extensions [9], AMD Platform Security Processor [1] and ARM TrustZone [8].

User space applications typically request operating system services through system calls, but the secure domain does not and should not contain one: developing even a minimal OS would require expanding the Trusted Computing Base (TCB) inside the isolated environment, leading to an increased probability of introducing bugs/vulnerabilities [13]. Furthermore, most of the operating system's features like disk and networking operations are processing untrusted input and do not belong to this isolated environment, since it would needlessly increase the attack surface [6].

Our work makes it possible to run existing applications inside the ARM TrustZone [8] secure environment. To do this, we developed a small microkernel that resides inside the secure domain, intercepts the system calls of the userspace programs running there and carefully proxies them over to the Rich OS, allowing them to run unmodified while maintaining its full feature set. As the source code does not require any changes, it offers an easy method for protecting an application from its operating system and minimizing the TCB.

For testing purposes, we took existing programs and tested them inside this trusted environment. We evaluate its performance by doing microbenchmarks of frequently-used system calls and comparing the proxied with the normal calls.

The paper is structured as follows: Sect. 2 offers some background on system calls and ARM TrustZone. Section 3 describes the security problem we are solving and thread model. Section 4 presents the architecture of or solution. Section 5 describes the implementation of our Linux-based prototype. Section 6 displays the evaluation results. Section 7 discusses some other published works related to ours. Finally, Sect. 8 concludes the paper.

2 Background

2.1 Userspace, Kernel and System Calls

Programs usually run inside the userspace, an unprivileged execution context designed to separate them from the other processes running on the machine. The operating system's kernel runs in a more privileged mode and fully controls process scheduling, memory allocation and access to the hardware peripherals.

Applications that wish to access privileged resources (e.g., process control, reading/writing files) must request those services from the underlying OS using a microprocessor-assisted system call.

On ARM CPUs, the user and kernel modes are separated using a Supervisor flag inside the processor's status register [7]. A program executing in userspace will have this flag cleared and has its access constrained to unprivileged resources only. When it needs a system service, it will issue a supervisor call (*svc*) instruction that switches the execution context to a privileged system call handler installed by the kernel. Parameters (such as the requested service, memory addresses etc.) may be passed before the call using the CPU registers.

During a system call, process execution is paused while the operating system works for the completion of the request, and a different process may be rescheduled (called preemption).

2.2   ARM TrustZone

ARM TrustZone [8] is a security extension for ARM microprocessors that introduces a trusted execution mode with hardware-protected regions where code and data are isolated from the normal operating system. The CPU's execution state may be in one of the following two domains: the Secure World, a higher privileged state which has access to the protected resources, and the Normal World, where the operating system and user applications will typically run. This mode is reflected by the NS (Non-Secure) bit inside a Secure Configuration Register (SCR). Both domains have User and Supervisor Modes, allowing for the implementation of a secure OS to manage multiple applications running inside the trusted environment. This architecture is illustrated in Fig. 1.

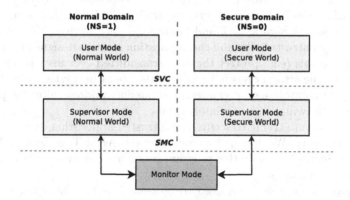

Fig. 1. TrustZone architecture

Changing between the two Worlds can be realized by using a new Secure Monitor Call instruction, or by using hardware exceptions (e.g. IRQ, FIQ) configured for that domain. Any of those methods will trigger a special exception handler in a Monitor Mode, which executes highly privileged code that can freely change the processor state between Trusted and Untrusted. The Monitor logic is implementation specific and is generally responsible for saving the current context (CPU registers, stack) and restoring the state to the new domain. This switching process is highly security sensitive and needs to have a small and rigorous implementation as to prevent exploits.

In order to support this separation, the processor's system and peripheral bus protocols received a supplementary bit, the NS (Non-Secure) flag, allowing the bus controllers to make authorization decisions based on it. Programs running inside the secure environment will have a private memory region, inaccessible from the Normal World by configuring TrustZone-aware bus controllers at boot time.

Another vital component is the TrustZone Aware Interrupt Controller. This adds new interrupt priority levels to implement secure transactions, protected against attacks from the Normal World.

Note that, while TrustZone may seem similar to a virtualization technology, it has a different purpose and interface, designed with security, simplicity and performance in mind. The virtual machine hypervisor must arbitrate shared hardware resource access such as physical memory and CPU cores, which translates to a software complexity that approaches that of typical operating systems, in opposition to the minimized TCB assumption of a trusted execution environment.

3   Problem Description

Our project provides a solution to secure a trusted application from a vulnerable Rich Operating System providing services required for its normal operation (for example, access to network, disk and human interface devices). These services are intrinsically untrustworthy and the application must be designed to be secure with regards to this (e.g., protect the data transmitted over insecure channels).

We assume the attacker has full access to the operating system kernel and all the resources it controls, e.g., it can read any memory address, alter the program execution flow at will, catch any interrupt etc.

The target we are trying to secure is the trusted application data's confidentiality and integrity. We do this by employing the ARM TrustZone technology described in Sect. 2 to isolate this program from the operating system (running it in the secure domain).

Normally, such applications need to be re-designed to be able to run in a trusted environment because they leverage on the operating system's services, and those and specific functionalities need to be ported/reimplemented inside the new environment. Nevertheless, doing this would increase the complexity of the Trusted Computing Base, defeating its purpose of being small and secure. Furthermore, many of the services required by the application are for handling untrusted data and have no need to be secured.

The correct solution would be to properly partition the program's code: fragments that handle confidential data need to be in the trusted domain, while the rest should remain in the unprivileged domain. However, this also requires extensive modifications of the program code, which is often unfeasible (e.g., for economic reasons).

Thus, we propose a solution that will make the usage of trusted execution environments more straightforward: implement a compatibility layer that makes it possible to run applications without any changes. The TCB will be greatly minimized from the exclusion of the Rich Operating System, and the developer can readily start to partition out the other insecure features.

For the security evaluation of our solution, we consider the hardware platform (ARM with Security Extensions) as trusted. The chip maker is assumed to have implemented proper safeguards against cache attacks, as documented inside the ARM development manual [7].

Another class of attacks possible on a trusted execution environment are Iago-type attacks [2]: the untrusted system call return values may be used to maliciously alter the control flow of the program, especially those used by memory management routines like *malloc()* that are returning addresses. This attack can be mitigated by implementing a firewall at the secure kernel level that validates the results and signals the errors. We chose another approach: by implementing all memory allocation functions as trusted services, as discussed in Sect. 4.

We note that denial of service attacks are out of scope in this paper: the Rich OS may refuse to respond to the supervisor calls (or even deny starting the program).

4   Architecture

Our system consists of two main components, each corresponding to one of the two security domains:

- the ***Trusted Microkernel*** that will supervise the applications running inside the Secure World, proxy their system calls to the insecure domain and check the results before sending them back to the program.
- the ***Untrusted Components***, running inside the Normal World and interfacing with the untrusted operating system to provide its services back to secure domain.

The **Trusted Microkernel** is a minimal operating system running inside the Secure World. When the machine first boots, it will be loaded first to securely initialize the TrustZone-aware memory bus and interrupt controllers and to install the Secure Monitor Code.

The physical memory is split in two segments: the first one is protected (only accessible from the trusted environment), while the remaining portion will be left to the Rich Operating System for managing. The Trusted Microkernel also reserves a couple of interrupts for its own use or for interception purposes, to be able to implement secure resource access (such as trusted input).

The microkernel will then boot the Rich Operating System (GNU/Linux) and wait for Secure Monitor Calls (SMC). These are issued for application loading requests, system call responses and resuming the trusted processes.

On the other side, the **Untrusted Components** integrates with the normal OS to schedule the processes, execute the system calls and send back the results. More specifically, those components are:

- the *Untrusted Application Wrapper*: for the operating system to be able to schedule the application and execute syscalls, it needs to have a corresponding process target; the wrapper is the program's counterpart that runs in the normal world and takes on this role;
- an *Untrusted Kernel Module*: since issuing a SMC requires supervisor privileges, the userspace programs are unable to communicate with the secure microkernel without help from the kernel; this is a minimalistic module that takes in requests from the userspace program (via Linux `ioctl` interface) and forwards them to the Secure World.

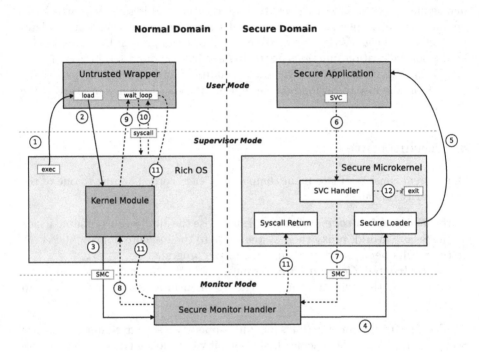

Fig. 2. The execution flow for secure applications

A typical execution flow is illustrated in Fig. 2:

1. The user opens the secure application: it will actually run the Wrapper executable in the untrusted domain, which includes the code and signature of the trusted program.
2. The Wrapper will send a program load request to the Secure Microkernel, indirectly, using the Untrusted Kernel Module.
3. The kernel module will copy the request packet to the Secure World shared memory region and run the SMC instruction.
4. The Secure Monitor saves the normal context, prepares the registers and stack for the secure microkernel and jumps to a service handler.

5. The microkernel parses the request, verifies the digitally signed code for the trusted application, sets up the user mode virtual memory structures to the secure regions and loads it then runs it.
6. When the applications needs to do a normal system call, it will setup the parameters on the registers/stack then call the SVC instruction.
7. The CPU then executes the trusted microkernel's Supervisor Call handler, which needs to analyze the system call, marshal its data to a RPC packet then do a SMC call.
8. The Monitor software does its context switching back to the untrusted kernel.
9. Our kernel module will detect a new request packet and schedule the wrapper for execution.
10. The wrapper program will read the packet and do the requested service call from the normal OS.
11. When this returns, it will encapsulate it in a response packet and sends it back through the Monitor, then to the microkernel and, finally, back the Secure Application.
12. This process (steps 6–11) may continue until the Secure Application issues an exit() call, which will free all resources from both Secure World and Normal World.

As we've seen, the wrapper is a normal program that first issues the secure application load request, then stays in a paused state (using a kernel call loop). It will only be scheduled when a system call request comes in: it will parse it and execute it on behalf of its Secure World sister.

The Untrusted Kernel Module needs to unmarshal the system call packets and copy the data to the userspace process's memory, so the wrapper program can build its service request. The same for the responses, in reverse (from userspace to kernel).

The Trusted Microkernel requires knowledge of all available Rich OS system calls, their parameters such as addresses, lengths and transfer directions (i.e., the ABI - Application Binary Interface). Supported system calls will have specific packing and unpacking code, with proper checks to defeat normal OS attacks. Here, we can also implement a call firewall and other complementary services e.g., seamless file encryption/decryption etc.

Most system calls are passed through to the Rich OS. However, several exceptions are made in order to maintain the security model of the system:

- all memory management functions (e.g. brk, mmap, discussed in Sect. 5) need to be re-implemented by the microkernel, in order to assign memory from the trusted region allocated at boot time only;
- the exit system call has a side effect in the microkernel: to clean up and free the application's resources;
- other special system calls may be intercepted to offer trusted services (e.g., random number generators).

5 Implementation

Our implementation is based on the GNU/Linux OS, an open-source project, with a well documented ABI.

The Trusted Microkernel was designed to be as simple as possible. It needs to do some platform initialization, initialize the Memory Management Unit for user-space application separation and implement the syscall proxying services as described in Sect. 4.

This resulted in a TCB of about $\approx$ 1500 lines of C code and $\approx$ 500 of ARM assembly instructions, excluding the cryptographic library used for digital signature verification (LibTomCrypt's RSA implementation) that had a large footprint (30 KB in binary form), but there is room for improvement.

We now describe some implementation-specific problems we had to overcome:

5.1 Linux Kernel Modifications

When the ARM system first boots, it starts the bootloader/operating system in the secure domain, so the first thing we needed to do was patch the kernel to be able to boot inside TrustZone's Normal World. A Linux v2.6.35 was used with several modifications made: to remove accesses to any secure world-specific registers (to let the microkernel handle the initialization of the platform) and to reserve physical memory for the secure domain.

Another modification we made was for the serial console driver to properly interoperate with the microkernel's exclusive usage of the same resource, so we implemented a new console driver that uses secure services (via SMC) to read/write to the console. As result, the serial device is a trusted input/output communication channel.

5.2 Linux System Calls

The Linux kernel has a large number of system calls available for the applications. We only took implemented marshalling procedures for a few common ones in order to proceed to test our solution on several sample applications.

The Linux kernel calling convention on ARM only uses registers $r0$–$r7$ for parameter passing, but some of those may be memory addresses (for example, read or write calls). As the untrusted operating system cannot read addresses from the Secure World, the microkernel will have to copy those buffers. Note that there are two possible data directions: input parameters require transferring the data from the secure application towards a Normal World region, and the output parameters (available when the syscall returns) need to be copied back to the Secure World. Those similarities allowed for shared code when implementing the ABI.

We also note that there are some syscalls receiving variable argument count and types based on some parameter (e.g., ioctl has multiple commands). Fortunately, they are few and they will have their own, separate procedures for marshalling.

As for the memory management calls that need to be implemented inside the Secure World, GNU/Linux programs use `mmap` and `brk` for requesting more virtual memory to be allocated (e.g., when using `malloc()`). Our microkernel has a minimalistic implementation using contiguous physical memory page allocation, but it can be extended if the applications require a more dynamic strategy.

5.3 Dynamic Libraries

For dynamic linking to work, the wrapper must implement ELF format parsing, analyze the loadable segments and send the code of the libraries and relocation metadata along with the main executable to the secure microkernel, which must use this information to do the loading. The libraries must also be verified for integrity because their code will reside inside the Secure World.

Unfortunately, dynamic loading is unsupported at this time and was left for future work. If the secure application uses any external libraries, they need to be linked statically into the executable (which we have done for our evaluated programs).

Table 1. System calls average latency table

Name	Standard (ms)	TrustZone (ms)	Overhead (%)
Getpid	0.58	49.33	8325%
Socket	12.6	61.5	384%
Write (256B)	29.60	114.27	386%
Write (512B)	51.92	153.19	295%

6   Evaluation

For evaluation, we used a Freescale/NXP i.MX53 development board with a Cortex-A8 CPU clocked at 500 MHz and 1 GB DDR3 memory.

We tested our implementation using several programs:

- sample C programs that read/write files;
- a telnet client;
- the Dropbear ssh client, which is using more advanced system calls (`newselect`, `ioctl`);

The applications were first analyzed statically for their system calls and had the marshalling code updated accordingly. As such, their functionality was unaffected when running inside the trusted environment.

Next, we did several benchmarks to evaluate the overhead added by our implementation.

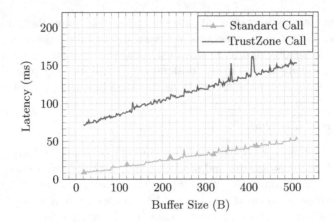

Fig. 3. Write call durations for different buffer sizes

All measurements were taken using the Performance Measuring Unit (PMU) capability of the processor. For this, we implemented a small driver with basic initialization, counter reset, start/stop and querying routines.

The results are presented in Table 1. As observed, there is a constant overhead of about ≈ 49 ms when forwarding the calls through our system. This mainly is due to the 4 context switches that need to be executed during the proxied call. This delay gets amortized when the typical duration of the system call is longer, as the case of the `write`.

For system calls that take pointers to buffers, the marshalling process needs to copy its contents, so the overhead will increase based on the amount of data that needs to be transferred through the TrustZone worlds barrier. We can see this relationship for `write` in Fig. 3.

7 Related Work

The trusted execution problem has been tackled by numerous other works. However, we will only discuss those that are applicable to our chosen platform (ARM TrustZone) and not, e.g., Intel SGX.

PrivateZone [10] also targets ARM hardware and consists of a framework that can be used by developers to run parts of their applications inside a TrustZone. However, the applications will need to be redesigned with this separation in mind, while our solution can be employed to run existing, unmodified programs.

VirtualGhost [3] has another take on the problem of protecting applications from vulnerable operating systems: by using compiler and run-time instrumentation on the OS kernel code (which requires it to be re-compiled using their toolchain). This eliminates the need for hardware security extensions, however, the TCB still includes the whole OS code (though instrumented) and will not get any smaller.

We also found a work with an approach similar to ours: TrustShadow [5] uses the ARM TrustZone platform and the same system call forwarding idea, creating a process (called "zombie") inside Normal World that gets used for system calls on behalf of the trusted app. The main difference is the fact that this process never gets scheduled by Linux: system calls are routed exclusively inside the kernel, requiring patches on its service handler and scheduler code. They also use the untrusted OS for allocating virtual memory inside the secure domain, with extra verifications to ensure that the allocated pages are protected and remain as such. In contrast, our solution implements simpler approaches: an allocation mechanism inside the microkernel and a fully schedulable untrusted process wrapper without any kernel modifications (except the loadable module).

Nonetheless, TrustShadow includes several features that we left out: Linux signalling (currently, we do not forward the signals received by the wrapper, but this can be implemented in the future) and secure floating point computation services (to avoid register value leakage to the untrusted OS).

8 Conclusion and Future Work

Our paper described a mechanism that enables the execution of existing applications into a trusted execution environment based on ARM TrustZone Security Extensions.

We have shown it can successfully load and execute the unmodified programs by using a secure microkernel doing system call proxying to the normal, untrusted OS, without compromising the security of the application (its private data remains private inside the trusted environment at all times). We have obtained a minimalistic implementation by using the Rich Operating System to perform the scheduling, while the trusted microkernel handles secure services (such as memory allocation).

Our system has a low TCB: only ≈ 1500 LOC, due to the simplicity of our implementation.

As future work, we need to extend the marshalling procedure to cover the majority of the system calls, to ensure compatibility with a greater range of applications. Other enhancements include forwarding signals and implementing more secure services inside the microkernel (such as floating point exceptions, as inspired by TrustShadow [5]).

We also want to do performance optimizations in order to minimize the base latency incurred by the syscall proxying layer, which is quite large at the moment: ≈ 49 ms.

Acknowledgments. This work was supported by a grant of Romanian Ministry of Research and Innovation, CCCDI - UEFISCDI, project number PN-III-P1-1.2-PCCDI-2017-0272/17PCCDI-2018, within PNCDI III.

Many thanks to Lucian Mogoșanu for early help on this project.

References

1. Advanced Micro Devices: AMD Platform Security. https://www.amd.com/en/technologies/security
2. Checkoway, S., Shacham, H.: Iago attacks: why the system call API is a bad untrusted RPC interface, vol. 41. ACM (2013)
3. Criswell, J., Dautenhahn, N., Adve, V.: Virtual ghost: protecting applications from hostile operating systems. ACM SIGARCH Comput. Arch. News **42**(1), 81–96 (2014)
4. Ekberg, J.E., Kostiainen, K., Asokan, N.: The untapped potential of trusted execution environments on mobile devices. IEEE Secur. Priv. **12**(4), 29–37 (2014)
5. Guan, L., et al.: Trustshadow: secure execution of unmodified applications with arm trustzone. In: Proceedings of the 15th Annual International Conference on Mobile Systems, Applications, and Services, pp. 488–501. ACM (2017)
6. Hendricks, J., Van Doorn, L.: Secure bootstrap is not enough: shoring up the trusted computing base. In: Proceedings of the 11th Workshop on ACM SIGOPS European Workshop, p. 11. ACM (2004)
7. Holdings, A.: Arm Architecture Manual. http://infocenter.arm.com/help/index.jsp?topic=/com.arm.doc.subset.architecture.reference/index.html
8. Holdings, A.: ARM TrustZone Security Extensions. https://developer.arm.com/technologies/trustzone
9. Intel: Intel SGX Software Guard Extensions. https://software.intel.com/en-us/sgx
10. Jang, J., et al.: Privatezone: providing a private execution environment using arm trustzone. IEEE Trans. Dependable Secur. Comput. **15**(5), 797–810 (2018)
11. Loscocco, P.A., Smalley, S.D., Muckelbauer, P.A., Taylor, R.C., Turner, S.J., Farrell, J.F.: The inevitability of failure: the flawed assumption of security in modern computing environments. In: Proceedings of the 21st National Information Systems Security Conference, vol. 10, pp. 303–314 (1998)
12. National Institute of Standards and Technology: National Vulnerability Database Statistics (2017). https://nvd.nist.gov/vuln/search/statistics
13. Rushby, J.M.: Design and verification of secure systems, vol. 15. ACM (1981)

Security Knowledge Management in Open Source Software Communities

Shao-Fang Wen$^{(\boxtimes)}$, Mazaher Kianpour$^{(\boxtimes)}$, and Basel Katt$^{(\boxtimes)}$

Norwegian University of Science and Technology, 2815 Gjøvik, Norway
{shao-fang.wen,mazaher.kianpour,basel.katt}@ntnu.no

Abstract. Open source software (OSS) communities are groups of individuals, technical or non-technical, interacting with collaborating peers in online communities of practices to develop OSS, solve particular software problems and exchange ideas. People join OSS communities with a different level of programming skills and experience and might lack formal, college-level software security training. There remains a lot of confusion in participants' mind as to what is secured code and what the project wants. Another problem is that the huge amount of available software security information nowadays has resulted in a form of information overload to software engineers, who usually finish studying it with no clue about how to apply those principles properly to their own applications. This leads to a knowledge gap between knowledge available and knowledge required to build secure applications in the context of software projects. Given the increased importance and complexity of OSS in today's world, lacking proper security knowledge to handle vulnerabilities in OSS development will result in breaches that are more serious in the future. The goal of this research work is to fill the knowledge gap by providing an artifact that would facilitate the effective security-knowledge transferring and learning in the context of OSS development. In this work-in-progress paper, we present our ongoing research work following design science research methodology on the domain problem identification and the development of the artifact.

Keywords: Software security · Open source software ·
Knowledge management

1 Introduction

Open source software (OSS) is based on the principle that software programs should be shared freely among users, giving them the possibility of introducing implementations and modifications [1]. To develop OSS, solve particular software problems and exchange ideas, numbers of technical and non-technical individuals interact with collaborating peers in online communities of practices [2–4]. The activities that these communities perform are usually called OSS projects. Because of its low-cost software solutions, and the openness and real collaboration of the software development process, OSS has become increasingly popular choice instead of closed source (proprietary) software: about 80% of companies run their operations on OSS [5] and 96% of applications utilize OSS as the software components [6].

© Springer Nature Switzerland AG 2019
J.-L. Lanet and C. Toma (Eds.): SecITC 2018, LNCS 11359, pp. 53–70, 2019.
https://doi.org/10.1007/978-3-030-12942-2_6

As OSS becomes an increasingly important part of our lives, researchers and security communities have spent numerous efforts on providing mechanisms of building security in OSS development [7]. However, the number of new vulnerabilities keeps increasing in today's OSS applications. The Blackduck 2017 Open Source Security and Risk Analysis report announced that 3623 new OSS vulnerabilities occurred in 2016 – almost 10 per day on average and a 10% increase from 2015 [6]. These known vulnerabilities open some of the most critical OSS projects to potential exploitation such as Heartbleed and Logjam (in OpenSSL); Quadrooter (in Android); Glibc Vulnerability (in Linux servers and web frameworks); NetUSB (in Linux kernel), and many others [8, 9]. The increasing quantity and severity of vulnerabilities in OSS have exposed the unique management and software security challenges in OSS communities.

People join OSS communities at different ages and have different backgrounds, capacities, and resources, as well as different objectives. They come from many disciplines and have different levels of programming skills and experience [10], and might lack formal, college-level software security training. When performing contribution, most project participants primarily focus on their immediate goals that usually involve functional requirements and performance [11], and then patch whatever bugs there may be when it's time for the next release or hotfix [12]. There remains a lot of confusion in participants' mind as to what is secured code and what the project wants. Another problem is that the domain knowledge of software security is quite vast and extensive [13]. The huge amount of software security information has resulted in a form of information overload to software engineers who usually finish studying it with no clue about how to apply those principles to their own applications, or with the feeling that security is so difficult to achieve, that they simply cast it aside [14]. Even be educated with software security practices before joining OSS projects these participants may fail to correlate the security knowledge with their projects and fix vulnerabilities in the code when given a chance. It especially relates to what is known as a knowledge gap between knowledge available and knowledge required to build secure applications in the context of software projects [15].

Given the increased importance and complexity of OSS in today's world, lacking proper security knowledge to handle vulnerabilities in OSS development will result in breaches that are more serious in the future. Our position is that there is a need by forging a solution to adaptively place the security knowledge in the appropriate context of the OSS development, i.e., to transfer the necessary security knowledge within the OSS community, meanwhile, to offer opportunities for learning security knowledge and skills to secure OSS products, which are developed, delivered and maintained by the community. The goal of this research work is to propose an artifact that would facilitate the effective security-knowledge transferring and learning in the context of OSS development. In this work-in-progress paper, we present our ongoing work on the domain problem investigation and the conceptual design of the artifact.

The rest of the paper is structured as follows: In Sect. 2, we present an overview of security knowledge management in software development. The research design is presented in Sect. 3. In Sect. 4, we present our initial study of security knowledge sharing and learning in OSS communities. Our proposed knowledge management application and the corresponding research steps are described in Sects. 5 and 6. Conclusions and future works are presented in Sect. 7.

2 Security Knowledge Management in the Software Development

Software security is more than just a security feature. Security features, such as password encryption and SSL (Secure Socket Layer) between the web server and a browser, are functions of an application to prevent malicious attacks. Security is an emergent, system-wide property of a software system, which means that one cannot presume to achieve a high level of security by simply introducing security-related features into the software [13, 16]. This is because most security problems arise from bugs during the development process [17–19]. Software security aims to avoid security errors in software by considering security aspects throughout the software development lifecycle (SDLC). To train software engineers on critical software security issues, security knowledge should be spread in an effective manner.

Knowledge Management has been defined as "the capability by which communities capture the knowledge that is critical to their success, constantly improve it, and make it available in the most effective manner to those who need it" [20]. Managing knowledge in software development is crucial to allow developers capturing, locating and sharing the knowledge of codes and methods throughout the project to leverage the competitive advantage. In order to increase development staffs' security knowledge, software project management needs to employ knowledge management mechanisms in encapsulating and spreading the emerging security discipline more efficiently in the software development process. As the software lifecycle unfolds, security-related knowledge could be directly applied with a knowledge-intensive best practice that can support software engineers prevent, spot and mitigate these security errors.

Despite this, our systematic literature review work [7] revealed that no research has been conducted focusing on the aspects of security knowledge management in OSS development. Studies in the areas of software construction and verification (Secure Architecture, Code Review, and Security Testing) are followed by researchers with more interests than governance, where education and training are the major activities. Secure architecture, code review, and security testing can help secure OSS products. However, due to the lack of research and other activities related to security knowledge management for OSS development, software security knowledge cannot be effectively spread within open source communities. Our research intends to fill this research gap by (a) empirically investigating the current situation and problems in the knowledge management of software security, (b) proposing and developing an application for adaptive security knowledge transferring and learning in OSS communities.

3 Research Design

In developing the security knowledge sharing and learning system adaptive in the context of OSS development, we applied the general methodology of Design Science Research (DSR) framework [21] (Fig. 1) to show how our research is both relevant and rigorous and contribute to the information system (IS) knowledge base by solving a rising security problem in OSS. DSR can be conducted when creating innovations and ideas that define technical capabilities and products through which the development process of artifacts can be accomplished effectively and efficiently [21, 22].

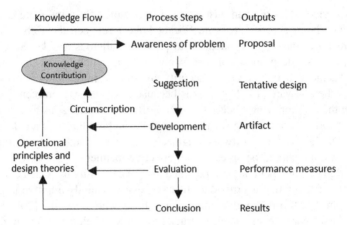

Fig. 1. Design research methodology [21]

4   A Study of the Research Domain Problem

At first, it is important to identify and establish the magnitude of the real-world problem, including technical and non-technical practices in our interests. In contrast to earlier researchers, which have focused on generic learning in OSS communities, our study aimed to observe OSS participants' perception of learning about software security knowledge. Our motivation for this study is not only to evaluate the knowledge sharing and learning mechanisms and the extent to which they may be viable and successful but also to gain insight into the security culture and project factors that affect software-security learning processes in OSS communities.

4.1   Study Method

To get an in-depth understanding of security knowledge sharing and learning behaviors surrounding everyday OSS development, an ethnographic approach was adopted. The ethnographic research can be classified as a qualitative research method that aims to study the cultural patterns and perspectives of participants in their natural settings [23, 24]. In empirical software engineering, ethnography provides an in-depth understanding of the socio-technical realities surrounding everyday software development practice [23] and highlights the significance of socio-technical issues in the design of software-intensive systems [24]. The knowledge gained can be used to improve processes, methods, and tools as well as to advance the observed security practices.

4.1.1   Case Selection

To get a broader understanding of the phenomena of interests, we set up the following criteria for the case selection: (1) the selected projects should be community driven;

(2) the selected projects should be as diverse as possible; (3) the projects use a wide range of communication tools within the communities. Table 1 gives an overview of the selected OSS projects. Having the selected sample cases that cover the range of the diversity of OSS communities is important to refine the phenomena being studied and improve the outcomes of this research endeavor.

Table 1. Overview of the selected projects

Project	Age	Software category	Programming language
A	3	Collaborative text editor	JavaScript
B	8	Content management system	PHP
C	5	Multimedia playback engine	C/C++

4.2 Data Collection

Since programming errors have been a major part of security vulnerabilities in software development [25], we dedicated our investigation in the knowledge sharing and learning about secure programming domain knowledge. Two data collection schemes were applied: observation and a semi-structured interview.

4.2.1 Observations

We participated in the selected projects as an observer to gain a close and intension familiar with the project members and understand the details and processes of the projects. The main idea of this approach is to observe developers performing the activities that they usually do in their daily jobs. To be more specific, observation consists of writing notes about developers' activities, events, interactions, tool usage, and any other phenomena. The digital objects (including source code repository, project documentation, mailing list, code review records, bug reports, and forum) were screened to collect any information related to secure programming. Information collected during the observation was recorded without distracting participants of communities. Observation is an important method to be used in this research because it allowed us to collect information about what learning tools the OSS participants used and how they used them. Moreover, it was a source of valuable insights to assist in a comprehensive understanding of the nature of the case data.

4.2.2 Semi-structure Interviews

As we wanted to get input from the OSS participants, while still allowing them to think freely to some extent, we chose to use a semi-structured interview as described by May [26]. Individual interviews were conducted with 13 participants in the selected three projects during the observation period. Participants with short (less than one year), medium (between 1 to 3 years) or long (more than 3 years) experience in the open source development were interviewed. Most of the interviewees did not want to disclose their identity and project name, thus, we did not represent their names in the finding. Due to the geographical distribution of the interviewees, all interviews were carried out via online communication software (Skype and Google Hangout). We had to accommodate all the interviewees' constraints in the setting of interviews.

All interviews were recorded and lasted approximately one hour. The questions were used to understand their experiences in OSS development and examine their perception of learning processes about secure programming in their OSS communities. In order to facilitate elaboration, certain possible follow up questions were prepared beforehand. As we suspected that the subjects would be unwilling to consider themselves behaving insecurely, we also asked about what other members would do. This also has the benefit of covering more subjects.

4.3 Data Analysis

Because this study deals with security issues in OSS development phenomenon, including both social and technical aspects, it is important to analyze and model the research context using system-holistic and socio-technical approaches. As Scacchi [27] points out, the meaning of OSS in the socio-technical context is broader than its technical definition and includes communities of practice, social culture, technical practices, processes, and organizational structures. In this study, we adopt a socio-technical system (STS) developed by Kowalski [28] to summarize and classify our findings. The STS model is depicted in Fig. 2. STS provides a structural analysis of the relationship between the social (cultural/ethical, structural/managerial) and technical elements (method/process and machine/technique) to give a complete overview of the status. Furthermore, the STS model allows the results to be categorized and presented in such a way that they are easy to understand by non-specialists.

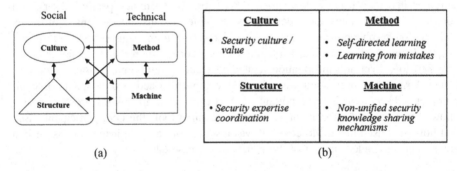

Fig. 2. (a) Socio-technical system [18], and (b) socio-technical analysis of research findings

4.3.1 Method Category

Method category of STS presents our findings regarding the learning process about secure programming knowledge. Our study firstly found that learning processes of secure programming for OSS developers are centered on informal-based and self-directed learning experiences. The openness and transparency of OSS projects provide an interesting setting for participants to exercise self-directed learning. In OSS development, participants usually first try to solve their problems themselves by the mean of available materials and if required by exploring the web: browsing documentations (guideline, wiki, FAQ, etc.), studying the source code and engaging in discussion threads. These internet resources have the advantage to provide the community with an information infrastructure for publishing and sharing description of software development in the form of hypertext, video, and a software artifact content indexes or directories.

Another learning process about secure programming in OSS communities is learning from mistakes. Our study found that OSS developers care more about making the software work eventually rather than trying to make it work at the very first time. When contributing to the projects, they mostly focus on their immediate goals that usually involve functional requirements and system performances and then patch whatever bugs there may be when it is time for the next release or hotfix. They have not considered the importance of a given function might have to the overall security of their application until they made mistakes and understand the consequence of the flaw. The learning ability from the mistakes become essential in this context. The process of code review is an important enabler for a developer to reflect their code, take corrective actions and build concrete coding experience. Not only members are opened about their mistakes, but they also share their experience as learning opportunities for others.

4.3.2 Structure Category

Structure category of STS presents the social elements is managerial and administrative perspectives. Security expertise coordination is the key element that fell into this category. Security expertise coordination is to combine explicit and tacit knowledge in all management and security expert decisions, and to get knowledge moved from individuals within the whole organization between different actors, and from tacit domain to explicit domain and also vice versa [33]. In this study, expertise coordination is manifested in the following two strategies: coordinating organizational structure and security infostructure.

Every member involves in OSS development should be concerned with software security, but it is inefficient to demand each participant taking care of all security aspects. The coordinating organizational structure serves as subject matter experts to ensure that security-related issues receive necessary attention in the community. Some OSS communities utilize security experts to define security requirements and best practices, help perform code reviews, and provides the necessary education for the software development staff. Through this structural mechanism, the security knowledge is able to gain valuable insights from the organization to facilitate strategic decision-making.

In the knowledge sharing process, infostructure serves as a role to provide rules, which govern the exchange between the actors on the network providing a set of cognitive resources (metaphors, common language) whereby people make sense of events on the network [34]. In the context of OSS development, developers meet face-to-face infrequently if at all, and coordinate their activity primarily by means of digital channels on the internet. A proper infostructure can help learners identify the location of the security information, knowing where an answer to a problem, and acquiring as much knowledge as possible.

4.3.3 Machine Category

A major problem we found is a lack of sufficient as well as efficient knowledge sharing mechanisms for secure programming in OSS communities. Based on the study, the security information is scattered over the community websites (source code, documentation, wiki, forum, conference pages, etc.), and the quantity of transferred knowledge is varied by projects. Finding and learning knowledge about secure programming becomes a key challenge that is highly dependent on the resources the community provides. However, they rarely address the security requirements in documentation to help drive the team to understand the prioritized security needs of the entire project. Newcomers feel that comprehending systems from exploring the website is hopeless, so they as well prefer to start with programming. They lose the learning opportunity about the security requirements of the project and being aware of the possible mistakes they may make in their code.

4.3.4 Culture Category

Security culture is the way our minds are programmed that will create different patterns of thinking, feeling, and actions for the security process [35]. As indicated in the Method category of STS, in the context of OSS development, developers enjoy contributing their code to the project for the fulfillment of functional requirements and performances. Secure software development is often left out from developer's heuristics. Subsequently, we observed that security culture and security knowledge sharing interact with each other in the OSS communities. Security culture decides how much security knowledge is disseminated within the community and what knowledge learners can learn; likewise, with more security knowledge sharing, it can help instill the value of security in the community, and the particular learning behaviors and actions can be expected among participants. The security culture backgrounds either at organizational or at the individual level have impacts on the amount of security knowledge transferred within the community, further, affecting participants' learning processes.

4.4 Suggestions from the Study of the Research Domain Problem

Based on the finding of our ethnographic observation in OSS projects, we have come to an outlook of an artifact that can address the explicated problems about security knowledge sharing and learning in OSS communities.

- The artifact should have the possibility to achieve the effectiveness of the learning process about software security in the open source software community by considering different socio-technical perspectives (Fig. 3).
- The artifact should be as a role of security expertise coordination, organizing and transferring useful security information, establishing rules and norms adaptive to the context of the OSS project.
- The artifact should offer opportunities for learning and self-development of software security knowledge with limited support from security experts or other peers.

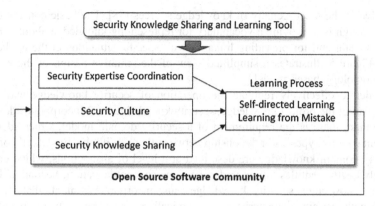

Fig. 3. Improving security learning process by considering different perspectives

5 A Proposed Security Knowledge Sharing and Learning Application

In this section, we present our proposed security knowledge sharing and learning application based on the observations and suggestions from the empirical study. The conceptual design depicted in Fig. 4 defines an abstract view of the application, which deals with the development of an ontology-driven web application for presenting software security knowledge in multiple formats. This application will provide a web-based environment that allows OSS participants or learners adaptively retrieve and present security knowledge content according to the context of the application developed by the project. In the following section, we describe three aspects of the application design: Context-sensitive ontology-based knowledge model, functional architecture, and system architecture of the application.

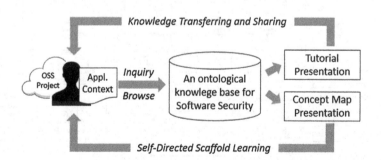

Fig. 4. Conceptual design of the application

5.1 The Context-Sensitive Ontology-Based Knowledge Model

Ontology facilitates capture and construction of domain knowledge and enables representation of skeletal knowledge to facilitate the integration of knowledge bases irrespective of the heterogeneity of knowledge sources [38]. The basic concept of our ontology design is to provide a vocabulary for representing knowledge about software security domain and for providing linkages with specific situations in the application context. Figure 5 illustrates a simplified view of the tentative design of the context-sensitive ontology-based model.

In order to effectively regulate the operation of security knowledge and be an essential part of the project knowledge, security knowledge must incorporate additional features. First, there is the requirement of a security domain model, which identifies fundamental entity types and relationship between them. With this model, all concepts of security domain knowledge are described at a level of abstractions, which enables cohesively treating entitles falling under the same conceptualization. Second and most important, knowledge, security knowledge must incorporate context, that is, to be modeled with certain characteristics of applications, such as software paradigms, programming languages and used technologies. The contextual information acts as a filter that defines, in a given context, what security knowledge pieces must be taken into account.

The main advantage of this ontology model is to share a common understanding of the structure of security knowledge along different SDLC activities and among different software development context to enable semantic interoperability. With this design, software engineers are allowed to find solutions to exceptional situations by searching for similar context. For example, a PHP web application designer can refer to other projects' security setup by looking for the same domain (subject area) and software technologies. The major terms used in the security domain ontology are explained in Table 2 while Table 3 lists the characteristics in the application context model.

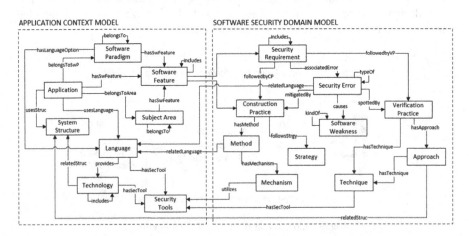

Fig. 5. A tentative design of the ontology-based context model

Table 2. The definition of major terms in security domain ontology

Class	Definition
Security requirement	A software security requirement can be defined as a software requirement needed to avoid a specific software security error during the development [43]
Construction practice	Construction practices focus on proactive activities for an organization to design and build secure software by default [44]
Verification practice	Software verification is to assure that software fully satisfies all the expected requirements [44], which typically include code review practices and security testing practices. Knowledge elements in verification practices are organized in two catalogs: Technique and Approach
Security error	A software security error is a tangible manifestation of a mistake in the software development artifacts of a piece of software that causes a software weakness [43, 45]
Software weakness	Software weaknesses are flaws, faults, bugs, vulnerabilities, and other errors in software implementation, code, design, or architecture that if left unaddressed could result in systems and networks being vulnerable to attack [46]

Table 3. Identified characteristics (classes) in the application context

Class	Definition	Example
Software paradigm	It represents the categories of software applications that share common development characteristics	Web application, desktop application, mobile application
Subject area	It represents domains that an application belongs	Banking, health, Travel
Software feature	It represents the essential elements of software with security concerns. The software feature is associated with the software paradigm and the subject area of the application	User authentication, credit card processing, file upload
Language	It represents programming language used to develop an application	C, C ++, Java, JavaScript, PHP
Technology	It represents the combination of frameworks or tools used to create an application. Technologies are built based on programming languages	Web framework (Symphony for PHP, Angular for JavaScript, etc.) toolkit, SDK
System structure	It represents the fundamental structure to operate the application	Database management system, runtime platform (MS Windows, Android)
Security tool	It represents a concrete solution to implement construction mechanisms or verification techniques	HTML Purifier, PHPUnit for PHP testing

5.2   Functional Architecture

The functional architecture (Fig. 6) illustrates the functionalities supported in the application, which are divided into two categories: knowledge presentation modules and system management modules. The knowledge representation module is to provide learners with learning materials. By making better use of the domain knowledge and contextual information, it is planned that the optimal materials are provided. The system management module is responsible for maintaining the ontology repository and loading knowledge content for the needs of the knowledge presentation. We give a brief for each module in below sections.

5.2.1   Query Module

Users can access the security knowledge through a query interface passing requests to a search engine. The input criteria can be constructed dynamically or use pre-configured question patterns.

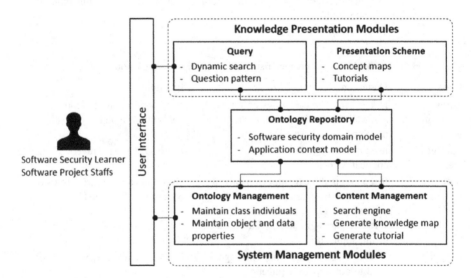

Fig. 6. The functional architecture of the proposed application.

5.2.2   Presentation Scheme Module

Regarding the knowledge presentation, two knowledge representation schemes are suggested in order to provide a navigation view and integrated information view of the knowledge items: concept maps and tutorials. Concept maps are the graphical representation of the knowledge items and their relationship. Concept maps can be used as primary sources for knowledge acquisition, adjunct aids to text processing, communication tools for organizing ideas, or retrieval cues [47]. In tutorials, knowledge content is presented as a form of static web pages, which are allowed users to browse the detailed information and relevant resources, such as sample code or URL links.

Ontology Management Module

Ontology management module is responsible for maintaining and loading data from the ontology, including specific individuals of classes, object properties, and data properties.

Content Management Function

Content management module acts as services to receive requests from users, to interact with ontology management functions, and to process and display the result set according to the requested knowledge presentation format.

5.3 Technical Architecture

Figure 7 provides an overview of our proposed architecture implementing the main feature of the application outlined above. The front-end has been designed as JSP pages and through them, the users can access the various modules and functions of the application. Clients can interact with the server (Apache Tomcat) using an HTTP request to a Java Servlet. The backend is implemented in Java and access to the ontology repository is provided through the Jena API[1], a Java framework for building semantic web applications. Jena provides extensive Java libraries for helping developers develop code that handles RDF, OWL, and SPARQL in line with published W3C recommendations[2]. Pellet[3] is an open source OWL DL (descriptive logic) for Java, which is used to infer relevant knowledge from the ontology defined in the OWL. Pellet can also be integrated with Jena or OWL API libraries.

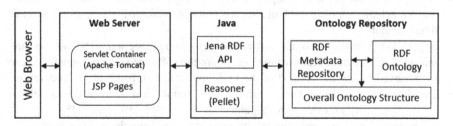

Fig. 7. The system architecture of the ontology-based web application.

6 Research Steps

Our research adopts Design Science Research (DSR) methodology, presented in Sect. 3, to form a development framework for our proposed artifact, a web-based security knowledge sharing and learning system in the OSS community. As the future work, we intend to carry out activities to facilitate the artifact development works using three DSR iterations (See Fig. 8). The detailed research steps are described in the following.

---

[1] https://jena.apache.org/.

[2] https://www.w3.org/2001/sw/.

[3] https://www.w3.org/2001/sw/wiki/Pellet.

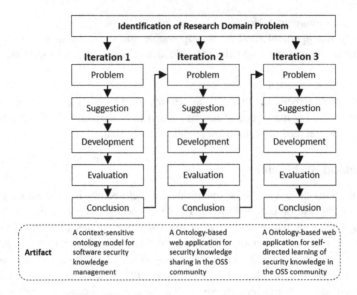

Fig. 8. Design science research iterations.

Iteration 1: Create a context-sensitive ontology for software security knowledge management.

- Awareness of the problem (Proposal): There is a gap between knowledge available and knowledge required to build secure software system in the context of OSS development.
- Suggestion (Tentative design): Software security knowledge should be modeled and managed in a context-sensitive manner where the software security knowledge can be retrieved taking the context of the OSS application in hand into consideration.
- Development (Artifact): Design of the new ontological knowledge model for software security knowledge management using Protégé OWL tool [48].
- Evaluation: To demonstrate the results and possibility from the development of the ontology, three web application vulnerabilities data will be modeled (Cross-site scripting, SQL injection and Cross-site request forgery). A compatible tool, SPARQL, to infer and to query on the ontology in OWL standard will be adopted.

Iteration 2: To create an ontology-based web application for security knowledge sharing in OSS communities.

- Awareness of the problem (Proposal): There lacks a unified security knowledge sharing tool in OSS communities.
- Suggestion (Tentative design): Design a web application with the proposed context-sensitive ontology, which supports distributing the necessary security knowledge within the OSS community.
- Development (Artifact): To implement the web application with the proposed application architecture presented in Fig. 6.

- Evaluation: Two experiments will be taken in this iteration:
  - The artifact will be tested with a number of individuals/students in academic settings in order to get feedback about system usability. The questionnaire will be designed to get the conception of the experiment subjects about the artifact.
  - The artifact will be tested in practices with members in 2 selected OSS communities. This experiment aims to testify the feasibility of security knowledge sharing using the artifact.

Iteration 3: To enhance the artifact from iteration 2 and provide features of self-directed learning for members in OSS communities.

- Awareness of the problem (Proposal): There exist different levels of security skills and experience among participants in the OSS community. The transferred security knowledge should be adaptive to the level of security knowledge of learners.
- Suggestion (Tentative design): The learning content should also be applicable to management and security readership more generally and should be appealing to all those who are concerned about software security in OSS communities.
- Development (Artifact): To adopt Concept Map in scaffold learning of software security knowledge.
- Evaluation: The artifact will be tested in practices with members in 3 selected OSS communities. The level of security knowledge is the independent variable. Questionnaires will be designed to test the level of security knowledge before and after using the artifact.

7   Conclusion and Future Works

In this paper, we present our ongoing research work in the field of security knowledge management in OSS communities. Learning software security is a difficult and challenging task since the domain is quite context-specific and the real project situation is necessary to apply the security concepts within the specific system. Identifying security knowledge that is applicable in a given context can become a major challenge for OSS participants. OSS communities cannot expect all its participants to be educated in software security before joining the project, and therefore must take some responsibility for educating both developers and users on potential security errors and the relevant mitigations. Although some OSS communities do have security experts and built-in security practices, many others do not. As a result, the issue of how to support developers or other learners reaching the required level of security knowledge to secure OSS development becomes an important topic.

As the future work, we intend to implement the proposed intelligent application and to evaluate its usability in educational paradigms and software development projects. Our ultimate goal is to provide open source software communities, a set of advanced services for efficiently handling and disseminating software security knowledge within the community.

References

1. Humes, L.L.: Communities of practice for open source software. In: Handbook of Research on Open Source Software: Technological, Economic, and Social Perspectives, pp. 610–623. IGI Global (2007)
2. Scacchi, W., et al.: Understanding free/open source software development processes. Softw. Process: Improv. Pract. **11**(2), 95–105 (2006)
3. Feller, J., Fitzgerald, B.: Understanding Open Source Software Development. Addison-Wesley, London (2002)
4. Feller, J., Finnegan, P., Kelly, D., MacNamara, M.: Developing open source software: a community-based analysis of research. In: Trauth, E.M., Howcroft, D., Butler, T., Fitzgerald, B., DeGross, J.I. (eds.) Social Inclusion: Societal and Organizational Implications for Information Systems. IIFIP, vol. 208, pp. 261–278. Springer, Boston, MA (2006). https://doi.org/10.1007/0-387-34588-4_18
5. NorthBridge: 2016 Future of Open Source Survey. http://www.northbridge.com/2016-future-open-source-survey-results
6. BlackDuck Software: 2017 Open Source Security and Risk Analysis. https://www.blackducksoftware.com/open-source-security-risk-analysis-2017
7. Wen, S.-F.: Software security in open source development: a systematic literature review. In: Proceedings of the 21st Conference of Open Innovations Association FRUCT, Helsinki, Finland (2017)
8. Pittenger, M.: Know your open source code. Netw. Secur. **2016**(5), 11–15 (2016)
9. Levy, J.: Top Open Source Security Vulnerabilities. WhiteSource Blog. https://www.whitesourcesoftware.com/whitesource-blog/open-source-security-vulnerability/. Accessed 22 June 2018
10. Agrawal, A., et al.: We Don't Need Another Hero? The Impact of "Heroes" on Software Development. arXiv preprint arXiv:1710.09055 (2017)
11. Benbya, H., Belbaly, N.: Understanding developers' motives in open source projects: a multi-theoretical framework (2010)
12. Jaatun, M.G., et al.: A lightweight approach to secure software engineering. In: A Multidisciplinary Introduction to Information Security, p. 183 (2011)
13. McGraw, G.: Software Security: Building Security In, vol. 1. Addison-Wesley Professional, Boston (2006)
14. Apvrille, A., Pourzandi, M.: Secure software development by example. IEEE Secur. Priv. **3**(4), 10–17 (2005)
15. Wen, S.-F.: Hyper contextual software security management for open source software. In: STPIS@ CAiSE (2016)
16. Mead, N.R., et al.: Software Security Engineering: A Guide for Project Managers. Addison-Wesley Professional, Boston (2004)
17. Viega, J., McGraw, G.R.: Building Secure Software: How to Avoid Security Problems the Right Way (2001)
18. Xie, J., Lipford, H.R., Chu, B.: Why do programmers make security errors? In: 2011 IEEE Symposium on Visual Languages and Human-Centric Computing (VL/HCC). IEEE (2011)
19. Graff, M., Van Wyk, K.R.: Secure Coding: Principles and Practices. O'Reilly Media, Inc., Sebastopol (2003)
20. Birkenkrahe, M.: How large multi-nationals manage their knowledge. Bus. Rev. **4**(2), 2–12 (2002)
21. Vaishnavi, V., Kuechler, W.: Design research in information systems (2004)

22. Von Alan, R.H., et al.: Design science in information systems research. MIS Q. **28**(1), 75–105 (2004)
23. Sharp, H., Dittrich, Y., de Souza, C.R.: The role of ethnographic studies in empirical software engineering. IEEE Trans. Softw. Eng. **42**(8), 786–804 (2016)
24. Baxter, G., Sommerville, I.: Socio-technical systems: from design methods to systems engineering. Interact. Comput. **23**(1), 4–17 (2011)
25. Kuhn, D.R., Raunak, M., Kacker, R.: An analysis of vulnerability trends, 2008–2016. In: 2017 IEEE International Conference on Software Quality, Reliability and Security Companion (QRS-C). IEEE (2017)
26. May, T.: Social Research. McGraw-Hill Education, New York (UK) (2011)
27. Scacchi, W.: Understanding the requirements for developing open source software systems. In: IEE Proceedings–Software. IET (2002)
28. Kowalski, S.: IT insecurity: a multi-discipline inquiry. Ph.D. thesis, Department of Computer and System Sciences, University of Stockholm and Royal Institute of Technology, Sweden (1994). ISBN 91-7153-207-2
29. Al Sabbagh, B., Kowalski, S.: A socio-technical framework for threat modeling a software supply chain. In: The 2013 Dewald Roode Workshop on Information Systems Security Research, Niagara Falls, New York, USA, 4–5 October 2013. International Federation for Information Processing (2013)
30. Bider, I., Kowalski, S.: A framework for synchronizing human behavior, processes and support systems using a socio-technical approach. In: Bider, I., et al. (eds.) BPMDS/EMMSAD -2014. LNBIP, vol. 175, pp. 109–123. Springer, Heidelberg (2014). https://doi.org/10.1007/978-3-662-43745-2_8
31. Karokola, G., Yngström, L., Kowalski, S.: Secure e-government services: a comparative analysis of e-government maturity models for the developing regions–the need for security services. Int. J. Electron. Gov. Res. (IJEGR) **8**(1), 1–25 (2012)
32. Wahlgren, G., Kowalski, S.: Evaluation of escalation maturity model for IT security risk management: a design science work in progress. In: The 2014 Dewald Roode Workshop on Information Systems Security Research, IFIP WG8.11/WG11.13. IFIP (2014)
33. Anttila, J., et al.: Fulfilling the needs for information security awareness and learning in information society. In: The 6th Annual Security Conference, Las Vegas (2007)
34. Pan, S.L., Scarbrough, H.: Knowledge management in practice: an exploratory case study. Technol. Anal. Strateg. Manag. **11**(3), 359–374 (1999)
35. Al Sabbagh, B., Kowalski, S.: Developing social metrics for security modeling the security culture of it workers individuals (case study). In: 2012 Mosharaka International Conference on Communications, Computers and Applications (MIC-CCA). IEEE (2012)
36. Gruber, T.R.: A translation approach to portable ontology specifications. Knowl. Acquisition **5**(2), 199–220 (1993)
37. Wand, Y., Storey, V.C., Weber, R.: An ontological analysis of the relationship construct in conceptual modeling. ACM Trans. Database Syst. (TODS) **24**(4), 494–528 (1999)
38. Gruber, T.R.: Toward principles for the design of ontologies used for knowledge sharing? Int. J. Hum. Comput. Stud. **43**(5–6), 907–928 (1995)
39. Uschold, M., Gruninger, M.: Ontologies: principles, methods and applications. Knowl. Eng. Rev. **11**(2), 93–136 (1996)
40. Noy, N.F., McGuinness, D.L.: Ontology development 101: a guide to creating your first ontology. Stanford Knowledge Systems Laboratory Technical Report KSL-01-05 and Stanford Medical Informatics Technical Report SMI-2001-0880, Stanford, CA (2001)
41. Wang, X., et al.: Semantic space: an infrastructure for smart spaces. IEEE Pervasive Comput. **3**(3), 32–39 (2004)
42. Gruninger, M.: Ontology: applications and design. Commun. ACM **45**(2), 39–41 (2002)

43. Khan, M.U.A., Zulkernine, M.: Quantifying security in secure software development phases. In: 32nd Annual IEEE International Computer Software and Applications, COMPSAC 2008. IEEE (2008)
44. Chandra, P.: The Software Assurance Maturity Model-A guide to building security into software development (2009)
45. Landwehr, C.E., et al.: A taxonomy of computer program security flaws. ACM Comput. Surv. (CSUR) 26(3), 211–254 (1994)
46. MITRE: Common Weakness Enumeration, Frequently Asked Questions. https://cwe.mitre.org/about/faq.html#A.1
47. O'donnell, A.M., Dansereau, D.F., Hall, R.H.: Knowledge maps as scaffolds for cognitive processing. Educ. Psychol. Rev. 14(1), 71–86 (2002)
48. Tudorache, T., et al.: WebProtégé: a collaborative ontology editor and knowledge acquisition tool for the web. Semant. Web 4(1), 89–99 (2013)

Formal Security Analysis of Cloud-Connected Industrial Control Systems

Tomas Kulik[✉], Peter W. V. Tran-Jørgensen, and Jalil Boudjadar

DIGIT, Department of Engineering, Aarhus University, Aarhus, Denmark
tomaskulik@eng.au.dk

Abstract. Industrial control systems are changing from *isolated* to *remotely accessible* cloud-connected architectures. Despite their advantages, these architectures introduce extra complexity, which makes it more difficult to ensure the security of these systems prior to deployment. One way to address this is by using formal methods to reason about the security properties of these systems during the early stages of development. Specifically, by analyzing security attacks and verifying that the corresponding mitigation strategies work as intended. In this paper, we present a formal framework for security analysis of cloud-connected industrial control systems. We consider several well-known attack scenarios and formally verify mitigation strategies for each of them. Our framework is mechanized using TLA+ in order to enable formal verification of security properties. Finally we demonstrate the applicability of our work using an industrial case study.

Keywords: Control systems · Cloud systems · Security · Formal verification · Model checking · TLA

1 Introduction

The computational and communication capabilities of cloud technologies are being leveraged to realize a wealth of new services across many application domains such as remote data collection, remote monitoring and software updates. This has contributed in shifting the architecture of industrial control systems from *isolated* to *remotely accessible* Internet-connected architectures where the different system components are viewed as services, accessible without requiring detailed knowledge of the underlying technologies and network topology [15]. This revolutionary migration comes with a cost in regards to the added system complexity, security threats and challenges [1,2,6,14,15,20]. From a control perspective, the threats include access to sensitive data, control software updates and, possibly, taking over the control of remote systems [9,12,20].

This work is supported by Manufacturing Academy of Denmark (MADE). For more information see http://www.made.dk/.

J.-L. Lanet and C. Toma (Eds.): SecITC 2018, LNCS 11359, pp. 71–84, 2019.
https://doi.org/10.1007/978-3-030-12942-2_7

The earlier a potential threat is detected the cheaper the mitigation will be [20]. One approach to detecting and mitigating threats early is by creating and analyzing system models, potential attack scenarios and mitigation strategies. This in turn supports *formal verification* of security properties [6,8]. In particular, by enabling verification of mitigation strategies, or in case of a failure, counter-example traces can be used to revise both the system behavior and mitigations.

During the last decade, the security analysis of cloud-connected industrial control systems has been investigated thoroughly in the state of the art [1, 2,6,14,15,20]. Different techniques have been proposed to cope with different attack patterns. Model-based design and formal methods offer promising ways to analyze the security properties of these systems [13].

In this paper we introduce a formal analysis framework for cloud-connected industrial control systems. Our primary contributions are as follows:

- Modular specification of the constituent components of cloud-connected industrial control systems.
- Specification of the behavior of several attack patterns.
- Development of mitigation strategies for each of the considered attacks.
- Formal verification of the immunity of the system against a given attack.
- Mechanization of the formal analysis framework in TLA+.

TLA+ [10] is a formal specification language for reasoning about concurrent and reactive systems. TLA+ is based on ordinary mathematics and Temporal Logic of Actions (TLA), a dialect of Linear Temporal Logic (LTL). In our work, we use TLA+ to mechanize the formal analysis framework in order to reason about security attacks and formally verify that the proposed mitigation strategies work as intended. Concretely, we describe system behavior, including attacks and mitigation strategies, using PlusCal [11]. PlusCal is an algorithm language based on TLA+ that enables specification of distributed systems or multiprocess algorithms. PlusCal algorithms can be automatically translated to TLA+ and validated using the TLC model checker. In our work we represent the constituent system components of a cloud-connected industrial control system as PlusCal processes. In addition, we specify desirable security properties using LTL and use the TLC model checker to verify them.

The rest of the paper is organized as follows: Sect. 2 presents the architecture and behavior of the considered system. Section 3 defines malicious firmware and and brute force attacks and introduces mitigations against these attacks. Section 4 demonstrates the formal analysis of the system with applied attacks and mitigation strategies. Section 5 presents related work. Finally, Sect. 6 concludes the paper and discusses future plans.

2   System Architecture and Behavior

This section describes the architecture and behavior of the systems we consider.

2.1   System Architecture

A cloud-connected industrial control system consists of (1) one or more clients that provide access to the system, (2) a cloud component used for executing requests from clients and a remote part of the system installed on a mobile platform consisting of (3) a gateway and (4) an operations terminal (OT). The full architecture is shown in Fig. 1.

The gateway acts as a data diode [9] that enables communication in one direction unless instructed otherwise. This communication restriction acts in such a way that the gateway always allows communication out of the remote mobile platform towards the cloud, while communication from the cloud is blocked in order to restrict remote

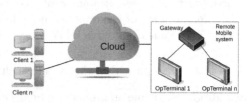

Fig. 1. System architecture of cloud connected industrial control system

access to the OT. However, the operator may decide to allow communication from the cloud to the mobile platform by toggling the access setting of the gateway.

OTs provide local access to the system directly on the mobile platform where these are installed. The OTs achieve this by providing connection to a network of microcontrollers. In this paper we abstract away these microcontrollers and focus on data flow from the OT. The system contains exactly one gateway connected to one or more OTs and a cloud service.

The client is a computer equipped with software that enables users to invoke operations that affect the OT via the cloud and gateway. Primary functions of the client include visualization of data collected from the OT and sending of firmware updates to the OT. The clients' access rights are identified by a client Id, a variable set during client deployment. The Id is validated each time the client makes a request towards the cloud, hence the client does not cache the Id validation between requests. This is to ensure that the Id can be invalidated at any time, which will prevent clients from accessing the system.

The cloud provides storage space for data obtained from the OT, communication relay between the OT and the client, and a trust authority for the client software to login to. The cloud is further split into two subsystems, the interactive cloud and the service cloud. The interactive cloud handles client requests as well as validation of client Ids. The service cloud, on the other hand, handles requests initiated by the OT. The data stored by the service cloud can be requested by the client via the interactive cloud.

2.2 System Behavior

We define the behavior of the system using a labeled transition system (LTS) [3] with a set of states S, initial state S_0 and a transition relation $\rightarrow$, given by a tuple $\langle S, S_0, \rightarrow \rangle$. The transitions are labeled by actions from an alphabet of actions and their respective guards. We further define the following notations:

- S refers to a set of states while s denotes a single state.
- S^x where $x \in \{c, i, s, d, o\}$ represents the set of states of client c, interactive cloud i, service cloud s, gateway d and OT o, respectively.
- A refers to a set of actions while a denotes a single action.
- $\mathcal{A}_{comp}$ refers to an alphabet of actions of a component as $\mathcal{A}_{comp} \subset A$
- V refers to a set of variables while v denotes a single variable.
- Z refers to a set of constants while z denotes a single constant.
- G refers to a set of guards while g denotes a single guard defined as
  $g \overset{\triangle}{=} v < z \mid v > z \mid v = z \mid g \vee g' \mid g \wedge g' \mid true \mid false.$
- $\rightarrow$ is a transition within the system such as $\rightarrow \in S^x \times G \times \mathcal{A}_x \times S^x$.

In addition, we define an immediate predecessor function $ImPrd$ to describe the source state of a transition targeting a given state:

$$ImPrd(s_j) \overset{\triangle}{=} s_i : \exists s_i \xrightarrow{g/a} s_j$$

We further define a function $Prdc$ to return a potential predecessor state of a given state:

$$Prdc(s_j) \overset{\triangle}{=} (\exists s_i : ImPrd(s_j) = s_i \vee \exists s : s_i \in Prdc(s) \wedge ImPrd(s) = s_j)$$

Finally, we define each system component template with parameters $\mathcal{P} : \mathcal{P} \subset 2^V$ and behavior β as:

$$Comp_T \overset{\triangle}{=} \langle \mathcal{P}, \beta \rangle : \beta = \langle s_0^{comp}, S^{comp}, \rightarrow \rangle \, and \rightarrow \in S^{comp} \times G \times \mathcal{A}_{comp} \times S^{comp}$$

Client. The client is able to perform a set of actions given by the alphabet $\mathcal{A}_C = \{RequestAccess, NotAuthorized, SendFWUpdate, AckUpdate, ViewData, ReceiveData\}$. Several clients actions are parameterized as shown in Fig. 2. We define client variables and guards as: $V^c = \{Id\} \, and \, G^c = \{Valid(Id)\}$.

The client template is instantiated as $Client = Client_T \langle Id \rangle$. In order for the client to be able to invoke actions within the cloud the Id must be valid. Other parameters of the transition actions are FW representing firmware, F_ID representing a unique firmware identifier, res representing the acknowledgment of firmware stored by the OT and $data$ representing the data returned by the cloud. We introduce a $Size(FW)$ function to determine the size of the firmware, $IntegValid(FW)$ predicate to determine if the firmware is genuine. Finally the signature of the firmware can be analyzed using a predicate $SigValid(FW)$.

The only action allowed from the client's initial states is *RequestAccess* which ensures validation of the client's identity. This leads to the following constraint on client behavior:

$$\rightarrow \in (s_0^c, RequestAccess, s^c) \cup (S^c \setminus s_0^c, \mathcal{A}_{C \setminus RequestAccess}, s^c)$$

The rest of clients transitions require the client to hold a valid identity. This constraint is expressed by the predicate $Valid(Id)$:

$$s_i^c \xrightarrow{Valid(Id)/SendFWUpdate(FW)} s_j^c$$

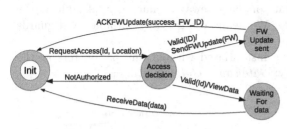

Fig. 2. Behavior model of the client

Interactive Cloud. The interactive cloud can perform a set of actions given by the alphabet $\mathcal{A}_I = \{GetData, ProvideData, GrantAccess, AlertClient, SendFW, AckUpdate\}$. Some of the alphabet actions are parametrized as shown in Fig. 3. The Interactive cloud variables and guards are: $V^i = \{\}$ and $G^i = \{InwardsOpen\}$.

The interactive cloud can be instantiated without passing any parameters as $ICloud = ICloud_T\langle\rangle$ as our system only considers a single unique interactive cloud. Some of the interactive cloud actions require acknowledgments when communicating with other system components. One of these actions is *SendFW*, which represents sending of firmware from the interactive cloud to the OT. For this reason we define a constraint on the transition relation:

$$\exists s_j : s_j \xrightarrow{AckUpdate(F\_ID,res)} s_k \text{ if } \exists s_i : s_i \in Prdc(s_j) : (s_i, SendFW(FW), s_j)$$

The interactive cloud holds a set of valid Ids: $ValidIds$, which is used to determine whether the client is allowed to invoke actions on the interactive cloud.

$$Valid(Id) \overset{\triangle}{=} \exists s_i : s_i \xrightarrow{GrantAccess(Id)} s_j \wedge Id \in ValidIds$$

Transitions within the interactive cloud that communicate towards the gateway are guarded by a read-only guard $InwardsOpen$, which ensures that the gateway allows inbound communication. An example of guarded transition is *SendFW* which represents sending of a firmware update to the OT via the gateway:

$$s_i^i \xrightarrow{InwardsOpen/SendFW(FW)} s_j^i$$

Service Cloud. The service cloud performs a set of actions given by the alphabet $\mathcal{A}_S = \{GetDataFromOT,$ $StoreData\}$. Some of the actions are parameterized as shown in Fig. 4b. The Service Cloud does not define any guards or variables and its template can be instantiated without passing any parameters as $SCloud = SCloud_T\langle\rangle$.

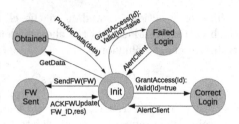

Fig. 3. Behavior model of the interactive cloud

Gateway. The gateway can perform a set of action given by the alphabet $\mathcal{A}_G = \{Open,\ Close\}$. Based on the state of the gateway a guard is applicable to the *Close* action as shown in Fig. 4a. We define the gateway variables and guards as: $V^d = \{\}$ and $G^d = \{InwardsOpen(s^d)\}$.

The gateway template can be instantiated without any parameters as the system only has a single gateway: $Gateway = Gateway_T\langle\rangle$.

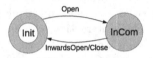

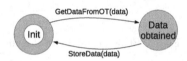

(a) Behavior model of the gateway   (b) Behavior model of the service cloud

Fig. 4. Gateway and service cloud behavior models

Operations Terminal. The OT can perform a set of actions given by the alphabet $\mathcal{A}_O = \{StoreData,\ CollectData,\ InsertUSB,\ StoreFW,\ SendData,\ ReceiveFW,\ InformCloud,\ Alert,\ AllowUSB\}$. Some of these actions can be parameterized as shown in Fig. 5. We define variables and guards for OT as: $V^o = \{Stor\}$ and $G^o = \{\}$. The OT template is instantiated with

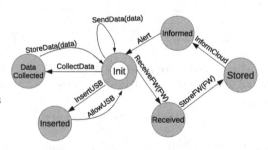

Fig. 5. Behavior model of the OT

instance attribute *Stor* which represents the space dedicated for storing of the firmware update as $OT = OT_T\langle Stor\rangle$. The transition representing the reception of firmware is:

$$s_i^o \xrightarrow{ReceiveFW(FW)} s_j^o$$

Table 1. Overview of selected synchronized transitions

Component action	Component compatible action	Description
Client $RequestAccess(Id)$	Interactive cloud $GrantAccess(Id)$	Client requesting access to the cloud
Client $SendFWUpdate(FW)$	Interactive cloud $SendFW(FW)$	Client sending firmware update to OT
Interactive cloud $AlertClient()$	Client $NotAuthorized()$	Cloud rejecting the Id of the client
Interactive cloud $SendFW(FW)$	Operations terminal $ReceiveFW(FW)$	Cloud sending firmware to operations terminal
Operations terminal $InformCloud(res, F\_ID)$	Interactive cloud $AckUpdate(res, F\_ID)$	Operations terminal sending result of update

System Behavior. The system behavior is formed by the parallel composition of component instances, which is defined as follows:

$$System \triangleq \langle \|_i\ Client\langle Id_i \rangle\ \|\ ICloud\ \|\ SCloud\ \|\ Gateway\ \|\|_j\ OT\langle Stor_j \rangle \rangle$$

Every time system execution advances it is either due to a transition of a single component instance or synchronization of two compatible component transitions. Table 1 presents the compatible actions we consider.

3 Attacks and Mitigations

Our framework requires an attack pattern as an input, hence it is focused on analysis of known attacks. Thus far we have analyzed the following attacks: uploading of malicious firmware, data theft, data tampering, data redirection, faking of client Ids as well as brute force authorization. However, due to space limitations, this section only covers the malicious firmware [5] and brute force authorization [2] attacks. Concretely, we formulate these attacks and the corresponding mitigation strategies using the definitions introduced in the previous sections. The remaining attacks are only briefly described: *data theft*: the data is acquired by a third party without this party being authorized to obtain this data. *data redirection*: the data flow is redirected to a different than intended sink by a malicious party. *faking of client Ids*: the client uses another known valid Id to increase its own privileges. Afterwards, in Sect. 4, we verify the mitigation strategies using formal analysis.

3.1 Malicious Firmware Attack and Mitigation

To execute the malicious firmware attack, the adversary creates a piece of firmware FW that either (1) does not contain a valid signature (2) is not considered genuine or (3) does not fit the firmware storage of the OT. Formally, we regard a piece of firmware FW as malicious if $\neg SigValid(FW) \vee \neg IntegValid(FW) \vee (Stor < Size(FW))$ holds. Now, to perform the attack, the adversary simply executes $SendFW(FW)$.

Once the firmware reaches the OT it must only be stored if it passes the necessary validation checks. In case there are problems with the firmware then this must be reflected by status as reported by the OT. Furthermore, the firmware status will only contain information about the firmware issue that is considered most severe: of highest concern are problems with the signature, then the firmware integrity, and finally storage related concerns. For this attack, the mitigation strategy entails performing these validation checks in order to ensure that malicious firmware is always rejected by the OT. That is, the firmware will only get stored by the OT if $SigValid(FW) \wedge IntegValid(FW) \wedge (storage \geq Size(FW))$ holds. To achieve this, we extend the OT alphabet with $VerifySig$, $VerifyIntegrity$ and $VerifySpace$ actions.

3.2   Brute Force Authorization Attack and Mitigation

For the brute force authorization attack, the adversary repeatedly tries to access the system by executing the $RequestAccess$ action using different client Ids in the hope that one them eventually will be valid. Assuming that it is sufficiently difficult for the adversary to make an educated guesses to find a valid Id, this attack can be mitigated by limiting the number of login attempts that the client is allowed to perform. To achieve this, we choose to suspend locations from which clients try to login using invalid Ids. Therefore, we extend the behavior of the interactive cloud with two new actions $MustSuspend$ and $Suspend$ defined as follows:

$$MustSuspend(Id) \triangleq Id \notin ValidIds$$

$$Suspend(Loc) \triangleq SuspendedLocs := SuspendedLocs \cup \{Loc\}$$

The former is used to decide whether the client's location must be suspended based on the client's Id, and the latter can be used to suspend locations. Finally, to prevent clients from sending and viewing data from suspended locations, we extend the actions $SendFWUpdate$ and $ViewData$ with the guard:

$$Susp(Loc) \triangleq Loc \in SuspendedLocs.$$

4   Formal Analysis

To perform tool-automated analysis of attacks and mitigation strategies, a TLA+ model has been created based on the behavioral definitions introduced above. In this model, the client, interactive cloud, service cloud, gateway and OT are modeled as individual TLA+ processes that communicate via global variables. In this Section we only show parts of the model that relate to the malicious firmware and brute force authorization attack. The full version of the model is publicly available via the references provided [19].

4.1   Case Study

As a case study[1] we are considering a system setup that consists of one client, one gateway, one interactive cloud, one service cloud and one OT. We choose to keep the setup simple as it is sufficient for our and industrial partners needs. This simple setup also limits the number of states produced by the model checker. The latter is necessary to make the verification process feasible and avoid state explosion.

The model is constructed in a way that allows us to analyze all attacks of interest within the scope of the setup. For example, how the system responds to requests from clients with both valid and invalid Ids. Or how the system handles both valid and malicious firmware updates. The model defines 20 properties that describe desirable security and liveness properties related to the attacks described in Sect. 3. These properties have been formally verified against the model using the TLC model checker. The verification process was performed on a standard laptop equipped with a 2,6 GHz dual core CPU, 16 GB of DDR 4 memory and a NVMe SSD running a Java 64 bit virtual machine. The model currently consists of 383 lines of PlusCal code that produce 1105 lines of TLA+. The TLC model checker generated a state space consisting of 187672 distinct states and verifying all 20 properties took approximately 3 min and 40 s.

4.2   Verifying the Malicious Firmware Attack Mitigation Strategy

Firmware is modeled as a structure that defines three boolean flags that describe whether the firmware has a valid signature, is considered genuine, and fits the OT's storage. Modeling firmware like this results in eight different pieces of firmware that the client could potentially send – all of which are contained in the set AllFirmware. The model accounts for all the different pieces of firmware by defining the firmware to send (clientFirmwareToSend) as being contained in AllFirmware as shown in Listing 1.1.

Listing 1.1. The client sending firmware to the OT (PlusCal)

```
fair process client = CLIENT begin
...
ClientBegin:
    either ClientSendFirmwareUpdate:
        with clientFirmwareToSend ∈ AllFirmware do
            clientFirmware := <<NextFirmwareTimestamp,
                                clientFirmwareToSend>>;
        end with;
    or ...
```

Other attacks are introduced in a similar way: the particular behavior that causes the attacks follows by expanding the "looseness" of the model in order to explore the complete state space.

---

[1] The industrial partner wishes to remain anonymous.

The OT performs different actions periodically such as processing firmware delivered by the gateway. In the model, guarding against malicious firmware is achieved by validating the firmware using the definitions `FirmwareIsGenuine`, `FirmwareHasValidSignature`, `FirmwareFitsStorage` and reporting the firmware status as explained in Sect. 3.1. The first part of the mitigation strategy (validating the signature of the firmware), as specified using PlusCal, is shown in Listing 1.2. After the firmware status has been determined, the OT sends a firmware acknowledgment to the gateway, which passes this acknowledgment on to the client cloud which delivers it to the client (the details of this has been omitted from the listing).

Listing 1.2. Processing of firmware received by the OT (PlusCal)

```
fair process ot = OT begin
OTBegin:
  ...
  OTReceiveFirmware:
    if gatewayDeliveredFirmware then
      if FirmwareHasValidSignature(clientFirmware) then
        OTFirmwareValidSignature:
          ... Perform integrity and size checks ...
      else
        OTFirmwareInvalidSignature:
          otFirmwareStatus :=
            FIRMWARE_STATUS_INVALID_SIGNATURE;
      end if;
      OTSendAck:
      ... send firmware acknowledgment ...
    end if;
  ...
```

To verify that this mitigation strategy works, it must be ensured that the firmware installed on the OT, including that on the storage device (if present), are valid (i.e. non-malicious). This property can be expressed using the following LTL predicate:

Listing 1.3. TLA property related to the malicious firmware attack

```
OTFirmwareAlwaysValid ≜
  □(FirmwareValid(otInstalledFirmware) ∧
    (otStorage ≠ NO_FIRMWARE ⇒ FirmwareValid(otStorage)))
```

Once this property is checked against the model, the model checker raises no errors. We therefore conclude that the mitigation strategy works as intended.

4.3 Verifying the Brute Force Attack Mitigation Strategy

The model has a notion of whether IDs are valid. The details of how IDs are represented, on the other hand, are of less importance, hence abstracted away. For these reasons, the model defines a single global variable that indicates whether the current client can be trusted: clientIdTrusted ∈ {**TRUE**, **FALSE**}. Related to this, the model defines the following three global flags:

- interactiveCloudLocationSuspended
- clientAuthorised
- interactiveCloudCheckedId

These variables indicate whether the current client location is suspended, the client is authorized and the client ID has been checked, respectively. Moreover, the last variable is a synchronization flag that the interactive cloud uses to signal to the client that the authorization process has finished.

From the adversary's perspective the brute force attack is successful when the client gets authorized, and the system must therefore prevent this. In addition, we wish to ensure that the system suspends locations from which brute force attacks are performed. The latter will reduce the number of attacks from the same location and make the attack more difficult to perform. This mitigation strategy, as specified using PlusCal, is shown in Listing 1.4.

Listing 1.4. Processing of login request by the interactive cloud (PlusCal)

```
fair process interactiveCloud = INTERACTIVE_CLOUD begin
...
InteractiveCloudBegin:
    await ClientRequestSent;
    if interactiveCloudLocationSuspended then
        clientAuthorised := FALSE;
        interactiveCloudCheckedId := TRUE;
    else
        if clientIdTrusted then
            ...handle client requests...
        else
            interactiveCloudLocationSuspended := TRUE;
            clientAuthorised := FALSE;
            interactiveCloudCheckedId := TRUE;
        end if;
    end if;
end process;
```

To verify that this mitigation strategy works it must be ensured that (1) clients with invalid IDs cannot access the system and (2) that locations are suspended due to unsuccessful login attempts. These two properties are confirmed to hold using the LTL predicates shown in Listing 1.5:

Listing 1.5. TLA properties related to the brute force authorization attack

```
InvalidIdsRejected ≜
    □(¬clientIdTrusted ⇒ ◇□(¬clientAuthorised))
LocationGetSuspended ≜
    □(¬clientIdTrusted ⇒ ◇□(clientCloudLocationSuspended))
```

5 Related Work

The community of researchers within the field of security of industrial control systems is embracing model-based approaches to security assessment and verification. This section presents relevant security analysis approaches for cloud-connected industrial control systems.

Wardell et al. introduce a formal framework for identifying security vulnerabilities in industrial control systems through modeling of malicious agents as potential attackers [20]. The underlying security is analyzed using model checking. However, in comparison to our work, no remedy/mitigation is presented to cope with potential attacks.

Gunawan et al. introduce a compositional security analysis framework to check system security and circumvent state space explosion [7]. The system components are individually analyzed against potential attacks. This leads to large scalability where only a subsystem is considered when analyzing a given attack pattern. By comparison we provide a framework suitable for analysis of collaborative attacks where a large set of system components is compromised/involved in the attack.

Ge et al. develop a modeling framework to assess the security of largely distributed/IoT systems [6]. The security is analyzed by assessing attack paths [16] against a set of well-defined security metrics. Based on the assessment outcomes, a library of defense strategies [4] can be evaluated against each attack in order to choose the most effective strategy. Compared to that, we provide for each attack pattern a single well-defined mitigation strategy.

Shrestha et al. use the NuSMV model checker to verify that the system model cannot reach undesirable states [17]. This is used to demonstrate the feasibility of model checking as a valuable tool for security assessment of control systems. However, compared to our work the method focuses on a local control loop within the system, rather than considering the system as a whole.

Ten et al. provide a framework to assess the security of distributed control systems [18]. Their framework combines areas of real-time monitoring, anomaly detection, impact analysis and mitigation strategies in order to prevent cyber attacks. Their framework uses an attack tree model in order to calculate a vulnerability score for the system. This approach differs from ours as we provide absolute guarantee, using model checking, that specific security properties hold.

Vulnerability assessments are used to identify where a system may be susceptible to attack [20]. In this paper, we introduce a formal security analysis framework for industrial control systems and analyze the cloud access-related security threats. Compared to the state of the art, whenever a potential successful attack is identified we do not change the system LTS specification. Instead we propose a mitigation process to handle it. This makes our framework flexible and extensible to cope with potential future attack patterns.

6 Conclusion and Future Work

This paper introduced a modeling and formal analysis framework for cyber security of cloud-connected industrial control systems. The system architecture we considered is based on a real industrial control system composed by a set of subcomponents, responsible for firmware updates, data collection and communication. We demonstrated a modular description of the system behavior including the firmware and communication. We conducted a formal analysis of the security properties of the system by executing scenarios where we exposed the system to attacks and introduced mitigation patterns to counteract these attacks. We demonstrated a mechanization of our framework using PlusCal with translation to TLA+, where the model checking has been carried out using the TLC model checker.

In the future we plan to extend our work with modeling of mitigation strategies based on industrial cyber-security standards. We wish to do this in order to ensure that the mitigation strategies follow recommended security practices.

References

1. Baker, T., Mackay, M., Shaheed, A., Aldawsari, B.: Security-oriented cloud platform for SOA-based SCADA. In: 2015 15th IEEE/ACM International Symposium on Cluster, Cloud and Grid Computing, pp. 961–970, May 2015. https://doi.org/10.1109/CCGrid.2015.37
2. Bekara, C.: Security issues and challenges for the IoT-based smart grid. Procedia Comput. Sci. **34**, 532–537 (2014). https://doi.org/10.1016/j.procs.2014.07.064, http://www.sciencedirect.com/science/article/pii/S1877050914009193. The 9th International Conference on Future Networks and Communications (FNC 2014)/The 11th International Conference on Mobile Systems and Pervasive Computing (MobiSPC 2014)/Affiliated Workshops
3. Bodeveix, J.-P., Boudjadar, A., Filali, M.: An alternative definition for timed automata composition. In: Bultan, T., Hsiung, P.-A. (eds.) ATVA 2011. LNCS, vol. 6996, pp. 105–119. Springer, Heidelberg (2011). https://doi.org/10.1007/978-3-642-24372-1_9
4. Chen, P., Cheng, S., Chen, K.: Information fusion to defend intentional attack in internet of things. IEEE Internet Things J. **1**(4), 337–348 (2014). https://doi.org/10.1109/JIOT.2014.2337018
5. Cui, A., Costello, M., Stolfo, S.J.: When firmware modifications attack: a case study of embedded exploitation. In: NDSS (2013)
6. Ge, M., Kim, D.S.: A framework for modeling and assessing security of the internet of things. In: 2015 IEEE 21st International Conference on Parallel and Distributed Systems (ICPADS), pp. 776–781 (2015). https://doi.org/10.1109/ICPADS.2015.102
7. Gunawan, L.A., Herrmann, P.: Compositional verification of application-level security properties. In: Jürjens, J., Livshits, B., Scandariato, R. (eds.) ESSoS 2013. LNCS, vol. 7781, pp. 75–90. Springer, Heidelberg (2013). https://doi.org/10.1007/978-3-642-36563-8_6
8. Hawblitzel, C., et al.: Ironclad apps: end-to-end security via automated full-system verification. In: Proceedings of the 11th USENIX Conference on Operating Systems Design and Implementation, OSDI 2014, pp. 165–181. USENIX Association, Berkeley (2014). http://dl.acm.org/citation.cfm?id=2685048.2685062

9. Jeon, B.S., Na, J.C.: A study of cyber security policy in industrial control system using data diodes. In: 2016 18th International Conference on Advanced Communication Technology (ICACT), pp. 314–317, January 2016. https://doi.org/10.1109/ICACT.2016.7423374

10. Lamport, L.: Specifying Systems: The TLA+ Language and Tools for Hardware and Software Engineers. Addison-Wesley Longman Publishing Co. Inc., Boston (2002)

11. Lamport, L.: The PlusCal algorithm language. In: Leucker, M., Morgan, C. (eds.) ICTAC 2009. LNCS, vol. 5684, pp. 36–60. Springer, Heidelberg (2009). https://doi.org/10.1007/978-3-642-03466-4_2

12. Miller, B., Rowe, D.: A survey SCADA of and critical infrastructure incidents. In: Proceedings of the 1st Annual Conference on Research in Information Technology, RIIT 2012, pp. 51–56. ACM, New York (2012). https://doi.org/10.1145/2380790.2380805

13. Pedroza, G., Apvrille, L., Knorreck, D.: AVATAR: a SysML environment for the formal verification of safety and security properties. In: 2011 11th Annual International Conference on New Technologies of Distributed Systems, pp. 1–10, May 2011. https://doi.org/10.1109/NOTERE.2011.5957992

14. Piggin, R.S.H.: Securing SCADA in the cloud: managing the risks to avoid the perfect storm. In: IET Conference Proceedings, pp. 1.2–1.2(1), January 2014. http://digital-library.theiet.org/content/conferences/10.1049/cp.2014.0535

15. Rong, C., Nguyen, S.T., Jaatun, M.G.: Beyond lightning: a survey on security challenges in cloud computing. Comput. Electr. Eng. **39**(1), 47–54 (2013). https://doi.org/10.1016/j.compeleceng.2012.04.015, http://www.sciencedirect.com/science/article/pii/S0045790612000870. Special issueon Recent Advanced Technologies and Theories for Grid and Cloud Computingand Bioengineering

16. Sheyner, O., Haines, J., Jha, S., Lippmann, R., Wing, J.M.: Automated generation and analysis of attack graphs. In: Proceedings 2002 IEEE Symposium on Security and Privacy, pp. 273–284, May 2002. https://doi.org/10.1109/SECPRI.2002.1004377

17. Shrestha, R., Mehrpouyan, H., Xu, D.: Model checking of security properties in industrial control systems (ICS). In: Proceedings of the Eighth ACM Conference on Data and Application Security and Privacy, CODASPY 2018, pp. 164–166. ACM, New York (2018). https://doi.org/10.1145/3176258.3176949

18. Ten, C., Manimaran, G., Liu, C.: Cybersecurity for Critical infrastructures: attack and defense modeling. IEEE Trans. Syst. Man Cybern. B Cybern. - Part A: Syst. Hum. **40**(4), 853–865 (2010). https://doi.org/10.1109/TSMCA.2010.2048028

19. Kulik, T., Peter W.V.: Tran-Jørgensen and Jalil Boudjadar: TLA+ model for security verification of industrial cloud-connected control system (2018). https://github.com/kuliktomas/industrial-control-system-model/blob/master/vehiclecloud.tla

20. Wardell, D.C., Mills, R.F., Peterson, G.L., Oxley, M.E.: A method for revealing and addressing security vulnerabilities in cyber-physical systems by modeling malicious agent interactions with formal verification. Procedia Comput. Sci. **95**, 24–31 (2016). https://doi.org/10.1016/j.procs.2016.09.289, http://www.sciencedirect.com/science/article/pii/S1877050916324619. Complex Adaptive Systems Los Angeles, CA November 2-4, 2016

A Hybrid Searchable Encryption Scheme for Cloud Computing

Stefania Loredana Nita[1(✉)] and Marius Iulian Mihailescu[2]

[1] Computer Science Department, University of Bucharest, Bucharest, Romania
stefanialoredanani@gmail.com
[2] RCL, Miami, FL, USA
marius.mihailescu@hotmail.com

Abstract. With the advances of technology, large amount of data is generated daily, which makes the traditional systems not to be able to handle such large quantities of data. A natural upgrade is to move to the cloud. In the last few years this was a trend adopted by an increasing number of organizations. Even an individual user uses the cloud in form of software as a service, for example, Google Drive, Google Docs, Microsoft OneDrive, Amazon Elastic Cloud etc. Also, a new trend is that smartphone manufacturers to provide a limited cloud storage in their own cloud for every user, storage used for data back-up or data storage. Extending the idea, an organization has much more data than an individual user and moving them to the cloud could be an advantage. But an organization or even an individual have sensitive documents stored on cloud and cloud computing brings many security challenges. A response to these challenges is searchable encryption, which allows searching for encrypted keywords over encrypted data on a server. In this paper, we propose a searchable encryption scheme, based on word suffix tree, in which we use two different algorithms to encrypt the keywords and documents.

Keywords: Searchable encryption · Suffix tree ·
Paillier cryptosystem · Okamoto-Uchiyama cryptosystem

1 Introduction

With advances of the technology, the amount of daily generated data is increasing fast. For example, the quantity of data produced every day in 2017 was 2.5 quintillion bytes, according to an IBM report [1]. In the last few years an increasing number of organizations moved their data into the cloud. Accessing the information is very easy: a user can access it from everywhere and anytime, all he/she needs is a good connection to the Internet. One of the advantages of the cloud is that the amount of the storage seems to be unlimited. On the other hand, the costs are decreased comparing to traditional approaches, because the maintenance and upgrades are supported by the cloud provider and the user

© Springer Nature Switzerland AG 2019
J.-L. Lanet and C. Toma (Eds.): SecITC 2018, LNCS 11359, pp. 85–96, 2019.
https://doi.org/10.1007/978-3-030-12942-2_8

pays as much as he/she uses the cloud resources. Another important feature is that the data stored in the cloud has back-ups and can be easily recovered. Lastly, the deployment is quick – just a few minutes, without needing additional installations or hardware settings.

As we have seen, adopting the cloud leads to many advantages, but let's look a little at the risks. Cloud computing is a very complex paradigm, containing many elements: networks, servers, virtual machines, software products and so on. The major concern about cloud computing is the security. Being such a complex paradigm, it inherits some security issues of its components. For example, shared infrastructure can propagate a security issue to all components that use that infrastructure. Another example is Denial-of-Service attacks, in which the users are impeded to access their data or applications.

A response to some of security challenges is searchable encryption. Let's suppose Alice has a set of documents that she wants to store in the cloud. Of course, Alice will encrypt her documents before storing them on the cloud. If she needs some particular documents from the cloud server, she would retrieve all documents from server, decrypt them, retrieve the desired documents, encrypt the documents again and store them back on the server. This process is time and resources consuming, so Alice has an idea. Before storing the documents to the cloud, she builds a secure index for every document and stores the indexes and encrypted documents on the server. When she needs a document, she will send a trapdoor to the server that contains the secure index for the desired document. The cloud server will search for the index, will select the document that matches to that index, and will send it to Alice. This is how searchable encryption (SE) works, and we can see that it allows searches of keywords/indexes over encrypted data. There are two types of SE schemes: those that use just a secret (private) key and those that use a pair of keys (public key, secret key). At its beginning, the preferred technique to create public-key SE schemes was to transform an identity-based encryption scheme into a SE scheme. Searchable encryption has many applications, for example in an email server.

In our scheme, we use two different cryptosystem to encrypt the keywords and the documents, namely Paillier encryption for keywords and Okamoto-Uchiyama for documents. The structure that will store the encrypted keywords is a word suffix tree. The suffix trees have applications in many areas, such as DNA sequencing. An advantage of the word suffix tree is that every word of the tree ends with a special symbol that marks the end of the word. We will associate to every encrypted document a unique special symbol and will use the above feature of the suffix trees to terminate the associated encrypted keywords in the word suffix tree. Then, extracting the desired document is easy: the encrypted keyword provided by the user is searched in the tree, then the documents having the identifier which terminates the encrypted keyword will be sent to the user.

The paper is organized as follows: in Sect. 2, we present the main concepts, constructions and algorithms used in our scheme, as they are proposed by their authors. In the next section, we describe our searchable encryption model based on the word suffix tree for searching keywords, and in the Sect. 4 we present an overview of the existing searchable encryption schemes. Finally, we present the conclusions of our study and briefly describe our future work.

2 Preliminaries

2.1 Cloud Computing

The National Institute of Standard and Technology (NIST) definition of the cloud computing is [2]:

"Cloud computing is a model for enabling ubiquitous, convenient, on-demand network access to a shared pool of configurable computing resources (e.g., networks, servers, storage, applications, and services) that can be rapidly provisioned and released with minimal management effort or service provider interaction."

The cloud computing types are [2,3]:

- Public cloud: it is used by the general public;
- Private cloud: it is used by a particular entity, but could be owned by a third party;
- Hybrid cloud: this is a combination between public cloud and private cloud. Some elements can be used by the general public and some elements are used just by a particular entity;
- Community cloud: this type of cloud is addressed to a community of users.

The main service models of the cloud are [2]: Software as a Service (SaaS), Platform as a Service (PaaS) and Infrastructure as a Service (IaaS). Every type of the service models provide the user different capabilities.

From the brief description of the cloud computing, we can see some advantages in adopting the cloud [2]: service on-demand, rapid elasticity, broadband network access, resource pooling, and measured services.

Even if adopting cloud computing has many advantages, a major concern exist, namely the security. In [4], the authors classified the cloud security challenges as follows:

- Communication level security challenges: these challenges arise due to the shared communication infrastructure, virtual network, configurations;
- Architectural level security challenges: these challenges arise due to the virtualization, data storage, web applications and APIs (Application User Interface), access control;
- Contractual and legal level security challenges: these challenges are non-technical, but they are also important, and arise due to the faulty service level agreements or even geographical placements of data owner and cloud provider.

2.2 Encryption Schemes

In our scheme, we will use two encryption algorithms: Paillier cryptosystem [5] and Okamoto-Uchiyama cryptosystem [6].

Paillier Cryptosystem [5]. This is a probabilistic asymmetric algorithm for the public-key cryptography. It consists in three algorithms: key generation (Algorithm 1), encryption (Algorithm 2) and decryption (Algorithm 3).

Algorithm 1. Paillier key generation algorithm
1. randomly generate primes p and q such that $\gcd(pq, (p-1)(q-1)) = 1$
2. $n \leftarrow pq$
3. $\lambda \leftarrow \operatorname{lcm}(p-1, q-1)$
4. randomly pick $g \in \mathbb{Z}_{n^2}^*$
5. $\mu \leftarrow (L(g^\lambda \mod n^2))^{-1} \mod n$
Output: $PK \leftarrow (n, g)$
$\qquad SK \leftarrow (\lambda, \mu)$

In the above algorithm, gcd represents the greatest common divisor and lcm represents the least common multiple. The L function is defined as $L(x) = \frac{x-1}{n}$. Also note that $\mathbb{Z}_{n^2}^*$ represents the group containing the integers $1, \ldots, n^2 - 1$.

Algorithm 2. Paillier encryption algorithm
Input: message $m, 0 \le m < n$
1. randomly pick r such that $0 < r < n$
2. $c \leftarrow g^m r^n \mod n^2$
Output: c

Algorithm 3. Paillier decryption algorithm
Input: ciphertext $c \in \mathbb{Z}_{n^2}^*$
1. $m \leftarrow L(c^\lambda \mod n^2)\mu \mod n$
Output: m

Okamoto-Uchiyama Cryptosystem. As Paillier cryptosystem, the Okamoto-Uchiyama is also public-key cryptosystem and contains the three algorithms: key generation (Algorithm 4), encryption (Algorithm 5) and decryption (Algorithm 6).

Algorithm 4. Okamoto-Uchiyama key generation algorithm
1. randomly generate primes p and q
2. $n \leftarrow p^2 q$
3. randomly pick $g \in (\mathbb{Z}/n\mathbb{Z})^*$ such that $g^{p-1} \neq 1 \mod p^2$
4. $h \leftarrow g^n \mod n$
Output: $PK \leftarrow (n, g, h)$
$\qquad SK \leftarrow (p, q)$

Algorithm 5. Okamoto-Uchiyama encryption algorithm
Input: message m
1. randomly pick $r \in \mathbb{Z}/n\mathbb{Z}$
2. $c \leftarrow g^m h^r \mod n$
Output: c

Algorithm 6. Okamoto-Uchiyama decryption algorithm
Input: ciphertext c
$1. m \leftarrow \frac{L(c^{p-1} \bmod p^2)}{L(g^{p-1} \bmod p^2)} \bmod p$
Output: m

For the above algorithms, the function L is also defined as $L(x) = \frac{x-1}{n}$ and $\mathbb{Z}/n\mathbb{Z}$ represents the multiplicative group of integers modulo n.

2.3 Searchable Encryption

Searchable encryption is an encryption technique that allows keywords search over the encrypted data. The main types of searchable encryption are [7]:

- *Symmetric searchable encryption (SSE)*: a private key is used. The plaintext is enciphered by the private key possessor, who also generates the keywords-based queries for searching and extracting the documents on the server.
- *Public-key Encryption with Keyword Search (PEKS)*: a pair of public key and private key is used. The public key is used by any user to generate encrypted data, but only the private key possessor can decrypt it and create the key word-based queries for searching and decrypting the documents on the server.

The entities evolved in these types of schemes are [8]:

- *Data owner.* The data owner wants to store a set of documents $D = (D_1, \ldots, D_n)$ and the associated keywords on a cloud server. The data owner encrypts the documents and keywords and then stores encrypted data on the cloud server.
- *Data user.* The data user is an authorized user who can submit keyword-based queries (called trapdoors) to the server in order to retrieve the documents that contain the keywords.
- *Cloud server.* It is the place where the data owner stores the encrypted data and the data users submits trapdoors. Also, the server makes searches on encrypted data. If it finds matches, then it sends the selected encrypted documents to the data user.

Our proposed scheme falls in the PEKS category, so in the following, we present the general algorithms for PEKS schemes [7,8]:

- KeyGen(λ) $\rightarrow$ (PK, SK): the input is a security parameter λ, and the output is a pair containing the public key PK and the secret key SK. The data owner run this algorithm in order to setup the scheme.
- Encryption(PK, D) $\rightarrow$ C: the input is the public key PK and a set of documents $D = (D_1, \ldots, D_n)$, and the output is the ciphertext $C = (C_1, \ldots, C_n)$. The algorithm is run by the data owner or data user.
- Trapdoor(SK, w) $\rightarrow$ t: the inputs are the secret key SK and the keyword w, and the output is the trapdoor t. The algorithm is run by the data user.

- Search(PK, c', t) → C': the inputs are the public key PK, the ciphertext c' of a keyword w' and the trapdoor t; the output is a set of documents C' that contains the keywords (note that the documents are encrypted). The algorithm searches for a keyword through all documents for discovering the set of documents that contains the keyword. It is performed by the cloud server.
- Decryption(SK, c_i) → D_i: the input is the secret key SK and the ciphertext c_i, and the output is the plain document D_i.

Note that the algorithms for SSE are the same, but just a secret key is used for both encryption and decryption, instead of a (public key, secret key) pair as in PEKS.

2.4   Word Suffix Tree

A word suffix tree is a particular type of suffix trees [9–11]. In the following, we will give the technical definition as it is presented in [12], where the authors adapted Ukkonen's construction algorithm for word suffix tree [11], obtaining linear complexity even in worst case.

Definition 1 (word suffix trie). *The word suffix trie of a string $w \in \Sigma_+$ is a trie which represents $Suffix_\Sigma(w)$.*

Definition 2 (word suffix tree). *The word suffix tree of a string $w \in \Sigma_+$ is a path-compressed trie which represents $Suffix_\Sigma(w)$.*

In the above definitions the term trie comes from retrieval data structure, the w represents a string, $\Sigma_+ = \Sigma^* \backslash \epsilon$ (Σ is a finite set of symbols, Σ^* is the set of strings over Σ and ϵ is the empty string), and the $Suffix_\Sigma(w)$ is the set of all suffixes of the w. In their approach, the authors used Deterministic Finite Automaton (DFA) in the initiation stage: for setting the *suffix link* (it is the result of a suffix function applied to a particular state) of the root as the initial state of the smallest DFA that accepts a dictionary Σ^* and the root of the tree as final state of the smallest DFA that accepts a dictionary Σ^*. As the construction algorithm contains many functions, we will not present it here, but in the below figure (Fig. 1) the construction process is presented, as described by the authors [12]. In our model, we will use word suffix tree and construction algorithm from [12] to generate it. Further, we will refer to the "word suffix tree" as simple "suffix tree".

3   The Proposed Model

Our proposed scheme is a PEKS scheme, in which we use the Paillier cryptosystem for the keywords and the Okamoto-Uchiyama cryptosystem for the documents.

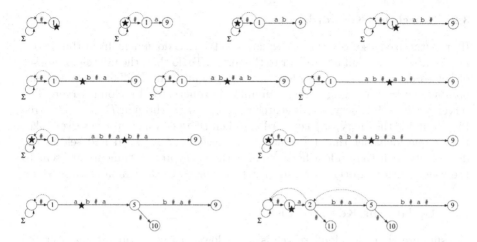

Fig. 1. The construction process of the string $w = ab\sharp ab\sharp a\sharp \in D = \{a, b\}^*$. The symbol $\sharp$ marks the end of preceding word and the star symbol $\star$ marks the location from which can be created a new edge [12].

3.1 Keywords Encryption and Documents Encryption

Let's suppose an entity A wants to store a set of documents $D = (D_1, \ldots, D_n)$, which are composed of words from Σ^*, on a cloud server. For every document D_i, A generates a unique identifier from a set of special symbols Γ (used only in this purpose) and extracts $m_i \geq 1$ keywords $kw^i = (kw_1^i, \ldots, kw_{m_i}^i) \in \Sigma_+$. Then, A encrypts the keywords using the Paillier cryptosystem and attaches to every encrypted keyword the unique identifier of the document to which belongs. Next, A generates the word suffix tree for the encrypted keywords and encrypts the documents using the Okamoto-Uchiyama cryptosystem. Finally, A stores the encrypted documents and the suffix tree of the encrypted keywords on the cloud server. Below, we present the overall algorithm described above.

Algorithm 7. Overall process of encryption
1. $c \leftarrow emptystring$
2. for $i \leftarrow 1, \ldots, n$
3. $s \leftarrow GenerateId(D_i)$
4. $kw_i \leftarrow ExtractKeywords(D_i)$
5. $c_i^j \leftarrow Paillier(kw_i^j)$
6. $c_i^{j'} \leftarrow Concat(c_i^j, s)$
7. $Concat(c, c_i^{j'})$
8. $C_i \leftarrow Okamoto(D_i)$
9. $C_i' \leftarrow Associate(C_i, s)$
10. $T \leftarrow Inenaga(c)$

11. send T to the cloud server
12. send $C \leftarrow (C_1', \ldots, C_n')$ to the cloud server

3.2 Search for Keywords

If an authorized user of entity A wants to retrieve a document from the server, he/she needs to submit a trapdoor to the server. To do that, the user chooses a set of keywords $w = (w_1, \ldots, w_k)$ and encrypts them, using Paillier cryptosystem, obtaining $c = (c_1, \ldots, c_k)$, then submits the query to the cloud server. The server receives the query, and it searches for $c_1, \ldots, c_k$ through T (the suffix tree that contains the encrypted keywords). When there is a match, the server takes the unique identifier that terminates each encrypted keyword and selects the documents with those identifiers. Finally, the encrypted documents are sent to the user, which will decrypt them, using the Okamoto-Uchiyama cryptosystem.

3.3 Update the Keyword List

We suppose that the cloud server is not allowed to make operations over the suffix tree T, other than search. To update the keywords list, firstly, the user needs to retrieve the suffix tree from the server. Then, the user needs to update the initial list of the encrypted keywords and construct again the suffix tree. Finally, the user submits the new suffix tree on the cloud server.

3.4 Adapted PEKS Algorithms

In the following, we adapt the PEKS algorithms to our model:

- KeyGen(λ) $\rightarrow$ (PK, SK): Chose λ, such that $\lambda = pq$, where p and q are primes. Run Algorithm 1 to obtain the keys for Paillier algorithm (PK$_P$, SK$_P$) and Algorithm 4 to obtain (PK$_O$, SK$_O$) for Okamoto-Uchiyama algorithm. The overall public key for our model is PK = (PK$_P$, PK$_O$) and SK = (SK$_P$, SK$_O$).
- Encryption(PK, D, kw) $\rightarrow$ (C, c): We adapted the encryption stage such that it supports the encryption of the keywords and the encryption of the documents, using different cryptosystems. Run the Algorithm 2, using PK and kw to obtain the encryption c of a keyword kw; run the Algorithm 5, using PK and D in order to obtain the encryption C of a document D.
- Trapdoor(PK, w) $\rightarrow$ t: in this algorithm it will be used also the public key PK, because we need to search an encrypted keyword using Paillier cryptosystem in a suffix tree of keywords obtained also using Paillier cryptosystem. Run Algorithm 2, using PK and w.
- Search(t, T) $\rightarrow$ C': PK is not used to search, the server just will apply the suffix tree search algorithm to find the associated encrypted documents $C' = (C'_1, \ldots, C'_k)$. If there is no such document, the server will send a proper message to the user, else it will send C' to the server.
- Decryption(SK, C'_i) $\rightarrow$ D_i: run Algorithm 6, using SK and C'_i in order to obtain the plain document D_i.

3.5   Complexity Analysis

Tree Construction. The suffix tree of the encrypted keywords contains the following encrypted keywords expressed for all n documents: $(kw^1{}_1, \ldots, kw^1{}_{m_1}), \ldots, (kw^n{}_1, \ldots, kw^n{}_{m_n})$. As the word suffix tree is constructed based on the concatenated keywords, let's denote the concatenation of all encrypted keywords with c. So, the number encrypted words in c will be:

$$\zeta := m_1 + m_2 + \ldots + m_n \tag{1}$$

The number of the edges and the numbers of the nodes of a tree gives the space complexity:

$$|V| + |E| = O(k), \tag{2}$$

where V is the set of the nodes, E is the set of the edges and k is the number of words that construct a tree. The edges of the word suffix tree used in our model contain labels of substrings of c (not just character by character), that will point to c [12]. Keeping this in mind and from Eqs. (1) and (2), we obtain that the construction space complexity of the suffix tree of the all encrypted keywords is $O(\zeta)$, so it is linear in the number of all encrypted keywords.

Further, the length of c is:

$$|c| = \tau := (|kw^1{}_1| + \ldots + |kw^1{}_{m_1}|) + \ldots + (|kw^n{}_1| + \ldots + |kw^n{}_{m_n}|) \tag{3}$$

As we used the method of the suffix tree construction presented in [12], the entire string c will be scanned, and the construction time complexity becomes linear in the length of the string. So, the time complexity to construct the suffix tree of the encrypted keywords will be $\Omega(\tau)$ (from Eq. (3)).

Search for the Keywords. Searching for an encrypted keyword c of the length l leads to a time complexity $\Omega(l)$ [12]. This is the best case, in which the user wants to find a set of documents based on just one keyword. But many times, a user is searching documents based on more keywords, let the number of them being n. So, in the worst case, the time complexity of search will be $\Omega(nl)$.

4   Related Work

In [13] it is proposed the first PEKS scheme. The basis of the scheme it is the attribute based encryption (IBE), where the message of the sender is encrypted using the public key of the receiver. The algorithms use two groups of prime order and two hash functions, it is PK-CKA2 secure, and the search complexity is linear in the number of keywords/document. Anyway, a secure channel needs to be used to send trapdoors.

In many studies, an often used approach is to transform an anonymous IBE scheme into a PEKS scheme. In [14] the authors proposed a general method through which an IBE could be transformed into a PEKS.

In [15] it is proposed a PEKS based on the Cocks IBE scheme, which is PK-CKA2 secure (namely, it respects SE definition). The search algorithm computes four Jacobi symbols, leading to a search time linear in the number of the ciphertexts. Anyway, the overhead of the communication and the storage is high.

In other studies, the researchers tried to eliminate the secure channel through which the trapdoors are sent from the sender to the server. In [16] the authors proposed a PEKS scheme in which the server has a pair of public and private keys, which allows it to search over the encrypted data.

Other studies focused on the Keyword Guessing Attack (KGA), since the keyword space is small. Based on this research, in [17] the authors proposed a scheme in which a random variable is used in the trapdoor computation that leads to an imperceptible trapdoor.

Looking at search perspective, the documents could be found based on more keywords, in the same run (ability called conjunctive keyword search). For example, in [18] the authors use a hidden vector encryption that allows arbitrary conjunctive search. The space complexity is high, because the authors use the composite order bilinear groups and the public key size requires a high cost. Anyway, the private key and the decryption operation require a minimum cost. In [19] it is proposed a new cryptographic primitive, namely witness-based searchable encryption, which ensures security against the KGA. In the construction, the authors use the smooth projective hash function and the building block.

In [20] the authors generate secure indexes based on a meta-data for every document, which are used to create a domain dictionary, used for searching on the encrypted data.

In [21] the authors propose a parallel SSE scheme that ensures forward privacy, namely, the server cannot detect if a new added document contains the keywords used in previous searches.

5   Conclusions and Future Work

In this paper we presented a searchable encryption scheme based on the word suffix tree.

Our construction uses two important cryptosystems to encrypt the keywords and the documents, respectively. We chosen two different encryption schemes, because even if an attacker analyses the keywords, the security of the documents is still ensured, because the keywords are encrypted different from the documents.

Both of encryption algorithms have homomorphic properties that allow to make operations directly on the encrypted data, without needing to retrieve the data from the server, decrypt it, make the desired operations on decrypted data, then encrypt the data again and send them back to the server. These additional steps are time and resources consuming.

In our future work, we will improve the proposed model to support operations directly over the encrypted data on the server, based on the homomorphic properties of the two cryptosystems. For example, the management of the keywords directly on the server: insert a key, update the suffix tree of keywords or delete a keyword. Regarding documents, the most difficult operation is to update an encrypted document on the server. Our future work contains a development direction, in which we will implement our proposed scheme and we will compare to existing solutions.

References

1. 10 Key marketing trends for 2017 and ideas for exceeding customer expectations. IBM Marketing Cloud (2017)
2. Mell, P., Grance, T.: The NIST definition of cloud computing (2011)
3. Chang, V., Bacigalupo, D., Wills, G., De Roure, D.: A categorisation of cloud computing business models. In: Proceedings of the 2010 10th IEEE/ACM International Conference on Cluster, Cloud and Grid Computing, pp. 509–512. IEEE Computer Society (2010)
4. Ali, M., Khan, S.U., Vasilakos, A.V.: Security in cloud computing: opportunities and challenges. Inf. Sci. **305**, 357–383 (2015)
5. Paillier, P.: Public-key cryptosystems based on composite degree residuosity classes. In: Stern, J. (ed.) EUROCRYPT 1999. LNCS, vol. 1592, pp. 223–238. Springer, Heidelberg (1999). https://doi.org/10.1007/3-540-48910-X_16
6. Okamoto, T., Uchiyama, S.: A new public-key cryptosystem as secure as factoring. In: Nyberg, K. (ed.) EUROCRYPT 1998. LNCS, vol. 1403, pp. 308–318. Springer, Heidelberg (1998). https://doi.org/10.1007/BFb0054135
7. Curtmola, R., Garay, J., Kamara, S., Ostrovsky, R.: Searchable symmetric encryption: improved definitions and efficient constructions. J. Comput. Secur. **19**(5), 895–934 (2011)
8. Wang, Y., Wang, J., Chen, X.: Secure searchable encryption: a survey. J. Commun. Inf. Netw. **1**(4), 52–65 (2016)
9. Weiner, P.: Linear pattern matching algorithms. In: 1973 IEEE Conference Record of 14th Annual Symposium on Switching and Automata Theory, SWAT 2008, pp. 1–11. IEEE (1973)
10. McCreight, E.M.: A space-economical suffix tree construction algorithm. J. ACM (JACM) **23**(2), 262–272 (1976)
11. Ukkonen, E.: Constructing suffix trees on-line in linear time. In: Proceedings of the IFIP 12th World Computer Congress on Algorithms, Software, Architecture-Information Processing 1992, pp. 484–492. North-Holland Publishing Co. (1992)
12. Inenaga, S., Takeda, M.: On-line linear-time construction of word suffix trees. In: Lewenstein, M., Valiente, G. (eds.) CPM 2006. LNCS, vol. 4009, pp. 60–71. Springer, Heidelberg (2006). https://doi.org/10.1007/11780441_7
13. Boneh, D., Di Crescenzo, G., Ostrovsky, R., Persiano, G.: Public key encryption with keyword search. In: Cachin, C., Camenisch, J.L. (eds.) EUROCRYPT 2004. LNCS, vol. 3027, pp. 506–522. Springer, Heidelberg (2004). https://doi.org/10.1007/978-3-540-24676-3_30
14. Abdalla, M., et al.: Searchable encryption revisited: consistency properties, relation to anonymous IBE, and extensions. J. Cryptol. **21**(3), 350–391 (2008)
15. Di Crescenzo, G., Saraswat, V.: Public key encryption with searchable keywords based on Jacobi symbols. In: Srinathan, K., Rangan, C.P., Yung, M. (eds.) INDOCRYPT 2007. LNCS, vol. 4859, pp. 282–296. Springer, Heidelberg (2007). https://doi.org/10.1007/978-3-540-77026-8_21

16. Baek, J., Safavi-Naini, R., Susilo, W.: Public key encryption with keyword search revisited. In: Gervasi, O., Murgante, B., Laganà, A., Taniar, D., Mun, Y., Gavrilova, M.L. (eds.) ICCSA 2008. LNCS, vol. 5072, pp. 1249–1259. Springer, Heidelberg (2008). https://doi.org/10.1007/978-3-540-69839-5_96
17. Rhee, H.S., Park, J.H., Susilo, W., Lee, D.H.: Trapdoor security in a searchable public-key encryption scheme with a designated tester. J. Syst. Softw. **83**(5), 763–771 (2010)
18. Boneh, D., Waters, B.: Conjunctive, subset, and range queries on encrypted data. In: Vadhan, S.P. (ed.) TCC 2007. LNCS, vol. 4392, pp. 535–554. Springer, Heidelberg (2007). https://doi.org/10.1007/978-3-540-70936-7_29
19. Ma, S., Mu, Y., Susilo, W., Yang, B.: Witness-based searchable encryption. Inf. Sci. **453**, 364–378 (2018)
20. Mahreen, S.K., Warsi, M.R., Neelam, S.K.: Domain dictionary-based metadata construction for search over encrypted cloud data. In: Singh, R., Choudhury, S., Gehlot, A. (eds.) Intelligent Communication, Control and Devices. AISC, vol. 624, pp. 661–669. Springer, Singapore (2018). https://doi.org/10.1007/978-981-10-5903-2_68
21. Etemad, M., Küpçü, A., Papamanthou, C., Evans, D.: Efficient dynamic searchable encryption with forward privacy. In: Proceedings on Privacy Enhancing Technologies, vol. 2018, no. 1, pp. 5–20 (2018)

Securing Cloud Storage by Transparent Biometric Cryptography

Leith Abed[1,2(✉)], Nathan Clarke[1,3], Bogdan Ghita[1],
and Abdulrahman Alruban[1,4]

[1] School of Computing, Electronics and Mathematics, Plymouth, UK
{Leith.Abed,N.Clarke,Bogdan.Ghita,
Abdulrahman.Alruban}@plymouth.ac.uk
[2] Middle Technical University, Baghdad, Iraq
[3] Security Research Institute, Edith Cowan University, Perth,
Western Australia, Australia
[4] Computer Sciences and Information Technology College,
Majmaah University, Majmaah, Saudi Arabia

Abstract. With the capability of storing huge volumes of data over the Internet, cloud storage has become a popular and desirable service for individuals and enterprises. The security issues, nevertheless, have been the intense debate within the cloud community. Given weak passwords, malicious attacks have been happened across a variety of well-known storage services (e.g. Dropbox and Google Drive) – resulting in loss the confidentiality. Although today's use of third-party cryptographic applications can independently encrypt data, it is arguably cumbersome to manually cipher/decipher each file and administer many keys. Biometric key generation can produce robust keys replacing the need to recall them. However, it still poses usability issues in terms of having to present biometric credentials each time a file needs to be encrypted/decrypted. Transparent biometrics seeks to eliminate the explicit interaction for verification and thereby remove the user inconvenience. This paper investigates the feasibility of key generation on the fly via transparent modalities including fingerprint, face and keystrokes. Sets of experiments using functional datasets reflecting a transparent fashion are conducted to determine the reliability of creating a 256-bit key via pattern classification. Practically, the proposed approach needs to create the correct key once a minute. In view of collecting numerous samples transparently, it is possible then to trade-off the false rejection against the false acceptance to tackle the high error. Accordingly, the average FAR was 0.9%, 0.02%, and 0.06% for fingerprint, face, and keystrokes respectively.

Keywords: Cloud storage · Biometric key generation · Transparent biometric

1 Introduction

Cloud computing is a sophisticated technology in the field of distributed systems providing services ranging from end-users applications, developers software platforms, to computing resources [1]. Amongst cloud computing services, cloud storage affords a capacity for remotely storing data, aimed at abstracting away the complexity of

© Springer Nature Switzerland AG 2019
J.-L. Lanet and C. Toma (Eds.): SecITC 2018, LNCS 11359, pp. 97–108, 2019.
https://doi.org/10.1007/978-3-030-12942-2_9

hardware maintenance and management. Customers also have ability to directly upload, download, update, remove, and share files via accessing their data from anywhere at all times [2]. With the rapid increase in the amount of digital information, cloud storage has been a predominant service for storing data over the Internet [3]. For instance, the services of Dropbox and Google Drive have more than 500 and 800 million active subscribers respectively [4]. Undoubtedly, cloud storage provides subscribers highly advantageous attributes including scalability, flexibility, accessibility, usability and data backup [5]. However, security issues have been the critical argument within the cloud community. Overall, cloud providers employ a number of security countermeasures, aiming at achieving robust security. Date in transit is secured by standard Internet security protocols, such as Transport Layer Security (TLS). Cryptographic techniques also encrypt data at rest to protect them from external attacks [6]. Accessing the stored data is granted by successful password verification [7]. If an attacker can obtain a verification credential, neither the security controls in transit nor at rest can combat that attack. This results in breaching data confidentiality – since the malicious access is considered to be genuine with successful verification. Passwords techniques have been the topic of intense debate in academia, and are arguably manifested to be poor [7, 8]. Subscribers often access cloud services by simple passwords. As such, a number of recent attacks have had significant impact. For instance, approximately 7 million Dropbox accounts were leaked illegally [9], and around 5 million Google Drive accounts were hacked in 2014 [10]. The selection of poor passwords arises when users are incapable of recalling, managing, and using complex passwords. With a view to handing the current security issues, many clients have sought to provide additional security through using third-party encryption tools to manually encrypt data prior to putting it into the cloud [11]. Illegitimate access to the cloud service will result in violating encrypted files which still require a secondary key – ideally for each and every file to breach them. Contrarily, these tools still bring usability issues in terms of having to manage a key for each file in addition to the login password. Subscribers also need to cipher/decipher each file manually, and this clearly leads to usability issues. Biometric key generation produces reliable and usable keys from biometrics [12] – where there is no need to remember complex passwords/keys. The application of bio-crypto key generation within cloud storage can offer the capacity to manage the security and privacy issues without incorporating any auxiliary applications. However, there are still some impairments related to the usability of the bio-crypto key and its security in reality. Users currently need to present their biometric modalities intrusively to encrypt data in practice; thus, it still presents a usability issue. The topic of transparent biometric, in which biometrics is non-intrusively acquired [13], introduces the opportunity to eradicate the usability issues of traditional biometric. This paper presents through experimentation a non-intrusive bio-cryptosystem to protect the privacy of the cloud storage data via encryption.

The remainder of the paper is structured as follows: Sect. 2 presents a literature review of the existing research to explore the biometric key generation approaches. Section 3 describes an innovative bio-crypto key generation approach. Section 4 illustrates the experimental methodology. A comprehensive evaluation and discussion are introduced in Sects. 5 and 6. The conclusion and future work are presented in Sect. 7.

2   Literature Review

Significant amounts of research have incorporated biometric and cryptography to present a biometric key generation schema that securely generates keys for security, aimed at solving the problems of poor and cumbersome passwords/secret keys [14]. The requirements of biometric key generation are secure management, revocation, performance, and diversity. While secure management ensures that the storage of important data will not affect the security, the revocation refers to the capability to cancel the key in case of hacking and reissue another one. The performance refers to the ability of generating a key for the genuine user only, and the diversity means that various keys can be created for different applications via the biometric modality [15, 16]. The fuzzy sketch and fuzzy extractor are amongst the most relevant biometric key generation approaches [17]. The former, fuzzy sketch extracts secure entity (latch construction) from the source template of the genuine user without any leakage of the template. The test template from the same user is presented to securely regenerate the same entity, and the verification will be valid if the entities are equal to a specific threshold. As such, Kanade et al. [18] proposed fuzzy sketch by xoring the iris features and a pseudo-code. The pseudo-code is constructed via encoding Hadamard and RS error correcting codes with a hashed outer random key. The outer key was used to verify that the generated fuzzy sketch belongs to the genuine user. Of course, the error correction codes are basically used to eliminate the biometric variations. The experiments performed on a public database from Iris Challenge Evaluations (ICE) demonstrated a 0.76% FRR and 0.096% FAR, with a total entropy of 94 bits. Sutcu et al. [19] introduced a fuzzy sketch using fingerprint and face. Having established the features, normalization and binarization techniques were employed to transform them from the real time into normal distributions. Afterwards, a similarity relation-based error correction code which was experimentally determined between the source and test features was applied to produce a uniform key. The secure sketch is constructed via calculating the difference between the error correction code and the multibiometric template. The databases of NIST for fingerprint and Essex Faces94 for face were used in experiments. The lower entropy for the fuzzy sketch was 39 bits at a performance of 2% FAR and 1.4% FRR.

The fuzzy exactor approach generates public data from the source sample that can create the key via the live sample of the same user. On enrolment, both the key and public data are extracted from the reference sample and only those public data are stored somewhere to be used at the time of authentication with the aim of regenerating the same key from the live sample. The public data storage should not aid adversaries to reveal any information about the secret key and/or the reference sample [17]. Li et al. [20] and Feng and Yuen [21] claimed that a fuzzy extractor could not be applied for some biometric modalities of high-dimensional geometric features, such as fingerprint and face. Accordingly, distance metrics reliant upon definitive threshold would be unable to determine the variances between the source and the test samples. As such, Li et al. [20] combined a number of error correction codes to determine the optimal method for tackling the variabilities. Furthermore, a probabilistic technique suggested by Sutcu et al. [22] was appropriately utilized in order to create the reliable key from the features. The experiments were performed by using the public database FVC02 DB2.

This research reported good results in terms of FAR and FRR which were 0% and 4.85% respectively. Contrarily, the length of the produced biometric key was 48-bit which can be hacked by guessing attack. In the same context, a neural network algorithm was exploited by Feng and Yuen [21] for identifying the discriminant features from the face modality. On enrolment, the neural perceptron trained the binary values of the high dimensional features to produce the most consistent bits and to set and store public data, such as the parameters of perceptron configuration that assist in regenerating the same features later if necessary. On verification, the neural network transforms the test face sample into the discriminant binary template by using the stored helper data. Consequently, the test template would be the same or near to the trained binary template. The experiments encouragingly demonstrated that the Genuine Acceptance Rate (GAR) was 96.38%. Interestingly, Chang [23] suggested non-static private key construction for the public key cryptosystem. The researcher exploited the keystroke technique and the RSA cryptographic approach for resolving the concerns of key management. The keystrokes were analyzed, and their features are trained via neural network to identify the generated random private key by RSA. On the key regeneration stage, the stored helper data (public key, random integer, transfer functions, weights) and the target keystroke features are utilized to generate the same random private key by reconfiguring the back-propagation algorithm. FRR and FAR were on average 5.25% and 9.61% consecutively.

From the above review, it is obvious that contributions tend to disregard numerous features to deal with fuzzy matching leading to badly impact the biometric entropy, which could result in brute-force attacks. Fuzzy matching requires a relatively consistent feature vector in order to reproduce the keys successfully. Unfortunately, with transparent biometrics, the nature of the biometric capture is far noisier, and this results in a more variable feature vector. Whilst Chang's approach presents a good way for encrypting/decrypting files, there are still specific flaws that can impact the system with regards to weak biometric entropy and using single weak modality (only keystrokes). As a result, the proposed approach in this paper will adopt the research of Chang to overcome its weaknesses and introduce a novel solution to resolve the existing concerns within cloud storage in terms of security and usability.

3   A Novel Bio-Crypto Key Generation Approach

The proposed approach seeks to develop a convenient and secure user-oriented cryptographic solution to further protect the data privacy of cloud storage by the subscribers themselves. This approach handles the shortcomings of the password login and removes the usability issues of the third-party cryptographic applications. The novel approach applies a transparent biometric technique to create a timely and repeatable bio-crypto key on the fly without storing it anywhere via extracting the reliable features. According to Chang [23], the pattern classification can be exploited towards achieving a biometric key generation scheme. In the machine learning field, this can be implemented via employing the multi-label classification problem. One of the methods to technically solve the problem of multi-label classification is an adapted algorithm approach. Backpropagation neural network is widely used to solve complex problems in pattern classification and achieved good performance [23]. As such, the approach of backpropagation algorithm is adapted for generating a long binary key from a transparent biometric technique. The innovative bio-crypto key generation scheme is depicted in Fig. 1.

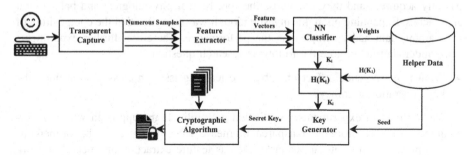

Fig. 1. The novel bio-crypto key generation scheme.

In the presented approach, the reference features would be trained by backpropagation to identify a multi-label random key. Then, only the weights in addition to the hashed key on training are stored as a helper data to reconfigure the network once again when generating the same key (master key) on encryption/decryption via the fresh features. As the target of the neural network is a binary random key of a k-bit length, the activation function of log-sigmoid is set at the output layer to produce a binary secret key and the tan-sigmoid at the hidden layer. As a result, the 1's labels would be ranked higher than the 0's labels reliant upon a specific threshold. Of course, the master key will be correct if its hash value equals the stored hashed key on enrolment. With numerous samples being acquired in a non-intrusive fashion, this verification procedure would allow to trade-off the FRR against FAR to generate the correct key. Within minute window of time, it is spontaneously possible to capture 6 samples. By applying the key verification, only one key is needed to be correct per minute. If the valid key is produced via one successful sample within that time window, the innovative approach would be effective even with 5 samples being rejected. Consequently, 1-minute key generation process is adopted to tackle the high error caused by the transparent collection. The last aspect of process is that an individual file seed stored also as a helper data is entered alongside the generated master key on encryption into a random key generator to produce document keys. Eventually, each document key is used to seamlessly encrypt each document within the cloud storage by a sophisticated cryptographic algorithm.

4 Experimental Methodology

The primary purpose of the experiment is to investigate whether transparent biometrics can be utilized within the presented key generation approach to produce a constant key. As such, experiments were developed and performed to empirically investigate the following research question:

- What is the reliability of regenerating a key material from a transparent biometric approach?

To address this question, three modalities were selected including fingerprint, face, and keystrokes. The reason of this selection is that all three modalities can be transparently acquired, and they are across the spectrum of physiological and behavioural approaches. Expanding upon this investigation, it was identified that the composition of the training data had an impact on the performance. Therefore, further experiments were undertaken to explore the following research question:

- What is the potential effect of imbalance learning issue in classification upon the key generation accuracy?

The first set of experiments investigated how reliable the approach was at generating the correct key from the transparent biometric. Accordingly, a number of methods were applied to carry out various tasks such as feature extraction and neural network configuration. Commercial algorithms were utilized to extract considerable and reliable features from the fingerprint and the face modalities. The features of the keystrokes were determined at the same time of data collection. In all experiments, the splitting approach of 50/50 was adopted to divide the samples into two groups: one for training the classifier, and the other for validating the performance of the classifier. In addition, the Feed Forward Multi-Layer Back-Propagation (FF-MLBP) for the classification problem was configured. Having conducted a number of trials in which the classification parameters were modified, the FF-MLBP settings of achieving the best performance were adopted as shown in Table 1.

Table 1. The parameters of the FF-MLBP neural network.

Modality	Input	Output	Hidden	Weights	Rounds
Fingerprint	516	256	386	200204	1000
Face	140	256	198	28372	1000
Keystrokes	60	256	158	10052	1000

The second series of experiments explored the effect of imbalance learning upon the key generation process. Training a small number of genuine samples versus large numbers of imposter samples can impact the effectiveness of the classifier in generating the key. Thus, it is believed that the overall performance of each modality was degraded because of using biased parameters. Accordingly, the random over-sampling was adopted to deal with imbalance training. By applying this method, random samples from the legitimate set were duplicated to be equal to the illegitimate set. For experimentation, functional datasets reflecting a transparent and unconstrained fashion were required. As such, realistic multimodal datasets (SDUMLA-HMT) introduced by Yin et al. [24] which included 106 users were employed for fingerprint and face. However, the GREYC keystrokes dataset [25] was satisfactorily chosen due to the absence of this modality within the SDUMLA-HMT. The SDUMLA-HMT (AES2501) [25] fingerprint dataset was selected since it is apparently more variable than the other fingerprint datasets, where the picture size clearly differed in various swiping processes. In addition, there is a significant variability within SDUMLA-HMT face dataset, where four facial variances (i.e. poses, lightings, face expressions and accessories) were taken to reflect real-life scenarios. The GREYC dataset included 133 users captured within different sessions and by two keyboards to present real variances. The accuracy of the key generation was evaluated by the FAR and FRR. The non-intrusive sample collection presents more variable feature vector leading to a higher error. The key generation process, therefore, was designed to be active through a fixed periodic manner. In this case, the correct key can be produced reliant upon the trade-off between the FRR and the FAR. As the encryption/decryption process is undertaken in a transparent fashion, many samples can be taken without inconveniencing the user. This allows the system to result in a tolerable high FRR, as long as the genuine user can generate the desired key via at least one successful sample within a predefined period of time. As such, a threshold was precisely determined on the basis which obtained the lowest FAR to ensure a valid key generation. The proposed approach operationally needs to create the correct key every minute. Practically, the system can transparently collect 6 samples per minute, and one sample at least should correctly create the wanted key. This argument accordingly confirms that the FRR rate of 83% is pretty acceptable in generating the non-intrusive key of 256-bit length, and simultaneously the FAR would be as minimal as possible.

5   Results and Analysis

On the whole, the results demonstrate that the generation of the repeatable key of 256-bit is fairly reliable to encrypt/decrypt the data in reality. Figure 2 manifests the performance of the key creation through fingerprint on imbalance training (experiment1). It is clear from the chart that the majority of participants generated the key with very limited forgery attempts, where the FRR and FAR rates ranged between 25%–75% and 0%–1.5% respectively. Contrarily, just under quarter of the population (15 users) failed to generate the key with 100% FRR, and this might be because of training pretty noisy samples besides the lack of the training samples (i.e. only 4 reference samples).

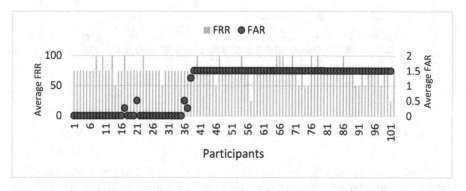

Fig. 2. The accuracy of the fingerprint key generation approach on imbalance learning.

The performance of the fingerprint key generation is relatively improved when balancing the legitimate and illegitimate spaces on training as illustrated in Fig. 3. It is obvious from the results that the vast majority of users achieved acceptable FRR and FAR figures; however, only 8 users cannot generate the key with 100% FRR. These results evidently reveal that the balance learning doses enhance the performance of the classifier in correctly generating the key of 256-bit length.

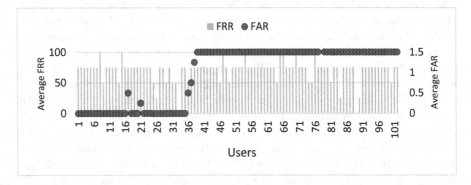

Fig. 3. The accuracy of the fingerprint key generation approach on balance learning.

The accuracy of generating the key from the face modality is very poor on imbalance training, where the whole population (except 2 users) was unable to generate the key (i.e. FRR was 96.05% on average). This could be because of training highly inconsistent facial samples in addition to the imbalance training classes (42 legitimate samples versus 3756 forgers' samples). However, the performance is noticeably improved on balance training as shown in Fig. 4.

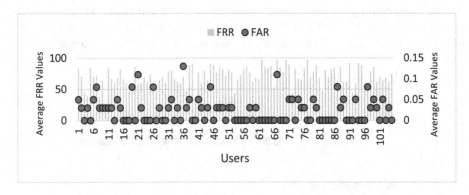

Fig. 4. The performance of the face key generation approach on balance learning.

According to the results, the majority of users succeeded to create the key with 0.02% FAR and 64.6% FRR on average due to the accurate classification. However, a quarter of the participants did not succeed to generate the key, where unsatisfactory FRR rates were accomplished – higher than 83%. This can be possible owing to the extreme variabilities of the face samples.

Figure 5 shows the performance of the key generation via keystrokes. The majority of users generated the key on imbalance learning, where the FAR and FRR figures ranged between 0%–0.13% and 10%–80% respectively. The possible interpretation is that the training of fairly acceptable 30 legitimate samples against 2970 illegitimate samples might be sufficient to accomplish a successful key generation. However, 91.66% FRR rate (very negative) on average was achieved by 18 users due to the potential of collecting pretty variant keystroke actions within overlapping intervals.

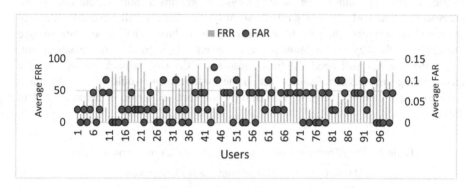

Fig. 5. The performance of the keystrokes key generation approach on imbalance learning.

On the other hand, the whole population had the capability to generate the wanted key through the keystrokes technique with a minimal illegitimacy access on balance training as outlined in Fig. 6. The experimental results reported very positive FRR and FAR rates on average which were 35.3% and 0.06% respectively. A possible explanation is that the accurate classification improved the key generation process overall – especially to those 18 users who failed to create the correct key during the time of training on imbalanced instances. Of course, whenever the FAR and FRR rates decrease, the reliability of the key generation process would be escalated.

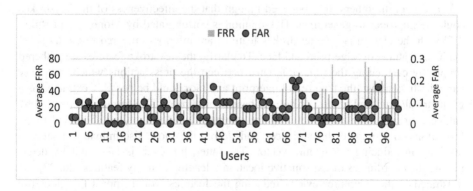

Fig. 6. The performance of the keystrokes key generation approach on balance training.

6   Discussion

Generally, the research findings demonstrate that a robust repeatable cryptographic key of 256-bit length can be positively generated from the selective transparent biometric modalities to encrypt/decrypt the data in reality. The classification conception is exploited to generate constant cryptographic keys through transparent biometric by using the training parameters and the fresh features. Consequently, high variations resultant by the non-intrusive collection would not overly impact the performance as the key is not squarely driven from the noisy features. At the same time, this perspective accomplished the necessity of including many features to reinforce the biometric entropy. The innovative bio-cryptosystem presents a more secure and usable encryption framework. With regards to security, the forgers will have difficulties in spoofing the acquired samples in a non-intrusive fashion. The helper data storage (weights) for the key regeneration process also ensures a good secure management, where the attacker still need the fresh features or the key to hack the system. By incorporating considerable features within the system, there would be a problematic issue to guess them by forgers. The entropy for each biometric is demonstrated in Table 2.

Table 2. The effective entropy (bit strength) for each biometric modality.

Modality	Fingerprint	Face	Keystrokes
Effective entropy	3956	1144	1504

In terms of usability, a convenient experience has been afforded for the cloud storage subscribers by applying transparent biometrics, where they no longer need to provide their credentials (e.g. biometrics, passwords and secret keys) to encrypt/decrypt the stored data. With numerous samples being collected transparently, the usability aspect would not affect the performance leading to eventually generate the wanted key as well as would allow the possibility of trading-off the FRR against the FAR. As such, the average FAR was 0.9%, 0.02%, and 0.06% for fingerprint, face, and keystrokes respectively. The key generation from the keystrokes modality is somewhat more effective than the others. It is believed though that the effectiveness of the keystrokes could be improper to generalize. This opinion is corroborated by Monrose and Rubin [26] with the claim that the keystrokes features are inferior compared to the transformational features of fingerprint and face. To clarify, the keystroke features are gathered simply by calculating the time difference between the press actions which are pretty variable. In contrast, the feature of fingerprint and face could be possibly extracted as a geometrical/structural feature or holistic-based coordinates. The former is extracted by engineering certain relations between the attributes besides applying additional transformations to eliminate the variances and derive the most discriminative feature – resulting in reducing the feature vector. The latter, however, is taken out by determining the coordinates of a distinctive location – leading to many features [26, 27]. As illustrated in the literature review, reducing the features would impact the biometric entropy factor and minimize the number of combination values of the feature vector. In this context, the bio-cryptosystem can be vulnerable to brute force attack. As such, this research adopted the holistic feature extraction within the fingerprint and face approaches which can be slightly less effective than the keystrokes to develop a robust trade-off between the security and accuracy.

7 Conclusion and Future Work

The existing security approaches within cloud storage are not providing sufficient security without introducing significant usability issues. Accordingly, this paper has proposed and manifested a novel transparent bio-crypto key generation approach to handle the shortcomings of the password login and removes the usability issues of the oriented cryptographic means. The results have empirically demonstrated that a reliable non-intrusive cryptographic key can be generated on the fly without storing it anywhere from the selective transparent modalities. Although the training of imbalanced legitimate and illegitimate classes has experimentally affected the key generation process, the results of balance learning have positively improved the performance in creating a reliable secret key. Future research will concentrate upon investigating the application of transparent multibiometric to maturely achieve secure and accurate cryptographic framework. A number of fusion techniques would be performed to determine the best system performance.

References

1. Kumar, N., Kushwaha, S.K., Kumar, A.: Cloud computing services and its application. Adv. Electron. Electric Eng. **4**, 107–112 (2011)
2. Columbus, L.: Roundup of cloud computing forecasts and market estimates, 2016. Forbes (2016)
3. Phillipson, C.: Cloud storage for business: 37 cloud experts reveal the top cloud storage mistakes they see companies make. http://www.docurated.com/all-things-productivity
4. Gildred, J.: Dropbox vs Google Drive: the Battle of the Titans, 30 August 2018. https://www.cloudwards.net/dropbox-vs-google-drive/
5. Behl, A., Behl, K.: An analysis of cloud computing security issues, pp. 109–114 (2012)
6. Galibus, T., Krasnoproshin, V.V., de Oliveira Albuquerque, R., de Freitas, E.P.: Elements of Cloud Storage Security Concepts, Designs and Optimized Practices (2016). https://www.researchgate.net/
7. Azam, A.S.M., Johnsson, M.: Mobile One Time Passwords and RC4 Encryption for Cloud Computing (2011)
8. Uludag, U., Pankanti, S., Prabhakar, S., Jain, A.K.: Biometric cryptosystems: issues and challenges. Proc. IEEE **92**(6), 948–960 (2004)
9. Kovach, S.: Nearly 7 Million Dropbox Passwords Have Been Hacked, 8 May 2015. http://www.businessinsider.com/
10. Vonnie: 5 million gmail passwords leaked today Here are 4 actions you need to take, 31 May 2015. http://www.fixedbyvonnie.com/
11. How to encrypt your files before uploading to Cloud Storage using CloudFogger, 5 May 2016. http://thehackernews.com/

12. Kanade, S., Petrovska-Delacrétaz, D., Dorizzi, B.: Multi-biometrics based cryptographic key regeneration scheme, pp. 1–7 (2009)
13. Clarke, N.: Transparent User Authentication: Biometrics. RFID and Behavioural Profiling. Springer, London (2011). https://doi.org/10.1007/978-0-85729-805-8
14. Rathgeb, C., Uhl, A.: A survey on biometric cryptosystems and cancelable biometrics. EURASIP J. Inf. Secur. **2011**(1), 1 (2011)
15. Kanade, S., Camara, D., Krichen, E., Petrovska-Delacrétaz, D., Dorizzi, B.: Three factor scheme for biometric-based cryptographic key regeneration using iris, pp. 59–64 (2008)
16. Jain, K., Nandakumar, K., Nagar, A.: Biometric template security. EURASIP J. Adv. Sig. Process. **2008**, 113 (2008)
17. Dodis, Y., Reyzin, L., Smith, A.: Fuzzy extractors: how to generate strong keys from biometrics and other noisy data. In: Cachin, C., Camenisch, J.L. (eds.) EUROCRYPT 2004. LNCS, vol. 3027, pp. 523–540. Springer, Heidelberg (2004). https://doi.org/10.1007/978-3-540-24676-3_31
18. Kanade, S., Camara, D., Petrovska-Delacrtaz, D., Dorizzi, B.: Application of biometrics to obtain high entropy cryptographic keys. World Acad. Sci. Eng. Tech. **52**, 330 (2009)
19. Sutcu, Y., Li, Q., Memon, N.: Secure biometric templates from fingerprint-face features, pp. 1–6 (2007)
20. Li, P., Yang, X., Qiao, H., Cao, K., Liu, E., Tian, J.: An effective biometric cryptosystem combining fingerprints with error correction codes. Expert Syst. Appl. **39**(7), 6562–6574 (2012)
21. Feng, Y.C., Yuen, P.C.: Binary discriminant analysis for generating binary face template. IEEE Trans. Inf. Forensics Secur. **7**(2), 613–624 (2012)
22. Sutcu, Y., Rane, S., Yedidia, J.S., Draper, S.C., Vetro, A.: Feature transformation of biometric templates for secure biometric systems based on error correcting codes, pp. 1–6 (2008)
23. Chang, T.-Y.: Dynamically generate a long-lived private key based on password keystroke features and neural network. Inf. Sci. **211**, 36–47 (2012)
24. Yin, Y., Liu, L., Sun, X.: SDUMLA-HMT: a multimodal biometric database. In: Sun, Z., Lai, J., Chen, X., Tan, T. (eds.) CCBR 2011. LNCS, vol. 7098, pp. 260–268. Springer, Heidelberg (2011). https://doi.org/10.1007/978-3-642-25449-9_33
25. Giot, R., El-Abed, M., Rosenberger, C.: Greyc keystroke: a benchmark for keystroke dynamics biometric systems, pp. 1–6 (2009)
26. Monrose, F., Rubin, A.D.: Keystroke dynamics as a biometric for authentication. Future Gener. Comput. Syst. **16**(4), 351–359 (2000)
27. Mohammadzade, H., Sayyafan, A., Ghojogh, B.: Pixel-level alignment of facial images for high accuracy recognition using ensemble of patches. JOSA A **35**(7), 1149–1159 (2018)

Examining the Use of Neural Networks for Intrusion Detection in Controller Area Networks

Camil Jichici[✉], Bogdan Groza, and Pal-Stefan Murvay

Faculty of Automatics and Computers, Politehnica University of Timisoara,
Timisoara, Romania
jichicicamil93@gmail.com,
{bogdan.groza,pal-stefan.murvay}@aut.upt.ro

Abstract. In the light of the recently reported attacks, in-vehicle security has become a major concern. Intrusion detection systems, common in computer networks, have been recently proposed for the in-vehicle buses as well. In this work we examine the performance of neural networks in detecting intrusions on the CAN bus. For the experiments we use a CAN trace that is extracted from a CANoe simulation for the commercial vehicle bus J1939 as well as a publicly available CAN dataset. Our results show good performance in detecting both replay and injection attacks, the former being harder to detect to their obvious similarity with the regular CAN frames. Nonetheless we discuss possibilities for integrating such detection mechanisms on automotive-grade embedded devices. The experimental results show that embedding the neural-network based intrusion detection mechanism on automotive-grade controllers is quite challenging due to large memory requirements and computational time. This suggests that dedicated hardware may be required for deploying such solutions in real-world vehicles.

Keywords: CAN bus · Vehicle security · Intrusion detection · Neural networks

1 Introduction and Related Work

Contemporary vehicles are easy targets in front of well motivated adversaries, this was well proved by recent research. The main cause for this vulnerability is the inherent lack of security on Controller Area Network (CAN) which was designed decades ago without adversaries in mind.

Recently, a strong body of research has been focusing on the use of cryptographic authentication for the CAN bus. This includes the use of regular cryptographic message authentication codes [4–6,19] but goes as far as using the physical layer to discard forged frames [10] or hide authentication bits in regular frames [24]. Attention is also payed to efficient allocation of signals in each frame [12]. Other works account for the physical layer in order to hide authentication

© Springer Nature Switzerland AG 2019
J.-L. Lanet and C. Toma (Eds.): SecITC 2018, LNCS 11359, pp. 109–125, 2019.
https://doi.org/10.1007/978-3-030-12942-2_10

bits within regular CAN bits or distinguish between nodes based on physical signal characteristics [2,3,15]. Other lines of work have been focusing in using characteristics of the physical layer to securely share a cryptographic key [7,14].

The design of intrusion detection mechanisms for CAN is an even more recent preoccupation. The use of entropy characteristics of the frames was explored by [16] and [13]. In [11], the authors propose an Intrusion Detection System (IDS) based on remote frames. The idea proposed by the authors is to send a remote frame and then stores the offset and time intervals between the remote frame and the response data frame. The experimental results demonstrated that offsets exists between normal frames and attack frames [11]. In [20] the authors show that the timestamps of messages can be used to detect attacks. Specialized detection sensors are used in [17]. Hardware measurements such as clock-shews [1] voltage thresholds or signal characteristics [3,15] may also set the stage for intrusion detection.

In [8] and [9] the authors propose an IDS based on deep neural networks. They use as input only the data-field of the CAN packet to detect the intrusion, which may not be sufficient to detect replay attacks (since replayed CAN frames are identical to genuine frames). In our proposal we use the timestamp of the CAN packet to circumvent this problem. A recurrent neural network is presented in [22]. The authors use two networks, one which is trained with the data packet and one which is trained with the CAN bus ID. A Markov Model is used in [18]. Finite-state automatons are used in [21] and multivariate time series in [23].

2   Background and Tools

In this section we discuss the adversary model then proceed to some background on neural networks and the tools that we use for evaluation.

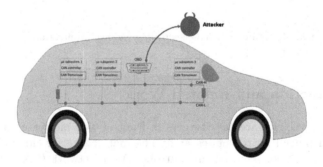

Fig. 1. Targeted scenario

2.1 Adversary Model

The setup that we address is depicted in Fig. 1. Here an adversary connects over the On-Board Diagnostics (OBD), via some compromised device and injects frames on the bus. Our work considers two types of attacks which are modelled on the CANoe trace:

1. Injection of random data, an attack in which a the malicious CAN frame is injected with the same identifier as a genuine frame but has data field that is randomly generated. The timestamp of the injected frame is a random time value between the timestamps of two regular CAN frames between which the injection takes place (we consider that this mimics a real-world attack scenario). The injection takes place at a random location in the regular trace. When analyzing traces for an attack on individual IDs, the injection occurs at random between two regular frames of the same ID. When analyzing the full trace, we consider that injection is again random, no later than few dozen frames from the genuine frame.
2. Replay of regular CAN frames, an attack in which the adversarial CAN frame has the same identifier and content. The frame has a random timestamp since it also mimics a real-world attack in which we assume that an adversary is replaying frames at random points in time. The injection is done at random locations, identical to the case of injection with random data.

Our adversary model is consistent with models from related work [11] where the authors define replay attacks and fuzzy attacks which are identical to our injections of random data. Additionally, in [11] the authors consider DoS attack by injecting the highest priority ID on the bus, i.e., 0x000h, but this attack is easy to detect since the ID does not occur in normal runs. Consequently we neglect this behaviours since detection would be trivial.

2.2 Neural Network Tools and Architecture

In our experiments we use both the Neural Network Toolbox made available by Matlab which is industry standard as well as an independent C++ implementation. The reason for using both these implementation is that the neural network toolset from Matlab is widely recognized for its performance and functionalities, however, for a microcontroller implementation an open-source C++ code is preferred. For this reason, the main results from the experimental section are done with Matlab but we also verified that similar results are obtain with the independent C++ code[1] which we also benchmark in the experimental section.

The Matlab toolbox provides plenty of algorithms and methods to solve classification problems. In particular, we used the *trainscg*, i.e., scaled conjugate gradient backpropagation, algorithm for training. The weights and bias values are updated by the algorithm using the scaled conjugate gradient method. The

---

[1] https://takinginitiative.wordpress.com/2008/04/23/basic-neural-network-tutorial-c-implementation-and-source-code/.

transfer function used between our layers is the hyperbolic tangent sigmoid transfer function *tansig* which returns a value in the range $[-1, 1]$. This function is recommended by the Matlab documentation as it offers good trade-offs where speed is important. The C++ implementation also uses the back-propagation algorithm and the a sigmoid function for activation.

For training and validation of the results, the dataset which we used is split in three parts:

1. training data (TD), which is the data used for training the network, i.e., updating the weights of the network,
2. validation data (VD), which is the data used to test how the neural network works with new data (this input is run at the end of each epoch),
3. test data (TsD) is used after the training phase (when the stop conditions are reached) and the correctness results are based on the output for this type of data.

We remark that in the C++ implementation the validation data is referred as generalization data and test data is referred as validation data. This is simply a naming convention since the role of the sets is obvious from the implementation.

An epoch sums over the running time of the entire training data set plus the generalization set. The neural network runs continuously until the stop conditions are met. We now discuss this conditions in Matlab. Since the training was in the order of minutes or less and the training stage is an off-line process which does not require a real-time response, we leave the *maximum amount of time*, one of the stop conditions for the training, set to ∞ which is the default. This allows stopping on one of the following conditions: (i) the *maximum epoch reached* (set to 1000), (ii) the *performance goal* is reached (set to 0), (iii) the performance gradient falls below the minimum gradient (set to 1e−06) or (iv) the validation performance has consecutively increased more than 6 times.

The independent C++ implementation had similar stopping conditions. For example, if the training set accuracy and generalization set accuracy is less than the desired accuracy, the network will run until the maximum epochs is reached. Otherwise, the *training set accuracy* (TSA) can be used as stop condition and this represents the number of CAN packets that are correctly classified, i.e.,

$$TSA = 100 \left(1 - \frac{NIC}{NT}\right)$$

where *NIC* is the number of incorrect results and *NT* the total number of CAN frames from the training set. Finally, another stop condition is the *generalization set accuracy* (GSA) which is identical to TSA, but computed on the generalization dataset.

The structure of the neural network consists in an input layer, a hidden layer and the output layer. These are shown in Fig. 2. The neural network input accounts for the data field, the identifier (29 bits, for extended CAN frame) and also the delay between consecutive timestamps of the same ID (Δt). Mathematically the data input vector $I \in \{0,1\}^{105}$ is described as: $I = \{b_0, b_1, b_2, ...b_{104}\}$ where bits $b_0...b_{11}$ represent the delay Δ_t, bits $b_{12}...b_{75}$ the 64-bit data field and bits $b_{76}...b_{104}$ the 29-bit identifier. The output $O \in \{0,1\}$ is given as: $O = \{b_0\}$ where

$$b_0 = \begin{cases} 1, \text{represents an attack frame} \\ 0, \text{represents a regular frame} \end{cases}$$

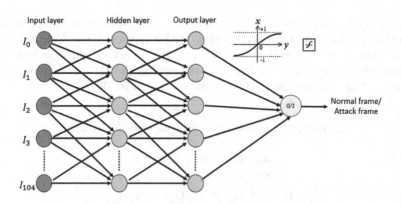

Fig. 2. Structure of the neural network

3 Experimental Results

In this section we first discuss metrics for performance evaluation then we proceed to concrete results on detection accuracy. Finally, we present results on computational performance on automotive-grade microcontrollers.

3.1 Metrics for Evaluating the Detection Rate

We evaluate success rate of the detection mechanism based on the usual four parameters: true positives (TP), i.e., the number of frames that are correctly reported as intrusions, true negatives (TN), i.e., the number of frames that are correctly reported as genuine, false positives (FP), i.e., the number of frames that are incorrectly reported as intrusions, and false negative (FN), i.e., the number of frames that are incorrectly reported as genuine. Based on these, we calculate the following: the sensitivity or the true positive rate $TPR = TP/(TP + FN)$, the false negative rate $FNR = FN/(TP + FN)$, the specificity or the true negative rate $TNR = TN/(TN + FP)$ and the fall-out or the false positive rate $FPR = FP/(FP + TN)$.

In addition to these, the validation set MSE (Mean Squared Error) is also used. This represents the average of the sum of the squared errors for each pattern in the validation set:

$$MSE = \frac{\sum_{i=0}^{n}(DesiredValue - ActualValue)^2}{n},$$

where n is the number of CAN frames from validation set.

3.2 Results on Detection Accuracy

We use a CANoe trace from a J1939 simulation. We compute the detection rates on portions of traces containing all packets with a particular CAN identifier. We consider three rates of injection: 5%, 10% and 20% of attack frames in the trace. For each injection rate we have five cases of splitting the data for training (TD), validation (VD) and testing (TsD). These are shown in Table 1.

Table 1. The five cases in which we split the dataset

I	60% TD	20% VD	20% TsD
II	40% TD	20% VD	40% TsD
III	20% TD	20% VD	60% TsD
IV	10% TD	10% VD	80% TsD
V	5% TD	5% VD	90% TsD

To begin with, we have conducted experiments on the real-world CAN bus data made public by the authors in [11]. The dataset includes traces for both regular network traffic and for the case of adversarial interventions. Unfortunately, for the later case, the traces do not have a mark to separate between injected frames and genuine frames. Consequently, we have only considered traces for fuzzy attacks and assumed that randomized frames are injections while the rest of the frames are genuine. The results, presented in Table 2, were excellent at almost 100% detection accuracy, but this is mostly due to the simplicity of the attack trace, e.g., the attack is carried on a single ID with low entropy. In what follows we complicate these experiments to test the limits of the neural network based detection.

Results on Single ID with Low vs. High Entropy. We now discuss detection rate on monitoring a single ID from our CANoe J1939 trace. Monitoring for a single ID is relevant as a baseline since it is expected that extending detection to all the IDs from the trace will require a larger neural network which in turn requires more computational power and storage space. Also, we note that in the trace that we use some of the IDs carry entropy that is close to 0, i.e., almost constant data-fields, while other frames have 12–13 bits of entropy. We present results

Table 2. Experimental results - efficiency rates regarding fuzzy attacks dataset

Inj.	Case	Neural network parameters				Results			
		Validation set max fail	Gradient	Validation set MSE	Nr. epochs	TN & TNR	TP & TPR	FP & FPR	FN & FNR
N/A	I	1	7.07e−07	9.6381e−07	24	2454	5586	2	0
						99.92%	100%	0.08%	0%
N/A	II	1	5.21e−07	7.5294e−04	31	5277	10806	2	0
						99.96%	100%	0.04%	0%
N/A	III	1	8.22e−07	7.4193e−07	28	7860	16266	2	0
						99.97%	100%	0.03%	0%
N/A	IV	1	6.08e−07	1.4023e−06	27	10462	21707	2	0
						99.98%	100%	0.02%	0%
N/A	V	1	6.49e−07	1.4732e−06	26	11827	24363	2	0
						99.98%	100%	0.02%	0%

for both these situations in Tables 3 and 4 for injections with random data. For replay attacks the results are available in Tables 5 and 6. Extended results on this dataset are deferred for the Appendix of this work in Tables 15, 16, 17 and 18. In case of injections with random data, for the higher entropy ID there is a slight increase in the false-negative rate, but detection rate is still close to 100% percents. For replay attacks, somewhat poorer results were obtained for the low-entropy ID. But the true negative rate stays at 100% while the true positive rate may occasionally drop to around 70%.

Table 3. Result on injections with random data over a low-entropy ID

Inj.	Case	Neural network parameters				Results			
		Validation set max fail	Gradient	Validation set MSE	Nr. epochs	TN & TNR	TP & TPR	FP & FPR	FN & FNR
20%	I	0	8.79e−07	1.0677e−07	29	7519	1518	0	0
						100%	100%	0%	0%
20%	II	0	9.23e−07	5.7362e−07	27	15079	2995	0	0
						100%	100%	0%	0%
20%	III	1	7.21e−07	1.7136e−06	26	22645	4466	0	0
						100%	100%	0%	0%
20%	IV	0	7.34e−07	1.1782e−06	31	30152	5996	0	0
						100%	100%	0%	0%
20%	V	1	8.12e−07	7.9371e−05	25	33871	6794	0	1
						100%	99.99%	0%	0.01%

Results on Full Trace. The results are now extended for attacks over the full trace as presented in Tables 7 and 8. In this case the attacks are carried by selecting a message at random from the trace and re-injecting it at some random point no later than a few dozen frames afterward. The data-field of the injected frame is either identical to the genuine one (replay attacks) or replaced by random data. The results start to degrade a bit as false-positives start to appear. Still, these

Table 4. Result on injections with random data over a high-entropy ID

Inj.	Case	Neural network parameters				Results			
		Validation set max fail	Gradient	Validation set MSE	Nr. epochs	TN & TNR	TP & TPR	FP & FPR	FN & FNR
20%	I	1	9.63e−07	3.7269e−07	28	7562	1475	0	0
						100%	100%	0%	0%
20%	II	1	9.57e−07	7.5004e−06	28	15093	2981	0	0
						100%	100%	0%	0%
20%	III	1	6.32e−07	3.281e−05	28	22645	4457	0	0
						100%	100%	0%	0%
20%	IV	0	8.27e−07	3.8664e−05	28	30161	5987	0	0
						100%	100%	0%	0%
20%	V	0	7.31e−07	5.3963e−06	29	33890	6774	0	2
						100%	99.97%	0%	0.03%

Table 5. Result on replay attacks over a low-entropy ID

Inj.	Case	Neural network parameters				Results			
		Validation set max fail	Gradient	Validation set MSE	Nr. epochs	TN & TNR	TP & TPR	FP & FPR	FN & FNR
20%	I	6	1.10e−03	2.9128e−04	26	7530	1507	0	0
						100%	100%	0%	0%
20%	II	6	2.32e−03	6.1636e−06	37	15086	2909	0	79
						100%	97.36%	0%	2.64%
20%	III	6	6.64e−04	6.0327e−03	33	22601	4297	0	213
						100%	95.28%	0%	4.72%
20%	IV	6	2.74e−03	4.3834e−03	16	30081	5639	0	428
						100%	92.95%	0%	7.05%
20%	V	6	4.23e−03	2.5314e−02	13	33886	5855	0	925
						100%	86.36%	0%	13.64%

Table 6. Result on replay attacks over a high-entropy ID

Inj.	Case	Neural network parameters				Results			
		Validation set max fail	Gradient	Validation set MSE	Nr. epochs	TN & TNR	TP & TPR	FP & FPR	FN & FNR
20%	I	6	9.61e−07	2.0248e−06	43	7557	1449	0	31
						100%	97.91%	0%	2.09%
20%	II	1	6.70e−07	3.7639e−03	45	15051	2992	0	31
						100%	98.97%	0%	1.03%
20%	III	6	6.64e−04	6.0327e−03	33	22592	4431	0	88
						100%	98.05%	0%	1.95%
20%	IV	1	8.85e−07	4.2954e−05	43	30147	5936	0	65
						100%	98.92%	0%	1.08%
20%	V	0	5.92e−07	1.8005e−05	42	33886	6585	0	195
						100%	97.12%	0%	2.88%

stay at several percents and only in case of 20% replays they increase to 13.83%. A bigger concern are the false negatives which also increase at almost 43.58% in case of 5% replays. This may be due to the low density of the training set since the rate drops at 17.64% as soon as the injection rate is increased at 20%.

Table 7. Results on injections with random over the full trace

Inj.	Case	Neural network parameters				Results			
		Validation set max fail	Gradient	Validation set MSE	Nr. epochs	TN & TNR	TP & TPR	FP & FPR	FN & FNR
5%	IV	1	9.15e−07	9.4955e−04	47	79842	3833	257	68
						99.68%	98.26%	0.32%	1.74%
5%	V	1	7.51e−07	8.2342e−04	50	89782	4368	269	81
						99.70%	98.18%	0.3%	1.82%
20%	IV	0	6.07e−07	1.6087e−03	48	80137	15552	288	23
						99.64%	99.85%	0.36%	0.15%
20%	V	1	8.34e−07	3.6169e−04	41	89850	17700	347	103
						99.62%	99.42%	0.38%	0.58%

Table 8. Results on replay attacks over the full trace

Inj.	Case	Neural network parameters				Results			
		Validation set max fail	Gradient	Validation set MSE	Nr. epochs	TN & TNR	TP & TPR	FP & FPR	FN & FNR
5%	IV	6	1.41e−02	1.8857e−02	213	78749	2445	1305	1501
						98.37%	61.96%	1.63%	38.04%
5%	V	6	3.47e−03	2.1721e−02	167	88401	2526	1622	1951
						98.20%	56.42%	1.80%	43.58%
20%	IV	6	2.01e−02	3.8511e−02	150	69220	12909	11106	2765
						86.17%	83.26%	13.83%	17.64%
20%	V	6	9.12e−03	3.7179e−02	158	80157	14430	10001	3412
						88.91%	80.88%	11.09%	19.12%

Results on Full Trace with Reduced Network Size. Reducing the network size is mandatory since the computational and memory load may be too high for automotive-grade controllers as we discuss in the next section. Tables 9 and 10 hold results for injections with random data and replays over the full trace with a network that has a hidden layer reduced to 1/4. Tables 11 and 12 hold the same results for a network with a hidden layer reduced to 1/16. As expected, the performance does degrade with a reduce network size. Still, the results are satisfactory at both 1/4 and 1/16 size of the hidden layer. Again the most significant degradation is for the false-negatives in case of replay attacks. This improves as soon as replays are increased to 20% suggesting the need for a bigger training set.

Results on a Longer Trace. Finally, we experiment with a longer trace of 500,000 frames. The objective was to determine if the longer trace will increase the false-positives rate. This however appears to remain stable and correlate only with the injection rate and learning time which was already obvious from the previous experiments. For brevity, the results are moved to Appendix A in Tables 19, 20 and 21 for injections with random data and Table 22 for replays.

Table 9. Results on injections with random data over the full trace at 1/4 hidden layer size

Inj.	Case	Neural network parameters				Results			
		Validation set max fail	Gradient	Validation set MSE	Nr. epochs	TN & TNR	TP & TPR	FP & FPR	FN & FNR
5%	IV	0	9.35e−07	4.9171e−04	45	79842	3846	257	67
						99.68%	98.28%	0.32%	1.72%
5%	V	1	4.60e−07	2.0366e−03	46	89665	4275	386	174
						99.57%	96.09%	0.43%	3.91%
20%	IV	6	5.42e−07	7.3191e−04	52	80153	15462	272	113
						99.66%	99.27%	0.34%	0.73%
20%	V	1	9.90e−07	1.0166e−03	50	89471	17695	726	108
						99.20%	99.39%	0.80%	0.61%

Table 10. Results on replay attacks over the full trace at 1/4 hidden layer size

Inj.	Case	Neural network parameters				Results			
		Validation set max fail	Gradient	Validation set MSE	Nr. epochs	TN & TNR	TP & TPR	FP & FPR	FN & FNR
5%	IV	6	8.93e−03	1.8363e−02	281	78719	2476	1335	1470
						98.33%	62.75%	1.67%	37.25%
5%	V	6	1.07e−02	1.8056e−02	214	89050	2711	973	1766
						98.92%	60.55%	1.08%	39.45%
20%	IV	6	1.82e−02	3.4832e−02	306	72010	12742	8316	2932
						89.65%	81.29%	10.35%	18.71%
20%	V	6	1.09e−02	3.4798e−02	154	84019	14046	6139	3796
						93.19%	78.72%	6.81%	21.28%

Table 11. Results on injections with random data over the full trace at 1/16 hidden layer size

Inj.	Case	Neural Network Parameters				Results			
		Validation set max fail	Gradient	Validation set MSE	Nr. epochs	TN & TNR	TP & TPR	FP & FPR	FN & FNR
5%	IV	6	1.79e−04	1.1984e−03	53	79818	3757	281	144
						99.65%	96.31%	0.35%	3.69%
5%	V	6	3.15e−05	1.6704e−03	39	89444	4229	607	220
						99.33%	95.06%	0.67%	4.94%
20%	IV	6	4.0e−05	1.1148e−03	42	80007	15401	418	174
						99.48%	98.88%	0.52%	1.12%
20%	V	6	7.50e−05	2.3672e−03	54	88763	17439	1434	364
						98.41%	97.96%	1.59%	2.04%

3.3 Computational Results

The successful deployment of an IDS in real life vehicular applications depends on the computational constraints of the embedded platforms employed in its implementation. We examine the computational performance of our proposal by measuring the runtime of the detection algorithm on three automotive grade platforms. The first, representing the low-performance device group, is a NXP

Table 12. Results on replay attacks over the full trace at 1/16 hidden layer size

Inj.	Case	Neural network parameters				Results			
		Validation set max fail	Gradient	Validation set MSE	Nr. epochs	TN & TNR	TP & TPR	FP & FPR	FN & FNR
5%	IV	6	7.86e−03	2.8314e−02	125	79528	1791	526	2155
						99.34%	45.39%	0.66%	54.61%
5%	V	6	4.45e−03	2.6876e−02	113	88184	1871	1839	2606
						97.96%	41.79%	2.04%	58.21%
20%	IV	6	1.35e−02	4.1603e−02	189	63747	12704	16579	2970
						79.36%	81.05%	20.64%	18.95%
20%	V	6	1.69e−02	4.5909e−02	202	74453	13068	15705	4774
						82.58%	73.24%	17.42%	26.76%

S12XF512 microcontroller. From the high performance sector we employed an Infineon AURIX TC297 microcontroller and a Renesas RH850/E1x. The S12XF chip comes with 32 KB of RAM, 512 KB of Flash and a 16 bit main core (a coprocessor is also available for reducing peripheral interrupt load) that can provide a top operating frequency of 50 MHz. On the other hand, the AURIX platform is equipped with 728 KB of RAM, 8 MB of Flash and three 32-bit cores running at up to 300 MHz. The Renesas platform which we evaluated using a dedicated simulator offers 352 KB of RAM and 4 MB of Flash and two 32 bit cores clocked at up to 320 MHz.

Our detection algorithm was implemented to run on a single-core using training data that is stored in the Flash memory. We assume that the weights are computed off-line and already available as a result of an initial training step. Three sets of weights were used in our tests corresponding to the network with a full size hidden layer, a hidden layer reduced to 1/4 and 1/16 respectively. Tests were made using set of weights stored both as single and double precision floating point values. Tables 13 and 14 holds the run-times measured for the detection algorithm in the analysed scenarios. We were unable to obtain results for running the detection algorithm on the S12XF platform with the full size hidden layer due to limitation in the employed compiler.

Table 13. Computational results on single precision floats

Platform	Full hidden layer	1/4 hidden layer	1/16 hidden layer
S12XF512	n/a	52.3 ms	13.22 ms
TC297	3.904 ms	899 μs	237.5 μs
RH850/E1x-FCC1	2.697 ms	667.1 μs	157.6 μs

As expected, the low-end platform bring on a considerable performance bottleneck making the deployment of the detection algorithm only feasible for a reduced neural network size and a CAN network with few nodes sending messages with high cycle times (i.e. greater than 100 ms). High performance platforms

Table 14. Computational results on double precision floats

Platform	Full hidden layer	1/4 hidden layer	1/16 hidden layer
S12XF512	n/a	110.5 ms	25.76 ms
TC297	15.26 ms	3.744 ms	822 μs
RH850/E1x-FCC1	2.680 ms	671.3 μs	162.73 μs

prove to be more suitable for implementing the detection algorithm. However, using the full version of the proposed neural network may still be problematic for handling CAN traffic with cycle times in the order of 10 s of milliseconds.

4 Conclusion

Neural networks prove to be effective in detecting intrusions on CAN but limitations exists. As expected, the results are split between the two types of attacks replay vs. modification attacks. For replay attacks detection rate is lower because injected frames are identical to genuine frames. In this case the time-stamp is the only indicator. In case of injections with random data, the attack is easily detected by the network. From the detection point of view, the results are satisfactory and neural networks looks like a promising mechanism for detecting intrusions on the CAN bus. The more significant problem comes from computational and storage requirements as neural networks do not appear suitable for low-end automotive-grade controllers. High-end controllers may cope with neural networks of reduced size, but computational demands are still high. Thus detection may not be always carried locally on each node, unless dedicated hardware is added. The solution may be to rely on gateways equipped with stronger cores that can filter traffic in real time. Such a solution may be subject of future investigations for us. Nonetheless, we plan as future work extending this evaluation over more complex real-world in-vehicle traces from CAN, CAN-FD and FlexRay.

Acknowledgement. This work was supported by a grant of Ministry of Research and Inovation, CNCS-UEFISCDI, project number PN-III-P1-1.1-TE-2016-1317, within PNCDI III (2018–2020).

A   Appendix - Results on Various Injection Rates over a Single ID and a Longer Trace of 500,000 Packets

Table 15. Result on injections with random data over a low-entropy ID

Inj.	Case	Neural network parameters				Results			
		Validation set max fail	Gradient	Validation set MSE	Nr. epochs	TN & TNR	TP & TPR	FP & FPR	FN & FNR
5%	I	0	7.88e−07	9.4077e−07	28	7537	370	0	0
						100%	100%	0%	0%
5%	II	0	9.36e−07	7.0086e−06	26	15078	736	0	0
						100%	100%	0%	0%
5%	III	1	7.64e−07	1.6502e−05	26	22603	1119	0	0
						100%	100%	0%	0%
5%	IV	1	9.78e−07	6.7137e−05	25	30113	1511	0	5
						100%	99.67%	0%	0.33%
5%	V	1	6.33e−07	8.5875e−05	25	33892	1683	0	8
						100%	99.53%	0%	0.47%
10%	I	6	7.95e−07	1.2784e−07	20	7562	721	0	0
						100%	100%	0%	0%
10%	II	0	7.17e−07	1.3031e−07	23	15073	1494	0	0
						100%	100%	0%	0%
10%	III	1	8.39e−07	1.0475e−06	27	22603	2248	0	0
						100%	100%	0%	0%
10%	IV	1	6.92e−07	2.5506e−05	25	30133	3002	0	0
						100%	100%	0%	0%
10%	V	1	7.53e−07	2.7009e−05	27	33892	3385	0	0
						100%	100%	0%	0%

Table 16. Result on injections with random data over a high-entropy ID

Inj.	Case	Neural network parameters				Results			
		Validation set max fail	Gradient	Validation set MSE	Nr. epochs	TN & TNR	TP & TPR	FP & FPR	FN & FNR
5%	I	0	9.73e−07	1.7407e−06	29	7535	372	0	0
						100%	100%	0%	0%
5%	II	0	8.36e−07	1.4209e−05	26	15068	746	0	0
						100%	100%	0%	0%
5%	III	1	6.65e−07	2.1e−05	29	22584	1136	0	2
						100%	99.82%	0%	0.18%
5%	IV	0	8.58e−07	1.6136e−04	27	30126	1498	0	5
						100%	99.67%	0%	0.33%
5%	V	0	6.57e−07	1.0028e−03	25	33898	1665	0	20
						100%	98.81%	0%	1.19%
10%	I	1	7.10e−07	1.2579e−06	26	7518	765	0	0
						100%	100%	0%	0%
10%	II	0	7.63e−07	2.8341e−06	25	15057	1510	0	0
						100%	100%	0%	0%
10%	III	1	8.85e−07	1.556e−05	20	22615	2234	0	2
						100%	99.91%	0%	0.09%
10%	IV	1	6.04e−07	7.2312e−07	17	30151	2983	0	1
						100%	99.97%	0%	0.03%
10%	V	0	7.23e−07	9.4239e−05	27	33884	3390	0	3
						100%	99.91%	0%	0.09%

Table 17. Result on replay attacks over a low-entropy ID

Inj.	Case	Neural network parameters				Results			
		Validation set max fail	Gradient	Validation set MSE	Nr. epochs	TN & TNR	TP & TPR	FP & FPR	FN & FNR
5%	I	6	1.59e−03	6.2598e−04	13	7561	346	0	0
						100%	100%	0%	0%
5%	II	6	5.11e−04	3.2658e−04	27	15082	693	0	39
						100%	94.67%	0%	5.33%
5%	III	6	7.18e−04	1.1147e−03	19	22618	1031	0	73
						100%	93.39%	0%	6.61%
5%	IV	6	5.87e−03	4.7389e−03	11	30132	1375	0	122
						100%	91.85%	0%	8.15%
5%	V	6	1.18e−03	1.9846e−02	14	33894	1308	0	381
						100%	77.44%	0%	22.26%
10%	I	6	4.98e−04	4.4403e−05	25	7549	734	0	0
						100%	100%	0%	0%
10%	II	6	6.35e−03	1.0116e−03	24	15081	1455	0	31
						100%	97.91%	0%	2.09%
10%	III	6	1.86e−03	7.7252e−04	16	22608	2126	0	117
						100%	94.78%	0%	5.22%
10%	IV	6	4.99e−03	8.5069e−03	13	30120	2803	0	212
						100%	92.97%	0%	7.03%
10%	V	6	1.69e−02	1.9815e−02	12	33882	2638	0	757
						100%	77.70%	0%	22.30%

Table 18. Result on replay attacks over a high-entropy ID

Inj.	Case	Neural network parameters				Results			
		Validation set max fail	Gradient	Validation set MSE	Nr. epochs	TN & TNR	TP & TPR	FP & FPR	FN & FNR
5%	I	0	9.62e−07	4.106e−08	42	7519	388	0	0
						100%	100%	0%	0%
5%	II	0	8.82e−07	6.7873e−08	47	15072	742	0	0
						100%	100%	0%	0%
5%	III	6	5.35e−05	4.8317e−05	43	22568	1154	0	0
						100%	100%	0%	0%
5%	IV	0	8.44e−07	8.9661e−08	53	30116	1458	0	55
						100%	96.36%	0%	3.64%
5%	V	6	1.35e−03	1.1116e−02	27	33875	1486	0	222
						100%	87%	0%	13%
10%	I	0	7.19e−07	4.7954e−08	51	7536	747	0	0
						100%	100%	0%	0%
10%	II	6	5.74e−04	1.8338-04	27	15068	1469	0	30
						100%	98%	0%	2%
10%	III	0	8.57e−07	4.0524e−08	48	22608	2126	0	117
						100%	94.96%	0%	5.04%
10%	IV	0	9.36e−07	1.5564e−08	68	30116	2831	0	188
						100%	93.77%	0%	6.23%
10%	V	6	3.33e−03	7.7698e−03	13	33877	3124	0	276
						100%	91.88%	0%	8.12%

Table 19. Results on injections with random data over a longer trace of 500,000 frames

Inj.	Case	Neural network parameters				Results			
		Validation set max fail	Gradient	Validation set MSE	Nr. epochs	TN & TNR	TP & TPR	FP & FPR	FN & FNR
5%	IV	1	9.04e−07	3.4937e−05	95	400193	19757	0	50
						100%	99.75%	0%	0.25%
5%	V	6	2.04e−05	6.4378e−03	53	450013	22302	93	92
						99.98%	99.59%	0.02%	0.41%
20%	IV	1	8.20e−07	6.1195e−05	58	401825	78159	0	16
						100%	99.98%	0%	0.02%
20%	V	0	7.50e−07	5.5172e−03	52	450822	89024	95	59
						99.98%	99.93%	0.02%	0.07%

Table 20. Results on injections with random data over a longer trace of 500,000 frames and 1/4 network size

Inj.	Case	Neural network parameters				Results			
		Validation set max fail	Gradient	Validation set MSE	Nr. epochs	TN & TNR	TP & TPR	FP & FPR	FN & FNR
5%	IV	1	9.04e−07	1.0093e−04	51	400193	19708	0	99
						100%	99.5%	0%	0.5%
5%	V	6	2.19e−04	6.357e−03	38	450014	22023	92	371
						99.98%	98.34%	0.02%	1.66%
20%	IV	1	8.35e−07	1.1475e−04	66	401825	78106	0	69
						100%	99.91%	0%	0.09%
20%	V	1	6.39e−07	5.5222e−03	50	450822	89007	95	76
						99.98%	99.91%	0.02%	0.09%

Table 21. Results on injections with random data over a longer trace of 500,000 frames and 1/16 network size

Inj.	Case	Neural network parameters				Results			
		Validation set max fail	Gradient	Validation set MSE	Nr. epochs	TN & TNR	TP & TPR	FP & FPR	FN & FNR
5%	IV	6	6.24e−05	1.3187e−04	62	400193	19677	0	130
						100%	99.34%	0%	0.66%
5%	V	6	1.41e−06	6.7372e−03	74	450013	22082	93	312
						99.98%	98.61%	0.02%	1.39%
20%	IV	6	1.28e−04	5.2868e−04	96	401825	77864	0	311
						100%	99.60%	0%	0.4%
20%	V	6	7.85e−05	5.0288e−03	63	450836	88707	81	376
						99.98%	99.58%	0.02%	0.42%

Table 22. Results on replay attacks over a longer trace of 500,000 frames

Inj.	Case	Neural network parameters				Results			
		Validation set max fail	Gradient	Validation set MSE	Nr. epochs	TN & TNR	TP & TPR	FP & FPR	FN & FNR
5%	IV	6	2.21e−02	2.6788e−02	79	399912	9267	122	10699
						99.97%	46.41%	0.03%	53.59%
5%	V	6	1.23e−02	3.3719e−02	62	449910	8981	160	13449
						99.96%	40.04%	0.04%	59.96%
20%	IV	6	6.93e−02	1.2133e−01	41	392552	35752	9215	42481
						97.71%	45.70%	2.29%	54.30%
20%	V	6	4.06e−02	6.7429e−02	78	329834	59553	121051	29562
						73.15%	66.83%	26.85%	33.17%

References

1. Cho, K.-T., Shin, K.G.: Fingerprinting electronic control units for vehicle intrusion detection. In: 25th USENIX Security Symposium (2016)
2. Choi, W., Jo, H.J., Woo, S., Chun, J.Y., Park, J., Lee, D.H.: Identifying ECUs using inimitable characteristics of signals in controller area networks. IEEE Trans. Veh. Technol. **67**(6), 4757–4770 (2018)
3. Choi, W., Joo, K., Jo, H.J., Park, M.C., Lee, D.H.: VoltageIDS: low-level communication characteristics for automotive intrusion detection system. IEEE Trans. Inf. Forensics Secur. **13**, 2114–2129 (2018)
4. Groza, B., Murvay, S., van Herrewege, A., Verbauwhede, I.: LiBrA-CAN: a lightweight broadcast authentication protocol for controller area networks. In: Pieprzyk, J., Sadeghi, A.R., Manulis, M. (eds.) CANS 2012. LNCS, vol. 7712, pp. 185–200. Springer, Heidelberg (2012). https://doi.org/10.1007/978-3-642-35404-5_15
5. Groza, B., Murvay, S.: Efficient protocols for secure broadcast in controller area networks. IEEE Trans. Ind. Inform. **9**(4), 2034–2042 (2013)
6. Hartkopp, O., Reuber, C., Schilling, R.: MaCAN-message authenticated CAN. In: 10th International Conference on Embedded Security in Cars (ESCAR 2012) (2012)
7. Jain, S., Guajardo, J.: Physical layer group key agreement for automotive controller area networks. In: Gierlichs, B., Poschmann, A.Y. (eds.) CHES 2016. LNCS, vol. 9813, pp. 85–105. Springer, Heidelberg (2016). https://doi.org/10.1007/978-3-662-53140-2_5
8. Kang, M.-J., Kang, J.-W.: Intrusion detection system using deep neural network for in-vehicle network security. PloS One **11**(6), e0155781 (2016)
9. Kang, M.-J., Kang, J.-W.: A novel intrusion detection method using deep neural network for in-vehicle network security. In: 2016 IEEE 83rd Vehicular Technology Conference (VTC Spring), pp. 1–5. IEEE (2016)
10. Kurachi, R., Matsubara, Y., Takada, H., Adachi, N., Miyashita, Y., Horihata, S.: CaCAN - centralized authentication system in CAN (controller area network). In: 14th International Conference on Embedded Security in Cars (ESCAR 2014) (2014)
11. Lee, H., Jeong, S.H., Kim, H.K.: OTIDS: a novel intrusion detection system for in-vehicle network by using remote frame. In: Privacy, Security and Trust (PST) 2017 (2017)

12. Lin, C.-W., Zhu, Q., Sangiovanni-Vincentelli, A.: Security-aware modeling and efficient mapping for CAN-based real-time distributed automotive systems. IEEE Embed. Syst. Lett. **7**(1), 11–14 (2015)
13. Marchetti, M., Stabili, D., Guido, A., Colajanni, M.: Evaluation of anomaly detection for in-vehicle networks through information-theoretic algorithms. In: Research and Technologies for Society and Industry Leveraging a Better Tomorrow (RTSI), pp. 1–6. IEEE (2016)
14. Mueller, A., Lothspeich, T.: Plug-and-secure communication for CAN. CAN Newsl. **4**, 10–14 (2015)
15. Murvay, P.-S., Groza, B.: Source identification using signal characteristics in controller area networks. IEEE Sig. Process. Lett. **21**(4), 395–399 (2014)
16. Müter, M., Asaj, N.: Entropy-based anomaly detection for in-vehicle networks. In: 2011 IEEE Intelligent Vehicles Symposium (IV), pp. 1110–1115. IEEE (2011)
17. Müter, M., Groll, A., Freiling, F.C.: A structured approach to anomaly detection for in-vehicle networks. In: 2010 Sixth International Conference on Information Assurance and Security (IAS), pp. 92–98. IEEE (2010)
18. Narayanan, S.N., Mittal, S., Joshi, A.: OBD_SecureAlert: an anomaly detection system for vehicles. In: 2016 IEEE International Conference on Smart Computing (SMARTCOMP), pp. 1–6. IEEE (2016)
19. Radu, A.-I., Garcia, F.D.: LeiA: a lightweight authentication protocol for CAN. In: Askoxylakis, I., Ioannidis, S., Katsikas, S., Meadows, C. (eds.) ESORICS 2016. LNCS, vol. 9879, pp. 283–300. Springer, Cham (2016). https://doi.org/10.1007/978-3-319-45741-3_15
20. Song, H.M., Kim, H.R., Kim, H.K.: Intrusion detection system based on the analysis of time intervals of CAN messages for in-vehicle network. In: 2016 International Conference on Information Networking (ICOIN), pp. 63–68. IEEE (2016)
21. Studnia, I., Alata, E., Nicomette, V., Kaâniche, M., Laarouchi, Y.: A language-based intrusion detection approach for automotive embedded networks. Int. J. Embed. Syst. **10**(1), 1–12 (2018)
22. Taylor, A., Leblanc, S., Japkowicz, N.: Anomaly detection in automobile control network data with long short-term memory networks. In: 2016 IEEE International Conference on Data Science and Advanced Analytics (DSAA), pp. 130–139. IEEE (2016)
23. Theissler, A.: Detecting known and unknown faults in automotive systems using ensemble-based anomaly detection. Knowl.-Based Syst. **123**, 163–173 (2017)
24. Van Herrewege, A., Singelee, D., Verbauwhede, I.: CANAuth-a simple, backward compatible broadcast authentication protocol for CAN bus. In: ECRYPT Workshop on Lightweight Cryptography, vol. 2011 (2011)

An Evaluation of OCR Systems Against Adversarial Machine Learning

Dan Sporici[✉], Mihai Chiroiu, and Dan Ciocîrlan

Bucharest, Romania
dan.sporici@cti.pub.ro

Abstract. Optical Character Recognition (OCR), while representing a significant progress in the field of computer vision can also contribute to malicious acts that imply automation. As an example, copycats of whole books use OCR technologies to eliminate the effort of typing by hand whenever a clear text version is not available; the same OCR process is also used by various bots in order to bypass CAPTCHA filters and gain access to certain functionalities. In this paper, we propose an approach for automatically converting text into unrecognizable characters for the OCR systems. This approach uses adversarial machine learning techniques, based on crafting inputs in an evolutionary manner, in order to adapt documents by performing a relatively small number of changes which should, in turn, make the text unrecognizable. We show that our mechanism can preserve the readability of text, while achieving great results against OCR services.

Keywords: Optical character recognition · Genetic algorithm · Adversarial machine learning

1 Introduction

Optical character recognition (OCR) [1–4] is a technology which performs character detection and classification from images, given as inputs, and provides access to a more accessible text-version. It is mainly used on scanned documents in order to convert them into electronic formats while also enabling the user to edit the original text. OCR implementations might vary but are typically based on image filtering algorithms, different heuristics or machine learning algorithms for character recognition (by classification).

OCR systems are commonly used in various implementations that perform automated requests (i.e.: various bots, bruteforce software, etc.). Many services, in order to prevent such actions, which can lead to resource depletion or even security breaches, will try to discover if the request was made by a human. This is usually implemented as an additional field which requires the sender to identify and type the characters found in a distorted image - this challenge is also known as CAPTCHA. Given the accuracy of the OCR systems, cleaner versions of CAPTCHA images will not always be able to separate human requests from

© Springer Nature Switzerland AG 2019
J.-L. Lanet and C. Toma (Eds.): SecITC 2018, LNCS 11359, pp. 126–141, 2019.
https://doi.org/10.1007/978-3-030-12942-2_11

automated requests (especially if the image goes through preprocessing stages). In addition, the strength of a CAPTCHA system is highly influenced by how distorted are the characters in the image which, on the other hand, will have an impact on readability.

OCR software also creates the following issue: it encourages the act of content stealing by making the whole process less time-consuming.

Existing attacks against OCR systems are of two types: (a) white-box attacks - which require information about the OCR engine's cost function. As an example, the adversary can try to locate the maximum value of the cost function (using gradient ascent) and therefore create images which have a very high chance of generating errors in the recognition process and finally leading to incorrect results; attempting to minimize a personal cost function in order to create targeted attacks is also a common strategy. This approach, while considerably faster than the evolutionary one, is not suitable since most professional OCR services will not provide access to such implementation details. (b) black-box attacks - where the attacker knows nothing about the recognition software [16,17]; these revolve around exploring what types of images achieve less accurate results from the OCR system and using them to craft inputs which aren't recognizable. They start with a set of images which contain noise added randomly; the images with the lowest noise and highest classification error are used to generate new adversary samples - in an evolutionary manner.

Both methods rely on adding noise to the original image; however noise's placement is an important factor. In [16], an image with 35% random noise makes Google's Cloud Vision platform return an incorrect result with a probability of 99%, but this also makes the text unreadable for humans. This type of attack is usually referenced as "evading classifiers" and is presented in [9,13–15,18].

In this paper we present a solution called Cyclops, which takes a noiseless image, alters a small number of pixels and generates samples that lead to incorrect classifications.

The main contributions of our work can be summarized as following:

- We created a framework that, given an image (e.g., page of a book), creates a similar one that withstands OCR systems.
- The first implementation of an attack using genetic algorithms against OCR systems. It guarantees relatively low noise densities in the altered images.
- It provides a different approach on solving the CAPTCHA's efficiency vs readability problem
- We show that the presented strategy preserves readability by evaluating it using more than 100 persons.
- We tested our attack against two of the most used OCR systems, the Google's Cloud Vision Service and Tesseract 4.0.
- Our solution perturbs below 7% of the text region and achieves better results than a 15% random (uniform) impulse noise approach.

The paper is organized as follows: In Sect. 2 we discuss about the OCR systems, while Sect. 3 presents the architecture of the obfuscation algorithm. Section 4 contains the details of our implementation and Sect. 5 will present the evaluation steps, with readable texts. In Sect. 6 we perform comparisons with similar systems; Sect. 7 summarizes our work.

2   Background

OCR can be seen as a classification problem: it takes an input (the image) and tries to place it in the most appropriate class (represented by a text character). The decisional process implies various comparisons with a set of known patterns or applying different heuristics. In this section we introduce some details of Tesseract 4.0 [1] which is an OCR engine developed by HP and later sponsored by Google.

Usually, the image given as input requires, besides a good resolution, various adjustments before it can be fed to the classifier; these adjustments consist in rotations, noise removal, contrast changing, normalization, etc. Right after the aforementioned actions, a binarization algorithm will be applied which will create a new black and white image. Tesseract will perform adaptive thresholding on the image in order to differentiate between background and text; studies revealed that providing grayscale inputs will lower the execution time and increase the accuracy [6]. Images deteriorated by noise are enhanced using different types of filters, applied using convolution matrices. Recent research [5] claims improved performance in removing impulse noise by mapping the image into a frequency spectrum and reconstructing parts of it using information from the adjacent pixels.

The OCR algorithm will try to locate regions of text and for each region it will attempt to discover baselines and meanlines in order to estimate the character's size (x-height). Each line is split into words and then each word is split into characters; when the confidence value of a whitespace is below a threshold, the space is marked as fuzzy and it will be evaluated again after the word recognition step. Each character is represented as a polygonal approximation of its outline, which is later compared to a group of known patterns. Each possible classification will also contain a confidence value which measures the difference between the input and the pattern.

Static character classification implies feature extraction using convolutional and deep belief neural networks; most features, if they're small, will match a template even when the character is damaged. This "shape classifier" is used as a backup procedure whenever the main Long Short-Term Memory (LSTM) neural network fails to deliver the proper text recognition.

Tesseract performs a two-step recognition using an adaptive classifier. After the first pass, each character which has a high confidence rating is used as training data for the current instance in order to increase the accuracy. The second pass will attempt to identify the remaining characters using the recently trained classifier.

The accuracy of the whole process at word-level is also improved by looking up the results in a dictionary. This method compensates for any errors which might have occurred during the recognition, if there exists a valid word that requires a relatively small number of changes.

3   Architecture

In this section we introduce the general work flow of our solution, which, given an image that contains text, outputs a modified version that withstands certain OCR systems. The implementation follows the list of simple steps presented in Fig. 1 and explained in this section.

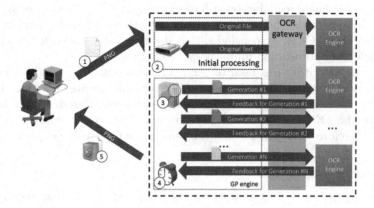

Fig. 1. Architecture

In phase #1, the user chooses the image that needs to be protected against an OCR system and sends it in a format supported by the current implementation (e.g. png, jpg, bmp). Next, the user must specify which OCR systems will be asked for feedback during the evolutionary process (e.g. creating a Tesseract-proof image requires feedback from Tesseract).

After receiving an image, the algorithm goes to phase #2: it stores the original data and queries the selected OCR engine. The returned text is presumed to be 100% correct so it will be used for comparisons in order to evaluate the efficiency of each generation.

During phase #3 the image goes through the Genetic Programming (GP) engine. New images, derived from the given input, are generated by applying small amounts of noise and observing how the OCR engine reacts to them. Each image is fed to the OCR system and the resulted texts are compared to the original text; the adversary samples that cause the highest changes at character level and contain the lowest amount of noise will be used to create a new generation of images, which will have a chance of achieving even higher scores. This process is repeated until the best image of the current generation achieves a satisfying score or until a fixed amount of time has passed.

Once an image achieved the required score (considering both the edit distance and the amount of noise) it goes to phase #4, the genetic algorithm halts and discards all the other images and releases any resources allocated for communicating with (or running) the OCR engine.

In phase #5, the final image is returned to the user, including the achieved score against the selected OCR system.

4 Implementation

In this section we will describe the general idea behind the implementation. Given an image as input, the objective is to add a small amount of noise so the image will remain readable yet still effective against OCR software. Without available noise patterns and information regarding the cost function implemented in Google's Cloud OCR, we concluded that the above objective can be classified as a search and optimization problem, on a blackbox.

A genetic algorithm was used to generate variations of the original image - each variation containing impulse noise. Multiple experiments on a local library called Tesseract revealed that high contrast impulse noise produces the largest change in the OCR engine's cost function with the lowest number of pixel changes, therefore we decided to use the same noise type in the experiment.

4.1 Genetic Algorithms

A genetic algorithm [7–9] is a metaheuristic/search algorithm that attempts to discover and optimize solutions for a given problem, without depending on a known error function and its gradient. The algorithm follows the basic principle of evolution - survival of the fittest - in this case, keeping only the solutions which seem to perform better in the current context. An advantage of the genetic algorithm is that it is relatively convenient to parallelize: we observe that multiple candidates from the same generation are independent and can be evaluated simultaneously. In addition, the parallelism can be extended to actions such as crossover and mutation.

Crossover implies picking 2 (or more) candidates and merging them into a new candidate. It simulates the idea that a new generation is formed with the characteristics of the most fit individuals thus creating a better population and generally increasing the average fitness value. Mutations are required in order to bring diversity and discover new traits which may or may not improve the fitness of a candidate. Newer generations might not produce better scores unless they also include the best candidates from the past, which are usually called elites. The elites will, subsequently, be replaced by newer candidates with higher scores.

Common yet renowned applications of the genetic algorithm include: attempting to simulate creativity in software without human intervention [10] or training artificial neural networks and finding optimal topologies in order to discover new strategies for playing certain games [11].

4.2 Implementation Details

We chose a score function which is directly proportional to the cost returned by the OCR engine and the Levenshtein distance [12] between the original text and what the OCR recognizes from the generated picture. This distance is calculated using only characters of interest (alphanumeric) thus discouraging the algorithm from resorting to simply inserting/editing punctuation marks.

During the tests on Google's Cloud OCR, the cost of each recognition was not available and the only useful feedback was the text itself. This led to an increase in the mutation rate and in the noise density in images (compared to Tesseract) because the granularity of the score function was rather "coarse". Therefore, instead of slowly adding noise and decreasing the confidence of the recognition system for a character and then changing it, we had to add a larger amount of noise that directly generated a change in the recognized text.

Most tests presented in this paper were performed by focusing on the edit distance and the cost returned by the OCR system (where available); noise quantity had a rather small contribution to the final score of a solution since the main goal was to initially generate an image that can cheat the targeted engine. In the final version, we rewrote the fitness function as following:

$$score(candidate) = \frac{edit\_distance^2}{current\_string\_length \times (noise\_cost + 1)} \tag{1}$$

Cyclops' goal is to generate images with improved noise signatures by using the best candidates from the current generation while also maintaining population diversity. Picking only the solutions with the best fitness values will drastically suppress the exploration step and accelerate convergence to a possibly suboptimal result, therefore we decided to implement a roulette-wheel selection, based on the score. It implies a certain randomness factor but assigns a higher probability for selection (and crossover) to the solutions with higher scores.

Various tests revealed that in this case, a merge-based crossover procedure is more beneficial than one which performs weighted arithmetic mean between the selected solutions. The problem with the arithmetic mean is that it produces colors with less powerful contrast between the background or the text (different nuances of gray) - these colors will not guarantee a change in the output of the OCR process and the genetic algorithm would get stuck.

The objective is to lower the classification accuracy with the smallest possible amount of noise therefore we chose the impulse noise model, which can be easily filtered by the human eye and yet provides a powerful contrast with the background color thus lowering the OCR engine's confidence. The procedure consists in selecting 2 candidates and creating an offspring - the color of each pixel of the offspring is decided by a weighted probability function:

$$P(pixel\_inherits\_color\_from\_parent_k) = \frac{score\_of\_parent_k}{\sum_{i=1}^{number\_of\_parents} score\_of\_parent_i} \tag{2}$$

This ensures that noise from the image with the higher score is more likely to be passed to the offspring. Because noise is applied region by region, crossover will be performed only using the pixels from the current editable area.

Running the algorithm without size constraints leads to a very large search space and brings additional difficulties in identifying the efficiency of the current mutation at pixel level. Performing mutations on the complete image will allow more noise variations and will lower the chance of discovering a group of modified pixels that contribute in the obfuscation process.

Our first idea consisted in grouping the characters into text rows and applying noise only in the regions which include these rows - one region at a time. New generations are created by mutating only the area enclosed by the current region, the number of offsprings being directly proportional to the score. This is a good approach and it generates good results but it's not very efficient when a small font size is used - simply because the number of pixels per character is not favorable. If a character is rendered using 20 pixels, altering 10 of them might take a toll on readability; but if the character is rendered using 200 pixels, changing 10 of them becomes negligible for the human eye yet it's still effective against OCR software.

We developed a strategy which aims to solve the problem of perturbing images which contain text written with a small font size. It focuses on directly exploiting the segmentation method by placing the editable regions between text rows; noise will not be inserted directly over the text but only above or below. It solves the problem of readability, reduces the search space even more, allows higher mutation rates and improves the overall execution time of the algorithm.

5   Evaluation

Local tests on Tesseract revealed that the location of noise is an important factor. We generated adversary samples for Google's Cloud Vision OCR service by configuring Cyclops to place noise directly over the text and attempting to optimize the location. We observed that this approach has a considerable impact on readability when smaller fonts are used - therefore we tried placing the noise between text rows (*artifacts mode*).

5.1   Tesseract

Tesseract provides the user with multiple *page segmentation methods*. We considered the test case where default/automatic segmentation mode is used.

During the tests against Tesseract, our objective was to discover the importance of placing the noise in almost optimal locations. Therefore, we applied perturbations to 2 images, with different fitness functions: one focused on maximizing the Levenshtein distance with relatively low amounts of noise while the other would do exactly the opposite. Figure 7 shows that with similar amounts of noise, we can achieve different Levenshtein distances thus justifying the existence of this optimization problem.

5.2   Google's Cloud Vision Service

In our tests, we measured the percentage of characters recognized by Google's OCR engine and the readability factor, according to the test participants.

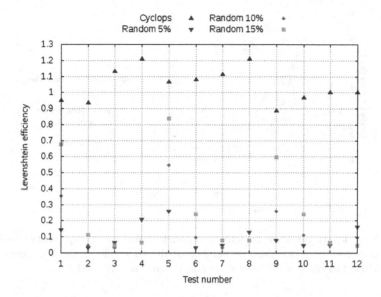

Fig. 2. Experimental results against Google's Cloud Vision OCR service. Levenshtein efficiency is calculated as the Levenshtein distance divided by the text's length (considering only alphanumeric characters).

In Fig. 2, we present the results of the tests performed using the following fonts: Arial $(1, 2, 3, 4)$, Times New Roman $(5, 6, 7, 8)$, Verdana $(9, 10, 11, 12)$ with the sizes 12 $(1, 5, 9)$, 21 $(2, 6, 10)$, 36 $(3, 7, 11)$ and 50 $(4, 8, 12)$.

Four sets of images were generated: the first by the genetic algorithm and the others by applying 5%, 10% and 15% impulse noise in a random, uniform manner [16]. There were 62 variations of each image that relied on random impulse noise - we used the average values during our comparison. The original image contains a clean high-contrast, black text on a white background - considered to be an ideal input for any OCR software. See Appendix (Fig. 6) for demos of adversarial samples.

The samples generated using our approach achieved a higher Levenshtein distance than the ones that used random impulse noise, while also requiring less noise thus performing better at maintaining readability.

Considering the whole image, we get noise densities between 0.4% and 3.5%; we can also notice that the noise distribution is not uniform (since it makes no sense perturbing pixels which are not near any text region). Therefore, we will consider only the area which contains text when evaluating the noise density of our adversary samples - which in this case falls below 7% (Fig. 3).

We observe that, for images generated by our program, the efficiency increases proportionally to the font's size - see Fig. 3. We can also notice that texts written with *Times New Roman* and a small font size are more challenging for the OCR system (both strategies - the random noise and the evolutionary approach - obtained a better efficiency factor on these).

134   D. Sporici et al.

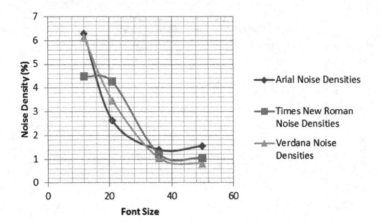

Fig. 3. Noise levels, classified by font type and font size values represented on Y are expressed as results of dividing the number of altered pixels by the total number of pixels included in the editable region (region which contains text).

Upon further investigations, we hypothesized that it should be easier to OCR-proof images which contain larger characters; the reason is that a larger font uses more pixels per character and this offers more freedom to the genetic algorithm when performing mutations. We illustrated this in Fig. 3, where we obtained different noise densities but similar Levenshtein distances.

We used the following formula to evaluate the noise efficiency in an adversary sample:

$$noise\_efficiency(candidate) = \frac{Levenshtein\_distance}{original\_text\_length \times (altered\_pixels + 1)} \tag{3}$$

While Fig. 4 proves the aforementioned concept, it also reveals that the random noise test set behaves in an opposite manner: noise efficiency grows when the font's size decreases. We can conclude that when the font's size is small enough, the genetic algorithm and the 15% random noise approach achieve similar noise efficiency values - basically, using a genetic algorithm becomes redundant.

5.3 Artifacts Mode: Applying Noise to Small-Sized Fonts

According to Fig. 4, applying noise right over the text will rapidly decrease readability when font's size also decreases. This strategy aims to solve the problem of perturbing images which contain text written with a small font size (i.e.: size 12 or lower). It focuses on directly exploiting the segmentation algorithm by placing the editable regions between text rows; noise will not be inserted directly over the text but only above or below. It can be considered an improvement since it solves the problem of readability, reduces the search space even more, allows higher mutation rates and improves the overall execution time of the algorithm.

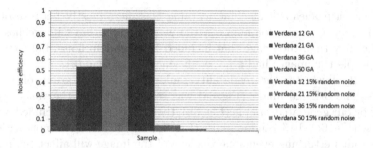

Fig. 4. Visual representation of the normalized noise efficiencies of the genetic algorithm and the 15% random noise approach, revealing the relationship between font's size and noise efficiency.

We tested this approach on Tesseract 4.0 and Google's Cloud Vision OCR service. Both tests proved successful as none of the original characters were identified by any OCR engine. Figure 5 shows an example of such adversary sample.

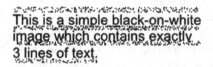

Fig. 5. Google's OCR service is unable to detect any character in this image - *Arial*, size 12.

5.4 Readability

In order to evaluate the readability factor, we considered the images which included text written with *Times New Roman*, size 21, because they achieved good results against Google's Cloud OCR service. Three types of images were used: the original, noiseless version (Fig. 6a), our adversary sample (Fig. 6b) and one image containing 10% random impulse noise (Fig. 6d). We divided the people into three groups: (a) original image with 43 participants, (b) Cyclops's image with 39 participants, and (c) 10% random noise image with 36 participants; and asked two questions: (1) *"How difficult is to read the text?"* with grades from 0 to 10, 0 meaning *"not at all"* and 10 for *"very difficult"*, and (2) *"How many characters you don't understand from the text?"*. We used the answers to determine how the people perceive the noise in the images.

Figure 8 reveals that people don't have a great difficulty in reading the texts found in the images. Only a small percentage of them found it difficult to read the characters from the generated sample image or from the 10% random noise image. In Fig. 9 is represented the noise efficiency against humans. It seems that humans are still ahead of machine learning classifiers mostly because of their low-filter capacity. Also, for humans, the genetic algorithm's image has lower noise efficiency than the image that included 10% random noise, but for almost 94% of people the images had a noise efficiency lower than 0.1.

Figure 10 illustrates the readability ranking made by a group of 114 participants. The original image (Fig. 6a) was selected first by the vast majority, followed by our generated sample (Fig. 6b), then the ones which included 5% random noise (Fig. 6c), 10% random noise (Fig. 6d) and 15% random noise (Fig. 6e). It seems that perturbing even small regions of the image will affect the reader's comfort.

6   Related Work

In [16] is proposed a black-box attack against classifiers in which the adversary doesn't have any knowledge about training data set or the output of the system. It only changes the input in a random manner. This attack is important because its only knowledge is the type of data given as input for the classifier. They use two types of noise: salt-and-pepper noise and gaussian noise. Their results claim that for 35% impulse noise the OCR service provided by Google always returns the wrong answer. Their average noise level for these attacks is 14.25%. The attack maintains the text recognizable by humans, but rather difficult to read. They also present a solution for this types of attacks. For the salt-and-pepper noise a weighted-average or median filter can be used and the gaussian noise can be reduced with a low pass filter. We tested their attack method against Google's Cloud OCR, and discovered that texts which contain many characters don't necessarily have a good percentage of unrecognizable characters. Our system uses less noise but applied in more critical locations for similar or improved outputs.

A different type of attack is presented in [17]. It is a black-box attack against machine learning classifiers, which considers that no knowledge about the system is available: architecture or training data. They introduce a machine learning substitute to simulate the attacked system and also lower the number of queries. This attack is important because it bypasses the usual defenses and a successful adversary sample has a high chance of working well against the targeted classifier. They propose a new type of attack by using a substitute neural network similar to the original classifier, training it with generated inputs and using the outputs obtained by querying the original network. It works because of the property of transferability between machine learning systems. They tested and claimed that deep neural networks (DNN) have a good transferability, when compared to other types of machine learning architectures. They use the attack against MetaMind, Google and Amazon with a success rate greater than 80%. It can be applied to our current algorithm but we presume that current OCR systems use, besides recurrent neural networks, more types of classifiers that perform preprocessing and segmentation which would be difficult to simulate exactly.

Another attack method is introduced in [9]. It implies using genetic programming to counter the effectiveness of machine learning classifiers (seen as blackboxes) for malware. It requires knowledge about input data and the output score. The 100% success rate of the attack shows that machine learning classifiers are not robust to such attacks and won't ensure optimal levels of protection. The procedure implies using genetic algorithms to modify PDF files so they will bypass two classifiers: PDFrate and Hidost. The process includes the following steps: (1) taking a PDF file with malicious content, (2) modifying the file's structure and metadata while maintaining its malicious behavior and (3) repeating the process until it is classified as a false negative. Their work is similar to ours, considering both attacks rely on evolutionary strategies - one of the key differences being the fact that they did not implement the crossover procedure.

7   Conclusion

Our work shows that Google's Cloud Vision implementation for text recognition can be deceived by using a local noise density below 7% - this method being effective on various font types and sizes. The noise ratio, is not guaranteed to be optimal and can be improved by increasing the size of the population and lowering the mutation rate.

We observed that OCR software, in general, is performing surprisingly well; a direct attack on the character's shape is not very efficient since it is still easily matched to the original pattern or corrected using the dictionary. Sometimes the OCR can successfully recognize the text that humans can't read; exploiting the segmentation method seems to represent a better approach.

People can bypass certain noise signatures better than OCR systems and the readability of texts is not affected for humans even with a 10% noise level. Robustness to noise becomes a more important topic, especially in the domain of computer vision since it has such a big impact.

In conclusion, this program aims to further exploit the vulnerability of OCR systems to noise in order to offer an additional layer of protection against both automated plagiarism. It also offers a more human-friendly idea of generating CAPTCHA images. Future work will focus on testing this approach against multiple OCR systems simultaneously and improving the algorithm in order to achieve similar effects with even lower noise densities.

Acknowledgements. This work was supported by a grant of Romanian Ministry of Research and Innovation, CCCDI - UEFISCDI, project number PN-III-P1-1.2-PCCDI-2017-0272/17PCCDI-2018, within PNCDI III.

A   Appendix

This is a simple black-on-white image which contains exactly 3 lines of text.

This is a simple black-on-white image which contains exactly 3 lines of text.

(a) Original Image   (b) Genetic Algorithm's Sample

This is a simple black-on-white image which contains exactly 3 lines of text.

This is a simple black-on-white image which contains exactly 3 lines of text.

(c) 5% Random Noise   (d) 10% Random Noise

This is a simple black-on-white image which contains exactly 3 lines of text.

(e) 15% Random Noise

Fig. 6. Adversary samples generated from an image - *Times New Roman*, size 21.

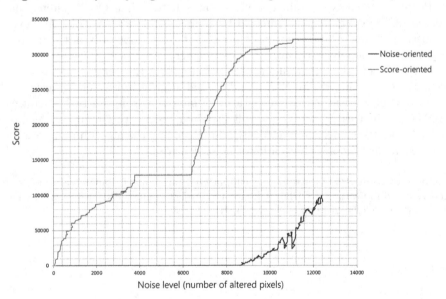

Fig. 7. Comparing 2 sets of images generated using the same program but with different fitness functions. In this case, the edit distance can be approximated by dividing the score by 1000. A larger score is desired since it implies a larger Levenshtein distance.

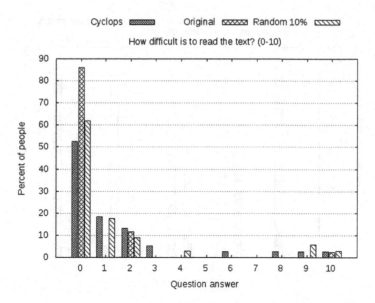

Fig. 8. The experimental result for the question: *"How difficult is to read the text? (1 - easy, 10 - hard)"*

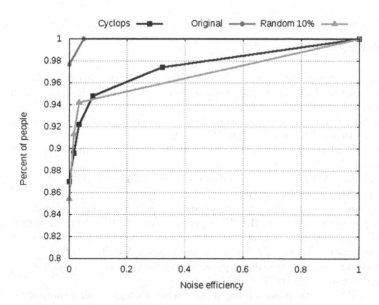

Fig. 9. The experimental result in a CDF for question: *"How many characters you don't understand from the text?"*

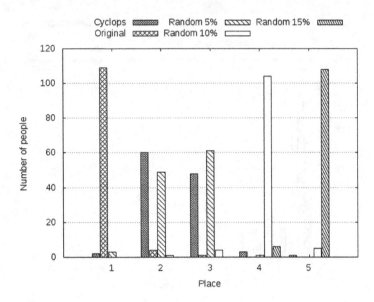

Fig. 10. Experimental results, given the task: *"Please rank the following images according to their readability"*.

References

1. Smith, R.: An overview of the Tesseract OCR engine. In: 2007 Ninth International Conference on Document Analysis and Recognition. ICDAR 2007, vol. 2. IEEE (2007)
2. Mori, S., Suen, C.Y., Yamamoto, K.: Historical review of OCR research and development. Proc. IEEE **80**(7), 1029–1058 (1992)
3. Mori, S., Nishida, H., Yamada, H.: Optical Character Recognition. Wiley, Hoboken (1999)
4. Chaudhuri, B.B., Pal, U.: A complete printed Bangla OCR system. Pattern Recogn. **31**(5), 531–549 (1998)
5. Hasegawa, M., et al.: Removal of salt-and-pepper noise using a high-precision frequency analysis approach. IEICE Trans. Inf. Syst. **100**(5), 1097–1105 (2017)
6. Patel, C., Patel, A., Patel, D.: Optical character recognition by open source OCR tool tesseract: a case study. Int. J. Comput. Appl. **55**(10) (2012)
7. Forrest, S.: Genetic algorithms: principles of natural selection applied to computation. Science **261**(5123), 872–878 (1993)
8. Koza, J.R.: Genetic programming as a means for programming computers by natural selection. Stat. Comput. **4**(2), 87–112 (1994)
9. Xu, W., Qi, Y., Evans, D.: Automatically evading classifiers. In: Proceedings of the 2016 Network and Distributed Systems Symposium (2016)
10. DiPaola, S., Gabora, L.: Incorporating characteristics of human creativity into an evolutionary art algorithm. Genet. Program. Evolvable Mach. **10**(2), 97–110 (2009)
11. Moriarty, D.E., Miikkulainen, R.: Discovering complex Othello strategies through evolutionary neural networks. Connect. Sci. **7**(3), 195–210 (1995)

12. Levenshtein, V.I.: Binary codes capable of correcting deletions, insertions, and reversals
13. Dalvi, N., et al.: Adversarial classification. In: Proceedings of the Tenth ACM SIGKDD International Conference on Knowledge Discovery and Data Mining. ACM (2004)
14. Lowd, D., Meek, C.: Adversarial learning. In: Proceedings of the Eleventh ACM SIGKDD International Conference on Knowledge Discovery in Data Mining. ACM (2005)
15. Laskov, P.: Practical evasion of a learning-based classifier: a case study. In: 2014 IEEE Symposium on Security and Privacy (SP). IEEE (2014)
16. Hosseini, H., Xiao, B., Poovendran, R.: Google's Cloud Vision API Is Not Robust To Noise. arXiv preprint arXiv:1704.05051 (2017)
17. Papernot, N., et al.: Practical black-box attacks against machine learning. In: Proceedings of the 2017 ACM on Asia Conference on Computer and Communications Security. ACM (2017)
18. Nguyen, A., Yosinski, J., Clune, J.: Deep neural networks are easily fooled: high confidence predictions for unrecognizable images. In: Proceedings of the IEEE Conference on Computer Vision and Pattern Recognition (2015)

Intrusion Detection and Classification with Autoencoded Deep Neural Network

Shahadate Rezvy[1]([✉])[iD], Miltos Petridis[1][iD], Aboubaker Lasebae[1][iD], and Tahmina Zebin[2][iD]

[1] Middlesex University, London, UK
{s.rezvy,M.Petridis,A.Lasebae}@mdx.ac.uk
[2] University of Manchester, Manchester, UK
tahmina.zebin@manchester.ac.uk

Abstract. A Network Intrusion Detection System is a critical component of every internet connected system due to likely attacks from both external and internal sources. A NIDS is used to detect network born attacks such as denial of service attacks, malware, and intruders that are operating within the system. Neural networks have become an increasingly popular solution for network intrusion detection. Their capability of learning complex patterns and behaviors make them a suitable solution for differentiating between normal traffic and network attacks. In this paper, we have applied a deep autoencoded dense neural network algorithm for detecting intrusion or attacks in network connection and evaluated the algorithm with the benchmark NSL-KDD dataset. Our results showed an excellent performance with an overall detection accuracy of 99.3% for Probe, Remote to Local, Denial of Service and User to Root type of attacks. We also presented a comparison with recent approaches used in literature which showed a substantial improvement in terms of accuracy and speed of detection with the proposed algorithm.

Keywords: Deep learning · Secure computing ·
Intrusion detection system · Autoencoder · Dense neural network

1 Introduction

Over the past few decades, the Internet has penetrated all aspects of our lives. Experts predict that by 2020 there would be 50 billion connected devices. As technology becomes more and more integrated, the challenge to keep the systems safe and away from vulnerability or attacks increases. Over the years we have seen an increase in hacks in banking systems, healthcare systems and many Internet of Things (IoT) devices [1]. These attacks cause billions of dollars in losses every year and loss of systems at crucial times. This has led to higher importance in cyber security specifically in the intrusion detection systems. A related challenge with most modern-day infrastructure is that data requirements pertaining to security are often an afterthought. It is assumed that this impacts

© Springer Nature Switzerland AG 2019
J.-L. Lanet and C. Toma (Eds.): SecITC 2018, LNCS 11359, pp. 142–156, 2019.
https://doi.org/10.1007/978-3-030-12942-2_12

the results of any machine learning algorithm applied towards the problem; however, an analysis contrasting the differences are yet to be seen. In addition to this, there is little research in the results of applying next level analysis using deep learning algorithms to determine if there is an improvement in accuracy versus its traditional machine learning counterparts. Deep learning (hierarchical learning) is part of a broader family of machine learning methods based on learning data representations, as opposed to task-specific algorithms. Recently, deep learning based methods have been successfully implemented in NIDS applications. Deep learning can substitute for manually designed feature extraction to create more secure firewall or intrusion detector [2].

In this work, we have proposed a data mining based hybrid intrusion detection system for distinguishing normal and intrusive events from the NSL-KDD dataset [3]. We focused on exploring low latency models while maintaining high accuracy by proposing a deep auto-encoded dense neural network (DNN) framework for effective intrusion detection. The NIDS using deep learning did alleviate the need of feature selection or feature engineering during the detection process. In our design, the autoencoder facilitated an unsupervised pre-tarining on the data to provide compressed and less noisy representation of the input space, while the final dense neural network functioned as the supervised classifier for our experimental intrusion detection scenario.

The remainder of this paper is organized as follows. Section 2 introduces the background literature in the recent development in intrusion detection systems using deep learning techniques, we then provide details on our parameter settings for the implemented model in Sect. 3. The performance of the developed model for attack classification is evaluated in Sect. 4. We also compared the results with some recent deep learning techniques appeared in the literature using the same dataset. Finally, the paper is concluded in Sect. 5 along with ideas for future work.

2   Background Literature

In recent years, machine learning has been widely applied to problems in detecting network attacks, particularly novel attacks. Given the landscape of the Internet, machine learning can be applied to handle the massive amounts of traffic to determine what is malicious or benign. NIDS are classifiers that differentiate unauthorized or anomalous traffic from authorized or normal traffic. Figure 1 shows an illustration of the proposed components for the NIDS implementation. As can be seen in the diagram, the network gateways and routers devices could potentially host an NIDS. In the recent past, researchers have investigated a wide variety of Machine Learning techniques to design intrusion detection systems for normal and attack classification. However the NIDS design community suffered from some major challenges as there are very few labeled traffic dataset from real networks for developing an NIDS. Additionally, effective feature selection from the Network Traffic dataset for anomaly detection is difficult. The features selected for one class of attack may not work well for other categories of attacks due to continuously changing and evolving attack scenarios.

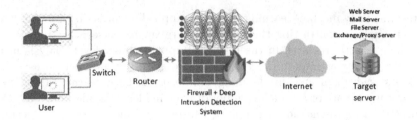

Fig. 1. Illustration of the proposed network intrusion detection system (NIDS)

Because of the lack of public data sets for network-based IDSs, we used the NSL-KDD dataset (which may not be a perfect representation of existing real networks) to compare different intrusion detection methods. However, traditional machine learning methods depend heavily on feature engineering, and extracting features is often time-consuming and complex. Thus, it is impractical to detect attacks with traditional machine learning methods in real-time applications [4]. To set our research in context, in the next subsection, we present a literature review on the intrusion detection systems that used deep learning techniques and the NSL-KDD dataset for their performance benchmarking.

Deep Machine Learning for Intrusion Detection: Neural networks have become an increasingly popular solution for network intrusion detection systems (NIDS). Their capability of learning complex patterns and behaviors make them a suitable solution for differentiating between normal traffic and network attacks [6]. One of the earliest work found in literature that used deep learning approach with Deep Belief Network (DBN) as a feature selector and Support Vector Machine (SVM) as a classifier was reported in [7]. This approach resulted in an accuracy of 92.84% when applied on training data of NSL-KDD dataset. We observed a use of Artificial neural networks (ANN) with enhanced resilient back-propagation for the design in Ref. [8]. This work also used the training dataset only by subdividing it in three parts (training (70%), validation (15%) and testing (15%)). The inclusion of the unlabeled data for testing resulted in a reduction of performance for this method. Reference [9] applied fuzzy clustering based ANN that resulted above 80% detection accuracy of with a low false positive rate. In [10], the work used an unsupervised greedy learning algorithm to learn similarity representations over the nonlinear and high-dimensional data in KDD dataset. The results show that four-hidden-layer Restricted Boltzmann machines can produce the higher accuracy in comparison with SVM and ANN. A deep Neural Network is essentially a multilayer perceptron, which was initially developed by stacking linear classifiers. The model is fed inputs, inputs get multiplied by weights and the passed into an activation function. The model uses backpropagation to adjust weights and increase accuracy. Deep Neural Networks with three or more hidden layers support higher generalization capability in comparison to ANN [11]. In [12], a deep belief network for malicious code detection method was reported that included an autoencoder based dimensionality reduction

Table 1. Attack types in the KDD Cup 1999 dataset [5]

Attack type	Description of the attack	Categories
Denial of Service (DoS)	A DoS attack is a type of attack in which the hacker makes a computing resources or memory too busy or too full to serve legitimate networking requests and hence denying users access to a machine	apache, back, land, mailbomb, neptune, pod, processtable, smurf, teardrop, udpstorm
Probe	Probing is an attack in which the hacker scans a machine or a networking device in order to determine weaknesses or vulnerabilities that may later be exploited so as to compromise the system	ipsweep, mscan, nmap, portsweep, saint, satan
Remote to Local (R2L)	A remote to user attack is an attack in which a user sends packets to a machine over the internet, which s/he does not have access to in order to expose the machines vulnerabilities and exploit privileges which a local user would have on the computer	ftpwrite, guesspassword, imap, multihop, named, phf, sendmail, snmpgetattack, snmpguess, warezmaster, worm, xlock, xsnoop, httptunnel
User to Root (U2R)	User to root attacks are exploitations in which the hacker starts off on the system with a normal user account and attempts to abuse vulnerabilities in the system in order to gain super user privileges	bufferoverflow, loadmodule, perl, rootkit, ps, sqlattack, xterm

technique. An accelerated deep architecture was introduced in Potluri et al. [13] to identify the abnormalities in the network data. They evaluated the performance of the model training related to different processor types and number of cores. Li et al. [14] presented an intrusion detection method using convolutional neural networks which adopts a novel representation learning method of graphic conversion. However, the model accuracy ranged from 79% to 81.57%

which did not justify the increased latency added by the representation learning of the feature space. In Ref. [15], Vinayakumar et al. reported various convolutional and recurrent neural network architectures for IDS implementation, however their results for under-represented remote to local (R2L) and user to root (U2R) attacks were very low. Shone et al. [1] reported a stacked non-symmetric deep auto-encoders with random forest classifier achieved an overall accuracy of 85.42%, with very poor performance on the R2L and U2R intrusion categories. A stacked autoencoder based implementation of NIDS by Farahnakian et al. [16] produced high accuracy (94.71%) and high detection rate (94.53%), however, these models could still be improved. The findings from our literature review have shown that despite the high detection accuracy being achieved, with most researchers still experimenting on combining various algorithms (e.g. training, optimisation, activation and classification) and layering approaches to produce the most accurate and efficient solution for a specific dataset.

In our research, we focused on exploring low latency models while maintaining high accuracy by proposing a hybrid deep neural network that includes an unsupervised pre-training using autoencoders to make the model more adaptive to the changes in the network traffic. We then used a dedicated supervised dense neural network structure for the final classification. In our design, we made sure the memory or processing power to train and execute machine learning models are within the capability of the routers processing power. We hence believe the model and work presented in this paper will serve towards the real time and low latency implementation of the NIDS models.

3   Data Pre-processing and Implementation of the Model

In this section, we further discuss on the technical details of our proposed deep learning based approach to increase the performance accuracy of the NSL-KDD benchmarking dataset. In the dataset, there are 41 different nominal, numeric and binary features extracted from a specific network connection. The 42nd column contains data about the label on the network access type (i.e. intrusion or normal). Table 1 summarizes the types of attacks or intrusion events available in the dataset. We have remapped the entire dataset to a five class scenario with four attack classes and one normal category for training and classification purposes. Further description on the features extracted in the dataset can be found in Ref. [17,18].

3.1   Data Pre-processing

The KDD dataset [5] has a huge number of redundant records, which causes the learning algorithms to be biased towards the frequent records, and thus prevent them from learning infrequent records which are usually more harmful to networks such as U2R and R2L attacks [18].

In this work, we have merged the training and test dataset from the KDD 1999 dataset and removed all duplicate records in data. We then intentionally added some duplicates in the R2L and U2R attack groups to have a increased representation of the smaller attack groups in the dataset. This in total constituted in 151063 instances of labelled data. We then separated 20% of the entire dataset as test set, the remaining 80% of the data was used for training and validation purpose.

We performed the following pre-processing on the NSL-KDD training and test sets:

- Encoding: As mentioned previously, the dataset contains different features with different value ranges. Hence, The dataset is preprocessed before applying autoencoded learning on it. Before using the data-set, we first convert the categorical features to numeric values. Categorical features such as protocol type, service and flag are encoded into numbered variables using one-hot (1-to-n) encoding. We have also applied log encoding on the large numerical features such as source bytes, destination bytes and duration to avoid any kind of biasing on the training due to their large values.
- Scaling and Normalization: All numeric features values are ranged between 0 and 1. We performed a min-max normalization on the feature vectors.

The output labels are one hot encoded. Therefore, the total number of input dimension is 122 after performing the above-mentioned steps and output dimension is 5 (4 attacksor intrusion types and 1 normal).

3.2   Proposed Model

Figure 2 illustrates the work flow and the proposed deep model architecture for the intrusion detection system. Similar to most existing deep learning research, our proposed classification model was implemented using python keras library [19] with TensorFlow back end. All of our evaluations were performed on a Windows machine with an Intel Xeon 3.60 GHz processor, 32 GB RAM and an NVIDIA GTX 1050 GPU.

We employed two main functional stages in our proposed model. An autoencoder based unsupervised pre-training layer and a supervised dense neural network for classification of the attack types for the NIDS. We describe our intuition for using these components in the system development in the coming subsections.

Unsupervised Pre-training with Autoencoder. An autoencoder is a type of artificial neural network used to learn efficient data representation in an unsupervised manner. In our proposed model, we have employed an autoencoder with an encoding and a decoding layer that has been trained to minimize the reconstruction error. This incorporated prior knowledge from the training set to effectively learn from the data itself and provide good performance. Such pre-training allow both the data for the current task and for previous related tasks to self-organize the learning system to build the learning system in a data driven fashion. We have fed the autoencoder with the features from the training

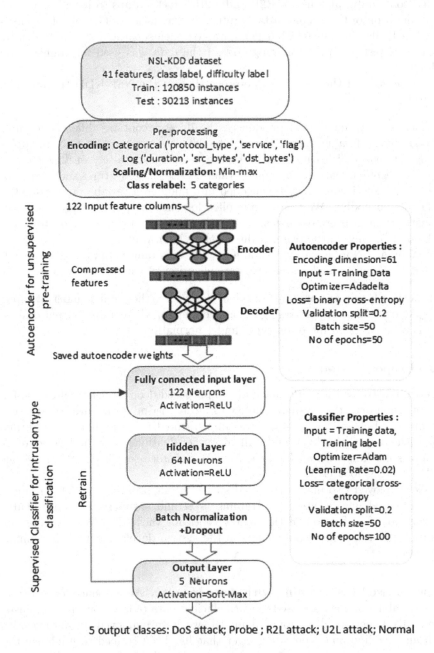

Fig. 2. Workflow and architecture of the proposed autoencoded dense neural network

dataset without labels (unsupervised). A set of compressed and robust feature is built at the end of this step. The encoder part of the autoencoder aims to compress input data into a low-dimensional representation, and there is a decoder part that reconstructs input data based on the low-dimension representation generated by the encoder.

For a given training dataset $X = \{x_1, x_2, ..., x_m\}$ with m samples or instances, where x_n is an n-dimensional feature vector, the encoder maps the input vector x_n to a hidden representation vector h_n through a deterministic mapping f_θ as given in (1)

$$h_n = f_\theta(x_n) = \sigma(Wx_n + b) \tag{1}$$

where W is a $p \times p$, p is the number of hidden units, b is a bias vector, θ is the mapping parameter set $\theta = \{W, b\}$. σ is sigmoid activation function.

The decoder maps back the resulting hidden representation h_n to a reconstructed p-dimensional vector y_n in input space.

$$y_i = g_\theta(h_n) = \sigma(Wh_n + b) \tag{2}$$

The goal of training the autoencoder is to minimize the difference between input and output. Therefore, a error function is calculated by the following equation:

$$E(x, y) = \frac{1}{m} \left\| \sum\nolimits_{i=1}^{m} (x_n - y_n) \right\|^2 \tag{3}$$

The main objective is to find the optimal parameters to minimize the difference between input and reconstructed output over the whole training set (m).

Supervised Classification with DNN. A three layer dense neural network is employed of a is trained by using the first auto-encoder, s output as inputs. This task sequence is retrained in a supervised manner with the class labels and the input feature given to the classifier. We have used a softmax activation layer as the output layer. The layer calculates the loss between the predicted values and the true values, and the weights in the network are adjusted according to the loss.

The simple *softmax* layer, which is placed at the final layer, can be defined as follows:

$$P(c|x) = \text{argmax}_{c \in C} \frac{\exp(x_{L-1}W_L + b_L)}{\sum_{k=1}^{N_C} \exp(x_{L-1}W_k)}, \tag{4}$$

where c is the number of classes, L is the last layer index, and N_C is the total number of class types including normal network connection and intrusion. After this stage, all layers are fine-tuned through back-propagation in a supervised way. In the test phase, the softmax layer outputs the probability of the predicted categories.

Figure 3 plots the performance of the network training process for 100 iterations. During training, we have used additional techniques such as dropout

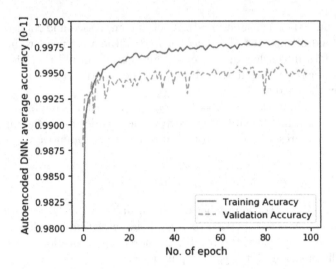

Fig. 3. Training and validation set accuracy over increasing number of epochs (training iterations)

and batch normalization to avoid over fitting and also to speedup the training process. The proposed algorithm achieves approximately 99% accuracy for the training set in 20 iterations which is four times faster if no dropout and batch normalization was employed. We used a five-fold cross-validation using 20% of the training data and the validation data set also achieves high overall accuracy with slight deviation over time. Potentially this allows a reduction in the training epochs required, and will be of vital importance for developing low-latency models and training future networks with bigger data sets. The proposed algorithm is summarized here in Algorithm 1.

4   Model Evaluation

The main aim of our designed model is to show that the intrusion detection system we designed using deep autoencoded neural network framework will maximize accuracy and minimize any falsely categorized values.

4.1   Model Evaluation Matrices

If True Positive (T_P) is the number of attacks classified rightly as attack; True Negative (T_N) is the number of normal events rightly classified normal; False Positive (F_P) is the number of normal events misclassified as attacks and False Negative (F_N) is the number of attacks misclassified as normal, we can define accuracy, recall, precision and F1 values of a model can be defined using the following equations [20].

Algorithm 1. Auto-encoded DNN training algorithm

Input: Taining dataset $X = \{x_1, x_2, ..., x_m\}$, Number of layers L
1 for $l \in [1, L]$ do;
2   Initialize $W_l = 0, W_l = 0, b_l = 0, b'_l = 0$;
   Encoding layer;
3   Calculate encoding or hidden representation using equation(1);
      $h_l = s(W_l x_{l1} + b_l)$;
   Decoding layer;
4   while not loss==stopping criteria do;
5   Compute y_l using equation (2);
6   Compute the loss function: binary cross-entropy;
7   Update layer parameters $\theta = \{W, b\}$;
8   end while;
9 end for;
   Classifier:Dense neural network, Soft-max activation at the output layer;
10 Initialize (W_{l+1}, b_{l+1}) at the supervised layer;
11 Calculate the labels for each sample x_n of the training dataset X;
12 Apply batch normalization and dropout for speeding up the calculation;
13 Perform back-propagation in a supervised manner to tune parameters of all
   layers, loss function categorical cross-entropy;
14 end;
   Output: Class labels

– Accuracy: It is an indicator of the total number of correct predictions provided
  by the model and defined as follows:

$$\text{Accuracy} = \frac{T_P + T_N}{T_P + T_N + F_P + F_N}. \tag{5}$$

– Recall, precision and F measure: Three of the most commonly used performance measures with F measure being the harmonic mean of recall and
  precision measures are defined as follows:

$$\text{Recall or True positive rate} = \frac{T_P}{T_P + F_N}. \tag{6}$$

$$\text{Precision} = \frac{T_P}{T_P + F_P}. \tag{7}$$

$$\text{F Measure} = \frac{2 * \text{Precision} * \text{Recall}}{\text{Precision} + \text{Recall}} \tag{8}$$

Figure 4 showed the class-wise receiver operating characteristic (ROC) for our
proposed model. The model produced highly accurate predictions for the classes
of the designed NIDS. We obtained a true positive rate (TPR) of above 99%

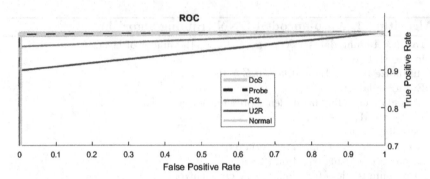

Fig. 4. Receiver operating characteristics for different classes (Color figure online)

for normal connection and DoS attack category. The model benefited from comparatively higher number of instances in these two categories. The TPR for the U2R (showed in red in Fig. 4) category was 89.2%, while R2L and Probe attack types had a TPR rate of 94.3% and 98.4% respectively. While compared with the ROC curve presented in Shone et al. [1], our model achieved much higher TPR values for the under-represented intrusion types R2L and U2R.

4.2   Confusion Matrix

We presented the confusion matrix plot in Fig. 5, for our model when evaluated with the test data set. The rows correspond to the predicted class (Output Class) and the columns correspond to the true class (Target Class). The diagonal cells in the confusion matrix correspond to observations that are correctly classified (T_P and T_N's). The off-diagonal cells correspond to incorrectly classified observations (F_P and F_N's). Both the number of observations and the percentage of the total number of observations are shown in each cell.

The column on the far right of the plot shows the percentages of all the examples predicted to belong to each class that are correctly and incorrectly classified. These values are often called the precision and false discovery rate respectively. The row at the bottom of the plot shows the percentages of all the examples belonging to each class that are correctly and incorrectly classified. These metrics are often called the recall and false negative rate, respectively. The cell in the bottom right of the plot shows the overall accuracy of the classifier which is 99.3% in our case.

To be noted, we have utilized builtin Matlab functions *plotroc (true class, predicted class)* and *plotconfusion (true class, predicted class)* for generating Figs. 4 and 5. Both true class and predicted class variables were one-hot encoded and imported from the python interface as .mat file for plotting purposes.

4.3   Comparison with Other Approaches

Our results showed an excellent performance with an overall detection accuracy of 99.3% for Probe, R2L, DoS and U2R type attacks. Table 2 summarizes the

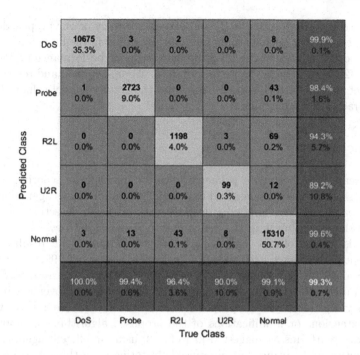

Fig. 5. Confusion matrix of the test dataset

Table 2. Quantitative comparison of the proposed method with other deep learning techniques for NSL-KDD 5-class intrusion detection

Learning method	Year	DoS (%)	Probe	R2L	U2R	Normal	Overall accuracy (%)
Self taught learning [21]	2016	-	-	-	-	-	75.76
Convolutional neural networks [14]	2017	-	-	-	-	-	81.57
Deep belief network (DBN) [1]	2018	87.96	72.97	0	0	95.64	80.58
CNN-3 layer [15]	2017	97.5	92.5	3.43	6.33	99.9	97.0
CNN 3 layer+LSTM [15]	2017	99.5	86.8	0.0	7.45	99.7	98.7
Deep neural network [13]	2016	97.7	89.8	13	39.6	95	93
Symmetric autoencoder (S-NDAE) [1]	2018	94.58	94.67	3.82	2.70	97.73	85.42
Stacked autoencoder [16]	2018	-	-	-	-	-	94.7
Proposed autoencoded DNN	2018	99.9	98.4	94.3	89.2	99.6	99.3

class-wise true positive rate (TPR) and overall accuracy of our proposed model with some concurrent deep learning methods presented in the literature. All previously reported models in the literature showed poor performance in detecting R2L and U2R type attacks due to lack of data. We up-sampled and restructured the dataset to deal with this discrepancy and the trained model achieved above 89% accuracy for all the classes.

5   Conclusions

Cyber threats have become a prime concern for information security. NIDS is one of the security mechanisms used to guard these applications against attacks. In this research, we have applied a deep network intrusion detection model and evaluated the algorithm with the benchmark NSL-KDD dataset. Currently, the algorithm is trained offline on high performance computer. Our results showed an excellent performance with an overall detection accuracy of 99.3% for Probe, R2L, DoS and U2R type of attacks. We also presented a comparison with recent approches used in literature which showed a substantial improvement in terms of accuracy and latency with proposed autoencoded DNN. In future, we will provide extensions or modifications of the proposed algorithm for mobile and IoT security platforms as suggested in Ref. [22] using intelligent agents such as soft computing and advanced unsupervised clustering algorithms. Because of the availability of deep learning libraries in python such as Keras and TensorFlow Lite [23], on-device machine learning inference is now possible with low latency. Hence, future models will cover a broader range of attacks, respond in real time and update itself over time. Future extension of this work will be to improve the detection accuracy and to reduce the rate of false negative and false positive rate in attack detection to improve the systems performance. In future, we will also continue our efforts for improvements to the approach and will apply the technique on similar but more recent and complex datasets such as Aegean Wi-Fi Intrusion Dataset (AWID) [24], UNSW-NB15 dataset [25].

References

1. Shone, N., Ngoc, T.N., Phai, V.D., et al.: A deep learning approach to network intrusion detection. IEEE Trans. Emerg. Top. Comput. Intell. **2**(1), 41–50 (2018)
2. Lee, B., Amaresh, S., Green, C., et al.: Comparative study of deep learning models for network intrusion detection. SMU Data Sci. Rev. **1**(1), Article 8 (2018)
3. NSL-KDD Dataset. http://www.unb.ca/cic/datasets/nsl.html
4. Liu, H., Lang, B., Liu, M., et al.: CNN and RNN based payload classification methods for attack detection. Knowl.-Based Syst. (2018)
5. McHugh, J.: Testing intrusion detection systems: a critique of the 1998 and 1999 DARPA intrusion detection system evaluations as performed by Lincoln Laboratory. ACM Trans. Inf. Syst. Secur. **3**(4), 262–294 (2000)
6. Mirsky, Y., Doitshman, T., Elovici, Y., et al.: Kitsune: an ensemble of autoencoders for online network intrusion detection. CoRR, vol. 1802.09089 (2018)

7. Salama, M.A., Eid, H.F., Ramadan, R.A., Darwish, A., Hassanien, A.E.: Hybrid intelligent intrusion detection scheme. In: Gaspar-Cunha, A., Takahashi, R., Schaefer, G., Costa, L. (eds.) Soft Computing in Industrial Applications. Advances in Intelligent and Soft Computing, vol. 96, pp. 293–303. Springer, Heidelberg (2011). https://doi.org/10.1007/978-3-642-20505-7_26

8. Naoum, R.S., Abid, N.A., Al-Sultani, Z.N.: An enhanced resilient backpropagation artificial neural network for intrusion detection system. Int. J. Comput. Sci. Netw. Secur. **12**, 11 (2012)

9. Pandeeswari, N., Kumar, G.: Anomaly detection system in cloud environment using fuzzy clustering based ANN. Mob. Netw. Appl. **21**(3), 494–505 (2016)

10. Gao, N., Gao, L., Gao, Q., et al.: An intrusion detection model based on deep belief networks. In: 2014 Second International Conference on Advanced Cloud and Big Data, pp. 247–252, November 2014

11. Kaynar, O., Yüksek, A.G., Görmez, Y., et al.: Intrusion detection with autoencoder based deep learning machine. In: 25th Signal Processing and Communications Applications Conference (SIU), pp. 1–4, May 2017

12. Li, Y., Ma, R., Jiao, R.: A hybrid malicious code detection method based on deep learning (2015)

13. Potluri, S., Diedrich, C.: Accelerated deep neural networks for enhanced intrusion detection system. In: 2016 IEEE 21st International Conference on Emerging Technologies and Factory Automation (ETFA), pp. 1–8, September 2016

14. Li, Z., Qin, Z., Huang, K., Yang, X., Ye, S.: Intrusion detection using convolutional neural networks for representation learning. In: Liu, D., Xie, S., Li, Y., Zhao, D., El-Alfy, E.S. (eds.) ICONIP 2017. LNCS, vol. 10638, pp. 858–866. Springer, Cham (2017). https://doi.org/10.1007/978-3-319-70139-4_87

15. Vinayakumar, R., Soman, K.P., Poornachandran, P.: Applying convolutional neural network for network intrusion detection. In: 2017 International Conference on Advances in Computing, Communications and Informatics (ICACCI), pp. 1222–1228, September 2017

16. Farahnakian, F., Heikkonen, J.: A deep auto-encoder based approach for intrusion detection system. In: 2018 18th International Conference on Advanced Communication Technology, pp. 1–6, February 2018

17. Dhanabal, L., Shantharajah, S.: A study on NSL-KDD dataset for intrusion detection system based on classification algorithms. Int. J. Adv. Res. Comput. Commun. Eng. **4**(6), 446–452 (2015)

18. Tavallaee, M., Bagheri, E., Lu, W., et al.: A detailed analysis of the KDD CUP 99 data set. In: 2009 IEEE Symposium on Computational Intelligence for Security and Defense Applications, pp. 1–6, July 2009

19. Chollet, F.: Keras: the python deep learning library (2013). https://keras.io/

20. Sokolova, M., Lapalme, G.: A systematic analysis of performance measures for classification tasks. Inf. Process. Manage. **45**(4), 427–437 (2009)

21. Javaid, A., Niyaz, Q., Sun, W., et al.: A deep learning approach for network intrusion detection system. In: Proceedings of the 9th EAI International Conference on Bio-inspired Information and Communications Technologies (Formerly BIONETICS), BICT 2015, New York City, United States, pp. 21–26. ICST (Institute for Computer Sciences, Social-Informatics and Telecommunications Engineering) (2016)

22. Abawajy, J., Huda, S., Sharmeen, S., et al.: Identifying cyber threats to mobile-IoT applications in edge computing paradigm. Future Gener. Comput. Syst. **89**, 525–538 (2018)

23. Tensorflow lite: A new mobile-specific library (2017). https://www.tensorflow.org/mobile/tflite/
24. Awid dataset - wireless security datasets project (2014). http://icsdweb.aegean.gr/awid/
25. Moustafa, N., Slay, J.: UNSW-NB15: a comprehensive data set for network intrusion detection systems (UNSW-NB15 network data set). In: 2015 Military Communications and Information Systems Conference (MilCIS), pp. 1–6, November 2015

Detecting Malicious Windows Commands Using Natural Language Processing Techniques

Muhammd Mudassar Yamin[✉] and Basel Katt[✉]

Norwegian University of Science and Technology,
Teknologivegen 22, 2815 Gjvik, Norway
{muhammad.m.yamin,basel.katt}@ntnu.no

Abstract. Windows command line arguments are used in administration of operating system through a CLI (command line interface). This command line interface gives access to multiple powerful system administration tools like PowerShell and WMIC. In an ideal scenario, access to CLI is restricted for malicious users, and the command line inputs are logged for forensic investigation. However, cyber criminals are implementing innovative command line obfuscation techniques to bypass those access restrictions and compromise system security. Traditional pattern matching techniques on obfuscated command line arguments are not suitable as detection mechanism due to the large search space presented in obfuscated command. In this work we used artificial intelligence driven natural language processing techniques for the classification of Windows command line as malicious or not. We implemented Multinomial Naive Bayes algorithm with neural network and trained it over a data set of malicious command line arguments. We evaluated the trained classifier in a real environment with both normal and malicious obfuscated command line argument and found our technique very effective in classifying malicious command line arguments with respect to false positives and performance.

Keywords: Command line obfuscation · Machine learning · Natural language processing

1 Introduction

Cyber arms race between attackers and defenders is in full swing. Attackers develop attack measures and defenders develop counter measures. With advent of modern SIEM (Security Information and Event Management), launching a successful cyber attack while avoiding detection by defenders becomes a difficult task. These SIEM solutions work by real time monitoring of system events and correlating events from multiples data sources for the identification of potential attacks. The SIEM solution is capable of detecting most traditional cyber attacks on a computer network. However, it solely relies on the information presented

© Springer Nature Switzerland AG 2019
J.-L. Lanet and C. Toma (Eds.): SecITC 2018, LNCS 11359, pp. 157–169, 2019.
https://doi.org/10.1007/978-3-030-12942-2_13

in event logs. Cyber attackers identified that if these event logs contain the attack information in an obfuscated manner then the SIEM solution detection mechanism will not be able to detect the attack.

This obfuscation of event information is achieved by obfuscation of command line arguments [8] used by attackers during the attack activity. The obfuscated command line was very difficult to detect by traditional pattern matching techniques, hence it bypasses through the defender's SIEM. To elaborate the problem more clearly, consider the very simple command line argument for opening calculator in Windows CMD.

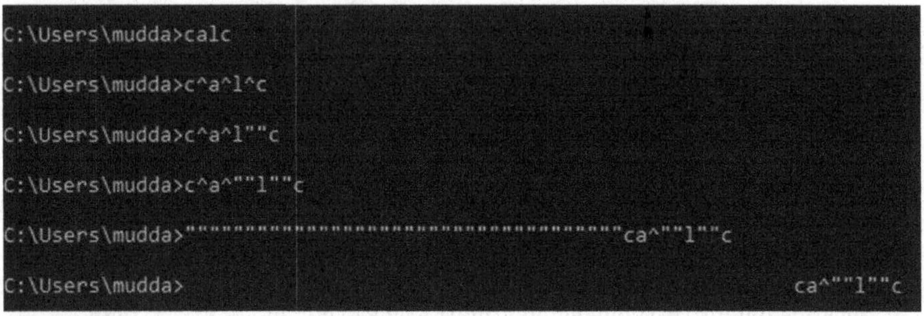

Fig. 1. Opening calculator in Windows CMD with multiple command line obfuscation techniques.

As seen in Fig. 1 the simple command line for opening a calculator can be obfuscated in many ways to avoid detection by an active SIEM solution. Usage of traditional pattern matching techniques in this type of scenario is not useful due to a new detection pattern required for each and every command. This leads us in to investigating other techniques used in the detection of patterns in such obscure data.

Research is being carried out in detecting Obfuscated Powershell command line arguments using NLP (Natural Language Processing) techniques. The Powershell command line obfuscation is automatically achieved by multiple attack tools like Powersploit [18]. However, new command line obfuscation techniques are starting to appear as highlighted by Fire eye [10]. The detection of such obfuscated commands in CMD is an ignored area in cyber security research.

In this paper, we used the NLP techniques on command line arguments for classifying the command lines as malicious or not. We developed our own data set of malicious command line argument by analyzing multiple online resources. We used that data set for the training of our classifier. Then we evaluated the classifier in real environment using both normal and obfuscated command lines. The rest of the paper is structured as follow. We first analyze the background of the problem and review the related literature. Then we discuss our malicious command line detection methodology. After that we present the evaluation results of our malicious command line detection methodology. Finally we present the conclusion and future work.

2   Background and Literature Review

2.1   Obfuscation

Source code obfuscation is a technique used to obscure application source code with random characters and functions while maintaining the original functionality of the program [1]. Obfuscation techniques are implemented to secure the application code from tempering and reverse engineering. However, these techniques are actively being used in virus and malware writers [2] to change and obscure the functionality of malicious programs and avoid detection by anti virus and anti malware programs. There are multiple types of obfuscation techniques, but the focus of this paper is obfuscation techniques of command line arguments, so only their details are given. There are two main types command line obfuscation techniques: Powershell and DoS code obfuscation. Details are given below:

- **Powershell Code Obfuscation**
  Powershell provides the ability to encode command and generate commands in run time. Attackers exploit this programming flexibility feature of Powershell for obfuscating malicious commands to evade detection. There are multiple techniques which are used for obfuscating Powershell command line arguments. Most of these techniques were introduced by Daniel Bohannon in 2016 with the tool "Invoke-Obfuscation" [9].
- **DoS Code Obfuscation**
  Microsoft Windows CMD have the feature for automatic command interpretation. CMD tries to execute the command even if it is not in a proper format. Attackers exploit this functionality to obfuscate the CMD commands to evade detection and launch new attacks. There are multiple techniques that are used for obfuscating CMD command line arguments. Most of these techniques were also introduced by Daniel Bohannon in 2018 with the tool "Invoke-DOSfuscation" [8].

2.2   Obfuscation in the Wild [10]

In June 2017 the financially-motivated FIN7 APT (Advance Persistence Threat) group (also known as Carbanak or Anunak) launched an attack with obfuscated CMD payloads [7] to evade detection by SIEM solutions. The APT group launched a spear phishing attack against United States securities and exchange commission. The attackers attached OLE (Object Linking Embedding) and LNK (Link) non executable files in the emails. These files in their code referred to CMD and when these files were opened, they executed CMD commands with obfuscated payload which resulted in persistence backdoor with a file less malware. Fireeye, [10] classified the 4 potential obfuscation techniques, which in total have thirteen sub categories. The classified techniques are given below:

1. **Obfuscating Binary Names**
   Attackers tamper with the binary name like changing name of CMD.exe to notepad.exe to evade detection this is achieved in two ways.

- **Environment Variable Sub-strings**
  It is possible to substitute environmental variable name with the command line executable name. Attackers exploits this functionality to evade detection.
- **For Loop Value Extraction**
  It is possible to construct for loops in command line arguments for automation tasks. Attackers exploit this functionality to generate and execute malicious command from a benign looking command.

2. **Character Insertion Obfuscation**
   Attackers insert special characters in the command line arguments to evade detection. This is achieved in four ways.
   - **Carets**
     ^ Used to obfuscate the command line arguments.
   - **Double Quotes**
     " Used to obfuscate the command line arguments.
   - **Parentheses**
     { } Used to obfuscate the command line arguments.
   - **Commas and Semicolons**
     , and ; used to obfuscate the command line arguments.

3. **Basic Payload Encoding**
   Attackers encode the command line arguments using different environment and custom variable present in the operating system to evade detection. This is achieved in three ways.
   - **Existing Environment Variables**
     Batch files of command line arguments can be encoded with help of existing environment variable present in Windows operating system.
   - **Custom Environment Variables**
     Whole batch files of command line arguments can be encoded by introducing new environment variable in Windows operating system and use them for encoding.
   - **Existing and Custom Environment Variables**
     Attackers combine both existing and new environment variable present in Windows operating system to encode the batch files.

4. **Advanced Payload Obfuscation**
   inserting command reversal code and replace special characters with normal characters to evade detection. This is achieved by four ways.
   - **Concatenation**
     Attackers concatenate a CMD level command line argument with a process level environment variable to evade detection.
   - **FORcoding**
     Attackers use loops in the command line arguments with combination of other obfuscation techniques to evade detection.
   - **Reversal**
     A FOR coding loop is used to generate a command from its reverse order and then execute it to evade detection.

- **FINcoding**
  Attackers use native sub string method of CMD to remove and replace delimiters with additional characters to generate a dynamic obfuscated command.

Attackers use the above mentioned techniques to obfuscate the command line arguments to very high levels. A very minimum obfuscation of net user command on Windows operating system using the above technique is shown in Fig. 2.

Fig. 2. Normal and obfuscated net user command

2.3   Current Obfuscation Detection Methodologies

Attempts are being made with collaboration of Microsoft to detect such attacks [3]. A deep CNN (Convolutional Neural Network) with combination of traditional NLP (Natural language processing techniques) was used for this purpose. The researchers focused on Powershell command line obfuscation detection and they published there research in April 2018. However the release of Invoke-DOSfuscation [8] tool which obfuscate CMD arguments instead of Powershell [9] argument in march 2018 created new attack vector, for which detection mechanisms still need to be developed.

Fireeye, in there commercial products, is also uses NLP techniques [11] for malicious obfuscation Windows command line detection. Fireeye has a large data set of malicious Powershell commands, logged and collected their customer systems. They used that data set for the training of a deep neural network based machine learning algorithm and achieved the accuracy of 99% in detecting malicious Powershell command line arguments.

In another scenario, researchers employed NLP techniques through Naive Bayes [6] algorithm for phising detection [5] The researchers used a machine learning classifier and trained the classifier over the data set of 1000 phishing emails. Their classifier only works on the textual data of the email not on the meta data. The textual data presents large obscure data. However, they achieved 98% accuracy in detecting phising emails.

As malicious obfuscated windows commands is a new attack vector in cyber security therefore very little research activities are performed on this topic. Researchers in another scenario of obfuscated malicious VBA macros detection [4] used five different classifiers SVM (Support Vector Machine), RF (Random Forest), MLP (Multi-Layer Perceptron), LDA (Linear Discriminant Analysis) and Naive Bayes (NB) classifier. Their results indicated that MLP achieved the best accuracy for obfuscation detection on some feature sets while not performed well on other feature sets as seen in Fig. 3.

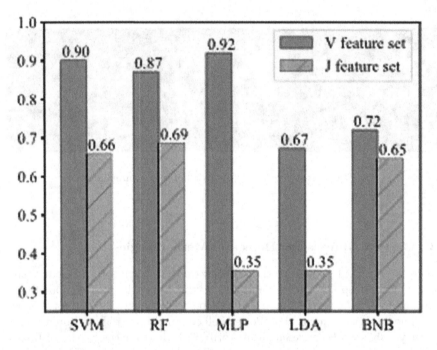

Fig. 3. Comparison of multiple machine learning classifier for detection of obfuscated malicious VBA macros [4]

2.4   Neural Network

ANN (Artificial neural networks) are inspired from neurons working of brain cell [12], ANN is composed of multiple interconnected artificial neurons, organized in multiple layers. A normal ANN contains a single layer for input and a single layer for output, one or more hidden layers are present between them for classification. When the neural network is deployed for classification of data the output was mostly in probabilities. A DNN (Deep Neural Network) [13] has more then one hidden layer between the input and output layer. A type of DNN architecture in CNN (Convolutional Neural Network) [14]. CNN is optimized for tasks in which input is given in raw format and the input requires minimum prepossessing which makes it ideal for the classification of obscure textual data.

3 Malicious Command Line Detection Methodology

The variance between the feature detection accuracy of NB is minimum compared to the rest of the classifier as seen in Fig. 3. From the previous discussion and through the literature review, we identified that NLP techniques through Naive Bayes [6] is the most commonly employed research methods of obfuscation detection. Based on [3, 4, 11] we decided to employ the same technique on our problem of malicious obfuscated Windows CMD commands detection. We chose one dimensional *Convolutional Neural Network* for text classification [3] with combination of *Multinomial Naive Bayes* classifier as we are going to classify malicious commands from large textual data [5].

3.1 Detection Classifier

We developed a 2-layer neuron (a hidden layer) and a malicious obfuscated command layer deep neural network for the classifier. As we are dealing with textual data so we implemented *Multinomial Naive Bayes* algorithm which uses multiple *Naive Bayes*, which is very effective in classification of objects from a noisy data source. However, it has few limitations, like it only gives a score on classification not a probability. It can only be applied on a positive sample data sets of required classification training data and negative sample data set will effect its accuracy of classification. Keeping all these limitation in mind we implemented our classifier. We used python with (NLTK) natural language processing toolkit [17] to develop the classifier. The developed neural network classifier is presented in Fig. 4.

3.2 Data Set

To train the classifier, we used Invoke-DOSfuscation samples obfuscated commands [8] as our training data. The sample contains a large collection of obfuscated DoS concatenated, reversed, for coded and fin coded commands, details of which is provided in Sect. 2.2. The sample was in text and evtx file format that required further processing, details of which is provided in Sect. 3.3. We also used the data set of post exploitation commands [19] and use them as test case for the verification of developed classifier. A raw form of a Data set sample of Invoke-DOSfuscation commands [8] can be seen in the Fig. 5.

3.3 Data Prepossessing

The data set which we used only contains the obfuscated commands. We manually performed classification on the data set. We created fourteen classes of CMD commands which are *blind files, system, networking, configs, finding important*

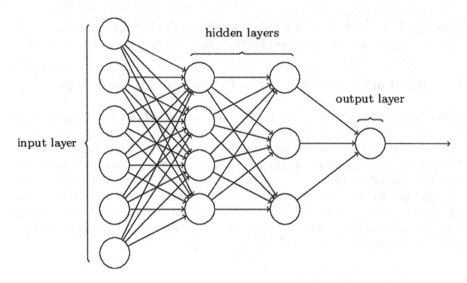

Fig. 4. Pictorial representation of developed classifier [15]

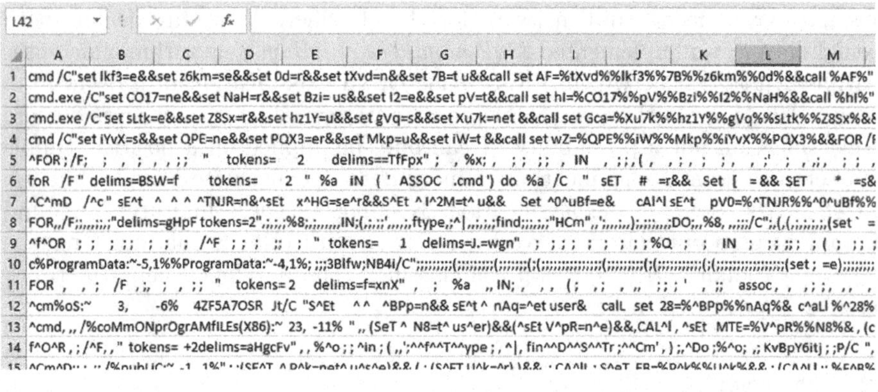

Fig. 5. Data set used for classifier training [8]

Files, files to pull, remote system access, auto start directories, binary planting, WMI, reg command exit, deleting logs, uninstalling software and *Powershell.* The classification based upon post exploitation command set of an attacker [19]. In our training data we specified the class type like system, deleting logs, powershell then we specified what the class contains, a command or an argument. We used only commands although our program can support single command line arguments as well. After that we specified the training commands on which the classifier should train on. A sample of classified data sources is shown in Fig. 6 of the source code.

The prepossessing could have been done automatically using an unsupervised classification such as a clustering algorithm suitable for the specificity of working

```
training_data.append({"class":"System", "commands":"fsutil fsinfo drives "})
training_data.append({"class":"Deleting Logs", "commands":"wevtutil el"})
training_data.append({"class":"Deleting Logs", "commands":"del %WINDIR%\*.log /a /s /q /f"})
training_data.append({"class":"Powershell", "commands":"`E`x`e`c`u`T`i`o`N`C`o`N`T`e`x`T}"})
```

Fig. 6. Data set classification in source code for training data

```
Training with 20 neurons, alpha:0.1, dropout:False
Input matrix: 32x69     Output matrix: 1x5
delta after 10000 iterations:0.015426917733242748
delta after 20000 iterations:0.01451529530641757
delta after 30000 iterations:0.01412455514301095
delta after 40000 iterations:0.0138954718572197
delta after 50000 iterations:0.013740812291282628
delta after 60000 iterations:0.013627535230054416
delta after 70000 iterations:0.0135400272982821
delta after 80000 iterations:0.01346983372762144
delta after 90000 iterations:0.013411928609035062
delta after 100000 iterations:0.013363113493269362
```

Fig. 7. Classifier in process training

data. However we wanted the classification to be compliant with SIEM solution rule set engines [16], therefore we performed the classification manually.

3.4 Training of the Classifier

Our hidden layers contain 20 neurons for easy adjustment of training data parameter, but it can vary depending upon the size of the data set. Our data set contains 10000 command lines for which it is suitable. The text processing in natural language processing requires intensive matrix manipulation. Therefore we used *numpy* [20] as it can perform matrix manipulation quite fast in comparison to other available libraries. We used *Sigmoid function* [21] as our activation function of neuron for high accuracy results. We iterated it and adjusted its parameters until false positive detection become very low. The final parameters on which we settled on hidden neurons are 20, *alpha* which is the learning rate parameter, is set to 0.1, *epochs* which is the learning data set size is set to 100000 and *drop-out* of randomly selected neurons during the training process is set to False. Figure 7 shows the in process training of the classifier on a relatively small data set.

4   Evaluation

As the work presented above is novel, we do not have any related work to compare our results with. Therefore we devised our own evaluation criteria. We classified normal and malicious obfuscated commands of different system functions.

Fig. 8. Un-obfuscated and obfuscated CMD command classification

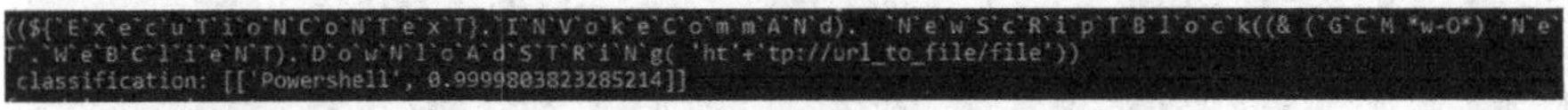

Fig. 9. Obfuscated Powershell command classification

– CMD obfuscated command
  "insert new row" command is detected in an obfuscated payload as shown in
  the Fig. 8
– Powershell obfuscated command
  Obfuscated Powershell command classification as shown in Fig. 9.

To properly evaluate our classifier we used post exploitation command
lines [19] un-obfuscated and obfuscated in our evaluation. A total of fourteen
types of commands are used for classification. It should be noted that we trained
the classifier on 10000 commands comprises of those fourteen classes and we used
2000s command comprises of those classes which is not the part of training data
set for the evaluation purposes. We sent 100 commands for each class to the
classifier, the classification of those commands by the classifier with respect to
true positive, false positive, false negative and detection precision percentage is
presented in Table 1.

We achieved an average precision of 96% in successful classification of malicious command line obfuscation on 14 types of commands. The most false positive classification occurred on uninstalling software commands. This is due to the
complex nature of these command. These commands includes many special characters on which our classifier is trained. Therefore it detected them malicious.
Some of the false positive test cases are given below:

– **Files To Pull**

  %WINDIR%\System32\drivers\etc\hosts

– **Remote System Access**

  net use \\ computername /user :DOMAINNAME\username password

Table 1. True positive, false positive, false negative and detection precision percentage of the developed classifier

ID	Class	True positive	False positive	False negative	Precision
1	Blind files	98	0	2	98%
2	System	99	1	0	99%
3	Networking	97	0	3	97%
4	Configs	96	3	1	96%
5	Finding important files	97	3	0	97%
6	Files to pull	94	5	1	94%
7	Remote system access	95	5	0	95%
8	Auto start directories	96	3	1	96%
9	Binary planting	96	4	0	96%
10	WMI	97	3	0	97%
11	Reg command exit	97	2	1	97%
12	Deleting logs	99	0	1	99%
13	Uninstalling software	93	7	0	93%
14	Powershell	95	5	0	95%

– **Uninstalling Software**

```
wmic product where name="XXX" call uninstall /Interactive:Off
```

– **Powershell**

```
app = Get-WmiObject -Class Win32_Product `
-Filter "Name = 'Software Name'"
```

5   Conclusion and Future Work

In this paper, we presented a technique for the detection of malicious obfuscated CMD commands. The problem of detecting such malicious obfuscated CMD commands has not been addressed before. We used natural language processing techniques developed for chat bots sentence classification to classify malicious obfuscated CMD commands. Our multinomial Naive Bayes with convolutional 2-layer neural network implementation performed exceptionally well and we achieved average classification score accuracy of 96%. It should be noted that these are the experimental result achieved. In a real world environment where million of logs coming every second to the classifier the accuracy may vary.

In future work, we are planning to integrate our obfuscated command line classification method with our exploit detection algorithm. Our exploit detection algorithm works by correlating multiple events on a system, which are executed.

Our obfuscated command line classification method will allow us to detect malicious exploits before the execution in Windows environment. In case the malicious command executed our exploit detection algorithm will eventually detect the exploit. We expect that combining machine learning techniques with event correlation algorithm will produce fruitful results.

References

1. Balakrishnan, A., Schulze, C.: Code Obfuscation Literature Survey. http://pages. cs.wisc.edu/~arinib/writeup.pdf. Accessed 1 Oct 2018
2. Konstantinou, E.: Metamorphic virus: analysis and detection. RHUL-MA-2008-02, Technical report of University of London, January 2008. http://www.rhul.ac.uk/ mathematics/techreports
3. Hendler, D., Kels, S., Rubin, A.: Detecting malicious PowerShell commands using deep neural networks. In: Proceedings of the 2018 on Asia Conference on Computer and Communications Security, pp. 187–197. ACM (2018)
4. Kim, S., Hong, S., Oh, J., Lee, H.: Obfuscated VBA macro detection using machine learning. In: 2018 48th Annual IEEE/IFIP International Conference on Dependable Systems and Networks (DSN), pp. 490–501. IEEE (2018)
5. Peng, T., Harris, I., Sawa, Y.: Detecting phishing attacks using natural language processing and machine learning. In: 2018 IEEE 12th International Conference on Semantic Computing (ICSC), pp. 300–301. IEEE (2018)
6. McCallum, A., Nigam, K.: A comparison of event models for naive bayes text classification. In: AAAI-98 Workshop on Learning for Text Categorization, vol. 752, no. 1, pp. 41–48 (1998)
7. FIN7 hacking group is switched to new techniques to evade detection. https:// securityaffairs.co/wordpress/64083/apt/fin7-new-techniques.html. Accessed 1 Oct 2018
8. Invoke-DOSfuscation. https://github.com/danielbohannon/Invoke-DOSfuscation. Accessed 1 Oct 2018
9. Invoke-Obfuscation. https://github.com/danielbohannon/Invoke-Obfuscation. Accessed 1 Oct 2018
10. DOSfuscation: Exploring the Depths of CMD.exe Obfuscation and Detection Techniques. https://www.fireeye.com/blog/threat-research/2018/03/dosfuscation-expl oring-obfuscation-and-detection-techniques.html. Accessed 1 Oct 2018
11. Malicious PowerShell Detection via Machine Learning. https://www.fireeye. com/blog/threat-research/2018/07/malicious-powershell-detection-via-machine-learning.html. Accessed 1 Oct 2018
12. Yegnanarayana, B.: Artificial Neural Networks. PHI Learning Pvt. Ltd. (2009)
13. Liu, W., Wang, Z., Liu, X., Zeng, N., Liu, Y., Alsaadi, F.E.: A survey of deep neural network architectures and their applications. Neurocomputing **234**, 11–26 (2017)
14. Lai, S., Xu, L., Liu, K., Zhao, J.: Recurrent convolutional neural networks for text classification. In: AAAI, vol. 333, pp. 2267–2273 (2015)
15. 2 Layer neural Network. https://blog.csdn.net/shebao3333/article/details/7873 9298. Accessed 1 Oct 2018
16. Detecting Lateral Movement through Tracking Event Logs (Version 2). https:// blog.jpcert.or.jp/2017/12/research-report-released-detecting-lateral-movement-through-tracking-event-logs-version-2.html. Accessed 22 Oct 2018

17. Natural language tool kit. https://www.nltk.org/. Accessed 1 Oct 2018
18. Powersploit. https://github.com/PowerShellMafia/PowerSploit. Accessed 1 Oct 2018
19. Windows Post Exploitation Command Execution. https://repo.zenk-security.com/. Accessed 1 Oct 2018
20. Nump. http://www.numpy.org/. Accessed 1 Oct 2018
21. Sigmoid Function. http://mathworld.wolfram.com/SigmoidFunction.html. Accessed 1 Oct 2018

Evolutionary Computation Algorithms for Detecting Known and Unknown Attacks

Hasanen Alyasiri[1(✉)], John A. Clark[2], and Daniel Kudenko[1]

[1] Department of Computer Science, University of York, York, UK
{hmha503,daniel.kudenko}@york.ac.uk
[2] Department of Computer Science, University of Sheffield, Sheffield, UK
john.clark@sheffield.ac.uk

Abstract. Threats against the internet and computer networks are becoming more sophisticated, with attackers using new attacks or modifying existing ones. Security teams have major difficulties in dealing with large numbers of continuously evolving threats. Various artificial intelligence algorithms have been deployed to analyse such threats. In this paper, we explore the use of Evolutionary Computation (EC) techniques to construct behavioural rules for characterising activities observed in a system. The EC framework evolves human readable solutions that provide an explanation of the logic behind its evolved decisions, offering a significant advantage over existing paradigms. We examine the potential application of these algorithms to detect known and unknown attacks. The experiments were conducted on modern datasets.

Keywords: Intrusion Detection System · Unknown attacks ·
Evolutionary computation

1 Introduction

The increasing use of online services in many domains has made them an attractive target for attack. Along with this popularity comes a serious risk of security breaches and securing services is now a major challenge for many organisations. Traditional protection tools, such as firewalls, security policies, prevention systems, access control and encryption have failed to protect networks and systems adequately from increasingly sophisticated attacks and malware [29]. The 2018 Akamai "state of the internet report" [1] shows an increase of 38% of web application attacks and 16% of Distributed Denial of Service (DDoS) attacks compared with 2017. Moreover, the APWG "phishing activity trends report" [4] stated that the number of phishing sites detected in the first quarter of 2018 was up 46% over the last quarter of 2017. These worrying trends demonstrate the need to develop and deploy new methods to enhance security.

"Intrusion detection is the process of monitoring the events occurring in a computer system or network and analysing them for signs of possible incidents, which are violations or imminent threats of violation of computer security

© Springer Nature Switzerland AG 2019
J.-L. Lanet and C. Toma (Eds.): SecITC 2018, LNCS 11359, pp. 170–184, 2019.
https://doi.org/10.1007/978-3-030-12942-2_14

policies, acceptable use policies, or standard security practices" [23]. An Intrusion Detection System (IDS) can help prevent or mitigate the effects of some threats. However, IDSs face various difficulties such as huge traffic volumes, unbalanced data distributions, difficulty distinguishing normal and abnormal behaviours, and constantly evolving environments [29]. Furthermore, unknown attacks (unseen variations of known attacks or new attacks) are emerging as one of the most serious threats to any system [6].

Various techniques from the discipline of Artificial Intelligence have been adopted to address this issue. In this study, we adopted various evolutionary computation (EC) approaches. These are inspired by evolution in nature and are well suited to addressing complex real-world problems. EC techniques have been used by researchers to tackle numerous intrusion detection tasks [29]. The EC approach has a number of attractive features, such as creating human readable and lightweight detection rules, and offering a collection of solutions with different trade-offs amongst conflicting objectives [24]. These features are significant for a security team as they often deal with resource-constrained applications [21]. In addition, EC offers an effective way of providing a framework to build computer programs automatically. It is often used when the desired solution is an 'expression' (typically a predicate or check) or program. Major advantages of the EC-based techniques are that no prior knowledge is needed about the statistical distribution of the data and they can operate directly on the data in its original form. EC discovers the most important discriminative features of a behaviour and the generated expressions (detection checks) can be used directly in the application environment. Genetic Programming (GP) [9], Grammatical Evolution (GE) [22] and Cartesian Genetic Programming (CGP) [13] are forms of EC suited to the synthesis of programs or expressions. In general, these techniques vary from one another primarily in how the individuals are represented. In this research, we use GP (a tree-based form), GE (a grammar-based form) and CGP (a graph-based form) as tools for synthesising an intrusion detection programs.

The remainder of this document is structured as follows. Section 2 gives an overview of related works. Section 3 introduces our proposed methods. Section 4 describes our experiments on the datasets and explains the results obtained. Section 5 examines how effectively our techniques can produce programs that can detect previously unknown attacks. Section 6 gives conclusions and indicates future work.

2   Related Work

EC is a branch of artificial intelligence widely used in the research of IDS. EC applies global optimization methods to solve the problem at hand. In the case of intrusion detection, the problem being solved is the detection of normal or intrusive events. Lu and Traore [10] investigated the use of GP to evolve rules whose aim is to discover novel or known network attacks. The initial population of rules was selected based on background knowledge from known attacks, and each rule can be represented as a parse tree. The algorithm was tested on the DARPA 1999 benchmark dataset. Their investigation showed how GP could identify novel intrusion signatures for previously unseen variations of known attacks (DoS attack subfamilies). Hansen et al. [7] investigated the potential of GP as an adaptive method for responding to the complexities of cyberterrorism, by increasing the detection rate of malicious intrusions, while at the same time, reducing the false positive rate. A machine code linear structure was used to encode the individuals. A subset of the KDD99 dataset was used in their experiment. GP produced directly executable programs that executed at the same speed as standard code. Orfila et al. [21] explored the application of GP for the detection of network attacks. They produced lightweight intrusion detection rules and simple patterns that can easily be understood by humans. Their experiments used internal enterprise traffic recorded at a medium-sized site from October 2004 through January 2005. The function set used provided more understandable semantics in relation to why an event is considered an intrusion. However, there is a need to include non-linear behaviour exploration in the solution space. Blasco et al. [5] guided the GP search by means of a fitness function based on recent advances in IDS evaluation, demonstrating that an intelligent use of GP is competitive in terms of effectiveness, efficiency and simplicity.

The contributions of our work are described below:

- Researchers often investigate a very limited number of attacks and make assumptions about the architectures of solutions. In this work, four widely different deployment environments containing modern sets of threats and their variants are investigated.
- We examine the detection of genuinely unseen attacks instead of only unseen variations of known attacks.
- In contrast to GP, GE has seen very limited application [28] and we know of no IDS applications of CGP by other researchers [3].

3   Proposed Methodology

Our intrusion detection synthesis approaches use a supervised learning module based on EC algorithms. Our rules will be expressed over features extracted from available datasets. Other researchers have already extracted features from these datasets as part of their attempts to derive intrusion detectors. We will start by the learning phase, and measure the performance of each generated feature relation (i.e. behavioural signature). The training phase finishes when either all instances are categorised correctly or else a maximum number of generations has been reached. Later the best-evolved programs feed into the testing phase to be evaluated. The basic architecture of our approach for producing programs is illustrated in Fig. 1.

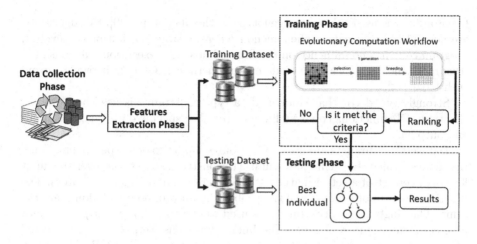

Fig. 1. Methodology framework.

3.1 Evolutionary Computation Based Classification Techniques

EC methods offer an effective way of providing a framework to build computer programs automatically. In general, an EC algorithm begins with creating a population consisting of individuals that represent potential solutions to the problem. Then individuals are evaluated to show how well each individual solves or comes near to solving the problem. The estimate of how far an individual is from solving the problem is captured by means of a 'cost function'. Thus we seek to minimise the cost function. The simulated evolutionary process seeks to evolve ever-fitter (lower cost) populations of candidate solutions, using operators inspired by biological metaphor, i.e. reproduction, such as crossover, mutation, and selection.

These three evolutionary operators are applied repeatedly until some termination criterion is met. Crossover causes solutions to be 'mated': two individuals exchange solution components to form 'offspring'. Mutation causes some component of a solution to spontaneously mutate, allowing it to take on values that are potentially not possessed currently by any candidate solution in the population.

Finally, selection determines which solutions go forward to form the next generation of the population. This implements some form of 'survival of the fittest' regime (fitter solutions have greater chances of going forward).

By repeatedly following the indicated cycle it is anticipated that later generations will have fitter individuals and hopefully the process will generate at least one that 'solves' the problem, or is otherwise acceptable.

The main difference between GP, GE and CGP is how candidate solutions are represented. Individuals are represented as trees in GP, linear genomes in GE, and as forms of directed acyclic graph in CGP. Another difference is the mapping process from the genotype to the phenotype. The GP parse tree is a direct mapping of the given composition functions and terminals [9]. Whereas CGP maps functions and terminals to an indexed graph [13]. In GE, a context-free grammar is used to map the genotype to the phenotype [20]. EC algorithms are susceptible to bloat, a phenomenon where a large portion of the evolved program code has no influence on the fitness but whose execution still consumes resources (and so typically extends execution times). CGP is known to avoid such bloat [12].

Strongly-typed GP that enforces data type constraints is used here [16]. In this type, GP functions could be limited to utilise specific data types (as input and output).

Datasets' feature sets are used as the source inputs to our experiments. Function nodes (which the techniques will use to construct expressions over the input features) consist of a set of mathematical, relational and logical operators. The functions used in order to define the problem in all proposed techniques are the same. The single input arity functions used were *sin*, *cos*, *log*, *log1p*, *sqrt*, *abs*, *exp*, *ceil*, *floor*, *tan* and *tanh*. The binary functions were $+$, $-$, $*$, protected $(/)$, *power*, *max*, *min*, *percent*, $>$, $\geq$, $\leq$, $<$, $=$, $\neq$, AND and OR. This set of functions allows individuals to be discriminated by linear and non-linear separation. Only relational and logical functions which return Boolean can be placed at the first level of GP and GE individuals requiring the 'if' statement to return Boolean value (i.e. normal vs. anomaly). CGP output nodes can be connected to any previous node [12]. In our implementation, we evolved two output nodes and we experimented decision-making process with various relational and logical functions. As a result, using greater than operator (i.e. $o0 > o1$) was found to give the highest performance.

The ECJ [11] toolkit is used for the GP and CGP implementations whereas GE was implemented using the package gramEvol [20]. Our experiments use a population size of 1000 with a maximum of 50 generations for both GP and GE experiments. CGP generally uses very small population sizes (i.e. 5) and a large number of generations [12]. The number of generations was 10,000, except for the modern DDoS dataset where a value of 2,000 was adopted. This is due to the fitness value stagnation after reaching 2,000 generation. The mutation rate used was 0.01. The maximum number of nodes was 500. There is no elitism operation performed in these implementations. These settings were determined via preliminary experimentation. The rest of the parameters were determined automatically by the packages.

3.2   Performance Measure

The effectiveness of proposed algorithms can be measured according to how malicious and normal behaviours are classified. Our datasets are labelled as normal or anomalous. We calculate the numbers of: true positives (TP), where malicious events are accurately classified as such; true negatives (TN), where normal events are classified as such; false positives (FP), where normal events are classified as malicious; and false negatives (FN), where malicious events are classified as normal. Both false classifications are problematic. FPs waste a great deal of time and can lead to loss of confidence and FNs are examples of the detector system not performing its primary task, i.e. they are attacks that go undetected.

Three derived performance metrics are used to assess our IDS detection rules. The Detection Rate (DR) ($\frac{TP}{(TP+FN)}$) indicates the fraction of real attacks that are detected; this is sometimes is referred to as Recall. Accuracy ($\frac{(TP+TN)}{(TN+TP+FN+FP)}$) defines the fraction of all instances (attacks or non-attacks) that are correctly classified. IDS experts consider both False Positive Rate (FPR) ($\frac{FP}{(FP+TN)}$) and False Negative Rate (FNR) ($\frac{FN}{(FN+TP)}$) to be as important as the detection accuracy. Finally, the False Alarm Rate (FAR) ($\frac{(FPR+FNR)}{2}$) gives the rate of misclassified instances.

3.3 Cost Function

The cost function measures how much an individual's performance deviates from the ideal. The cost function used in our experiments is defined as:

$$Fitness = (\frac{TP - Anomaly\ Count}{Anomaly\ Count})^2 + (\frac{TN - Normal\ Count}{Normal\ Count})^2 \qquad (1)$$

When classification is perfect the cost is 0. Many other reasonable cost functions are possible.

4 Experiment

The performance of proposed techniques has been evaluated using four different datasets. These datasets are fully labelled, containing realistic normal and malicious scenarios. There are three types of extracted feature: numeric, symbolic and binary. Using EC approaches has notable benefits as they can deal with input data in its raw form without pre-processing and without assuming any prior distribution. However, we did not employ all sets of features available; processing symbolic features such as protocol type, packet type and flag fields would have significantly increased the complexity of the learning process. Also, some attributes are changing constantly such as IP addresses and port numbers. This occurs for many reasons, malicious (e.g. spoofed by attackers) and legitimate (with the aim of hiding by proxies to protect privacy). Any synthesised detectors relying on these attributes may not generalize well in real world applications [8].

4.1 Description of the Benchmark Datasets

The **Kyoto 2006+ dataset** covers more than three years of real traffic data, over the period between November 2006 and August 2009, collected from both honeypots and regular servers that were deployed at Kyoto University. The main known cyber threats that researchers observed in their honeypots were

Trojans, Worms, Phishing attacks, Email spams and Shellcodes. There is also a percentage of unknown threats that did not activate any IDS alarms, and yet included shellcodes. They have extracted 24 significant features from the raw traffic data obtained by honeypot systems. The final feature set that we used for this study comprised: duration, service, source-bytes, destination-bytes, count, same-srv-rate, serror-rate, srv-serror-rate, dst-host-count, dst-host-srv-count, dst-host-same-src-port-rate, dst-host-serror-rate and dst-host-srv-serror-rate. More details on the features names, types, possible values and descriptions are given in [26]. For the experiments on the Kyoto 2006+ dataset, we evaluated our frameworks on the dataset collected on the 27, 28, 29, 30 and 31 August 2009. We selected 152,460 samples randomly. Our dataset is split into 70% for training and 30% for testing.

Our phishing oriented dataset is the **Phishing websites dataset** produced by Mohammad et al. published in UCI repository [14]. These websites are created with the aim of seizing users' private information such as usernames, passwords and social security numbers [15]. The dataset consists of 11055 websites samples. It has 4898 examples labelled as phishing websites whereas the remaining examples are labelled as genuine websites. Most of this dataset's attributes are binary (0, 1) or ternary (0, 1, −1) where the values are 1, 0, and −1 refer to legitimate, suspicious, and phishing respectively. This dataset contains 30 features in four main categories that have proved to be sound and effective in predicting phishing websites. For further details about each category and its features can be found in [14,15]. The dataset is divided randomly into 80% for training and 20% for testing.

The **UNSW-NB15 dataset** from the Cyber Range Lab of the Australian Centre for Cyber Security (ACCS) is also used. In this dataset, a mix of real modern normal activities and attack behaviours were generated. This dataset contains over 2 million sample data elements from two different simulation periods. In UNSW-NB15, there are nine categories of attacks [17]:

1. Fuzzers: a technique where the attacker tries to uncover new and unknown vulnerabilities in a program, operating system, or network by feeding it with the widest possible range of unexpected inputs of random data to make it crash.
2. Analysis: a variety of intrusions that penetrate web applications via ports (e.g., port scans), emails (e.g., spam), and web scripts (e.g., HTML files).
3. Backdoor: attacks in which the attacker attempts bypassing a stealthy normal authentication, securing unauthorized remote access to a device, and locating the entrance to plain text.
4. Denial of Service (DoS): an intrusion that causes computer resources to be so heavily used as to prevent the authorized requests from accessing a device or service.
5. Exploit: a sequence of instructions that takes advantage of a glitch, bug, or vulnerability to be caused by an unintentional or unsuspected behaviour on a host or network.
6. Generic: an attack that works against all block-cipher employing a hash function to collision with no consideration to the structure of the block-cipher.

7. Reconnaissance: can be defined as a probe; an attack that gathers information about a computer network to evade its security controls.
8. Shellcode: an attack in which the attacker penetrates a piece of code starting from a shell to control the compromised machine.
9. Worm: an attack whereby the attacker replicates itself in order to spread on other computers. Often, it uses a computer network to spread itself, depending on the security failures on the target computer to access it.

For each network packet 47 different features have been extracted. These features are classified into five groups: flow features, basic features, content features, time features and additional generated features. Only features with numeric values (i.e. integer, float and binary) are used; there are 39 of them. For more details about each group and features refer to [17,19]. The portion of UNSW-NB15 dataset detailed in [17] is used for training and testing.

Modern DDoS dataset which contains contemporary type of DDoS attack. A network simulator (NS2) was utilized to generate this dataset where it simulated different types of attack targeting application and network layers. The collected dataset contains four types of DDoS attack as below [2]:

1. Smurf is a network traffic effected by spoofing IP addresses in a network for sending a massive amount of Internet Control Message Protocol (ICMP) echo request packets to the target server. With enough ICMP responses forwarded, the target machine is brought down.
2. User Datagram Protocol (UDP) flood is network layer attack on the UDP connectionless protocol. The intruders dispatch a great number UDP packets to overwhelm the target server.
3. SQL Injection DDOS is an application layer attack, where intruders begin from the client side, a web browser for instance, by inserting a malicious code element (i.e. SQL statement) and forwarding it to the server-side database. This code will be executed indefinitely making the service unavailable for legitimate clients.
4. HTTP flood is a type of application layer attack. HTTP flood attacks are volumetric attacks, where attackers send what seem to be legitimate HTTP GET or POST requests for a web server or application. The attackers act as a legitimate user repeatedly requesting http services.

In this dataset, 27 features were extracted from each network packet. The final feature set that we used in our experiment are pkt-id, pkt-size, seq-number, fid, number-of-pkt, number-of-byte, pkt-in, pkt-out, pkt-r, pkt-delay-node, pkt-rate, byte-rate, pkt-avg-size, utilization, pkt-delay, pkt-send-time, pkt-reserved-time, first-pkt-sent and last-pkt-reseved. For more details refer to [2]. To obtain realistic results and splitting the dataset into 34% testing and 66% training.

4.2 Results

For each evolved program, we calculate its detection rate (DR), False Alarm Rate (FAR) and Accuracy (Acc). To obtain a statistically significant measure that does not depend on the initial random seed, the results for our proposed algorithms correspond to the average of 20 independent runs. The results from the testing phase are presented in Table 1.

Table 1. The Performance of GP, GE and CGP (%)

Dataset	GP			GE			CGP		
	DR	FAR	Acc	DR	FAR	Acc	DR	FAR	Acc
Kyoto 2006+	98.78	1.64	98.42	98.79	1.88	98.22	99.65	0.70	99.35
Phishing website	85.63	11.47	88.87	83.64	12.65	87.78	89.99	8.31	91.88
UNSW-NB15	90.67	19.19	81.80	88.50	24.34	76.95	94.20	13.46	87.31
Modern DDoS	87.39	7.15	97.15	86.76	8.14	95.88	87.38	7.13	97.19

Some conclusions can be drawn from these results. CGP outperformed GP and GE especially on the UNSW-NB15 dataset which was the more complex one. GP showed a better performance compared to GE in almost all cases. The worst performance in the detection rate achieved by each algorithm was on the phishing websites dataset and the modern DDoS dataset.

This may be due to the difference between dataset collecting environment and the kind of threats. In addition, the results suggest that is because of both datasets nature. Features with ternary values (i.e. 1, 0 and -1) represented phishing websites dataset. Whereas the unbalanced distribution of the modern DDoS dataset since the number of normal events is much higher than the number of malicious events. This issue could be addressed by improving the fitness function, e.g. assigning different weights to TP and TN. However, we treated both classes equally important in this implementation.

Some of best individuals output evolved by the proposed methods taken from the UNSW-NB15 dataset experiment are presented in Fig. 2. An advantage of proposed algorithms is the representation of the evolved solution. Examining the evolved output can provide useful insights into how the algorithm learns to solve the given problem. Also, it can be seen that GP algorithm selected 7 out of 39 features to construct it best individual. Whereas both GE and CGP algorithms utilized 6 features only to generate their outputs.

Any reduction in the solution size that is able to provide a given overall performance is necessary for the computational efficiency of the IDS. Consequently, if normal and attacks activities are accurately detected with lightweight processing, it becomes feasible to the security team to carry out other actions (e.g. IP blocking) in real time.

5   Evolutionary Computation Techniques for Detecting Unknown Attacks

With each passing year, the volume and variety of attacks has dramatically increased [27]. To test the robustness of our proposed approaches, we have

GP: (AND (AND (AND (AND (>= (abs sttl) smeansz) (>= (abs sttl) smeansz)) (AND (>= ct_state_ttl (max ct_state_ttl synack)) (>= (abs sttl) (/ tcprtt is_sm_ips_ports)))) (< ct_srv_src smeansz))(> (log1p sttl) (max ct_state_ttl synack)))

GE: (percent(ct_srv_dst, dttl - (power(trans_depth, abs (ct_ftp_cmd)) + tanh(floor(dload)))) <= ct_dst_sport_ltm

CGP: o0 = log (ceil (exp (* (tan ct_state_ttl) (!= swin is_sm_ips_ports))))
     o1 = min ct_srv_dst (power ct_dst_src_ltm (tan dur))

Fig. 2. Proposed methods output.

ensured that the attack types in the training dataset are different from those in the testing dataset. This will allow us to determine whether learned characteristics of known attacks are of use in detecting previously unseen attacks. In this implementation, the detecting of previously unseen variations of known attacks (i.e. subfamilies) and unseen attacks are both tested. The same GP, GE and CGP framework settings from the previous investigation were adopted here. Twenty independent runs were performed and the results of the best run in each case is reported. The detection of attacks present in the testing dataset and absent from the training dataset indicates the potential to detect novel attacks.

First we use the training and testing dataset of the modern DDoS dataset, which includes 4 subfamilies of DDoS attack. Table 2 presents the new distribution of this dataset where only network layer DDoS attacks appear in the training dataset (i.e. Smurf and UDP Flood). Application layer DDoS attacks (i.e. SIDDOS and HTTP Flood) appear only in the testing dataset. These attacks instances were removed from the training and added to the testing dataset.

Table 2. Attack distribution for modern DDoS dataset

Attack name	Attack traffic in training set	Attack traffic in testing set
Smurf	8,341	4,249
UDP Flood	132,441	68,903
SIDDOS	0	6,665
HTTP Flood	0	4,110
Total records	140,782	83,927

The distributions of testing results are given in Fig. 3 of DR, FAR and Acc measurements respectively for 20 runs form each method. From these results, it would suggest that both CGP and GP are performing similarly to each other and better than the GE algorithm.

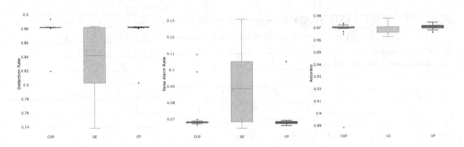

Fig. 3. Distribution of performance measurements of each algorithm applied to modern DDoS dataset.

The number of detected attacks by the best-evolved program is presented in Table 3. Although Smurf attack was included in the training dataset, it was the most challenging attack class to classify for the proposed algorithms. This is due to the nature of this attack [2]. However, frameworks such as Multilayer Perceptron, Random Forest, Decision Tree, Nave Bayes and Support Vector Machine in [2,25] achieved a lower detection rate for Smurf attacks than the results reported here. The proof of concept implementation shows the proposed approaches can detect application layer attacks especially the HTTP Flood, which are absent from the training dataset.

Table 3. Detection percentage of unseen variants of attack

Attack name	GP		GE		CGP	
	No. of attack detected	DR (%)	No. of attack detected	DR (%)	No. of attack detected	DR (%)
Smurf	1,552	36.52	1,539	36.22	1,552	36.52
UDP Flood	62,015	90	61,981	89.95	62,023	90.01
SIDDOS	6,310	94.67	6,315	94.74	6,313	94.71
HTTP Flood	4,110	100	4,110	100	4,110	100
Total records	73,987	88.15	73,945	88.10	73,998	88.16

The UNSW-NB15 dataset was adopted for the unseen attacks experiment. As presented in Table 4, there were nine types of attacks only five types are present in the training. We randomly selected 4 attack types (i.e. Analysis, Backdoor, Shellcode and Worms), removed their training instances and added them to the testing dataset.

The distributions of UNSW-NB15 dataset testing results of 20 runs are given in Fig. 4. We can see clearly how each algorithm performed in terms of DR, FAR and Acc. The presented results showed that CGP approach achieved better overall performance than the other techniques. Whereas GP performed better than GE algorithm.

Table 4. Attack distribution for UNSW-NB15 dataset

Attack name	Attack traffic in training set	Attack traffic in testing set
Analysis	0	2,677
Backdoor	0	2,329
DoS	12,264	4,089
Exploits	33,393	11,132
Fuzzers	18,184	6,062
Generic	40,000	18,871
Reconnaissance	10,491	3,496
Shellcode	0	1,511
Worms	0	174
Total records	114,332	50,341

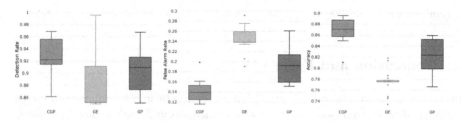

Fig. 4. Distribution of performance measurements of each algorithm applied to UNSW-NB15 dataset.

The attack detection percentage from the best-evolved programs are summarised in Table 5. As we can see, proposed algorithms were able to recognise unseen attacks effectively. CGP achieved the highest detection rate of unknown attacks except for the Shellcode attack where GP performed slightly better. GE was the lowest among them. Although the Fuzzers attack was present in the training phase, the algorithms have achieved the lowest detection rate compared to other known and unknown attacks. This is due to lower variances among some malicious records and normal records in the UNSW-NB15 dataset [18]. However, the proposed techniques have achieved a higher attack detection rate than [18] but with lower normal records classification percentage. Moving forward, these variations in the behaviour towards attacks make it possible to combine these signatures and store them together in an IDS database.

Table 5. Detection percentage of unseen attacks

Attack name	GP		GE		CGP	
	No. of attack detected	DR (%)	No. of attack detected	DR (%)	No. of attack detected	DR (%)
Analysis	2,290	85.54	2,450	91.52	2,674	99.88
Backdoor	2,254	96.77	2,237	96.04	2,297	98.62
DoS	3,970	97.08	3,951	96.62	4,033	98.63
Exploits	10,671	95.85	10,530	94.59	10,966	98.50
Fuzzers	5,240	86.44	3,576	58.99	4,853	80.05
Generic	18,811	99.68	18,782	99.52	18,855	99.91
Reconnaissance	3,442	98.45	3,340	95.53	3,439	98.36
Shellcode	1,487	98.41	1,425	94.30	1,472	97.41
Worms	165	94.82	169	97.12	172	98.85
Total records	48,330	96.00	46,460	92.29	48,761	96.86

6   Conclusion and Future Work

In this paper, we show that evolutionary computation techniques can discover predicates over features that distinguish normal and malicious events. One interesting feature of these approaches is the ability to evolve a detector that can detect a wide range of attacks. In addition, the experimental results demonstrated that our proposed approaches have successfully classified unknown attacks that the systems were not trained on. These results suggest that proposed methods generalize well based on similarity to known attacks. GP, GE and CGP emerged as reliable predictors for finding previously unseen attacks/sub-families of known attacks. In general, CGP was the best performing paradigm compared to GP and GE.

Based on experience in many other domains, we anticipate that a *collection* of detectors might well provide a means of achieving practical detection goals. In machine learning, such collections of primitive elements (e.g. detectors or classifiers) are termed ensembles and we aim to synthesise such combination using EC approaches.

Acknowledgements. Hasanan Alyasiri would like to thank the Iraqi Ministry of Higher Education and Scientific Research and the University of Kufa for supporting his PhD study. John Clark is supported by the EPSRC DAASE Programme Grant EP/J017515/1.

References

1. Akamai: state of the internet report (2018). https://www.akamai.com/
2. Alkasassbeh, M., Al-Naymat, G., Hassanat, A.B., Almseidin, M.: Detecting distributed denial of service attacks using data mining techniques. Int. J. Adv. Comput. Sci. Appl. **7**(1), 436–445 (2016)
3. Alyasiri, H., Clark, J., Kudenko, D.: Applying cartesian genetic programming to evolve rules for intrusion detection system. In: Proceedings of the 10th International Joint Conference on Computational Intelligence, IJCCI, vol. 1, pp. 176–183 (2018)
4. APWG: Phishing activity trends report (2018). https://www.antiphishing.org/
5. Blasco, J., Orfila, A., Ribagorda, A.: Improving network intrusion detection by means of domain-aware genetic programming. In: 2010 International Conference on Availability, Reliability, and Security, ARES 2010, pp. 327–332. IEEE (2010)
6. Cisco: 2018 annual cybersecurity report. https://www.cisco.com/
7. Hansen, J.V., Lowry, P.B., Meservy, R.D., McDonald, D.M.: Genetic programming for prevention of cyberterrorism through dynamic and evolving intrusion detection. Decis. Support Syst. **43**(4), 1362–1374 (2007)
8. Khanchi, S., Vahdat, A., Heywood, M.I., Zincir-Heywood, A.N.: On botnet detection with genetic programming under streaming data label budgets and class imbalance. Swarm Evol. Comput. **39**, 123–140 (2018)
9. Koza, J.R.: Genetic Programming: On the Programming of Computers by Means of Natural Selection, vol. 1. MIT Press, Cambridge (1992)
10. Lu, W., Traore, I.: Detecting new forms of network intrusion using genetic programming. Comput. Intell. **20**(3), 475–494 (2004)
11. Luke, S.: ECJ evolutionary computation library (1998). http://cs.gmu.edu/~eclab/projects/ecj/
12. Miller, J.F.: Cartesian genetic programming. In: Miller, J. (ed.) Cartesian Genetic Programming. Natural Computing Series, pp. 17–34. Springer, Heidelberg (2011). https://doi.org/10.1007/978-3-642-17310-3_2
13. Miller, J.F., Thomson, P.: Cartesian genetic programming. In: Poli, R., Banzhaf, W., Langdon, W.B., Miller, J., Nordin, P., Fogarty, T.C. (eds.) EuroGP 2000. LNCS, vol. 1802, pp. 121–132. Springer, Heidelberg (2000). https://doi.org/10.1007/978-3-540-46239-2_9
14. Mohammad, R.M., McCluskey, L., Thabtah, F.: UCI machine learning repository: phishing websites data set (2015). https://archive.ics.uci.edu/ml/datasets/Phishing+Websites. Accessed 14 May 2016
15. Mohammad, R.M., Thabtah, F., McCluskey, L.: Intelligent rule-based phishing websites classification. IET Inf. Secur. **8**(3), 153–160 (2014)
16. Montana, D.J.: Strongly typed genetic programming. Evol. Comput. **3**(2), 199–230 (1995)
17. Moustafa, N., Slay, J.: The evaluation of network anomaly detection systems: statistical analysis of the UNSW-NB15 data set and the comparison with the KDD99 data set. Inf. Secur. J. Global Perspect. **25**(1–3), 18–31 (2016)
18. Moustafa, N., Slay, J., Creech, G.: Novel geometric area analysis technique for anomaly detection using trapezoidal area estimation on large-scale networks. IEEE Trans. Big Data (2017)
19. Moustafa, N., Slay, J.: UNSW-NB15: a comprehensive data set for network intrusion detection systems (UNSW-NB15 network data set). In: 2015 Military Communications and Information Systems Conference (MilCIS), pp. 1–6. IEEE (2015)

20. Noorian, F., de Silva, A.M., Leong, P.H.: gramEvol: grammatical evolution in R. J. Stat. Softw. **71** (2015)
21. Orfila, A., Estevez-Tapiador, J.M., Ribagorda, A.: Evolving high-speed, easy-to-understand network intrusion detection rules with genetic programming. In: Giacobini, M., et al. (eds.) EvoWorkshops 2009. LNCS, vol. 5484, pp. 93–98. Springer, Heidelberg (2009). https://doi.org/10.1007/978-3-642-01129-0_11
22. Ryan, C., Collins, J.J., Neill, M.O.: Grammatical evolution: evolving programs for an arbitrary language. In: Banzhaf, W., Poli, R., Schoenauer, M., Fogarty, T.C. (eds.) EuroGP 1998. LNCS, vol. 1391, pp. 83–96. Springer, Heidelberg (1998). https://doi.org/10.1007/BFb0055930
23. Scarfone, K., Mell, P.: Guide to intrusion detection and prevention systems (IDPS). NIST special publication, vol. 800, no. 2007, p. 94 (2007)
24. Sen, S.: A survey of intrusion detection systems using evolutionary computation. In: Bio-inspired Computation in Telecommunications, pp. 73–94 (2015)
25. Sofi, I., Mahajan, A., Mansotra, V.: Machine learning techniques used for the detection and analysis of modern types of DDoS attacks. Learning **4**(06), 1085–1092 (2017)
26. Song, J., Takakura, H., Okabe, Y., Eto, M., Inoue, D., Nakao, K.: Statistical analysis of honeypot data and building of Kyoto 2006+ dataset for NIDS evaluation. In: Proceedings of the First Workshop on Building Analysis Datasets and Gathering Experience Returns for Security, pp. 29–36. ACM (2011)
27. Symantec: Internet security threat report (2018). https://www.symantec.com/
28. Wilson, D., Kaur, D.: Using grammatical evolution for evolving intrusion detection rules. WSEAS Trans. Syst. **6**(2), 346 (2007)
29. Wu, S.X., Banzhaf, W.: The use of computational intelligence in intrusion detection systems: A review. Appl. Soft Comput. **10**(1), 1–35 (2010)

Assuring Privacy in Surfing the Internet

Stefan Bodoarca and Mihai-Lica Pura⁽✉⁾

Military Technical Academy, 050141 Bucharest, Romania
bodoarcastefan@yahoo.ro, mihai.pura@mta.ro

Abstract. On-line security is a very important aspect of Internet browsing, so a lot of research has been targeting confidentiality, integrity,
authentication, non-repudiation and availability of on-line services. But
another aspect that is at least equally important has been rather
neglected: Internet privacy. On-line tracking can be used for legitimate
purposes (e.g. preventing illegitimate login attempts), but it also invades
the privacy of the users. This paper focuses on browser fingerprinting,
which is the least known threat to privacy among Internet users, presenting it in detail, from definition to the possible countermeasures. Some
software models built inside the so called *crypto-for-privacy* are also
described. The paper also presents a Chrome extension that has been
developed in order to obfuscate *third party tracking*. The browser fingerprint of a device has been consistently changed, assuring a balanced
trade-off between privacy and usability.

Keywords: Privacy · Internet security · Browser fingerprinting

1 Introduction

Computer security is a field whose actuality is unquestionable and the point of
interest of many researchers. In the article *The Moral Character of Cryptographic
Work* [1], presented at Asiacrypt 2015, Auckland, New Zealand, Phillip Rogaway
draws attention upon the moral and ethical implications associated with this
kind of research. The author emphasizes the famous Russel-Einstein manifesto,
which speaks about the present threat to all mankind, namely, nuclear weapons,
makes an appeal to humanity, and highlights that science should be a good for
all people, reminding us two things: first, that technical work itself can have
political implications; and second, that some scientists, in response, explicitly
assume political roles.

The author states that a scientist gets involved in what can be called implicit
politics, because his technical work can influence power relations. Politics is
about power - who has more and of what type. The nuclear bomb is the final
expression of coercion; it embodies politics. So, science and technical work usually involve politics. The ways technological advancement are obtained and how
these advancement are used, for good or for bad purposes, are as important as
the results themselves. Although cryptographic ideas are largely mathematical,

© Springer Nature Switzerland AG 2019
J.-L. Lanet and C. Toma (Eds.): SecITC 2018, LNCS 11359, pp. 185–203, 2019.
https://doi.org/10.1007/978-3-030-12942-2_15

this does not make them apolitical, cryptography being deeply related to the political area. According to the author "a scientist can engage in *overt* politics through the mechanisms of activism and participatory democracy". The rule, hypothetically, argues that scientists have an obligation to select the work that promotes the social good, or, ultimately, to refrain from the work that has negative implications for mankind or the environment. The obligations stems from three basic truths: the work of scientists and engineers transforms society; this transformation may be good or bad; what they accomplish is quite difficult for other people to understand, so they have to present an essential perspective on things for the general public. This also applies to information security and to the research conducted in this field.

A 2013 essay [2] by Arvind Narayanan suggests a taxonomy for cryptographic work: *crypto-for-security* and *crypto-for-privacy*. *Crypto-for-security* is the cryptography that has commercial purposes. It's the cryptography in TLS, credit cards and mobile phones. *Crypto-for-privacy* has social or political objectives. Here the author distinguishes between *pragmatic crypto* - which is about trying to use cryptography to retain our predigital privacy - and *cypherpunk crypto* - part of the cryptography that could be used to precipitate sweeping social or political reforms. In the author's opinion, *crypto-for-security* has done well, but *crypto-for-privacy* has failed badly.

The issue of keeping privacy while on-line has been addressed in terms of multiple attack vectors (*cookies* - as an active method for tracking users, *browser fingerprinting* - as a passive and active method for collecting device specific information, IP - through which a user can be located), both theoretically and through practical implementations. These vectors can be used solely or in association in order to identify an on-line user. This paper presents a field where privacy concerns have been mostly neglected (by the end-users, but also by the scientists) and were little research has been done in order to fix the problems: browser fingerprinting. As a contribution to the *crypto-for-privacy* field, the paper also describes a tool designed to cover the gaps and assure a high level of on-line privacy, under the form of a Google Chrome extension. Some software models with similar purposes are also presented.

The rest of the paper is organized as follows. Section 2 describes browser fingerprinting, its possible usages (legitimate and illegitimate), and the specifics for Google Chrome browser, one of the most used currently available browsers. The third section depicts several countermeasures to this technique, highlighting there advantages and disadvantages. Section 4 describes the Google Chrome extension that has been developed to eliminate the possibility of browser fingerprinting. The fifth section presents an evaluation of the developed extension, using dedicated web-sites measuring the fingerprint of a browser, while on-line. Section 6 presents the related work. The last section contains some conclusions and future work directions.

2 Browser Fingerprinting

2.1 General Presentation

A **browser fingerprint** is defined as a set of information regarding a user's device obtained from the hardware as well from the operating system, browser and its configuration [3]. The process of collecting these information through a web browser in oder to create a fingerprint for a certain device is called *browser fingerprinting*; a script running into the browser can be used to collect information from public interfaces - APIs - and from HTTP headers onto a server. Unlike other tracking methods (e.g. cookies) browser fingerprinting is considered non-traceable given the fact that it does not require any information stored into the browser. If a fingerprint contains enough information, it is likely to be unique to the device and therefore can be used totally or partially to identify a visitor on a site, thanks to the device characteristics that are exposed [3].

In regard to cookies, browsers provide control mechanisms that allow the user to decide when and how the cookies are used; the user can install an extension to manage the cookies a he pleases [3].

Browser fingerprinting can be considered as being on the opposite side of the identification spectrum because it is not part of any web standard. There is no built-in mechanism to allow or refuse executing fingerprint scripts. The privacy implications are very strong because users have no easy way to control this technique. They must configure the browsers accurately or install the right extension to prevent the disclosure of too much information. Any website that a user contacts when surfing the web has the tools to build a complete fingerprint of a device and identify it. Finally, it should be noted that fingerprints do not replace cookies. They complement each other as they can be used in parallel to provide very extensive means of identification [3].

A browser fingerprint is not compiled from just on source, but from multiple ones, so that it can be as complete as possible.

First of all, the server acquires information from the first interaction with the client. According to RFC references on HTTP[1], the browser sends additional headers to the server, so that the server can adapt the response based on the client's requests. Such headers contain information about the types of formats and encodings supported by the browsers, as well as the platform of the device or the user's preferred language [3]. This interaction is also known as "passive fingerprinting".

In contrast to the above, there is also "active fingerprinting" that is based on running some scripts in the browser for information gathering. With JavaScript, the following information can be collected: **list of plug-ins** - through the *navigator.plugins* property, **platform** - through the *navigator.platform* property, **cookies enabled** - through the *navigator.cookieEnabled* property, **do not track** - through the *navigator.doNotTrack* property, **timezone, screen resolution and color depth** through the *window* object, if **local and session storage** are

---

[1] RFC 2616 - Hypertext Transfer Protocol - HTTP/1.1. https://tools.ietf.org/html/rfc2616.

available, **use of an ad blocker**, images that are rendered differently depending on the device through **Canvas (2D)** and **WebGL (3D)**, **WebGL Vendor and renderer**, information obtained through the **AudioContext** API, **battery level**, etc.

In conclusion, a fingerprint is not just a collection of device-specific information. It reflects the actual set of components that are running on the device.

2.2   Usage

Browser fingerprinting can provide much detail about a device's configuration. The use of collected information can be divided into two main categories [3]:

- **Negative or destructive:** A third party can (1) attack the device of a user by identifying a known vulnerability, or (2) it can track a user without having his consent.
- **Positive:** Users can be warned if their devices are not up to date and can be recommended for specific updates. The security of on-line services can also be enhanced by verifying the authenticity of a device and the fact that it is known by the system.

In the next paragraphs, the negative usage of fingerprints will be described in more detail.

Attack on the Devices of the Users. A browser fingerprint can be analyzed and the installed components can be compared with a database such as CVE (Common Vulnerabilities and Exposures)[2], so that security vulnerabilities be discerned [3]. From this point attackers can prepare the perfect payload to target a specific device, knowing its vulnerabilities in advance. For example, through the *navigator.plugins* property, one can see if a device is running an outdated version of the Flash plug-in. At the time of writing the *AmIUnique* study, the CVE database recorded 1006 Flash vulnerabilities, more than 84% of which were considered critical, including the most recent ones[3]. If the Flash Player is not up to date, users may be exposed to serious security risks, since any attacker in the on-line environment could run malicious code on their device [3].

Attack on the Privacy of the Users. Because browser fingerprinting can uniquely identify a device on the web, the implications on privacy are important. By collecting fingerprints from multiple websites, a third party can recognize a user and can correlate his browsing activity within and across sessions. Most importantly, the user has no control over the collection process because

---

[2] Common Vulnerabilities and Exposures - The Standard for Information Security Vulnerability Names. https://cve.mitre.org/.

[3] Adobe Flash Player: List of security vulnerabilities. https://www.cvedetails.com/vulnerability-list/vendor_id-53/product_id-6761/Adobe-Flash-Player.html.

it is completely transparent, since the tracking scripts are silent and are being executed in the background [3].

In [4], Peter Eckersley highlights in detail how fingerprinting can a be a threat to web privacy:

- **Fingerprints as Global Identifiers:** If a fingerprinting algorithm provides enough information that a group of users is easily identified, then the created fingerprint for each user can be used as a global identifier [3]; such an identifier could be assimilated to a non-removable cookie, so that only a substantial change in the browser configuration may alter the formed fingerprint. A unique fingerprint makes the identification through other mechanisms such as cookies and IP address unnecessary. Users using a VPN are also vulnerable to browser fingerprinting, since the VPN masks the IP and does not modify the browser information [3].
- **Fingerprint + IP address as Cookie Regenerators:** Adobe's Flash LSO supercookies can be used to regenerate normal cookies that have been deleted or to link the previous ID of a cookie to the new assigned ID [3]. Deleted cookies can also be regenerated when a browser fingerprint is used in conjunction with a fixed IP address. Researchers have noticed that any existing storage mechanism in the browser, such as Flash local storage [5], HTML5 Web storage [6] or IndexedDB [7], can be used to regenerate cookies. Browser fingerprinting can be added to this list, but since the detection accuracy varies greatly between devices, it is necessary to use another source of information, such as the IP address, to have a high probability of identifying the right device [3].
- **Fingerprint + IP address in the Absence of Cookies:** Fingerprints can differentiate between the machines that are behind the same IP, even if cookies are blocked entirely by those devices [3].

The next paragraphs will describe the positive usage of fingerprints.

Fraud Prevention. Another use of fingerprinting is to improve on-line security by checking the contents of a fingerprint. Since there are many dependencies between the collected attributes, it is possible to check whether a fingerprint has been modified or matches the device it is supposed to belong to. For example, the platform on which the device is running appears clearly in attributes such as *user-agent* or the *navigator.platform* property. However, the platform can also be obtained from other attributes such as verifying file extensions in the plug-ins list, or by checking the presence of OS-specific fonts. For example fraudsters can change their IP address, delete cookies and use scripts to randomize the device attributes, but if there is a mismatch in the presented fingerprint (e.g. *navigator.platform* differs from the same property obtained from the plug-ins list) they can be easily stopped from accessing a specific server [3].

Augmented Authentication. Browser fingerprinting also comes as a solution that can enhance password-based authentication. By checking the fingerprint of a device when logged in, a system can very easily block unauthorized access from a new or unknown device. For example, if a system notices that it is accessed from an iPhone, while the legitimate user is logging on from an Android, then the system may report and may require additional authentication information.

Moreover, the browser fingerprinting has the advantage of being completely transparent to the user, thus not adding shortcomings during the logging process [3].

2.3 Google Chrome Specifics

The privacy policy[4] of Google Chrome, one of the most used web browsers[5], states the following: "When you're not signed in to a Google Account, we store the information we collect with unique identifiers tied to the browser, application, or device you're using". and "We collect information about the apps, browsers, and devices you use to access Google services, which helps us provide features like automatic product updates and dimming your screen if your battery runs low". The last example: "The information we collect includes unique identifiers, browser type and settings, device type and settings, operating system, mobile network information including carrier name and phone number, and application version number... We also allow specific partners to collect information from your browser or device for advertising and measurement purposes using their own cookies or similar technologies".

It should be clearly enough that browser fingerprinting has been adopted on a very large scale. This is an ongoing threat to on-line privacy and many users don't know about the real harm they are facing while surfing the Internet. It should also be noted that not all browsers give free access to all the device specific information. For example, any script can query for the WebGL Vendor and Renderer values on Chrome, while Firefox requires a privileged context activated by a browser flag to unmask the real values (it returns "Mozilla" in an unprivileged context) [3].

The above paragraphs give the reason of choosing Google Chrome as the target environment of the developed tool, as it is the browser with the most exposure from the point of view of on-line fingerprinting.

3 Countermeasures to Browser Fingerprinting

This section describes some techniques and solutions that aim to minimize the effects of browser fingerprinting. The goal is to improve users privacy by preventing unwanted tracking. There is no ultimate approach that can prevent fingerprinting while keeping the richness of a modern web browser. Designing a strong defense requires a balance between privacy and usability, which is not that easy to obtain.

---

[4] Google Privacy & Terms. https://policies.google.com/privacy.

[5] Usage share of web browsers. https://en.wikipedia.org/wiki/Usage_share_of_web_browsers.

3.1   Increasing Device Diversity

The first defense method used to alleviate browser fingerprinting is increasing the diversity of devices so that real fingerprints are hidden in the noise. The intuition behind this method is that third parties rely on fingerprint stability to be able to link a fingerprint to a device. By sending random or predefined values instead of real ones, the collected fingerprints would be so different and unstable that a tracking company is unable to identify devices on the web [3].

While this approach seems strong in theory, in reality it is much more complicated. Instead of improving users' privacy, some tools make tracking easier by displaying a much more distinctive fingerprint. There are many extensions in Chrome and Firefox that can mimic or change the values collected by scripts. One such extension for Firefox is Random Agent Spoofer[6]; this extension changes the browser profiles at an interval defined by the user. Nikiforakis et al. demonstrate that this extension does not cover all the possibilities when it comes to discovering the true identity of a browser [9]. First of all, this extension does not cover completely the modified objects. Thus, the extension changes the *navigator.UserAgent* property, but it does not modify other objects such as *platform* or *appName*. This lack of coverage is an opportunity for the discovery of the real values that were supposedly hidden by the extension. Some extensions generate configurations whose attributes do not match. For example, the *user-agent* of a browser indicating that it is running on a Linux OS, while the *navigator.platform* property suggesting a Windows OS. Furthermore, while most attributes are collected by JavaScript, HTTP headers or plug-ins like Flash can be used to gather more information. Thus, although some extensions change HTTP headers, these do not change the same values that are accessible through JavaScript [9].

In conclusion, while the idea of changing values seems promising, the constant evolution of browsers, combined with a strong link between attributes, prevent this approach from being recommended. In order to address the shortcomings of the above mentioned extensions, the scientific community turned to other approaches.

One of the approaches, belonging to Christof Ferreira Torres, Hugo Jonker and Sjou Mauw, is called *FP-Block* [10]. In their article, and also in the implementation of the *FP-Block* as a Firefox extension, the on-line tracking was divided in two categories: *regular tracking* and *third-party tracking*. By *regular tracking*, they mean tracking for fraud prevention purposes, by identifying illegitimate usage attempts, suggesting related content, and better targeting of ads.

They add that some companies offer services included in a large number of sites. Examples of such services are social sharing buttons, popular JavaScript libraries, and popular web analytics services. Due to these integrations,

---

[6] Random Agent Spoofer - Firefox extension. https://addons.mozilla.org/firefox/addon/random-agent-spoofer/.

companies can track users across large portions of the Internet. They give, for example, Facebook's *Like* button. A site gets this button by including a code that triggers the user's browser to contact the Facebook server to download the button. Browsers always say where the request originated (the HTTP Referrer field), so a browser will tell Facebook exactly which URL triggered the request each time. This allows Facebook to track users over the web, whether a user has a Facebook account or not. The authors call this type of tracking *third-party tracking*. This type of tracking can be done by both HTTP cookies and fingerprinting.

They state that existing methods that combat fingerprinting mechanisms also have an impact on the user experience. In the authors' opinion, one needs to found a method that provides a better balance between the user experience (meaning less impact on the desired content) and the tracking that is taking place. They address this through the concept of *web identity*: the set of browser features that can be collected through fingerprinting. A web identity is generated for the main site visited (e.g., bbc.com) and that identity is then used in all interactions that take place with embedded elements (e.g., videos, social buttons, etc.). If the user visits a different site (e.g. cnn.com), a different identity is used (web identity for cnn.com). Thus, a third party contained on both sites will first see the web identity for bbc.com and later the web identity for cnn.com. Since it has been ensured that the two generated identities are distinct, the two visits can no longer be correlated with their fingerprint. The described method is depicted in Fig. 1 and represents the theoretical model of the *FP-Block* tool.

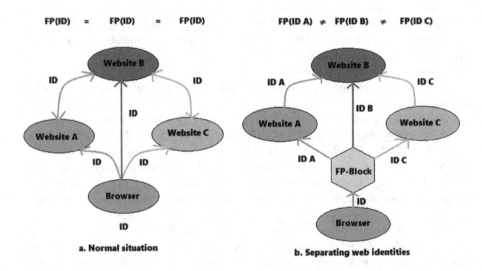

Fig. 1. Third-party fingerprinting

3.2 Presenting a Homogeneous Fingerprint

Another defense mechanism is to make all devices on the web present the same fingerprint. This approach is chosen by the Tor browser[7] also known as TBB (the Tor Browser Bundle) which connects to the Tor network.

The Tor network while preventing an attacker to find the real IP of a client, does not change the content of a HTTP request, thus the identity of the user can be discovered when a cookie ID or a browser fingerprint is present in the payload. So, the Tor browser was developed to address this problem. Two sets of requirements are inherent to the Tor Browser: the *Security requirements* (which make sure that the browser is properly configured to use the Tor network) and the *Privacy requirements*, which resolve the link that could be made between two sites. A section called *Cross-Origin Fingerprinting Unlinkability*, included by the *Privacy requirements*, addresses browser fingerprinting. An analysis presented in the design document[8] of the Tor Browser tries to establish which defense mechanism, whether randomization or uniformity, is more efficient against fingerprinting. Some good reasons are brought for using uniformity (or a single fingerprint) for the Tor browser:

- **Evaluation and measurement difficulties:** The benefits of randomization are difficult to be assessed objectively and may create a false sense of security, given the fact that fingerprinting algorithms can ignore randomized information; at the same time, a more stable fingerprinting could be created by eliminating randomness, modeling it or making it an average [3].
- **Randomization attributes related to hardware:** Browser attributes are easy to be changed compared to hardware attributes which cannot be modified so easily. Enough randomness is necessary so that the browser could be perceived like other devices and hardware properties are to be blurred so they would not provide identification information [3].
- **Usability issues:** When the browser attributes are changed extensively, the user experience may be negatively impacted given the fact that he will no longer receive web pages adapted to the technologies supported by his browser [3].
- **Performance costs:** Performance costs are increased by randomization, given the fact that fingerprinting surfaces increases over time [3].
- **Increased vulnerability surface:** Improper randomization could be the cause of the appearance of some new fingerprinting vectors, that may be used by third parties to aid fingerprinting [3].

For all these reasons, Tor developers opted for the strategy based on uniformity. They modified the Firefox browser incorporating protection against known fingerprinting vectors. The design document lists 24 changes introduced

---

[7] Tor Browser - Tor Project Official website. https://www.torproject.org/projects/torbrowser.html.

[8] The Design and Implementation of the Tor Browser [DRAFT] - Tor Project Official website. https://www.torproject.org/projects/torbrowser/design/.

in the Tor browser. It's worth mentioning blocking the Canvas and WebGL APIs, removing plug-ins completely, introducing a default font to prevent fingerprinting vectors based on font enumeration, and changing the user-agent along with HTTP headers. Whether a user uses Windows, Mac or Linux, the Tor browser will always say that the device is running a Windows operating system.

3.3   Decreasing the Surface of Browser APIs

Reducing the available APIs in the browser means reducing the information that can be collected through a tracking script. This can be done by disabling plug-ins so that fingerprinting vectors (e.g. Flash or Silverlight) will not be available to provide information regarding the device [3].

Another method is to avoid running tracking scripts; the settings of the browser include the possibility of stopping JavaScript. The downside of this method is the result obtained by the user, meaning a static and non-functional on-line environment for most services.

Another approach is to use ad and tracker blockers extensions that block scripts and domains based on a blacklist. When a page is loaded, the extension analyzes its content, and if it finds a script or a domain present in the list, it will block it. The most popular extensions of this type are Adblock Plus[9], Ghostery[10], uBlock Origin[11] and Disconnect[12]. These extensions use different methods to update domain lists and scripts, which means it may take some time for a new script to be detected and blocked [3].

One last resort is to disable browser features and APIs to prevent trackers from using them. In this way, tracking scripts cannot collect information to help them differentiate between devices. For example, an extension such as CanvasBlocker[13] for Firefox can block the entire Canvas API. Thus, a script will not be able to collect information and interact with this API. The extension provides other methods for sites to display images (write functions are allowed), while blocking functions like *toDataURL* so scripts can not access the contents of an image. Another example is the Brave browser[14] that includes fingerprint protection. If enabled, the following APIs are blocked: Canvas, WebGL, AudioContext, WebRTC against IP leakage and Battery Status. It should be also noted that the Tor browser implicitly blocks APIs such as Canvas or WebGL [3].

---

[9] Adblock Plus Official website. https://adblockplus.org/.

[10] Ghostery Official website. https://www.ghostery.com/.

[11] uBlock Origin - An efficient blocker for Chromium and Firefox. Fast and lean. https://github.com/gorhill/uBlock.

[12] Disconnect Official website. https://disconnect.me/.

[13] CanvasBlocker - Firefox extension to block the Canvas API. https://addons.mozilla.org/fr/firefox/addon/canvasblocker/.

[14] Brave Official website - Browse faster and safer with Brave. https://brave.com/.

4   Google Chrome Extension for Privacy in Surfing the Internet

The developed Chrome extension aims to improve privacy while surfing the Internet. The application has three basic features: deleting cookies and browsing data, creating and viewing web identities, and changing the IP by redirecting the traffic to the Tor network.

The presentation of the general architecture of a Google Chrome extension is out of the scope of this paper. For information on this topic please see[15].

4.1   Description of Components

The extension provides four main functionalities, which will be described in the next subsections:

- Cookie management,
- Web identity management,
- Proxy management,
- Browsing data deletion.

Cookie Management. This feature provides the user the following possibilities: he can delete cookies for all domains, for a single domain or only a certain cookie. He can view each cookie individually, search for private domain cookies, synchronize cookies, and block them for third parties or for all domains.

Because "there is growing awareness among web users that HTTP cookies are a serious threat to privacy, and many people now block, limit or periodically delete them" [4] we considered opportunely that our tool would include some functionalities addressing the **cookie management**.

When viewing a cookie, the information displayed is represented by the cookie properties from[16].

Web Identity Management. The user can view the web identities attributed to each accessed domain. He can stop JavaScript for all domains or specifically for a certain domain, can stop the canvas API on all domains or just for a certain domain. He can delete the identity for a domain, or all of the existing identities. For each domain, the user can view the created identity and other changes affecting that domain.

It is worth mentioning that the web profiles used for building the web identities are the same as the ones used by the *Random User Agent*[17] Firefox extension, meaning that a real database of browser profiles is being used. This means that

---

[15] Chrome Extensions Overview. https://developer.chrome.com/extensions/overview.

[16] Chrome Extensions Cookies. https://developer.chrome.com/extensions/cookies.

[17] dillbyrne - random-agent-spoofer. https://github.com/dillbyrne/random-agent-spoofer/blob/master/data/json/useragents.json.

the resulted fingerprint is **consistent** for at least two reasons: (1) because a real database represents the starting point for making a new fingerprint, and (2) because all the attributes spoofed at the same time with HTTP headers (e.g. *platform* from the User-Agent header) have also been modified at the Javascript level (e.g. *navigator.platform*). The mentioned Firefox extension does not provide consistency at the JavaScript level, even if it uses real browser profiles, as it has been demonstrated by Nikiforakis et al. [9]. The developed tool comes with the advantage of covering the shortcomings that this Firefox extension presents.

When viewing a web identity, the most important information showed in the interface is depicted in Table 1.

Table 1. Web identity properties

Attribute	Value	Action
Description	Browser Class - Linux/Windows/Mac/Unix	No
User-Agent	HTTP User-Agent	Spoof
Accept	HTTP Accept	Spoof
Content encoding	HTTP Accept-Encoding	Spoof
Content language	HTTP Accept-Language	Spoof
Mime types	navigator.mimeTypes =""	Spoof
List of plug-ins	navigator.plugins =""	Spoof
Timezone offset	getTimezoneOffset() overridden	Spoof
Battery	Undefined	Blocked
Get_Battery	Undefined	Blocked
AudioContext	No	Blocked
WebKit-AudioContext	No	Blocked
Platform	navigator.platform	Spoof
Screen resolution	screen.width x screen.height x screen.pixelDepth	Spoof
Canvas	No	Blocked/allowed
WebGL	No	Blocked
Plug-ins	No	All blocked
Location, Popups, Notifications, Microphone, Camera	No	All blocked
Javascript	No	Blocked/allowed
Protocol	http/https	No
Requests	3rd party requests	No

Proxy Management and Browsing Data Deletion. This functionality allows the user to connect to the Tor network. In order for the user to successfully connect, it is necessary to run the "tor.exe" program - Expert Bundle[18] -

---

[18] Expert Bundle - Tor Project Official website. https://www.torproject.org/download/download.html.en.

made available by the Tor project. This program connects to the Tor network and creates different circuits through which it transmits the data.

In the context of this feature, since a connection through the Tor network has been made available, it has been considered appropriate to suggest a few steps that should be followed for a safer navigation on this network: stopping JavaScript and starting it only when necessary, using an extension to prevent leakage through WebRTC, using the HTTPS Everywhere[19] and the Duck-DuckGo search engine[20], which is also the search engine used by default by the Tor browser, and **deleting all browsing data**, which can be done from the interface provided - App Cache, Cache, Downloads, History, IndexedDB, Passwords, Plugin Data, Serivce Workers, WebSql, Cookies, FileSystems, FormData, LocalStorage were targeted as sources that hold users information.

The feature of **browsing data deletion** is very important because "researchers have already observed in the wild that any browser storage mechanisms [...], can be used to "respawn" HTTP cookies" [3]. For this reason all the browsing data provided by the Chrome API could be a possible source for information about users. Moreover, because all the plug-ins were blocked, storage mechanisms like Flash local storage [5] cannot be used anymore.

4.2   Implementation Details

Changing the Canvas API

As defined by the W3C specification of Canvas 2D[21], the "2D Context provides objects, methods, and properties to draw and manipulate graphics on a canvas drawing surface". Users can draw and animate any number of shapes and they can render textual content directly in the browser, by using the graphics capabilities of the device. With regards to fingerprinting, any script can create an HTML canvas element and interact with it through a *CanvasRenderingContext2D* object. Once an image has been rendered, the *getDataUrl()* function can be called to represent the image through a string, allowing devices to be easily compared.

It is worth mentioning that an image can be collected without ever being presented to the user, because a canvas element can be invisible for the whole duration of the rendering process [3].

Regarding this API two changes has been made. First, "noise" has been added by modifying *toDataURL()*, *toBlob()* and *getImageData()* functions, and then the entire API has been blocked (the functions for rendering and reading the image). The first change takes place regardless of the user's option. For each web identity a "noise" field has been defined - a random integer number. If a script performs canvas fingerprinting obtaining a hash from a picture, the result will be a very distinctive one (almost unique compared to other known

---

[19] HTTPS Everywhere. https://www.eff.org/https-everywhere.

[20] Duck Duck Go. https://duckduckgo.com/.

[21] HTML Canvas 2D Context - W3C Recommendation 19 November 2015. https://www.w3.org/TR/2dcontext/.

"hashes"), but it will not provide information that can lead to the identification of the browser or of the operating system, because of the "noise" added in the reading functions. Moreover, even if this random value is very distinctive, in the context of the approached model (**web identities** and *regular tracking* from [10]), this is not a drawback: even if a domain can recognize the user, when a new request will be performed to another domain, another "noise" value will be used (the "noise" related to that domain), and so the two "hashes" obtained through canvas fingerprinting cannot be correlated. The approached model focuses on linkability between different sites, not on distinguishing users on one site.

The second change occurs when the user explicitly blocks the canvas API. Blocking the entire API prevents reading any information that could be obtained by fingerprinting.

Modifying the Requests and the Responses

The developed extension intercepts and modifies all outgoing requests and incoming responses.

For the **outgoing requests**, the existing web identity for the domain is first retrieved, or, if none exists, a new web identity is generated and stored. Second, the HTTP headers - User-Agent, Accept, Accept-Encoding, Accept-Language - are set according to this web identity.

For the **incoming responses**, the E-Tag headers has been deleted (which are intended to aid caching), because they can easily be exploited to track users [10].

5   Qualitative Evaluation

The developed extension has been tested on the sites of the *Panopticlick* [4] and *AmIUnique*[22] [3] projects.

For the first test case, when the extension is not activated, the fingerprint on the two websites has the same values for the same attributes, differences exist where the approach/algorithm differs between the two projects. For example **canvas** fingerprinting and **WebGL** fingerprinting - the *AmIUnique* [3] project provides information obtained directly through fingerprinting (a picture for the canvas and the vendor, respectively the type of graphics card for WebGL), while the *Panopticlick* [4] project creates a "hash" on the information obtained from the two APIs.

For the second test case, two fingerprints result from the fingerprinting of the two sites. For example, on the first test site [3] the browser is recognized as a Chrome 51, while on the second site [4] the browser is seen as a Firefox 45. This is just an example, the resulting fingerprints being fully compliant with the specific web identities of the two domains, identities that can also be viewed at the interface level.

This theoretical model for the results is depicted in Fig. 2.

---

[22] Am I Unique? https://amiunique.org/.

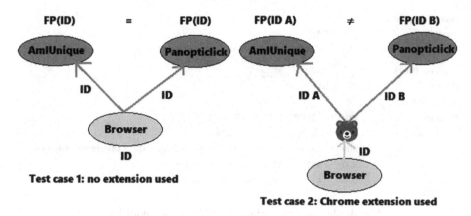

Fig. 2. Test of generating different web identities

Adding noise for the canvas API was tested on the **browserleaks.com** domain. In Fig. 3 it can be noticed that after the canvas fingerprinting, the browser and the operating system running on the device can be determined, while in Fig. 4, after the addition of "noise", it can be seen that the obtained signature is unique, which prevents finding the type of browser and operating system. Basically, the signature can no longer be found among other known signatures of existing browsers and operating systems.

Your Fingerprint :

Signature	✓ 81E42236
Uniqueness	99.28% (1855 of 258561 user agents have the same signature)
Image File Details :	BrowserLeaks.com `<canvas>` 1.0
File Size	4689 bytes
Number of Colors	209
PNG Hash	B2522922E7860375635A13B552A960FD

PNG Headers	Chunk :	Length :	CRC :	Content :
	IHDR	13	477A703E	PNG image header: 220x30, 8 bits/sample, truecolor+alp
	IDAT	4632	81E42236	PNG image data
	IEND	0	AE426082	end-of-image marker

Browser Statistics :

Looking at your signature, it's very likely that your web-browser is **Chrome** and your operating system is **Windows**.

Fig. 3. Canvas fingerprinting - no noise

The changing of the IP was tested on sites that return the current IP and user location. After proxy activation, the current IP is changed. After a few minutes if the test is resumed on the **browserleaks.com** for example, it can be observed an IP from a different country than was previously obtained, which means that the traffic was redirected through another circuit of the Tor network.

Your Fingerprint :

Signature	✓ BE780351			
Uniqueness	100% (0 of 258561 user agents have the same signature)			
Image File Details :	BrowserLeaks.com <canvas> 1.0			
File Size	4590 bytes			
Number of Colors	190			
PNG Hash	6910C475C57F35B6C32151F35777E99E			
PNG Headers	Chunk :	Length :	CRC :	Content :
	IHDR	13	477A703E	PNG image header: 220x30, 8 bits/sample, truecolor+alp
	IDAT	4533	BE780351	PNG image data
	IEND	0	AE426082	end-of-image marker

Fig. 4. Canvas fingerprinting - with "noise" addition

6   Related Work

The *AmIUnique* [3] project adds two important contributions to the defense methods used against fingerprinting. The first one is called *Blink*, and it's a software that works at the operating system level. At the time of running, the program assembles selected components from a multitude of thousands (plug-ins, fonts, browsers, operating systems) and gets a new fingerprint for each browsing session. Since Blink is based on real components, it does not show the problem of incomplete coverage encountered in many solutions, the fingerprints being authentic. The problem with this solution is that it occupies much of the HDD space. The second solution is called *FPRandom* and works at the browser level. By modifying the code for Firefox, the authors have introduced randomness into some browser functions so that they provide different results for each browsing session. In this way, functions are considered unstable for tracking and can not be used for fingerprinting. Among the changes made with this solution, it is worth mentioning the modification of the Canvas and AudioContext APIs.

DCB (Disguised Chromium Browser) [8] is a solution designed by Baumann et al. through which the browser language, the screen resolution, the user-agent, the time and date, the list of fonts and the list of plug-ins are changed. When this modified browser launches, it contacts the main server that "maintains a database of real world fingerprinting features to enforce a robust browser configuration on the client". One of the two following strategies is then applied:

- 1:N One Browser, Many Configurations - Every time DCB starts, the browser configuration is changed, hiding at the same time the actual browser and system configuration.
- N:1 Many Browsers, One Configuration - A single fingerprint is adopted for a given period of time by several devices connected to the central server. This way, a third party will not be able to uniquely identify a device as they will all look the same to a tracker. Devices are organized in groups of configurations that share similar values to avoid contradiction in exhibited fingerprints.

Even if it has already been mentioned, the *FP-Block* [10] project can be recalled, as it represents the core idea of the developed extension. When the browser connects to a new domain, a new web identity, for this particular domain, is generated (i.e. a new fingerprint). If at some point the domain will be again encountered, the fingerprint associated with it will be returned. The intuition is that third parties will see different fingerprints on each site they are embedded so that tracking is hampered.

Tor Browser can also be remained as its developers have made some very strong modifications to limit browser fingerprinting as much as possible. If users stick with the default browser fingerprint that most users share, it provides the strongest protection against known fingerprinting techniques. However, if one starts to deviate from the unique fingerprint that the browser builds, the user may end up being more visible and more easily traceable than with a standard browser.

Even if some more recent studies [11] showed that the effectiveness of browser fingerprinting as a tracking and identification technique at a large scale (meaning not on some dedicated websites as the one of Panopticlick [4] and AmIUnique [3] projects) is much smaller than has previously been demonstrated by the Eckersley et al. [4] in 2010 and Laperdix et al. [3] in 2017, this technique still remains a threat for user's privacy. In this context, it is worth reminding that the developed tool does not concentrate on *regular tracking* [10], the browser fingerprinting area having the purpose to obfuscate *third-party tracking* [10]. The most important aspect of the developed extension is the combination between **cookie management**, a **browser fingerprinting countermeasure** and the **IP hiding** through the Tor network. These areas used together have the purpose to limit the harmful combination of browser fingerprinting, cookies and IP presented in Subsect. 2.2.

7   Conclusions and Future Work

In addition to identifying users through cookies and IP, methods known by most on-line users, it has been pointed out, through the mentioned studies, that the browser fingerprinting is a reality. It has been shown that a lot of different information can be collected through public APIs: from browser version to operating system, GPU details and other device information.

This paper does not focus on how the amount of information obtained through fingerprinting is calculated, but, as a result of the fact that fingerprinting is a real problem, it focuses mainly on explaining the uses of this technique and the types of existing defense methods, with the aim of developing a tool for assuring privacy on the Internet while browsing with Google Chrome browser.

The Chrome extension is a prototype that can be further developed. Specifically, with regard to the cookie area, most existing types of super cookies can be studied in order to clearly identify them. The developed tool provides a mechanism for deleting the browsing data, but at the moment it can not be said with certainty that a particular super cookie has been deleted or if has ever existed.

Furthermore, functionalities can be made available to the user in order to be able to modify the attributes of a cookie. With respect to browser fingerprinting surface, new APIs that can provide identification information should be searched. At the same time, displaying all the APIs present in the browser (which are known as fingerprinting sources of information) should be made available to the user. A feature can be added to stop automatic browser updates and request the user's permission for them. It is important for the user to know at each moment and as clearly as possible what APIs are activated when browsing the Internet.

According to the presented defense techniques, it has been considered appropriate to combine the increase of diversity with the decrease of the APIs' available surface in the browser.

The developed extension is a useful tool not necessarily for scientists, computer engineers, etc. because in most cases they are capable of assuring a safe work environment when surfing the Internet, but for those users who are not computer scientists, but who are interested in their privacy, because it can be easily managed and installed in the browser. Moreover, this paper aimed to inform and raise awareness of the threat that the browser fingerprinting represents.

The developed tool can be found at: https://github.com/StefanBodoarca/BFingerprinting.

References

1. Rogaway, P.: Department of Computer Science University of California, Davis, USA rogaway@cs.ucdavis.edu. The Moral Character of Cryptographic Work, December 2015
2. Narayanan, A.: What happened to the crypto dream? Part 1. IEEE Secur. Privacy Mag. 11(2), 75–76 (2013). Part 2 in IEEE Secur. Privacy Mag. 11(3), 68–71 (2013)
3. Laperdrix, P.: Browser Fingerprinting: Exploring Device Diversity to Augment Authentication and Build Client-Side Countermeasures. Computer Science [cs]. INSA Rennes (2017)
4. Eckersley, P.: How unique is your web browser? In: Atallah, M.J., Hopper, N.J. (eds.) PETS 2010. LNCS, vol. 6205, pp. 1–18. Springer, Heidelberg (2010). https://doi.org/10.1007/978-3-642-14527-8_1
5. Soltani, A., Canty, S., Mayo, Q., Thomas, L., Hoofnagle, C.J.: Flash cookies and privacy. In: AAAI Spring Symposium: Intelligent Information Privacy Management, vol. 2010, pp. 158–163 (2010)
6. Ayenson, M.D., Wambach, D.J., Soltani, A., Good, N., Hoofnagle, C.J.: Flash cookies and privacy II: Now with HTML5 and ETag respawning (2011)
7. Acar, G., Eubank, C., Englehardt, S., Juarez, M., Narayanan, A., Diaz, C.: The web never forgets: persistent tracking mechanisms in the wild. In: Proceedings of the 2014 ACM SIGSAC Conference on Computer and Communications Security, CCS 2014, pp. 674–689. ACM, New York (2014)
8. Baumann, P., Katzenbeisser, S., Stopczynski, M., Tews, E.: Disguised chromium browser: robust browser, flash and canvas fingerprinting protection. In: Proceedings of the 2016 ACM on Workshop on Privacy in the Electronic Society, WPES 2016, pp. 37–46. ACM, New York (2016)

9. Nikiforakis, N., Kapravelos, A., Joosen, W., Kruegel, C., Piessens, F., Vigna, G.: Cookieless monster: exploring the ecosystem of web-based device fingerprinting. In: Proceedings of the 2013 IEEE Symposium on Security and Privacy, SP 2013, pp. 541–555. IEEE Computer Society, Washington, DC (2013)

10. Torres, C.F., Jonker, H., Mauw, S.: *FP-Block*: usable web privacy by controlling browser fingerprinting. In: Pernul, G., Ryan, P.Y.A., Weippl, E. (eds.) ESORICS 2015. LNCS, vol. 9327, pp. 3–19. Springer, Cham (2015). https://doi.org/10.1007/978-3-319-24177-7_1

11. Gómez-Boix, A., Laperdrix, P., Baudry, B.: Hiding in the crowd: an analysis of the effectiveness of browser fingerprinting at large scale. In: WWW2018 - TheWebConf 2018: 27th International World Wide Web Conference, Lyon, France, April 2018, pp. 1–10 (2018)

Roaming Interface Signaling Security for LTE Networks

Isha Singh[1]([⊠])(iD), Silke Holtmanns[1]([⊠])(iD), and Raimo Kantola[2]

[1] Nokia Bell Labs, Espoo, Finland
isha.singh@nokia.com, silke.holtmanns@nokia-bell-labs.com
[2] Aalto University, Helsinki, Finland
raimo.kantola@aalto.fi

Abstract. A consistent effort has been made to provide fast, secure and uninterrupted mobile connectivity around the world. Mobile network operators use the private Interconnection network (IPX) to communicate with each other and with other service providers for international roaming and a large range of services. In LTE/4G, many core network nodes are involved in the communication and connection setup for the subscriber in roaming scenarios. Currently, Diameter based protocols and the S9 interface are rolled out on the IPX network. We analyze the roaming interface (S9) in the LTE networks which is used for communicating charging, service control and QoS control signaling messages. This research explores Diameter Protocol features for the charging mechanisms and describes how manipulation in policy control and charging rules can influence the subscriber plan and services. The concept has been implemented and tested using a specification conformant LTE emulator. To mitigate the attack we will describe approaches and protection strategies that can be deployed.

Keywords: LTE · Diameter · Interoperability · IPX · S9 · CCR · CCA · RAR · RAA

1 Introduction

Ubiquitous LTE deployment has brought Mobile Network Operators (MNOs) to strategically support global roaming connectivity [26]. The common objective of all the service providers, supporting roaming, is to deliver traffic and services securely and in an efficient manner. All subscribers demand to have uninterrupted services and Internet connectivity even when traveling around the world.

The LTE core network is a complex environment, and, for roaming purposes, it is connected to the Interconnection Network (IPX) [15]. Switching from voice centric to data centric [6] services presents even more opportunities for hackers to attack higher value services and m-commerce transactions [19]. The adoption of IT (Information Technology) type of protocols and the opening up of networks to all kind of services and to the Internet accelerate this trend. This

© Springer Nature Switzerland AG 2019
J.-L. Lanet and C. Toma (Eds.): SecITC 2018, LNCS 11359, pp. 204–217, 2019.
https://doi.org/10.1007/978-3-030-12942-2_16

changing environment requires a fine-grained approach towards network security and fraud detection. This paper aims to ensure that mobile traffic analysis can be performed quickly and accurately on the relevant data to minimize risk and make the LTE wireless network a less attractive target for hackers and cyber-criminals.

A standardized means of communication is followed in telecom networks. Despite being run by different operators and manufactured by different vendors, they adhere to the same standards set by the 3rd Generation Partnership Project 3GPP[1]/GSMA[2]/IETF[3] to enable interoperability between different devices and networks across the globe.

Security is part of the 3GPP standards, but, in general, communications between core network elements are regarded as trustworthy or secured by Network Domain Security (NDS). On the other hand, due to the fact that the roaming network was a closed fully private network, those security measures were commonly not deployed. Since the IPX network is nowadays a huge network with about 2000 participants from all over the globe, misconfiguration and potential compromises exist and offer attack vectors for all kind of malicious actors.

Mobile networks need to be able to identify their subscribers to provide roaming over IPX. A subscriber of any mobile network service provider is identified at any geographical location by any network operator through the International Mobile Subscriber Identity (IMSI). It is a fifteen digit number, where the first three digits represent the mobile country code (MCC), the second three digits represent the mobile network code (MNC) and the last nine digits represent the mobile subscriber identification number (MSIN) [3]. When a subscriber is out of the geographical range of its home MNO, the mobile phone searches for connectivity to the available mobile networks. At this moment, the services are provided by the MNO, which has a roaming agreement with the home MNO of the subscriber [15]. This process is transparent for the subscriber, a subscriber just enables the roaming facility on the mobile device, and the rest of the process is handled among the MNO's directly. The two MNO's share information about the type of services to be provided to the subscriber by the visited network. The visited network collects the subscription plan of the subscriber from the home network through the policy control and charging rules (PCC) messages over S9 interface [4]. Accordingly, the visited network provides services to the subscriber, which includes data, SMS (Short Message Service) and calls.

This paper discusses the LTE roaming interface vulnerabilities over S9 interface. We have demonstrated how the Policy Control and Charging (PCC) rules can be manipulated, while they are communicated over S9 interface.

We have organized the rest of the paper as follows: Sect. 2 describes the related work including recent security breaches. Section 3 briefly explains the background of LTE roaming including IPX, Diameter protocol, S9 interface and

---

[1] www.3gpp.org.

[2] www.gsma.com.

[3] www.ietf.org.

PCC rules. In Sect. 4 we discuss test setup for proof of concept and experiment. Section 5 outlines the step by step implementation of the attack. In Sect. 6 we discuss the results obtained and countermeasures. Finally, Sect. 7 concludes the paper.

2 Related Work

LTE roaming requires roaming agreements, user data management, accounting and billing flow, fraud detection and counteraction, invoicing and settlements [22].

Impacts of LTE roaming are discussed in research paper [26] at initial level. LTE security is mainly focused on identity theft, VoIP (Voice over IP) fraud, viruses and DDoS (Distributed Denial of Service) attacks. Research [5] on LTE roaming scenarios predicts the potential of attack on the LTE roaming network. The white paper [27] insists on identifying a security system for fraud management. Unmanaged interconnection for International Mobile Roaming is detailed by [21]. The author has analyzed the drawback of adopting unmanaged international mobile data roaming. Detailed security architecture is discussed by [7] as per 3GPP specifications, and it discusses on solution to 4G fraud detection by using Data Analytics. Constant training and retaining of the whole system for secure network is the proposed methodology.

Security attacks and fraud activities are always persistent. Security researcher teams have to work one step ahead to diagnose possible attacks and fix them beforehand. The possible Diameter interconnection attacks in LTE network are briefly described in Table 1.

Table 1. Known attacks on Diameter based interfaces

Diameter based interfaces	Type of attack
Sh	IMSI Retrieval, User Data Request (UDR) [22]
S6a	Inter-Subscriber-Data-Request, DoS [16]
S6a	Cancel-Location-Request, DoS [13,26]
S6a	Update-Location-Request, DoS [14,23]
S6a	Delete-Subscriber Data-Request, DoS [7,25]
S6a	Purge-UE-Request, DoS [16]
S6a	Inter-Subscriber-Data-Request [15]
Sh	Location Tracking, UDR [14,22]

The communication among the MNO's and interoperability issues with LTE [24], highlight the roaming across LTE and 2G/3G. The issue here raised is roaming and interworking between two different domains. The interoperability issue is not just limited to the LTE but a relevant study discusses performance management between host and customer networks in upcoming 5G and Internet networks [20].

In this paper we are able to show the concept of LTE roaming along with the possible procedure to change the credit control signaling messages.

3   LTE Roaming

LTE roaming aims to allow compatibility with another network when the user is out of the geographical range of their HPMN (Home Public Mobile Network).

The roaming architecture for LTE [11] defines how the user traffic is routed and what procedure the two MNOs follow to communicate. The two PMN's have predefined agreements. In LTE, QoS based charging is introduced and additional charging parameters like data usage and duration are included in the billing procedure at the roaming interconnection [9]. There can be multiple roaming scenarios as per GSMA [11] specifications based on the two PMNs (Public Mobile Network) agreements i.e. between the subscribers Home-PMN (HPMN) and the Visited-PMN (VPMN). LTE roaming is defined in two forms.

- **Home Routed Roaming:** It is widely used in 2G/3G networks and enables subscribers to access the roaming network through the home network and gateways [9]. This roaming scenario is used over SS7 Protocol and the billing and QoS controls are managed by Home Public Land Mobile Network (HPLMN).
- **Local Breakout Roaming:** It is specially designed for the LTE network by using Diameter Protocol. In this type of roaming the Visited Policy and Charging Rules Function (VPCRF) is supposed to obtain the Policy Control and Charging (PCC) rules of the subscriber from the Home Policy and Charging Rules Function (HPCRF) over the S9 interface [9]. This enables the visited network to offer to the inbound roamer the same kind of service experience as he has in his home network.

There exist direct and IPX based interconnections between two MNO's.

The Fig. 3 describes a simplified view of the LTE roaming interconnections. The two networks are named as Home Public Land Mobile Network (HPLMN) and Visited Public Land Mobile Network (VPLMN). For LTE roaming S9 interface in Fig. 3 between the home Policy and Charging Rules Function (hPCRF) and visited Policy and Charging Rules Function (vPCRF) is used for control signaling. User traffic is represented by green line and in case of LTE uses visited network services [9].

When a LTE subscriber visits a roaming location, the VPCRF communicates to the HPCRF for the subscription details over the S9 interconnection as shown in the Fig. 3. Diameter Protocol is used for messaging. As per 3GPP TS 29.215 [1] specifications the Fig. 1 details the messages between the VPCRF and HPCRF. The communication starts with the Credit Control Request (CCR) message from the VPCRF and the HPCRF responds with the Credit Control Answer (CCA). This is for session initiation. The second phase messages are the Re-Authentication Request (RAR) and Re-Authentication Answer (RAA) messages. The third block of messages contains the session termination.

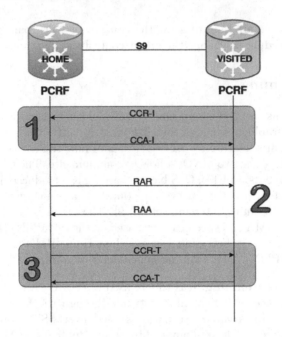

Fig. 1. Message flow over S9 interface

3.1 IPX

The Internet Protocol (IP) Packet eXchange (IPX) networks are operated and managed by a third party and cover the interconnected networks of IPX providers and roaming exchange providers [10]. IPX is designed to support multiple service providers in a secure and business sustainable way.

An IPX connection endpoint can be connected to multiple operators based on the roaming agreements among them. This is helpful in reducing roaming costs of an operator, e.g. by choosing the cheapest route for a customer. Also, there exist roaming aggregators, which have a large range of contracts and a service provider can just make contract with that entity, and, in turn they get connected to all the partners of that aggregator. IPX groups the traffic into classes, and offers Class of Service (CoS), which prioritizes the data packets based on the subscribed [17] services.

3.2 Diameter

Diameter protocol is widely used in LTE interfaces. Information used for interconnection between the visited and home networks, subscription and authentication data for visited network access, and policy and charging control information are communicated when roaming [18] (Fig. 2).

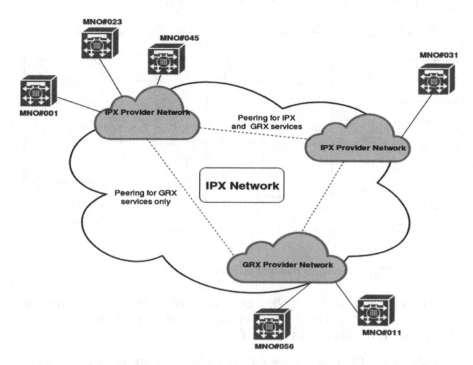

Fig. 2. IPX Network adapted from [8]

The Diameter Base Protocol [11] defines two types of Diameter agents.

- Diameter Relay Agent (DRA): It is used to establish a session over S9 interface. It is present in the IPX network. It is not responsible to inspect the actual Diameter messages it will just route the received message based on the information found in the message, like Application ID and Destination-Realm.
- Diameter Edge Agent (DEA): It is considered as the only point from where the operator network can be accessed in or out.

The Diameter roaming architecture in Fig. 3 shows the Diameter Edge agent at the Home Public Land Mobile Network (HPLMN) and Visitor Public Land Mobile Network (VPLMA). S9 interface is used for communicating Policy Control and Charging (PCC) rules. This communication can be done directly or through an IPX network.

3.3 PCC Rules

The 3GPP Policy Control and Charging rule specifications [4] have defined functions of PCC rules. In brief the PCC rules are responsible for detecting the packets as per Service Data Flow (SDF). This includes the SDF filters that select

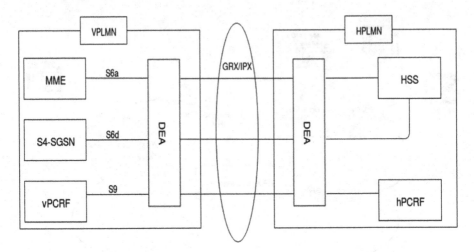

Fig. 3. Diameter roaming architecture adapted from [11]

the traffic for which the rule applies. PCC rules also provides effective charging parameters per SDF and communicate policy control for the SDF.

There are two types of PCC rules [4]

- **Predefined PCC rules:** These rules are defined and are not meant to change in Policy and Charging Enforcement Function (PCEF) and can be activated and deactivated as per the requirement by Policy and Charging Rule Function (PCRF).
- **Dynamic PCC rules:** These rules are dynamically generated by PCRF and provided to PCEF via Gx interface. These rules can be installed, modified and removed at any time.

The operators define the PCC rules as per their contracts with the subscribers, also called mobile subscription plans. Table 2 summaries the fields of a PCC rule.

Table 2. PCC rules fields

Field	Detail
Rule name	It is the name of the rule being communicated
Service identifier	It identifies the services SDF provides
Service data flow filter(s)	Differentiate the traffic for which the rules have to be applied
Gate status	Responsible to move the packets on uplink or downlink direction
QoS parameters	These parameter define the class of the traffic
Charging parameters	Define the prepaid or post paid billing methods
Monitoring key	It is used for usage monitoring

4   Test Setup

It is challenging to practically perform tests on theoretically proven facts. The S9 interface is rolled out currently but practically, not all deployment possibilities have been considered. The standards defining the policies have left space for individual implementation. Theoretical vulnerabilities figured out in a protocol defined by specific standards may or may not exist in practice. The flaw may be totally or partially covered by other protocols running in parallel with the so-called vulnerable protocol. Also there is a possibility that those unspecified details in the standards are implemented by the MNO's. The laboratory tests we conducted are based on an LTE emulator.

4.1   LTE Emulator

LTE emulator models all LTE nodes. It is a Linux based software implementation of 3GPP/LTE network elements. It is functionally a standard Nokia product which provides required real-time aspects and offers real physical interfaces towards other network elements or terminals, using either emulated or real products. When changing a parameter value we can see the corresponding system changes in the form of log files. Both user plane and control plane traffic can be generated on the emulator. Diameter protocol signaling packets can be captured using Wireshark. The LTE emulator consists of all the nodes and interfaces as mentioned in 3GPP specifications [2]. The Fig. 4 includes the nodes we have used for our test setup.

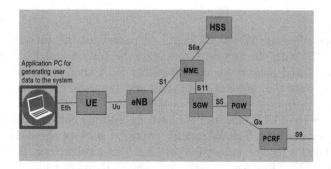

Fig. 4. LTE emulator

4.2   Subscribers Data Plans

A subscriber is assigned to a particular mobile subscription plan at the home location (HPLMN). The subscriber is provided services accordingly and PCC rules are updated accordingly. If the subscriber is at the visited network, the PCC rules are transfered from the HPCRF to the VPCRF through the S9 interface. If we consider a subscriber 'A' with the subscription details in Table 3, and

Table 3. 'A' subscription plan

Fields	Attributes
Plan	SMART15
Data volume	15 GB
Network	LTE 4G
Charging	Off line

Table 4. 'B' subscription plan

Fields	Attributes
Plan	Simple
Data volume	10 MB
Network	UMTS 3G
Charging	On line

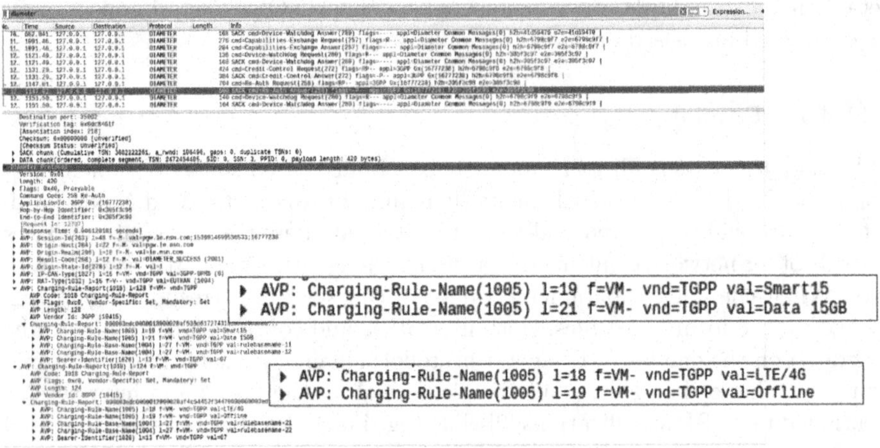

Fig. 5. Diameter packet for subscriber 'A'

the Fig. 5 describes the Wireshark captured packet for the subscriber 'A' and a subscriber 'B' with the subscription details in Table 4 and Fig. 6 shows the Wireshark captured packets for the subscriber B. A single attribute change in the plan can effect the operator credit risk and the subscriber's dissatisfaction e.g. through a degradation of service quality.

With the help of LTE emulator we have successfully changed the PCC rules for the two subscribers. The Wireshark captured packets show the Attribute Value Pair (AVP) for the subscriber 'A' Fig. 5 and subscriber 'B' Fig. 6. The packet is the RAA (Re- Authentication Answer) message which has the AVP that defines the PCC rules.

5   Step by Step Implementation of the Attack

The User Equipment (UE) when in roaming state and the visited network operator node - Visited Policy Control and Reinforcement Function (VPCRF) communicate to the home network operator node called Home Policy Control and Reinforcement Function (HPCRF).

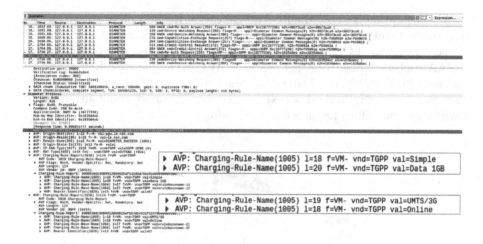

Fig. 6. Diameter packet for subscriber 'B'

The attacker can steal the PCC rules of a good subscription and manipulate an inexpensive subscription e.g. prepaid to a good one e.g. post paid flat-rate. The inexpensive subscription can enjoy then all the services without paying for them. The loss will be covered by the home network operator or a dispute must be settled.

The first step for an attacker is to obtain a 'sample' PCC rule. For that he has two possibilities: The Fig. 7 mentions the credit control request (CCR) from the VPCRF to HPCRF. The attacker may request for the PCC rules from the HPCRF for a specific IMSI. The HPCRF responds with the credit control answer message and the communication is established.

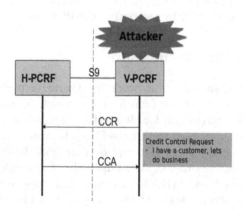

Fig. 7. Messaging between VPCRF (Attacker) and HPCRF

Another option is to use the Re-Authentication Request message, which also gives the PCC rule. In this paper we have used Re-Authentication Answer (RAA) messages to get the PCC rules. The Wireshark captured Diameter traffic consists of RAA packets. These RAA packets have AVP: Charging-Rule-Report, which has the field AVP: (PCC). These PCC rules can be modified and therefore the user may have unauthorized access to services. This may result in access to services without billing i.e. in a fraud scenario.

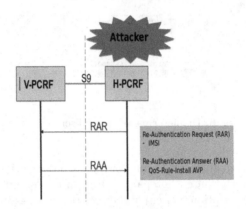

Fig. 8. Messaging between HPCRF (Attacker) and VPCRF

The next step is to place a good set of PCC rules into a subscription that the attacker wants to "upgrade" using the RAR messages which contain the PCC rules. As shown in Fig. 8 now the attacker pretends to be the HPCRF to the VPCRF and communicates the manipulated PCC rules through RAR messages.

The same method can be deployed to deny service e.g. turning the attack into a Denial of Service attack by restricting the PCC content.

6   Results and Countermeasures

The weaknesses of the security framework the Diameter protocol acts in have been tested for the Gx interface (which is a network internal interface) and similar tests have been carried out for S9 interface (which is a roaming interface). The LTE emulator setup is used to test the Policy Charging and Control (PCC) messages, which define the users subscription plan and the service he can use. A successful change in the order of Attribute Value Pairs (AVPs) is possible in the Re-Authentication Answer (RAA) messages. This may result in a successful change of the allowed service descriptions and by that in a fraud or DoS attempt. The end result of such an attack can effect the subscribers for unaccepted changes in the subscription plan, which might pose in particular a risk for IoT, where companies may have a large subscription base with flat-rate contracts and there is no user noticing any strange change in the subscription.

To overcome LTE roaming frauds and have a secure, trusted roaming partnership, GSMA purposed a guideline for operators how to enhance their network security for roaming. This work was done in cooperation with GSMA to improve pro-actively the overall security of mobile networks. GSMA, for example, recommends to place at the edge of the network nodes and firewalls that are "diameter aware". There is a range of checks such a node can make:

- Is the sending node from a roaming partner.
- Can the subscriber really travel in that time such a distance (velocity check).
- Blocking of messages that come from own domain.
- Separation of inbound roamers and own customers.

Also, configuration guidelines and recommendations are given e.g. not to have Diameter interfaces open, when not needed. In addition, the Near Real Time Roaming Data Exchange (NRTRDE) is a GSMA [12] initiative to fight against the roaming fraud. It allows the operators to check the NRTRDE incoming and outgoing data as per GSMA TD.32 specifications. It helps the operators to speed up the roaming fraud response by several hours.

7   Conclusion

This paper demonstrates a way to access and manipulate the credit controls and QoS of the mobile network subscribers. Since commercializing LTE roaming worldwide is still at an early stage, there is a lack of real time test scenario. Firewalls can be a solution. A more persistent and smart solution we purpose is using Machine Learning. The data over roaming interface through Diameter Protocol can be monitored for anomaly detection and upon any suspicion, we can immediately warn the Evolved Packet Core (EPC) and policy management node to cross validate the interconnections. This work is useful for MNOs and IPX providers and this work can also be extended to the IoT and 5G network security.

Acknowledgements. We thank to the European Union's Horizon 2020 research and innovation programme for funding this project under grant agreement No. 737422 of the SCOTT project and Nokia Bell Labs for providing this platform.

References

1. 3GGP: 3GPP TS 29.215 version 9.9.0 release 9. https://www.etsi.org/deliver/etsi_ts/129200_129299/129215/09.09.00_60/ts_129215v090900p.pdf
2. 3GGP: Evolved Packet Core. http://www.3gpp.org/technologies/keywords-acronyms/100-the-evolved-packet-core
3. 3GGP: Numbering, addressing and identification. http://www.qtc.jp/3GPP/Specs/23003-3e0.pdf
4. 3GGP: Policy and Charging Control 3GPP TS 29.212 version 12.6.0 release 12. https://www.etsi.org/deliver/etsi_ts/129200_129299/129212/12.06.00_60/ts_129212v120600p.pdf

5. Cichonski, J., Franklin, J.M., Bartock, M.: Guide to LTE security. Technical report, NIST SP 800–187, National Institute of Standards and Technology, Gaithersburg, MD, December 2017. https://doi.org/10.6028/NIST.SP.800-187. https://nvlpubs.nist.gov/nistpubs/SpecialPublications/NIST.SP.800-187.pdf, 00002
6. Ferrus, R., Sallent, O., Baldini, G., Goratti, L.: LTE: the technology driver for future public safety communications. IEEE Commun. Mag. **51**(10), 154–161 (2013). https://doi.org/10.1109/MCOM.2013.6619579
7. Forsberg, D., Horn, G., Moeller, W.D., Niemi, V.: LTE Security. Wiley, Hoboken (2012). Google-Books-ID: 9wTs815ii70C, 00097
8. GSMA: Guidelines for IPX Provider networks. https://www.gsma.com/newsroom/wp-content/uploads//IR.34-v14.0-3.pdf
9. GSMA: International roaming explained. https://www.gsma.com/latinamerica/wp-content/uploads/2012/08/GSMA-Mobile-roaming-web-English.pdf
10. GSMA: IPX White Paper. https://www.gsma.com/publicpolicy/wp-content/uploads/2012/03/ipxwp12.pdf
11. GSMA: IR.88 - LTE and EPC Roaming Guidelines. https://www.gsma.com/newsroom/wp-content/uploads//IR.88v18.0.pdf
12. GSMA: NRTRDE. http://www.archclearing.com/html/Service/FraudandRevenue Assurance/NRTRDE/NRTRDE.htm
13. Holtmanns, S.: Mobile Data Interception from the Interconnection Link. https://media.ccc.de/v/34c3-8879-mobile_data_interception_from_the_interconnection_link
14. Holtmanns, S.: Interconnection Security-SS7 and Diameter, December 2017. https://www.youtube.com/watch?v=GczSCWRWyCk
15. Holtmanns, S., Nokia Bell Labs, Karakaari 13, 01620 Espoo, Finland: interconnection security standards - we are all connected. J. ICT Stand. **4**(1), 1–18 (2016). https://doi.org/10.13052/jicts2245-800X.411. http://www.riverpublishers.com/journal_read_html_article.php?j=JICTS/4/1/1, 0000
16. Holtmanns, S., Oliver, I.: SMS and one-time-password interception in LTE networks (2017). https://www.semanticscholar.org/paper/SMS-and-one-time-password-interception-in-LTE-Holtmanns-Oliver/d53b731b979697cab9bd9963956 3be0a10f3530a, 00003
17. Huawei: LTE International Roaming Whitepaper. http://carrier.huawei.com/en/technical-topics/core-network/lte-roaming-whitepaper
18. IETF: Diameter Base Protocol. https://tools.ietf.org/html/rfc3588
19. Ivan, I., Milodin, D., Zamfiroiu, A.: Security of M-Commerce transactions. http://store.ectap.ro/articole/880.pdf
20. Kantola, R., Kabir, H., Loiseau, P.: Cooperation and end-to-end in the internet. Int. J. Commun. Syst. **30**(12), e3268 (2017). https://doi.org/10.1002/dac.3268. https://onlinelibrary.wiley.com/doi/abs/10.1002/dac.3268, e3268 IJCS-15-0043.R4
21. Kumar, K.R.R.: International mobile data roaming: managed or unmanaged? In: 2010 9th Conference of Telecommunication, Media and Internet, pp. 1–9, June 2010. https://doi.org/10.1109/CTTE.2010.5557699, 00004
22. Mashukov, S.: Diameter security: an auditor's viewpoint. J. ICT Stand. **5**(1), 53–68 (2017). https://doi.org/10.13052/jicts2245-800X.513. https://riverpublishers.com/journalreadhtmlarticle.php?j=JICTS/5/1/3, 00000
23. Rupprecht, D., Dabrowski, A., Holz, T., Weippl, E., Pöpper, C.: On security research towards future mobile network generations. arXiv:1710.08932 [cs], October 2017, 00006

24. Sanyal, R.: Challenges in interoperability and roaming between LTE - legacy core for mobility management, routing, real time charging. In: 2011 Technical Symposium at ITU Telecom World (ITU WT), pp. 116–122, October 2011
25. Holtmanns, S., Kotte, B., Rao, S.: Detach Me Not - DoS Attacks Against 4G Cellular Users Worldwide from your Desk. https://www.blackhat.com/eu-16/speakers/Dr-Silke-Holtmanns.html
26. Syniverse Technologies: Preparing for LTE Roaming. https://pdfs.semanticscholar.org/presentation/7a09/50e6a2679ad03948b259445852797206247e.pdf
27. Tata Communications: Fighting Fraud on 4G. https://www.tatacommunications.com/sites/default/files/MOB-LTE-Fraud-WP-87299.pdf

Limited Proxying for Content Filtering Based on X.509 Proxy Certificate Profile

Islam Faisal[✉] and Sherif El-Kassas[✉]

Computer Science and Engineering Department,
The American University in Cairo, Cairo, Egypt
{islamfm,sherif}@aucegypt.edu

Abstract. Use of proxy servers to filter content is very critical in achieving both personal and enterprise security. A common practice to perform this task is by allowing a man-in-the-middle to intercept the traffic unconditionally and act as a proxy between the client and the server. While this method is good enough for unencrypted HTTP connections, it is not a good practice in encrypted HTTPS (SSL/TLS) connections. In this paper, we introduce an access-controlled limited proxying framework to allow HTTPS content filtering based on the Internet X.509 Public Key Infrastructure (PKI) Proxy Certificate Profile. Limited proxying allows the client and the server to decide which content can be accessed by a proxy to avoid compromise of sensitive content. The proposed framework grants the user full control to grant or revoke specific proxy privileges which enhances the user's privacy online. We also define and argue about the security properties of the framework as well as some practical considerations for its implementation.

Keywords: Proxy servers · Content filtering ·
Proxy certificate profile · Privacy

1 Introduction

Content filtering is used extensively to achieve different tasks. For example, content filtering systems are used by parents to filter inappropriate content [27,45], by anti-malware systems such as [7] to filter content in order to ensure enterprise or personal security, and by governments for surveillance and censorship [8,17].

There exist different types of content control systems [40] such as email filtering [1,6], DNS-based filtering [4], network-based filtering, and web proxy filtering [40].

In HTTP proxy filtering, the client does not connect directly to the server, yet, the network is configured to allow (or force) users to connect to HTTP servers via a *proxy server*. This man-in-the-middle approach is sometimes used

I. Faisal's travel to the SECITC conference is supported by AUC's Undergraduate Research Office grant UG#1810898.

J.-L. Lanet and C. Toma (Eds.): SecITC 2018, LNCS 11359, pp. 218–233, 2019.
https://doi.org/10.1007/978-3-030-12942-2_17

for the same purposes to filter connections to HTTPS servers. However, this approach doesn't differentiate between legitimate proxying approved by users and forged SSL certificate attacks initiated against users. Moreover, this interception exposes the security of the SSL/TLS protocol[1] and can result in severe consequences [19,31,33]. This motivates the need for a framework that legalizes the use of HTTPS proxy servers so that a clear distinction is made between accountable proxying and unauthorized attacks.

Contributions. The following contributions are included in this paper:

- We introduce a use case and a policy language for the X.509 Proxy Certificate Profile described in RFC 3820 [49] to enable limited proxying capabilities for the task of web content filtering.
- We propose a framework and practical advise for the mechanism of verifying the identity and privileges of content filtering systems and handling sensitive data on connections established with a principal identifying by a proxy certificate. This privacy-enhancing framework gives the user full control to grant or revoke specific proxy privileges.
- We discuss the security properties of the proposed framework and demonstrate an application as well as practical considerations when implementing in the real world.

Outline. The rest of the paper is organized as follows. Section 2 explains the necessary background and related work. Then, Sect. 3 defines the threat model, system requirements, and the proposed framework. Then, Sect. 4 discusses the security properties, applications, and practical advise for implementation. Finally, Sect. 5 concludes the paper and introduces the future directions.

2   Background and Related Work

2.1   Content Filtering Systems

Content filtering systems are systems that inspect web content and/or web URLs for removing or blocking unwanted content [40]. These systems vary in both the method and the application. Nowadays, most content filtering systems use machine learning or artificial intelligence [28,44] to rule out unwanted content. Some systems also use this in combination with a list of unwanted websites [40] such as Google's safe browsing API[2]. Content filtering is used at scale for a wide variety of applications such as:

- Parental access control to block adult or unsafe content [27,45]
- Malware detection by antivirus software such as Symantec WebFilter[3]
- Government mass survelliance and content censorship [8,17].

---

[1] In this paper's scope, we are not interested in differentiating between SSL and TLS connections. Unless clearly stated or suffixed by a version number, we consider both terms as a method to communicate encrypted web traffic payload.

[2] https://developers.google.com/safe-browsing/.

[3] https://www.symantec.com/products/webfilter-intelligent-services.

2.2 HTTPS Interception

The two standard protocols to encrypt HTTP traffic are *Secure Sockets Layer (SSL)* [25] and its successor *Transport Layer Security (TLS)* [13–15,46]. When the TLS protocol was introduced [15], it was assumed that all the functionalities reside on the connection endpoints. Middlebox network security solutions are not "legal" under this assumption, so middleboxes resort to going around the protocol. *HTTPS interception* refers to the common man-in-the-middle (MITM) attack done by inserting a middlebox between the HTTPS client and server which is demonstrated in Fig. 1. Intercepting HTTPS traffic using this naive MITM approach is not recommended [19] because it can severely reduce connection security. In the literature, multiple alternatives to naive interception were proposed [19] such as:

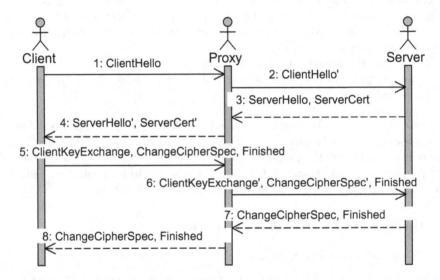

Fig. 1. Man-in-The-Middle HTTPS handshake interception by a proxy: The proxy intercepts the connection by creating two client-server connections with the original parties. Usually, a new *certificate authority (CA)* is added on the client side to trust that "forged" SERVERCERT' certificate. Messages transmitted by the proxy are colored in red and a prime is added to distinguish possibly altered messages. In addition to the fact that the proxy will use a "forged" certificate, this approach is not safe and can degrade security because the proxy can use out-dated TLS versions or weak cipher suites [19]. (Color figure online)

1. **HTTP 2.0 Explicit Trusted Proxy RFC** [36]: This very simple solution requires middleboxes to explicitly notify the client of the interception.
2. **TLS Proxy Server Extension** [37]: This extends the idea of explicit proxy in HTTP to HTTPS, requiring the proxy to indicate the interception, and to additionally relay proxy-server session information back to the client.

3. **Multi-context TLS (mcTLS)** [41]: This approach introduced an extended version of TLS that requires endpoints to explicitly specify permitted middleboxes in order to securely authenticate each hop and cryptographically control exactly what data middleboxes can access. This protocol, however, was proven to be insecure because it lacked formal analysis [3].

4. **BlindBox** [47]: In this approach, instead of thinking how to "legitimately" insert the proxy, the proxy is just let to observe the traffic in its encrypted form and advise what to do after performing *deep packet inspection (DPI)* over encrypted traffic.

5. **Hardware-Assisted Middleboxes** [11,18,26,29,35,43,48]: These systems leverage the use of trusted hardware such as Intel's *Software Guard Extensions (SGX)* [2,10,30,38] to support the middlebox's functionality and security properties.

6. **Formally verified accountable proxying** [3]: This paper introduced a new notion of security for middleboxes intercepting the TLS connections called *Authenticated and Confidential Channel Establishment with Accountable Proxies (ACCE-AP)*. They use this formal model to show the insecurity of existing middlebox techniques such as [41] and introduce a formally verified *ACCE-AP*-secure framework for accountable proxying.

Our method is different from prior work in the sense that it employs an access-control strategy by properly delegating an honest proxy via proxy certificates [49] without reliance on trusted hardware. Except for relaying back the server certificate along with the proxy certificate to the client and adding extra restrictive checks, we don't modify the handshakes of the TLS. Additionally, our method is independent of the TLS version used and doesn't require much software updates to the connection endpoints.

2.3   Analyzing SSL Certificates

It is not a good practice to blindly trust an SSL certificate. Many problems including private keys compromise, and forged SSL certificates can arise in the wild. For example, [31] analyzed SSL certificates from a sample collected via a research network as well as active websites and found that over 40% of their sample exhibit broken certificate chains. In a study done by Facebook [33], it was found that 0.2% of the SSL connections sampled from a small portion of Facebook traffic were tampered with forged SSL certificates, most of them related to antivirus software and corporate-scale content filters. Although some of those "forged" certificates are issued based on the user's consent, it is not a good idea to pool an attacker and a legitimate antivirus in the same pool.

2.4   Proxy Certificate Profile

The concept of *computational grids* [22] has emerged in the late 90's to support high performance computing needs. The Globus project [23] was introduced to enable the construction of computational grids providing pervasive, dependable, and consistent access to high-performance computational resources, despite geographical distribution of both resources and users. As these computational grids grew and became popular, their security concerns grew rapidly as well. [24] was one of the earliest efforts to introduce security requirements, develop a security policy and corresponding security architecture for computing grids. This came with an implementation within the Globus metacomputing toolkit [23]. Later, the implementation was separated as an online repository credentials management system called *MyProxy*[4] [42] which was later proposed as IETF RFC 3820 [49]. RFC 3820[5] defines a certificate profile based on the Internet X.509 Public Key Infrastructure defined in RFC 3280 [32] and updated in RFC 5280 [9].

Terminology. We list some useful terms from RFC 3820 [49] and RFC 5280 [9] that will be helpful in describing the proposed framework later:

- *Certificate Authority (CA):* An authority that is authorized to certify entities by certificates upon which the relying parties can depend.
- *End Entity Certificate (EEC):* Sometimes called *Public Key Certificate (PKC)*; An X.509 Public Key Certificate issued to an end entity, such as a user or a service, by a CA.
- *Proxy Certificate (PC):* A PKC with special fields issued by an end entity delegating some of its priveligies to another entity.
- *Proxy Issuer (PI):* An entity with an End Entity Certificate or Proxy Certificate that issues a Proxy Certificate.
- *Attribute Certificate (AC):* Sometimes called *Authorization Certificate*; (defined in RFC 3281 [21] which was obsoleted by RFC 5755 [20]) A certificate that contains the attributes associated with an end entity. While a PKC is used as a proof of identity, the AC is used as a proof of authorization.
- *Attribute Authority (AA):* (defined in RFC 3281 [21] which was obsoleted by RFC 5755 [20]) An authority that can issue attribute certificates.
- *Certificate Revocation List (CRL):* A list of certificates that were revoked before their expiry dates. Certificates in this list should not be trusted by relying parties.

Proxy certificates are associated with a public and private key pair that is separate from its holder's EEC. A proxy certificate can only sign other proxy certificates. The *relying party* is the party who is interested in verifying the validity of the certificate. For example, in a TLS connection where a server provides a server certificate, a relying party can be the client's web browser.

This profile adds the extension listed in Listing 1.1 which introduces the following proxy certificate fields:

1. *pCPathLenConstraint*: An integer that defines the delegation depth for a certain proxy.

---

[4] http://grid.ncsa.illinois.edu/myproxy/.

[5] Although dating back to 2004, this is the most updated version of the RFC to our knowledge.

2. *policyLanguage*: An identifier for the language used in interpreting the policy field. The RFC encourages acquiring an *object identifier* (OID) for these languages.
3. *policy*: The delegation policy from the issuer to the proxy that specified the scope of the privileges being delegated to the proxy.

Listing 1.1. ProxyCertInfo Extension Definition From [49] defined in the *Abstract Syntax Notation One (ASN.1)* [34]

```
1   — The ProxyCertInfo Extension
2       ProxyCertInfoExtension    ::= SEQUENCE {
3           pCPathLenConstraint
                ProxyCertPathLengthConstraint OPTIONAL,
4           proxyPolicy              ProxyPolicy
5       }
6
7       ProxyCertPathLengthConstraint  ::= INTEGER
8       ProxyPolicy  ::= SEQUENCE {
9           policyLanguage           OBJECT IDENTIFIER,
10          policy                   OCTET STRING OPTIONAL
11      }
```

Issuing a Proxy Certificate. To issue a proxy certificate, first a new public and private key pair is generated. A request for a PC is created. The proxy issuer verifies that the PC request is valid by checking that the PC fields are appropriately set. If the fields are appropriately set, the PI signs the PC using the private key of either an associated EEC or a PC. A PI may use the *pCPathLenConstraint* field of the *proxyCertInfo* to limit subsequent delegation of this PC. If it is set to zero, the proxy's delegated privileges can not be delegated further.

Verifying a Proxy Certificate. Verifying a request made using a proxy certificate is the responsibility of the relying party. Definition 1 gives the conditions to validate the path of a proxy certificate. It has to be used in conjunction with path validation of EEC as in RFC 5280. In Definition 2, the conditions for a valid proxy certificate are stated. These definitions are mentioned here because they are slightly different from RFC 3820 in the sense that we allow a proxy issuer to revoke a proxy certificate by publishing it to a CRL.

Definition 1. *A path containing a succession of proxy certificates* $\{C_1, \ldots, C_n\}$ *is valid if:*

1. *C_1 is a valid proxy certificate issued by a valid end entity certificate[6]*

---

[6] We don't describe how to verify an end entity certificate in this definition. Verifying an EEC is done in accordance with RFC 5280.

2. $\forall\, x \in \{1, \ldots, n-1\}$, the subject of certificate C_x is the issuer of the proxy certificate C_{x+1}
3. $\forall\, x \in \{1, \ldots, n\}$, C_x is valid at the time in question (not expired nor revoked).
4. $\forall\, x \in \{1, \ldots, n-1\}$, if C_x contains a pCPathLenConstraint field, then $n - x \leq$ pCPathLenConstraint.

Definition 2. Let $\{C_1, \ldots, C_n\}$ be a path of proxy certificates with policies written in the policy language policyLanguage and C_0 be the parent EEC of C_1. A request Q made via proxy certificate C_n is considered valid by a relying party R if it satisfies the following conditions:

1. $\{C_1, \ldots, C_n\}$ is a valid path of proxy certificates
2. R can interpret policyLanguage
3. Q is allowed under C_n's policy
4. If the proxy issuer of C_n is an EEC, then R must authorize this PI to perform Q
5. If the proxy issuer of C_n is a PC, then either (i) R authorizes the owner of C_{n-1} to perform Q, or (ii) C_{n-1} inherits the right to perform Q by a parent proxy certificate C_{n-2}. This right is verified recursively using this definition by checking if Q made via C_{n-2} is considered valid by the relying party R.

If the request is not valid, it is up to the relying party to either deny it or act as if no proxy certificate was provided.

3   Proposed Framework

3.1   Threat Model

We assume the attacker has the capabilities of the Dolev-Yao active attacker model [16]. This attacker can eavesdrop, delete, replace, re-transmit, and delay messages that honest parties communicate over the network. They can also send any message over the network. We assume the security of private keys and private communication channels as well as perfect cryptography. We assume that the proxy server is a trusted party and won't collude or tamper with the traffic. We don't consider the process of certifying entities and its socioeconomics. However, in Sect. 4.3, we give advice on bringing this method to the real world with some consideration to these factors.

3.2   Security Requirements

The client-proxy and proxy-server connections must conform to the security requirements of an HTTPS connection. Besides these requirements, the proposed framework has to satisfy some requirements that we list below and argue about their validity in Sect. 4:

1. **Authorized Proxying:** Proxy connections are only accepted from proxies with a valid EEC and PC.

2. **Limited Proxying:** The client and the server have control over what pages or parts of traffic can be shared with the proxy. This is based on:
   (a) Proxy Trust Level
   (b) Content Sensitivity.
3. **Proxy Detection:** Both the client and the server must be able to detect and distinguish between direct client-server connections and connections established via an intermediate proxy.
4. **Limited-Depth Proxying:** The depth of the chain of proxy certificates is controlled by the entity delegating the proxy.
5. **Certificate Path Validation:** The relying party can trace the path of the delegation and verify that the delegation is legitimate.

3.3   Limited Proxying Framework

We propose a framework for providing access-controlled content filtering services based on the proxy certificate profile defined in Sect. 2.4. The framework definition includes defining a filtering-specific access-control policy language, processes for issuing and verifying proxy certificates, and the handshakes used to create the client-proxy and proxy-server connections.

Content Filtering Policy Language. We define a policy language in the proxy certificate profile that is suitable to the task of content filtering. This policy can be used to determine if the proxy is allowed to visit the content they are trying to visit. The policy in this policy language is defined as the concatenation of:

1. A integer representing the *trust level* associated with that proxy certificate.
2. A list of allowed and disallowed domains that the proxy can visit on behalf of the user.
3. A set of allowed cipher suites to be used by the proxy.

We elaborate more on this definition in Appendix A. Given a certain content on one of the proxy's allowed domains, the server, can determine if the proxy can serve this content based on the trust level of the proxy server and the sensitivity of the content. For example, a high-quality anti-virus can be trusted more than a cheap parental-control software.

Managing End Entity Certificates. Similar to the X.509 PKI, the identities of all entities including clients, servers, and proxies is verified using EEC. The issuance of an identity certificate is done typically via one of the trusted certificate authorities. An example is the free, automated, and open-source certificate authority *Let's Encrypt*[7]. Proxies are required to identify by an identity end entity certificate that is different from the proxy certificate issued by the

---

[7] https://letsencrypt.org/.

corresponding client proxy issuer. An end entity certificate serves as the proxy's long-term identity, while a proxy certificate is a proof of delegation issued by every client. In the framework, a proxy can't function if their EEC is expired or revoked even if their PC is valid.

Managing Proxy Certificates. Proxy certificates are issued by a proxy issuer, which is in our case either the client or another proxy server. The proxy certificate is issued using the procedure described in Sect. 2.4 while making sure the certificate request conforms to the policy language defined previously by including these fields:

– Proxy depth
– The policy fields (trust level, allowed and disallowed domains, allowed cipher suites) or customized privileges identifier in the case of use of a customized policy language.

To validate a proxy certificate by the relying party, the conditions in Definitions 1 and 2 mentioned in Sect. 2.4 have to be satisfied besides the following language-specific conditions if the proxy issuer is already a proxy:

1. The trust level is at most as privileged as the parent proxy.
2. The set of allowed domains is a subset of the parent proxy's allowed domains.
3. The set of disallowed domains is a superset of the parent proxy's disallowed domains.
4. The cipher suites set is a subset of the parent proxy's cipher suites.

Revoking Proxy Certificates. At any point in time, the client may decide to revoke a proxy certificate they have issued at a point in time before its expiry date. To do so, they publish the certificate to a certificate revocation list (CRL) as explained in Sect. 2.4. A note is given on the practicality of this process in Sect. 4.3.

Establishing Proxy Connections. As illustrated in Fig. 2, to establish a full proxy connection, the proxy creates two connections; one to the client initiated by the client and one to the server initiated by the proxy on behalf of the client as follows:

1. **Client-Proxy Connection**: The client initiates a connection to the proxy server using their EEC and the proxy uses their PC and EEC. The user uses Definition 2 to determine if this connection request is valid based on the validity of the proxy's introduced proxy certificate and based on that the client decides whether to proceed.
2. **Server-Proxy Connection**: The proxy initiates a connection to the server identifying by its EEC and PC while the server identifies by a typical X.509 certificate as in RFC 5280. Here, we mandate that the proxy notifies the server that the connection is a proxy-type connection and that the proxy

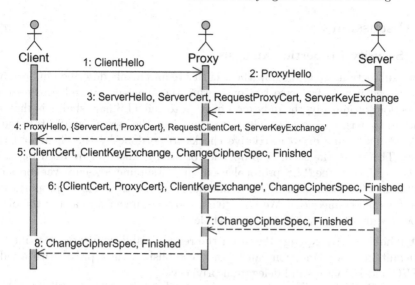

Fig. 2. HTTPS interception Handshake in the proposed framework: Note that the proxy relays back the server certificate information in step 4.

provides their proxy certificate which will be considered the client certificate in this proxy-server TLS connection. The proxy has also to use one of the cipher suites required by the client in the policy language. In Sect. 4.3, we give a note on the practicality of verifying the client credentials. The server here must verify that the cipher suite being used is one of the suites given in the proxy certificate.

Relaying Server Certificate Information. When establishing the proxy-server connection, we require the proxy to relay back the server certificate information to the user (step 4 in Fig. 2). The client uses the certificate information to decide if they want to proceed with the connection. As explained in Sect. 3.1, it is assumed that the proxy is an honest principal who will relay the certificate information as is. The client can decide then based on their trusted certificate authorities whether to accept the relayed server certificate.

Sharing Content via Proxy. After establishing both connections successfully, the client tunnels their data to the server via the proxy. For each payload the client wishes to send, they decide based on the trust level of the connected proxy if they want to send this specific content over the proxy connection. The server does the same by selectively deciding which content to send over via the proxy.

4 Discussion

4.1 Security Properties Analysis

In this subsection, we argue how the security requirements described in Sect. 3.2 are satisfied in this framework. Considering the client-proxy and proxy-server connections atomically, the only modification to the TLS handshakes is that we mandate that the proxy relays back to the client the server certificate (step 4 in Fig. 2) and some extra restrictive checks to be done by the client and the server. Therefore, the security properties of each connection by itself depends on the version of the TLS protocol used, and assuming a secure version such as TLS 1.3 [46], both proxy connections don't expose the security properties of the individual connections. We now give a short argument for each of the other properties about the framework as a whole:

1. **Authorized Proxying:** Based on the request validity criteria described in Definition 2, a connection can be only established via a proxy with a valid EEC and PC with valid delegation privileges.
2. **Proxy Detection:** The proxy connection is done via a proxy certificate which is distinguishable from an EEC. A relying entity can clearly determine if the connection is direct or via a proxy.
3. **Limited Proxying:** In the proxy certificate fields, the level of trust and allowed domains to be accessed is specified. The relying party (client or server) can choose what content to share over a proxy server based on these fields.
4. **Limited-Depth Proxying:** The depth of delegation is specified in the proxy certificate field pCPathLenConstraint as described in RFC 3820 and enforced in the certificate issuance and validation processes.
5. **Certificate Path Validation:** The framework uses the path validity criteria described in Definition 1 which relies on the chain of trust principle. This enables the relying user to trace the trail of certificates up to a root certificate they trust.

4.2 Applications

This framework has the typical applications mentioned in Sect. 2.1 that a content filtering system can perform. We demonstrate an application of our framework by the following example from the enterprise security domain.

Enterprise Content Filtering. For a company X to use the proposed framework to do company-wide content filtering using the proxy server Y to achieve enterprise security, one strategy can be as follows. The company employees can issue a proxy certificate to the company with a depth greater than 1. The company can then use this proxy certificate to subsequently delegate the content filtering proxy Y to act as a proxy between the employee and the requested web service. When the employees start surfing the web, they will find that their connections are being tunneled through Y as instructed by X. Since this path can be validated up to the client's EEC, the client can trust this connection as long as the other request validity conditions are satisfied.

4.3   Practical Considerations

Server-Side Proxy Certificates. In our framework, we chose to let the proxy issuer be the client. In some cases, it may be important for the server to selectively determine which proxies can be used to access their services and therefore requiring issuing proxy certificates from both the client and the server.

Trusting Proxy Certificates. In today's world, most HTTPS connections are done without providing a client certificate or caring about its validity. Although it is crucial for the client to verify that the proxy certificate is valid, it may be an overhead for the server to verify client-issued proxy certificates, specially that not all normal users own trusted end entity certificates. In this case, a server may choose to deal with the proxy connection as if it were a direct connection and leaving the choice of what content is shareable over the proxy to the client. One more issue is the normal users' ability to publish revoked proxy certificate serial numbers to a global CRL that web servers rely on. While this may be hard in practice, we still include it in the framework design for completeness.

Relaying Server Certificate Information. In the proposed framework, relaying the server certificate information back to the user provides the user with finer control on the certificates they want to trust. Not only that the proxy has to trust the server certificate, but also the client has to give their final approval via their own chain of trust.

Limitations. Although we have been struggling to distinguish between an attacker and a legitimate proxy, it doesn't mean that this method eliminates the risks associated with practical use of SSL certificates in the wild mentioned in Sect. 2.3 such as forged, expired, or misconfigured SSL certificates.

5   Conclusions

We have proposed a novel method to establish proxy connections for content-filtering purposes between clients and web services. The proposed framework establishes an access-controlled limited proxying method that enhances the privacy of the users online. We have also analyzed the security properties and some practical considerations of this framework and demonstrated how it can be applied in the domain of enterprise security as an application.

In the future, we want to consider the applicability of this method to the recent TLS 1.3 protocol draft [46]. It is also interesting to verify our security requirements using formal methods such as ProVerif[8] [5] or Tamarin Prover[9] [39] by extending existing formal models such as [12]. We are also interested in implementing this framework by adding software support to the participating parties; clients, proxies, and servers.

---

[8] http://prosecco.gforge.inria.fr/personal/bblanche/proverif/.

[9] https://tamarin-prover.github.io/.

Appendix A Content Filtering Policy Language

In the proposed framework, we have defined a policy language to be used with the proxy certificate profile. In this section, we list the structure of that language.

The policy field of the proxy certificate extension is encoded as a string in the field *policy* in Listing 1.1. This string is an encoding of the structure listed in Listing 1.2. This structure is defined in the *Abstract Syntax Notation One (ASN.1)* [34] which is a standard interface description language. The structure consists of the fields mentioned in Sect. 3.3.

Listing 1.2. The definition of the policy structure in the ASN.1 notation before encoding.

```
1  FilteringPolicy  ::=  SEQUENCE {
2      allowedDomains        SEQUENCE( SIZE ( 0 . . 2 5 5 ) )  OF OCTET
           STRING,
3      disallowedDomains     SEQUENCE( SIZE ( 1 . . 2 5 5 ) )  OF OCTET
           STRING,
4      cipherSuites          SEQUENCE( SIZE ( 1 . . 1 0 0 ) )  OF
           CipherSuite ,
5      -- Assuming there is an enum of type CipherSuite
           already defined .
6      trustLevel            INTEGER( 0 . . 1 0 0 0 )
7  }
```

References

1. Almomani, A., Gupta, B., Atawneh, S., Meulenberg, A., Almomani, E.: A survey of phishing email filtering techniques. IEEE Commun. Surv. Tutor. **15**(4), 2070–2090 (2013)
2. Anati, I., Gueron, S., Johnson, S., Scarlata, V.: Innovative technology for CPU based attestation and sealing. In: Proceedings of the 2nd International Workshop on Hardware and Architectural Support for Security and Privacy, vol. 13. ACM, New York (2013)
3. Bhargavan, K., Boureanu, I., Delignat-Lavaud, A., Fouque, P., Onete, C.: A formal treatment of accountable proxying over TLS. In: 2018 IEEE Symposium on Security and Privacy (SP), pp. 799–816, May 2018. https://doi.org/10.1109/SP.2018.00021
4. Bilge, L., Kirda, E., Kruegel, C., Balduzzi, M.: EXPOSURE: finding malicious domains using passive DNS analysis. In: NDSS (2011)
5. Blanchet, B.: An efficient cryptographic protocol verifier based on prolog rules. In: Proceedings of the 14th IEEE Workshop on Computer Security Foundations, CSFW 2001, p. 82. IEEE Computer Society, Washington, DC (2001). http://dl.acm.org/citation.cfm?id=872752.873511
6. Blanzieri, E., Bryl, A.: A survey of learning-based techniques of email spam filtering. Artif. Intell. Rev. **29**(1), 63–92 (2008)
7. Canali, D., Cova, M., Vigna, G., Kruegel, C.: Prophiler: a fast filter for the large-scale detection of malicious web pages. In: Proceedings of the 20th International Conference on World Wide Web, WWW 2011, pp. 197–206. ACM, New York (2011). https://doi.org/10.1145/1963405.1963436

8. Chen, T.M., Wang, V.: Web filtering and censoring. Computer **43**(3), 94–97 (2010). https://doi.org/10.1109/MC.2010.84
9. Cooper, D., Santesson, S., Farrell, S., Boeyen, S., Housley, R., Polk, W.: Internet X.509 public key infrastructure certificate and certificate revocation list (CRL) profile. RFC 5280, RFC Editor, May 2008. http://www.rfc-editor.org/rfc/rfc5280.txt
10. Costan, V., Devadas, S.: Intel SGX explained. IACR Cryptology ePrint Archive 2016(086), 1–118 (2016)
11. Coughlin, M., Keller, E., Wustrow, E.: Trusted click: overcoming security issues of NFV in the cloud. In: Proceedings of the ACM International Workshop on Security in Software Defined Networks & Network Function Virtualization, SDN-NFVSec 2017, pp. 31–36. ACM, New York (2017). https://doi.org/10.1145/3040992.3040994
12. Cremers, C., Horvat, M., Hoyland, J., Scott, S., van der Merwe, T.: A comprehensive symbolic analysis of TLS 1.3. In: Proceedings of the 2017 ACM SIGSAC Conference on Computer and Communications Security, CCS 2017, pp. 1773–1788. ACM, New York (2017). https://doi.org/10.1145/3133956.3134063
13. Dierks, T., Rescorla, E.: The transport layer security (TLS) protocol version 1.1. RFC 4346, RFC Editor, April 2006. http://www.rfc-editor.org/rfc/rfc4346.txt
14. Dierks, T., Rescorla, E.: The transport layer security (TLS) protocol version 1.2. RFC 5246, RFC Editor, August 2008. http://www.rfc-editor.org/rfc/rfc5246.txt
15. Dierks, T., Allen, C.: The TLS protocol version 1.0. RFC 2246, RFC Editor, January 1999. http://www.rfc-editor.org/rfc/rfc2246.txt
16. Dolev, D., Yao, A.C.: On the security of public key protocols. In: Proceedings of the 22nd Annual Symposium on Foundations of Computer Science, SFCS 1981, pp. 350–357. IEEE Computer Society, Washington, DC (1981). https://doi.org/10.1109/SFCS.1981.32
17. Dornseif, M.: Government mandated blocking of foreign web content. arXiv preprint arXiv:cs/0404005 (2004)
18. Duan, H., Yuan, X., Wang, C.: LightBox: SGX-assisted secure network functions at near-native speed. CoRR abs/1706.06261 (2017). http://arxiv.org/abs/1706.06261
19. Durumeric, Z., et al.: The security impact of https interception. In: Proceedings of the Network and Distributed System Security Symposium (NDSS) (2017)
20. Farrell, S., Housley, R., Turner, S.: An internet attribute certificate profile for authorization. RFC 5755, RFC Editor, January 2010
21. Farrell, S., Housley, R.: An internet attribute certificate profile for authorization. RFC 3281, RFC Editor, April 2002. http://www.rfc-editor.org/rfc/rfc3281.txt
22. Foster, I., Kesselman, C.: Computational Grids: The Future of High Performance Distributed Computing. Morgan Kaufmann, Los Altos (1998)
23. Foster, I., Kesselman, C.: The globus project: a status report. In: 1998 Proceedings of the Seventh Heterogeneous Computing Workshop (HCW 1998), pp. 4–18, March 1998. https://doi.org/10.1109/HCW.1998.666541
24. Foster, I., Kesselman, C., Tsudik, G., Tuecke, S.: A security architecture for computational grids. In: Proceedings of the 5th ACM Conference on Computer and Communications Security, CCS 1998, pp. 83–92. ACM, New York (1998). https://doi.org/10.1145/288090.288111
25. Freier, A., Karlton, P., Kocher, P.: The secure sockets layer (SSL) protocol version 3.0. RFC 6101, RFC Editor, August 2011. http://www.rfc-editor.org/rfc/rfc6101.txt

26. Goltzsche, D., et al.: Endbox: scalable middlebox functions using client-side trusted execution. In: Proceedings of the 48th International Conference on Dependable Systems and Networks, DSN, vol. 18 (2018)

27. Hammami, M., Chahir, Y., Chen, L.: WebGuard: web based adult content detection and filtering system. In: Proceedings IEEE/WIC International Conference on Web Intelligence (WI 2003), pp. 574–578, October 2003. https://doi.org/10.1109/WI.2003.1241271

28. Hammami, M., Chahir, Y., Chen, L.: WebGuard: a web filtering engine combining textual, structural, and visual content-based analysis. IEEE Trans. Knowl. Data Eng. **18**(2), 272–284 (2006). https://doi.org/10.1109/TKDE.2006.34

29. Han, J., Kim, S., Ha, J., Han, D.: SGX-Box: enabling visibility on encrypted traffic using a secure middlebox module. In: Proceedings of the First Asia-Pacific Workshop on Networking, APNet 2017, pp. 99–105. ACM, New York (2017). https://doi.org/10.1145/3106989.3106994

30. Hoekstra, M., Lal, R., Pappachan, P., Phegade, V., Del Cuvillo, J.: Using innovative instructions to create trustworthy software solutions. In: HASP@ ISCA, p. 11 (2013)

31. Holz, R., Braun, L., Kammenhuber, N., Carle, G.: The SSL landscape: a thorough analysis of the X.509 PKI using active and passive measurements. In: Proceedings of the 2011 ACM SIGCOMM Conference on Internet Measurement Conference, IMC 2011, pp. 427–444. ACM, New York (2011). https://doi.org/10.1145/2068816.2068856

32. Housley, R., Ford, W., Polk, T., Solo, D.: Internet X.509 public key infrastructure certificate and certificate revocation list (CRL) Profile. RFC 3280, RFC Editor, April 2002. http://www.rfc-editor.org/rfc/rfc3280.txt

33. Huang, L.S., Rice, A., Ellingsen, E., Jackson, C.: Analyzing forged SSL certificates in the wild. In: 2014 IEEE Symposium on Security and Privacy, pp. 83–97, May 2014. https://doi.org/10.1109/SP.2014.13

34. Abstract Syntax Notation One (ASN.1): Specification of basic notation. Standard, International Telecommunication Union, August 2015

35. Kuvaiskii, D., Chakrabarti, S., Vij, M.: Snort intrusion detection system with Intel software guard extension (Intel SGX). CoRR abs/1802.00508 (2018). http://arxiv.org/abs/1802.00508

36. Loreto, S., Mattsson, J., Skog, R., Spaak, H., Druta, D., Hafeez, M.: Explicit trusted proxy in HTTP/2.0. Internet-Draft draft-loreto-httpbis-trusted-proxy20-01, IETF Secretariat, February 2014. http://www.ietf.org/internet-drafts/draft-loreto-httpbis-trusted-proxy20-01.txt

37. McGrew, D., Wing, D., Gladstone, P.: TLS proxy server extension. Internet-Draft draft-mcgrew-tls-proxy-server-01, IETF Secretariat, July 2012. http://www.ietf.org/internet-drafts/draft-mcgrew-tls-proxy-server-01.txt

38. McKeen, F., et al.: Innovative instructions and software model for isolated execution. In: HASP@ ISCA, p. 10 (2013)

39. Meier, S., Schmidt, B., Cremers, C., Basin, D.: The TAMARIN prover for the symbolic analysis of security protocols. In: Sharygina, N., Veith, H. (eds.) CAV 2013. LNCS, vol. 8044, pp. 696–701. Springer, Heidelberg (2013). https://doi.org/10.1007/978-3-642-39799-8_48

40. Murdoch, S.J., Anderson, R.: Tools and technology of internet filtering. Access Denied: Pract. Policy Glob. Internet Filter. **1**(1), 58 (2008)

41. Naylor, D., et al.: Multi-context TLS (mcTLS): enabling secure in-network functionality in TLS. In: Proceedings of the 2015 ACM Conference on Special Interest Group on Data Communication, SIGCOMM 2015, pp. 199–212. ACM, New York (2015). https://doi.org/10.1145/2785956.2787482

42. Novotny, J., Tuecke, S., Welch, V.: An online credential repository for the grid: MyProxy. In: Proceedings 10th IEEE International Symposium on High Performance Distributed Computing, pp. 104–111 (2001). https://doi.org/10.1109/HPDC.2001.945181

43. Poddar, R., Lan, C., Popa, R.A., Ratnasamy, S.: SafeBricks: shielding network functions in the cloud. In: 15th USENIX Symposium on Networked Systems Design and Implementation (NSDI 2018), Renton, WA (2018)

44. Polpinij, J., Chotthanom, A., Sibunruang, C., Chamchong, R., Puangpronpitag, S.: Content-based text classifiers for pornographic web filtering. In: 2006 IEEE International Conference on Systems, Man and Cybernetics, vol. 2, pp. 1481–1485, October 2006. https://doi.org/10.1109/ICSMC.2006.384926

45. Polpinij, J., Sibunruang, C., Paungpronpitag, S., Chamchong, R., Chotthanom, A.: A web pornography patrol system by content-based analysis: in particular text and image. In: 2008 IEEE International Conference on Systems, Man and Cybernetics, pp. 500–505, October 2008. https://doi.org/10.1109/ICSMC.2008.4811326

46. Rescorla, E.: The transport layer security (TLS) protocol version 1.3. RFC 8446, RFC Editor, August 2018

47. Sherry, J., Lan, C., Popa, R.A., Ratnasamy, S.: BlindBox: deep packet inspection over encrypted traffic. In: Proceedings of the 2015 ACM Conference on Special Interest Group on Data Communication, SIGCOMM 2015, pp. 213–226. ACM, New York (2015). https://doi.org/10.1145/2785956.2787502

48. Trach, B., Krohmer, A., Gregor, F., Arnautov, S., Bhatotia, P., Fetzer, C.: ShieldBox: secure middleboxes using shielded execution. In: Proceedings of the Symposium on SDN Research, SOSR 2018, pp. 2:1–2:14. ACM, New York (2018). https://doi.org/10.1145/3185467.3185469

49. Tuecke, S., Welch, V., Pearlman, D.E.L., Thompson, M.: Internet X.509 public key infrastructure (PKI) proxy certificate profile. RFC 3820, RFC Editor, June 2004. http://www.rfc-editor.org/rfc/rfc3820.txt

Anomaly-Based Network Intrusion Detection Using Wavelets and Adversarial Autoencoders

Samir Puuska$^{(\boxtimes)}$, Tero Kokkonen, Janne Alatalo, and Eppu Heilimo

Institute of Information Technology, JAMK University of Applied Sciences,
Jyväskylä, Finland
{samir.puuska,tero.kokkonen,janne.alatalo,eppu.heilimo}@jamk.fi

Abstract. The number of intrusions and attacks against data networks and networked systems increases constantly, while encryption has made it more difficult to inspect network traffic and classify it as malicious. In this paper, an anomaly-based intrusion detection system using Haar wavelet transforms in combination with an adversarial autoencoder was developed for detecting malicious TLS-encrypted Internet traffic. Data containing legitimate, as well as advanced malicious traffic was collected from a large-scale cyber exercise and used in the analysis. Based on the findings and domain expertise, a set of features for distinguishing modern malware from packet timing analysis were chosen and evaluated. Performance of the adversarial autoencoder was compared with a traditional autoencoder. The results indicate that the adversarial model performs better than the traditional autoencoder. In addition, a machine learning pipeline capable of analyzing traffic in near real time was developed for data analysis.

Keywords: Adversarial autoencoder · Intrusion detection · Anomaly detection · Haar wavelets

1 Introduction

The Internet is becoming more secure as encryption becomes more ubiquitous and new standards are adopted. Web pages and other related assets that make up modern web applications are more often transferred using Transport Layer Security (TLS). In addition to providing security to end users, it also allows malicious actors to leverage encryption for evading detection. Therefore, it is extremely important to know the situation of your own valuable assets in the network. For accomplishing that task, one must maintain good visibility into the network, despite of increasing encryption.

Artificial intelligence (AI) and its applications for cyber security are active and growing research fields. Pham et al. compared various machine learning techniques commonly used for intrusion detection [20], while Dhingra et al. outlined

© Springer Nature Switzerland AG 2019
J.-L. Lanet and C. Toma (Eds.): SecITC 2018, LNCS 11359, pp. 234–246, 2019.
https://doi.org/10.1007/978-3-030-12942-2_18

several different application areas and challenges for AI in the enterprise information security landscape [6]. Hendler et al. used neural networks for detecting malicious PowerShell commands [9]. Various novel approaches, such as neural immune detectors, Short-Term Memory Recurrent Neural Networks, and Stacked Auto-Encoders (SAE) have also been studied for attack detection [13,14,25]. Intrusion detection systems (IDS) can be divided into anomaly-based detection (anomaly detection) and signature-based detection (misuse detection). Anomaly detection has capability to detect unknown attack patterns; however, anomaly detection usually generates a large amount of false positive indications [19].

Modern intrusions and malware are tasked from the Internet by malicious actors using so-called command and control (C2) channels. Modern malware utilizes various techniques, such as encryption and steganography, for avoiding the detection of communication with a C2 server. TLS is an extremely good way of hiding the command and control traffic because it has become almost ubiquitous, and the recent efforts at hardening TLS infrastructure, such as certificate preloading or easily obtainable free legitimate certificates, have made certificate bumping and other deep inspection methods unreliable. This paper focuses on malware that utilizes TLS for evasion.

This paper presents an anomaly detection -based IDS that leverage Haar wavelet transforms and Adversarial Autoencoders (AA). First, the reasoning about selected features and methods is presented. Next, the implemented solution and validation results are shown. Finally, future research topics are given along with a discussion.

2   Feature Engineering and Selection

Feature selection is the key element in anomaly detection, determining the maximal effectiveness of the detection capability. Chandola et al. [4], and Sommer et al. [22] both listed several challenges in applying machine learning to anomaly detection. One of the challenges they mentioned is how to select features that actually vary between legitimate and malicious traffic, and defining an effective boundary between them. They also noted that when a malicious actor is involved, the adversary is able to adapt.

Due to the increasing ratio of encrypted traffic, the features cannot utilize the payload of the network packets. In the Internet Protocol (IP) packets, the fields cannot be encrypted and are available for feature engineering. Packet timings, and TLS connection parameters, such as handshake parameter negotiation, are also available.

Networks and Internet traffic are not static in volume or content. They experience considerable variance depending on many factors such as workday cycles, scheduled software updates, or changes in workforce structure. More formally, time series based on our features are non-stationary.

The aim of feature selection is to use as much feature engineering as possible to filter out variances in data that are known to be irrelevant. In addition, the features used must not be readily attacker controlled or circumvented.

2.1   TLS Fingerprints

In the TLS handshake the client and server agree what cryptographic suites they will use. The client sends its preferred suites in preferred order in a package dubbed "ClientHello" [21]. The order, number, and types of these suites vary considerably between web browsers, desktop applications and other programs, thus forming a sort of fingerprint.

Common malware and various APT-simulation tools, such as CobaltStrike[1], Empire[2], and Meterpreter[3], were analysed. It was discovered that their TLS handshakes were either unique or different than legitimate programs. Specific versions of Firefox browsers used in Kali Linux[4], a well known penetration testing tool collection, was also detected. This is in line with previous research; for example, Husák et al. obtained similar results when fingerprinting applications [10]. Although preliminary look into this feature gave extremely positive results, it is also something that the adversary may choose to change, as e.g. TOR meek[5] does. The feature is still useful in a limited manner, it groups applications reliably and only the most sophisticated adversary can tailor the malware traffic to look like the one a particular target organization is using. It should be noted that e.g. PowerShell environment, often used for running malicious code, does not allow the scripts to select preferred suites. We did not use TLS fingerprints in the neural network input data.

The malware used in this research was tasked to beacon to the C2 server from several hours to days. After that the malware was used to perform various malicious activities, such as listing processes, transferring files, taking screenshots, and for further lateral movement on the internal networks. First infection was achieved using either phishing e-mails, or custom-made zero-day exploits.

2.2   Network Flows and Time Series

Network flows form a natural time series, especially when considering those made with Transmission Control Protocol (TCP). Depending on the application, these flows will vary with respect to duration, number of packets transmitted and received, and periodicity, among other characterizing statistics. As previously stated, these time series are non-stationary. This is partly due to the inherent nature of TCP flows, as well as the aim to keep once-negotiated tunnels up for subsequent data transfer, rather than renegotiate. This is also true for TLS, which in virtually any application, runs on top of TCP.

There are several well-know legitimate use cases for TLS encrypted connections. The most ubiquitous one is the World Wide Web; virtually every major

---

[1] https://www.cobaltstrike.com/.
[2] https://www.powershellempire.com/.
[3] https://www.offensive-security.com/metasploit-unleashed/about-meterpreter/.
[4] https://www.kali.org/.
[5] https://trac.torproject.org/projects/tor/wiki/doc/meek.

web application is accessible or mandates the use of TLS. Virtual Private Networks (VPN) may also be deployed on top of TLS. Compared to the web browsing, these connections can be longer-lived, and their activity is more varying. The third major category is desktop applications, which use TLS to connect securely to their back-ends which may reside either on an internal network or the Internet.

As for malware, TLS provides a practical channel for communicating with Command and Control (C2) servers. It blends in easily with legitimate network traffic, and in many deployments is permitted through firewalls. However, these connections are not usually similar to the legitimate use cases. In the analyzed malware and APT tools, the connections were very short-lived when there were no instructions available for them in their C2 server. When they are tasked to e.g. transfer files or take screenshots, the connections looked different. Based on these observations it was concluded that an aggregation of TLS connections using the IP address or Server Name Indication (SNI) record, the result will form a descriptive time series usable for anomaly detection. This series can be constructed from packet timings and sizes made into an impulse signal, where received packets have negative values, sent packets positive values and where the impulse values are the packet sizes.

2.3   Analysis Using Haar Wavelets

There are many options for characterizing a time series. It is important to use a representation that retains the essential features for the classification task at hand without overfitting the data. By considering overfitting also at this stage, the input to the classification algorithm can be made less noisy. Due to the non-stationary nature of our data, the methods at our disposal are somewhat limited. The differing lengths of the series also needs to be addressed.

There are two main categories for mathematical time series representations, data-adaptive and non data-adaptive [15]. Haar wavelets [8], a non data-adaptive representation, was chosen. The transform contains both time and frequency elements, and is therefore advantageous for data which is both non-stationary and sparse [3,5].

Figure 1 illustrates the result of decomposition as it is used in this study. The image represents eight of the lowest frequency coefficient layers from the wavelet transformation result. Brighter areas represent higher coefficient values and the black areas have coefficients values very close to zero. The number of coefficient samples doubles on each layer when more layers are taken. The new layers represent higher and higher frequencies. The solution is designed to examine the long, low frequency traffic patterns so it is safe to discard the high frequency layers. In this study, only the eight coefficient layers that represent the lowest frequencies are kept.

(a) Legitimate web browser traffic to an authentication portal.

(b) Malicious traffic caused by a CobaltStrike beacon.

Fig. 1. Wavelet decomposition, illustrated here with scalograms, for both legitimate and malicious TLS traffic samples.

2.4 Adversarial Autoencoders

The wavelet transform provides a starting point for anomaly detection. However, the comparison of the decomposition results is a non-trivial task. There are no obvious ways to assign probabilities to real-valued time series or their transformations in this dataset.

Autoencoders are constructed using artificial neural networks that attempt to reconstruct their input using a relatively small hidden (latent) layer, in a fashion similar to the Principal Component Analysis. Adversarial autoencoders have several desired properties for anomaly detection, especially in our use case. Adversarial autoencoders (AA) combine ideas from traditional autoencoders and generative adversarial networks, turning autoencoders into generative models. AAs are suitable for unsupervised learning, or they can also be used in supervised or semi-supervised fashion [7,17]. Their advantage over traditional AAs is the ability to influence what distribution the hidden layer should approximate. This allows the model to learn additional variance that is not present in the training data, making it less likely overfitted. Adversarial autoencoders use generative adversarial neural networks for regulating the distribution of the autoencoder's latent space (the latent). The encoder of the network is trained to fool the discriminator by generating vectors similar to the chosen distribution, while the discriminator is trained to determine if the sample is generated or from the chosen distribution. Meanwhile, the decoder is trained to reconstruct the input data from the latent space. [17] The reconstruction loss and generation loss are optimized for each batch using separate optimizers, hence the calculated gradients are applied in turns.

Figure 2 shows the general architecture of the neural network design developed during this research. It is based on the architecture proposed by Makhzani

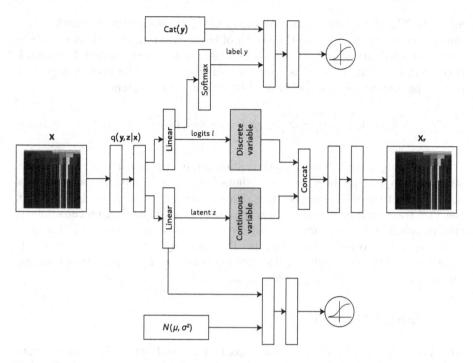

Fig. 2. The general architecture of the neural network design used in this research. The encoder's outputs latent z and label y are enforced to match the selected distributions by establishing a two-player adversarial min-max game between the discriminator and the generator/encoder [17]. The circles represent adversarial loss, while X_r represents the reconstruction.

et al. [17]. The AA variant in this study (TLS-AAE) is trained unsupervised, and regularized with a continuous distribution. This allows the TLS-AA to better reconstruct input variants not present in the training dataset, resulting in a lower reconstruction error than a traditional autoencoder. Although the reconstruction of the new variants is beneficial for reducing the number of false positives, the network might learn to reconstruct anomalies as well. To counter the unwanted variants, a one-hot categorical distribution was imposed into softmax of the latent, dividing the latent space into clusters of continuous distributions. The amount of clusters can be set using a parameter, that is 20 in this study. The number of clusters does not determine or depend on the labels or classes the network can predict. The TLS-AAE, trained in an unsupervised fashion, uses the classes as a way to utilize the latent space more efficiently.

By utilizing the discrete variable y, the TLS-AAE can output what it considers the best cluster for each input. The clusters are used in a cost function; the cost function is added to the cluster variable (logits l), and it penalizes small Euclidean distances between any two points belonging to different clusters. If the distance between cluster boundaries is over a chosen threshold, it is set to zero.

Since the TLS-AAE uses a Gaussian distribution as the continuous distribution, the cluster threshold is set to the length of three standard deviations to ensure that the probability of outlier variants between clusters is minimized. Equation 1 is the cost function, where C is a set containing point sets for each cluster, and $d_{\min}$ is the desired minimum distance between any two clusters.

$$L(C, d_{\min}) = \frac{1}{|C|} \sum_{x \in C_i} \sum_{y \in C_j, \ i \neq j} \max \left\{ 0, d_{\min} - ||x - y||^2 \right\} \tag{1}$$

By utilizing several different optimization targets the latent space can be constructed to approximate what the authors believe are reasonable assumptions about the nature of TLS connections. This reasoning stems from the idea that the TLS traffic can be divided into several categories depending on the application responsible for generating it; web browsing, music streaming services, and malware should form distinct clusters. The anomaly detection is done by calculating the squared Euclidean distance between the input and output image. Squared error magnifies larger errors while disregards small ones.

3   Analysis Pipeline

The TLS-AAE was implemented as a part of an analysis pipeline for evaluating real-world performance and suitability. The implementation was made using open source software frameworks. The pipeline works in any network where the traffic can be mirrored for the analysis system for inspection. Figure 3 illustrates the architecture of the pipeline. The line consists of two main components, the preprocessing pipeline and the machine learning model.

3.1   Data Processing

In the start of the pipeline, a slightly modified version of Suricata IDS software [23] was used for constructing network flows from the individual mirrored packets. The modification to Suricata software was made for collecting individual packet timings for each flow.

The main pipeline functionality was implemented using Apache Kafka [1] as a message queue. Suricata was configured to send the flows to one of the Kafka topics. From there, the flows are consumed using Apache Spark [2] platform running a custom preprocessing and feature extraction script. The extracted features are then sent back to Kafka, and delivered to the machine learning algorithm. In the final step of the pipeline the TLS-AAE returns the anomaly scores back to Kafka, after predicting the anomaly score.

The Apache Spark platform was used for extracting the needed features from flows. It was used for flow filtering, flow aggregation, and wavelet calculation by writing a custom script. The script filters all the flows that are not TLS traffic and aggregates the flows using a time window. The aggregation joins flows in a specified time window using source IP, destination IP, destination port and JA3 hash[6]. The JA3 hash is used in aggregation to separate different applications on a host.

The flows include the timing and size information for every packet. Packet timings are reduced from microseconds to seconds in accuracy to reduce unnecessary computational complexity. The packet timings and sizes are made into an impulse signal, where the received packets have negative values, sent packets positive values, the impulse values being the packet sizes. The signal is zero-padded from both ends so that the length of the signal is power of two and the minimum length is reached. The minimum length of the signal depends on how many layers from the wavelet transformation are needed.

The wavelet transform is calculated for the signal using the Haar mother wavelet. Only the last N layers of the transform result are maintained so that all the results are of the same size regardless of the original signal length. The wavelet result is then transformed to an $X \times Y$ matrix. The transformation is made so that the results are easy to visualize. Absolute values are taken from the coefficients and the matrix values are normalized per matrix. The matrix is made in a way that each detail coefficient value populates equal amount of elements in the matrix. Figure 1 shows the matrix transformation visualized as an image. The color in the image represents the element value. The lower squares in the image represent the higher frequencies and the position from the left represents in which time the frequency has happened in the signal.

The results are sent back to Kafka where the machine learning algorithm can consume it and produce the anomaly score as the result.

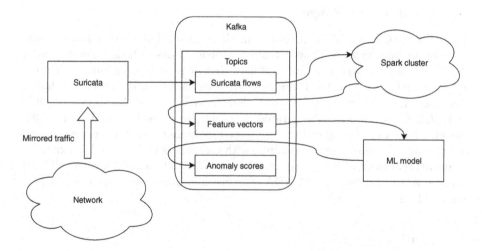

Fig. 3. Architecture of the implemented IDS solution

---

[6] https://github.com/salesforce/ja3.

3.2   Dataset

A relevant and modern dataset is required for training, testing, and evaluating a IDS solution. Although some public datasets, such as the DARPA intrusion detection evaluation dataset [16] exists, they tend to be dated and not suitable for modern research. They lack both up-to-date cyber attacks, and modern traffic profile.

Since 2013 the Finnish national cyber security exercise has been conducted using the RGCE Cyber Range. In 2018 the exercise was organized by The Ministry of Defence, The Security Committee, and JAMK University of Applied Sciences. The exercise is a large-scale live cyber security exercise, with more than 100 individuals from different national security authorities exercising cooperation during the cyber incidents [18].

The data set used in this study was created from network traffic captured during the exercise. The whole traffic capture, at full packet level, consists of over 100,000,000 network flows from which a subset of 56,408,665 flows were captured from a place where anomaly traffic was present. This subset was used to create the training and testing data sets. The data set contains 729,998 flows that are TLS traffic, of which 665 flows are malicious.

The flows contain both human and auto-generated web browsing traffic, authentication portal logins, automatic updates of software, e-mail protocols that use TLS, and other common benign activity. Malicious flows were generated by Meterpreter, Empire, or CobaltStrike.

3.3   RGCE Cyber Range

The Realistic Global Cyber Environment (RGCE) is a holistic cyber range suitable for various tasks such as training, exercises, research and development. RGCE mimics the structure and traffic of real Internet. For example, ISP tiers are emulated using real hardware and structure. Network distances and latencies reflect those in real world, up to including packet losses. The network traffic of RGCE Cyber Range is generated according to a realistic end user traffic model, which augments the traffic generated by humans. RGCE includes industry specific organization environments, with complex deployments. For example, financial organization, electricity company and Internet service providers all have realistic AD infrastructure, SCADA systems, and other specialized production assets [11,12].

4   Results

The evaluation of the performance was made by using the receiver operating characteristic (ROC) curve by plotting the true positive rate (TPR) to y-axis and false positive rate (FPR) to x-axis [24]. Overall, the following characteristics were considered: TPR, FPR, and accuracy [19,24].

For evaluation of TLS-AAE, the prediction results were compared against a traditional autoencoder. The performance characteristics are listed in Table 1 and ROC curves are plotted in Fig. 4.

The results indicate that the TLS-AAE achieves similar TPR as the plain counterpart. However, the FPR is considerably lower, resulting in better accu-

Table 1. Performance characteristics

Method	TPR	FPR	Accuracy
TLS-AAE	95%	36%	65%
Plain autoencoder	97%	47%	55%

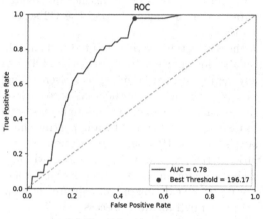

(a) Traditional autoencoder

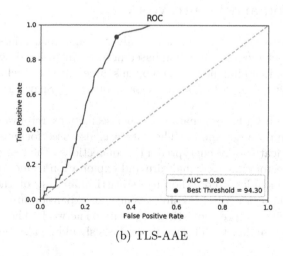

(b) TLS-AAE

Fig. 4. Receiver operating characteristic curves for both plain autoencoder and the TLS-AAE. Best thresholds are based on the best ratio.

racy. The input image of the autoencoder is 128 × 128 pixels and the grayscale values vary between 0 and 255 integers. Both autoencoders have two dense layers of 2048 units in both encoder and decoder. The bottleneck of the adversarial autoencoder consists of 10 dimensional latent and 20 dimensional cluster linearly activated variables. For consistency, the traditional autoencoders latent is 30 dimensional. The output of the decoder uses sigmoid activation to map the decoded values between 0 and 1.

5 Discussion

Based on the findings, the Haar wavelet transform seems to provide adequate representation on the nature of the TLS connections in the dataset, allowing categorization. Time window aggregation of distinct but related TLS flows captures malicious programs that infrequently poll the C2 server, opening a new TLS connection each time.

Considering that the connections were encrypted and only the size and timing information was available for analysis, the unsupervised TLS-AAE was able to construct a relatively representative latent space. Even though the dataset is relatively extensive in size, the variance of the flows is constricted. The relatively high false positive rate is partly explained by non-malicious outliers. The number of false positives can be drastically lowered by augmenting the results with other means of traffic analysis, such as IP/domain reputation.

The modified Suricata IDS, Spark, Kafka, and TensorFlow – in combination – proved to be a working base for an IDS solution. As Suricata can either process live mirrored traffic or replay an existing packet capture, developing models using the platform is relatively straightforward process.

6 Conclusion and Future Work

In this study Haar wavelet transforms and adversarial autoencoders were applied for constructing an anomaly detection based network intrusion detection system. For evaluation, a data pipeline based on open source software, including Suricata IDS, TensorFlow framework, Kafka message bus, and Spark framework, was constructed.

Network data from Finnish national cyber security exercise was used for the evaluation of the proposed model. The data was also used for finding and engineering suitable features for encrypted TLS connections. The test data included various attack vectors made by malware and exploitation frameworks.

Future work includes a more thorough statistical analysis on the TLS-AAE's latent space and its structure. Possible avenues of expansion are combining the current model with a more sophisticated predictor network. The wavelet transform and its applicability for TLS traffic analysis should be also further studied.

Acknowledgment. This research project is funded by MATINE - The Scientific Advisory Board for Defence.

References

1. Apache Kafka: Apache kafka a distributed streaming platform. https://kafka.apache.org/. Accessed 31 Aug 2018
2. Apache Spark: Apache Spark lightning-fast unified analytics engine. https://spark.apache.org/ Accessed 31 Aug 2018
3. Chan, K., Fu, W.: Efficient time series matching by wavelets. In: Proceedings 15th International Conference on Data Engineering (Cat. No. 99CB36337), pp. 126–133, March 1999. https://doi.org/10.1109/ICDE.1999.754915
4. Chandola, V., Banerjee, A., Kumar, V.: Anomaly detection: a survey. ACM Comput. Surv. **41**(3), 15:1–15:58 (2009). https://doi.org/10.1145/1541880.1541882
5. Daubechies, I.: The wavelet transform, time-frequency localization and signal analysis. IEEE Trans. Inf. Theory **36**(5), 961–1005 (1990). https://doi.org/10.1109/18.57199
6. Dhingra, M., Jain, M., Jadon, R.S.: Role of artificial intelligence in enterprise information security: a review. In: 2016 Fourth International Conference on Parallel, Distributed and Grid Computing (PDGC), pp. 188–191, December 2016. https://doi.org/10.1109/PDGC.2016.7913142
7. Goodfellow, I., et al.: Generative adversarial nets. In: Ghahramani, Z., Welling, M., Cortes, C., Lawrence, N.D., Weinberger, K.Q. (eds.) Advances in Neural Information Processing Systems, vol. 27, pp. 2672–2680. Curran Associates, Inc. (2014)
8. Haar, A.: Zur theorie der orthogonalen funktionensysteme. Mathematische Annalen **69**(3), 331–371 (1910). https://doi.org/10.1007/BF01456326
9. Hendler, D., Kels, S., Rubin, A.: Detecting malicious powershell commands using deep neural networks. In: Proceedings of the 2018 on Asia Conference on Computer and Communications Security, ASIACCS 2018, pp. 187–197. ACM, New York (2018). https://doi.org/10.1145/3196494.3196511
10. Husák, M., Čermák, M., Jirsík, T., Čeleda, P.: HTTPS traffic analysis and client identification using passive SSL/TLS fingerprinting. EURASIP J. Inf. Secur. **2016**(1), 6 (2016). https://doi.org/10.1186/s13635-016-0030-7
11. JAMK University of Applied Sciences, Institute of Information Technology, JYV-SECTEC: Rgce cyber range. http://www.jyvsectec.fi/en/rgce/. Accessed 23 Aug 2018
12. Kokkonen, T., Puuska, S.: Blue team communication and reporting for enhancing situational awareness from white team perspective in cyber security exercises. In: Galinina, O., Andreev, S., Balandin, S., Koucheryavy, Y. (eds.) NEW2AN/ruSMART -2018. LNCS, vol. 11118, pp. 277–288. Springer, Cham (2018). https://doi.org/10.1007/978-3-030-01168-0_26
13. Komar, M., et al.: High performance adaptive system for cyber attacks detection. In: 2017 9th IEEE International Conference on Intelligent Data Acquisition and Advanced Computing Systems: Technology and Applications (IDAACS), vol. 2, pp. 853–858, September 2017. https://doi.org/10.1109/IDAACS.2017.8095208
14. Le, T., Kim, J., Kim, H.: An effective intrusion detection classifier using long short-term memory with gradient descent optimization. In: 2017 International Conference on Platform Technology and Service (PlatCon), pp. 1–6, February 2017. https://doi.org/10.1109/PlatCon.2017.7883684
15. Lin, J., Keogh, E., Lonardi, S., Chiu, B.: A symbolic representation of time series, with implications for streaming algorithms. In: Proceedings of the 8th ACM SIGMOD Workshop on Research Issues in Data Mining and Knowledge Discovery, DMKD 2003, pp. 2–11. ACM, New York (2003). https://doi.org/10.1145/882082.882086

16. Lippmann, R.P., et al.: Evaluating intrusion detection systems: the 1998 DARPA off-line intrusion detection evaluation. In: Proceedings DARPA Information Survivability Conference and Exposition, DISCEX 2000, vol. 2, pp. 12–26, January 2000. https://doi.org/10.1109/DISCEX.2000.821506

17. Makhzani, A., Shlens, J., Jaitly, N., Goodfellow, I.: Adversarial autoencoders. In: International Conference on Learning Representations (2016). http://arxiv.org/abs/1511.05644

18. Ministry of Defence Finland: The national cyber security exercises is organised in Jyväskylä - Kansallinen kyberturvallisuusharjoitus kyha18 järjestetään Jyväskylässä, official bulletin 11th of May 2018, May 2018. https://valtioneuvosto.fi/artikkeli/-/asset_publisher/kansallinen-kyberturvallisuusharjoitus-kyha18-jarjestetaan-jyvaskylassa. Accessed 23 Aug 2018

19. Mokarian, A., Faraahi, A., Delavar, A.G.: False positives reduction techniques in intrusion detection systems-a review. IJCSNS Int. J. Comput. Sci. Netw. Secur. **13**(10), 128–134 (2013)

20. Pham, T.S., Hoang, T.H., Vu, V.C.: Machine learning techniques for web intrusion detection – a comparison. In: 2016 Eighth International Conference on Knowledge and Systems Engineering (KSE), pp. 291–297, October 2016. https://doi.org/10.1109/KSE.2016.7758069

21. Rescorla, E., Dierks, T.: The Transport Layer Security (TLS) Protocol Version 1.2. RFC 5246, August 2008. https://doi.org/10.17487/RFC5246

22. Sommer, R., Paxson, V.: Outside the closed world: on using machine learning for network intrusion detection. In: 2010 IEEE Symposium on Security and Privacy, pp. 305–316, May 2010. https://doi.org/10.1109/SP.2010.25

23. Suricata: Suricata Open Source IDS/IPS/NSM engine. https://suricata-ids.org/. Accessed 31 Aug 2018

24. Suyal, P., Pant, J., Dwivedi, A., Lohani, M.C.: Performance evaluation of rough set based classification models to intrusion detection system. In: 2016 2nd International Conference on Advances in Computing, Communication, Automation (ICACCA) (Fall), pp. 1–6, September 2016. https://doi.org/10.1109/ICACCAF.2016.7748991

25. Vartouni, A.M., Kashi, S.S., Teshnehlab, M.: An anomaly detection method to detect web attacks using stacked auto-encoder. In: 2018 6th Iranian Joint Congress on Fuzzy and Intelligent Systems (CFIS), pp. 131–134, February 2018. https://doi.org/10.1109/CFIS.2018.8336654

Analysis and Evaluation of Dynamic Feature-Based Malware Detection Methods

Arzu Gorgulu Kakisim$^{(\boxtimes)}$, Mert Nar, Necmettin Carkaci,
and Ibrahim Sogukpinar

Gebze Technical University, 41400 Kocaeli, Turkey
{arzukakisim,m.nar,ncarkaci,ispinar}@gtu.edu.tr

Abstract. While increasing the threat of malware for information systems, researchers strive to find alternative malware detection methods based on static, dynamic and hybrid analysis. Due to obfuscation techniques to bypass the static analysis, dynamic methods become more useful to detect malware. Therefore, most of the researches focus on dynamic behavior analysis of malicious software. In this work, our main objective is to find more discriminative dynamic features to detect malware executables by analyzing different dynamic features with common malware detection approaches. Moreover, we analyze separately different features obtained in dynamic analysis, such as API-call, usage system library and operations, to observe the contributions of these features to malware detection and classification success. For this purpose, we evaluate the performance of some dynamic feature-based malware detection and classification approaches using four data sets that contain real and synthetic malware executables.

Keywords: Malware detection · Dynamic analysis ·
Polymorphic/metamorphic malware · API-call · Usage system library ·
Behavior-based analysis

1 Introduction

With the spreading of digitalization in the world, the number of attacks using malicious codes have increased dramatically. According to the AV technical report 2017/18, the number of new malware reached 121.7 Million in 2017 and 34.9 million in the first quarter of 2018 [1]. Therefore, malware detection becomes important research topic for computer and information technology systems.

Most of malware detection systems generally use static techniques such as signature-based and anomaly-based detection techniques. Some systems make a signature matching to determine whether a program is a virus while some systems try to find anomalies from the code structure. To understand of the code structure, static methods examine malware programs without running them [3]. They aim to find distinctive features from the API-calls, [4], opcode structures

© Springer Nature Switzerland AG 2019
J.-L. Lanet and C. Toma (Eds.): SecITC 2018, LNCS 11359, pp. 247–258, 2019.
https://doi.org/10.1007/978-3-030-12942-2_19

[5] and control flow graphs [6] of the malware programs. However, new generation malware executables can modify their signatures or structures by applying obfuscation techniques like polymorphism, oligomorphism, metamorphism and encryption [2] to bypass static analysis. For instance, metamorphic malware executables have ability to change their content, size, and signature by using disassembler, code analyzer, code transformer and assembler in order to create their mutants. Therefore, static methods can be ineffective to detect these new generation executables. Dynamic-based malware detection come into prominence because it is more resistant against code obfuscations.

In dynamic analysis, malware behavior is monitored by tracing its Windows API-calls and network interactions by executing the malware in a virtual environment. To detect malicious behavior, these monitored API-call information are used by the dynamic malware detection methods. API-call information contains the function names, parameters and return values of an executable. Dynamic methods try to extract distinctive features to identify malware programs using the frequency and sequence of API-calls [11–14]. API-call frequency may indicate how important an API-call for a malware, while API-call sequence indicates the knowledge about how important consecutive behaviors of the malware. In addition, some dynamic methods [17] utilize additional behaviors executed during API calls. These additional information (mutex, dynamic-link library, file operation etc.) can give valuable information about malware.

In this work, our main objective is to compare the performance of different common malware detection approaches by using different features obtained by dynamic analysis. We analyze different dynamic-based features separately to observe the contributions of these features to malware detection and classification success. Therefore, we extract most common dynamic features such as API calls, usage of system libraries and operations for mutexes, registries, and files. We aim to obtain more discriminative dynamic-based feature subsets from many features with a feature selection process. In this work, the detection performance of the metamorphic malware families is also evaluated. Therefore, different metamorphic and real malware executables have been collected to test performance of the approaches on accuracy. In addition, we aim to test the effect of the number of malware samples and the effect of the number of malware families on the performance of the compared approaches. For this reason, we have created four data with different characteristics.

The rest of this work is organized as follows. Section 2 presents the related works for the malware detection. In Sect. 3, common dynamic features with common dynamic approaches are presented. The experimental results and discussion are given in Sect. 4. Conclusion and future works are explained in Sect. 5.

2 Related Works

While increasing the threat of malware for information systems, researchers try to find alternative malware detection methods. To determine whether the unknown software poses a threat for a system, the efficient and effective way is to analyze behavior of the software. Behavior analysis covers the observation and indication of all activities executed by the software, hence allowing to catch any malicious one [7]. Many studies have applied dynamic analysis techniques which monitor behaviors of the programs by executing in safe environment. Bayer et al. [8] propose a method which aim at capturing common behaviors of malware programs by analyzing a huge number of malware mutation files. Bai et al. [9] propose a dynamic malware detection scheme based on the frequency of API-calls. Hansen et al. [10] analyze the API-call frequencies and API-call sequences of the malware executables by monitoring API-calls. Shaid et al. [11] propose a method which creates malware behavior images by mapping API-calls to colors in order to detect malware variants. Pektas [12] proposes an API-call sequence-based detection method by applying online machine learning algorithms. In [13], function call sequences are used with Hidden Markov Model to classify malware. In [14], API-call sequences are used with sequence alignment algorithms. Non-critical API-functions are eliminated to improve efficiency of the detection algorithms. In [15,16], text-mining algorithms are applied on the API-call sequences. In [15], some operation, location and parameter information of each API-call are analyzed to identify malware behavior. Udayakumar et al. [17] focus on analysis of unsafe dynamic linked libraries loaded by portable executable files. In [18], a hybrid approach is proposed to extract common features of malware instances using both static and dynamic analysis. Choi et al. [18] propose a hybrid approach that extracts common features of malware instances using both static and dynamic analysis. They utilize dynamic-link libraries and functions that are called by API-calls. Gandotra et al. [19] use the frequency of system operations which are activated by portable executables to identify malicious instances.

3   Dynamic Analysis and Detection Methods

In this section, we give brief information about dynamic malware analysis and detection approaches which we focus on in this work.

3.1   Dynamic Behaviors of Malware

Dynamic Analysis. Dynamic analysis is performed by observing the actions of a program while the program is running on a real or safe environment. With dynamic analysis, the behaviors, functionality and indicators of the program, that allow us to decide whether a program is malicious or not, can be identified. The process of dynamic analysis consists of three steps: to setup and disinfect an environment, to execute the malware, and to monitor and log malware behaviors. The log files provide detail information about files that are opened, accessed or called. There are two ways of performing dynamic analysis; manual or automatic analysis. In manual dynamic analysis, a debugger is generally used for tracing malware samples [21]. However, this process is time-consuming due to tracing all execution step by step [12]. In addition, the information obtained with manual analysis is not suitable applying learning algorithms such as data mining and machine learning [22]. In automatic dynamic analysis, tracing of the program behaviors is performed by some typical tools such as CWSandbox [23] and Cuckoo [24]. These tools take a file as input and execute it in virtual environment. Program executables can be analyzed dynamically in two ways: function call monitoring and information flow tracking. During the function call monitoring, the tool captures the function calls by calling hook function. Hooking function is a technic that allows to intercept function calls [7]. Another way of performing automatic dynamic analysis is to track information flow. With information flow tracking, how the program operates the data is monitored during the execution of the program. To track target data, data is labeled [25].

API-Calls. Application programming interface (API) is a procedure provided by the operating system [26]. API functions can be divided into six distinct categories according to core-functionality: network management, memory management, registry operations, file I/O, processor and threads, and socket [15]. To consume base services to access resources such as file systems, processes and windows registry, application programs execute the API functions [16]. Therefore, significant clues can be obtained about behavior of the applications by analyzing the arguments, definitions, purposes and results of API functions [26]. To extract dynamic characteristics of a program, most dynamic approaches use API-call sequences by tracing each function call in sequence [9].

Usage System Library. Executing a portable executable (PE) file cause at least one process to begin. In virtual environment, executable files are analyzed in process level. Processes are monitored while PE file executes. It is observed that processes load some system files or dynamic linked libraries (DLL) such as KERNEL32.DLL, NTDLL.DLL and USER32.DLL. These system files cohesively contain API functions which allow accessing system resources including files, registry, mutex, processes, network information etc. In windows system, the interface which provides these functions is WIN32 API. In PE file format which windows executable is in, there is section for API functions called by the executable and their corresponding DLL; namely Import Address Table (IAT). This data structure is an array of pointers to make API functions be called [23]. Files and DLLs perform operations which serve functionality around duty of DLL belonged [15]. During execution of the program, dynamic sequential features can be obtained by monitoring the system libraries. This sequential data can be used to find meaningful patterns to analyze behaviors of malicious or benign programs.

Operations. Applications implement some operations such as file operation, registry key operations and network operations by calling API functions [28]. In virtual environment, it is possible to monitor these effects dynamically. Instead of taking API-call as a feature set, some malware detection approaches focus on these dynamic operations. Operations can be divided into twelve classes:

file failed, file opened, file created, file read, file exists, file deleted, registry key opened, registry key deleted, registry key read, DLL loaded, file written and directory enumerated [6]. To analyze the program behavior, the knowledge of how many times an operation has been performed can be an important information.

3.2   Malware Detection Methods Based on Dynamic Analysis

Feature Extraction. In dynamic malware analysis, malicious files are executed in an isolated virtual environment for monitoring and capturing any malicious activity. In order to be able to decide whether an executable is malware or benign, descriptive and distinctive patterns are extracted from executables in a learning phase. Various data mining techniques can be applied to represent a feature space belonging to dynamic behaviors, to select valuable attributes and to classify the files as malware or benign. One of the most frequently used feature extraction methods is the term and inverse term frequency (TF-IDF) [27], when an attribute is characterized as discrete and frequency-based [28]. TF-IDF is frequently used to represent dynamic-based features of malware [20,21,29]. TF of a term (for example, an API-call) for a file is the number of times this term appears in the API-call sequence of the file. It indicates how frequently an API-call occurs in the executable. IDF is computed as the logarithm of the ratio number of the samples in the corpus to the number of the samples where the specific API-call appears. High IDF value of an API-call indicates that this API-call occurs in relatively few documents. Given a file collection D, a term t, and an individual file $d \in D$, TF-IDF value is calculated as given in Eq. 1 where, $f_{t,d}$ is the number of times t appears in d, $f_{t,D}$ is the number of files in which t appears in D, and $|D|$ is the size of the file collection.

$$TF - IDF(t,d) = f_{t,d} * log(|D|/f_{t,D}) \qquad (1)$$

TF-IDF approach does not consider the sequences of terms. For instance, API-call sequence of a malware file can be important to understand the behavior of program [30]. Therefore, the n-gram model [31] is extensively used for representation of API-call sequences [10,11,30]. N-gram is a contiguous sequence

API Call Sequence
GetModuleHandle, GetProcAddress, RegEnumKeyEx, LoadLibrary, VirtualAllocEx, RegCreateKeyEx

2-Gram
GetModuleHandle-GetProcAddress, GetProcAddress-RegEnumKeyEx, RegEnumKeyEx-LoadLibrary, LoadLibrary-VirtualAllocEx, VirtualAllocEx-RegCreateKeyEx

3-Gram
GetModuleHandle-GeProcAddress-RegEnumKeyEx, GetProcAddress-RegEnumKeyEx-LoadLibrary, RegEnumKeyEx-LoadLibrary-VirtualAllocEx, LoadLibrary-VirtualAllocEx-RegCreateKeyEx

Fig. 1. The n-gram sample representation

of n terms which appears in the file. With n-gram method, common consecutive terms between malware samples can be identified. Bi-gram (2-gram) is the most common usage of n-gram because extracting three-gram, four-gram etc. of API-call sequence is time-consuming. The n-gram sample representation for an API-call sequence is given in Fig. 1. The frequencies of the bi-grams can be valuable to distinguish malware or benign files. In addition, some classification algorithms which models sequential data (e.g. Hidden Markov Model (HMM)) can be executed on the bi-grams.

Detection and Classification Methods. Malware detection and classification methods can be used to detect benign and malware using a set of observations based on a set of attributes. On the other hand, these methods are used in order to classify unknown malware executables into either known malware families because malware developers use different techniques as polymorphism and metamorphism to generate a group of malware programs, which originates from a single source code. Various machine-learning methods like Decision Tree, Random Forest, Support Vector Machine and Hidden Markov Model have been used for malware detection and classification [32,37]. Each method builds a classification model from an input data set. Decision Tree builds a classification model in the form of a tree structure by learning simple decision rules extracted from the features of input data. In a decision tree, each interior node represents a data attribute, each leaf represents an outcome and each edge corresponds to a decision rule. Random forest (RF) is an ensemble learning method, which constructs decision tree classifiers on various subsets of the input data. Support Vector Machine (SVM) is a classifier based on concept of decision hyperplanes. It learns an optimal decision boundary, which categorizes the input data. In order to model sequential data, one of the most commonly used methods is Hidden Markov Model (HMM) [32]. HMM is a statistical analysis method which is used for sequential data. Its greatest strength is take into consideration of hidden structure in given sequence while forming the model. It takes observations sequences and estimate hidden states and their transition probabilities. Then model generated with observation sequences calculates the probability of sequences by using hidden states and probability distributions. We observed API-call sequences to form HMM [33,34].

4   Experimental Results and Discussion

In this section, we evaluate dynamic attributes-based some malware detection and classification approaches on four datasets which contain real and synthetic malware executables.

4.1   Datasets and Experimental Setup

We use four different datasets with varying size, which includes different malware families. We select samples of malware and benign files which run in windows operating systems. We created some metamorphic malwares known as Next Generation Virus construction kit (NGVCK), Phalcon-Skism Mass-Produced Code

Generator (PSMPC), Generation Virus Constructor (G2), Metamorphic Worm (MWOR) using malware generation toolkits [35,36]. PSMPC was created in 1992 by the Dark Angel. It is script-driven constructor kit that generates metamorphic viruses whose decryption routines and structures change in variants. G2 viruses are produced as viral assembler source of different virus types. It is an enhanced version of the PSMPC code generator with more option for construction. NGVCK has a rather advanced Assembly source-morphing engine which was introduced in 2001 by the virus writer, SnakeByte. NGVCK is a Win32 application producing viruses that creates have random function ordering, junk code insertion, and user-defined encryption methods. MWOR constructs worms whose main purpose is to spoil statistical analysis. These worms inject junk codes into their code per each infection. The real malware executables, called VXHeaven [35], is used. Malware executables in VXHEAVEN have been labeled as virus, rootkit, trojan etc. In this work, to compare the performance of the methods on the unknown malware data set which consist of different types of malware, we labelled all VXHeaven executables as unknown malware. CYGWIN, WINDOWS 7 and WINDOWS 10 program and OS files were collected for benign samples. We created two datasets with varying characteristic. These datasets are described in Table 1. All benign samples are defined as a benign class. Malware from different families are each defined as a different class. To measure the effect of dataset size on the accuracy of our test, we use two more datasets at different scales created from these datasets. A dataset C of 600 samples and a dataset D of 900 samples were created from Dataset A and Dataset B respectively, with a sample count of 100 for benign and malware types.

Table 1. Dataset description.

| | Dataset A (4-class) | | Dataset B (6-class) | |
	Types	Counts	Types	Counts
Benign	CYGWIN	2000	CYGWIN	2000
	WINDOWS 7	1032	WINDOWS 7	1032
	WINDOWS 10	1825	WINDOWS 10	1825
			APPS	2000
Malware	NGVCK	2000	NGVCK	2000
	G2	2000	G2	2000
	MWOR	701	MWOR	701
			PSMPC	2000
			VXHEAVEN	2000

In our experiments, we select four classifiers known as Hidden Markov Model (HMM), Support Vector Machine (SVM), Decision Tree (J48), and Random Forest (RF). WEKA tool [38] is used for applying these classifiers. The default parameters of these classification methods were used as provides in the WEKA library. To obtain more valuable features, a correlation based-feature selection (FS) method [39] is used. The results show that the FS method is useful to increase the detection performance at lower dimension.

The effectiveness of the dynamic approaches is compared in terms of accuracy. To ascertain the validity of the approaches and to create test and train set, we use ten-fold cross validation. Dynamic malware features are obtained by using Cuckoo sandbox tool [24].

We set up a virtual machine by using VirtualBox to simulate Windows 7 and we run each executable in VirtualBox by requesting from cuckoo Web API. We write codes to automatize this process in Python. After producing report file for each executable, we extract some dynamic features, which are given in detail in Sect. 3. The process of general dynamic analysis is given in Fig. 2.

4.2   Experimental Result

In this section, we investigate the performances of malware detection and classification approaches based on different dynamic features. To analyze how the detection rates of the approaches change when different malware families and benign types are used, we use different datasets, which are described in Sect. 4.1. To measure the difference of the approaches on datasets varying scale, the experiments were repeated on two more datasets with different sample count. Finally, we compare the detection performances of the approaches in terms of malware detection and family classification.

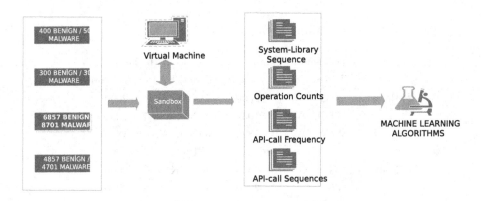

Fig. 2. The architecture of general dynamic analysis

The accuracy results of malware detection are given in Table 2. Malware programs are detected 100% correctly for the USL approach with only three features for Dataset C. In similar manner, high accuracy values are obtained with USL for other datasets. For other datasets, the best results are obtained by API-Bigram. The family classification performances of the approaches are given in Table 2. According to the results, API-Bigram approach and API-Frequency approach give the best performance for all dataset. RF is the most effective classifier for these approaches. One of the most important results was obtained by Operations approach with FS. A success rate of 97.17% was achieved with only two attributes for Dataset C. Similarly, for other data sets, the accuracy values obtained from this method are close to the accuracy values of the most successful approaches. Compared with other methods, an effective result was not obtained by the USL for family classification. Moreover, as the number of bi-gram features is quite high, classification process for USL-Bigram has not been achieved for Dataset B.

Table 2. The accuracy results for malware detection and family classification.

Dataset	# of Att.	Methods	Malware detection				Family classification			
			HMM	SVM	J48	RF	HMM	SVM	J48	RF
C 300/300 4-class	99	API-Freq.	-	97.33	96.83	97.17	-	**97.33**	97.17	**97.33**
	4	API-Freq.+FS	-	92.17	96.83	97.17	-	96.83	97.17	97.17
	1399	API-Bigram	90.64	97.33	97.00	97.33	96.61	97.17	97.17	**97.33**
	6	API-Bigram+FS	-	97.17	97.00	97.33	-	96.83	96.67	96.67
	367	USL-Bigram	-	**100**	**100**	**100**	-	85.83	86.00	86.00
	3	USL-Bigram+FS	-	**100**	**100**	**100**	-	86.00	86.00	86.00
	16	Operations	-	96.83	97.00	97.00	-	96.83	97.00	97.00
	2	Operations+FS	-	90.50	97.17	97.17	-	81.67	97.17	97.17
D 400/500 6-class	226	API-Freq.	-	92.22	93.78	94.00	-	91.22	92.78	**94.00**
	8	API-Freq.+FS	-	84.33	93.33	94.22	-	92.00	90.89	92.00
	5518	API-Bigram	93.38	93.78	91.89	**95.00**	92.51	91.56	92.67	**94.00**
	16	API-Bigram+FS	-	82.78	91.89	92.33	-	89.78	91.33	92.89
	1510	USL-Bigram	-	91.89	92.56	93.33	-	70.67	71.44	72.56
	7	USL-Bigram+FS	-	93.33	90.33	93.22	-	70.67	70.22	70.78
	16	Operations	-	92.22	93.78	94.00	-	83.33	90.56	91.22
	4	Operations+FS	-	92.22	93.33	94.22	-	74.44	90.11	90.44
A 4857/4701 4-class	131	API-Freq.	-	96.92	97.13	97.29	-	96.87	**97.29**	**97.29**
	7	API-Freq.+FS	-	96.93	96.90	96.95	-	96.98	96.97	96.93
	1557	API-Bigram	-	**97.98**	97.27	96.29	-	96.90	97.28	**97.29**
	7	API-Bigram+FS	-	96.89	96.93	96.97	-	96.78	96.75	96.76
	4412	USL-Bigram	-	96.34	96.78	96.33	-	89.07	89.56	-
	50	USL-Bigram+FS	-	96.80	96.78	96.78	-	89.52	89.44	89.52
	16	Operations	-	96.79	96.78	96.74	-	96.77	96.77	96.78
	3	Operations+FS	-	96.78	96.79	96.82	-	96.83	96.81	96.81
B 6857/8701 6-class	271	API-Freq.	-	90.56	95.21	96.04	-	89.72	94.75	95.73
	17	API-Freq.+FS	-	91.72	93.90	94.50	-	90.38	92.77	93.73
	12982	API-Bigram	-	90.54	95.60	**96.30**	-	88.42	95.19	**96.01**
	21	API-Bigram+FS	-	89.65	88.53	89.88	-	91.09	93.10	93.45
	-	USL-Bigram	-	-	-	-	-	-	-	-
	-	USL-Bigram+FS	-	-	-	-	-	-	-	-
	16	Operations	-	91.69	94.68	95.60	-	89.69	92.47	93.77
	6	Operations+FS	-	92.81	94.49	94.65	-	90.45	91.97	92.71

4.3   Discussion and Evaluation

It is seen in Table 2 that the number of features is increased as the number of samples increases. The number of bi-grams increases considerably depending on the number of samples. However, by applying the feature selection algorithm, it is observed that high success rates are achieved with very few features. By analyzing these selected attributes from different dynamic feature set, a new feature representation can be provided to increase the malware detection performance. When comparing the results of Dataset A and Dataset B or the results of Dataset C and D, a difference of about 2 to 4% was observed between the values of their obtained accuracy rates. The main reason for this is that VXHeaven executables are included in the classification process. VXHeaven samples decrease the total classification accuracy for Dataset D and Dataset B because they cannot be classified correctly. VXheaven dataset contains many different types of malwares such as virus, rootkit, trojan, metamorphic malwares and unknown viruses. Therefore, discovering common patterns for all VXheaven samples becomes particularly difficult for family classification. According to the results, the best accuracy values are obtained by conducting Random Forest classifier. The HMM method yields a lower performance compared to other methods. In addition, the memory and time consumption increase when HMM is applied for huge number of samples.

5   Conclusion and Future Works

While increasing number of malware and sophisticated functions of that codes, static analysis cannot be detecting them with high accuracy. Because advanced malware writers use obfuscation and cryptographic techniques to conceal their properties to make harder detection of malware. Behavioral properties of malware can be used to increase detection rate of malware by using dynamic analysis techniques. In this work, our goal is to find best dynamic features to develop efficient detection method for malware. Therefore, we have constructed a dataset by collecting benign and malicious codes. Dynamic properties like API Calls and operations are analyzed using sandbox tools. Those properties have been used to detect malwares using different machine learning methods like Random Forest (RM), Support Vector Machine (SVM), Decision Tree (J48) and Hidden Markov Model (HMM). We will use those results to develop a hybrid method for malware detection with higher accuracy and performance. In addition, our data set will be opened for researcher to make more research about malware.

Acknowledgment. This work was supported by the Scientific and Technological Research Council of Turkey (TUBITAK), Grant No: ARDEB-116E624.

References

1. AV-Test GmbH AV-Test malware statistics Technical report 2017. https://www. av-test.org. Accessed 18 Oct 2018
2. Rad, B.B., Masrom, M., Ibrahim, S.: Camouflage in malware: from encryption to metamorphism. Int. J. Comput. Sci. Netw. Secur. 12(8), 74–83 (2012)
3. Szor, P., Ferrie, P.: Hunting for metamorphic. In: Virus Bulletin Conference, pp. 123–144, Abingdon (2001)
4. Han, K.S., Kang, B., Im, E.G.: Malware classification using instruction frequencies. In: Proceedings of the 2011 ACM Symposium on Research in Applied Computation, pp. 298–300. ACM (2011)
5. Lee, J., Jeong, K., Lee, H.: Detecting metamorphic malwares using code graphs. In: Proceedings of the 2010 ACM Symposium on Applied Computing, pp. 1970–1977. ACM (2010)
6. Alam, S., Sogukpinar, I., Traore, I., Horspool, R.N.: Sliding window and control flow weight for metamorphic malware detection. J. Comput. Virol. Hacking Tech. 11(2), 75–88 (2015)
7. Egele, M., Scholte, T., Kirda, E., Kruegel, C.: A survey on automated dynamic malware-analysis techniques and tools. ACM Comput. Surv. (CSUR) 44(2), 6 (2012)
8. Bayer, U., Kirda, E., Kruegel, C.: Improving the efficiency of dynamic malware analysis. In: Proceedings of the 2010 ACM Symposium on Applied Computing, pp. 1871–1878. ACM (2010)
9. Bai, J., An, Z., Zou, Z., Mu, S.: A dynamic malware detection approach by mining the frequency of API calls. In: Applied Mechanics and Materials, vol. 519–520, pp. 309–312 (2014)
10. Hansen, S.S., Larsen, T.M.T., Stevanovic, M., Pedersen, J.M.: An approach for detection and family classification of malware based on behavioral analysis. In: 2016 International Conference on Computing, Networking and Communications (ICNC), pp. 1–5. IEEE (2016)
11. Shaid, S.Z.M., Maarof, M.A.: Malware behavior image for malware variant identification. In: 2014 International Symposium on Biometrics and Security Technologies (ISBAST), pp. 238–243. IEEE (2014)
12. Pektaş, A.: Behavior based malware classification using online machine learning. Doctoral dissertation, Grenoble Alpes (2015)
13. Imran, M., Afzal, M.T., Qadir, M.A.: Using hidden Markov model for dynamic malware analysis: first impressions. In: 2015 12th International Conference on Fuzzy Systems and Knowledge Discovery (FSKD), pp. 816–821. IEEE (2015)
14. Ki, Y., Kim, E., Kim, H.K.: A novel approach to detect malware based on API call sequence analysis. Int. J. Distrib. Sens. Netw. 11(6), 659101 (2015)
15. Choudhary, S.P., Vidyarthi, M.D.: A simple method for detection of metamorphic malware using dynamic analysis and text mining. Procedia Comput. Sci. 54, 265–270 (2015)
16. Yu, B., Fang, Y., Yang, Q., Tang, Y., Liu, L.: A survey of malware behavior description and analysis. Front. Inf. Technol. Electr. Eng. 19(5), 583–603 (2018)
17. Udayakumar, N., Anandaselvi, S., Subbulakshmi, T.: Dynamic malware analysis using machine learning algorithm. In: 2017 International Conference on Intelligent Sustainable Systems (ICISS), pp. 795–800. IEEE (2017)

18. Choi, Y.H., Han, B.J., Bae, B.C., Oh, H.G., Sohn, K.W.: Toward extracting malware features for classification using static and dynamic analysis. In: 2012 8th International Conference on Computing and Networking Technology (ICCNT), pp. 126–129. IEEE (2012)

19. Gandotra, E., Bansal, D., Sofat, S.: Zero-day malware detection. In: 2016 Sixth International Symposium on Embedded Computing and System Design (ISED), pp. 171–175. IEEE (2016)

20. Firdausi, I., Erwin, A., Nugroho, A.S.: Analysis of machine learning techniques used in behavior-based malware detection. In: 2010 Second International Conference on Advances in Computing, Control and Telecommu-nication Technologies (ACT), pp. 201–203. IEEE (2010)

21. Sikorski, M., Honig, A.: Practical Malware Analysis: The Hands-On Guide to Dissecting Malicious Software. No Starch Press, San Francisco (2012)

22. Arends, J., Kerstin, I.: Malware Analysis (2018)

23. Willems, C., Holz, T., Freiling, F.: Toward automated dynamic malware analysis using cwsandbox. IEEE Secur. Priv. 5(2) (2007)

24. The Cuckoo sandbox. http://www.cuckoosandbox.org/. Accessed 18 Oct 2018

25. Denning, D.E., Denning, P.J.: Certification of programs for secure information flow. Commun. ACM 20(7), 504–513 (1977)

26. Windows API Index. Tech Article 2018. https://docs.microsoft.com/en-us/windows/desktop/apiindex/windows-api-list. Accessed 18 Oct 2018

27. Aizawa, A.: An information-theoretic perspective of TF-IDF measures. Inf. Process. Manage. 39(1), 45–65 (2003)

28. Nair, V.P., Jain, H., Golecha, Y.K., Gaur, M.S., Laxmi, V.: MEDUSA: MEtamorphic malware dynamic analysis usingsignature from API. In: Proceedings of the 3rd International Conference on Security of Information and Networks, pp. 263–269. ACM (2010)

29. Kim, C. W.: NtMalDetect: A Machine Learning Approach to Malware Detection Using Native API System Calls. arXiv preprint arXiv:1802.05412 (2018)

30. Eskandari, M., Khorshidpur, Z., Hashemi, S.: To incorporate sequential dynamic features in malware detection engines. In: Intelligence and Security Informatics Conference (EISIC) 2012 European, pp. 46–52. IEEE (2012)

31. Cavnar, W.B., Trenkle, J.M.: N-gram-based text categorization. Ann Arbor MI 48113(2), 161–175 (1994)

32. Stamp, M.: A Revealing Introduction to Hidden Markov Models. Department of Computer Science, San Jose State University, pp. 26–56 (2004)

33. Damodaran, A., Di Troia, F., Visaggio, C.A., Austin, T.H., Stamp, M.: A comparison of static, dynamic, and hybrid analysis for malware detection. J. Comput. Virol. Hacking Tech. 13(1), 1–12 (2017)

34. Wong, W., Stamp, M.: Hunting for metamorphic engines. J. Comput. Virol. 2(3), 211–229 (2006)

35. Heavens, VX.: http://83.133.184.251/virensimulation.org/. Accessed 18 Oct 2018

36. Sridhara, S.M., Stamp, M.: Metamorphic worm that carries its own morphing engine. J. Comput. Virol. Hacking Tech. 9(2), 49–58 (2013)

37. Souri, A., Hosseini, R.: A state-of-the-art survey of malware detection approaches using data mining techniques. Hum.-centric Comput. Inf. Sci. 8(1), 3 (2018)

38. WekaTool. https://www.cs.waikato.ac.nz/ml/weka/. Accessed 18 Oct 2018

39. Hall, M.A.: Correlation-based feature subset selection for machine learning. Thesis sub-mitted in partial fulfillment of the requirements of the degree of Doctor of Philosophy at the University of Waikato (1998)

Trends in Design of Ransomware Viruses

Vlad Constantin Craciun[1,2(✉)], Andrei Mogage[1,2(✉)], and Emil Simion[3(✉)]

[1] Department of Computer Science, UAIC IASI, Iaşi, Romania
{vcraciun, mogage.andrei.catalin}@info.uaic.ro
[2] Bitdefender, Bucharest, Romania
{vcraciun,amogage}@bitdefender.com
[3] University Politehnica of Bucharest, Bucharest, Romania
emil.simion@upb.ro

Abstract. The ransomware nightmare is taking over the internet, impacting common users, small businesses and large ones. The interest and investment which is pushed into this market each month, tell us a few things about the evolution of both technical and social engineering, along with what is to expect in the short-coming future from them. In this paper, we analyze how ransomware programs developed in the last few years and how they were released in certain market segments throughout the deep web via RaaS (Ransomware as a Service), exploits or SPAM, while learning from their own mistakes to bring profit to the next level. We also highlight a set of mistakes that were made, which allowed for total or partial recovery of the encrypted data. We also consider the ransomware authors preference for specific encryption types, encryption key exchange mechanisms and some edge cases of encryption, which may prove to be exploitable in the near future.

Keywords: Cyber threat · Ransomware · Cryptography · Cyber security

1 Introduction

Ransomware is a term used to define the set of computer threats which demand for a ransom. They can demand for a ransom by making users believe they have a problem, damaging their data (crypto-lockers), or by denying the access to their computers (screen-locker).

This research is an overview of trends, used in the design of ransomware (crypto-lockers), based on about 150 different families in 2017 and about 100 families in 2018 (up to October), totaling up to 50k samples. The actual number of ransomware is actually much larger, however our limit derives from the limited number of samples per family, chosen for study, which do not exceeds a few hundreds on average. In Appendix A, we present a set of most relevant ransomware families analyzed for this study. Since 2013, when threat authors start focusing on this type of malware, the various forms of ransomware which proved to not survive (bad-jokes, screen-lockers), were just filtered out. Our research

J.-L. Lanet and C. Toma (Eds.): SecITC 2018, LNCS 11359, pp. 259–272, 2019.
https://doi.org/10.1007/978-3-030-12942-2_20

only targets the crypto-locker version of the ransomware, as it proved to be the most outstanding.

As most binary threats today use a wide range of tricks to exhibit their analysis (both static and dynamic), most of the times, analyzing such a threat requires human intervention to guide the execution into revealing what lies behind the encryption design and how payment works. Static and dynamic binary analysis are two of the required skills for cyber-threat researchers and we find at the moment, a wide range of tools which attempt to automate this analysis process, through emulation, binary instrumentation, decompilation, taint-analysis or symbolic execution. Because ransomware creators, usually improve their skills in time, the built malware families also change into slightly changed versions of the same threat. These updates range from obfuscation level, to design level of encryption or spreading.

A ransomware will inform its victim about the damages it has done, through ransom notes. Some of these ransom notes only show an email address to contact, while others have a well designed onion page to automate the payments and assist users with the decryption process. Among the total families involved in our research, we have seen:

– A big percent of ransomware adding an additional extension to the encrypted files;
– A small percent of ransomware changing the entire filename;
– A very small percent of ransomware not touching the file name at all.

This research does not focus on prevention, but on presenting a larger picture on the entire ransomware phenomenon, including, but not limited to, latest trends.

2   State of the Art

A report [15] from Symantec, back in 2012, shows a few numbers on how distributed was this threat until then, how quickly a single family got to compromise multiple computers and how their earnings varied at that time. In a more recent paper [5], Dean F. Sittig and Hardeep Singh, discuss about the problems these threats pose to hospitals and propose a few prevention mechanisms. Some similar reviews were released in the last few years [1,2], which deal with ransomware prior to 2017, or use a smaller number of families and samples for their study. As these threats become pandemic in the last few years, there was a huge reaction from the security community and there are a couple of researches [3,4,6–8,10] which provide prevention or remediation solutions. We also base our investigation both on publicly available technical papers like [9] and our internal technical papers, which dissect these threats, revealing every possible piece of code to be of interest. For instance, Bitdefender was the only one to provide a decryption tool for the first version of GandCrab[1] in March 2018, while we had never released a public technical paper on the subject.

---

[1] https://labs.bitdefender.com/2018/02/gandcrab-ransomware-decryption-tool-available-for-free/.

3   Spreading Mechanisms

Table 1 highlights the current spreading mechanisms of ransomware as concluded on the 250 chosen families, between 2017 and 2018. Because there is a huge number of ransomware families in each section, we briefly provide a few ransomware names for each of them.

Table 1. Spreading mechanisms

Spreading mechanism	Ransomware name
SPAM	GandCrab, Cerber, Nemucod
RDP brute-force	Crysis, GlobeImposter, SamSam, LockCrypt
Exploit kits	Hermes, GandCrab, Magniber, Cerber
OS exploit	WannaCry, NotPetya, BadRabbit, SynAck
BotNet, RaaS	Satan, Scarab, GandCrab, UIWIX

Various means of distribution of infection have been seen throughout the entire ransomware phenomenon. One of the easiest and most common way is via SPAM. This includes fraud emails, which contain malicious scripts, VB macros within Office documents (Fig. 1[2]), or URLs to malicious applications, which get downloaded and executed on a target PC.

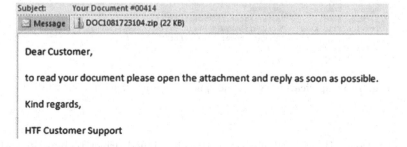

Fig. 1. SPAM email delivering GandCrab samples

A method of distribution which occurred especially among ransomware families as Crysis, GlobeImposter, SamSam, or LockCrypt, is brute-forcing the credentials through RDP (Remote Desktop Protocol) sessions (Fig. 2).

Once the attacker obtained access, it would manually disable any security product and then manually run the malicious samples. This also occurs in various

---

[2] https://www.fortinet.com/blog/threat-research/gandcrab-2-1-ransomware-on-the-rise-with-new-spam-campaign.html.

```
1/23/2018 1:38:33 PM.755   An account failed to log on.
4/1/2017 9:01:13 AM.027    An account failed to log on.
4/11/2017 11:35:55 AM.9    An account failed to log on.
1/23/2018 2:55:26 PM.269   An account failed to log on.
1/23/2018 3:38:07 PM.755   An account failed to log on.
4/1/2017 8:47:45 AM.707    An account failed to log on.
```

Fig. 2. A set of log on failed login attempts, taken from an terminal affected by Crysis ransomware

cases of botnets and/or coin-miners. What is interesting is that only on various occasions any of these techniques are part of an Advanced Persistent Threat, meaning that the attackers are interested in making as many victims as possible, without restricting their attack to a specific zone or victim. A few exception have been seen on some ransomware which will not infect victims based on geographic location (i.e. GandCrab excepts Russia IPs). Since spring of 2017, we have seen an increase in this trend, where hackers are ready to bring down security products on target machines, prior to execution of the ransomware. These attacks however, take places in 99% of cases, on computers belonging to companies, because companies are most probable to pay the ransom if they lack some backup solution. Two of the most common ways to get rid of a potential installed security product, are:

```
A service was installed in the system.
Subject:
        Security ID:          S-1-5-21-272638160-2255198395-2554806501-1129
        Account Name:         
        Account Domain:       
        Service Name:         ProcessHackerDRZUASRTEEFSUET
        Service File Name:    "C:\Users\        \Music\taskmgr\x64\ProcessHacker.exe" -ras
                              "ProcessHackerDRZUASRTEEFSUET"
        Service Type:         0x10
        Service Start Type:   3
```

Fig. 3. An application event, showing that processhacker was installed

– Using ProcessHacker, which has a digitally signed driver to bypass most of the security products, protection mechanisms;
– Forcing a security product removal with it's own uninstall tool[3].

Another frequent method is to exploit various security flaws found at software, operating system or hardware levels. A famous example is WannaCry ransomware, which would be distributed via EternalBlue exploit. This was based on a vulnerability at the Samba protocol, which allowed an attacker to inject malicious code remotely, through a kernel heap corruption. Another example is

---

[3] https://www.bleepingcomputer.com/news/security/the-avcrypt-ransomware-tries-to-uninstall-your-av-software.

```
cmd.exe /C sc config "MBAMService" start= disabled & sc stop "MBAMService" & sc de
lete "MBAMService";
```

```
cmd.exe /C wmic product where ( Vendor like "%Emsisoft%" ) call uninstall /nointer
active & shutdown /a & shutdown /a & shutdown /a;
```

Fig. 4. WMI script in AVCrypt ransomware

the second version of SynAck ransomware, which uses Process Doppelgänging[4] technique. This involves replacing the memory of a legitimate process through exploiting some Windows built-in functions (NTFS transactions – in this case) and how the Windows loader works. Both of them are based on fileless malware attacks (Figs. 3 and 4).

A trend in automating the monetizing system is to have a RaaS (Ransomware as a Service) for your ransomware, so common people will enroll to make money with a given ransomware. The existence of these services, as observed until now, are merely a safe noise level isolating the layer of ransomware creators from the threats themselves and leave these RaaS users to a front-line of exposed human actors, for a small percent of incomes.

More ransomware make use of strong cloud polymorphic services to better protect their payloads. These packers were first seen in bot-nets like Emotet[5] and we now see them on ransomware as GlobeImposter, GandCrab, Crysis, etc. Recent bot-nets just became a service providers for other threat creators and some of them like CoreBot are able to tell ransomware owners if the systems they infected, belong to companies or end users, in order to deploy the ransomware where their owners are guaranteed a high percent for the ransom payment. By the fall of 2017 we have seen a mix between crypto currency miners and ransomware and UIWIX is such a ransomware which at that time got deployed in certain conditions by Adylkuzz coinminer which among others like it, used the EternalBlue SMB exploit to spread in local area networks.

4   Encryption Algorithms

As concluded from our research, most of the ransomware are using standard algorithms both for encryption (Ex: AES, RSA, Blowfish, RC4) and hashing (SHA256, MD5). What is interesting is that there is a high percent (above 80%) of those who prefer standard libraries, such as OS API or OpenSSL over those choosing for slightly changed implementations of Salsa, ChaCha, or AES-512.

We identify about 5 different encryption key exchange mechanisms among all ransomware families:

---

[4] https://www.blackhat.com/docs/eu-17/materials/eu-17-Liberman-Lost-In-Transaction-Process-Doppelganging.pdf.

[5] https://media.scmagazine.com/documents/225/bae_qbot_report_56053.pdf.

1. Downloading a secret key/key-stream, to globally encrypt all user files. Usually the download servers are brought up by the ransomware owner, only for a short time-frame;
2. Creating a random key to encrypt all user files and uploading it to a server. The server database in these cases can only be captured, helped by authorities;
3. Using a constant shipped key. This is the most easy way to recover the key by reverse-engineering the binary sample;
4. Using a shipped RSA public key to encrypt random generated AES keys used for file-encryption. More recently, we saw a layered approach for the RSA key usage;
5. Using ECDH method, where keys are derived from a master key like TeslaCrypt V3 did (only a few cases).

There is a small number of ransomware which prefer to upload or download their keys, because it is difficult for the author to ensure that the server will be online at the time of encryption. Cyber-criminals will not risk to get discovered by the authorities by leaving public-available servers which could be sized for investigations. They also cannot risk to encrypt user files without making sure that they can correlate a key with an affected user. However, we have a few such cases described in Table 2 and one of them will be further described in **Corner cases** section. The recent approach, designed in GandCrab ransomware works as follows:

1. Ransomware queries an IP for a .bit domain name in a custom DNS server, using nslookup.
2. If the DNS server happens to be online, the nslookup replies with the IP address of the .bit domain.
3. Ransomware posts a short user-info data on the obtained IP address and begins to encrypt the files using the public shipped RSA key.

Table 2. Ransomware-hacker key sharing mechanism

Ransomware name	Key exchange	Encryption
ACCDFISA	Upload	Password protected rar SFX archives
HiddenTear	Upload	AES256
LockCrypt	Download	Custom block-cypher

There is a higher preference for local key generation instead of using a key obtained by other means, which we will discuss soon, due to its increased security and transparency for ransomware creators. Many of the ransomware who locally generate the encryption key are either using some secure key generator algorithms available in OS API or OpenSSL, deriving a SECP elliptic curve master key, or using an insecure key generator, which can lead to a breakable key as seen in Table 3.

Table 3. Ransomware using weak key generator or weak encryption

Ransomware name	Encryption	Key
OpenToYou	RC4	Hardcoded Plain-text key
Annabelle	AES	Hardcoded Plain-text key
Nemucod	Cyclic XOR	Hardcoded Plain-text key
Amnesia	AES128, CBC	Time (C rand() function)
Globe V3	AES256, ECB	Time (C rand() function)
Nemesis	AES256/512, ECB,CBC	Time (C rand() function)
Xorist	TEA / XOR	Time (C rand() function)
Xmas	CUSTOM	Time (C rand() function)
LeChiffre	BlowFish	Hardcoded and User-Info
Petya	Salsa20	secp192k1

The ransomware families using slightly changed encryption algorithms, usually prefer easy to revert light XOR operations or RC4 encryption with low-security key generators or even worse, with plain-text keys. Table 3, Figs. 5 and 6 reveals something about the encryption mechanisms available in Nemucod and OpenToYou ransomware. The recovery of files affected by these ransomware is possible not because of the weak-keys involved, but because the encryption algorithms are breakable. For OpenToYou ransomware, it is sufficient to have a pair of encrypted and not encrypted files to recover all the affected files, because we know that RC4 function, actually applies a xor operation between a key-stream and the actual data allowing the recovery of the key-stream from a pair of {encrypted, original} pieces of data.

We already know that for RC4 encryption, the following affirmations will lead us to decrypt any file starting from a pair of encrypted and not encrypted files, because the Key Stream can be computed using two different methods:

$$RC4 = \{P, KS, KSA, I, O\}$$
$$P - password$$
$$KS - \text{Key Stream}$$
$$KSA - \text{Key Stream Generator Algorithm}$$
$$I - \text{Input data}$$
$$O - \text{Output data}$$

Given the above description and knowing that $KS = KSA(P)$, we can encrypt I with KS, obtaining $O = KS \oplus I$. However having I and O can lead us to a valid KS, without knowing P, because $KS = O \oplus I$.

Most of the ransomware families nowadays will choose for RSA/ECDH key exchange mechanisms because they are more secure. They also ease the entire key-exchange mechanism, providing the hacker with a map of user IDs and RSA keys used for encryption. The ransomware authors only require for the affected

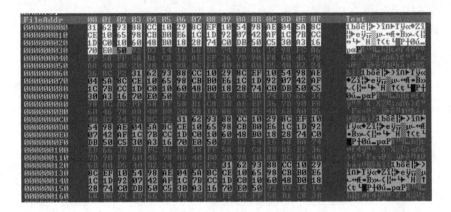

Fig. 5. Nemucod rolling key

Fig. 6. Block of zero encrypted bytes with RC4 (OpenToYou)

users ID, to get their correct decryption keys. There are a lot of sub-cases of using this type of keys, but all of them fall back to the same mechanism of having RSA to encrypt some symmetric encryption keys and not the actual user data. Most of the RSA keys range from 1024 to 4096 bits and there are a few mistakes of keys less than 1024 bit which have been broken so far (TeslaCrypt V1/V2). Among the ransomware using RSA keys, we have seen about three slightly different layered approaches, considered by ransomware so far:

1. shipped RSA public key to encrypt a global AES key. AES key is used to encrypt the user data;
2. shipped RSA public key to encrypt random AES keys, AES key is generated for each file to be encrypted;
3. shipped RSA public key A to encrypt another random generated RSA private key B. The RSA public key B is used to encrypt random AES keys for each file. The encrypted RSA private key B is stored locally, ready to upload and decrypt on ransomware-owner servers.

The third layered RSA method is actually used by the WannaCry ransomware. The ransomware owners secure that way their private keys and do not expose them to users paying the ransom, making the recovery of private key A, impossible. This is a multi layer RSA introduced to deal with cases where an affected user paying the ransom could share the received private keys with other users affected by the same binary. Troldesh/Crysis ransomware creators, for instance will provide a binary file containing a RSA private key after paying the ransom, which will actually decrypt about 15 different sub-versions. Those who run these businesses are aware of the fact that multiple users can get affected by the same ransomware binary, so they need a way to keep secret their keys when users pay the ransom and the same time to minimize the hacker-user interaction or their servers availability. Table 4 reveals a couple of ransomware, using the RSA key encryption with their preference for one of the above mentioned RSA layered methods.

Table 4. RSA key count/threat

Ransomware name	RSA layering index
Troldesh/Crysis	1
GlobeImposter	2
WannaCry	3
Rapid	3

There are a few ransomware families which use ECDH for key exchange. We tend to consider any ransomware using RSA or ECDH to be unbreakable, however about 2 years ago in May 2016, a researcher found that TeslaCrypt ransomware (first two versions) which used ECDH, was breakable because of the key encoding mechanism. We believe that authors wanted to store 1024 bit public keys inside the encrypted files, but they actually stored the 1024 bit key as ASCII hex, reducing the keys to 512 bit. Some of these keys are breakable in about seconds using factoring tools like Yafu[6] and Msieve[7]. The authors updated this weakness in their 3rd and 4th ransomware versions. While Fig. 7 reveals an actual 512 bit hex-ASCII key stored in an encrypted file of TeslaCrypt V2, Fig. 8 is a snapshot taken from an actual factorization of that key. The time 03:52:12 means that the factorization was possible in about 4 h.

To ensure that file recovery is not possible and the ransomware will execute in most operating system environments, ransomware owners must be aware of the environment where encryption will take place, how it looks like and how can be tuned to help them with the encryption. On Windows operating systems, a ransomware will make sure that all vss shadow copies are cleared, prior to encryption. This service ensures that lost data can be recovered if the disk has enough free space. Other ransomware like GobeImposter which are more recently, tend to auto-cleanup the hacker intervention and remove some event-logs and RDP logs after the execution ends. The environment is most of the time vulnerable to certain behaviors, be them on application level (MS Office Word memory corruption CVE-2018-0802), administrative weakness (unauthorized installation of

---

[6] https://sites.google.com/site/bbuhrow/.

[7] https://github.com/radii/msieve.

Fig. 7. 512 bit public ECDH session key - TeslaCrypt

```
Msieve v. 1.52 (SVN 958)
Mon Jun 27 21:16:27 2016
random seeds: 827f7e10 64a7d24e
factoring
4827120231746941627277871122529816642282088401040156708805731338505538063829718699894
751449816730588996387548521007853946714364905056199367398690986361785 (154 digits)
p1 factor: 5
p2 factor: 11
p2 factor: 19
p2 factor: 41
p2 factor: 79
p2 factor: 79
p5 factor: 30773
p10 factor: 1764861389
prp11 factor: 24606022423
prp34 factor: 3285322147279992991707207373888759
prp38 factor: 18440853927954741005957446698775339637
prp51 factor: 222973341931983505688879056180168807955140071025721
elapsed time 03:52:12
```

Fig. 8. Factoring the above key with Yafu on a i7 CPU, 8 threads at 2.70 GHz

WMI scripts/services, unauthorized uninstall of security products), or in kernel mode level, like MS17-010 first exploited by WannaCry back in 2017.

5　Common Ransomware Mistakes

One major observation found among the entire ransomware phenomenon is that the authors or attackers rarely have good or even decent cryptography knowledge. Various indicators were found to support this claim:

- ransomware such as Xmas, Xorist, Bart, Globe generate an encryption key for AES using the random() function from C. This leads to an easy recoverable key, by having a generation space of 2^{32} bits, which can be brute-forced in a reasonable time.
- Encryption using CBC mode having the Initialization Vector equal to 0. While this does not always support the key recovery, it makes the encryption process

less secure[8] and, in combination with the previous point, makes the recovery process even faster.

- Flawed implementation: some authors try manually to implement an encryption scheme and do not take all security measures, resulting in a possible exploitable scheme. Such a case can be seen in some versions of Nemesis ransomware, where the author tried to implement a version of AES based on 512 bits length of both encrypted block and key. A similar case is the first version of Petya (Red Petya) which implemented a custom Salsa20, explained in [12] which uses 32 bit words in the proposed design, but only 16 bit words in Red Petya implementation, because the boot-loader, encrypting disk sectors, worked in 16 bit mode. The authors patched this issue in Green Petya and more recent versions like BadRabbit which use 32 bit boot-loader code.
- Using a static key and a basic encryption scheme with little or no cryptographic properties. Such an example can be found in PCLock, Nemucod, OpenToYou, where a static key was used in a basic XOR scheme.
- Using simple, exploitable verifications: Cryp0l0cker, for instance, used to make a request on *blockchain.info* using a hardcoded BTC address in order to check whether the victim has paid. Once it received the confirmation, it started to decrypt the files. Therefore, manually modifying the address to one which already has the minimum of request bitcoins, will trick the ransomware into decrypting the files.
- Exploitable services: once the ransom payment has been completed, some ransomware would query a service where they would send the user key and download the decryption. Therefore, anyone who knew a victim's key could make the request and obtain the decryption key.
- Damaging the files: cases have been seen where the ransomware would faulty encrypt or write the encrypted data and, therefore, make the data irrecoverable. GandCrab, for instance, would use the SetFilePointer in order to move the file pointer to overwrite the clear data with the encrypted one. However, the lpDistanceToMoveHigh parameter, which specifies **"A pointer to the high order 32-bits of the signed 64-bit distance to move"** wasn't used, which causes a function failure if the purpose is to move the pointer more than 2 GB. Therefore, the file pointer would not be properly moved and data would be lost.
- Memory persistence: Some ransomware generate a local key which will be used to encrypt the entire system and will be kept in memory for the entire process. However, some of them will continue scanning for new files indefinitely. Therefore, anyone with system access can dump the entire memory of the process and obtain the key from there.

6   Cryptographic Corner Cases

We believe that the ransomware encryption touches a few corner-cases which can be exploited both by the up-coming technologies and math development the

---

[8] https://courses.csail.mit.edu/6.857/2014/files/18-das-gopal-king-venkatraman-IV-equals-zero-security.pdf.

same time. We will refer to 2 special cases of encryption, based on RSA1024 keys which might be breakable in the near future and some custom encryption mechanisms which could be broken using tools like Z3 Theorem Prover / Solver.

1. RSA1024 keys can already be broken using special hardware like SHARK explained in [11]. the problem is that the hardware implementation requires a costly financial investment ($20-30 M) and the time is not too short with all this.
   We also presume that quantum computing along with mathematical advancements will make these keys easy to break in the near future.
2. Custom encryption using Theorem Prover/Solver
   A couple of threats (LockCrypt ransomware, ShadowPad botnet) are using block-chain encryption based on 64 bit keys or pairs of 32 bit keys. Our research using Z3 Solver from Microsoft, proves that knowing the first 16-32 bytes of the output can lead to a corresponding equation system which might give us the decryption key without actually attempting a full brute-force.

As quantum computing becomes more approachable, the problem of quantum cryptography arises. Despite the fact that a theoretical theorem has proven that a quantum computer cannot perform general arbitrary computation, it can be used to access specific quantum states and perform operations that are similar. As theoretically proven, a quantum computer is much faster than a classical one can be used to attack many of current encryption schemes.

To prevent this, researchers are working on post-quantum or quantum-resistant cryptography [13], which present the possibility of developing encryption mechanisms, which are secure against quantum attacks. A way of sharing an encryption key through a quantum network is via quantum key distribution [14], which allows sharing a key between two parties without having to rely on a third one. Current popular schemes are not resistant to quantum attacks mainly because they rely on difficult mathematical problems, such as discrete logarithm, integer factorization, elliptic-curve discrete logarithm, quadratic residuosity problems.

However, once quantum cryptography will be practically implementable, everything we currently know as security will change dramatically. Obviously, the malicious software will be changed as well. Therefore, this brings the possibility of quantum malware or, more closer to the subject, quantum ransomware. One can only assume what such a concept implies at this point in time. Despite the security measures that will be taken, it is highly possible that the quantum computer will be somehow exploitable. Therefore, an attacker might build a quantum malware that performs similarly to a ransomware, but based on quantum cryptography. Other quantum scenarios involve changes of quantum states through "illegally" entaglements, approaching what we would call quantum DDoS.

7   Conclusions

In this paper we evaluated how ransomwres got more powerful over the last few years, growing along with their creators skills set. They became one of the biggest sources of revenue, helped by the security technologies developing in parallel and one of their biggest advantage is the crypto currency system, which allows their owners to be anonymous, while extorting large network infrastructures. The ransomware authors seem to keep up with the ongoing security products and studying their weak points, are able to fast shift the deployment, or the way they got to be executed on target machines. The more the security systems improve, the more "smart" ransomware spreading and infecting techniques become. As previously mentioned, once quantum computers can be used, more or less, in practical issues, the entire industry might change. We are aware that most of the affected users nowadays, will most probable be able to recover their files in the short coming future, but at the cost of time. Social engineering taking place in this field, forces both companies and end-users to get skilled in knowing how things evolve in an electronic world, and from our point of view, this process accelerates the way the people will get educated, forced by this trial and error path.

A   Ransomware Families Set

ACCDFISA, Amnesia, Annabelle, BadRabbit, Bart, Cerber, Crypt0l0cker, GandCrab, Globe, GlobeImposter, Hermes, HiddenTear, LeChiffre, LockCrypt, Magniber, Nemucod, NotPetya, OpenToYou, PCLock, Petya, Rapid, SamSam, Satan, Scarab, SynAck, TeslaCrypt, Troldesh, UIWIX, WannaCry, Xmas, Xorist

References

1. Kharraz, A., Robertson, W., Balzarotti, D., Bilge, L., Kirda, E.: Cutting the gordian knot: a look under the hood of ransomware attacks. In: Almgren, M., Gulisano, V., Maggi, F. (eds.) Detection of Intrusions and Malware, and Vulnerability Assessment DIMVA 2015. LNCS, vol. 9148, pp. 3–24. Springer, Cham (2015). https://doi.org/10.1007/978-3-319-20550-2_1
2. Gazet, A.: Comparative analysis of various ransomware virii. J. Comput. Virol. **6**(1), 77–90 (2010)
3. Scaife, N., Carter, N., Traynor, P., Butler, K.R.B.: Cryptolock (and drop it): stopping ransomware attacks on user data. In: IEEE 36th International Conference on Distributed Computing Systems (ICDCS) (2016)
4. Kharaz. A., et al.: UNVEIL: a large-scale, automated approach to detecting ransomware. In: 25th USENIX Security Symposium (USENIX Security 2016), pp. 757–772, Austin, TX, USENIX Association (2016). ISBN: 978-1-931971-32-4
5. Sittig, D.F., Singh, H.: A socio-technical approach to preventing, mitigating, and recovering from ransomware attacks. Appl. Clin. Inf. **7**(2), 624–632 (2016). PMC. Web. 1 October 2018
6. Kolodenker, E., Koch, W., Stringhini, G., Egele, M.: PayBreak: defense against cryptographic ransomware. In: Proceedings of the 2017 ACM on Asia Conference on Computer and Communications Security, pp. 599–611 (2017)
7. Gómez-Hernández, J.A., Álvarez González, L., García-Teodoro, P.: R-Locker: Thwarting ransomware action through a honeyfile-based approach. Comput. Secur. **73**, 389–398 (2018)

8. Andronio, N., Zanero, S., Maggi, F.: HELDROID: dissecting and detecting mobile ransomware. In: Bos, H., Monrose, F., Blanc, G. (eds.) RAID 2015. LNCS, vol. 9404, pp. 382–404. Springer, Cham (2015). https://doi.org/10.1007/978-3-319-26362-5_18
9. Lemmou, Y., Souidi, E.M.: Inside gandcrab ransomware. In: Camenisch, J., Papadimitratos, P. (eds.) CANS 2018. LNCS, vol. 11124, pp. 154–174. Springer, Cham (2018). https://doi.org/10.1007/978-3-030-00434-7_8
10. Young, A.L., Yung, M.M.: Cryptovirology: extortion-based security threats and countermeasures. In: Proceedings of the 17th IEEE Symposium on Security and Privacy, pp. 129–141. IEEE, May 1996
11. Kleinjung, T., et al.: Factorization of a 768-bit RSA modulus. In: Rabin, T. (ed.) CRYPTO 2010. LNCS, vol. 6223, pp. 333–350. Springer, Heidelberg (2010). https://doi.org/10.1007/978-3-642-14623-7_18
12. Bernstein, D.J.: The salsa20 family of stream ciphers. In: Robshaw, M., Billet, O. (eds.) New Stream Cipher Designs. LNCS, vol. 4986, pp. 84–97. Springer, Heidelberg (2008). https://doi.org/10.1007/978-3-540-68351-3_8
13. Aditya, J., Shankar Rao, P.: Quantum Cryptography
14. Lo, H.-K., Ma, X., Chen, K.: Decoy state quantum key distribution. Phys. Rev. Lett. **94**, 230504 (2005). (See also "Archived copy". Archived from the original on 24 December 2015. Retrieved 6 February 2016.)
15. O'Gorman, G., McDonald, G.: Ransomware: a growing menace

Efficient Implementation of the SHA-512 Hash Function for 8-Bit AVR Microcontrollers

Hao Cheng[1], Daniel Dinu[2], and Johann Großschädl[1(✉)]

[1] CSC and SnT, University of Luxembourg,
6, Avenue de la Fonte, 4364 Esch-sur-Alzette, Luxembourg
hao.cheng.001@student.uni.lu, johann.groszschaedl@uni.lu
[2] Bradley Department of Electrical and Computer Engineering, Virginia Tech,
Blacksburg, VA 24061, USA
ddinu@vt.edu

Abstract. SHA-512 is a member of the SHA-2 family of cryptographic hash algorithms that is based on a Davies-Mayer compression function operating on eight 64-bit words to produce a 512-bit digest. It provides strong resistance to collision and preimage attacks, and is assumed to remain secure in the dawning era of quantum computers. However, the compression function of SHA-512 is challenging to implement on small 8 and 16-bit microcontrollers because of their limited register space and the fact that 64-bit rotations are generally slow on such devices. In this paper, we present the first highly-optimized Assembler implementation of SHA-512 for the ATmega family of 8-bit AVR microcontrollers. We introduce a special optimization technique for the compression function based on a duplication of the eight working variables so that they can be more efficiently loaded from RAM via the indirect addressing mode with displacement (using the `ldd` and `std` instruction). In this way, we were able to achieve high performance without unrolling the main loop of the compression function, thereby keeping the code size small. When executed on an 8-bit AVR ATmega128 microcontroller, the compression function takes slightly less than 60k clock cycles, which corresponds to a compression rate of roughly 467 cycles per byte. The binary code size of the full SHA-512 implementation providing a standard Init-Update-Final (IUF) interface amounts to approximately 3.5 kB.

Keywords: Internet of Things (IoT) · Lightweight cryptography ·
AVR microcontroller · Software optimization · Performance evaluation

1 Introduction

A cryptographic hash function takes data of arbitrary form and size as input to produce a fixed-length output of typically between 160 and 512 bits that can be seen as a "digital fingerprint" of the data [15]. Hash functions play a major role

© Springer Nature Switzerland AG 2019
J.-L. Lanet and C. Toma (Eds.): SecITC 2018, LNCS 11359, pp. 273–287, 2019.
https://doi.org/10.1007/978-3-030-12942-2_21

in IT security and serve a wide variety of purposes, ranging from verifying the integrity of data (e.g. messages, documents, software) over securing the storage of sensitive credentials (e.g. passwords, credit card numbers) to realizing proof-of-work systems for digital currencies. In addition, hash functions are essential building blocks of digital signature schemes, key derivation functions, message authentication codes, and pseudo-random number generators. The design and analysis of cryptographic hash functions has been an active area of research in the past 30 years that yielded not only a large body of new algorithms but also many insights on the security of existing ones. Among the most important and commonly-used hash functions are the members of the SHA-2 family, which are approved by the NIST [17] and many other standardization bodies around the world. The SHA-2 family consists of six hash functions providing varying levels of security with digests ranging from 224 to 512 bits. However, only two of the six members, namely SHA-256 and SHA-512, can be seen as "original" designs since the other four are just variants of them with different initial hash values and truncated digests. SHA-256 and SHA-512 share many properties; they are both based on the Merkle-Damgård structure with a Davies-Meyer compression function that is solely composed of Boolean operations (bitwise AND, bitwise XOR), modular additions, as well as rotations (resp. shifts). These operations are performed on eight working variables, each of which has a length of 32 bits in SHA-256 and 64 bits in SHA-512.

The enormous expansion of the Internet of Things (IoT) in recent years has initiated a strong interest in *lightweight cryptography*, a relatively new subfield of cryptography dealing with (i) the design of novel cryptographic algorithms tailored to extremely constrained environments, and (ii) the efficient and secure implementation of cryptographic algorithms with the objective to minimize the execution time and resource requirements (e.g. power consumption and silicon area in the case of hardware implementation, and RAM footprint and code size when implemented in software) [1]. Optimization techniques to make SHA-256 suitable for resource-constrained IoT devices have been actively researched in the past 10 years and numerous lightweight implementations in both hardware [8] and software [4,19] were reported in the literature. Balasch et al. describe in [4] an optimized Assembler implementation of SHA-256 for the 8-bit AVR platform that achieves a hash rate of 532 cycles per byte when hashing a 500-byte message on an ATtiny45 microcontroller. The to-date fastest SHA-256 software for an 8-bit processor was introduced by Osvik in [19] and reaches an execution time of 21440 cycles for the compression function alone, which corresponds to a compression rate of 335 cycles per byte. These results show that SHA-256 is difficult to implement efficiently on small 8-bit microcontrollers, mainly due to the severely limited register space of these platforms, which is not sufficient to accommodate the working variables *and* provide storage for temporary values or pointers to access RAM. Furthermore, rotations are generally slow on these processors since they do not feature dedicated rotation hardware, which means rotating an 8-bit register by n bits takes (at least) n clock cycles.

SHA-512 is even more challenging to implement on small microcontrollers than SHA-256 since each of the eight working variables has a length of 64 bits instead of 32 bits, which doubles the register pressure. To our knowledge, it has never been attempted before to optimize SHA-512 in Assembly language for an 8-bit microcontroller since the scientific literature does not provide any results and also public repositories like GitHub do not contain any source codes. This is quite surprising since SHA-512 is one of the most important hash functions and especially popular on 64-bit platforms, where it significantly outperforms SHA-256 [12]. It is expected that the (relative) importance of SHA-512 versus SHA-256 will increase in the future, not only in the realm of high-performance computing but also in the IoT, mainly for two reasons. The first reason is the emergence of *EdDSA*, a state-of-the-art signature scheme using elliptic curves in twisted Edwards form [6]. EdDSA is most commonly instantiated with a curve that is birationally equivalent to Curve25519, providing a security level of approximately 128 bits, and SHA-512 as hash function, which is assumed to have 256 bits of security against collision attacks [14]. While it is common practice to choose elliptic curves and hash functions of roughly equivalent security, the designers of EdDSA decided to deviate from this practice and utilize a double-size hash function in order to "help alleviate concerns regarding hash function security" [6]. EdDSA comes with a number of features that make it attractive for resource-limited IoT devices, most notably the outstanding efficiency of the underlying elliptic-curve arithmetic. Speed-optimized EdDSA implementations for the 8-bit AVR platform are described in [13,16], but these implementations are mainly tuned towards fast arithmetic (i.e. fast scalar multiplication) and do not contain any Assembler optimizations for SHA-512.

The second reason why SHA-512 can be expected to increase in importance compared to SHA-256 is the emerging threat of *quantum cryptanalysis*. Some 20 years ago, Grover [11] introduced a quantum algorithm for finding a specific entry in an unsorted database of size n with complexity $\mathcal{O}(2^{n/2})$, providing (in theory) a quadratic speedup compared to classical exhaustive search. Grover's algorithm is believed to have an effect on cryptanalysis; for example, it could be applied to find the secret key used by an n-bit block cipher or a preimage of an n-bit hash value in $\sqrt{n}$ steps. Brassard et al. [7] proposed a quantum algorithm for generic collision search based on Grover's technique that needs to perform only $\mathcal{O}(2^{n/3})$ quantum evaluations of a hash function, but requires a very large amount of memory. Recently, Chailloux et al. [9] put forward a novel quantum algorithm for finding collisions with a quantum-query complexity and also time complexity of $\mathcal{O}(2^{2n/5})$, a quantum-memory complexity of just $\mathcal{O}(n)$ qbits, and a classical memory complexity of $\mathcal{O}(2^{n/5})$ bits. However, Bernstein [5] disputes the complexity analysis given in [9] and argues that all of the currently-known quantum algorithms for collision search are, in fact, less cost-effective than the best classical (i.e. pre-quantum) technique when execution time and hardware cost are considered appropriately. Nonetheless, the NIST published in [18] an assessment of the impact of quantum computers on present-day cryptographic algorithms according to which hash functions may need a larger output. In the context of the SHA-2 family, this obviously suggests to use a hash function with a digest length of more than 256 bits, i.e. SHA-384 or SHA-512, when 128 bits of security against collision attacks are needed. Since research in quantum cryptanalysis is still in its infancy, it seems prudent to err on the safe side and deploy SHA-512 in applications that require long-term security[1].

In this paper, we introduce a carefully-optimized Assembler implementation of the SHA-512 hash function for 8-bit AVR microcontrollers, in particular the ATmega series. As mentioned before, we are not aware of previous publications concerned with implementation and optimization aspects of SHA-512 on small 8-bit platforms. Therefore, it is not known how to optimize SHA-512 for these resource-constrained microcontrollers and what execution time can be reached with hand-written Assembler code. The present paper intends to answer these questions and describes two software optimization techniques that allow one to achieve significant performance gains compared to standard C implementations compiled with avr-gcc. Our first optimization technique aims to accelerate the four sigma operations, especially the rotations (resp. shifts) of 64-bit operands they perform. The other optimization speeds up the memory accesses that have to be carried out during the computation of the SHA-512 compression function by exploiting the indirect addressing mode with displacement (offset), which is supported by the AVR architecture. Combining both optimization techniques enabled our Assembler implementation of the compression function to outperform C code compiled with optimization level -o2 by a factor of 4.42.

2   Overview of SHA-512

SHA-512 is a member of the NIST-standardized SHA-2 family of cryptographic hash functions that produces a 512-bit digest and, therefore, provides 256 bits of security against collisions [17]. The input message can have a length of up to $2^{128} - 1$ bits and is processed in blocks of 1024 bits. Like other members of the SHA-2 family, SHA-512 is based on the well-known Merkle-Damgård structure with a Davies-Meyer compression function that uses solely Boolean operations (i.e. bitwise AND, XOR, OR, and NOT), modular additions, as well as shifts and rotations. All operations are applied to 64-bit words.

SHA-512 consists of two stages: preprocessing and hash computation. In the former stage, the eight *working variables*, denoted as a, b, c, d, e, f, g, and h in [17], are initialized to certain fixed constants. Furthermore, the input message is padded and then divided into 1024-bit blocks. The actual hash computation passes each message block (represented by 16 words m_0, m_1, ... m_{15} of 64 bits each) through a *message schedule* (illustrated in Fig. 1) to expand them to 80 words w_i with $0 \leq i \leq 79$. Then, the eight working variables are updated using a *compression function* that consists of 80 rounds. A round of the compression function is exemplarily depicted in Fig. 2. The processing of a 1024-bit message

---

[1] A common example of a class of IoT devices with long-term security requirements are smart meters because they are expected to reach lifetimes of between 10 and 25 years (according to [22, Table 2]) without requiring regular maintenance.

block results in eight 64-bit intermediate hash values. After the whole message has been processed, the 512-bit digest is generated by simply concatenating the eight intermediate hash values.

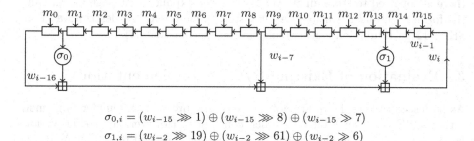

$$\sigma_{0,i} = (w_{i-15} \ggg 1) \oplus (w_{i-15} \ggg 8) \oplus (w_{i-15} \gg 7)$$
$$\sigma_{1,i} = (w_{i-2} \ggg 19) \oplus (w_{i-2} \ggg 61) \oplus (w_{i-2} \gg 6)$$
$$w_i = w_{i-16} \boxplus \sigma_{0,i} \boxplus w_{i-7} \boxplus \sigma_{1,i}$$

Fig. 1. The message schedule of SHA-512.

Each round of the compression function consists of seven modular additions of 64-bit words and four relatively more costly operations: *Maj* (Majority) and *Ch* (Choice) are composed of a sequence of bitwise operations (mainly logical AND and XOR), whereas the two sigma operations Σ_0, Σ_1 perform XORs and rotations of a 64-bit word by a fixed amount of bit-positions. Furthermore, in each round i of the compression function, the set of eight working variables is rotated word-wise. The word k_i in Fig. 2 is one of eighty 64-bit constants.

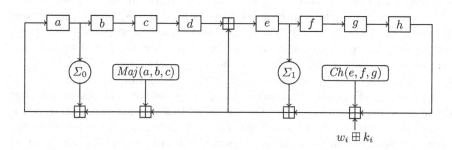

$$\Sigma_{0,i} = (a_i \ggg 28) \oplus (a_i \ggg 34) \oplus (a_i \ggg 39)$$
$$Maj_i = (a_i \wedge b_i) \oplus (a_i \wedge c_i) \oplus (b_i \wedge c_i)$$
$$t_{2,i} = \Sigma_{0,i} \boxplus Maj_i$$
$$\Sigma_{1,i} = (e_i \ggg 14) \oplus (e_i \ggg 18) \oplus (e_i \ggg 41)$$
$$Ch_i = (e_i \wedge f_i) \oplus (\bar{e}_i \wedge g_i)$$
$$t_{1,i} = h_i \boxplus \Sigma_{1,i} \boxplus Ch_i \boxplus k_i \boxplus w_i$$
$$(h_{i+1}, g_{i+1}, f_{i+1}, e_{i+1}) = (g_i, f_i, e_i, d_i \boxplus t_{1,i})$$
$$(d_{i+1}, c_{i+1}, b_{i+1}, a_{i+1}) = (c_i, b_i, a_i, t_{1,i} \boxplus t_{2,i})$$

Fig. 2. A round of the SHA-512 compression function.

As pointed out in [17, Sect. 6.1.3], the message schedule can either be pre-computed (so that the expanded message block is available before starting the first round of the compression function) or executed "on the fly" in an iterative fashion, e.g. 16 words at a time. The latter method is more RAM-friendly since there is not need to store all 80 words w_i of the expanded message block, while the former approach is usually a bit faster. A more detailed description of the SHA-512 hash function can be found in the specification [17].

3   Evaluation of Existing C/C++ Implementations

As indicated in Sect. 1, we are not aware of any previous Assembler implementation of SHA-512 for 8-bit AVR microcontrollers. However, there exist various lightweight C/C++ implementations that can be compiled to run on AVR.

3.1   8-Bit AVR Architecture

The popular AVR architecture was originally developed by Atmel Corporation (now part of Microchip Technology, Inc.) on basis of the RISC philosophy and a modified Harvard memory model. Its latest revision supports 129 instructions altogether, the vast majority of which have a fixed length of two bytes [2]. The register file is relatively large and contains 32 general-purpose working registers (named R0 to R31) of 8-bit width that are directly connected to the Arithmetic Logic Unit (ALU). Standard arithmetic/logical instructions have a two-address format, which means they can read two 8-bit operands independently from two of the working registers and write the result back to one of them. Since AVR is a "Harvard-based" architecture, it uses separate memories, buses, and address spaces for program and data to maximize performance and parallelism. Three pairs of working registers can operate as 16-bit pointers (X, Y, and Z) to access data memory, whereby five addressing modes are supported. Furthermore, the pointer Z can be used to read from (and write to) program memory.

The specific AVR microcontroller on which we simulated the execution time of our SHA-512 software is the ATmega128 [3]. It features a two-stage pipeline capable to execute an instruction while the next instruction is fetched from the program memory. Conventional ALU instructions take one clock cycle, whereas load/store instructions from/to data memory have a latency of two cycles. The memory sub-system includes 128 kB flash memory and 4 kB SRAM.

3.2   Performance Analysis

At the beginning of our research effort towards high-speed SHA-512 hashing on 8-bit AVR mircontrollers was a careful analysis of some existing open-source C and C++ implementations, including the SHA-512 software contained in the Arduino Cryptography Library [20]. We compiled the source codes with version 5.4.0 of avr-gcc (optimization option -o2) and determined the execution times through simulations using the ATmega128 as target platform [3]. The SHA-512 implementation from the Arduino Cryptography Library needs 1341398 cycles to compute the digest of a 500-byte message, which corresponds to a hash rate of 2683 cycles per byte. We also evaluated a couple of other C implementations that were available on source-code repositories like GitHub and found them to be very similar in terms of performance. In addition, we searched the literature for lightweight SHA-512 software, but did not discover any recent (i.e. less than five years old) publications with implementation results for AVR. However, we came across a paper by Wenzel-Brenner et al. [21] from 2012 that analyzes the performance of several hash algorithms, including a C implementation of SHA-512, on an ATmega1284P. They reported a hash rate of more than 8000 cycles per byte when hashing a long message, but this result should taken with some caution because it was obtained with a now-outdated version of avr-gcc that is not state-of-the-art anymore. For comparison, the to-date best implementation of SHA-256 was written in AVR Assembly language and reaches a compression rate of 335 cycles per byte [19]. These results immediately prompt the question of why the compiler-generated code for SHA-512 is approximately eight times less efficient than the hand-optimized Assembler code for SHA-256. In order to answer this question, we inspected the Assembler output generated by avr-gcc and found two reasons for the rather poor performance of SHA-512. First, the four sigma operations are much slower than they could be because avr-gcc uses the "generic" rotation functions for 64-bit words from libgcc. Second, the code generated by avr-gcc contains an unnecessarily large number of load and store instructions due to register spills, which could be massively reduced by means of a sophisticated register allocation strategy. What makes things even worse is that many of these load/store operations involve costly address arithmetic.

The four sigma operations have a major impact on the overall performance of the SHA-512 compression function. In essence, they comprise a few rotations of 64-bit words by a fixed number of bit-positions and logical XOR operations [17]. Rotations are generally slow on 8-bit AVR microcontrollers since, unlike to ARM processors, they do not feature a dedicated functional unit that could execute rotations by several bit-positions in a single clock cycle. Therefore, all multi-bit rotations need to be composed of several rotations by one bit. Whenever avr-gcc discovers a rotation of a 64-bit word in C code, it implements this rotation using functions named `rotldi3` (to rotate left) or `rotrdi3` (to rotate right), which are part of the avr-gcc low-level runtime library libgcc. Both are generic rotation functions that consist of two loops; the first loop performs one or more bytewise rotations (by simply copying the content of registers via the `mov` instruction [2]) and the second loop a sequence of bitwise rotations. When rotating by n bits, then the first loop is iterated (at most) $\lfloor n/8 \rfloor$ times and the second loop (n mod 8) times. Unfortunately, it seems avr-gcc is not capable to "globally" optimize the sigma operations since it just calls `rotldi3`/`rotrdi3` to perform the rotations and then executes `eor` instructions without taking into account that the bytewise rotations and XORs can be merged. We describe in Subsect. 4.1 hand-written Assembler implementations of the sigma operations that reduce the execution time significantly compared to C code.

Another reason for the relatively poor performance of C implementations is that each of the eight working variables has a length if 64 bits, which amounts to 64 bytes altogether. However, the register file of an AVR microcontroller can accommodate only 32 bytes, i.e. just half of the size of all working variables. In addition, it has to be taken into account that not every register can be used to store working variables since some registers are needed for temporary variables or to hold the 16-bit pointers. Thus, it is only possible to keep (at most) three 64-bit words in the register file at any time, which implies the majority of the working variables has to be kept in RAM rather than in registers. Our analysis of the Assembler code generated by avr-gcc showed that the register allocation strategy is far from ideal, which causes a massive number of memory accesses (i.e. loads and stores) that could be avoided. Most of these loads/stores require further instructions for address (i.e. pointer) arithmetic. Particularly costly in terms of memory accesses is the word-wise cyclic rotation of the set of working variables, which, as explained in Sect. 2, has to be carried out in each iteration of the compression function. However, it is possible to completely avoid these word-wise rotations by (partially) unrolling the main loop and replicating the loop body eight times. This unrolling enables one to accomplish the word-wise rotation in an implicit (i.e. "hard-coded") way by simply adapting the order in which the eight working variables are accessed. Unfortunately, the performance gained by this technique has to be paid with a significant increase of code size due to the loop unrolling. We present in Subsect. 4.2 a new approach to reduce the cost of the word-wise rotations that increases the code size only slightly.

4   Our Assembler Implementation

In the following, we present the Assembler optimizations we developed to speed up the sigma operations and memory accesses of the compression function.

4.1   Optimization of the Sigma Operations

Our decision to develop Assembler optimizations for the four sigma operations σ_0, σ_1, Σ_0, and Σ_1, which are used in the SHA-512 compression function, was motivated by the high potential for improvement we identified by analyzing the Assembler code generated by avr-gcc and comparing it with the best-optimized implementations of rotations on 8-bit AVR from [10]. In short, our strategy to speed up the sigma operations was to minimize the overall number of bitwise rotations and to "merge" the bytewise rotations with XORs.

The only rotation instructions supported by the 8-bit AVR architecture are rotations of 8-bit operands by one bit to the left (rol) and right (ror). Therefore, rotations of 8-bit words by other amounts, and also rotations of operands that are longer than eight bits, have to be carried out by executing a sequence of 1-bit rotations and other instructions [10]. For example, a 1-bit left-rotation of a 64-bit operand consists of a 1-bit logical left-shift (lsl), followed by seven 1-bit left-rotations through carry (`rol`), and an addition with carry (`adc`). The over-all execution time of this sequence of instructions is nine clock cycles (see [10, p. 251] for further details). A rotation of a 64-bit operand by n bits, where $1 < n < 8$, can be computed by repeating n times the sequence of instructions for rotating a 64-bit quantity by one bit in the same direction. However, it has to be pointed out that a left-rotation and a right-rotation by one and the same number of bits can have different execution times. For example, a right-rotation of a 64-bit operand by one bit requires ten cycles, which is one cycle more than what is needed for a left-rotation. Consequently, it makes sense to compare the two possible options for a rotation, namely rotation by n bits to the left versus rotation by $(64 - n)$ bits to the right, to select the most efficient one [10].

By combining our efficient implementations of the rotations with the XORs performed in each of the four sigma operations, we were able to further reduce the execution time of the compression function. Our basic idea is to exploit the fact that a bytewise rotation of a 64-bit operand can be executed for free when it is XORed with another 64-bit operand. More concretely, an operation of the form $x = x \oplus (y \ggg 8)$ can be performed with just eight `eor` instructions on an AVR processor by simply XORing the bytes of x and y in such a way that the bytewise rotation is "implicitly" carried out. This approach can also be applied for rotations by other amounts. For example, the operation $x = x \oplus (y \ggg 7)$ is normally implemented as a bitwise rotation to the left by one bit (which takes nine clock cycles), followed by a bytewise right-rotation (also nine cycles), and an XOR (eight cycles). However, by integrating the bytewise right-rotation into the XOR, the total execution time decreases to 17 clock cycles. Similar savings in execution time are possible when rotations by a larger number of bits have to be performed since our idea also works for multiples of eight bits.

The "small" sigma operations σ_0, σ_1 are used in the message schedule, while the "big" sigma operations Σ_0, Σ_1 are essential components of the compression function. They can be expressed through the following formulae [17].

$$\sigma_0 = (x \ggg 1) \oplus (x \ggg 8) \oplus (x \gg 7)$$
$$\sigma_1 = (x \ggg 19) \oplus (x \ggg 61) \oplus (x \gg 6)$$
$$\Sigma_0 = (x \ggg 28) \oplus (x \ggg 34) \oplus (x \ggg 39)$$
$$\Sigma_1 = (x \ggg 14) \oplus (x \ggg 18) \oplus (x \ggg 41)$$

By applying the optimization techniques described above, the formulae for the four sigma operations can be rewritten to clearly show the bitwise and bytewise rotations and whether they go to the left or to the right. Rotations by amounts that are multiple of eight, marked in green, are executed implicitly (i.e. merged into a 64-bit XOR operation) and do not increase the execution time.

$$\sigma_0 = (x \ggg 1) \oplus (x \ggg 8) \oplus (((x \lll 1) \ggg 8) \wedge (2^{57} - 1))$$
$$\sigma_1 = (((x \lll 2) \ggg 8) \wedge t) \oplus ((x \lll 2) \lll 1) \oplus ((((x \lll 2) \lll 1) \lll 2) \ggg 24)$$
$$\Sigma_0 = ((x \ggg 40) \lll 1) \oplus ((x \ggg 2) \ggg 32) \oplus (((x \ggg 2) \ggg 2) \ggg 24)$$
$$\Sigma_1 = ((x \ggg 16) \lll 2) \oplus ((x \ggg 1) \ggg 40) \oplus (((x \ggg 1) \ggg 1) \ggg 16)$$

Table 1. Execution time and code size of the sigma operations on the ATmega128.

Operation	Assembler		C language	
	Time (cycles)	Code size (bytes)	Time (cycles)	Code size (bytes)
σ_0	41	82	525	168
σ_1	71	142	399	168
Σ_0	71	142	431	168
Σ_1	58	116	521	168

We implemented the four sigma operations in AVR Assembly language using the optimized formulae given above. The value of t on the right side of the formula for σ_1 is $2^{58} - 1$ so that it can be used to mask off the six most-significant bits of a 64-bit operand. Our implementations perform the rotations by a multiple of eight bit-positions implicitly (i.e. "merged" into an XOR); only the rotations by less than eight bits to the left or right are actually executed. Table 1 shows the execution time and code size of our optimized Assembler implementations and that obtained by compiling C code for the sigma functions. The C sources were compiled with avr-gcc, which uses generic rotation functions from the low-level runtime library libgcc, such as `rotldi`, to rotate a 64-bit operand. Our results show that the optimized Assembler implementations are between 5.6 and 12.8 times faster and up to 2.04 times smaller than their C counterparts.

4.2 Optimization of the Memory Accesses

As analyzed in Subsect. 3.2, one of the reasons for the suboptimal performance of the binary code generated by the avr-gcc compiler is an unnecessarily large number of memory access to load or store the eight working variables (or parts of them) from/to the SRAM. Especially costly is the word-wise rotation of the set of working variables that has to be carried out during each iteration of the compression function as is explained in Sect. 2 and illustrated in Fig. 2. Some implementations unroll (or partially unroll) the loops to avoid these word-wise rotation, which comes at the expense of increased code size. To overcome this problem, we developed a special optimization strategy that maintains two sets of working variables in SRAM (i.e. we "duplicate" the eight working variables) and intensively uses the indirect addressing mode with displacement [2] of the AVR architecture to avoid the word-wise rotation in each iteration *without* the need to unroll the main loop of the compression function. In this way, we were able to achieve both high performance and small code size.

The indirect addressing mode with displacement is one of several modes to address data in SRAM and can be used with the 16-bit pointer registers Y and Z. This mode forms the actual address by adding a "displacement" (sometimes called *offset*) to the content of a pointer register. In AVR, the displacement is a 6-bit constant that is embedded into the instruction word (i.e. the maximum displacement is 63). Other embedded RISC architectures like ARM are more flexible since the displacement (or offset) does not need to be constant but can

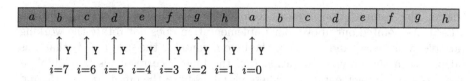

Fig. 3. Graphical representation of the "duplicated" set of working variables stored in an array of 128 bytes. (Color figure online)

also be a variable stored in a general-purpose register. Two AVR instructions that support indirect addressing with displacement are `ldd` and `std`, which can be used to efficiently access a given element of an array when its index is fixed and known a priori (i.e. at compile time). Concretely, when pointer Y holds the start address of a byte-array S, then the Assembler statement `ldd r4,Y+2` can be used to load $S[2]$ (i.e. the third byte of the array S) to register `r4`, whereby the pointer Y itself does not get modified in any way.

Our optimized Assembler implementation of the compression function uses two sets of working variables to simplify the address calculations. At the beginning (i.e. before the very first iteration), the second set is simply a copy of the first one, which means both sets are identical. The two sets are stored in a byte array S of length 128 bytes in SRAM in such a way that the first set occupies the upper half of the array (i.e. the bytes from $S[64]$ to $S[127]$) and the second set the lower half ($S[0]$ to $S[63]$). Figure 3 illustrates the byte array S with the first set of working variables colored in green on the right side and the second set in blue on the left side. We use pointer-register Y to access the array. In the very first iteration (i.e. in the iteration with loop-counter $i = 0$), Y contains the start address of working variable a of the first set (i.e. the least-significant byte of the green a), which is the address of $S[64]$. All eight working variables of the first (green) set can be conveniently accessed via the indirect addressing mode with displacement since the offset will never be bigger than 63. Thanks to this addressing mode, no costly address arithmetic needs to be performed to obtain the actual addresses of the bytes of the working variables. Our implementation first computes the Maj operation, which requires to load the working variables a, b, and c from the green set. The offsets for these three working variables are 0–7, 8–15, and 16–23, respectively. Thereafter, Σ_0, Ch, and Σ_1 are computed and finally the temporary values t_1 and t_2. In a "conventional" implementation of the compression function (i.e. an implementation that actually performs the word-wise rotation of the set of working variables), the sum $t_1 + t_2$ is assigned to a and the sum $d + t_1$ to e (see Sect. 2). However, our implementation does not perform a word-wise rotation and, therefore, $d + t_1$ is written to the green d and $t_1 + t_2$ to the blue h. The last step is to decrement Y by eight.

At the beginning of the second iteration (i.e. the iteration where $i = 1$), the pointer-register Y contains the address of the least-significant byte of the blue h, i.e. the address of $S[56]$. The second iteration is carried out quite similar to the first iteration, which means we start with computing the Maj operation as before. This computation requires to load the blue h and the green a, b from SRAM. As pointed out above, our implementation does not rotate the working variables word-wise, and therefore the blue h contains the sum $t_1 + t_2$ that was calculated in the previous iteration (i.e. the blue h corresponds to variable a in a "rotated" implementation). These variables have the offsets 0–7, 8–15, and 16–23, respectively, exactly like in the first iteration. Also Σ_0, Ch, and Σ_1 are computed in the same fashion as above. At the end of the second iteration, the pointer register Y is again decremented by eight. Subsequent iterations are also performed in this way. It is important to understand that in each iteration, the offsets used to access the bytes of the working variables are always the same as in the first iteration, only the base address in Y is different. In this way, we can avoid the word-wise rotations without loop unrolling. However, after eight iterations, the two sets of working variables must be "synchronized," which means the second (blue) set has to be copied to the first (green) set so that both sets are identical again. Fortunately, this duplication of the variables is only needed in every eighth iteration; therefore, it is much more efficient than rotating the set of working variables word-wise in each iteration. The only drawback of this approach is a slight increase in RAM consumption (by 64 bytes) since two sets of working variables are needed.

5   Results and Comparison

We developed besides the AVR Assembler implementation of the compression function also a C version based on the same optimization techniques using two sets of working variables. All other parts of the SHA-512 algorithm, such as the padding, were written only in C since they are not really performance-critical [19]. Our software provides both a high-level and a low-level API, whereby the former consists of just a single function, namely sha512_hash. The low-level API, on the other hand, comes with the standard IUF (init, update, final) functions that allow for hashing of very large or fragmented data without the need to have the full data in SRAM.

We used Atmel Studio v7.0 as development environment with an extension that provides the 8-bit AVR GNU toolchain including avr-gcc version 5.4.0. All execution times reported in this section were determined with the help of the cycle-accurate instruction set simulator of Atmel Studio, whereby we used the ATmega128 microcontroller as target device. We simulated the execution time of the Assembler version and the C version of the compression function alone and also the time required to hash a 500-byte message so that we can compare our results with those from previous papers such as [4]. The latter performance test was carried out with the help of the high-level API by simply calling the sha512_hash function. Our simulations gave an execution time of 59768 cycles for the AVR-Assembler version of the compression function and 264133 cycles for the C implementation. In both cases, the function call overhead is included in the specified cycle count. These execution times represent compression rates of approximately 467 and 2064 cycles per byte, respectively, which means the

Table 2. Performance (i.e. hash rate when hashing a 500-byte message) and code size of different hash functions on the ATmega128.

Reference	Algorithm	Impl.	Hash rate (cyc/byte)	Code size (bytes)
This paper	SHA-512	C	2654	4610
This paper	SHA-512	C+Asm	611	3460
Weatherley [20]	SHA-512	C++	2683	8072
Osvik [19]	SHA-256 (CP)	Asm	335	2720
Balasch et al. [4]	SHA-256	Asm	532	1090
Balasch et al. [4]	Blake (256 bit)	Asm	562	1166
Balasch et al. [4]	Grøstl (256 bit)	Asm	686	1400
Balasch et al. [4]	Keccak (256 bit)	Asm	1432	868
Balasch et al. [4]	Photon (256 bit)	Asm	6210	1244

Assembler implementation outperforms the C version by a factor of 4.42. We also simulated the execution time of the compression function of the SHA-512 software contained in the Arduino Cryptography Library [20] and found it to be slightly slower than our own C implementation.

When hashing a message of length 500 bytes (using the high-level function sha512_hash), we obtained an overall execution time of 1327132 cycles for the "pure" C implementation and 305303 cycles for the Assembler version. These two cycle counts translate to hash rates of approximately 611 and 2654 cycles per byte, respectively, which means the Assembler optimizations we proposed yield a speed-up by a factor of about 4.34 over the C code. The hash rates are significantly worse than the compression rates, which is mainly because of the padding. Normally, a 500-byte message fits into four 128-byte blocks, but due to padding, the compression function gets executed five times altogether. If we would hash e.g. a 620-byte message, we get exactly the same execution time as for a 500-byte message (since in both cases the compression function is called five times), but the hash rate is much better because the cycle count is divided by 620 instead of 500. Table 2 compares our results with that of a few previous SHA-2 implementations and three SHA-3 candidates from [4]. It is remarkable that our Assembler version of the SHA-512 hash algorithm is only slightly less efficient than Balasch et al.'s Assembler implementation of SHA-256 [4], even though using a 500-byte message for benchmarking favors SHA-256 over SHA-512. Namely, as pointed out before, hashing 500 bytes with SHA-512 requires five calls of the compression function (whereby each time a 128-byte block gets processed), but in the case of SHA-256 the compression function is only called eight times (to process 64 bytes each time). When we hash a 620-byte message instead of the 500-byte message, then our SHA-512 software actually achieves a *better* hash rate than the SHA-256 implementation of Balasch et al.

The code size of our implementation, including both the high-level function sha512_hash and the low-level functions init, update, final, along with the compression function (in Assembler), amounts to 3460 bytes. The compression function alone has a size of 2206 bytes and occupies 158 bytes on the stack.

6 Conclusions

We demonstrated that the execution time of SHA-512 on 8-bit AVR microcontrollers can be significantly improved through hand-optimized Assembler code for the compression function. Our implementation of the compression function takes 59768 clock cycles on an ATmega128 microcontroller, which corresponds to a compression rate of approximately 467 cycles per byte. For comparison, an implementation in C compiled with avr-gcc 5.4.0 is about 4.42 times slower as it requires 264133 cycles (i.e. roughly 2064 cycles per byte). Hashing a 500-byte message with and without Assembler optimizations takes 305303 and 1327132 cycles, respectively, which represents a nearly 4.35-fold difference in execution time. We achieved this performance gain through a careful optimization of the four sigma operations and by minimizing the cost of memory (SRAM) accesses via a novel approach that duplicates the working variables but does not require loop unrolling. The latter optimization technique can potentially be applied in various other contexts beyond the acceleration of SHA-512 on AVR. It can be easily adapted to other architectures that feature an indirect addressing mode (e.g. MSP430, ARM) and may be useful for other cryptosystems that perform word-wise rotation of working variables or a state. We hope that our work will contribute to a more wide-spread deployment of SHA-512 (and cryptosystems that use SHA-512, in particular EdDSA) on constrained IoT devices.

Acknowledgements. The research described in this paper was supported, in part, by the Internet Privatstiftung Österreich via the Netidee programme.

References

1. Alippi, C., Bogdanov, A., Regazzoni, F.: Lightweight cryptography for constrained devices. In: Proceedings of the 14th International Symposium on Integrated Circuits (ISIC 2014), pp. 144–147. IEEE (2014)
2. Atmel Corporation: 8-bit AVR instruction set. User guide (2008). http://www.atmel.com/dyn/resources/prod_documents/doc0856.pdf
3. Atmel Corporation: 8-bit AVR microcontroller with 128K bytes in-system programmable flash: ATmega128, ATmega128L. Datasheet (2008). http://www.atmel.com/dyn/resources/prod_documents/doc2467.pdf
4. Balasch, J., et al.: Compact implementation and performance evaluation of hash functions in attiny devices. In: Mangard, S. (ed.) CARDIS 2012. LNCS, vol. 7771, pp. 158–172. Springer, Heidelberg (2013). https://doi.org/10.1007/978-3-642-37288-9_11
5. Bernstein, D.J.: Quantum algorithms to find collisions. The cr.yp.to blog (2017). http://blog.cr.yp.to/20171017-collisions.html

6. Bernstein, D.J., Duif, N., Lange, T., Schwabe, P., Yang, B.-Y.: High-speed high-security signatures. In: Preneel, B., Takagi, T. (eds.) CHES 2011. LNCS, vol. 6917, pp. 124–142. Springer, Heidelberg (2011). https://doi.org/10.1007/978-3-642-23951-9_9

7. Brassard, G., Høyer, P., Tapp, A.: Quantum cryptanalysis of hash and claw-free functions. In: Lucchesi, C.L., Moura, A.V. (eds.) LATIN 1998. LNCS, vol. 1380, pp. 163–169. Springer, Heidelberg (1998). https://doi.org/10.1007/BFb0054319

8. Cao, X., O'Neill, M.: Application-oriented SHA-256 hardware design for low-cost RFID. In: Proceedings of the 45th IEEE International Symposium on Circuits and Systems (ISCAS 2012), pp. 1412–1415. IEEE (2012)

9. Chailloux, A., Naya-Plasencia, M., Schrottenloher, A.: An efficient quantum collision search algorithm and implications on symmetric cryptography. In: Takagi, T., Peyrin, T. (eds.) ASIACRYPT 2017. LNCS, vol. 10625, pp. 211–240. Springer, Cham (2017). https://doi.org/10.1007/978-3-319-70697-9_8

10. Dinu, D.: Efficient and secure implementations of lightweight symmetric cryptographic primitives. Ph.D. thesis, University of Luxembourg (2017)

11. Grover, L.K.: A fast quantum mechanical algorithm for database search. In: Miller, G.L. (ed.) Proceedings of the 28th Annual ACM Symposium on the Theory of Computing (STOC 1996), pp. 212–219. ACM Press, New York (1996)

12. Gueron, S., Johnson, S., Walker, J.: SHA-512/256. Cryptology ePrint Archive, Report 2010/548 (2010). http://eprint.iacr.org/2010/548

13. Hutter, M., Schwabe, P.: NaCl on 8-bit AVR microcontrollers. In: Youssef, A., Nitaj, A., Hassanien, A.E. (eds.) AFRICACRYPT 2013. LNCS, vol. 7918, pp. 156–172. Springer, Heidelberg (2013). https://doi.org/10.1007/978-3-642-38553-7_9

14. Josefsson, S., Liusvaara, I.: Edwards-curve digital signature algorithm (EdDSA). Internet Research Task Force, Crypto Forum Research Group, RFC 8032, January 2017

15. Menezes, A.J., van Oorschot, P.C., Vanstone, S.A.: Handbook of Applied Cryptography. Discrete Mathematics and Its Applications. CRC Press, Boca Raton (1996)

16. Nascimento, E., López, J., Dahab, R.: Efficient and secure elliptic curve cryptography for 8-bit AVR microcontrollers. In: Chakraborty, R.S., Schwabe, P., Solworth, J. (eds.) SPACE 2015. LNCS, vol. 9354, pp. 289–309. Springer, Cham (2015). https://doi.org/10.1007/978-3-319-24126-5_17

17. National Institute of Standards and Technology (NIST): Secure hash standard (SHS). Federal Information Processing Standards Publication 180–4, August 2015. https://doi.org/10.6028/NIST.FIPS.180-4

18. National Institute of Standards and Technology (NIST): Report on post-quantum cryptography. Internal Report 8105, April 2016. https://doi.org/10.6028/NIST.IR.8105

19. Osvik, D.A.: Fast embedded software hashing. Cryptology ePrint Archive, Report 2012/156 (2012). http://eprint.iacr.org/2012/156

20. Weatherley, R.: Arduino Cryptography Library. Source code (2018). http://github.com/rweather/arduinolibs

21. Wenzel-Benner, C., Gräf, J., Pham, J., Kaps, J.-P.: XBX benchmarking results January 2012. In: Proceedings of the 3rd SHA-3 Candidates Conference (2012)

22. Zhou, S., Brown, M.A.: Smart meter deployment in Europe: a comparative case study on the impacts of national policy schemes. J. Clean. Prod. **144**, 22–32 (2017)

Secure IoT Supply Chain Management Solution Using Blockchain and Smart Contracts Technology

Cristian Toma[1]([✉]) [iD], Bogdan Talpiga[2]([✉]), Catalin Boja[1]([✉]),
Marius Popa[1]([✉]), Bogdan Iancu[1]([✉]), and Madalina Zurini[1]([✉])

[1] Department of Economic Informatics and Cybernetics,
The Bucharest University of Economic Studies, Bucharest, Romania
{cristian.toma,catalin.boja,marius.popa,
bogdan.iancu}@ie.ase.ro, madalina.zurini@csie.ase.ro
[2] ICT | Cyber Security Master Program, The Bucharest University of Economic
Studies, Bucharest, Romania
bogdantalpiga93@gmail.com
http://www.ase.ro, http://ism.ase.ro

Abstract. Supply Chain has played a key role in developing the corporate processes and significantly improved the way they interconnect one to each other. In the last decades, the Supply Chain Management has attracted the attention of academic research, in the scope of improving or creating better solution for coordinating the flaws that undergo a supply chain. Last research in the area have focused on the integration properties of the Supply Chains. This is due to the globalization effects over the worldwide economy. The study of the integration creates the knowledge and the infrastructure needed for the networks of interdependent corporations, in order to provide a more dynamic demand and supply of products and services. The paper presents a solution by using the block chain and smart contracts technologies within IoT – Internet of Things environment.

Keywords: Blockchain · IoT · Ethereum · Supply chain · Logistics · Solidity · DApp · Smart contract

1 Introduction

The supply chain represents how a producer turns the raw materials into finite goods or services to meet the client's request. There can be several steps along the way of a supply chain, and sometimes, the sites can be distributed all along the globe. The globalization and the desire of big manufacturers to reduce costs emphasize this approach mode.

The economy is profoundly affected by disruptions in supply chains, and since this can be speeded in different areas, risks become greater. For example, Japan's earthquake and resultant tsunami damaged enough ports and airports to halt 20% of the world's supply of semiconductor equipment and materials. The necessity to control all the steps involved in a supply chain led to complex solutions called supply chain management.

© Springer Nature Switzerland AG 2019
J.-L. Lanet and C. Toma (Eds.): SecITC 2018, LNCS 11359, pp. 288–299, 2019.
https://doi.org/10.1007/978-3-030-12942-2_22

For better results, they integrate diverse area of research and development, such as industrial engineering, system engineering, logistics, information technology and marketing. The basic phases that a supply chain management solution needs to manage are the flows alignment, that means keeping the money, information and other materials flowing up and down the supply chain, integration of distinct functions, like purchasing and logistics, processes coordination, and managing resources. Because the customers' expectations are always increasing, the world becomes "smaller" with the raise of globalization and attacks over the internet or other information technology related channels are increasing, the evolution of a new architecture in supply chain management need to arise [3, 10, 12].

2 IoT SCM Problem

The IoT (Internet of Things) SCM (Supply Chain Management) solutions are using a mix of proprietary and open communications protocols and technologies and are strongly depended by the current system's actors.

The paper presents a solution that meets this requirement using less resources and thus reducing the costs. It provides some new features addressed on the agenda of supply chain issues and is built on top of an already existing infrastructure, called Blockchain. Figure 1 presents the use case for the problem formulation:

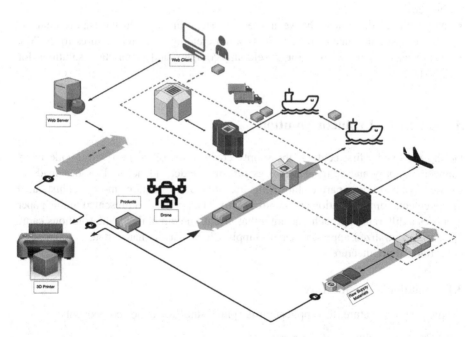

Fig. 1. A use case for the supply chain management solution applied into the for the Internet of Things field

A common use case is the following (from the upper left using reverse clock-wise direction of the Fig. 1):

- An end-user via web application is ordering a product from an e-commerce web site.
- The web site is storing the request and trigger the product manufacturing since the user is paying a part of the product.
- The 3D printer is printing the product and when it is ready, the drone is automatically collecting the products for various orders and are placing them into the containers.
- The transport containers are moved from the warehouse to the first transporter by having an IoT Blockchain smart contract to be fulfilled with certain conditions (e.g. the temperature, the humidity, etc.). The IoT is specific because of the transportation containers which have different sensors.
- Once, first transporter is moving the product to another transporter keeping the proper conditions, with parts of the smart contract fulfilled, then is receiving the crypto-currencies corresponding to its service.
- Finally, the product is hitting the end-user and the final payment for the transportation is done by the end-user.

This new architecture needs to address and resolve some of the next issues:

- With the development of the information technology and the way that people purchase products and services, the amount of data that are exchanged and need to be stored and process during the supply chain becomes big. This leads to even bigger costs.
- Multicultural differences between sites and steps involved in the supply chain is another issue that needs to be address when creating new architectures for SCMs.
- These leads to huge costs for developing complex and proprietary solutions for SCMs.

3 IoT SCM Problem Solution

During the twenty-first century, the supply chain has evolved into world-wide interconnected supply-and-demand networks full of interdependencies. This fact leads to smarter collaborative partnerships, big manufacturers require more sophisticated management, communication and control [4, 6]. The application presented in this paper proposes a different approach, meaning that, if until now mainly all the solutions came up with a centralized approach, Open Supply Chain – as its name states - proposes a decentralized architecture.

3.1 Solution's Architecture

To provide this feature, the application is spitted into two major components:

(a) The core backbone of the application.
(b) The consumers, represented by IoT devices.

The core backbone of the application is composed of two smart contracts, written in Solidity - a set of instructions that manage the exchange of value. These smart contracts are deployed on a test network, called TestRPC (for the demo purposes, Ropsten and Rinkeby test networks have been used), playing the role of the "BlockChain".

This backbone provides all the services needed by the second category, in the use of recording every state of the product and the transporter, and creating some rules between them, which they are automatically enforced to respect.

Figure 2 shows the Secure IoT SCM Components Diagram:

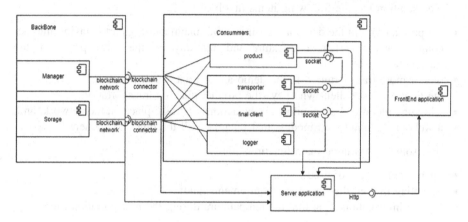

Fig. 2. Secure IoT SCM blockchain components diagram

The first smart contract provides the following utilities:

1. Setting and retrieving the public key of each node that take part in the contract.
2. Broadcasting bid requests, emitted by the product, in the search for transporters that could take him from one point to another.
3. The functionality by which a transporter can place its bid, for a chosen product.
4. The utility functions providing the caller the blockchain address of the previous and the next node involved in the smart contract.
5. It offers the product the free choice over the best suited transporter on a desired route, based on its own criteria.
6. The possibility offered to the product to log details about the temperature during transportation time.
7. A hierarchy type representation of the transporters, based on their scoring, and also an inter-nal function that calculates the scoring for each transporter based on the way that they respected the terms agreed with the product.
8. The functionality by which the current node can exchange the product that is in his posses-sion to the next one.
9. Authentication functionalities.
10. Utility by which value, represented here by some tokens, is transferred from an account to another.

The second smart contract provides some extra storage functionalities: stores the email of the client that is supposed to receive the product, for authentication purpose, stores each node's exposed interface (<IP>:<PORT>). The second piece of the architecture is made up by the clients that use the backbone. A good intro and understanding of the Bitcoin blockchain and technology [1, 5] and the Ethereum system and the smart contracts [2, 8, 12, 13] will help the reader in understanding the underlying mechanisms at developer level. An example of the parts of the smart contract in Solidity used into the demo for this paper is in the Annex of this paper.

The solution has the following items involved:

- the product(s) – in the demo a mini-industrial manufacturing part is taking into account (it needs certain temperature and humidity for the entire period of the transportation);
- one or more transporters – in the demo are at least 2 transporters;
- the final end-user client who pays the product plus the transportation;
- a logging module, that monitors all the actions that take place on the network, and;
- a web-application based module that integrates all the other components.

The solution has three main functionalities:

- open a bid for the desired route,
- accepting the bid that suites its requirements, and;
- log the information regarding the temperature during the transportation time.

The transporter interacts with the BlockChain, having the next key functions: listen if there is a new bid opened, check if he can accomplish the requested requirements, and place his bid. If his bid is accepted, then he must transport the product, in conformity with the contract agreed.

The final client is a Node script that runs on a server machine. It has the role to accept connections from the last transporter, in the scope of mutual authentication. It represents the last step in the process, mapping the physical client that requested the product.

The last component is the web-based application. It represents the actual online store, from where users can purchase goods. It has a frontend side, which makes calls to the server application running in the backend side. This server is also connected to the Block-chain network, listening to informative events emitted for the final client, and in the same time, communicates with the product script and with the final client script, linking the physical demands, requested by the external user, with the logical demands, requested by these scripts.

3.2 Application Data Flow

Data are exchanged between all the participants in the application. There are two main sections of data flow that may be distinguished:

(a) Data exchanged using the Blockchain.
(b) Data exchange between web application and peers involved in blockchain network.

Figure 3 shows the UML Activity diagram for the user-web application and blockchain interaction:

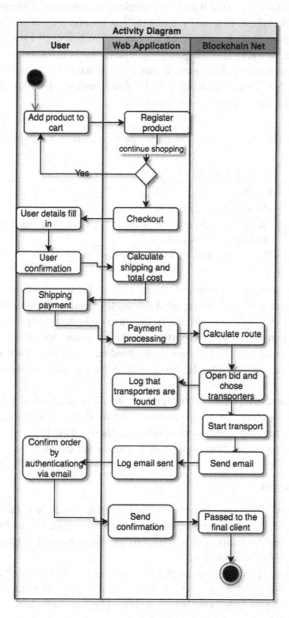

Activity Diagram

| User | Web Application | Blockchain Net |

- Add product to cart
- Register product
- continue shopping
- Yes
- User details fill in
- Checkout
- User confirmation
- Calculate shipping and total cost
- Shipping payment
- Payment processing
- Calculate route
- Log that transporters are found
- Open bid and chose transporters
- Start transport
- Confirm order by authentication via email
- Log email sent
- Send email
- Send confirmation
- Passed to the final client

Fig. 3. The data flow for the user-web application and blockchain interaction as the UML Activity diagram

The protocol used for sending and receiving data on the Blockchain network is called JSON-RPC. It is a light-weight form of a remote procedure call protocol. It is transport agnostic, meaning that it can be used over HTTP, over sockets, in the same process or over other message passing environment. There are two ways of exchanging data using Blockchain. The first way is via sending transactions. Through transaction, the state of the Blockchain is actually updated. The second way of sending data using the network, is via events. A smart contract can define and emit events, broadcasting them to the entire network. It is the job of the client that is involved in the process, to create a listener for that specific event, a process it accordingly.

The Table 1 shows the interactions of the peers registered to the blockchain network which can be decomposed in four phases.

Table 1. The interactions stages of the peers registered to the blockchain network

Phases	Stage description
Phase 1	The bidding
Phase 2	The start of the transport
Phase 3	The actual transportation phase and passing the product from one transporter to another
Phase 4	The reception of the product by the final client

This stage contains the opening of a new request for transportation and receiving bids for that request. After analyzing all the bids, the product chooses the best bid for each section, then send it to the contract, in the form of an accepting response. This one forwards the response to the transporter, using the event approach. After the first transporter starts its way to the destination, the product is notified by the smart contract. When receiving the notification, the product starts to log the temperature at a given interval.

When one transporter reaches the end of its section, there is taking place the exchange of the product, from the current one to the next transporter. The final transporter, when arriving at the destination, is authenticating the final user and, if he proves to be who he claims, the product is passed to the client.

3.3   Security Issues

Regarding security, there are two main angles from which we must analyze the application. One of them is the cryptographic utilities provided by the blockchain, and the other is the confidentiality and integrity of the data changed between nodes, in a peer to peer type of communication.

First, blockchain provides immutability. This means that each transaction, once recorded, is there for good. This property, very useful in any value transferring system, is achieved using the so called one-way functions. Each new block of transactions that must be added to the ledger, has a field that represents the result of a hash function between the same field of the previews block and the hash of current block. This implies that each block depends on the previews one, which provides his previous one, and so on. In these mode, tempering data from blocks that are already registered in the blockchain is practically impossible.

Second, one of the core functionalities of the blockchain is strong cryptography. Every network participant has his own private keys. Every transaction made by a participant has assigned this key, that acts like a kind of digital signature. In this way, every modification on a transaction already registered in blockchain will make the signature invalid and every peer in the network will know that something happened. In this way, further damage is prevented.

At the application level, the communication between the nodes involved in the process, should also be secured and authenticated. This implies the fact that the smart contract needs to do some validations before mediating data transfer. First, the smart contract should keep an internal list of all the participants involved in the supply chain. When a product agrees a trans-porter, it is automatically added to this list, in the proper order. The smart contract is built to deal with multiple products, having multiple transporters. To accomplish this, it uses an internal structure, called dictionary, or map. In this way, for every product address, it is assigned a list of transporter addresses, and the final address being the one of the final client.

One of the biggest issue regarding security was the authentication of the giving and receiving nodes. In the real world, an attacker could easily impersonate one or the other, tricking the counterparty to receive another product, or to steal the product. Since blockchain doesn't pro-vide data confidentiality, mutual authentication had to be done in a hybrid mode, meaning that each peer is connected to the smart contract via the blockchain network, and in the same time is communication with the counterparty peer using sockets.

Before booting, each node connected to the network creates a pair of ECIES keys (Elliptic Curve Integrated Encryption Scheme). After the keys are created, each peer uploads its public key to the network. This step is vital in the process of mutual authentication.

When two nodes try to make the exchange of the product, one of them must initiate the authentication process. First, the initiating node has to find the blockchain address of the counterparty, using functions provided by the smart contract. After receiving the address, it must find out the network IP and PORT on which the other node has opened a socket. This is done using again functionalities provided by the smart contract. Next step is initiating the socket connection. This implies a client-server architecture, in which the initiator represents the client, and the counterparty represents the server.

The initiator creates a random challenge. The challenge is first sent to the smart contract, in con-junction with the address of the peer that must be authenticated. The smart contract stores this challenge into an internal dictionary, so that no one can access the content of the it. Meanwhile, on the initiator side, the challenge is encrypted with the counterparty's public key, retrieved from the network. The encrypted message is sent to the other peer, which decrypts the challenge, only if it has the correct private key.

After the decryption, the receiving peer does the same steps as the initiator. It creates a random challenge, that is sent to the smart contract and bound with the initiator's address, then it encrypts this challenge with the initiator's public key and sends the output to the later.

Figure 4 shows the authentication flow as the UML Activity diagram:

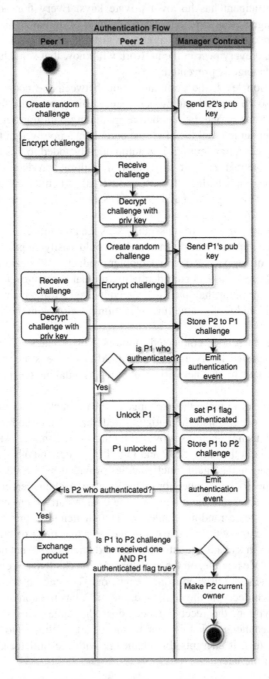

Fig. 4. The authentication activity diagram

Next, the receiving peer sends the received challenge to the smart contract, which tries to find if the value registered in its internal dictionary, for the address of the sender of this transaction, matches the value received. If yes, then the receiving peer is authenticated, and an event is emitted by the contract in the whole network. When receiving the event, the initiator submits its own received challenge, and the smart contract does the same validations.

4 Conclusions

Supply chain management is a key problem in our modern economy. Thus, improving the solutions offered up until now, to meet the customers' needs and the suppliers' capabilities is vital for keeping up and running the economic system at its fast dynamics.

There are a lot of points that need to be improved, such as transparency, speed, reliability, interoperability, and as our world becomes more digitalized and the risk of cyber-attacks in-creases drastically, security is making its way up to the top challenges.

Combining blockchain, IoT, software development and proper architecture, it is resolved a list of issues found in the real SCMs as can be seen in Table 2:

Table 2. Issues in real SCMs

Issue	Description
Transparency	More and more customers and providers want to track and see the status of their products. As a real use case, we could think of groceries bought from a super market. Usually, we must trust the producers and the vendors by their own word, and very often we find out that they hide some things. Using the application described, one can see all the phases and changes made upon the groceries that he/she buys. This leads us to the lifetime of the data
Life time of data	This is another issue that is resolved. Usually, a private SCM solution comes up with costly archival databases, that are very hard to maintain. Open Supply Chain comes with an alternative solution, built on top of blockchain, that is less ex-pensive and the data are stored forever
Accessibility and scalability	These are important for the reliability. The customer would like to see the product's status at any time. In the digitalized economy, every minute is important. In traditional and centralized SCM's, if the central unit is down for only a few moments, there are big loses. But Open Supply Chain, having a decentralized architecture, doesn't have a single point of failure or attack. This way, the accessibility is maximum and the solution is always running
Security	The reception of the product by the final client should be secure in terms of privacy and confidentiality. More than this, the customer identity theft and the customer impersonation must be avoided

The secured supply chain management presented in this paper tried to address some of the real-world issues and implemented the solutions, to prove that there are ways that can be used to diminish the risks in this area.

Acknowledgment. This work was supported by a grant of the Romanian Ministry of Research and Innovation, CCCDI UEFISCDI, project number PN-III-P1-1.2-PCCDI-2017-0272/Avantgarde Technology Hub for Advanced Security (ATLAS), within PNCDI III.

Annex – Parts of the Solidity Smart Contract for SCM Demo

Example of the parts of a Smart Contract for the IoT SCM Blockchain solution – manager.sol:

```solidity
pragma solidity ^0.4.4;
contract manager2 {
    address admin;
    mapping (address => string) challanges;
    function manager2() public payable {
        admin = msg.sender;
        balance[admin] = 100000000000;
    }
    struct transporter{
        address transporterAddress;
        uint price;
        uint time;
        uint temp;
        bool isAccepted;
        bool agreed;
        uint pointA;
        uint pointB;
        uint256 startTime;
    }
    mapping (address => uint) balance;
    mapping (address => transporter[]) productWay;
    mapping (address => uint) currentOwner;
    mapping (address => uint) startIndex;
    mapping (address => bool) unlock;
    mapping (address => string) pubKeys;
    mapping (address => uint) scoringMap;

    event LogChallange(address from, string challange, uint id);
    event LogTransporterAdded(address product, address transporter, uint poz, uint pointA,
    uint pointB, uint id);
    event LogTransporterChanges(address product, address transporter, uint poz, uint price,
    uint temp, uint time, uint id);
    event LogProductChanges(address product, address trans-porter, uint poz, uint price, uint
    temp, uint time, uint id);
    event LogBeginTransport(address transport, uint id);
    event LogArivedAtFinalClient( uint id);

    ...
    function setPubKey(string key) public returns (bool){
        LogDebug('Set the pub key', idSeq++);
        pubKeys[msg.sender] = key;
        return true;
    }
    ...
```

References

1. Antonopoulos, A.M.: Mastering Bitcoin, 2nd edn. O'Reilly Media, Inc., Sebastopol (2017). ISBN 9781491954379
2. Antonopoulos, A.M., Wood, G.: Mastering Ethereum - Building Smart Contracts and DApps. O'Reilly Media, Inc., Sebastopol (2018). https://covers.oreillystatic.com/images/0636920056072/rc_lrg.jpg
3. Christidis, K., Devetsikiotis, M.: Blockchains and smart contracts for the internet of things. IEEE Access (2016). https://doi.org/10.1109/access.2016.2566339
4. Brynjolfsson, E., McAfee, A.: The Second Machine Age (2014)
5. Nakamoto, S.: Bitcoin: a peer-to-peer electronic cash system (2008). https://bitcoin.org/bitcoin.pdf
6. Christopher, M.: Logistics and Supply Chain Management. Financial Times Publishing, Upper Saddle River (1992)
7. Narayanan, A., Bonneau, J., Felten, E., Miller, A., Goldfeder, S.: Bitcoin and Cryptocurrency Technologies: A Comprehensive Introduction. Princeton University Press, Princeton (2016)
8. Dannen, C.: The EVM. In: Introducing Ethereum and Solidity: Foundations of Cryptocurrency and Blockchain Programming for Beginners. Apress (2017)
9. AT&T: What you need to know about IoT platforms (2017)
10. Supply Chain. https://www.thebalance.com/what-is-the-supply-chain-3305677
11. O'Dowd, A., Ramakrishna, V., Novotny, P., Gaur, N., Desrosiers, L., Baset, S.: Hands-On Blockchain with Hyperledger. E-Packt Publishing House, Birmingham (2018). ISBN 9781788994521
12. IBM Blockchain. https://www.ibm.com/blogs/blockchain/2017/12/blockchain-security-what-keeps-your-transaction-data-safe/
13. Solidity Smart Contracts. https://blockgeeks.com/guides/solidity/
14. Ethereum. https://www.ethereum.org

ADvoCATE: A Consent Management Platform for Personal Data Processing in the IoT Using Blockchain Technology

Konstantinos Rantos[1]([envelope]), George Drosatos[2], Konstantinos Demertzis[1], Christos Ilioudis[3], Alexandros Papanikolaou[3], and Antonios Kritsas[1]

[1] Department of Computer and Informatics Engineering,
Eastern Macedonia and Thrace Institute of Technology, Kavala, Greece
{krantos,kdemertzis,ankrits}@teiemt.gr
[2] Department of Electrical and Computer Engineering,
Democritus University of Thrace, Xanthi, Greece
gdrosato@ee.duth.gr
[3] Department of Information Technology,
Alexander Technological Educational Institute of Thessaloniki,
Thessaloniki, Greece
iliou@it.teithe.gr, alxpapanikolaou@gmail.com

Abstract. The value of personal data generated and managed by smart devices which comprise the Internet of Things (IoT) is unquestionable. The EU General Data Protection Regulation (GDPR) that has been recently put in force, sets the cornerstones regarding the collection and processing of personal data, for the benefit of Data Subjects and Controllers. However, applying this regulation to the IoT ecosystem is not a trivial task. This paper proposes ADvoCATE, a user-centric solution that allows data subjects to easily control consents regarding access to their personal data in the IoT ecosystem and exercise their rights defined by GDPR. It also assists Data Controllers and Processors to meet GDPR requirements. A blockchain infrastructure ensures the integrity of personal data processing consents, while the quality thereof is evaluated by an intelligence service. Finally, we present some preliminary details of a partial implementation of the proposed framework.

Keywords: Privacy · Internet of Things · GDPR ·
Consents management · Blockchain · Policy-based access control ·
Data privacy ontology

1 Introduction

The rapid growth of the number of deployed Internet of Things (IoT) devices that collect personal data from the user's environment is bound to threaten users' privacy. These devices share data that can be used to monitor users activities, status and characteristics, create user profiles – with or without their consent

© Springer Nature Switzerland AG 2019
J.-L. Lanet and C. Toma (Eds.): SecITC 2018, LNCS 11359, pp. 300–313, 2019.
https://doi.org/10.1007/978-3-030-12942-2_23

– and make automated decisions. Most of the users will experience significant challenges regarding the protection of their personal data in the IoT ecosystem, which mainly originate from the fact that the average user does not understand how these data are being collected and used. At the same time, the majority of the IoT users are particularly concerned about the exposure of their personal data, they consider privacy an important issue in the IoT and want to have personal control of their personal data. These concerns have also been highlighted in a global survey contacted by Fortinet regarding key issues pertaining to the Internet of Things (IoT) [11].

The General Data Protection Regulation (GDPR) [10], which has recently set new rules for how companies can share EU citizens' personal data, significantly addresses the above concerns and influences user-centric privacy solutions and research directions regarding privacy in the IoT ecosystem [21]. Compliance with the GDPR requirements in the IoT world, and especially in applications related to smart health and smart homes, typically requires data controllers to obtain and manage appropriate users' consents[1].

ADvoCATE aims to provide an environment to help users retain control over their personal data in the IoT ecosystem, in line with the GDPR requirements. Following a user-centric approach, the framework aims to satisfy the main GDPR requirements according to which data controllers will, among others, be able to request data subjects' consents and inform them in a transparent and unambiguous manner about (a) personal data to be managed and the sources of origin, (b) the purposes, time periods and legal basis of the processing, (c) the entity(ies) that will process it, and (d) recipients or categories of data recipients.

Similarly, data subjects, in line with the GDPR requirements [10], will (a) be informed about requests for processing their personal data, (b) be able to create privacy preferences, define specific data processing rules and give their consent, (c) have the opportunity to exercise their rights in terms of access, correction, deletion, restriction, and object to the processing, and (d) be aware of the security and quality of the licenses/consents they have given.

Moreover, ADvoCATE utilizes blockchain technology to protect the integrity and versioning of users' consents while an intelligence component analyses policy data to detect conflicts in a data subject's policy and provides recommendations to data subjects to further protect them from unwittingly exposing their personal data. This paper extends the work published in [19] and presents the details of our prototype implementation.

The remainder of this paper is organized as follows. Section 2 describes the related work. Section 3 specifies the proposed framework and its components. Section 4 presents a preliminary implementation details, while Sect. 5 concludes this paper and presents suggestions for future work.

---

[1] The regulation defines additional lawful bases for personal data processing that do not require users' consents, such as for the protection of data subjects' vital interests. These are out of the scope of ADvoCATE as they do not require user interaction.

2   Related Work

The need to give users the ability to control their personal data generated by IoT devices in their personal environment is widely recognised [20]. The European Research Cluster on the Internet of Things (IERC) also points this need with an extra emphasis on the GDPR [12]. However, user's privacy protection in the IoT is not an easy task [26]. One of the ways to address the privacy challenges is to find appropriate ways to apply policy-based access control. This has been recognised as an important research opportunity by IERC and other researchers in the field [21, 22].

The framework proposed in [3], allows users to define their privacy preferences for the IoT devices with which they interact. Communications are performed via a central blockchain-connected gateway, which ensures that the transmitted data is in accordance with the user's preferences. Blockchain technology is employed to protect and manage the privacy preferences that each user of the system has set, ensuring that no sensitive data has been gained without their consent.

The use of Blockchain gateways is also suggested in [4], where the setup is customised for use with IoT scenarios. In particular, the same account can be used for connecting to different Blockchain-enabled gateways rather than having to register to each gateway, which is a very practical approach. These gateways effectively play the role of mediators, handling the various requests/responses to/from the devices accordingly.

Ongoing research efforts regarding user-centric security and privacy in IoT, such as the UPRISE-IoT project [14], consider users' behaviour and context to elevate protection in a privacy-preserving manner. Apart from enabling the user to fine-tune the level of privacy it also makes them aware about what information is being protected as well as the value of the aforementioned information. Good practices to be taken into account for obtaining user's consent for IoT applications in the healthcare sector are also proposed in [17].

The work presented in [6] involves the use of a semi-autonomous context-aware agent, which takes decisions on behalf of the user. The agent takes into account context, behaviour and a community-based reputation system in order to reach a decision. Despite the fact that the system allows the user to retain control, it may be the case that it may fail to choose the intended privacy options in cases that fall outside the observed behaviour.

The EnCoRe project [9], has also developed mechanisms in which subjects can set consent policies and manage them. However, EnCoRe was not designed for the IoT ecosystem. Instead it was centered on employee data on an organisational context and on how user's privacy policy is enforced within the organization. The framework proposed in the present work borrows certain aspects of the EnCoRe solution, adapted to the IoT environment, while adopting enhanced GDPR-compliant ontologies to provide a solid mechanism for managing data subjects' consents.

ADvoCATE addresses the challenges of privacy protection in the IoT, particularly with regards to the management of consents, as required by the GDPR, and tries to fill a considerable gap in this area. It permits users to manage their consents and formulate policies for the distribution of their personal data, taking into account the corresponding recommendations provided by the platform. Likewise, it provides data controllers with a useful tool to facilitate their compliance with the GDPR.

3   Proposed Architecture

The ADvoCATE approach concerns a series of sensors in the user's environment that gather data related to the data subject. Such environments could be a patient health monitoring system, activity monitoring sensors or even a smart home. The usage of a portable device, such as a smartphone, provides data subjects with a user-friendly environment to interact and manage their consents and their personal data disposal policy. Furthermore, it provides a way for data controllers to communicate with data subjects and acquire the necessary consents. Figure 1 presents our proposed architecture and it is focused, for simplicity reasons, on health ecosystems and smart cities. In this architecture, ADvoCATE is visualised as a cloud service platform, that consists of the functional components described in the following sections, while their interaction during the creation of a new consent is presented in Fig. 2.

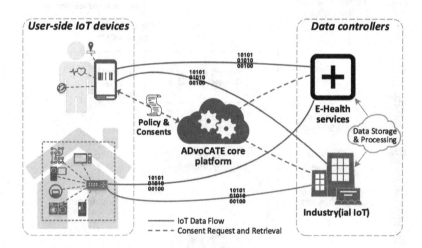

Fig. 1. ADvoCATE infrastructure.

3.1   Consent Management Component

The *consent management* component is responsible for managing users' personal data disposal policies and their respective consents, including generation, updates and withdrawals. These generic, domain-specific, or context-based privacy policies consists of a set of rules that correspond to data subjects' consents

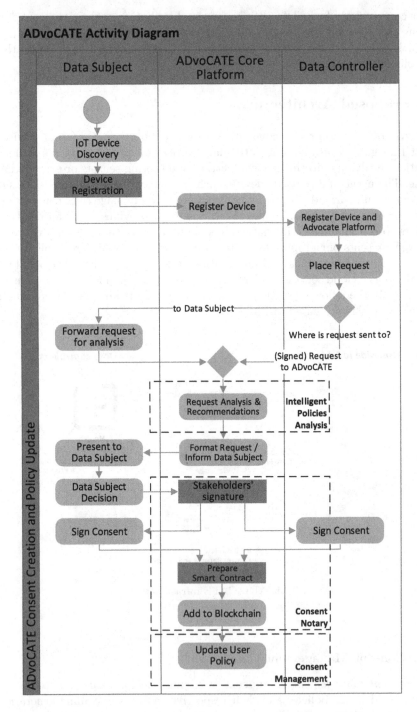

Fig. 2. Interaction of ADvoCATE components during creation of new consents.

and can be formulated as a result of requests submitted by data controllers for access to certain IoT data and for fixed processing purposes and periods, in accordance with the GDPR requirements.

One of the main challenges in establishing such a mechanism that is used across multiple sectors in the IoT ecosystem is to secure the semantic interoperability of the information exchanged among data subjects and controllers. The procedure to place requests, grant permissions and formulate policies requires that it is based on common rules for defining personal data sets and the use thereof, fine-grained privacy preferences, and access privileges. The grounds of this mechanism are data privacy ontologies, which ensure that data controller access requests are displayed to data subjects in a unified and clear manner. ADvoCATE adopted the ontology defined in [1], which models data protection requirements to facilitate data controllers in achieving the desired GDPR compliance.

In ADvoCATE, ontologies also facilitate intelligence policies analysis, as described in Sect. 3.3, and the specification of enforceable privacy policies. This suggests that policy description is based on clearly defined policy languages, such as the eXtensible Access Control Markup Language (XACML), to help the decision-making process. Using policies that conform to a widely adopted policy language standard, such as XACML, offers many advantages that have been also demonstrated by EnCoRe project [9] which has adopted XACML for enforcing policy based access control.

However, adopting a single ontology from ADvoCATE does not preclude the use of competitive or even similar ontologies by participating data controllers. In this case, ontology-matching mechanisms should be developed to reduce semantic gaps among different overlapping representations of the same data privacy-related information [18]. Such mechanisms include those based on machine learning which provide reliable and accurate matching results [8] and those based on a semi-supervised learning approach [27].

3.2 Consent Notary Component

To ensure the integrity, non-repudiation and validity of data subjects' consents and data controllers' commitments, ADvoCATE core platform adopted digital signatures and the usage of blockchain technology. Blockchain technology was firstly introduced to secure transactions in Bitcoin cryptocurrency [15] and nowadays has a wide range of applications to IoT [5], smart contracts and digital content distribution [25], and even to the biomedical domain [13]. The component that acts as mediator between the *consent management* component and a blockchain infrastructure is the *consent notary* component. It ensures that the created consents (and the respective policies) are up-to-date, they protect user's privacy and are protected against unauthorized or malicious attempts to repudiate or modify them.

The concept of smart contracts introduced by Ethereum [2] is our main focus in the ADvoCATE. A smart contract defines the rules and penalties around an agreement, like a conventional one, and also automatically imposes these obligations. In Bitcoin [15] and Ethereum [2], all the transactions with the blockchain are publicly available and verifiable, yet there is no direct connection to the identities of the participating entities. In ADvoCATE, the consents are also digitally signed by the contracting parties to provide non-repudiation. Moreover, in order to ensure their anonymity, only the consents' hashed version are deployed to a blockchain infrastructure.

Figure 3 presents the workflow of the *consent notary* component which works as follows. As a first step, the *consent notary* component receives as entry the agreed consent from the *consent management* component. This consent could be a new one, an update of an existing one which modifies the respective policies among the parties, or a withdrawal notice. Afterwards, both the data subject and the data controller are requested to independently sign the data subject's consent. These signatures can be later used in a dispute, if necessary. Subsequently, the hash (e.g. SHA-256 or Keccak-256 hash function utilised by Ethereum [2]) of both digital signatures is submitted in the blockchain infrastructure using a *smart contract*.

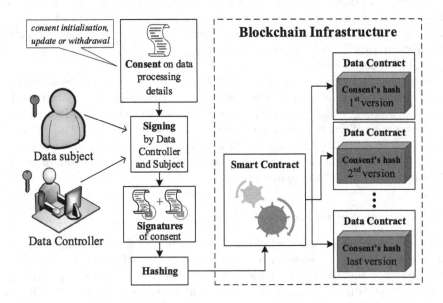

Fig. 3. The workflow of the consent notary component.

The *smart contract* between a data controller and a data subject represents a specific consent (initial, updated or withdrawal) for a particular IoT device, and is deployed in the blockchain that holds the initial consent. Thus, the *smart contract* is responsible for managing each new update of the initial consent or even its final withdrawal while a different version of the consent is represented as a *data contract*. This structure of the smart contract allows verifying whether a specific consent is the last version of it. Apart from the consents' integrity, the usage of a blockchain infrastructure guarantees the versioning and the withdrawal of consents. Finally, the current version of the signed consent with the corresponding signatures is returned by the *consent notary* component to the *consent management* component, together with the address of the *smart contract* on the blockchain.

At any later time, the data subject and the data controller (or any other authorised third-party) can verify the validity of the consent: (i) by validating the digital signatures on the consent, and (ii) by retrieving the relevant data contract (i.e., the latest version) from the blockchain infrastructure through the smart contract and comparing the retrieved hash with a new hash of the consent digital signatures. The utilisation of a blockchain infrastructure is important for our platform to secure the given consents and validation of all versions thereof, in a public verifiable and distributed way without a single trusted third-party. The digital consents with the corresponding signatures are stored for each contracting party on ADvoCATE platform, while the blockchain infrastructure is only responsible for managing the hashes of them. The smart contracts are deployed using the private key of the platform for digitally signing the transactions in the blockchain. The privacy of data subjects is preserved by utilising this information distribution among the parties and only the contracting parties know data subjects' identity without any leaks from the blockchain infrastructure.

3.3   Intelligence Component

The *intelligence* component is an innovative hybrid computational intelligence framework that combines an Intelligent Policies Analysis Mechanism (IPAM) to distinguish contradictory or conflicting rules/policies of a user's consents and an Intelligent Recommendation Mechanism (IReMe) to endorse in real-time adaptive intelligent policies or rules for the users' privacy strategies.

Intelligent Policies Analysis Mechanism. The Intelligent Policies Analysis Mechanism (IPAM) utilizes intelligent adaptive technologies to identify contradictory or conflicting rules and policies related to the disposal of private information and ensure that these cannot be used for user profiling. These rules or policies concern application-side information, such as the option "Forget me" (in accordance with GDPR), notifications to third-parties for deletion, exporting data, re-requesting or updating consent, encrypting data during transfer, implementing pseudonymisation, options about the available checkboxes in the consents, putting fields in the registration/profile form that are not needed, etc. This information does not concern the disclosure of data for the purpose of assessing personal aspects about a natural person, their habits, location, personal interests and other personal information, and do not compose a centralised entity that threatens users' privacy.

To achieve this, we use Fuzzy Cognitive Maps (FCM). FCM is a method used to achieve and represent the underlying knowledge, it supports causal knowledge in reasoning process and belongs to the neuro-fuzzy systems. The latter aim to solve decision-making problems and to model/simulate sophisticated environments. Learning algorithms have been proposed for training and updating FCMs weights based primarily on ideas derived from recurrent artificial neural networks and fuzzy logic. Additionally, the learning algorithms are used to decrease the human intervention by suggesting automated FCM candidates, activating only the most relevant concepts at any time of execution, or even making models more transparent and dynamic [7]. The IPAM supervises the overall privacy of users by generating adaptive and automated rules or capabilities. In order to achieve this control, the proposed intelligence mechanism is responsible for monitoring any changes to the user's privacy statement that disturb the overall privacy based on a mapping of the agreements.

Intelligent Recommendation Mechanism. The Intelligent Recommendation Mechanism (IReMe) is a machine learning framework used for recommending personalised rules in real-time. It provides adapted, real-time and personalised information to protect users' privacy by applying an advanced machine learning method called Cognitive Filtering (CF) [24]. It makes automated estimates and predictions by gathering specific non-private information from the user. The CF approach recommends rules based on an evaluation or comparison between the contents of the items and the user's consents. The content of each item is characterised as a set of terms or descriptors. The user's consents are depicted by the same terms and created by examining the content of the items that have been already inspected by the user.

In the IReMe, we use a hybrid process that includes neighborhood-based CF and content-based filtering, which is a vigorous model-based method that expands and improves the superiority of recommendations [23]. The purpose of this mechanism is to achieve more personalised intelligent policy rules and real-time recommendations for the users' privacy strategies to avoid any privacy leakages. Furthermore, this mechanism is more flexible in the sense that it works better when the user's space is large, it scales well with unrelated items, it is easy to implement and does not involve sophisticated tuning parameters.

4   Reference Implementation

A reference implementation for the device registration and the consent management component, based on cutting edge technologies such as Node.js[2] and MongoDB[3] and the ontology defined in [1], can be found in https://github.com/AnthonyK95/adplatform.

The user-friendly interface allows registered users to add new devices and manage them together with the corresponding consents. Moreover, the platform supports the presentation of vendors' requests, policies analysis and the collection of consents to create or update a smart contract. When this sequence is

---

[2] https://nodejs.org.
[3] https://www.mongodb.org.

finished, the platform creates a new smart contract or update an existing one that is already deployed in the blockchain.

New personal devices can be registered by providing the device name, serial number and type of device. The platform stores the provided information to the database using the pre-built schema shown below, and the registered device is assigned by the platform a unique ID.

```
1  # Advocate Device:
2    "_id":"5b02939aee297917f42c052",
3    "owner":"5af3a64f2848d418c425e80f",
4    "deviceID":741,
5    "vendorID":"IoT Electronics",
6    "deviceType":"Lamp",
7    "__v":0
```

After the successful registration of a new device, the vendor gets a notification about it with the corresponding device ID, namely 'deviceID'. The vendor's id, namely 'vendorID', located at the serial number of the device, allows the platform to identify the corresponding vendor.

The vendor creates a contract request with all the necessary data privacy information, such as processing purposes and recipients, and sends it to the user. Note that this will most likely be an automated process for the vendor. Moreover, this functionality can be expanded to allow any company or organization to request access to IoT devices, e.g. of specific type. The json-formatted request contains the following information.

```
1  {
2    "PersonalData":"Uptime data collected periodically",
3    "Retention":"We are going to collect data
4                until August 5 2019",
5    "Purpose":"Identify potential bugs",
6    "EURecipient":"We are going to share the
7                data with Wayne Enterprise,",
8    "NonEURecipient":"We are not going to share
9                your data with Non-Eu Recipients",
10   "AutomatedProcessing": false,
11   "Profiling": false,
12   "ManualProcessing": false
13 }
```

The request is displayed on the user's device as shown in Fig. 4, while the user's response initiates the creation of an instance of a contract which will keep all the requested data and the user's consent in a database entry shown below.

```
1  {
2    "_id":"5b1ff382af6c5810d00a6512",
3    "PersonalData":{"Uptime data collected periodically"},
4    "Purpose":{"Identify potential bugs"},
5    "Response":{"Agreed to Data: Uptime data will be
6                collected periodically Purpose: First Purpose"},
7    "Controller":"5afd5c52a6399d1f641ca922",
8    "deviceID":"5b1ff382af6c5810d00a6512",
9    "deviceType":"humidity sensor",
10   "Status":"Confirmed",
11   "Retention":"Data collected until August 5 2019",
12   "EURecipient":"We are going to share your data with Wayne
13                Enterprise",
14   "NonEURecipient":"We are not going to share your data with
15                Non-Eu Recipients",
```

```
16      "Company_Signature":"a243b69f8df1bec4ecfccd512405...",
17      "Client_Signature":"9ed7776be1c79395504af0c8e57e...",
18      "ID_Transaction":"a243b69f8df1bec4ec...",
19      "AutomatedProcessing":true,
20      "Profiling":false,
21      "ManualProcessing":false,
22      "__v":0
23  }
```

Fig. 4. Pending requests on user's device.

The source code of the smart contract that is shown in Contract 1 is written in Solidity language[4], and represents what is deployed to the Ethereum blockchain infrastructure per device. This contract manages all user's consents for a specific device and can be updated or even withdrawn over time. More specifically, the platform supports four basic functions: the first one adds new consents (initial, updated or withdrawal) for a data controller, the second function returns the hash of the last consent for a data controller, the third returns the time that a specific consent was given to a data controller and the fourth function returns all the consents that are given to a specific data controller over time. The cost analysis of this contract at the time of our experiments on 19 September 2018 (1 Ether = 179.78€) using average price of 'gas' 14 Gwei (1 Gwei = 1 M Nanoether) is: deployment cost - 1.03€, initial consent to a data controller - 0.22€ and updating or withdrawing consent - 0.18€.

---

[4] https://solidity.readthedocs.io.

Contract 1. Smart contract of a consent per device of user.

```
 1: pragma solidity ^0.4.23;
 2: contract ConsentPerUserDevice{
 3:   mapping (bytes32=>ConsentVersion) controller;
      //the address of the ADvoCATE platform
 4:   address private advocate = 0x583031d1113ad414f02576bd6afabfb302140225;
 5:   bytes32 userHash = 0xd35f61ad141d7b92f4c17e609ef394292ca0e9341942c55...;
 6:   bytes32 deviceHash = 0xa018a0957ed590aeb053fa0561ea90453e260eca1846f...;

 7:   struct ConsentVersion{
 8:     bytes32[ ] consentHash;
 9:     mapping (bytes32=>uint256) timeStamp;
10:   }

      //Function 1: add new consent for a data controller
11:   function addConsent(bytes32 _ctlhash, bytes32 _csthash) public{
12:     require(msg.sender == advocate); //only the owner can add new values
13:     controller[_ctlhash].consentHash.push(_csthash);
14:     controller[_ctlhash].timeStamp[_csthash]=now;
15:   }

      //Function 2: return the hash of the last consent for a data controller
16:   function getLastConsent(bytes32 _ctlhash) view public returns(bytes32){
17:     if(controller[_ctlhash].consentHash.length==0) return 0;
18:     else return controller[_ctlhash].consentHash[controller[_ctlhash].consentHash.length-1];
19:   }

      //Function 3: return the time of consent for a data controller
20:   function getTime(bytes32 _ctlhash, bytes32 _csthash) view public returns(uint256){
21:     return controller[_ctlhash].timeStamp[_csthash];
22:   }

      //Function 4: return all the consents for a data controller
23:   function getAll(bytes32 _ctlhash) view public returns(bytes32[ ]){
24:     return controller[_ctlhash].consentHash;
25:   }
26: }
```

5   Conclusions and Future Work

In this work, we proposed a framework that covers a major emerging need regarding the privacy of users in the IoT ecosystem. This work in progress sets the foundations for creating trust relationships among data controllers and subjects towards an IoT ecosystem compliant with the GDPR. The goal is to develop a user-centric solution that will allow data subjects to shape and manage the policies of their consents as a response to unambiguous access requests placed by data controllers. Additionally, the proposed approach utilises blockchain technology to support the consents' integrity, non-repudiation and versioning in a publicly verifiable manner. The cost of blockchain usage could be transferred to the data controllers that would gain the benefits of the aggregated knowledge from the management of personal data. Additionally, a private blockchain network maintained by all the data controllers and other data regulators (such as in [16]) could be established to minimize this cost. Finally, an intelligence component analyses incoming requests to identify policy rules conflicts regarding personal data disposal and assists users make the right decisions.

312   K. Rantos et al.

As future work, we intend to explore further the issues surrounding each of the components that make up the proposed framework with an emphasis on the improvement of GDPR-compliant data privacy ontologies and the *intelligence* component. Furthermore, we aim to consider the use of policies, generated by the proposed system, in policy-based access control systems, which will complement a personal data management solution in the IoT ecosystem.

References

1. Bartolini, C., Muthuri, R., Santos, C.: Using ontologies to model data protection requirements in workflows. In: Otake, M., Kurahashi, S., Ota, Y., Satoh, K., Bekki, D. (eds.) New Frontiers in Artificial Intelligence, vol. 10091, pp. 233–248. Springer, Cham (2017). https://doi.org/10.1007/978-3-319-50953-2_17
2. Buterin, V.: A next-generation smart contract and decentralized application platform (n.d.). https://github.com/ethereum/wiki/wiki/White-Paper. Accessed 02 Oct 2018
3. Cha, S.C., Chen, J.F., Su, C., Yeh, K.H.: A blockchain connected gateway for BLE-based devices in the Internet of Things. IEEE Access **PP**(99), 1–1 (2018). https://doi.org/10.1109/ACCESS.2018.2799942
4. Cha, S.C., Tsai, T.Y., Peng, W.C., Huang, T.C., Hsu, T.Y.: Privacy-aware and blockchain connected gateways for users to access legacy IoT devices. In: 2017 IEEE 6th Global Conference on Consumer Electronics (GCCE), pp. 1–3, October 2017. https://doi.org/10.1109/GCCE.2017.8229327
5. Conoscenti, M., Vetrò, A., Martin, J.C.D.: Blockchain for the Internet of Things: a systematic literature review. In: 2016 IEEE/ACS 13th International Conference of Computer Systems and Applications (AICCSA), pp. 1–6, November 2016. https://doi.org/10.1109/AICCSA.2016.7945805
6. Copigneaux, B.: Semi-autonomous, context-aware, agent using behaviour modelling and reputation systems to authorize data operation in the Internet of Things. In: 2014 IEEE World Forum on Internet of Things (WF-IoT), pp. 411–416, March 2014. https://doi.org/10.1109/WF-IoT.2014.6803201
7. Demertzis, K., Iliadis, L.S., Anezakis, V.D.: An innovative soft computing system for smart energy grids cybersecurity. Adv. Build. Energy Res. **12**(1), 3–24 (2018). https://doi.org/10.1080/17512549.2017.1325401
8. Eckert, K., Meilicke, C., Stuckenschmidt, H.: Improving ontology matching using meta-level learning. In: Aroyo, L., et al. (eds.) ESWC 2009. LNCS, vol. 5554, pp. 158–172. Springer, Heidelberg (2009). https://doi.org/10.1007/978-3-642-02121-3_15
9. EnCoRe Project: Ensuring consent and revocation (2010). www.hpl.hp.com/breweb/encoreproject/. Accessed 02 Oct 2018
10. European Parliament and Council: Regulation (EU) 2016/679 of 27 April 2016 on the protection of natural persons with regard to the processing of personal data and on the free movement of such data, and repealing Directive 95/46/EC (General Data Protection Regulation). Official Journal of the European Union (Apr 2016), http://eur-lex.europa.eu/legal-content/en/TXT/?uri=CELEX%3A32016R0679
11. Fortinet Inc.: Fortinet reveals "Internet of Things: connected home" survey results (2014). https://www.fortinet.com/corporate/about-us/newsroom/press-releases/2014/internet-of-things.html. Accessed 02 Oct 2018

12. IERC: European Research Cluster on the Internet of Things, Internet of Things: IoT governance, privacy and security issues (2015). http://www.internet-of-things-research.eu/pdf/IERC_Position_Paper_IoT_Governance_Privacy_Security_Final.pdf. Accessed 02 Oct 2018

13. Kleinaki, A.S., Mytis-Gkometh, P., Drosatos, G., Efraimidis, P.S., Kaldoudi, E.: A blockchain-based notarization service for biomedical knowledge retrieval. Comput. Struct. Biotechnol. J. **16**, 288–297 (2018). https://doi.org/10.1016/j.csbj.2018.08.002

14. Musolesi, M.: UPRISE-IoT: User-centric PRIvacy & Security in IoT (2017). http://gtr.rcuk.ac.uk/projects?ref=EP%2FP016278%2F1. Accessed 02 Oct 2018

15. Nakamoto, S.: Bitcoin: a peer-to-peer electronic cash system (2008). https://bitcoin.org/bitcoin.pdf. Accessed 02 Oct 2018

16. Nugent, T., Upton, D., Cimpoesu, M.: Improving data transparency in clinical trials using blockchain smart contracts. F1000Research **5**, 2541 (2016). https://doi.org/10.12688/f1000research.9756.1

17. O'Connor, Y., Rowan, W., Lynch, L., Heavin, C.: Privacy by design: informed consent and internet of things for smart health. Procedia Comput. Sci. **113**, 653–658 (2017). https://doi.org/10.1016/j.procs.2017.08.329

18. Otero-Cerdeira, L., Rodríguez-Martínez, F.J., Gómez-Rodríguez, A.: Ontology matching. Expert Syst. Appl. **42**(2), 949–971 (2015). https://doi.org/10.1016/j.eswa.2014.08.032

19. Rantos, K., Drosatos, G., Demertzis, K., Ilioudis, C., Papanikolaou, A.: Blockchain-based consents management for personal data processing in the IoT ecosystem. In: 15th International Conference on Security and Cryptography (SECRYPT 2018), part of ICETE, pp. 572–577. SciTePress, Porto (2018). https://doi.org/10.5220/0006911005720577

20. Russell, B., Garlat, C., Lingenfelter, D.: Security guidance for early adopters of the Internet of Things (IoT). White paper, Cloud Security Alliance, April 2015

21. Sicari, S., Rizzardi, A., Grieco, L.A., Coen-Porisini, A.: Security, privacy and trust in Internet of Things: the road ahead. Comput. Netw. **76**, 146–164 (2015). https://doi.org/10.1016/j.comnet.2014.11.008

22. Stankovic, J.A.: Research directions for the Internet of Things. IEEE Internet Things J. **1**(1), 3–9 (2014). https://doi.org/10.1109/JIOT.2014.2312291

23. Shih, Y.-Y., Liu, D.-R.: Hybrid recommendation approaches: collaborative filtering via valuable content information, p. 217b. IEEE (2005). https://doi.org/10.1109/HICSS.2005.302

24. Yang, Z., Wu, B., Zheng, K., Wang, X., Lei, L.: A survey of collaborative filtering-based recommender systems for mobile internet applications. IEEE Access **4**, 3273–3287 (2016). https://doi.org/10.1109/ACCESS.2016.2573314

25. Yli-Huumo, J., Ko, D., Choi, S., Park, S., Smolander, K.: Where is current research on blockchain technology?—A systematic review. PLoS ONE **11**(10), e0163477 (2016). https://doi.org/10.1371/journal.pone.0163477

26. Zhang, Z.K., Cho, M.C.Y., Wang, C.W., Hsu, C.W., Chen, C.K., Shieh, S.: IoT security: ongoing challenges and research opportunities. In: 7th International Conference on Service-Oriented Computing and Applications, pp. 230–234. IEEE, November 2014. https://doi.org/10.1109/SOCA.2014.58

27. Zhu, X., Ghahramani, Z., Lafferty, J.: Semi-supervised learning using Gaussian fields and harmonic functions. In: IN ICML, pp. 912–919 (2003)

Development of the Unified Security Requirements of PUFs During the Standardization Process

Nicolas Bruneau[1], Jean-Luc Danger[2], Adrien Facon[1,3], Sylvain Guilley[1,2,3(✉)],
Soshi Hamaguchi[4], Yohei Hori[5], Yousung Kang[6], and Alexander Schaub[2]

[1] Secure-IC S.A.S., 15 Rue Claude Chappe, Bât. B, 35 510 Cesson-Sévigné, France
`sylvain.guilley@secure-ic.com`
[2] LTCI, Télécom ParisTech, Université Paris-Saclay, 75 013 Paris, France
[3] École Normale Supérieure, Paris, France
[4] Cosmos Corporation, Mie, Japan
[5] National Institute of Advanced Industrial Science and Technology (AIST), Ibaraki, Japan
[6] ETRI, Daejeon, Korea

Abstract. This paper accounts for some scientific aspects related to the international standardization process about physically unclonable functions (PUFs), through the drafting of ISO/IEC 20897 project. The primary motivation for this standard project is to structure and expand the market of PUFs, as solutions for non-tamperable electronic chips identifiers.

While drafting the documents and discussing with international experts, the topic of PUF also gained much maturity. This article accounts how scientific structuration of the PUF as a field of embedded systems security has been emerging as a byproduct. First, the standardization has allowed to merge two redundant security requirements (namely *diffuseness* and *unpredictability*) into one (namely *randomness*), which in addition better suits all kinds of PUFs. As another contribution, the standardization process made it possible to match unambiguous and consistent tests with the security requirements. Furthermore, the process revealed that tests can be seen as *estimators* from their theoretic expressions, the so-called *stochastic models*.

1 Introduction

Security is an enabler for the expansion of our digital society. The trend is all the more important with the settling of Internet of Things (IoT). Communicating parties become not only humans but also machines, and without surprise, there are today more machines than humans on our planet. Typically, each human uses many machines to service him personally. Besides, some mutualized infrastructures also leverage on IoT or Machine-To-Machine (M2M) objects.

In this context, it is crucial to attest of the identity of parties. Indeed, communicating with unidentified IoT objects can lead to malware infection and can

© Springer Nature Switzerland AG 2019
J.-L. Lanet and C. Toma (Eds.): SecITC 2018, LNCS 11359, pp. 314–330, 2019.
https://doi.org/10.1007/978-3-030-12942-2_24

of course be subverted by attackers to build attacks. Most simple attacks consist in masquerade, that is malevolent situation whereby one device pretends it is another one. These vulnerabilities are the premise of building botnets. Beyond these attacks, which target individual devices, the issue propagates to service providers. With the possibility of such device impersonation, the cloud operators happen to exchange and receive information from unreliable sources. Consequently, the information manipulated by the cloud is thus unreliable too. However, it is known that big data market can only thrive provided the collected data can be relied on. This is captured by the attribute "veracity" of big data characterization in 5Vs (Volume, Velocity, Variety, Veracity, and Value).

Therefore, trustworthy identification is paramount. Besides, it is also important to safeguard other immaterial assets, such as data confidentiality (for privacy concerns) and program authentication (in the case of software updates). All these properties are part and parcel of the scope of *security* requirements.

Security Technologies. Security is thus an important aspect of digital communications. It must thus be addressed rigorously. Building security from a technical point of view requires the collaboration of various technologies, including:

- cryptographic algorithms, which implement building blocks for confidentiality (through encryption), integrity (through hash functions) and authentication (through message authentication codes and/or digital signatures),
- sensitive security parameters[1] management, which consists in their generating, in ensuring their protection while they are in memory (in use or backed-up), and in warranting their erasure when they shall be disposed of,
- proving the correctness of the implementation, since bugs are known to be devastating in their exploitation [13], included but not limited by cyber-attacks,
- checking for the absence of side-channels in cryptographic implementations, which can be revealed by timing biases in micro-architectural behaviors, or by effects related to reliability issues in Double Data Rate (DDR) modules [15,17] or in FLASH memories [3] (collectively being known as *RowHammer* attacks).

The complexity of implementing such security technologies has led to many attacks, which leverage on inconsistent interaction between primitives. Typical examples are authenticated encryption using AES-CBC with AES-based CMAC, which natively does not provide authentication, or compression oracles, whereby the combination of compression and use of MAC-then-encrypt paradigm makes it possible to extract plaintext bytes just by analyzing the size of the encrypted data.

---

[1] Sensitive security parameters (SSPs) consist either in critical security parameters (CSPs) or public security parameters (PSPs). CSPs shall be kept secret. Examples are nonces, long-term and ephemeral keys. PSPs are public, but shall not be chosen. Examples are initialization vectors.

Specificities of Standardization in Security. Because of this complexity and in order to prevent the thrive of so numerous attacks, security mechanisms have been standardized. Standardization ensures that the design and the choice of cryptographic primitives are done without errors (trivially) leading to attacks.

But standardization goes beyond simplification of choice regarding security algorithms. It also simplifies the understanding of the whole solution, thereby provided a more clear vision of the design rationale. This is important because the adoption of security can be considered as trust delegation into a security standard. Therefore, standardized solutions give more confidence in the fact that no security issue will happen. As a matter of facts (recall Snowden affair), one of the risks is about backdoors in security protocols. It is indeed cynical to invest in a security solution which actually helps attackers hack your devices.

Another aspect related to security is that the Devil lays in the details. In particular, unintentional vulnerabilities might be injected while implementing cryptographic solutions. Typically, side-channels (i.e., non-functional albeit adversarially observable behaviors) might leak information about the secrets. This includes timing, cache hit/miss patterns, power consumption, electromagnetic field radiation, etc.

Scope of the Paper. In this article, we survey the role of standardization for Physically Unclonable Functions (PUFs) as a key generation technology. Such technology is a cornerstone, since cryptography bases itself on the principle that all the design can be made public, whilst the only secrecy lays in the key, according to a doctrine which is known as the Auguste Kerckhoffs law.

In particular, we detail the service which is expected from the PUFs, derive security requirements, and expose ways to test and evaluate them. These aspects are part and parcel of the mandatory normative features of project ISO/IEC 20897.

Outline and Contributions. The rest of the paper is organized as follows. First of all, we provide the reader with a high-level description of PUFs. This topic is addressed in Sect. 2. In this section, we stress the progress which has been made during standardization process concerning the definition of independent features of PUFs of seemingly different nature. Our main contribution lays in Sect. 3. We here account for a remarkable progress in the modelization of PUFs, namely the duality between challenges and responses. Based on this achievement, we enunciate clearly in this Sect. 3 the unified security requirements for PUFs. Eventually, we explain in Sect. 4 how to test and/or evaluate whether or not security requirements are met, and how, in a given device. Conclusions are in Sect. 5.

2   Description of a PUF

A PUF is a function implemented in a device that is produced or configured with the security objective that random fluctuations in the production process lead to different behaviours and are hard to reproduce physically.

This means that a PUF generates data which do not result from a read access in a Non Volatile Memory (NVM). Indeed, no data are stored in the PUF during its whole life cycle.

2.1 Towards a Standard Related to PUFs

The international standards of PUFs are discussed in ISO/IEC 20897-1 and 20897-2 [12]: the former deals with the security requirements and the latter deals with the test and evaluation methods of PUFs. The documents of the standards are edited within ISO/IEC JTC 1/SC 27/WG 3. Notice that the contents of this paper concerns only the authors, and is not endorsed by ISO/IEC.

There have been many PUF variants reported so far [1,2], and excerpt of technologies taken from a selection of published academic papers is reported below:

- Optical PUF [20],
- Coating PUF [28],
- SRAM PUF [9],
- Glitch PUF [27],
- Arbiter PUF [6,19],
- Loop PUF [4],
- Memory contention PUF [8],
- Oxide rupture PUF [29],
- Transistor voltage threshold [26].

All those very different structures aim at providing a similar service to the final users. Namely, they all implement a function which is hard if not impossible to copy. All those objects are covered by the scope of ISO 20897-1/-2 drafts.

2.2 Parameters of PUF

A PUF is, by definition, a function. The input parameters are termed challenges, and output parameters are termed responses.

In this paper we focus on so-called silicon PUFs. Their challenges and responses are digital, i.e., consist in bitstrings. Precisely, PUFs obtain digital(ized) responses by amplifying analog signals from physical properties of tiny imperfections of the device implementation. This property allows PUFs to be unclonable.

The goal of standardization is to provide portable metrics along with tests and evaluation methods which are comparable whilst they embrace a wide array of very different PUF technologies. The effort to be carried out is thus to abstract away all peculiarities inherent to various PUF technologies. The method to do so is to think about the services expected by a PUF in general, without referring to any implementation specific choice.

It is customary in the literature to classify PUFs as either *weak* or *strong*. A weak PUF has no input, but usually a (unique) response of large size. A strong

PUF has many inputs, but usually short responses in size. As the standardization process has revealed, this classification is a bit caricatural. A softer classification will be introduced in Sect. 3.1.

We provide here-after some useful notations.

The responses from multiple PUFs are arranged into a cube as Fig. 1 shows. The repetitive calls to a PUF are illustrated in Fig. 2. The single small cube describes a 1-bit response from a PUF. The three axes of the cube and the time are described hereafter, as directions:

- **direction B**: "#bit" shows the bit length of the response obtained from a single challenge. In a 1-bit response PUF, e.g., arbiter PUF, the dimension B collapses.
- **direction C**: "#challenge" shows the number of different challenges given to a PUF. In a no-challenge PUF (or, more rigorously, a one-challenge PUF, see discussion in Sect. 3.1), e.g., SRAM PUF, the dimension C collapses.
- **direction D**: "#PUF" shows the number of different PUF devices under test.
- **direction T**: "#query" shows the number of query iterations under the fixed PUF device and challenge.

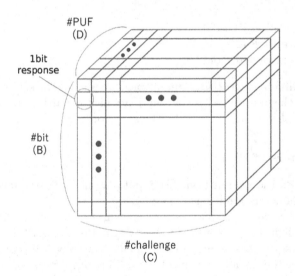

Fig. 1. The three dimensions involved in the PUFs entropy metrics

2.3   Use-Cases of PUFs

By definition, a PUF is a "non-stored sensitive security parameter". Therefore, PUFs can be used to fulfill different needs where non-tamperability is a strong requirement.

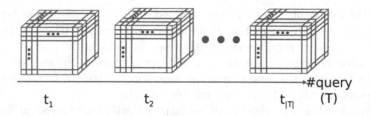

$$t_1 \qquad\qquad t_2 \qquad\qquad t_{|T|} \quad \#\text{query}\ (T)$$

Fig. 2. Illustration of the PUF repetitive usage, involved in the PUF steadiness metric

A first use-case consists in using the value of the PUF as a private data, which can play the role of some secret key, known by nobody (neither by the designer nor by the tester nor by the firmware developer, etc.). Therefore, such solution solves the problem of key management, as each device handles its own key.

A second use-case consists in device unfalsifiable identification. The PUF is used as a public identifier, which shall therefore be non-tamperable.

A third use-case consists in device authentication. This application is demanding more security than the plain identification, as the protocol shall be protected against replay attacks. Therefore, in this use-case, a subset of PUF's challenges and responses is saved and this whitelist enables future interactive attestation that the device is genuine. The scenario is referred to as challenge-response protocol (CRP).

Yet a forth use-case consists simply in generating randomness: this can consist in the replacement of an unavailable true random number generator, or for a source of random numbers, which can be reseeded (as if `srand(0)` is called before a sequence of several `rand()` in a software implementation). For this purpose, a list of selected challenges is queried, and the associated responses are taken as random source unique to the device under consideration.

2.4 PUF Life-Cycle

The usual steps involved in the life-cycle of a PUF are depicted in Fig. 3 for the exemplar use-cases presented in Sect. 2.3. The design must first be realized, and then it is sent to the silicon foundry for fabrication. Most PUFs are becoming unique as soon as they are fabricated. However, some PUFs are prepared by the foundry, but must be "revealed" later on (like a photographic picture after exposition). For example, the oxide rupture PUF [29] is not operational right after fabrication, but becomes operational subsequent to some locking process. Besides, some PUFs are not steady by nature, and for them to be of practical use, their overall steadiness must be improved by removing those entropy sources which are the less steady. This step consists in so-called helper data extraction. At this stage, the PUF is ready to be used, except for the authentication protocol. Indeed, it requires first to register all challenge-response pairs which will be used later on to attest of the PUF identity. All those steps are carried out in a safe environment, typically the PUF designers factory, hence no risk of attacks.

From this stage on, the PUFs are deployed in their *operational environment*: responses are gathered, to either build a key, an identifier (ID), a response to compare to formerly registered challenge-response pairs in the case of authentication protocols, or responses for static entropy gathering. Notice that most of the PUFs require a response correction step, which attempts to remove errors in the responses when they are not reliable enough.

Notice that Fig. 3 presents optional steps (which can be removed for some instances of PUF if they do not jeopardize security requirements) between braces.

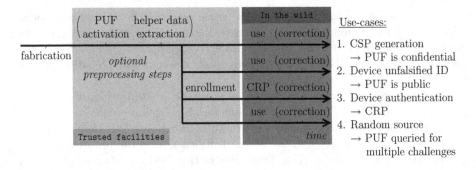

Fig. 3. Life cycle of a PUF in four use-cases

3 Security Requirements

One of the virtues of the standardization process has been to clarify and to unite the vision of PUFs, as diverse as they are. In particular, we account in Sect. 3.1 for the symmetrical role of challenges and responses, and then introduce in Sect. 3.2 a consistent list of security requirements which apply equally to any PUF avatars.

3.1 Duality Between Challenges and Responses

It has been highlighted earlier in Sect. 2.2 that the PUFs are varied in terms of number of challenges and responses. However, there is a way to unify this notion, by analyzing the tradeoff between number of challenges and of responses.

Actually, we would like to introduce a transformation from a PUF with a given number of challenge and response bits into a PUF with other such parameters. In this respect, we highlight a broader interpretation which allows to derive a **duality** notion between response number of bits and challenge number of bits. It is indeed possible to trade some response bits for some challenge bits. Let us introduce here-after the transformation.

Sub-selection to Trade Large Response Bitwidth for Short Challenge Bitwidth. Let us model an SRAM by a module with no input (or equivalently, an input of 0 bitwidth), and an output word on 2^n bits; notice that memories of maximum capacity always contain a number of bits which is a power of 2, since the n-bit address is fully decoded. Thus, the address bitwidth is zero[2] and the data read out has a bitwidth of 2^n bits. The SRAM can also be seen as two memories of 2^{n-1} bits each, or four memories memories of 2^{n-2} bits each, etc. Those tradeoffs are illustrated for $n = 8$ in Fig. 4. The Table 1 explains how such tradeoffs work in general.

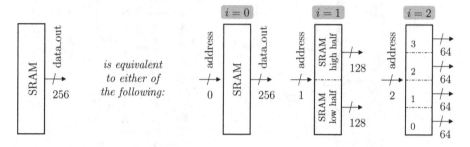

Fig. 4. Transformation of 0-bit address (challenge) with 2^n-bit unique output data (response) into equivalent i-bit challenges with (2^{n-i})-bit responses, for $i \in \{0, 1, 2\}$ and for $n = 8$

Table 1. Tradeoff between challenges (addresses) and response number of bits per input for an SRAM-PUF

Number of inputs	Number of outputs
$1 = 2^0$	2^n
$2 = 2^1$	2^{n-1}
$4 = 2^2$	2^{n-2}
$\vdots$	$\vdots$
2^n	$1 = 2^0$

Actually, most SRAM modules are already partitioned in banks, hence the contents of Fig. 4 is fairly natural. For instance, for small sizes, it is not uncommon to have so-called *cuts of RAM* of 32 bytes, that is 5-bit addresses and data out on 8 bits. This is the equivalent of a memory with no address and size $8 \times 2^5 = 2^8$, i.e., with 256 data (single bit) outputted.

---

[2] To be accurate, there is thus $2^0 = 1$ input, which is consequently constant.

A similar situation is encountered for Look-up-Tables (LUTs) or Block RAMs (BRAMs) in FPGAs, which can have multiple form factors. See the example depicted in Fig. 5 of a 4-LUT (memory of 4 input bits and 1 output bit) which is equivalent to two 3-LUTs.

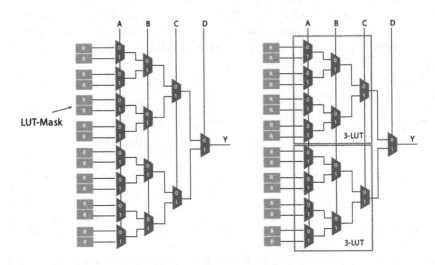

Fig. 5. Architecture of a 4-LUT, equivalent to two 3-LUTs (diagram courtesy of Altera [5])

Repeating to Trade Numerous Challenges for Short Responses. Let us model an arbiter-PUF [19] by a module with an input of n bits and a single-bit response, which can be seen as a word on $1\ (=2^0)$ bit. The challenge is seen as an integer c comprised between 0 and $2^n - 1$ and the reponse r is seen as an integer comprised between 0 and 1. Challenges drive conditional switches $\left(\begin{smallmatrix}1\\0\end{smallmatrix}\raisebox{-1mm}{\framebox{$\times$}}\raisebox{-2mm}{$\uparrow$}\right)$, and responses are produced by an arbiter, as fair as possible, e.g., using an RS-latch:

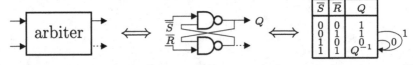

The Fig. 6 for $i \in \{0, 1, 2\}$ shows how to turn this mono-bit response PUF into an equivalent PUF with challenges on $(n - i)$ bits and responses on 2^i bits. Notice that this figure represents a *sequential protocol*, where the same n-bit arbiter-PUF is called 2^i times in a row. The resulting quantitative tradeoff is given in Table 2.

Summary of the Duality Between Response Number of Bits and the Number of Challenges. For both SRAM-PUF and arbiter-PUF, the trade-off between the

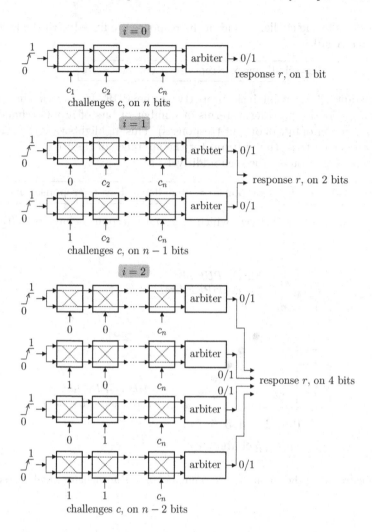

Fig. 6. Transformation of n-bit challenge with 1-bit response into equivalent $(n-i)$-bit challenges with 2^i-bit responses, for $i \in \{0,1,2\}$

Table 2. Tradeoff between challenges (addresses) and response number of bits per input for an arbiter-PUF

Number of inputs	Number of outputs
2^n	$1 = 2^0$
2^{n-1}	$2 = 2^1$
2^{n-2}	$4 = 2^2$
$\vdots$	$\vdots$
$1 = 2^0$	2^n

number of bits in the challenge and in the response are linked with the following **conservation rule**:

$$\#\text{challenge} \times \#\text{reponse} = \text{volume} = 2^n.$$

The constant 2^n is an intrinsic property of the PUF. It stays unchanged as its "aspect ratio" is changing in terms of number of bits of inputs (challenges) traded for number of bits of output (responses). This highlights that the constant 2^n can be referred to as the **volume** (or the **surface**) of the PUF.

The same equation can be seen additively, as:

$$\log_2(\#\text{challenge}) + \log_2(\#\text{reponse}) = \#\text{challenge\_bits} + \#\text{reponse\_bits} = n.$$

The Fig. 7 summarizes this law, which takes into account behaviors of Tables 1 and 2.

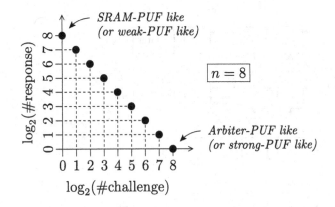

Fig. 7. Illustration of the duality between number of bits in challenges and in responses

3.2 List of Metrics (Security Requirements)

The definition and the explanation of security requirements for PUFs are given here-after:

- **Steadiness**[3]: it is a measurement of stability of PUF responses in time. This metric can be seen as a *safety* requirement. However, PUFs with unsteady responses could be prone to prediction attacks (if the response is very biased) or to related keys attacks.

---

[3] Notice that *steadiness* is a word reserved for stability of a given PUF response corresponding to a fixed challenge. The synonymous terms *reliability*, *reproducibility* and *stability* are not preferred. In particular, "reliability" is discarded as it would make some confusion regarding the metric related to the yield in the CMOS manufacturing processes.

- **Randomness:** it assesses how unpredictable are PUF responses when considering a collection of response bits under all the possible challenges. The obtained *intra-PUF* bitstring shall be, ideally, unpredictable. Such security requirement attests of the PUF unclonability.
- **Uniqueness:** it estimates how different are any two pairs of different PUFs. This *inter-PUF* metric is required to quantify in which respect the fab is unable to generate clones of PUFs.
- **Unpredictability:** it estimates how hard it is to predict the responses of an $(n + 1)^{\text{th}}$ PUF knowing all previous n instances. This metric relates to randomness, but is more pragmatic as it involves machine learning or *ad hoc* tests.
- **Unclonability:** this metric makes sure no easy exploitable bias exist in the PUF architecture, by design. The goal of this security requirement is to valide for the absence of trap or backdoor in the PUF rationale.

Impact of Input and Output Bits Duality on the PUF Metrics. As shown in Sect. 3.1, the same metric can be used to measure the *randomness* with respect to challenges (aka *diffuseness*) and with respect to response bits (aka *unpredictability*). Therefore, trading bits of challenge for bits of response, or vice-versa, does not affect the properties of the PUF. We say that the transformation of PUF form-factor change is iso-metric, i.e., it does not modify its randomness metric. Thus, the transformation is safe, and can be applied at the convenience of the user without compromising the randomness of the PUF. We say that randomness consists in computing entropy "in the C-B plane".

4   Tests and Evaluations

The security requirements defined in Sect. 3 have some value only provided one has a means to attest that a device indeed implements them. There are two methods to do so: *test* and *evaluation*.

In testing philosophy, an automatic procedure is launched to check each and any security requirement. This allows for fast and reproducing checking. However, subtle issues (e.g., corner cases, weak vulnerabilities, problems not covered by the test suite, etc.) could inadvertently pass successfully through the test.

This explains why testing is complemented by the evaluation philosophy. Evaluation is conducted by an expert, who attempts to think out-of-the-box in a view to derive attacks. This expert defines a couple of attack paths, performs a quotation (i.e., scores which reflect the cost of the attacks) for them, selects and realizes the attack of lowest quotation.

4.1   Well Established Tests

The tests base themselves on a *metric*. For the tests to be consistent even in heterogeneous conditions, the metric must be generic. The idea is that the metric must suit to a variety of PUFs.

Entropy is a metric which can compare data of various nature. The output of discussions at standardization committee meetings is to use this very same metric for different security requirements. The method is termed "**multiple data, one same metric**". This enables consistency within metrics, and simplifies the test of security requirements. Notice that the entropy for the steadiness is simply $H_2(\text{BER}) = -\text{BER} \log_2 \text{BER} - (1 - \text{BER}) \log_2(1 - \text{BER})$, where BER is the bit error rate. The BER is laying between 0 and 1, and its value can be interpreted as follows:

- when $0 \leqslant \text{BER} < 1/2$, the bit is most of the time correct;
- when $1/2 < \text{BER} \leqslant 1$, the bit is most of the time incorrect – it behaves the same as if the bit is actually inverted, with BER corresponding to the previous case ($0 \leqslant \text{BER} < 1/2$);
- when $\text{BER} = 1/2$, the PUF is actually a perfect TRNG (True Random Number Generator).

Therefore, in practice, it is assumed that $0 \leqslant \text{BER} < 1/2$. As the function $p \mapsto H_2(p)$ is strictly increasing on interval $[0, 1/2[$, it is equivalent to minimize the entropy $H_2(\text{BER})$ and to minimize the BER itself.

Remark 1. Notice that metrics different from entropy might be misleading. For instance, measuring the randomness by average Hamming distances can hide some weaknesses in terms of security level. For instance, as a motivating example, let us consider the following 8-bit responses to three challenges:

- R1: $(10101100)_2$
- R2: $(01101100)_2$
- R3: $(10100011)_2$

Those responses are balanced (bitstrings with as many 0s as 1s). But their Hamming distances (d_H) are not balanced, since:

- $d_H(\text{R1}, \text{R2}) = 2$,
- $d_H(\text{R2}, \text{R3}) = 6$,
- $d_H(\text{R3}, \text{R1}) = 4$.

However, the average Hamming distance is $(2 + 6 + 4)/3 = 4$, which might give a false confidence that responses to different challenges are "independent" (random).

Only one security requirement cannot be tested, namely *physical unclonability*.

4.2   Well Established Evaluations

Evaluation is required for those security requirements which cannot be tested, because they cannot be decided based on measured data. This happens for requirements which are *"negative"*: this means that the security requires *not to* verify a property.

This holds for instance for "unclonability". One aspect of unclonability could be termed "supervised" unclonability: the attacker manages to predict responses from unseen challenges, after having seen enough responses from known challenges. This metric, termed *mathematical unclonability*, can be estimated as the entropy in the C-B space, hence can be turned into a test.

However, *physical unclonability*, consists in evaluating the difficulty of fabricating a PUF that has the same CRPs as a specific PUF. This task can only be achieved by a thorough qualitative analysis of the PUF design.

4.3   Further Tests and Evaluations

The tests described in Sect. 4.1 and the evaluations described in Sect. 4.2 are natural. Still, some more "specialized" (if not bespoke) methods can be leveraged for challenging more drastically the security requirements.

Regarding tests, entropy can also be *characterized* (instead of *estimated*) by some testsuites (e.g., DieHard [16], NIST FIPS 140-2 [25], FIPS SP 800-90 [18], FIPS SP 800-22 [22], BSI AIS31 [14], ISO/IEC 18031 [10] and companion 20543 project [11], etc.). This has been suggested already by several papers, such as [7,21]. Still, it is important those tests adhere to the principle: **multiple data, one same testsuite**

Still regarding tests, machine learning (ML) of challenge and response pairs has been shown to be able to predict with good accuracy responses from unseen challenges [21]. Thus, the general-purpose entropy metric can be traded for crafted tools, e.g., using ML, or any taylored distinguisher. Still, for consistency reasons, this analysis shall adhere to the principle: **multiple data, one same distinguisher**. For the sake of clarification, the equivalent of *randomness* when trading entropy for ML tools is referred to as *unpredictability* (or alternatively: *mathematical unclonability*).

4.4   Conclusion on Tests and Evaluations

The current *statu quo* on tests and evaluations is recalled in Table 3.

The steadiness is evaluated by the entropy of BER, and shall be minimized. The corresponding test would be to check for the balanced, that is situations where BER $\approx 1/2$. However, for PUFs, the ideal situation is when BER ≈ 0, therefore classical tests are ignored.

On the contrary, randomness and uniqueness can rely on tests since their entropy metric shall be maximized. Regarding ML test, we expect that:

- high entropy goes hand in hand with passing of all tests and failure of ML
- low entropy goes hand in hand with failing of all tests and success of ML
- intermediate situations might exist, such as machine learning to succeed, but still high entropy; though, in this case, one expects the entropy to be still less than expected (e.g., 127 instead of 128 for a randomness on 128 bits).

Table 3. Current *statu quo* on relevant tests and evaluations for PUFs

Metric	Mathematical tests (with data)			Rationale evaluation (without data)
	Entropy	Tests	ML	
Steadiness	Entropy in T dimension	No	No	No
Randomness	Entropy in B-C plane	Yes	No	No
Uniqueness	Entropy in D dimension	Yes	No	No
Unpredictability[a]	No		No	Yes	No
Unclonability[b]	No		No	No	Yes

[a]**Unpredictability** is also called **mathematical unclonability**
[b]**Unclonability** is also called **physical unclonability**

Each metric is thus related to entropy. The entropy can be *estimated*, albeit with limited precision, since a PUF can only be queried a finite number of times. Therefore, it is reassuring to employ for PUF metrics *estimations* of *abstract random metrics*, through *stochastic models* (see e.g., [23] for steadiness and [24] for entropy metrics).

5   Conclusions

The standardization process on PUFs has allowed to clarify security requirements. For instance, *diffuseness* (variability in the dimension of the challenges) and *unpredictability* (variability in the dimension of the response bits) are related requirements, which both concern the *randomness* of one instance of the PUF at one instant of time. Besides, diffuseness is not suitable for PUFs without challenges, where the unpredictability is irrelevant for those PUFs with only one bit of response. Our analysis has showed that a notion of randomness can encompass both diffuseness and unpredictability, thereby solving the case. Besides, we showed how randomness can be addressed both by a metric and machine learning tools.

Acknowledgments. This work was partly supported by both Institute for Information & communications Technology Promotion (IITP) grant funded by the Korea government (MSIT) (No. 2016-0-00399, Study on secure key hiding technology for IoT devices [KeyHAS Project]) and the project commissioned by the Japanese New Energy and Industrial Technology Development Organization (NEDO).

References

1. Halak, B.: Physically Unclonable Functions—From Basic Design Principles to Advanced Hardware Security Applications. Springer, Cham (2018). https://doi.org/10.1007/978-3-319-76804-5
2. Böhm, C., Hofer, M.: Physical Unclonable Functions in Theory and Practice. Springer, New York (2012). https://doi.org/10.1007/978-1-4614-5040-5

3. Cai, Y., Ghose, S., Luo, Y., Mai, K., Mutlu, O., Haratsch, E.F.: Vulnerabilities in MLC NAND flash memory programming: experimental analysis, exploits, and mitigation techniques. In: 2017 IEEE International Symposium on High Performance Computer Architecture, HPCA 2017, Austin, TX, USA, 4–8 February 2017, pp. 49–60. IEEE Computer Society (2017)
4. Cherif, Z., Danger, J.-L., Guilley, S., Bossuet, L.: An easy-to-design PUF based on a single oscillator: the loop PUF. In: DSD,Çeşme, Izmir, Turkey, 5–8 September 2012 (2012). (Online PDF)
5. Altera Corporation: White paper: FPGA architecture, July 2006. ver. 1.0. https://www.altera.com/content/dam/altera-www/global/en_US/pdfs/literature/wp/wp-01003.pdf. Accessed 19 Apr 2018
6. Gassend, B., Clarke, D.E., van Dijk, M., Devadas, S.: Silicon physical random functions. In: Atluri, V. (ed.) Proceedings of the 9th ACM Conference on Computer and Communications Security, CCS 2002, Washington, DC, USA, 18–22 November 2002, pp. 148–160. ACM (2002)
7. Guilley, S., El Housni, Y.: Random numbers generation: tests and attacks. In: 2018 Workshop on Fault Diagnosis and Tolerance in Cryptography, FDTC 2018, Amsterdam, Netherlands, 13 September 2018. IEEE Computer Society (2018)
8. Güneysu, T.: Using data contention in dual-ported memories for security applications. Signal Process. Syst. **67**(1), 15–29 (2012)
9. Holcomb, D.E., Burleson, W.P., Fu, K.: Power-up SRAM state as an identifying fingerprint and source of true random numbers. IEEE Trans. Comput. **58**(9), 1198–1210 (2009)
10. ISO/IEC JTC 1/SC27/WG2. ISO/IEC 18031:2011 - Information technology - Security techniques - Random bit generation
11. ISO/IEC JTC 1/SC27/WG3. ISO/IEC DIS 20543 - Information technology - Security techniques - Test and analysis methods for random bit generators within ISO/IEC 19790 and ISO/IEC 15408
12. ISO/IEC NP 20897. Information technology - Security techniques - Security requirements, test and evaluation methods for physically unclonable functions for generating nonstored security parameters. http://www.iso.org/iso/home/store/catalogue_tc/catalogue_detail.htm?csnumber=69403
13. Joye, M., Tunstall, M. (eds.): Fault Analysis in Cryptography. Information Security and Cryptography. Springer, Heidelberg (2012). https://doi.org/10.1007/978-3-642-29656-7. ISBN 978-3-642-29655-0
14. Killmann, W., Schindler, W.: A proposal for: functionality classes for random number generators, September 2011. https://www.bsi.bund.de/SharedDocs/Downloads/DE/BSI/Zertifizierung/Interpretationen/AIS_31_Functionality_classes_for_random_number_generators_e.pdf?__blob=publicationFile
15. Kim, Y., et al.: Flipping bits in memory without accessing them: an experimental study of DRAM disturbance errors. In: ACM/IEEE 41st International Symposium on Computer Architecture, ISCA 2014, Minneapolis, MN, USA, 14–18 June 2014, pp. 361–372. IEEE Computer Society (2014)
16. Marsaglia, G.: The Marsaglia random number CDROM including the diehard battery of tests of randomness. Web site at the Department of Statistics, Florida State University, Tallahassee, FL, USA (1995)
17. Mutlu, O.: The RowHammer problem and other issues we may face as memory becomes denser. In: Atienza, D., Di Natale, G. (eds.) Design, Automation and Test in Europe Conference and Exhibition, DATE 2017, Lausanne, Switzerland, 27–31 March 2017, pp. 1116–1121. IEEE (2017)

18. NIST. Recommendation for the entropy sources used for random bit generation (2012). http://csrc.nist.gov/publications/drafts/800-90/draft-sp800-90b.pdf
19. Pappu, R., Recht, B., Taylor, J., Gershenfeld, N.: Physical one-way functions. Science **297**(5589), 2026–2030 (2002). https://doi.org/10.1126/science.1074376
20. Pappu, R.S.: Physical one-way functions. Ph.D. thesis, Massachusetts Institute of Technology, March 2001
21. Rührmair, U., Sehnke, F., Sölter, J., Dror, G., Devadas, S., Schmidhuber, J.: Modeling attacks on physical unclonable functions. In: Al-Shaer, E., Keromytis, A.D., Shmatikov, V. (eds.) Proceedings of the 17th ACM Conference on Computer and Communications Security, CCS 2010, Chicago, Illinois, USA, 4–8 October 2010, pp. 237–249. ACM (2010)
22. Rukhin, A., et al.: A statistical test suite for the validation of random number generators and pseudo random number generators for cryptographic applications, April 2010. https://nvlpubs.nist.gov/nistpubs/legacy/sp/nistspecialpublication800-22r1a.pdf
23. Schaub, A., Danger, J.-L., Guilley, S., Rioul, O.: An improved analysis of reliability and entropy for delay PUFs. In: Novotný, M., Konofaos, N., Skavhaug, A. (eds.) 21st Euromicro Conference on Digital System Design, DSD 2018, Prague, Czech Republic, 29–31 August 2018, pp. 553–560. IEEE Computer Society (2018)
24. Schaub, A., Rioul, O., Boutros, J.J., Danger, J.-L., Guilley, S.: Challenge codes for physically unclonable functions with Gaussian delays: a maximum entropy problem. In: Latin American Week on Coding and Information, UNICAMP - Campinas, Brazil, 22–27 July 2018 (2018). LAWCI
25. NIST FIPS (Federal Information Processing Standards). Security Requirements for Cryptographic Modules publication 140-2, 25 May 2001. http://csrc.nist.gov/publications/fips/fips140-2/fips1402.pdf
26. Su, Y., Holleman, J., Otis, B.P.: A digital 1.6 pJ/bit chip identification circuit using process variations. IEEE J. Solid-State Circuits **43**(1), 69–77 (2008)
27. Suzuki, D., Shimizu, K.: The glitch PUF: a new delay-PUF architecture exploiting glitch shapes. In: Mangard, S., Standaert, F.-X. (eds.) CHES 2010. LNCS, vol. 6225, pp. 366–382. Springer, Heidelberg (2010). https://doi.org/10.1007/978-3-642-15031-9_25
28. Tuyls, P., Škoric, B., Kevenaar, T.: Security with Noisy Data: On Private Biometrics, Secure Key Storage and Anti-Counterfeiting, 1st edn. Springer, New York (2007). https://doi.org/10.1007/978-1-84628-984-2. ISBN 978-1-84628-983-5
29. Wu, M.-Y., et al.: A PUF scheme using competing oxide rupture with bit error rate approaching zero. In: 2018 IEEE International Solid-State Circuits Conference, ISSCC 2018, San Francisco, CA, USA, 11–15 February 2018, pp. 130–132. IEEE (2018)

A PUF-Based Destructive Private Mutual Authentication RFID Protocol

Cristian Hristea and Ferucio Laurenţiu Ţiplea(✉)

Department of Computer Science, Alexandru Ioan Cuza University of Iaşi,
Iaşi, Romania
cristi.hristea@gmail.com, ferucio.tiplea@uaic.ro

Abstract. We propose the first stateful RFID protocol that offers mutual authentication and provides destructive privacy, in the Vaudenay model. In order to achieve destructive privacy we use Physically Unclonable Functions (PUFs) to assure that the internal secret of the tag remains hidden against an adversary with invasive capabilities. The proposed protocol avoids the use of pseudo random generators on tags, and provides scalability by offering a constant authentication time. For the mitigation of desynchronization attacks we propose a mechanism, on reader level, that thwarts them.

1   Introduction

Radio Frequency Identification (RFID) technology enables wireless identification of objects or persons in a wide range of applications: access control, logistics and supply chain visibility and management, (item level inventory, tool, attendee, IT asses) tracking, kiosks, library systems, interactive marketing, real-time location systems, national IDs management, patient care management and so on.

The ecosystem of a RFID setting consists of a *server*, a *reader*, and a *tag* which is a cheap resource constrained device capable of identifying an object that it is attached to. Given the heterogeneous use of the technology, there are ample concerns about impersonating (*security*) and tracking (*privacy*) tags. Thus, the need for authentication protocols capable to assure the security and privacy of the users, whilst remaining lightweight enough to fit on tags. Alongside the development of such protocols, there are several works [3,7–9,13,19] that have contributed to the development of a formal framework for the evaluation of RFID protocols. The model in [19], completed with [13], contains both a comprehensive description of RFID systems and the associated security goals, as well as a complete presentation of the interaction between an attacker and an RFID scheme. Based on the ability of the attacker to learn the internal secrets of a tag, i.e. *corruption*, and whether a certain instance of the protocol has successfully been completed, the model distinguishes eight classes of adversaries against the privacy property. In the process of developing a protocol, this granularity offers an appropriate selection of an application dependent privacy level, with the first level describing an adversary that cannot corrupt a tag and does not determine

© Springer Nature Switzerland AG 2019
J.-L. Lanet and C. Toma (Eds.): SecITC 2018, LNCS 11359, pp. 331–343, 2019.
https://doi.org/10.1007/978-3-030-12942-2_25

the result of an authentication session (*narrow-weak*) and the strongest level (*wide-strong*) allowing the attacker to freely corrupt tags and learn whether a protocol instance succeeded.

Contribution. In this paper we construct the first stateful (i.e., the tag has a persistent updatable state shared with the reader) protocol that offers mutual authentication and provides destructive privacy. We prove our protocol to be secure and private in the Vaudenay model [19]. In order to achieve destructive privacy we build upon the efforts of [10,15,16] and use a PUF embedded in each tag to assure that the internal secret of the tag remains hidden against an adversary with invasive capabilities. A PUF is a lightweight construction capable of uniquely identifying a device, whilst offering a tamper-evident behavior [12]. This characteristic is consistent with the destructive privacy experiment, that considers a tag destroyed after corruption. The proposed protocol also aims at providing scalability by offering a constant authentication time and avoids the use of pseudo-random generators on tags that can be considered a potential security risk [2] in low cost RFID tags. For the mitigation of desynchronization attacks, specific to protocol constructions with a reader-tag shared state [6,14,18], we propose a mechanism, on reader level, that thwarts them.

Paper structure. The paper consists of seven sections, the first one being the introduction. In Sect. 2 we review the state of the art of RFID authentication protocols that provide destructive privacy. We introduce in Sects. 3 and 4 the basic terminology and notation used throughout the paper. Our protocol is presented in Sect. 5, while its security and privacy analysis is provided in Sect. 6. We conclude the paper in the last section.

2   Related Work

The first destructive private RFID authentication protocol with a full security proof based on the model from [19] has been proposed in [15,16]. The authors enriched the weak-private RFID protocol in [19] with *ideal PUFs* on tags. As a result, each tag accommodates a random number generator, a pseudo-random function (PRF) $F = (F_K)$, a PUF, and a secret S on which the PUF is to be evaluated. A round of the protocol debuts with the reader sending the tag a nonce a. The tag, on the receipt of a, generates a nonce b, retrieves the secret key $K = PUF(S)$, computes $c = F_K(a, b)$, and sends back b and c. On the receipt of b and c, the reader evaluates the tag response by exhaustively searching for a database entry that satisfies $c = F_K(a, b)$ (this time, $F_K(a, b)$ is computed by reader using the the database entry that must contain a key K). According to whether the equality "$c = F_K(a, b)$" holds or not, the reader authenticates or not the tag. This protocol does not assure reader authentication (but only tag authentication) and is not scalable with respect to the number of tags (i.e., the time needed to find the tag in the database is linear in the size of the database).

It was also shown in [11] that the protocol discussed above is not secure if the adversary has access to the tag's volatile memory. To solve this problem, the authors of [11] proposed a new protocol where the tag's PUF generates two keys in a row: when the first key is used, it is deleted and only then the second key is generated. Therefore, the trick is that the volatile memory contains only one of the two keys at a given time.

In [10], the authors describe a destructive private mutual authentication protocol designed for *offline* RFID systems. As opposed to an *online* RFID system, where a reader cannot be corrupted and is considered connected at all times with the central database, an offline system contains multiple readers that function without a direct link to the database and are prone to corruption. This feature is captured by adding an oracle to the model from [19], $CorruptReader(R_i)$, that allows an adversary to corrupt a reader R_i. Privacy achieved in this setting is denoted as *privacy+*. The proposed protocol makes use of a random number generator, a hash function and an ideal PUF. In order to thwart adversaries capable of corrupting a tag during a protocol execution (i.e., reading the contents of the tag's volatile memory), the authors use the same approach as in [5] (and later used in [1]): the PUF is called twice on two distinct challenges. After the first PUF query, the answer is hashed together with other protocol information (the hash result is stored in a temporary variable), and then the answer is deleted from volatile memory. The PUF is queried a second time, the response and the previous hash are subsequently hashed, which creates the values used for tag and reader authentication. When a destructive adversary corrupts the tag during protocol execution, based on the assumption that the PUF is destroyed upon corruption, he can either obtain the first PUF result or the second. Thus the tag is protected from cloning and privacy leakage. As in [15,16], the reader has to exhaustively search its database for the authentication of a single tag.

A mutual authentication, destructive private protocol was developed in [1]. As a framework for proving privacy, the authors use [19] enriched with the $Timer(\pi)$ oracle from [4], that returns the duration of the reader computation during the identification process. Following the same line of thinking as in [5,10,11], destructive privacy is assured using two secret PUF values that are never in the volatile memory at the same time. The functions used in the protocol are a random number generator, a hash function H, and a PUF. In the setup of the RFID scheme, a random state S is generated for the reader. The internal state of the tag (shared with the reader) is comprised of an ID and two PUF challenges a and b. The tag has an additional value c that satisfies the equation $c = S \oplus PUF(a) \oplus PUF(b)$. The conversation is initiated by the reader who sends a random generated number $r_1 \in \{0,1\}^l$. The tag generates $r_2 \in \{0,1\}^l$, computes $M_1 = H(r_1, r_2, a)$, $M_2 = H(r_2, r_1, 1) \oplus ID$, $h = H(r_2, 1, 2)$, and, in a second stage process, $k = S \oplus r_2$ (to avoid the secret exposure). Upon receiving M_1, M_2, and k, the reader will extract r_2 and ID from k and $M2$, respectively. Using the entry associated with ID, the tag is authenticated if $M_2 = H(r_1, r_2, a)$. For reader authentication, r_3 is generated and used to compute $M_3 = H(H(r_2, 1, 2), r_3, b)$. The tag authenticates the reader if $M_3 = H(h, r_3, b)$. Although the protocol is scalable, it becomes vulnerable when considering adversaries that have access to the random tapes of the tag pseudo random generation (which is a plausible assumption). In [2] it is shown that the protocol achieves no privacy when the adversary can predict the random value r_2. This attack is possible due to the protocol structure that assumes that r_2 is secret.

3   Basic Definitions and Notation

Throughout this paper we will use *probabilistic polynomial time* (PPT) algorithms $\mathcal{A}$ as defined in [17]. If $\mathcal{O}$ is an oracle we will use $\mathcal{A}^{\mathcal{O}}$ to denote that $\mathcal{A}$ has oracle access to $\mathcal{O}$. When the oracle $\mathcal{O}$ implements some function f, we will simply write $\mathcal{A}^f$ to denote that $\mathcal{A}$ has oracle access to f. This means that whenever $\mathcal{A}$ sends a value x to the oracle, it gets back $f(x)$.

If A is a set, then $a \leftarrow A$ means that a is uniformly at random chosen from A. If $\mathcal{A}$ is a probabilistic algorithm, then $a \leftarrow \mathcal{A}$ means that a is an output of $\mathcal{A}$ for some given input. Throughout this paper, λ will be used to denote a security parameter.

A *pseudo-random function* (PRF) is a family of functions with the property that if we randomly choose a function from this family then its input-output behavior is computationally indistinguishable from that of a random function. To be more precise, consider and fix two polynomials ℓ_1 and ℓ_2 with positive values. Then, define a family of functions as a construction $F = (F_\lambda)_{\lambda \in \mathbb{N}}$, where F_λ is a set of functions from $\{0,1\}^{\ell_1(\lambda)}$ to $\{0,1\}^{\ell_2(\lambda)}$, for all λ. We use U_λ for the set of all functions from $\{0,1\}^{\ell_1(\lambda)}$ to $\{0,1\}^{\ell_2(\lambda)}$, and $U = (U_\lambda)_{\lambda \in \mathbb{N}}$.

Two families $F = (F_\lambda)_{\lambda \in \mathbb{N}}$ and $G = (G_\lambda)_{\lambda \in \mathbb{N}}$ of functions are called *computationally indistinguishable* if, for any PPT algorithm $\mathcal{A}$ with oracle access to functions, its *advantage*

$$Adv^{prf}_{\mathcal{A},F,G}(\lambda) = |P(1 \leftarrow \mathcal{A}^f(1^\lambda) : f \leftarrow F_\lambda) - P(1 \leftarrow \mathcal{A}^g(1^\lambda) : g \leftarrow G_\lambda)|$$

is negligible (as a functions of λ).

$F = (F_\lambda)_{\lambda \in \mathbb{N}}$ is called a *pseudo-random function* if it is:

1. *Efficiently computable*: there exists a deterministic polynomial-time algorithm that on input λ, $f \in F_\lambda$, and $x \in \{0,1\}^{\ell_1(\lambda)}$, returns $f(x)$;
2. *Pseudo-random*: F is computationally indistinguishable from U.

In order to show that F is a PRF, we assume the existence of a *challenger* $\mathcal{C}$ that plays the following security game with an adversary (PPT algorithm) $\mathcal{A}$:

1. $\mathcal{C}$ randomly chooses $b \leftarrow \{0,1\}$;
2. if $b = 1$ then $\mathcal{C}$ randomly chooses $f \leftarrow F_\lambda$; otherwise, $\mathcal{C}$ randomly chooses $f \leftarrow U_\lambda$;
3. $\mathcal{C}$ provides oracle access to f for $\mathcal{A}$;
4. At some point, $\mathcal{A}$ outputs a bit b'.

The adversary wins the game if $b' = b$. Now, one can see that F is a PRF if it is efficiently computable and the probability to win the above security game is negligible, for all adversaries.

A *physically unclonable function* (PUF) can be seen as a physical object that, when queried with a challenge x generates a response y that depends on both x and the specific physical properties of the object. PUFs are typically assumed to be physically unclonable (it is infeasible to produce two PUFs that cannot be distinguished based on their challenge/response behavior), unpredictable (it is infeasible to predict the response to an unknown challenge), and tamper-evident (any attempt to physically access the PUF irreversible changes the challenge/response behavior).

Unfortunately, PUFs are subject to noise induced by the operating conditions, such as supply voltage or ambient temperature. Therefore, PUFs return slightly different responses when queried with the same challenge multiple times. However, from a theoretical point of view it is assumed that PUFs return a similar response when queried with the same challenge multiple times (this is usually called robustness).

Based on these, we adopt here the concept of an *ideal PUF* slightly different than in [16]. Namely, an *ideal PUF* is a physical object with a challenge/response behavior that implements a function $P : \{0,1\}^p \rightarrow \{0,1\}^k$, where p and k are of polynomial size in λ, such that:

1. P is computationally indistinguishable from U_λ;
2. Any attempt to physically tamper with the object implementing P results in destruction of P (P cannot be evaluated any more).

4 RFID Systems

We use Vaudenay's approach [13,19] to model and reason about *RFID systems*. According to [13,19], an RFID system consists of a *reader* $\mathcal{R}$ and a polynomial number of tags $\mathcal{T}$. The reader is a powerful transceiver[1] device whose task is to identify legitimate tags and to reject all other incoming communication. For this, the reader has associated a database DB that stores information about tags. It is assumed that the communication between reader and the database is secure. A tag is a transponder[2] device with much more limited computation capabilities than the reader. Depending on tag, it can perform simple logic operations, symmetric-key or even public-key cryptography. Each tag is identified by an identifier and its memory may contain some information usually referred to as the *tag's state*. A tag is considered *legitimate* when it is registered in the reader's database.

From a formal point of view [13], a RFID system consists of three PPT algorithms, $\mathcal{S} = (SetupR, SetupT, Ident)$, where:

1. $SetupR(\lambda) \rightarrow (pk, sk, DB)$ sets up the reader. It inputs a security parameter λ and outputs a public/private key pair (pk, sk) and an empty database DB. pk is public, while sk is kept secret by reader;

---

[1] Contraction from transmitter and receiver.

[2] Contraction from transmitter and responder.

2. $SetupT(pk, ID) \rightarrow (K, S)$ inputs the public key pk and an identity ID and outputs a secret key K and a tag state S. Thus, this algorithm creates a tag with identity ID and initial state S, and stores the pair (ID, K) in DB;
3. $Ident(T_{ID} : S; \mathcal{R} : sk, DB; * : pk) \rightarrow (T_{ID} : -, \mathcal{R} : out_{\mathcal{R}})$ is an interactive protocol between reader (with its sk and DB) and a tag T_{ID} (with its state S). When the protocol terminates, $\mathcal{R}$ returns either the identity ID, meaning that T_{ID} is legitimate, or $\perp$ to indicate that T_{ID} is not legitimate.

The adversary model views the tags as divided into two distinct classes: tags that are in the proximity of the adversary, referred to as *drawn tags*, and tags outside the adversary's reach, referred to as *free tags*. The adversary can intercept and manipulate the conversation between the reader and the drawn tags. The oracles the adversary has access to are:

$CreateTag^b(ID)$: creates a tag with the identifier ID by calling the algorithm $SetupT(pk, ID)$ to generate a pair (K, S). If $b = 1$, the tag is considered legitimate and (ID, K) is added in DB; otherwise ($b = 0$), the tag is considered illegitimate and nothing is added to DB;

$DrawTag(\delta) \rightarrow (vtag_1, b_1, \ldots, vtag_n, b_n)$: chooses n tags from the set of free tags according to the distribution δ and moves them to the list of drawn tags. n fresh identifiers $vtag_1, \ldots, vtag_n$ are used to anonymously refer to these tags. Information on whether these tags are legitimate ($b_i = 1$) or not ($b_i = 0$) are also provided. The $DrawTag$ oracle manages a secret look-up table that keeps track of the real tag identifier ID_i referred to by $vtag_i$;

$Free(vtag)$: removes the tag referred to by $vtag$ from the set of drawn tags and inserts it into the free set. Moreover, following [9], we assume that before inserting the tag into the set of free tags, a random number of complete protocol instances occur between the tag and the reader, aiming to re-randomize the tag state (in this way, consecutive corruption of the tag does not reveal any information);

$Launch() \rightarrow \pi$: launches a new protocol instance π;

$SendReader(m, \pi)$: outputs the reader's answer when the message m is sent to the reader as part of the protocol instance π;

$SendTag(m, vtag)$: outputs the tag's answer when the message m is sent to the tag referred to by $vtag$;

$Result(\pi)$: returns 1 if the protocol instance π concluded with a successful authentication and 0 otherwise;

$Corrupt(vtag) \rightarrow S$: returns the internal state of the tag pointed to by $vtag$ (the internal state does not include temporary information).

By the ability to corrupt tags and availability to information, the adversaries are classified into:

- *Weak adversaries*: they do not have access to the $Corrupt$ oracle;
- *Forward adversaries*: if they access the $Corrupt$ oracle, then they can only access the $Corrupt$ oracle;
- *Destructive adversaries*: if the adversary queried $Corrupt(vtag)$, then no oracle for $vtag$ can further be queried (that is, $vtag$ is destroyed);

- *Strong adversaries*: there are no restrictions on the use of oracles;
- *Narrow adversaries*: they cannot access the *Result* oracle.

Correctness, *security*, and *privacy* are three main issues that have to be discussed with respect to RFID protocols.

Correctness [13] describes the honest behavior of the tags and reader. More precisely, an RFID system is correct if for any λ, any $(pk, sk, DB) \in SetupR(\lambda)$, and any $(K, S) \in SetupT(pk.ID)$, it holds with overwhelming probability that $Ident(\mathcal{T}_{ID} : S; \mathcal{R} : sk, DB; * : pk) \to (\mathcal{T}_{ID} : -, \mathcal{R} : ID)$.

Security of RFID systems [13] embraces two aspects: *tag authentication* and *reader authentication*.

The experiment for tag authentication, denoted $RFID^{t\text{-}auth}_{\mathcal{A},\mathcal{S}}(\lambda)$, involves an RFID scheme $\mathcal{S}$ and an adversary $\mathcal{A}$ that tries to make the reader to identify some legitimate tag in some protocol instance. To avoid trivial man-in-the-middle attacks, it is assumed that $\mathcal{A}$ computes at least one message without knowing tag's secrets. The advantage of $\mathcal{A}$ in the experiment $RFID^{t\text{-}auth}_{\mathcal{A},\mathcal{S}}(\lambda)$ is defined as

$$Adv^{t\text{-}auth}_{\mathcal{A},\mathcal{S}}(\lambda) = Pr(RFID^{t\text{-}auth}_{\mathcal{A},\mathcal{S}}(\lambda) = 1)$$

An RFID scheme $\mathcal{S}$ achieves tag authentication if $Adv^{t\text{-}auth}_{\mathcal{A},\mathcal{S}}$ is negligible, for any strong adversary $\mathcal{A}$.

The experiment for reader authentication, denoted $RFID^{r\text{-}auth}_{\mathcal{A},\mathcal{S}}(\lambda)$, is quite similar to that above. The main difference is that the adversary $\mathcal{A}$ tries to make some legitimate tag to authenticate the reader. As above, it is assumed that $\mathcal{A}$ computes at least one message that makes the tag to authenticate the reader. An RFID scheme $\mathcal{S}$ achieves reader authentication if the advantage of $\mathcal{A}$, $Adv^{r\text{-}auth}_{\mathcal{A},\mathcal{S}}$, is negligible, for any strong adversary $\mathcal{A}$ (the advantage of $\mathcal{A}$ is defined as above, by using $RFID^{r\text{-}auth}_{\mathcal{A},\mathcal{S}}(\lambda)$ instead of $RFID^{t\text{-}auth}_{\mathcal{A},\mathcal{S}}(\lambda)$).

Privacy for RFID systems [13] captures anonymity and untraceability. It basically means that an adversary cannot learn anything new from intercepting the communication between a tag and the reader. To model this, the concept of a *blinder* is introduced [13], which is a PPT algorithm $\mathcal{B}$ that simulates the communication between tags and reader without knowing their secrets. Now, there are two cases for an adversary $\mathcal{A}$:

1. $\mathcal{A}$ interacts with the RFID system making use of all the oracles that are allowed by the class the adversary belongs to (in this case, the answer to the oracle queries are based on the secrets known to tags and reader);
2. $\mathcal{A}$ interacts with the RFID system making use of all the oracles that are allowed by the class the adversary belongs to, except that the queries to *Lunch*, *SendReader*, *SendTag*, and *Result* are redirected to and answered by the blinder $\mathcal{B}$.

The privacy experiment obtained in this way is denoted $RFID^{priv-b}_{\mathcal{A},\mathcal{S},\mathcal{B}}(\lambda)$, where $b = 0$ corresponds to the first case above, and $b = 1$ corresponds to the second case. The *advantage* of $\mathcal{A}$ is

$$Adv^{prv}_{\mathcal{A},\mathcal{S},\mathcal{B}}(\lambda) = \mid P(RFID^{priv-0}_{\mathcal{A},\mathcal{S},\mathcal{B}}(\lambda) = 1) - P(RFID^{priv-1}_{\mathcal{A},\mathcal{S},\mathcal{B}}(\lambda) = 1) \mid$$

The advantage of $\mathcal{A}$ acts like an indirect measure of the information leaked by the RFID system to the adversary $\mathcal{A}$: the more information is leaked, the more likely $\mathcal{A}$ will distinguish between the two worlds (cases).

An RFID system achieves privacy for a class $\mathcal{C}$ of adversaries if for any adversary $\mathcal{A} \in \mathcal{C}$ there exists a blinder $\mathcal{B}$ such that $Adv^{prv}_{\mathcal{A},\mathcal{S},\mathcal{B}}(\lambda)$ is negligible. When $\mathcal{C}$ is the class of destructive adversaries and the protocol achieves privacy for $\mathcal{C}$, we will also say that the protocol is *destructive private*.

5   The Protocol

In order to obtain a destructive private authentication RFID protocol, the authors of [15,16] endowed tags with (ideal) PUFs to generate private keys for PRFs. Using the same generic idea, we propose an authentication RFID protocol that has the following properties:

1. it is destructive private;
2. it provides mutual authentication;
3. tags are not equipped with pseudo-random generators;
4. it is scalable.

As far as we know, our protocol is the first one that meets these four features (except for the first property, all the other three properties are not met by the protocol in [15,16]).

For the description of the protocol we consider $\lambda \in \mathbb{N}$ a security parameter and a PRF function $F = (F_K)_{K \in \{0,1\}^k}$, where $F_K : \{0,1\}^{\ell_1} \to \{0,1\}^{\ell_2}$ for all K, and k, ℓ_1, and ℓ_2 are of polynomial size in λ. The protocol requires that each tag is equipped with a (unique) PUF $P : \{0,1\}^p \to \{0,1\}^k$, where p is of polynomial size in λ too. It is also assumed that each tag has the capacity of computing F.

The internal state of each tag consists of triples (s, S_1, S_2), where $s \in \{0,1\}^p$ is a random seed needed to evaluate the PUF, and $S_1, S_2 \in \{0,1\}^{\ell_1}$ are two updatable secrets of the tag.

The reader maintains a database DB with entries for all legitimate tags. Each entry is a vector (ID, S_1, S_2, K), where ID is the tag's identity, (s, S_1, S_2) is the (current) tag's state for some s, and $K = P(s)$, where P is the tag's PUF. When the tag is registered, (s, S_1, S_2) is the initial state of the tag.

The mutual authentication protocol between tag and reader that we propose is illustrated in Table 1.

The protocol is initiated by the reader which sends a generic and constant *hello* message to the tag. The tag computes $K = P(s)$, responds with $M_0 = F_K(S_2 \oplus hello)$, and erases K. The value M_0 acts as a static identifier until the

Table 1. RFID mutual authentication protocol

Reader (DB)		**Tag** (s, S_1, S_2)
	$\xrightarrow{\quad hello \quad}$	$K = P(s)$
		$M_0 = F_K(S_2 \oplus hello)$
If $\not\exists (ID, S_1, S_2, K) \in DB$	$\xleftarrow{\quad M_0 \quad}$	Erase K
s.t. $M_0 = F_K(S_2 \oplus hello)$		
then halt ("invalid tag")		
else		
$S_{1,new}, S_{2,new} \leftarrow \{0,1\}^{\ell_1}$		
$M_1 = S_1 \oplus S_{1,new}$		
$M_2 = S_2 \oplus S_{2,new}$		
$M_3 = F_K(S_{1,new})$		
$M_4 = F_K(S_{2,new})$	$\xrightarrow{\ M_1, M_2, M_3, M_4\ }$	$K = P(s)$
		$S_{1,new} = M_1 \oplus S_1$
		$S_{2,new} = M_2 \oplus S_2$
		If $M_3 = F_K(S_{1,new})$ &
		$M_4 = F_K(S_{2,new})$
		then
		auth. reader
		$M_5 = F_K(S_{1,new} \oplus hello)$
		$S_1 := S_{1,new}, S_2 := S_{2,new}$
		else
		$M_5 = \bot$
If $M_5 = F_K(S_{1,new} \oplus hello)$	$\xleftarrow{\quad M_5 \quad}$	Erase K
then		
return ID (auth. tag)		
$S_1 := S_{1,new}, S_2 := S_{2,new}$		

internal state is replaced. The reader checks the database entries until it finds one (ID, S_1', S_2', K') such that $M_0 = F_{K'}(S_2' \oplus hello)$. In such a case, the reader identifies the tag; otherwise, if no such entry is found, the reader rejects the tag and halts the protocol. When the tag is identified, it must be the case that $K' = K$, $S_2' = S_2$, and $S_1' = S_1$ with overwhelming probability.

Assuming that the tag is identified, the reader randomly generates two new secrets $S_{1,new}$ and $S_{2,new}$, and sends them to the tag by means of M_1 and M_2 ("authenticated" by M_3 and M_4).

When the tag receives these messages, it recovers $S_{1,new}$ and $S_{2,new}$, computes the key $K = P(s)$, and checks them by means of the equality $M_3 = F_K(S_{1,new})$ and $M_4 = F_K(S_{2,new})$. If the two equalities hold, the tag authenticates the reader, computes $M_5 = F_K(S_{1,new} \oplus hello)$, and updates its state to $(s, S_{1,new}, S_{2,new})$. Otherwise, the tag computes only $M_5 = \bot$. Finally, M_5 is sent to the reader and the key K is erased.

If the reader checks successfully the equality "$M_5 = F_K(S_{1,new} \oplus hello)$", then the tag is authenticated and the reader state is updated. Otherwise, the current state is kept.

Scalability. To achieve a constant tag authentication time, the following idea can be implemented at the reader level. Each item (ID, S_1, S_2, K) in the database is expanded to (ID, S_1, S_2, K, M_0), where $M_0 = F_K(S_2 \oplus hello)$. Then, the database is sorted by M_0.

When the reader receives M_0, it performs a binary search in the database to find an item (ID, S_1, S_2, K, M_0). The protocol follows its normal way as described above. Finally, when the reader authenticates the tag it removes the tuple (ID, S_1, S_2, K, M_0) and inserts the tuple $(ID, S_{1,new}, S_{2,new}, K, M_{0,new})$, where $M_{0,new} = F_K(S_{2,new} \oplus hello)$, in the corresponding position so that the database still remains sorted.

In this way, the reader searches the database in time $\mathcal{O}(\log d)$, where d is the database size. Remark that this is possible due to the fact that the reader opens the communication with tags by the same constant *hello*.

Desynchronization. Remark that some desynchronization between reader and tag may occur: the tag authenticates the reader but the equality "$M_5 = F_K(S_{1,new} \oplus hello)$" does not hold. This can be caused by the first three communication steps with negligible probability. Therefore, in such a case of desynchronization, the reader only identifies the tag but does not authenticate it, the tag authenticates the reader and updates the state while the reader maintains the older tag state.

A standard way to "partially" solve this desynchronization problem would be to allow the reader to maintain a list of the last entries, but at most m, for each tag (m is a fixed parameter):

$$(ID, S_1, S_2, K, S_2^1, S_2^1, \ldots, S_1^i, S_2^i, \perp)$$

The meaning of such a list is that the reader sent (S_1^1, S_2^1) to the tag but the authentication failed, then it sent (S_1^2, S_2^2) and again the authentication failed and so on. The last pair sent by reader was (S_1^i, S_2^i), where $i < m$. If the authentication fails again when $i = m - 1$, the reader may remove the tag from its database. Otherwise, if the authentication succeeds (when $i < m$), the reader updates the corresponding entry by removing all unsuccessful attempts and maintaining only the last one (which has the form $(ID, S_{1,new}, S_{2,new}, K)$).

The security of this extended version of the protocol is in fact the same to the plain one described in Table 1 and so we will focus only on the plain version of the protocol.

6   Security and Privacy Analysis

Correctness. Assuming that the reader and the tag are legitimate, they will share initially the same information S_1, S_2, and $K = P(s)$. As the PUF P is ideal, the reader and the tag will exchange exactly the same new values $S_{1,new}$ and $S_{2,new}$, and they will authenticate each other. This means that the protocol is correct.

Security and Privacy. We will now present the security and privacy results for our protocol (due to the space limitation we only sketch the proofs).

Theorem 1. *The protocol in Table 1 achieves tag authentication, provided that F is a PRF and the tags are endowed with ideal PUFs.*

Proof Idea. Assume that the protocol does not achieve tag authentication, and let $\mathcal{A}$ be an adversary that has non-negligible advantage over the protocol, with respect to the tag authentication property. We will show that there exists a PPT algorithm $\mathcal{A}'$ that can break the pseudo-randomness property of the function F. The main idea is the next one. Let $\mathcal{C}$ be a challenger for the pseudo-randomness security game of the function F. $\mathcal{C}$ chooses at random a key K^* and will answer all queries submitted by $\mathcal{A}'$ with respect to F_{K^*}. The algorithm $\mathcal{A}'$, which knows F but does not know K^*, will run the adversary $\mathcal{A}$ on the protocol, providing it with all the oracle answers. When $\mathcal{A}$ succeeds in authenticating some tag ID^* to the reader, $\mathcal{A}'$ will use the information obtained from $\mathcal{A}$ to answer some challenge of $\mathcal{C}$, with non-negligible probability. □

Theorem 2. *The protocol in Table 1 achieves reader authentication, provided that F is a PRF and the tags are endowed with ideal PUFs.*

Proof Idea. It follows a similar line to the proof of Theorem 1. □

Theorem 3. *The protocol in Table 1 achieves destructive privacy, provided that F is a PRF and the tags are endowed with ideal PUFs.*

Proof Idea. We will show that for any destructive adversary $\mathcal{A}$ there exists a blinder $\mathcal{B}$ such that the advantage of distinguishing the blinder is negligible i.e. $\mathcal{A}$ is trivial. The blinder $\mathcal{B}$ will answer the *Lunch, SendReader, SendTag,* and *Result* oracles without knowing the secrets of the tags or reader. We use a sequence of six games $G_0, \ldots, G_5$, where G_0 is the real scheme without the blinder, G_1 replaces the secret K with a randomly chosen secret (as opposed to be PUF generated), and $G_2, \ldots, G_5$ introduce the oracles one by one. We prove that the advantage of distinguishing between two consecutive games is negligible, thus distinguishing between the real scheme (G_0) and the blinder (G_5) has a negligible probability. Therefore the protocol achieves destructive privacy. □

7   Conclusions

In this paper we have presented the first stateful protocol that provides mutual authentication for RFID systems and achieves destructive privacy. We have proven our protocol to be secure and private under the Vaudenay model. The protocol is constructed using a PRF and an idealised PUF representation. In order to avoid security issues of random number generators in low cost RFID technology and reduce the size of the protocol, we do not employ a RNG in our protocol. On the reader side, the scheme offers scalability through constant time identification using a precomputed identification message.

References

1. Akgün, M., Çaglayan, M.U.: Providing destructive privacy and scalability in RFID systems using PUFs. Ad Hoc Netw. **32**(C), 32–42 (2015)
2. Arslan, A., Kardaş, S., Çolak, S.A., Ertürk, S.: Are RNGs Achilles' heel of RFID security and privacy protocols? Wirel. Pers. Commun. **100**(4), 1355–1375 (2018)
3. Avoine, G., Carpent, X., Martin, B.: Strong authentication and strong integrity (SASI) is not that strong. In: Ors Yalcin, S.B. (ed.) RFIDSec 2010. LNCS, vol. 6370, pp. 50–64. Springer, Heidelberg (2010). https://doi.org/10.1007/978-3-642-16822-2_5
4. Avoine, G., Coisel, I., Martin, T.: Time measurement threatens privacy-friendly RFID authentication protocols. In: Ors Yalcin, S.B. (ed.) RFIDSec 2010. LNCS, vol. 6370, pp. 138–157. Springer, Heidelberg (2010). https://doi.org/10.1007/978-3-642-16822-2_13
5. Bringer, J., Chabanne, H., Icart, T.: Improved privacy of the tree-based hash protocols using physically unclonable function. In: Ostrovsky, R., De Prisco, R., Visconti, I. (eds.) SCN 2008. LNCS, vol. 5229, pp. 77–91. Springer, Heidelberg (2008). https://doi.org/10.1007/978-3-540-85855-3_6
6. Canard, S., Coisel, I.: Data synchronization in privacy-preserving RFID authentication schemes. In: Conference on RFID Security (2008)
7. Canard, S., Coisel, I., Etrog, J., Girault, M.: Privacy-preserving RFID systems: model and constructions (2010). https://eprint.iacr.org/2010/405.pdf
8. Hermans, J., Pashalidis, A., Vercauteren, F., Preneel, B.: A new RFID privacy model. In: Atluri, V., Diaz, C. (eds.) ESORICS 2011. LNCS, vol. 6879, pp. 568–587. Springer, Heidelberg (2011). https://doi.org/10.1007/978-3-642-23822-2_31
9. Hermans, J., Peeters, R., Preneel, B.: Proper RFID privacy: model and protocols. IEEE Trans. Mobile Comput. **13**(12), 2888–2902 (2014)
10. Kardaş, S., Çelik, S., Yildiz, M., Levi, A.: PUF-enhanced offline RFID security and privacy. J. Netw. Comput. Appl. **35**(6), 2059–2067 (2012)
11. Kardaş, S., Kiraz, M.S., Bingöl, M.A., Demirci, H.: A novel RFID distance bounding protocol based on physically unclonable functions. In: Juels, A., Paar, C. (eds.) RFIDSec 2011. LNCS, vol. 7055, pp. 78–93. Springer, Heidelberg (2012). https://doi.org/10.1007/978-3-642-25286-0_6
12. Maes, R.: Physically Unclonable Functions: Constructions, Properties and Applications. Springer, Heidelberg (2013). https://doi.org/10.1007/978-3-642-41395-7
13. Paise, R.-I., Vaudenay, S.: Mutual authentication in RFID: security and privacy. In: Proceedings of the 2008 ACM Symposium on Information, Computer and Communications Security, ASIACCS 2008, pp. 292–299. ACM, New York (2008)
14. Peris-Lopez, P., Hernandez-Castro, J.C., Tapiador, J.M.E., Ribagorda, A.: Advances in ultralightweight cryptography for low-cost RFID tags: Gossamer protocol. In: Chung, K.-I., Sohn, K., Yung, M. (eds.) WISA 2008. LNCS, vol. 5379, pp. 56–68. Springer, Heidelberg (2009). https://doi.org/10.1007/978-3-642-00306-6_5

15. Sadeghi, A.-R., Visconti, I., Wachsmann, C.: Enhancing RFID security and privacy by physically unclonable functions. In: Sadeghi, A.R., Naccache, D. (eds.) Towards Hardware-Intrinsic Security. Information Security and Cryptography, pp. 281–305. Springer, Heidelberg (2010). https://doi.org/10.1007/978-3-642-14452-3_13
16. Sadeghi, A.-R., Visconti, I., Wachsmann, C.: PUF-enhanced RFID security and privacy. In: Workshop on Secure Component and System Identification (SECSI), vol. 110 (2010)
17. Sipser, M.: Introduction to the Theory of Computation. Cengage Learning, Boston (2012)
18. Van Deursen, T., Radomirovic, S.: Attacks on RFID protocols (2008). http://eprint.iacr.org/2008/310
19. Vaudenay, S.: On privacy models for RFID. In: Kurosawa, K. (ed.) ASIACRYPT 2007. LNCS, vol. 4833, pp. 68–87. Springer, Heidelberg (2007). https://doi.org/10.1007/978-3-540-76900-2_5

Weakened Random Oracle Models
with Target Prefix

Masayuki Tezuka$^{(\boxtimes)}$, Yusuke Yoshida, and Keisuke Tanaka

Tokyo Institute of Technology, Tokyo, Japan
tezuka.m.ac@m.titech.ac.jp

Abstract. Weakened random oracle models (WROMs) are variants of
the random oracle model (ROM). The WROMs have the random oracle
and the additional oracle which breaks some property of a hash function. Analyzing the security of cryptographic schemes in WROMs, we
can specify the property of a hash function on which the security of
cryptographic schemes depends.

Liskov (SAC'06) proposed WROMs and later Numayama *et al.*
(PKC'08) formalized them as CT-ROM, SPT-ROM, and FPT-ROM. In
each model, there is the additional oracle to break collision resistance,
second preimage resistance, preimage resistance respectively. Tan and
Wong (ACISP'12) proposed the generalized FPT-ROM (GFPT-ROM)
which intended to capture the chosen prefix collision attack suggested
by Stevens *et al.* (EUROCRYPT'07).

In this paper, in order to analyze the security of cryptographic schemes
more precisely, we formalize GFPT-ROM and propose additional three
WROMs which capture the chosen prefix collision attack and its variants. In particular, we focus on signature schemes such as RSA-FDH, its
variants, and DSA, in order to understand essential roles of WROMs in
their security proofs.

Keywords: Weakened random oracle model · WROM · RSA-FDH ·
DSA · Chosen prefix collision attack

1 Introduction

A hash function is often used for cryptographic schemes. The security of these
schemes is often proved in the random oracle model (ROM) [1]. In this model, a
hash function is regarded as an ideal random function. Instead of computing a
hash value, all the parties can query the random oracle $\mathcal{RO}$ to get the hash value.
Compared to the standard model, it is easier to design efficient cryptographic
schemes with the provable security.

Supported in part by Input Output Hong Kong, Nomura Research Institute,
NTT Secure Platform Laboratories, Mitsubishi Electric, I-System, JST CREST
JPMJCR14D6, JST OPERA and JSPS KAKENHI 16H01705, 17H01695.

J.-L. Lanet and C. Toma (Eds.): SecITC 2018, LNCS 11359, pp. 344–357, 2019.
https://doi.org/10.1007/978-3-030-12942-2_26

When we implement a cryptographic scheme, the random oracle is replaced by a hash function. However, when a hash function is attacked, there is a problem whether the security of the cryptographic scheme proven in ROM can be guaranteed or not. For example, RSA-Full-Domain-Hash (RSA-FDH) [3] satisfies the existential unforgeability against chosen message attacks (EUF-CMA) security in ROM. However, when a collision (m, m') satisfying $h(m) = h(m')$ and $m \neq m'$ is found for the hash function h, and the adversary get a valid signature $\sigma = \mathbf{Sign}(m)$, the adversary can generate a valid forgery (m', σ). It can be seen that the security of RSA-FDH depends on the collision resistance property of a hash function. Stevens, Bursztein, Karpman, Albertini, and Markov [14] found a collision of SHA-1 [19] in 2017. Hence, the security of RSA-FDH implemented with SHA-1 is not completely guaranteed.

Stevens, Lenstra, and de Weger [15] proposed the chosen prefix collision attack that was used to find a collision of MD5 [13]. Moreover, the idea of this attack was used to find the collision of SHA-1 [19]. Analyzing the security of cryptographic schemes against the chosen prefix collision attack is meaningful as it serves as a criterion.

Weakened Random Oracle Models. Liskov [10] introduced the idea of weakened random oracle models (WROMs). Each model has the additional oracle that breaks the specific property of a hash function. For instance, assuming that the oracle which returns the collision is added, we can capture the situation where the collision is found.

Pasini and Vaudenay [12] used the Liskov's idea to consider the security of Hash-and-Sign signature schemes in the random oracle model with the additional oracle which returns the first preimage.

Numayama, Isshiki, Tanaka [11] formalized the Liskov's idea as three types of WROMs: The collision tractable ROM (CT-ROM), the second preimage tractable ROM (SPT-ROM), and the first preimage tractable ROM (FPT-ROM). Each model has the additional oracle $\mathcal{CO}$, $\mathcal{SPO}$, $\mathcal{FPO}$, respectively:

- $\mathcal{CO}()$: It picks x randomly and uniformly returns a collision (x, x') such that $x \neq x'$ and $h(x) = h(x')$.
- $\mathcal{SPO}(x)$: Given an input x, it uniformly returns x' such that $x \neq x'$ and $h(x) = h(x')$.
- $\mathcal{FPO}(y)$: Given an input y, it uniformly returns x such that $h(x) = y$.

Since Liskov's models considered only compression functions, these oracles are different from that of Liskov's model in following respects. $\mathcal{CO}$ does not provide a collision if there is no x' such that $x \neq x'$ and $h(x) = h(x')$ for x. $\mathcal{SPO}$ (resp. $\mathcal{FPO}$) does not provide x' (resp. x) if there is no x' (resp. x) such that $h(x) = h(x')$ (resp. $h(x) = y$). Numayama et al. analyzed the EUF-CMA security of RSA-FDH and its variant in WROMs.

Kawachi, Numayama, Tanaka, and Xagawa [8] analyzed the indistinguishability against adaptive chosen ciphertext attacks (IND-CCA2) security of RSA-OAEP [2], the Fujisaki-Okamoto conversion (FO) [5] and its variants in WROMs.

They showed RSA-OAEP encryption scheme is IND-CCA2 secure even in FPT-ROM.

The Chosen Prefix Collision Attack. Stevens, Lenstra and de Weger [15] proposed the chosen prefix collision attack which cannot be caught by FPT-ROM. In this attack, we decide a pair (P, P') of prefixes beforehand and find a collision $(P||S, P'||S')$. Using this attack against MD5 [13], an adversary can find a target collision by making roughly 2^{49} calls to the internal compression function.

Moreover, Stevens, Sotirov, Appelbaum, Lenstra, Molnar, Osvik and de Weger [16] succeeded in reducing the number of calls to the internal compression function to find a collision to 2^{16} by setting $P = P'$.

To capture the chosen prefix attack, Tan and Wong [17] proposed the generalized FPT-ROM (GFPT-ROM). This model has the additional oracle $\mathcal{GFPO}$.

- $\mathcal{GFPO}(y, r)$: Given an input (y, r), it uniformly returns $x = m||r$ such that $h(m||r) = y$.

They showed RSA-PFDH$^{\oplus}$ [11] is not EUF-CMA secure in GFPT-ROM. Moreover, they proposed a generic transformation of Hash-and-Sign signature schemes. If the original scheme is secure in ROM, the converted scheme is secure in GFPT-ROM. They proposed RSA-FDH^{+} by using this transformation for RSA-FDH.

Our Contributions. Thanks to transformation proposed by Tan and Wong [17], constructing a secure scheme in WROMs is not a serious problem. But the security against the chosen prefix collision attack of standard signature schemes have not been clarified. We analyze the EUF-CMA security of standard signature schemes against chosen prefix collision attacks. Our analysis of these schemes in WROMs provides a more precise security indication against chosen prefix collision attacks.

In order to analyze the security against chosen prefix collision attacks in more detail, we extend the idea of [17]. Consequently, we obtain common-CP-CT-ROM and CP-CT-ROM from CT-ROM, and CP-SPT-ROM from SPT-ROM.
common-CP-CT-ROM captures the case of $P = P'$ in the chosen prefix collision attack, CP-CT-ROM captures the chosen prefix collision attack, and CP-SPT-ROM captures a variation of this attack that we decide $(P||S, P')$ beforehand and find a collision $(P||S, P'||S')$.

The analysis results in these WROMs are given in Table 1. Models become weaker as it goes right of the table. The security in a weaker model indicates the scheme is secure against stronger attacks to hash functions. Table 1 shows RSA-PFDH and RSA-PFDH$^{\oplus}$ are secure in CP-CT-ROM, but not secure in CP-SPT-ROM. The analysis result of RSA-PFDH$^{\oplus}$ in Table 1 indicate even if a cryptographic scheme is secure in SPT-ROM or FPT-ROM, it may not be secure in CP-SPT-ROM.

In 2018, Jager, Kakvi and May [6] prove that RSASSA-PKCS-v1.5 [7] is EUF-CMA secure in ROM under the RSA assumption. RSASSA-PKCS-v1.5 and DSA [9] are not analyzed using WROMs in previous works [11,17]. We show that both signature schemes are not EUF-CMA secure in both CT-ROM and common-CP-CT-ROM.

Related Works. Unruh [18] proposed ROM with oracle-independent auxiliary inputs. In this model, an adversary $\mathcal{A}$ consists of $(\mathcal{A}_1, \mathcal{A}_2)$. The first step, computationally unbounded $\mathcal{A}_1$ can full access to $\mathcal{RO}$ and store information (e.g collisions) in the string z. In the second step, z is passed to the bounded running time adversary $\mathcal{A}_2$ who can access to $\mathcal{RO}$. Unruh showed that RSA-OAEP encryption scheme is IND-CCA2 secure in ROM with oracle-independent auxiliary inputs. The situation captured by WROMs and ROM with oracle-independent auxiliary inputs are different. The relevance between WROMs and ROM with oracle-independent auxiliary inputs is not still clear. In particular, even if a cryptographic scheme is insecure in ROM with oracle-independent auxiliary inputs, it is not clear whether it is secure in WROMs or not. Hence it is worth anlyzing cryptographic schemes with WROMs.

Table 1. The EUF-CMA security of signature schemes

Schemes\Models	ROM	CT-ROM [11]		SPT-ROM [11]	FPT-ROM [11]
		common-CP-CT-ROM Definition 7	CP-CT-ROM Definition 8	CP-SPT-ROM Definition 9	CP-FPT-ROM [17]
RSA-FDH [3]	✓ [3]	× [11]		×	×
		× Theorem 1	×	×	×
RSA-PFDH [4]	✓	✓ [11]		× [11]	×
		✓	✓ Theorem 2	× Theorem 3	×
RSA-PFDH$^{\oplus}$ [11]	✓	✓		✓	✓ [11]
		✓	✓ Theorem 4	× Theorem 5	× [17]
RSA-FDH$^+$ [17]	✓	✓		✓	✓ [17]
		✓	✓	✓	✓ [17]
RSASSA- PKCS-v1.5 [7]	✓ [6]	× Theorem 6		×	×
		× Theorem 7	×	×	×
DSA [9]	✓ [20]	× Theorem 8		×	×
		× Theorem 9	×	×	×

✓: Secure, ×: Insecure

2   Preliminaries

Let k be a security parameter. A function $f(k)$ is negligible in k if $f(k) \leq 2^{-\omega(\log k)}$. **PPT** stands for probabilistic polynomial time. For strings m and r, $|m|$ is the bit length of m and $m\|r$ is the concatenation of m and r. For a finite set S, $s \xleftarrow{\$} S$ denotes choosing an element from S uniformly at random. Let $y \leftarrow \mathcal{A}(x)$ be the output of algorithm $\mathcal{A}$ on input x.

2.1   A Digital Signature Scheme

We review a digital signature scheme and the EUF-CMA security.

Definition 1 (A digital signature scheme). *A digital signature scheme Π over the message space M is a triple $\Pi = (\mathbf{Gen}, \mathbf{Sign}, \mathbf{Verify})$ of $\mathbf{PPT}$ algorithms:*

- **Gen**: *Given a security parameter 1^k, return a keypair (sk, vk).*
- **Sign**: *Given a signing key sk and a message $m \in M$, return a signature σ.*
- **Verify**: *Given a verification key vk, a message m and a signature σ, return either 1 (Accept) or 0 (Reject).*

Correctness. *For all $k \in \mathbb{N}$, $(sk, vk) \leftarrow \mathbf{Gen}(1^k)$, $m \in M$, we require*

$$\mathbf{Verify}(vk, m, \mathbf{Sign}(sk, m)) = 1.$$

Definition 2 (EUF-CMA). *The EUF-CMA security of a digital signature scheme Π is defined by the following EUF-CMA game between a challenger C and $\mathbf{PPT}$ adversary $\mathcal{A}$.*

- *C produces a keypair $(sk, vk) \leftarrow \mathbf{Gen}(1^k)$, and gives the vk to $\mathcal{A}$.*
- *$\mathcal{A}$ makes a number of signing queries m to C. Then, C signs it as $\sigma \leftarrow \mathbf{Sign}(sk, m)$, and sends σ to $\mathcal{A}$.*
- *$\mathcal{A}$ outputs a message m^* and its signature σ^*.*

A digital signature scheme satisfies the EUF-CMA security if for all $\mathbf{PPT}$ adversaries $\mathcal{A}$, the following advantage of $\mathcal{A}$:

$$Adv_{\Pi, \mathcal{A}}^{\text{EUF-CMA}} = \Pr[\mathbf{Verify}(pk, m^*, \sigma^*) = 1 \land m^* \text{ is not queried to signing}]$$

is negligible in k.

2.2   Security Notions of a Hash Function

Security notions of a hash function are as follows.

- Collision resistance:
  It is hard to find a pair (x, x') of inputs such that $h(x) = h(x')$.
- Second preimage resistance:
  Given an input x, it is hard to find a second preimage $x' \neq x$ such that $h(x) = h(x')$.
- First preimage resistance:
  Given a hash value y, it is hard to find a preimage x such that $h(x) = y$.

2.3   WROMs Proposed by Numayama et al. [11]

Let ℓ be polynomial in k, $X = \{0,1\}^{\ell}$, $Y = \{0,1\}^{k}$, $h : X \to Y$ a random function, and $\mathbb{T}_{h} = \{(x, h(x)) \mid x \in X\}$ the table which defines the correspondence between the inputs and outputs of h. We define $\mathsf{ROM}_{(\ell,k)}$. To make a more rigorous discussion, we introduce subscript (ℓ, k) in the definition, which make explicit that the length of the input of h is ℓ and the length of the output of h is k.

Definition 3 ($\mathsf{ROM}_{(\ell,k)}$). *The random oracle model $\mathsf{ROM}_{(\ell,k)}$ is the model that all parties can query the random oracle $\mathcal{RO}^{h}$.*

- **Random oracle $\mathcal{RO}^{h}(x)$**
  Given an input x, the random oracle returns y such that $(x, y) \in \mathbb{T}_{h}$.

Now, we review $\mathsf{CT\text{-}ROM}_{(\ell,k)}$, $\mathsf{SPT\text{-}ROM}_{(\ell,k)}$ and $\mathsf{FPT\text{-}ROM}_{(\ell,k)}$ which are defined by Numayama *et al.* [11].

Definition 4 ($\mathsf{CT\text{-}ROM}_{(\ell,k)}$ [11]). *The collision tractable random oracle model $\mathsf{CT\text{-}ROM}_{(\ell,k)}$ is the model that all parties can query $\mathcal{RO}^{h}$ and the collision oracle $\mathcal{CO}^{h}$.*

- **Collision oracle $\mathcal{CO}^{h}()$**
  The collision oracle picks one entry $(x, y) \in \mathbb{T}_{h}$ uniformly at random. If there is any other entry $(x', y) \in \mathbb{T}_{h}$ then it picks such an entry (x', y) uniformly at random and returns (x, x'). Otherwise, it returns $\perp$.

In $\mathsf{CT\text{-}ROM}_{(\ell,k)}$, we can capture the situation where the collision resistance property is broken.

Definition 5 ($\mathsf{SPT\text{-}ROM}_{(\ell,k)}$ [11]). *The second preimage tractable random oracle model $\mathsf{SPT\text{-}ROM}_{(\ell,k)}$ is the model that all parties can query $\mathcal{RO}^{h}$ and the second preimage oracle $\mathcal{SPO}^{h}$.*

- **Second preimage oracle $\mathcal{SPO}^{h}(x)$**
  Given an input x, let y be the hash value of x (i.e., $(x, y) \in \mathbb{T}_{h}$). If there is any other entry $(x', y) \in \mathbb{T}_{h}$ such that $x' \neq x$, then second preimage oracle returns x' uniformly at random. Otherwise, it returns $\perp$.

In $\mathsf{SPT\text{-}ROM}_{(\ell,k)}$, we can capture the situation where the second preimage resistance property is broken.

Definition 6 ($\mathsf{FPT\text{-}ROM}_{(\ell,k)}$ [11]). *The first preimage tractable random oracle model $\mathsf{FPT\text{-}ROM}_{(\ell,k)}$ is the model that all parties can query $\mathcal{RO}^{h}$ and the first preimage oracle $\mathcal{FPO}^{h}$.*

- **First preimage oracle $\mathcal{FPO}^{h}(y)$**
  Given an input y, if there is any entry $(x, y) \in \mathbb{T}_{h}$ then the first preimage oracle returns such x uniformly at random. Otherwise, it returns $\perp$.

In $\mathsf{FPT\text{-}ROM}_{(\ell,k)}$, we can capture the situation where the preimage resistance property is broken.

3   WROMs Against Chosen Prefix Collision Attacks

In this section, we propose WROMs which capture the chosen prefix collision attack and its variants. Let ℓ and t be polynomials in k, $M = \{0,1\}^\ell$, $R = \{0,1\}^t$, $X = M \times R$, $Y = \{0,1\}^k$, $h : X \to Y$ a random function, and $\mathbb{T}_h = \{(x, h(x)) \mid x \in X\}$ the table which defines the correspondence between the inputs and outputs of the function h. To make a more rigorous discussion, we introduce subscript (ℓ, t, k) in the definition, which make explicit that the length of the input of the function is ℓ, the length of the prefix is t, and the length of the output is k.

Definition 7 (common-CP-CT-ROM$_{(\ell,t,k)}$). *The common chosen prefix collision tractable random oracle model* common-CP-CT-ROM$_{(\ell,t,k)}$ *is the model that all parties can query* $\mathcal{RO}^h$ *and the common chosen prefix collision oracle* $\mathcal{COMMON\text{-}CP\text{-}CO}^h$.

- **Common chosen prefix collision oracle** $\mathcal{COMMON\text{-}CP\text{-}CO}^h(r)$
  Given an input r ($|r| = t$), the common chosen prefix collision oracle picks one entry $(m\|r, y) \in \mathbb{T}_h$ uniformly at random. If there is any other entry $(m'\|r, y) \in \mathbb{T}_h$ then it picks such an entry $(m'\|r, y)$ uniformly at random and returns $(m\|r, m'\|r)$. Otherwise, it returns $\bot$.

In common-CP-CT-ROM$_{(\ell,t,k)}$, we can capture the case of $P = P'$ of the chosen prefix collision attack.

Definition 8 (CP-CT-ROM$_{(\ell,t,k)}$). *The chosen prefix collision tractable random oracle model* CP-CT-ROM$_{(\ell,t,k)}$ *is the model that all parties can query* $\mathcal{RO}^h$ *and the chosen prefix collision oracle* $\mathcal{CP\text{-}CO}^h$.

- **Chosen prefix collision oracle** $\mathcal{CP\text{-}CO}^h(r, r')$
  Given an input (r, r') ($|r| = |r'| = t$), the chosen prefix collision oracle first picks one entry $(m\|r, y) \in \mathbb{T}_h$ uniformly at random. If there is any other entry $(m'\|r', y) \in \mathbb{T}_h$ then it picks such an entry $(m'\|r', y)$ uniformly at random and returns $(m\|r, m'\|r')$. Otherwise, it returns $\bot$.

In CP-CT-ROM$_{(\ell,t,k)}$, we can capture the chosen prefix collision attack.

Definition 9 (CP-SPT-ROM$_{(\ell,t,k)}$). *The chosen prefix second preimage tractable random oracle model* CP-SPT-ROM$_{(\ell,t,k)}$ *is the model that all parties can query* $\mathcal{RO}^h$ *and the chosen prefix second preimage oracle* $\mathcal{CP\text{-}SPO}^h$.

- **Chosen prefix second preimage oracle** $\mathcal{CP\text{-}SPO}^h(x, r')$
  Given an input (x, r') ($|x| = \ell + t, |r'| = t$), let y be the hash value of x (i.e., $(x, y) \in \mathbb{T}_h$). If there is any other entry $(m'\|r', y) \in \mathbb{T}_h$ such that $m'\|r' \neq x$, then the chosen prefix second preimage oracle returns $m'\|r'$ uniformly at random. Otherwise, it returns $\bot$.

In CP-SPT-ROM$_{(\ell,t,k)}$, we can capture a variation of the chosen prefix collision attack that we decide $(P||S, P')$ beforehand and find a collision $(P||S, P'||S')$.

In order to treat GFPT-ROM [17] in a similar manner to above models, we rename it to CP-FPT-ROM$_{(\ell,t,k)}$.

Definition 10 (CP-FPT-ROM$_{(\ell,t,k)}$). *The chosen prefix first preimage tractable random oracle model* CP-FPT-ROM$_{(\ell,t,k)}$ *is the model that all parties can query* $\mathcal{RO}^h$ *and the chosen prefix first preimage oracle* $\mathcal{CP}\text{-}\mathcal{FPO}^h$.

- **Chosen prefix first preimage oracle** $\mathcal{CP}\text{-}\mathcal{FPO}^h(y, r)$
  Given an input (y, r) $(|y| = k, |r| = t)$, *if there is an entry* $(m||r, y) \in \mathbb{T}_h$ *then the chosen prefix first preimage oracle returns such* $m||r$ *uniformly at random. Otherwise, it returns* $\bot$.

By Definitions 7, 8, 9, 10, following relations between WROMs hold.

- If a cryptographic scheme is secure in CP-CT-ROM$_{(\ell,t,k)}$, then it is secure in common-CP-CT-ROM$_{(\ell,t,k)}$.
- If a cryptographic scheme is secure in CP-SPT-ROM$_{(\ell,t,k)}$, then it is secure in CP-CT-ROM$_{(\ell,t,k)}$.
- If a cryptographic scheme is secure in CP-FPT-ROM$_{(\ell,t,k)}$, then it is secure in CP-SPT-ROM$_{(\ell,t,k)}$.

Intuition of Simulating WROMs. In ROM, the reduction algorithm simulates $\mathcal{RO}^h$ using a table $\mathbb{T}$ which has entries (x, y) representing that the hash value of x is y. In WROMs, the reduction algorithm must simulate the additional oracle. In CT-ROM$_{(\ell,k)}$, SPT-ROM$_{(\ell,k)}$ and FPT-ROM$_{(\ell,k)}$, the behavior of the additional oracle depends on the number of preimages. The reduction algorithm uses $\mathbb{T}$ and a table $\mathbb{L}$. The table $\mathbb{L}$ has entries (y, n) representing that y has n preimages. In common-CP-CT-ROM$_{(\ell,t,k)}$, CP-CT-ROM$_{(\ell,t,k)}$, CP-SPT-ROM$_{(\ell,t,k)}$ and CP-FPT-ROM$_{(\ell,t,k)}$, the behavior of the additional oracle depends on not only the number of preimages but also prefixes. The reduction algorithm simulates the additional oracle by adding an entry for prefix r to tables $\mathbb{T}$ and $\mathbb{L}$. Concretely, $\mathbb{T}$ has entries $((m, r), y)$ representing that a hash value of $m||r$ is y and $\mathbb{L}$ has entries $((y, r), n)$ representing that y has n preimages which have the prefix r. We will describe technical details in the full version of this paper.

4   The Security of Signature Schemes in WROMs

In this section, we argue the EUF-CMA security of signature schemes in WROMs. We will describe the proof of security analyses of signature schemes in the full version of this paper. We recall the RSA assumption.

Definition 11 (RSA generator). *The RSA generator* **RSA**, *which on input* 1^k, *randomly chooses distinct $k/2$-bit primes p, q and computes $N = pq$ and* $\phi = (p-1)(q-1)$. *It randomly picks $e \xleftarrow{\$} \mathbb{Z}_{\phi(N)}$ and computes d such that* $ed = 1 \bmod \phi(N)$. *The RSA generator outputs* (N, e, d).

Assumption 1 (RSA assumption). *A polynomial-time machine $\mathcal{A}$ is said to solve the RSA problem if given an RSA instance (N, e, z) where N, e is generated by $\mathsf{RSA}(1^k)$ and $z \xleftarrow{\$} \mathbb{Z}_N^*$, it outputs $z^{1/e} \bmod N$ with non-negligible probability. The RSA assumption is that there is no **PPT** machine that solves the RSA problem.*

4.1 RSA-FDH

Let ℓ be a polynomial in k, $M = \{0,1\}^\ell$ the message space, and $h : \{0,1\}^\ell \to \{0,1\}^k$ a hash function. RSA-FDH [3] is described as follows (Table 2).

Table 2. RSA-FDH

Gen(1^k)	Sign(sk, m)	Verify(vk, m, σ)
$(N, e, d) \leftarrow \mathbf{RSA}(1^k)$	$y \leftarrow h(m)$	$y \leftarrow \sigma^e \bmod N$
$vk \leftarrow (N, e)$	$\sigma \leftarrow y^d \bmod N$	if $h(m) = y$
$sk \leftarrow (N, d)$	return σ	return 1
return (vk, sk)		else
		return 0

Theorem 1. *In* common-CP-CT-ROM$_{(\ell_1, t_1, k)}$ *($\ell_1 + t_1 = \ell$), there exists a* **PPT** *query machine $\mathcal{A}$ that breaks RSA-FDH by making queries to the signing oracle and $\mathcal{COMMON\text{-}CP\text{-}CO}^h$ with probability at least $1 - e^{(1-2^{\ell_1})/2^k}$.*

4.2 RSA-PFDH

Let ℓ and k_1 be polynomials in k, $M = \{0,1\}^\ell$ the message space, and $h : \{0,1\}^{\ell+k_1} \to \{0,1\}^k$ a hash function. RSA-PFDH [4] is described as follows (Table 3).

Table 3. RSA-PFDH

Gen(1^k)	Sign(sk, m)	Verify(vk, m, σ)
$(N, e, d) \leftarrow \mathbf{RSA}(1^k)$	$r \xleftarrow{\$} \{0,1\}^{k_1}$	parse σ as (r, x)
$vk \leftarrow (N, e)$	$y \leftarrow h(m\|r)$	$y \leftarrow x^e \bmod N$
$sk \leftarrow (N, d)$	$x \leftarrow y^d \bmod N$	if $h(m\|r) = y$
return (vk, sk)	$\sigma \leftarrow (r, x)$	return 1
	return σ	else
		return 0

In WROMs defined in this paper, the following facts were further clarified.

Theorem 2. *In* CP-CT-ROM$_{(\ell_1,t_1,k)}$ *($\ell_1 + t_1 = \ell + k_1$), for all* **PPT** *oracle query machines* $\mathcal{B}$ *that break* RSA-PFDH *with probability* ϵ_{euf} *by making* q_{sign}, q_h *and* q_{sc} *queries to the signing oracle,* $\mathcal{RO}^h$, *and* CP-CO^h *respectively. There exists a* **PPT** *machine* $\mathcal{A}$ *that solves the RSA problem with* ϵ_{rsa} *such that*

$$\epsilon_{euf} \leq \epsilon_{rsa} + \frac{1}{2^k} + \frac{q_{sign}Q_2}{2^{k_1}} + Q_1 \times p_{\mathbf{prefixRO}^h}$$

where $Q_1 = q_{sign} + q_h + q_{sc}$, $Q_2 = q_{sign} + q_h + 2q_{sc}$ *and*

$$p_{\mathbf{prefixRO}^h} \leq \begin{cases} \frac{\ln 2^k}{\ln\ln 2^k}\frac{10Q_2}{2^k} + \frac{1}{(2^k)^2} + \frac{Q_2}{2^k} & (\ell_1 \geq k) \\ \frac{\ln 2^k}{\ln\ln 2^k}\frac{10Q_2}{2^{\ell_1}} + \frac{1}{(2^k)^2} + \frac{Q_2}{2^k} & (\ell_1 < k). \end{cases}$$

Theorem 3. *In* CP-SPT-ROM$_{(\ell,k_1,k)}$, *there exists a* **PPT** *oracle query machine* $\mathcal{A}$ *that breaks* RSA-PFDH *by making queries to the signing oracle and* CP-SPO^h *with probability at least* $1 - e^{(1-2^\ell)/2^k}$. *If* $\ell \geq k \geq 2$, $\mathcal{A}$ *outputs a valid forgery with probability at least* $1 - e^{-1/2}$.

4.3 RSA-PFDH$^\oplus$

Let ℓ be a polynomial in k, $M = \{0,1\}^\ell$ the message space, and $h : \{0,1\}^{\ell+k} \rightarrow \{0,1\}^k$ a hash function. RSA-PFDH$^\oplus$ [11] is described as follows (Table 4).

Table 4. RSA-PFDH$^\oplus$

Gen(1^k)	Sign(sk, m)	Verify(vk, m, σ)
$(N, e, d) \leftarrow \mathbf{RSA}(1^k)$	$r \overset{\$}{\leftarrow} \{0,1\}^k$	parse σ as (r, x)
$vk \leftarrow (N, e)$	$w \leftarrow h(m\|r)$	$y \leftarrow x^e \bmod N$
$sk \leftarrow (N, d)$	$y \leftarrow w \oplus r$	$w \leftarrow h(m\|r)$
return (vk, sk)	$x \leftarrow y^d \bmod N$	if $w \oplus r = y$
	$\sigma \leftarrow (r, x)$	return 1
	return σ)	else
		return 0

Theorem 4. *In* CP-CT-ROM$_{(\ell_1,t_1,k)}$ *($\ell_1 + t_1 = \ell + k$), for all* **PPT** *oracle query machines* $\mathcal{B}$ *that break* RSA-PFDH$^\oplus$ *with probability* ϵ_{euf} *by making* q_{sign}, q_h *and* q_{sc} *queries to the signing oracle,* $\mathcal{RO}^h$, *and* CP-CO^h, *respectively. There exists a* **PPT** *machine* $\mathcal{A}$ *that solves the RSA problem with* ϵ_{rsa} *such that*

$$\epsilon_{euf} \leq \epsilon_{rsa} + \frac{1}{2^k} + \frac{q_{sign}Q_2}{2^{k_1}} + Q_1 \times p_{\mathbf{prefixRO}^h}$$

where $Q_1 = q_{sign} + q_h + q_{sc}$, $Q_2 = q_{sign} + q_h + 2q_{sc}$ *and*

$$p_{\mathbf{prefixRO}^h} \leq \begin{cases} \frac{\ln 2^k}{\ln\ln 2^k}\frac{10Q_2}{2^k} + \frac{1}{(2^k)^2} + \frac{Q_2}{2^k} & (\ell_1 \geq k) \\ \frac{\ln 2^k}{\ln\ln 2^k}\frac{10Q_2}{2^{\ell_1}} + \frac{1}{(2^k)^2} + \frac{Q_2}{2^k} & (\ell_1 < k). \end{cases}$$

Theorem 5. *In* CP-SPT-ROM$_{(\ell,k,k)}$, *there exists a* **PPT** *oracle query machine* $\mathcal{A}$ *that breaks* RSA-PFDH$^{\oplus}$ *by making queries to the signing oracle and the chosen prefix second preimage oracle for h with probability at least* $1 - e^{(1-2^{\ell})/2^k}$.

4.4 RSASSA-PKCS-v1.5

We discuss RSASSA-PKCS-v1.5 [7]. To simplify the discussion, exclude detailed settings and treat octet strings as binary strings. Let ℓ, k_1, and k_2 be polynomials in k, and c a constant which is determined by the type of hash function when implementing RSASSA-PKCS-v1.5. Let $M = \{0,1\}^{\ell}$ be the message space and $h : \{0,1\}^{\ell} \to \{0,1\}^{k_2}$ a hash function. Let s be a fixed binary string of length k_1. The *HashAlgID* represent the type of hash function when implementing RSASSA-PKCS-v1.5 in a specific binary string of length c. The *HashAlgID* and the string s are published in advance. Let $k = k_1 + c + k_2$. RSASSA-PKCS-v1.5 is described as follows (Table 5).

Table 5. RSASSA-PKCS-v1.5

Gen(1^k)	Sign(sk, m)	Verify(vk, m^*, σ^*)
$(N, e, d) \leftarrow \mathbf{RSA}(1^k)$	$w \leftarrow h(m)$	$y^* \leftarrow (\sigma^*)^e \bmod N$
$vk \leftarrow (N, e)$	$y \leftarrow s \| HashAlgID \| w$	parse y^* as $s^* \| HashAlgID^* \| w^*$
$sk \leftarrow (N, d)$	$x \leftarrow y^d \bmod N$	if $s^* \| HashAlgID^* \neq s \| HashAlgID$
return (vk, sk)	$\sigma \leftarrow x$	return 0
	return σ	if $h(m^*) = w^*$
		return 1
		else
		return 0

Theorem 6. *In* CT-ROM$_{(\ell,k_2)}$, *there exists a* **PPT** *oracle query machine* $\mathcal{A}$ *that breaks* RSASSA-PKCS-v1.5 *by making queries to the signing oracle and* $\mathcal{CO}^h$ *with probability at least* $1 - e^{(1-2^{\ell})/2^{k_2}}$.

Theorem 7. *In* common-CP-CT-ROM$_{(\ell_1, t_1, k_2)}$ $(\ell_1 + t_1 = \ell)$, *there exists a* **PPT** *oracle query machine* $\mathcal{A}$ *that breaks* RSASSA-PKCS-v1.5 *by making queries to the signing oracle and* $\mathcal{COMMON}$-$\mathcal{CP}$-$\mathcal{CO}^h$ *with probability at least* $1 - e^{(1-2^{\ell_1})/2^{k_2}}$.

4.5 DSA

We discuss DSA [9]. We recall the DSA setup algorithm **DSA**.

Definition 12 (DSA setup). *The DSA setup algorithm* **DSA**, *which on input* 1^k, *randomly chooses a k-bit prime q and a j-bit prime such that* $q|(p-1)$ *(j is polynomial in k). It chooses an* $x \in \{1, \ldots, p-1\}$ *such that* $x^{(p-1)/q} \not\equiv 1 \bmod p$ *and sets* $g = x^{(p-1)/q} \bmod p$. *The DSA setup algorithm outputs* (p, q, g).

Table 6. DSA

Gen(1^k)	Sign(sk, m)	Verify(vk, m, σ)
$(p, q, g) \leftarrow \mathbf{DSA}(1^k)$	$k \xleftarrow{\$} [0, q-1]$	parse σ as (r, s)
$x \xleftarrow{\$} \{0, \ldots, q-1\}$	$r \leftarrow (g^k \bmod p) \bmod q$	$w \leftarrow s^{-1} \bmod q$
$y \leftarrow g^x$	$z \leftarrow h(m)$	$z \leftarrow h(m)$
$vk \leftarrow (p, q, g, y)$	$s \leftarrow (k^{-1}(z + xr)) \bmod q$	$u_1 \leftarrow zw \bmod q, u_2 \leftarrow rw \bmod q$
$sk \leftarrow (p, q, g, x)$	$\sigma \leftarrow (r, s)$	$v \leftarrow g^{u_1} y^{u_2} \bmod q$
return (vk, sk)	return σ	if $v = r$
		return 1
		else
		return 0

Let ℓ be a polynomial in k, $M = \{0, 1\}^\ell$ the message space, and $h : \{0, 1\}^{\ell+k} \to \{0, 1\}^k$ a hash function. DSA is described as follows (Table 6).

Theorem 8. *In* CT-ROM$_{(\ell+k,k)}$, *there exists a* **PPT** *oracle query machine* $\mathcal{A}$ *that breaks* DSA *by making queries to the signing oracle and* $\mathcal{CO}^h$ *with probability at least* $1 - e^{(1 - 2^{\ell+k})/2^k}$.

Theorem 9. *In* common-CP-CT-ROM$_{(\ell_1, k_1, k)}$ $(\ell_1 + k_1 = \ell + k)$, *there exists a* **PPT** *oracle query machine* $\mathcal{A}$ *that breaks* DSA *by making queries to the signing oracle and* $\mathcal{COMMON\text{-}CP\text{-}CO}^h$ *with probability at least* $1 - e^{(1 - 2^{\ell_1})/2^k}$.

5   Conclusion

In this paper, we analyze the security of standard signature schemes against chosen prefix collision attacks by defining three WROMs. Our analysis of these schemes in WROMs provides a more precise security indication against chosen prefix attacks. We showed RSA-PFDH and RSA-PFDH$^\oplus$ are EUF-CMA secure in CP-CT-ROM, but not secure in CP-SPT-ROM. We also showed that RSASSA-PKCS-v1.5 and DSA are not EUF-CMA secure in both CT-ROM and common-CP-CT-ROM.

When discussing the security in CP-CT-ROM$_{(\ell,t,k)}$, we fixed the length of the prefix ℓ. Studying the case of variable length is a future work. There are practical signature schemes and encryption schemes which have not been analyzed in WROMs. The security analysis of these schemes in WROMs is also an interesting future work.

Acknowledgement. We are grateful to Kazuo Ohta (University of Electro-Communications) and Shiho Moriai (National Institute of Information and Communications Technology) for giving us the opportunity to do this research. We would also like to thank anonymous referees for their constructive comments.

References

1. Bellare, M., Rogaway, P.: Random oracles are practical: a paradigm for designing efficient protocols. In: CCS 1993, Proceedings of the 1st ACM Conference on Computer and Communications Security, Fairfax, Virginia, USA, November 3–5, 1993, pp. 62–73 (1993)
2. Bellare, M., Rogaway, P.: Optimal asymmetric encryption. In: De Santis, A. (ed.) EUROCRYPT 1994. LNCS, vol. 950, pp. 92–111. Springer, Heidelberg (1995). https://doi.org/10.1007/BFb0053428
3. Bellare, M., Rogaway, P.: The exact security of digital signatures-how to sign with RSA and Rabin. In: Maurer, U. (ed.) EUROCRYPT 1996. LNCS, vol. 1070, pp. 399–416. Springer, Heidelberg (1996). https://doi.org/10.1007/3-540-68339-9_34
4. Coron, J.-S.: Optimal security proofs for PSS and other signature schemes. In: Knudsen, L.R. (ed.) EUROCRYPT 2002. LNCS, vol. 2332, pp. 272–287. Springer, Heidelberg (2002). https://doi.org/10.1007/3-540-46035-7_18
5. Fujisaki, E., Okamoto, T.: Secure integration of asymmetric and symmetric encryption schemes. In: Wiener, M. (ed.) CRYPTO 1999. LNCS, vol. 1666, pp. 537–554. Springer, Heidelberg (1999). https://doi.org/10.1007/3-540-48405-1_34
6. Jager, T., Kakvi, S.A., May, A.: On the security of the PKCS#1 v1.5 signature scheme. In: Proceedings of the 2018 ACM SIGSAC Conference on Computer and Communications Security, CCS 2018, Toronto, ON, Canada, October 15–19, 2018, pp. 1195–1208 (2018)
7. Jonsson, J., Moriarty, K., Kaliski, B., Rusch, A.: PKCS# 1: RSA cryptography specifications version 2.2. RFC 8017, RFC Editor, United States (2016)
8. Kawachi, A., Numayama, A., Tanaka, K., Xagawa, K.: Security of encryption schemes in weakened random oracle models. In: Nguyen, P.Q., Pointcheval, D. (eds.) PKC 2010. LNCS, vol. 6056, pp. 403–419. Springer, Heidelberg (2010). https://doi.org/10.1007/978-3-642-13013-7_24
9. Kerry, C.F., Romine, C.: FIPS PUB 186-4 Digital Signature Standard (DSS) (2013)
10. Liskov, M.: Constructing an ideal hash function from weak ideal compression functions. In: Biham, E., Youssef, A.M. (eds.) SAC 2006. LNCS, vol. 4356, pp. 358–375. Springer, Heidelberg (2007). https://doi.org/10.1007/978-3-540-74462-7_25
11. Numayama, A., Isshiki, T., Tanaka, K.: Security of digital signature schemes in weakened random oracle models. In: Cramer, R. (ed.) PKC 2008. LNCS, vol. 4939, pp. 268–287. Springer, Heidelberg (2008). https://doi.org/10.1007/978-3-540-78440-1_16
12. Pasini, S., Vaudenay, S.: Hash-and-sign with weak hashing made secure. In: Pieprzyk, J., Ghodosi, H., Dawson, E. (eds.) ACISP 2007. LNCS, vol. 4586, pp. 338–354. Springer, Heidelberg (2007). https://doi.org/10.1007/978-3-540-73458-1_25
13. Rivest, R.: The MD5 Message-Digest Algorithm. RFC 1321, RFC Editor, United States (1992)
14. Stevens, M., Bursztein, E., Karpman, P., Albertini, A., Markov, Y.: The first collision for full SHA-1. In: Katz, J., Shacham, H. (eds.) CRYPTO 2017. LNCS, vol. 10401, pp. 570–596. Springer, Cham (2017). https://doi.org/10.1007/978-3-319-63688-7_19
15. Stevens, M., Lenstra, A., de Weger, B.: Chosen-prefix collisions for MD5 and colliding X.509 certificates for different identities. In: Naor, M. (ed.) EUROCRYPT 2007. LNCS, vol. 4515, pp. 1–22. Springer, Heidelberg (2007). https://doi.org/10.1007/978-3-540-72540-4_1

16. Stevens, M., et al.: Short chosen-prefix collisions for MD5 and the creation of a rogue CA certificate. In: Halevi, S. (ed.) CRYPTO 2009. LNCS, vol. 5677, pp. 55–69. Springer, Heidelberg (2009). https://doi.org/10.1007/978-3-642-03356-8_4

17. Tan, X., Wong, D.S.: Generalized first pre-image tractable random oracle model and signature schemes. In: Susilo, W., Mu, Y., Seberry, J. (eds.) ACISP 2012. LNCS, vol. 7372, pp. 247–260. Springer, Heidelberg (2012). https://doi.org/10.1007/978-3-642-31448-3_19

18. Unruh, D.: Random oracles and auxiliary input. In: Menezes, A. (ed.) CRYPTO 2007. LNCS, vol. 4622, pp. 205–223. Springer, Heidelberg (2007). https://doi.org/10.1007/978-3-540-74143-5_12

19. U.S. Department of Commerce/National Institute of Standards and Technology. FIPS PUB 180-2, Secure Hash Standard (SHS) (2002)

20. Vaudenay, S.: The security of DSA and ECDSA. In: Desmedt, Y.G. (ed.) PKC 2003. LNCS, vol. 2567, pp. 309–323. Springer, Heidelberg (2003). https://doi.org/10.1007/3-540-36288-6_23

An Improved Algorithm for Iterative Matrix-Vector Multiplications over Finite Fields

Ceyda Mangır[1]([⊠]) [iD], Murat Cenk[1] [iD], and Murat Manguoğlu[1,2]

[1] Institute of Applied Mathematics, METU, Ankara, Turkey
{e150893,mcenk}@metu.edu.tr
[2] Department of Computer Engineering, METU, Ankara, Turkey
manguoglu@ceng.metu.edu.tr

Abstract. Cryptographic computations such as factoring integers and computing discrete logarithms over finite fields require solving a large system of linear equations. When dealing with such systems iterative approaches such as Wiedemann or Lanczos are used. Both methods are based on the computation of a Krylov subspace in which the computational cost is often dominated by successive matrix-vector products. We introduce a new algorithm for computing iterative matrix-vector multiplications over finite fields. The proposed algorithm consists of two stages. The first stage (preprocessing) sorts the elements of the matrix row by row in ascending order and produces permutation tables. After preprocessing, many consecutive multiplications can be performed by the second stage of the algorithm using sequential additions on vector elements by the guidance of the permutation tables. We show that the preprocessing cost of the proposed algorithm can easily be amortized after several matrix-vector multiplications are performed. We implemented the algorithm using the C++ programming language and compared the performance with a classical method. The proposed algorithm exhibits significant improvement between 35% and 67%.

Keywords: Matrix-vector multiplication · Index calculus algorithm · Wiedemann · Lanczos

1 Introduction

The problem of solving a large sparse system of linear equations over finite fields arises in different areas such as computer algebra, number theory, and cryptography. In cryptographic computations, factoring integers and solving discrete logarithms over finite fields are two well-known problems that require solving a large system of linear equations [1,3,7–9]. In [5], the results on solving 768-bit prime field discrete logarithm were reported. For solving this problem, the number field sieve algorithm produced a system of linear equation of dimension approximately 23 million and the block Wiedemann algorithm was used to solve

ⓒ Springer Nature Switzerland AG 2019
J.-L. Lanet and C. Toma (Eds.): SecITC 2018, LNCS 11359, pp. 358–367, 2019.
https://doi.org/10.1007/978-3-030-12942-2_27

this system. Similarly, in [4], the factorization of a 768-bit number using the number field sieve method was presented. The size of the matrix in that work is approximately 190 million of total weight 27 million, i.e., there are 144 non-zeros per row.

Two of the widely used methods for solving a system of linear equations in cryptographic computations are the methods of Wiedemann [2,10] and Lanczos [6] (including their block variants). These methods compute the successive matrix-vector products $A^t v$ where A is an $n \times n$ matrix, v is an $n \times 1$ vector, and $t = 1, \ldots, m$ for a positive integer m. In the case of the matrices that arise from integer factorization or discrete logarithm computation, A is a highly sparse non-square matrix. Thus for each t, a sparse matrix-vector multiplication (SpMV) is calculated. The numerical community has widely studied the performance of SpMV particularly exploiting the matrix structures since SpMV requires as much memory access as arithmetic operations and on modern processors, data access is a major challenge for good performance. However, for cryptographic purposes, multiple precision arithmetic is used which is considerably slower than the arithmetic using numbers that fit entirely within processor registers. Although simple algorithms exist for multiple- precision addition, subtraction and comparison, the multiplication and modular reduction are more complex.

In this work, we propose an algorithm for computing such iterative matrix-vector products. The proposed algorithm includes two stages. The first stage sorts the rows of the matrix and then the multiplications of a matrix by a vector are performed using additions in the second stage. The proposed algorithm has advantages especially when the index calculus family of algorithms is used since they require modular multiplications and using additions results in slow changes in the entries. We have shown that the proposed algorithm leads to improved running time over the classical result up to 67%.

The rest of the paper is organized as follows: In Sect. 2 the explanation of the two stages of the proposed algorithm namely preprocessing and permutational matrix-vector multiplication (PMVM) are given along with pseudocodes and a running example. In Sect. 3 complexity analysis of the algorithms are explained. In addition, the performance comparison between the proposed algorithm and the classical algorithm is given.

2   Permutational Matrix-Vector Multiplication (PMVM) with Preprocessing

We present a new algorithm for computing matrix-vector multiplications over prime fields. The algorithm consists of two stages. The first one is the preprocessing stage which constructs the permutation tables. The second stage is the actual matrix-vector multiplication using the permutation tables.

When solving a large sparse system of equations iterative methods such as Wiedeman or Lanczos algorithms are preferred. While Wiedemann algorithm calculates $2n$ iterative matrix-vector multiplications $A^t v$ for $1 \leq t \leq 2n$, n

iterative matrix-vector multiplications of the same type are computed within Lanczos algorithm over finite fields. Both methods have large iteration counts when index calculus algorithms are considered since n can be millions as referred in [4,5].

The underlying idea behind the proposed algorithm can be understood by rearranging the vector-vector multiplications that are employed for each row of the matrix. Let the ith row vector of $n \times n$ matrix A be $a = \{a_0, a_1, \cdots, a_{n-1}\}$ and let s_1 be the index of the smallest entry of a. If we multiply a with an n-vector $v = \{v_0, v_1, \cdots, v_{n-1}\}$ then the product $a.v^T = a_0 v_0 + a_1 v_1 + \cdots + a_{n-1} v_{n-1}$ can be written as:

$$av^T = (a_0 - a_{s_1})v_0 + a_{s_1}v_0 + (a_1 - a_{s_1})v_1 + a_{s_1}v_1 + \cdots + a_{s_1}v_j + \cdots$$
$$+(a_{n-1} - a_{s_1})v_{n-1} + a_{s_1}v_{n-1}$$
$$= a_{s_1} \sum_{j=0}^{n-1} v_j + \sum_{\substack{j=0 \\ j \neq s_1}}^{n-1} (a_j - a_{s_1})v_j$$

If the smallest element in the set $\{a_j - a_{s_1} | j = 0, 1, \cdots, n-1 \, and \, j \neq s_1\}$ is $a_{s_2} - a_{s_1}$ then the product can be rearranged as:

$$av^T = a_{s_1} \sum_{j=0}^{n-1} v_j + (a_{s_2} - a_{s_1}) \sum_{\substack{j=0 \\ j \neq s_1}}^{n-1} v_j + \sum_{\substack{j=0 \\ j \notin \{s_1, s_2\}}}^{n-1} (a_j - a_{s_2})v_j$$

In the same way, by picking the smallest element and excluding it from the last summation, the equality becomes:

$$av^T = a_{s_1} \sum_{j=0}^{n-1} v_j + (a_{s_2} - a_{s_1}) \sum_{\substack{j=0 \\ j \neq s_1}}^{n-1} v_j + (a_{s_3} - a_{s_2}) \sum_{\substack{j=0 \\ j \notin \{s_1, s_2\}}}^{n-1} v_j + \cdots$$
$$+(a_{s_{n-2}} - a_{s_{n-3}})(v_{s_{n-2}} + v_{s_{n-1}}) + (a_{s_{n-1}} - a_{s_{n-2}})v_{s_{n-1}} \qquad (1)$$

Above rearrangement can be regarded as the first step and successive steps can be applied until the subtractions $(a_{s_k} - a_{s_{k-1}})$ are minimized to zero. The algorithm for this process is separated into two stages as the subtraction on matrix entries given in Sect. 2.1 namely the preprocessing stage and the vector additions given in Sect. 2.2 namely the PMVM stage.

In the preprocessing stage of the proposed algorithm, the entries of the matrix are sorted in order to make the subtraction operations in (1) sequential. As soon as a matrix entry is subtracted from the preceding entry, the corresponding element in the vector should be excluded from the addition. Therefore the same sorting permutation is applied to the vector in PMVM stage.

2.1   The Preprocessing Stage

In this stage, the input matrix is processed row by row. Each row is sorted in ascending order and then minimized by applying sequential subtractions until the desired number of nonzero elements $\bar{z}$ is left at the row. The main objective of the preprocessing stage is to save the permuted indices of the sorted row into a table in every sorting step. Each row vector A_i of the $m \times n$ matrix A has $(c_i + 1)$ number of permutation tables P_i. How the value $\bar{z}$ is chosen is discussed in Sect. 3. Algorithm 1 shows the pseudocode for preprocessing and Table 1 gives an example of an application of the algorithm to a 3×3 matrix.

Algorithm 1. The Preprocessing Algorithm

    Input: $m \times n$ matrix A

    Output: Permutation table P, the number of permutations per row c_i, preprocessed matrix A^P

1: **for** $i \leftarrow 0, m - 1$ **do**
2:     $c_i \leftarrow 0, sort \leftarrow true, \bar{z} \leftarrow$ the number of nonzero elements left
3:     **while** $sort$ is $true$ **do**
4:         $A_i \leftarrow$ the elements of A_i sorted in ascending order
5:         $z_i \leftarrow$ index of first nonzero element
6:         $P_{i,c_i} \leftarrow$ the permutation of the indices of the nonzero elements
7:         **if** $z_i < (n - \bar{z})$ **then**
8:             **for** $j \leftarrow n - 1, z_i + 1$ **do**
9:                 $A_{i,j} \leftarrow A_{i,j} - A_{i,j-1}$
10:        **end for**
11:            $c_i \leftarrow c_i + 1$
12:        **else**
13:            $sort \leftarrow false$
14:        **end if**
15:     **end while**
16: **end for**
17: $A^P \leftarrow A$

An example of a preprocessing stage is given in Table 1 for the inputs $m = n = 3$, $\bar{z} = 1$ and $A = \begin{bmatrix} 3 & 1 & 4 \\ 0 & 2 & 1 \\ 1 & 4 & 0 \end{bmatrix}$. The first column shows the indices of the rows of the matrix A and the second column c_i is the number of permutations produced for the row until the current step. When the last sort is applied for a row then the total number of permutations i.e. sorts will be $c_i + 1$. In the columns titled as *After Sorting*, the sorted row A_i, the index of the first non-zero element z_i and the resulting permutation P_{i,c_i} are given. *After Subtraction* column presents the ith row of A after consequent subtractions over the elements of sorted A_i are applied. For example, the first row of the table, $A_0 = \begin{bmatrix} 3 & 1 & 4 \end{bmatrix}$ is sorted and the vector $\begin{bmatrix} 1 & 3 & 4 \end{bmatrix}$ is revealed. The index of first non-zero element encountered in sorted A_i is 0 thus $z_i = 0$ and the permutation produced by sorting is $\begin{bmatrix} 1 & 0 & 2 \end{bmatrix}$. Since the required number of non-zero elements for ending the preprocessing of a row is $\bar{z} = 1$ and we have no non-zero elements then the subtraction step is applied. Beginning with the last element, the previous element is subtracted. As a result A_i becomes $\begin{bmatrix} 1 & (3-1) & (4-3) \end{bmatrix} = \begin{bmatrix} 1 & 2 & 1 \end{bmatrix}$ and the preprocessing continues with the next sorting step. When c_0 becomes 3, the A_0 is reduced to the vector $\begin{bmatrix} 0 & 0 & 1 \end{bmatrix}$ and the desired number of non-zero elements is reached.

Table 1. An example for Algorithm 1

i	c_i	A_i	After sorting			After subtraction	A_i^P
			A_i	z_i	P_{i,c_i}	A_i	
0	0	$\begin{bmatrix} 3 & 1 & 4 \end{bmatrix}$	$\begin{bmatrix} 1 & 3 & 4 \end{bmatrix}$	0	$\begin{bmatrix} 1 & 0 & 2 \end{bmatrix}$	$\begin{bmatrix} 1 & 2 & 1 \end{bmatrix}$	
	1	$\begin{bmatrix} 1 & 2 & 1 \end{bmatrix}$	$\begin{bmatrix} 1 & 1 & 2 \end{bmatrix}$	0	$\begin{bmatrix} 0 & 2 & 1 \end{bmatrix}$	$\begin{bmatrix} 1 & 0 & 1 \end{bmatrix}$	
	2	$\begin{bmatrix} 1 & 0 & 1 \end{bmatrix}$	$\begin{bmatrix} 0 & 1 & 1 \end{bmatrix}$	1	$\begin{bmatrix} 0 & 2 \end{bmatrix}$	$\begin{bmatrix} 0 & 1 & 0 \end{bmatrix}$	
	3	$\begin{bmatrix} 0 & 1 & 0 \end{bmatrix}$	$\begin{bmatrix} 0 & 0 & 1 \end{bmatrix}$	2	$\begin{bmatrix} 1 \end{bmatrix}$		$\begin{bmatrix} 0 & 0 & 1 \end{bmatrix}$
1	0	$\begin{bmatrix} 0 & 2 & 1 \end{bmatrix}$	$\begin{bmatrix} 0 & 1 & 2 \end{bmatrix}$	1	$\begin{bmatrix} 2 & 1 \end{bmatrix}$	$\begin{bmatrix} 0 & 1 & 1 \end{bmatrix}$	
	1	$\begin{bmatrix} 0 & 1 & 1 \end{bmatrix}$	$\begin{bmatrix} 0 & 1 & 1 \end{bmatrix}$	1	$\begin{bmatrix} 1 & 2 \end{bmatrix}$	$\begin{bmatrix} 0 & 1 & 0 \end{bmatrix}$	
	2	$\begin{bmatrix} 0 & 1 & 0 \end{bmatrix}$	$\begin{bmatrix} 0 & 0 & 1 \end{bmatrix}$	2	$\begin{bmatrix} 1 \end{bmatrix}$		$\begin{bmatrix} 0 & 0 & 1 \end{bmatrix}$
2	0	$\begin{bmatrix} 1 & 4 & 0 \end{bmatrix}$	$\begin{bmatrix} 0 & 1 & 4 \end{bmatrix}$	1	$\begin{bmatrix} 0 & 1 \end{bmatrix}$	$\begin{bmatrix} 0 & 1 & 3 \end{bmatrix}$	
	1	$\begin{bmatrix} 0 & 1 & 3 \end{bmatrix}$	$\begin{bmatrix} 0 & 1 & 3 \end{bmatrix}$	1	$\begin{bmatrix} 1 & 2 \end{bmatrix}$	$\begin{bmatrix} 0 & 1 & 2 \end{bmatrix}$	
	2	$\begin{bmatrix} 0 & 1 & 2 \end{bmatrix}$	$\begin{bmatrix} 0 & 1 & 2 \end{bmatrix}$	1	$\begin{bmatrix} 1 & 2 \end{bmatrix}$	$\begin{bmatrix} 0 & 1 & 1 \end{bmatrix}$	
	3	$\begin{bmatrix} 0 & 1 & 1 \end{bmatrix}$	$\begin{bmatrix} 0 & 1 & 1 \end{bmatrix}$	1	$\begin{bmatrix} 1 & 2 \end{bmatrix}$	$\begin{bmatrix} 0 & 0 & 1 \end{bmatrix}$	
	4	$\begin{bmatrix} 0 & 0 & 1 \end{bmatrix}$	$\begin{bmatrix} 0 & 0 & 1 \end{bmatrix}$	2	$\begin{bmatrix} 1 \end{bmatrix}$		$\begin{bmatrix} 0 & 0 & 1 \end{bmatrix}$

2.2 The PMVM Stage

$A.v = u$ is computed by successively permuting v according to permutation tables P_{i,c_i} constructed at preprocessing stage and adding the permuted elements consecutively. Algorithm 2 shows how PMVM stage works.

An example of a PMVM stage is given in Table 2. $Av = u$ is calculated over $GF(11)$ for $v = \begin{bmatrix} 4 & 10 & 8 \end{bmatrix}^T$ using permutation tables coming from Table 1. The notation '$\varnothing$' is used for unused vector entries. The first and second column in Table 2 show the indices i and c_i of the permutation tables, the other columns show the permutation that will be applied and the vector after permutation and addition. For instance, the first permutation $P_{0,0} = \begin{bmatrix} 1 & 0 & 2 \end{bmatrix}$ is applied to vector $\begin{bmatrix} 4 & 10 & 8 \end{bmatrix}$ The permuted vector is $\begin{bmatrix} 10 & 4 & 8 \end{bmatrix}$. After adding the elements over $GF(11)$ successively, the vector becomes $\begin{bmatrix} 0 & 1 & 8 \end{bmatrix}$. The result of the product $u = \begin{bmatrix} 10 & 6 & 0 \end{bmatrix}$ is given at last column.

Algorithm 2. The PMVM Algorithm

Input: Preprocessed matrix A^P, Permutation table P, the number of permutations per row c_i, $n-$vector v

Output: $n-$vector $u = Av$

1: **for** $i \leftarrow 0, m - 1$ **do**
2:     $w \leftarrow v$
3:     $A^P \leftarrow$ Preprocessed A
4:     **for** $j \leftarrow 0, c_i$ **do**
5:        $w \leftarrow w$ is permuted according to $P_{i,j}$
6:        **for** $l \leftarrow (n - 2), (n-($the number of elements in $P_{i,j})$ **do**
7:           $w_l \leftarrow w_l + w_{l+1}$
8:        **end for**
9:     **end for**
10:    $u_i \leftarrow 0$
11:    **for** $j \leftarrow 0, \bar{z}$ **do**
12:       $u_i \leftarrow u_i + (w_{n-1-j} * A^P_{n-1-j})$
13:    **end for**
14:
15: **end for**

Table 2. An example for Algorithm 2

i	c_i	w_i	Permutation		Addition	u_i
			P_{i,c_i}	w_i	w_i	
0	0	[4 10 8]	[1 0 2]	[10 4 8]	[0 1 8]	
	1	[0 1 8]	[0 2 1]	[0 8 1]	[9 9 1]	
	2	[9 9 1]	[0 2]	[∅ 9 1]	[∅ 10 1]	
	3	[∅ 10 1]	[1]	[∅ ∅ 10]		10
1	0	[4 10 8]	[2 1]	[∅ 8 10]	[∅ 7 10]	
	1	[∅ 7 10]	[1 2]	[∅ 7 10]	[∅ 6 10]	
	2	[∅ 6 10]	[1]	[∅ ∅ 6]		6
2	0	[4 10 8]	[0 1]	[∅ 4 10]	[∅ 3 10]	
	1	[∅ 3 10]	[1 2]	[∅ 3 10]	[∅ 2 10]	
	2	[∅ 2 10]	[1 2]	[∅ 2 10]	[∅ 1 10]	
	3	[∅ 1 10]	[1 2]	[∅ 1 10]	[∅ 0 10]	
	4	[∅ 0 10]	[1]	[∅ ∅ 0]		0

3   Analysis of the Algorithm and the Performance Tests

The number of sorts for each row A_i determines the number of permutation tables P_i to be used in PMVM algorithm. When the differences between the successive entries $(a_{s_i} - a_{s_{i-1}})$ become equal to each other, the preprocessing of a row terminates after a sort. So if it is possible to choose entries which are very close to each other then the amount of the sorts and the running time of the algorithm decreases. Yet for most of the systems, it may not be possible to produce a matrix with appropriate entries. However, matrices with this property are encountered in the linear algebra phase of index calculus family of algorithms.

In general, the index calculus algorithms employ a sieving phase which reveals a matrix A such that each row in A is an exponent vector. For example, the index calculus algorithm chooses a random a and calculates $g^a \in GF(p)$. If $B = \{p_1, p_2, \cdots, p_\ell\}$ is a factor base and g^a can be written as the product of prime powers in B then exponents coming from the prime factorization constitute a row of A. Since $a < p$ then the exponents and consequently the entries of A are limited by the size of the prime p. Despite the huge sizes of the matrices for large primes, their sparsity makes the number of nonzero elements per row and the maximum value of that row close to each other. According to the experimental results if n is much larger than p then the preprocessing terminates earlier.

The properties of the matrices that we are dealing with in index calculus algorithms give us an opinion about how many additions we will be calculating in PMVM stage and these properties are revealed by the preprocessing stage. At worst case, $(c_i + 1)n$ additions are computed in PMVM stage. However according to the sparsity of the matrices only $\bar{z}$ element of the $n-$vector will be affected in the first step and the number of elements that are affected decreases rapidly. Therefore the performance of PMVM algorithm becomes faster than classical matrix-vector multiplication (CMVM) algorithm in which each row vector of the $m \times n$ matrix is multiplied with the n-vector. Thus CMVM needs n multiplications and $n - 1$ additions per row.

If the running time of the proposed algorithm is analyzed by means of single matrix-vector multiplication then preprocessing step dominates the overall time. However, as iteration count grows the algorithm becomes faster than the classical method since the preprocessing stage is done once for a given problem and the iteration count does not affect the time consumed by preprocessing, therefore, can be easily amortized. The PMVM stage is applied for all iterations involved and in order to gain efficiency the running time of this stage should be less than the ordinary matrix-vector multiplication for at least $t < n$ counts. This goal is achieved by using successive additions instead of multiplications. Another advantage of the proposed method is in the computation of modular reductions when operating over finite fields. Since PMVM stage applies additions instead of multiplications, the values grow slower thus less modular reductions are needed.

Table 3 shows the performance comparison between the classical matrix-vector multiplication algorithm (CMVM) and the proposed algorithm (PMVM with preprocessing) for one and 100 iterations, i.e., for computing Av and $A^t v$ for $t = 1, \cdots, 100$. We generated $n \times n$-matrices and n-vectors are randomly using

SageMath for given parameters. The 4096×4096 and 8192×8192 matrices with 0.01, 0.05, 0.1 sparsity (represented as $\bar{z}/n$ in the second column of the Table 3) and 256, 512, 1024 maximum entry values (represented as b in the third column of the Table) are tested. Also the 256 bit, 512 bit and 1024 bit prime numbers are obtained from SageMath and the vectors of sizes 4096 and 8192 are generated over prime fields $GF(p_1)$, $GF(p_2)$ and $GF(p_3)$.

The results are obtained on a single core of a 3.7 GHz Xeon E3-1281 processor. Each algorithm is programmed using the C++ programming language and compiled with the Visual Studio 2012 Compiler. Mpir library is used for multiple-precision calculations and compressed row storage (CRS) format is used to store sparse matrices. The same kind of optimizations is implemented on both methods in order to gain fair running times.

Table 3. Time required (in Seconds) by PMVM and CMVM for various n and b, and amortization of preprocessing cost if multiple iterations are performed. Note that Total indicates the total required time by PMVM including the preprocessing time.

n	$\bar{z}/n$	b	Time for preprocessing (s)	Time for 1 iteration (s)			Time for 100 iterations (s)		
				PMVM	Total	CMVM	PMVM	Total	CMVM
4096	0.01	256	0.174	0.02	0.194	0.05	1.902	2.076	4.518
		512	0.196	0.034	0.23	0.066	3.114	3.31	6.360
		1024	0.224	0.062	0.286	0.099	6.007	6.231	9.698
	0.05	256	1.370	0.062	1.432	0.233	6.070	7.44	22.905
		512	1.460	0.101	1.561	0.318	9.798	11.258	30.680
		1024	1.533	0.175	1.708	0.474	17.577	19.11	47.645
	0.1	256	3.801	0.108	3.909	0.380	10.288	14.089	36.214
		512	4.461	0.173	4.634	0.518	17.250	21.711	49.978
		1024	4.772	0.316	5.088	0.841	31.388	36.16	84.855
8192	0.01	256	0.759	0.066	0.825	0.204	6.233	6.992	19.891
		512	0.802	0.106	0.908	0.267	10.014	10.816	26.829
		1024	0.868	0.184	1.052	0.401	18.012	18.88	39.318
	0.05	256	7.921	0.215	8.136	0.926	21.889	29.81	91.504
		512	9.258	0.378	9.636	1.250	36.594	45.852	132.918
		1024	9.956	0.661	10.617	1.897	64.618	74.574	190.222
	0.1	256	24.970	0.371	25.341	1.458	36.881	61.851	145.877
		512	28.702	0.621	29.323	2.043	62.399	91.101	200.995
		1024	34.798	1.169	35.967	3.354	115.413	150.211	336.239

As can be seen from Table 3, the PMVM algorithm without preprocessing is faster than CMVM for both one and 100 iterations. However, PMVM algorithm is not enough to implement a whole matrix-vector multiplication. The Preprocessing should be done in order to produce permutation tables that are going to be used in PMVM stage. When a single iteration is considered, the total time representing the sum of running times of PMVM and preprocessing stages is bigger than the running time of CMVM. When the matrix grows larger the gap between the total time and CMVM for single iteration grows either. But for multiple iterations that gap decreases and finally PMVM with preprocessing becomes faster than CMVM. We obtain improvements between 35% and 67% for 100 iterations. As iteration count increases, the time spent for preprocessing becomes negligible.

4   Conclusion

In this paper, we proposed a new algorithm for computing iterative sparse matrix-vector multiplications over finite fields. The new algorithm consists of a preprocessing stage which is run once for a given problem and a second stage for calculating iterative multiplications. The algorithm has advantages over the classical method by means of computational performance. The use of additions instead of multiplications and computing less modular reductions make the algorithm more efficient. We obtained improvements between 35% and 67% in comparative performance results. In the future, the preprocessing stage of the algorithm can be parallelized and this can lead to better performance results for single matrix-vector multiplication.

References

1. Adleman, L.M., DeMarrais, J.: A subexponential algorithm for discrete logarithms over all finite fields. In: Stinson, D.R. (ed.) CRYPTO 1993. LNCS, vol. 773, pp. 147–158. Springer, Heidelberg (1994). https://doi.org/10.1007/3-540-48329-2_13
2. Coppersmith, D.: Solving homogeneous linear equations over GF(2) via block Wiedemann algorithm. Math. Comput. **62**(205), 333–350 (1994). https://doi.org/10.1090/S0025-5718-1994-1192970-7
3. Joux, A.: Algorithmic Cryptanalysis, 1st edn. Chapman & Hall/CRC, Boca Raton (2009). https://doi.org/10.1007/3-540-48329-2_13
4. Kleinjung, T., et al.: Factorization of a 768-bit RSA modulus. In: Rabin, T. (ed.) CRYPTO 2010. LNCS, vol. 6223, pp. 333–350. Springer, Heidelberg (2010). https://doi.org/10.1007/978-3-642-14623-7_18
5. Kleinjung, T., Diem, C., Lenstra, A.K., Priplata, C., Stahlke, C.: Computation of a 768-bit prime field discrete logarithm. In: Coron, J.-S., Nielsen, J.B. (eds.) EUROCRYPT 2017. LNCS, vol. 10210, pp. 185–201. Springer, Cham (2017). https://doi.org/10.1007/978-3-319-56620-7_7
6. Montgomery, P.L.: A block lanczos algorithm for finding dependencies over GF(2). In: Guillou, L.C., Quisquater, J.-J. (eds.) EUROCRYPT 1995. LNCS, vol. 921, pp. 106–120. Springer, Heidelberg (1995). https://doi.org/10.1007/3-540-49264-X_9
7. Odlyzko, A.M.: Discrete logarithms in finite fields and their cryptographic significance. In: Beth, T., Cot, N., Ingemarsson, I. (eds.) EUROCRYPT 1984. LNCS, vol. 209, pp. 224–314. Springer, Heidelberg (1985). https://doi.org/10.1007/3-540-39757-4_20

8. Pomerance, C.: The quadratic sieve factoring algorithm. In: Beth, T., Cot, N., Ingemarsson, I. (eds.) EUROCRYPT 1984. LNCS, vol. 209, pp. 169–182. Springer, Heidelberg (1985). https://doi.org/10.1007/3-540-39757-4_17

9. Pomerance, C.: A tale of two sieves. Not. Am. Math. Soc. **43**, 1473–1485 (1996)

10. Wiedemann, D.H.: Solving sparse linear equations over finite fields. IEEE Trans. Inf. Theor. **32**(1), 54–62 (1986). https://doi.org/10.1109/TIT.1986.1057137

On the Security of Jhanwar-Barua Identity-Based Encryption Scheme

Adrian G. Schipor$^{(\boxtimes)}$

Department of Computer Science, "Al. I. Cuza" University of Iași,
700506 Iași, Romania
aschipor@info.uaic.ro

Abstract. In [3], Jhanwar and Barua presented an improvement of the Boneh-Gentry-Hamburg (BGH) scheme. In addition to reducing the time complexity of the algorithm to find a solution of the equation $ax^2 + Sy^2 \equiv 1 \bmod n$, their scheme reduces the number of equations to be solved by combining existing solutions. In [2], Susilo et al. extended the Jhanwar-Barua scheme, reducing more the number of equations to be solved. This paper presents a security flaw that appears in both schemes and shows that they are not IND-ID-CPA secure.

1 Intoduction

Identity Based Encryption (IBE) is a type of public key encryption in which the public key can be any arbitrary string. It has been proposed in 1984 by Adi Shamir [6]. Although the idea was presented a long time ago, the first IBE scheme was proposed relatively recently, in 2001, when Boneh and Franklin developed an IBE scheme based on elliptic curves [4]. Soon after, Clifford Cocks developed another IBE scheme [7], based on Quadratic Residuosity Problem (QRA). However, the Cocks scheme is impractical to use because it encrypts one bit by $2 \log n$ bits.

In [1], Boneh, Gentry and Hamburg proposed an IBE scheme (BGH) that encrypts a bit by multiplying it by a random Jacobi symbol, so the ciphertext expansion is much smaller than the ciphertext expansion of the Cocks scheme. However, the time complexity is not as good. In order to encrypt or decrypt a bit, a solution of the equation $ax^2 + Sy^2 \equiv 1 \bmod n$ is needed, where a represents the hashed identity and S is a quadratic residue *modulo n*. Two polynomials, f and g, that satisfy the property that $g(s) = 2y + 2$ and $f(r) = rx + 1$ have the same Jacobi symbol, for every square root s of S and every square root r of a, are used: the Jacobi symbol of $g(s)$ is used for encryption and the Jacobi symbol of $f(r)$ is used for decryption. The main bottleneck of the BGH scheme is the complexity of the algorithm that finds a solution of the equation $ax^2 + Sy^2 \equiv 1 \bmod n$.

Jhanwar and Barua proposed in [3] an efficient algorithm for finding such a solution, together with a modified version of the BGH scheme that uses that algorithm. The resulting scheme is more time efficient than the BGH scheme, but the ciphertext expansion is bigger. This is because the algorithm for finding

© Springer Nature Switzerland AG 2019
J.-L. Lanet and C. Toma (Eds.): SecITC 2018, LNCS 11359, pp. 368–375, 2019.
https://doi.org/10.1007/978-3-030-12942-2_28

a solution is probabilistic, so it is not guaranteed that it will find the same solution on both encryption and decryption of a bit. Also, their scheme reduces the number of equations to be solved at encryption and doesn't need to solve any equation at decryption. In [2], Susilo et al. presents an improvement of the Jhanwar-Barua scheme, reducing more the number of equation needed to be solved at encryption. This paper presents a security flaw which affects both schemes.

2 Preliminaries

2.1 IBE Scheme

An IBE scheme $\mathcal{E}$ consists of four randomized algorithms [3]:

- **Setup**(λ): takes as input a security parameter λ and returns the system's public parameters PP and the master secret key msk. The system's public parameters PP are publicly known, and the master secret key msk is known only to a third party, "Private Key Generator" (PKG).
- **Keygen**(PP, msk, id): takes as input the system's public parameters PP, the master secret key msk and an arbitrary identity $id \in \{0,1\}^*$ and returns the private key d associated with the identity id.
- **Encrypt**(PP, id, m): takes as input the system's public parameters PP, an identity id and a message $m \in \{0,1\}^*$ and returns the ciphertext c, that represents the encryption of the message m.
- **Decrypt**(PP, c, d): takes as input the system's public parameters PP, a ciphertext $c \in \{0,1\}^*$ and a private key d and returns the decrypted message m, or $\perp$ if the ciphertext is not valid.

2.2 The IND-ID-CPA Security Model

Boneh and Franklin extended the security notion of indistinguishability against chosen plaintext attack (IND-CPA) to identity-based encryption schemes [4]. The resulting security model (IND-ID-CPA) is defined as the following game between a challenger $\mathcal{C}$ and a PPT adversary $\mathcal{A}$.

IND-ID-CPA game:

1. The challenger $\mathcal{C}$ runs the **Setup** algorithm with a security parameter λ. It publishes the system's public parameters PP to the adversary $\mathcal{A}$ and keeps the master secret key msk for itself.
2. The adversary performs (adaptively) private key extraction queries for the identities $id_1, ..., id_k$. The challenger runs the **Extraction** algorithm and sends to the adversary the private keys $d_{id_1}, ..., d_{id_k}$ corresponding to the received identities.

3. The adversary makes one challenge query. It selects two equal length messages m_0, m_1 and a public key id_{Ch} (that didn't appeared in the previous phase) and sends them to the challenger.
4. The challenger picks a random bit $b \in \{0, 1\}$ and sends $c = m_b$ as a challenge to the adversary.
5. The adversary performs more private key extraction queries for the identities $id_{k+1}, ..., id_n$ and receives from the challenger the corresponding private keys $d_{id_{k+1}}, ..., d_{id_n}$. The only constraint is that id_i $(k + 1 \le i \le n)$ is not equal to id_{Ch}.
6. Finally, the adversary outputs a guess $b' \in \{0, 1\}$ for the value of b.

The advantage of the adversary $\mathcal{A}$ against an IBE scheme is defined as the following function of the security parameter λ:

$$Adv_{IBE,\mathcal{A}}^{IND-ID-CPA}(\lambda) = Pr[b' = b] - \frac{1}{2}$$

Definition 1. *An IBE scheme is IND-ID-CPA secure if $Adv_{IBE,\mathcal{A}}^{IND-ID-CPA}(\lambda)$ is a negligible function for all PPT adversaries $\mathcal{A}$.*

2.3 Jacobi Symbols and the QR Assumption

Let p be an odd prime. For any integer a, the Legendre symbol $\left(\dfrac{a}{p}\right)$ is defined as follows:

$$\left(\frac{a}{p}\right) = \begin{cases} 0, & \text{if } a \equiv 0 \bmod p \\ 1, & \text{if } a \text{ is a quadratic residue mod } p \\ -1, & \text{if } a \text{ is a quadratic non-residue mod } p. \end{cases}$$

Let $N = p_1 p_2 ... p_k$ be the product of k odd primes (not necessarily distinct). For any integer a, the Jacobi symbol $\left(\dfrac{a}{N}\right)$ is defined as the product of the Legendre symbols corresponding to the prime factors of N:

$$\left(\frac{a}{N}\right) = \left(\frac{a}{p_1}\right)\left(\frac{a}{p_2}\right)...\left(\frac{a}{p_k}\right).$$

For a positive integer N, let $J(N)$ be the following set:

$$J(N) = \{a \in \mathbb{Z}_N \mid \left(\frac{a}{N}\right) = 1\}.$$

The set of residues *modulo* N is defined as:

$$QR(N) = \{a \in \mathbb{Z}_N \mid gcd(a, N) = 1 \wedge x^2 \equiv a \bmod N \text{ has a solution}\}.$$

Definition 2. *Let $RSAgen(\lambda)$ be a PPT algorithm that generates two equal size primes p and q. The Quadratic Residuosity (QR) Assumption holds for $RSAgen(\lambda)$ if given a tuple (N, V), where $N = pq$ and $V \in J(N)$, there is no polynomial time algorithm which can determine if $V \in QR(N)$ or $V \in J(N) \setminus QR(N)$ with non-negligible probability.*

2.4   The Jhanwar-Barua Scheme

The scheme uses the following probabilistic algorithm for finding a solution of the equation $ax^2 + Sy^2 \equiv 1 \bmod N$, where S is a quadratic residue *modulo* N [3]:

1. Randomly choose $t \in \mathbb{Z}_N^*$ such that $a + St^2 \in \mathbb{Z}_N^*$.
2. Output $x_0 = \frac{-2st}{a+St^2}$, $y_0 = \frac{a-St^2}{s(a+St^2)}$.

In addition to this algorithm, the following product formula is used [3]:

Lemma 1. *Let (x_i, y_i) be a solution to $ax^2 + S_i y^2 \equiv 1 \bmod N$ for $i = 1, 2$. Then (x_3, y_3) is a solution to*

$$ax^2 + S_1 S_2 y^2 \equiv 1 \bmod N$$

where $x_3 = \frac{x_1+x_2}{a x_1 x_2 + 1}$ and $y_3 = \frac{y_1 y_2}{a x_1 x_2 + 1}$.

Also, the scheme uses two functions $f(r) = rx + 1$ and $g(s) = 2sy + 2$ that satisfies the property that the Jacobi symbol of $f(r)$ equals the Jacobi symbol of $g(s)$ for every square root s of S and every square root r of a.

The JB scheme is detailed below:

- **Setup(λ):** Generate two primes, p and q, and let $N = pq$. Choose a random element $u \in J(N) \setminus QR(N)$ and a hash function $H : \mathcal{ID} \mapsto J(N)$. The system's public parameters PP are (N, u, H). The master secret key msk is the factorization of N and a secret key K for a pseudorandom function $F_K : \mathcal{ID} \mapsto \{0, 1, 2, 3\}$.
- **Keygen(PP, msk, id):** Set $R = H(id) \in J(N)$ and $w = F_K(id) \in \{0, 1, 2, 3\}$. Choose $a \in \{0, 1\}$ such that $u^a R \in QR(N)$. Let $\{z_0, z_1, z_2, z_3\}$ be the four square roots of $u^a R \in \mathbb{Z}_N$. Outputs the private key $r = z_w$.
- **Encrypt(PP, id, m):** The following algorithm is used to encrypt a message $m \in \{-1, 1\}^l$:

$$k \leftarrow \sqrt{l}, \; R \leftarrow H(id) \in J(N)$$

    for $i \in [1, l]$ **do**
        if $i \leq k$ **then**

$$s_i \in \mathbb{Z}_N^*, \; S = s_i^2 \bmod N$$
$$(x_i, y_i) \leftarrow Rx_i^2 + S_i y_i^2 \equiv 1 \bmod N$$
$$(\bar{x}_i, \bar{y}_i) \leftarrow uR\bar{x}_i^2 + S_i \bar{y}_i^2 \equiv 1 \bmod N$$
$$c_i \leftarrow m_i \cdot \left(\frac{2 y_i s_i + 2}{N} \right)$$
$$\bar{c}_i \leftarrow m_i \cdot \left(\frac{2 \bar{y}_i s_i + 2}{N} \right)$$

        else

$$(j_1, j_2) \leftarrow i = k \cdot j_1 + j_2$$
$$y_{j_1, j_2} \leftarrow \frac{y_{j_1} y_{j_2}}{R x_{j_1} x_{j_2} + 1}, \; \bar{y}_{j_1, j_2} \leftarrow \frac{\bar{y}_{j_1} \bar{y}_{j_2}}{u R \bar{x}_{j_1} \bar{x}_{j_2} + 1}$$
$$c_i \leftarrow m_i \cdot \left(\frac{2 y_{j_1, j_2} s_{j_1} s_{j_2} + 2}{N} \right)$$
$$\bar{c}_i \leftarrow m_i \cdot \left(\frac{2 \bar{y}_{j_1, j_2} s_{j_1} s_{j_2} + 2}{N} \right)$$

    end if
$$c \leftarrow [c_1, c_2, ..., c_l], \quad \bar{c} \leftarrow [\bar{c}_1, \bar{c}_2, ..., \bar{c}_l]$$
$$x \leftarrow [x_1, x_2, ..., x_k], \quad \bar{x} \leftarrow [\bar{x}_1, \bar{x}_2, ..., \bar{x}_k]$$
    end for

The resulted ciphertext is $C \leftarrow (c, \bar{c}, x, \bar{x})$.

- **Decrypt**(PP, C, r): To decrypt the ciphertext C using the private key r, the following algorithm is used:

    for $i \in [1, l]$ do
      if $r^2 = R$ then
        if $i > k$ then
          $(j_1, j_2) \leftarrow i = k \cdot j_1 + j_2$
          $x_i \leftarrow \frac{x_{j_1} + x_{j_2}}{R x_{j_1} x_{j_2} + 1}$
        end if
        $m_i \leftarrow c_i \cdot \left(\frac{x_i r + 1}{N} \right)$
      end if
      if $r^2 = uR$ then
        if $i > k$ then
          $(j_1, j_2) \leftarrow i = k \cdot j_1 + j_2$
          $\bar{x}_i \leftarrow \frac{\bar{x}_{j_1} + \bar{x}_{j_2}}{u R \bar{x}_{j_1} \bar{x}_{j_2} + 1}$
        end if
        $m_i \leftarrow \bar{c}_i \cdot \left(\frac{\bar{x}_i r + 1}{N} \right)$
      end if
    end for

Susilo et al. extended the Jhanwar-Barua scheme, reducing the number of equations needed to be solved. They claim that having the Jacobi symbols $\left(\frac{2 y_{j_1} s_{j_1} + 2}{N} \right)$ and $\left(\frac{2 y_{j_2} s_{j_2} + 2}{N} \right)$ is hard to find the value of $\left(\frac{2 y_{j_1, j_2} s_{j_1} s_{j_2} + 2}{N} \right)$ [2], saying that Damgård proved that [5]. However, because some values are publicly known, this is not a hard problem, as it will be seen in the next section.

3   The Security Flaw

Because the algorithm used for solving the equations is probabilistic, $(x_i, ..., x_k)$ and $(\bar{x}_i, ..., \bar{x}_k)$ are added to the ciphertext so they are publicly known. Thus, if R is a quadratic residue *modulo* N, the following property holds:

$$\left(\frac{r x_{j_1, j_2} + 1}{N} \right) = \left(\frac{r x_{j_1} + 1}{N} \right) \left(\frac{r x_{j_2} + 1}{N} \right) (R x_{j_1} x_{j_2} + 1)^{-1} \tag{1}$$

Because x_{j_1, j_2} is composed we have:

$$r x_{j_1, j_2} + 1 = r(x_{j_1} + x_{j_2})(R x_{j_1} x_{j_2} + 1)^{-1} + 1.$$

But

$$(r x_{j_1} + 1)(r x_{j_2} + 1) = r^2 x_{j_1} x_{j_2} + r x_{j_1} + r x_{j_2} + 1$$
$$= R x_{j_1} x_{j_2} + 1 + r(x_{j_1} + x_{j_2})$$

and if we multiply this with $(Rx_{j_1}x_{j_2} + 1)^{-1}$ we obtain

$$(rx_{j_1} + 1)(rx_{j_2} + 1)(Rx_{j_1}x_{j_2} + 1)^{-1} = r(x_{j_1} + x_{j_2})(Rx_{j_1}x_{j_2} + 1)^{-1} + 1,$$

so the Jacobi symbol $\left(\frac{(rx_{j_1}+1)(rx_{j_2}+1)(Rx_{j_1}x_{j_2}+1)^{-1}}{N} \right) = \left(\frac{rx_{j_1,j_2}+1}{N} \right)$. x_{j_1} and x_{j_2} are publicly known, so anyone can compute this Jacobi symbol. This proves the property (1).

We know that $\left(\frac{g(s)}{N} \right) = \left(\frac{f(r)}{N} \right)$, so

$$\left(\frac{2y_{j_1}s_{j_1} + 2}{N} \right) = \left(\frac{rx_{j_1} + 1}{N} \right),$$

$$\left(\frac{2y_{j_2}s_{j_2} + 2}{N} \right) = \left(\frac{rx_{j_2} + 1}{N} \right),$$

$$\left(\frac{2y_{j_1,j_2}s_{j_1}s_{j_2} + 2}{N} \right) = \left(\frac{rx_{j_1,j_2} + 1}{N} \right),$$

thus, when R is a quadratic residue, we have:

$$\left(\frac{2y_{j_1,j_2}s_{j_1}s_{j_2} + 2}{N} \right) = \left(\frac{2y_{j_1}s_{j_1} + 2}{N} \right) \left(\frac{2y_{j_2}s_{j_2} + 2}{N} \right)(Rx_{j_1}x_{j_2} + 1)^{-1} \quad (2)$$

But what happens when R is not a quadratic residue? The property (2) holds even if R is not a quadratic residue *modulo N*:

$$2y_{j_1,j_2}s_{j_1}s_{j_2} + 2 = 2y_{j_1}s_{j_1}y_{j_2}s_{j_2}(Rx_{j_1}x_{j_2} + 1)^{-1} + 2$$

$$= 2\frac{R - S_{j_1}t_{j_1}^2}{s_{j_1}(R + S_{j_1}t_{j_1}^2)}s_{j_1}\frac{R - S_{j_2}t_{j_2}^2}{s_{j_2}(R + S_{j_2}t_{j_2}^2)}s_{j_2}(Rx_{j_1}x_{j_2} + 1)^{-1} + 2$$

$$= \frac{2(R - S_{j_1}t_{j_1}^2)(R - S_{j_2}t_{j_2}^2)}{(R + S_{j_1}t_{j_1}^2)(R + S_{j_2}t_{j_2}^2)(Rx_{j_1}x_{j_2} + 1)} + 2$$

Let $d = (R + S_{j_1}t_{j_1}^2)(R + S_{j_2}t_{j_2}^2)(Rx_{j_1}x_{j_2} + 1)$. Then, $2(R - S_{j_1}t_{j_1}^2)(R - S_{j_2}t_{j_2}^2) * d^{-1} + 2 =$

$$= 2(R - S_{j_1}t_{j_1}^2)(R - S_{j_2}t_{j_2}^2)d^{-1} +$$

$$+ 2(R + S_{j_1}t_{j_1}^2)(R + S_{j_2}t_{j_2}^2)(R\frac{-2s_{j_1}t_{j_1}}{R + S_{j_1}t_{j_1}^2}\frac{-2s_{j_2}t_{j_2}}{R + S_{j_2}t_{j_2}^2} + 1)d^{-1}$$

$$= 2(R - S_{j_1}t_{j_1}^2)(R - S_{j_2}t_{j_2}^2)d^{-1} +$$

$$+ 2(R + S_{j_1}t_{j_1}^2)(R + S_{j_2}t_{j_2}^2)\frac{4Rs_{j_1}t_{j_1}s_{j_2}t_{j_2} + (R + S_{j_1}t_{j_1}^2)(R + S_{j_2}t_{j_2}^2)}{(R + S_{j_1}t_{j_1}^2)(R + S_{j_2}t_{j_2}^2)}d^{-1}$$

$$= 2(R - S_{j_1}t_{j_1}^2)(R - S_{j_2}t_{j_2}^2)d^{-1} +$$

$$+ (8Rs_{j_1}t_{j_1}s_{j_2}t_{j_2} + 2(R + S_{j_1}t_{j_1}^2)(R + S_{j_2}t_{j_2}^2))d^{-1}$$

$$= (2R^2 - 2R(S_{j_1}t_{j_1}^2 + S_{j_2}t_{j_2}^2) + 2S_{j_1}S_{j_2}t_{j_1}^2t_{j_2}^2)d^{-1} +$$

$$+ (8Rs_{j_1}t_{j_1}s_{j_2}t_{j_2} + 2R^2 + 2R(S_{j_1}t_{j_1}^2 + S_{j_2}t_{j_2}^2) + 2S_{j_1}S_{j_2}t_{j_1}^2t_{j_2}^2)d^{-1}$$
$$= (8Rs_{j_1}t_{j_1}s_{j_2}t_{j_2} + 4R^2 + 4S_{j_1}S_{j_2}t_{j_1}^2t_{j_2}^2)d^{-1}$$
$$= (4(R^2 + 2Rs_{j_1}s_{j_2}t_{j_1}t_{j_2} + S_{j_1}S_{j_2}t_{j_1}^2t_{j_2}^2))d^{-1}$$
$$= 4(R + s_{j_1}s_{j_2}t_{j_1}t_{j_2})^2d^{-1},$$

and

$$(2y_{j_1}s_{j_1} + 2)(2y_{j_2}s_{j_2} + 2) = \left(\frac{2(R - S_{j_1}t_{j_1}^2)}{s_{j_1}(R + S_{j_1}t_{j_1}^2)}s_{j_1} + 2 \right) \left(\frac{2(R - S_{j_2}t_{j_2}^2)}{s_{j_2}(R + S_{j_2}t_{j_2}^2)}s_{j_2} + 2 \right)$$

$$= \frac{16R^2}{(R + S_{j_1}t_{j_1}^2)(R + S_{j_2}t_{j_2}^2)},$$

so

$$\left(\frac{(2y_{j_1}s_{j_1} + 2)(2y_{j_2}s_{j_2} + 2)(Rx_{j_1}x_{j_2} + 1)^{-1}}{N} \right) = \left(\frac{2y_{j_1,j_2}s_{j_1}s_{j_2} + 2}{N} \right)$$

even if R is not a residue *modulo* N. This proves that Jhanwar-Barua scheme is not IND-ID-CPA secure. An adversary chooses two messages m_1, m_2 with $m_{1_{j_1}} = m_{2_{j_1}}$, $m_{1_{j_2}} = m_{2_{j_2}}$ and $m_{1_{j_1,j_2}} \neq m_{2_{j_1,j_2}}$, and sends them to the challenger. The challenger randomly picks one, encrypts it and sends it back to the adversary. The adversary can say with non-negligible probability which message has been encrypted: he obtains the Jacobi symbols $\left(\frac{g(s_{j_1})}{N} \right)$, $\left(\frac{g(s_{j_2})}{N} \right)$ used for encrypting the bits j_1, j_2 and computes $\left(\frac{g(s_{j_1}s_{j_2})}{N} \right) = \left(\frac{g(s_{j_1})}{N} \right) \left(\frac{g(s_{j_2})}{N} \right) (Rx_{j_1}x_{j_2} + 1)^{-1}$, so he can decrypt the ith bit, $i = kj_1 + j_2$. Because $m_{1_i} \neq m_{2_i}$ the adversary can say which message has been encrypted. It doesn't matter which component of the ciphertext he chooses for calculating this because the property (2) holds in both cases. This proves that the Jhanwar-Barua scheme is not IND-ID-CPA secure. Also, the scheme proposed by Susilo et al. has the same security flaw.

4   Conclusion

This paper presents a security flaw that affects the Jhanwar-Barua scheme and it's extension proposed in [2]. Although Susilo et al. pointed that Jhanwar-Barua scheme is not IND-ID-CPA secure, their demonstration is based on the fact that some bits are encrypted using the same solution. However, even if their scheme solves that problem, the security flaw presented in this paper remains.

Acknowledgment. I wish to thank to my supervisor, Prof. Dr. Ferucio Laurenţiu Ţiplea, for helping me by deducing the property (2) from the Sect. 3 (the case when R is not a quadratic residue), after the practical tests told us that the property should hold.

References

1. Boneh, D., Gentry, C., Hamburg, M.: Space-efficient identity based encryption without pairings. In: Proceedings of the 48th Annual IEEE Symposium on Foundations of Computer Science, FOCS 2007, pp. 647–657. IEEE Computer Society, Washington (2007)
2. Elashry, I., Mu, Y., Susilo, W.: Jhanwar-Barua's identity-based encryption revisited. In: Au, M.H., Carminati, B., Kuo, C.-C.J. (eds.) NSS 2014. LNCS, vol. 8792, pp. 271–284. Springer, Cham (2014). https://doi.org/10.1007/978-3-319-11698-3_21
3. Jhanwar, M.P., Barua, R.: A variant of Boneh-Gentry-Hamburg's pairing-free identity based encryption scheme. In: Yung, M., Liu, P., Lin, D. (eds.) Inscrypt 2008. LNCS, vol. 5487, pp. 314–331. Springer, Heidelberg (2009). https://doi.org/10.1007/978-3-642-01440-6_25
4. Boneh, D., Franklin, M.: Identity-based encryption from the Weil pairing. In: Kilian, J. (ed.) CRYPTO 2001. LNCS, vol. 2139, pp. 213–229. Springer, Heidelberg (2001). https://doi.org/10.1007/3-540-44647-8_13
5. Damgård, I.B.: On the randomness of legendre and jacobi sequences. In: Goldwasser, S. (ed.) CRYPTO 1988. LNCS, vol. 403, pp. 163–172. Springer, New York (1990). https://doi.org/10.1007/0-387-34799-2_13
6. Shamir, A.: Identity-based cryptosystems and signature schemes. In: Blakley, G.R., Chaum, D. (eds.) CRYPTO 1984. LNCS, vol. 196, pp. 47–53. Springer, Heidelberg (1985). https://doi.org/10.1007/3-540-39568-7_5
7. Cocks, C.: An identity based encryption scheme based on quadratic residues. In: Honary, B. (ed.) Cryptography and Coding 2001. LNCS, vol. 2260, pp. 360–363. Springer, Heidelberg (2001). https://doi.org/10.1007/3-540-45325-3_32

Vulnerabilities of the McEliece Variants Based on Polar Codes

Vlad Drăgoi[1,2]([⊠]) [iD], Valeriu Beiu[1] [iD], and Dominic Bucerzan[1] [iD]

[1] "Aurel Vlaicu" University of Arad, Arad, Romania
{vlad.dragoi,valeriu.beiu,dominic.bucerzan}@uav.ro
[2] Normandie University, LITIS, 76821 Mont-Saint-Aignan, France
vlad-florin.dragoi@univ-rouen.fr

Abstract. Several variants of the McEliece public key encryption scheme present interesting properties for post-quantum cryptography. In this article we pursue a study of one potential variation, namely the McEliece scheme based on polar codes, and, more generally, based on any weakly decreasing monomial code. Recently, both polar as well as Reed-Muller codes were redefined using a polynomial formalism using different partial orders on the set of monomials over the ring of polynomials of m variables with coefficients in $\mathbb{F}_2$. We use this approach to study the star product of two weakly decreasing monomial codes and determine its dimension. With these results at hand, we will identify particular types of weakly decreasing monomial codes for which the star product allows for an efficient distinguisher. These results support our quest for efficient key recovery attacks against these variants of the McEliece scheme.

Keywords: Post-quantum cryptography ·
McEliece public key encryption scheme · Polar code ·
Square code attack · Decreasing monomial code

1 Introduction

A major threat to existing public key cryptography is represented by the steady advances in quantum computing (QC), which are laying the foundations of quantum information processing (QIP). In the last decade big strides were made by QC, a research topic supported financially by a plethora of national and international initiatives, both public and private. Rigetti has just announced in September 2018 their new Quantum Cloud Services (QCS) platform, as well as a US$ 1M prize for the first demonstration of Quantum Advantage (on a real world application). In August 2018 the US National Science Foundation released a new program solicitation for foundries working on novel quantum materials and devices. The National Quantum Initiative Act is also worth mentioning. In particular, the latest bills S.3143 (Senate) and H.R.6227 (House) are mentioning NIST (US$ 400M), NSF (US$ 250M), together with NASA and DOE. In parallel, Google AI Quantum Team has released an open source library for testing quantum circuits and announced OpenFermion-Cirq for quantum chemistry simulations.

© Springer Nature Switzerland AG 2019
J.-L. Lanet and C. Toma (Eds.): SecITC 2018, LNCS 11359, pp. 376–390, 2019.
https://doi.org/10.1007/978-3-030-12942-2_29

The QC idea was put forward by Richard Feynman, in 1982 [23]. Afterwards it was boosted by a seminal article of Peter Shor [42], which showed how prime factors of large numbers could be computed in polynomial time on a quantum computer. The potential of breaking almost all the public key cryptographic infrastructure has very strongly motivated the search for alternate solutions (to those based on the difficulty of number theoretical problems). This is why and how post-quantum cryptography has emerged. Currently, the main competing candidates are: lattice-based, code-based, hash-based and multivariate cryptography. The need for new public key cryptography (PKC) standards is obviously supported by the NIST [12] through their post-quantum cryptography (PQC) standardization process. The first PQC Standardization Conference took place in April 2018, and, out of 64 submissions, the majority were lattice- and code-based schemes.

Code-based encryption schemes [29] are as old as RSA [37]. The first one was introduced by Robert McEliece in [29]. The scheme relies on the decoding capability of binary Goppa codes, while having stronger security arguments (we mention here the syndrome decoding problem, which is NP-hard [7] for random linear codes) than the RSA. The main disadvantage of McEliece's solution was its larger key size, which made it unpractical. Plenty of efforts aimed to reduce the key size, e.g., by choosing other code families which either have a better decoding capacity, or exhibit compact descriptions (e.g., quasi-cyclic or quasi-dyadic). Among these we mention the Niederreiter scheme based on GRS codes [32], Sidelniko's scheme based on Reed-Muller codes [42], the McEliece variant using algebraic geometry codes [25], QC-LDPC codes [2,3], Wild Goppa codes [8], Srivastava codes [35], QC-MDPC codes [31], polar codes [24,41]. Many of these variants were successfully cryptanalyzed using more or less efficient algorithms that exploit the structure of the underlying codes. Typically there are two main directions for cryptanalysis: either build structural attacks, or use algebraic attacks. Their aim is to solve a well-known problem, namely the code equivalence problem.

The first type of attacks tries to solve this problem by exploiting the structure of the minimum weight codewords [4,30], or by using square code techniques [13,14,33,43]. In general square code techniques are more efficient than attacks using the structure of the minimum weight codewords. The main reason is that in order to compute the set of all minimum weight codewords one would typically use a variant of the Information Set Decoding algorithm [6,10,18,27,28,36]. The complexity of this algorithm is roughly exponential in the weight of the codewords to be found, when the weight is sublinear in n [11] (n being the code length). In contrast, computing the square code has a complexity which is polynomial in n.

The second type of attacks relies mostly on using Grobner basis to solve a polynomial system obtained from the public key and a potentially good basis for decoding [21,22]. In many cases, additional techniques are used for reducing the complexity of computing the Grobner basis, like, e.g., folding techniques [20]. All of these aspects are summarized in articles such as [9,17,34,40].

Our Contribution. In this article we use the algebraic formalism proposed in [5] to analyze the structure of the square code of a weakly decreasing monomial code. Informally, our first result can be summarized as follows: Given two weakly decreasing sets I and J and their maximum monomials $I_{\max_{\preceq_w}}$ and $J_{\max_{\preceq_w}}$, the star product code $\mathscr{C}(I) \star \mathscr{C}(J)$ is a weakly decreasing monomial code given by the weakly decreasing intervals $[1, f_i g_j]$ with $f_i \in I_{\max_{\preceq_w}}$ and $g_j \in J_{\max_{\preceq_w}}$. This result is rather large, in the sense that it also holds for decreasing monomial codes, as any decreasing monomial code is a weakly decreasing monomial code. In particular, two well-known families of codes, namely polar and Reed-Muller codes, are following this result.

Our second result is represented by a closed form formula for computing the cardinality of a weakly decreasing set I, given a set of non-comparable monomials that defines the weakly decreasing intervals for I. The formula will allows us to compute the dimension of the square code of a weakly decreasing monomial code. This result is immediately applicable to proving that a weakly decreasing monomial code is distinguishable from a random linear code. This application can be used in a code-based cryptographic context to distinguish a McEliece variant based on weakly decreasing monomial codes from one based on random linear codes.

Even though there is no direct cryptanalysis flowing from the distinguisher, the results reported here allow us to envision such attacks. In particular, this technique could be adapted to any weakly decreasing monomial code, similarly to the approach of Chisnov and Borodin [13] for Reed-Muller codes. However, the conditions related to the permutation group of the square code seem to make the attack a bit more complex for random weakly decreasing monomial codes (as compared to Reed-Muller codes). Nevertheless, we expect that, in the near future, our results could provide the building blocks for such attacks.

Outline of the article. This article is structured in four sections as follows. Section 2 briefly introduces coding theory and code-based cryptography. Towards the end of this section we present the two code families of relevance to this paper, namely the Reed-Muller and the polar codes. Afterwards, it is Sect. 3 that delves into the main part of this article. This section starts by explaining the algebraic formalism necessary for proving the results. These are followed by detailing the structure of the star product of two weakly decreasing monomial codes. Computing the dimension of a weakly decreasing monomial code given the set of maximum monomials represents the next step. These results allow us to propose several types of weakly decreasing monomial codes for which the dimension of the square code enables an efficient distinguisher. Finally, Sect. 4 is concluding while also hinting on how this work might be carried on.

2 The McEliece Variant Based on Polar Codes

2.1 Main Tools from Coding Theory

Besides basic definitions from coding theory we will need a few more explanations.

The intersection between a code $\mathscr{C}$ and its dual is called the *Hull* of $\mathscr{C}$

$$\mathcal{H}(\mathscr{C}) = \mathscr{C} \cap \mathscr{C}^{\perp}.$$

A code $\mathscr{C}$ with dimension $k \leq n/2$ is called *weakly self-dual* if $\mathcal{H}(\mathscr{C}) = \mathscr{C} \subset \mathscr{C}^{\perp}$ and *self-dual* if $\mathcal{H}(\mathscr{C}) = \mathscr{C} = \mathscr{C}^{\perp}$ (in this case $k = n/2$).

The component-wise product of two codewords $\boldsymbol{x}$ and $\boldsymbol{y} \in \mathbb{F}_2^n$ is defined as

$$\boldsymbol{x} \star \boldsymbol{y} \stackrel{\text{def}}{=} (x_1 y_1, \ldots, x_n y_n) \in \mathbb{F}_2^n. \tag{1}$$

For $i \in \{1, 2\}$ let $\mathscr{C}_i$ be a $[n, k_i, d_i]$ binary linear code. Then, the star product code of $\mathscr{C}_1$ and $\mathscr{C}_2$ is the binary linear code defined as

$$\mathscr{C}_1 \star \mathscr{C}_2 \stackrel{\text{def}}{=} \operatorname{Span}_{\mathbb{F}_2} \{ \boldsymbol{c}_1 \star \boldsymbol{c}_2 \mid \boldsymbol{c}_1 \in \mathscr{C}_1 \text{ and } \boldsymbol{c}_2 \in \mathscr{C}_2 \}. \tag{2}$$

It is known that the dimension of the star product code is

$$\dim (\mathscr{C}_1 \star \mathscr{C}_2) \leq \min \left\{ n, k_1 k_2 - \binom{\dim (\mathscr{C}_1 \cap \mathscr{C}_2)}{2} \right\}. \tag{3}$$

Definition 1 (Permutation group of a code). *Let $\mathscr{C}$ be a $[n, k, d]$ binary linear code and $\pi \in \mathfrak{S}_n$. We denote by $\boldsymbol{x}^{\pi} = (x_{\pi^{-1}(i)})_{1 \leq i \leq n}$ the vector $\boldsymbol{x}$ permuted by π. $\mathscr{C}^{\pi} = \{ \boldsymbol{c}^{\pi} \mid \boldsymbol{c} \in \mathscr{C} \}$ denotes the permuted code of $\mathscr{C}$. Then the permutation group of a code is*

$$\operatorname{Perm}(\mathscr{C}) \stackrel{\text{def}}{=} \{ \pi \in \mathfrak{S}_n \mid \mathscr{C}^{\pi} = \mathscr{C} \}$$

Proposition 1. *Let $\mathscr{C}$ be a binary linear code $[n, k, d]$ and $\operatorname{Perm}(\mathscr{C})$ be its permutation group. Then we have that*

$$\operatorname{Perm}(\mathscr{C}) = \operatorname{Perm}(\mathscr{C}^{\perp}) \quad \text{and} \quad \operatorname{Perm}(\mathscr{C}) \subseteq \operatorname{Perm}(\mathscr{C}^2). \tag{4}$$

2.2 The McEliece Public Key Encryption Scheme

The McEliece public key encryption scheme [29] is composed of three algorithms: *key generation* (KeyGen), *encryption* (Encrypt) and *decryption* (Decrypt). KeyGen picks a generator matrix for an $[n, k]$ code $\mathscr{C}$ that can correct t errors, a random invertible matrix $\boldsymbol{S}$ and a permutation $\boldsymbol{P}$. It computes $\boldsymbol{G}_{\text{pub}} \stackrel{\text{def}}{=} \boldsymbol{SGP}$, and outputs $\mathsf{pk} = (\boldsymbol{G}_{\text{pub}}, t)$ and $\mathsf{sk} = (\boldsymbol{S}, \boldsymbol{P})$.

To encrypt a message $\boldsymbol{m}$, the Encrypt function generates a random error-vector $\boldsymbol{e}$ of weight $|\boldsymbol{e}| \leq t$ and computes the cyphertext $\boldsymbol{z} = \boldsymbol{m} \boldsymbol{G}_{\text{pub}} \oplus \boldsymbol{e}$. The decryption takes as input a ciphertext $\boldsymbol{z}$ and the private key sk and outputs the corresponding message $\boldsymbol{m}$.

To verify the correctness of the scheme we can verify

$$\mathsf{Decrypt}(\mathsf{Encrypt}(\boldsymbol{m}, \mathsf{pk}), \mathsf{sk}) = \boldsymbol{m}.$$

2.3   Polar and Reed-Muller Codes

Algebraic Formalism. Polar and Reed-Muller codes can be described using a unified algebraic formalism. For doing that we will use the following notations

- The ambient space is the polynomial ring

$$\mathbb{R}_m = \mathbb{F}_2[x_0, x_1, \ldots, x_{m-1}]/(x_0^2 - x_0, \ldots, x_{m-1}^2 - x_{m-1});$$

- Codes that are studied here have length $n = 2^m$;
- Any binary vector $\boldsymbol{u} \in \mathbb{F}_2^m$ is denoted by $\boldsymbol{u} = (u_0, \ldots, u_{m-1})$, where u_{m-1} is the most significant bit.

To any element $\boldsymbol{u} \in \mathbb{F}_2^m$ we will associate an integer $u \in \mathbb{Z}$ defined as $u = \sum_{i=0}^{m-1} u_i 2^i$ (the elements of $\mathbb{F}_2^m$ will be ordered in decreasing index order). With this convention at hand, we can now define the evaluation function of polynomials, as follows. Let $g \in \mathbb{R}_m$ and order the elements in $\mathbb{F}_2^m$ with respect to the decreasing index order, then define

$$\begin{aligned} \mathbb{R}_m &\to & \mathbb{F}_2^n \\ g &\mapsto & \mathsf{ev}(g) = \big(g(\boldsymbol{u})\big)_{\boldsymbol{u} \in \mathbb{F}_2^m} \end{aligned}.$$

An important part in the formalism will be played by monomials.

Notation 1. *We denote by $\boldsymbol{x^i}$ the monomial $x_0^{i_0} \cdots x_{m-1}^{i_{m-1}}$, where $\boldsymbol{i} \in \mathbb{F}_2^m$. We also denote the set of monomials*

$$\mathcal{M}_m \overset{def}{=} \big\{ \boldsymbol{x^i} \mid \boldsymbol{i} = (i_0, \ldots, i_{m-1}) \in \mathbb{F}_2^m \big\}.$$

For any monomial $g \in \mathcal{M}_m$ of degree $1 \leq s \leq m$ we use the notation $g = x_{l_1} \ldots x_{l_s}$ where $0 \leq l_1 < l_2 \cdots < l_s \leq m - 1$. We also denote the support of a monomial by $\mathrm{ind}(g) = \{l_1 \ldots, l_s\}$.

Definition 2. *Let $I \subseteq \mathbb{R}_m$ be a finite set of polynomials in m variables. The linear code defined by I is the vector subspace $\mathscr{C}(I) \subseteq \mathbb{F}_2^n$ generated by $\{\mathsf{ev}(f) \mid f \in I\}$.*

These codes are called polynomial codes (see [16]), and when $I \subset \mathcal{M}_m$ we call $\mathscr{C}(I)$ a monomial code. The Reed-Muller code $\mathscr{R}(r, m)$ is a monomial code with dimension $k = \sum_{i=0}^{r} \binom{m}{i}$, defined as $\mathscr{R}(r, m) \overset{def}{=} \big\{ \mathsf{ev}(g) | g \in \mathbb{R}_m, \deg g \leq r \big\}$, in [26].

Polar Codes. Defining polar codes through this algebraic formalism has already been mentioned in [16]. We will give here only part of the details (i.e., those supporting this article). Polar codes are devised for a specific communication channel, a fact that makes them of interest as they achieve the capacity of that channel, for any binary discrete memoryless channel [1]. In order to define polar codes, Arikan introduced [1] two synthetic channels derived from the initial communication channel W

$$W^-(y_1, y_2 | u_2) \overset{\text{def}}{=} \frac{1}{2} \sum_{u_1 \in \mathbb{F}_2} W(y_1 | u_1) W(y_2 | u_1 \oplus u_2)$$

$$W^+(y_1, y_2, u_2 | u_1) \overset{\text{def}}{=} \frac{1}{2} W(y_1 | u_1) W(y_2 | u_1 \oplus u_2).$$

We will associate to any monomial $g \in \mathcal{M}_m$ the synthetic channel $W^g = W^{v_{m-1} \cdots v_0}$, where $v_i = -$ if $x_i | g$, and $v_i = +$ otherwise. The idea behind polar codes is to order the synthetic channels with respect to a figure-of-merit, and select the most reliable ones. One of the most common figures-of-merit used for this aim is the Bhattacharyya parameter of a channel W, that is

$$\mathcal{B}(W) = \sum_{y \in \mathcal{Y}} \sqrt{W(y|0) W(y|1)}. \tag{5}$$

Small values of the Bhattacharyya parameter are a good indicator that the corresponding channel is reliable. Hence, a channel W^f is more reliable than the channel W^g if $\mathcal{B}(W^f) \leq \mathcal{B}(W^g)$. Now we can define.

Definition 3. *The polar code of length $n = 2^m$ and dimension k devised for a channel W is the monomial code $\mathscr{C}(I)$ where I is the set of k monomials in $\mathcal{M}_m$ which take the k smallest values $\mathcal{B}(W^g)$ among all g in $\mathcal{M}_m$.*

3 Structural Attacks and Distinguisher Against Decreasing Monomial Codes

3.1 Introduction

Both the polar code based variant [41] and the Reed-Muller variant [42] were successfully cryptanalyzed using the structure of the minimum weight codewords in [4], and respectively in [30]. The complexity of these attacks was dominated by the complexity of the computation of the set of minimum weight codewords, which is exponential in the weight of the codewords. Hence, a more efficient cryptanalysis against the Reed-Muller variant using the square code attack was proposed in [13].

A key ingredient of the cryptanalysis of Shreska and Kim scheme [41] was based on the observation that polar codes are decreasing monomial codes. This implies a particular order $\preceq$ on the set of monomials in $\mathcal{M}_m$ (see [5,16]).

Definition 4. *Let f and g be two monomials in $\mathcal{M}_m$. Then $f \preceq_w g$ if and only if $f | g$. Also, we say that $f \preceq g$ if: (i) when $\deg(f) = \deg(g) = s$ we have $\forall\ 1 \leq \ell \leq s\ \ i_\ell \leq j_\ell$, where $f = x_{i_1} \ldots x_{i_s}$, $g = x_{j_1} \ldots x_{j_s}$; (ii) when $\deg(f) < \deg(g)$ we have $f \preceq g$ iff $\exists g^* \in \mathcal{M}_m$ s.t. $f \preceq g^* \preceq_w g$.*

Definition 5. *Let f and g be two monomials in $\mathcal{M}_m$ such that $f \preceq_w g$ and $I \subset \mathcal{M}_m$.*

- We define the closed interval $[f, g]_{\preceq_w}$ with respect to the partial order $\preceq_w$ as the set of monomials $h \in \mathcal{M}_m$ such that $f \preceq_w h \preceq_w g$.
- The set I is called a weakly decreasing set if and only if $(f \in I$ and $g \preceq_w f)$ implies $g \in I$.
- Let I be a weakly decreasing set. We define the subset of maximum monomials of I

$$I_{\max_{\preceq_w}} = \{f \in I \mid \not\exists g \in I, g \neq f \text{ s.t. } f \preceq_w g\}.$$

These definitions can be naturally extended to $\preceq$, and in this case we will simply call a set I decreasing. We will also call $\mathscr{C}(I)$ a weakly decreasing monomial code when I is a weakly decreasing set, respectively a decreasing monomial code when I is a decreasing set. Notice that, by definition, any decreasing set I is a weakly decreasing set. However, the set of maximum monomials might be different for $\preceq$ and $\preceq_w$. A particular example when an interval is both decreasing and weakly decreasing is $[1, x_0 \ldots x_t]_{\preceq} = [1, x_0 \ldots x_t]_{\preceq_w}$.

Theorem 2. *Polar codes and Reed-Muller codes are decreasing monomial codes. For $\mathscr{R}(r, m)$ we have*

$$\mathscr{R}(r, m) = \mathscr{C}([1, x_{m-r} \cdots x_{m-1}]_{\preceq}) = \mathscr{C}\left(\cup_{\deg(g)=r}[1, g]_{\preceq_w}\right).$$

Duality Properties

Let us begin by defining the *multiplicative complement* of a monomial $g \in \mathcal{M}_m$ as $\check{g} \overset{\text{def}}{=} \dfrac{x_0 \ldots x_{m-1}}{g}$. By extension, for any $I \subseteq \mathcal{M}_m$, we define $\check{I} = \{\check{f} : f \in I\}$.

Proposition 2. *Let $\mathscr{C}(I)$ be a weakly decreasing monomial code. Then its dual is a weakly decreasing monomial code given by*

$$\mathscr{C}(I)^{\perp} = \mathscr{C}(\mathcal{M}_m \setminus \check{I}).$$

Corollary 1.

$$\mathscr{R}(r, m)^{\perp} = \mathscr{R}(m - r - 1, m).$$

3.2 Star Product and Square Code of Weakly Decreasing Monomial Codes

Proposition 3. *Let I and J be two monomial sets and let IJ be the product set, more exactly $IJ \overset{\text{def}}{=} \{fg, f \in I \text{ and } g \in J\}$. Then we have*

$$\mathscr{C}(I) \star \mathscr{C}(J) = \mathscr{C}(IJ).$$

Proof. The componentwise product of the vectors $\mathsf{ev}(f)$ and $\mathsf{ev}(g)$, where $f, g \in \mathcal{M}_m$ equals the evaluation vector of fg, namely

$$\mathsf{ev}(f) \star \mathsf{ev}(g) = \mathsf{ev}(fg). \tag{6}$$

From (6) and (2) we obtain the desired result.

Corollary 2. *Let* $(\mathbb{R}_m, +, \cdot, \cdot)$ *be the algebra of polynomials in* m *variables (where "$\cdot$" represents the usual multiplication), and let* $(\mathbb{F}_2^n, +, \cdot, \star)$ *be the algebra of* n *length binary vectors, equipped with the star product operation. Then the* ev *function defines an isomorphism of algebras.*

Proposition 4. *Let* l *and* s *be two positive integers and* $(f_i)_{1 \leq i \leq l}$ *and* $(g_j)_{1 \leq j \leq s}$ *be two sequences of noncomparable monomials. Let* $I = \bigcup_{1 \leq i \leq l} [1, f_i]_{\preceq w}$ *and* $J = \bigcup_{1 \leq j \leq s} [1, g_j]_{\preceq w}$, *be two weakly decreasing sets. Then*

$$\mathscr{C}(I) \star \mathscr{C}(J) = \mathscr{C}\left(\cup_{\substack{1 \leq i \leq l \\ 1 \leq j \leq s}} [1, f_i g_j]_{\preceq w}\right).$$

Corollary 3.
$$\mathscr{R}(r_1, m) \star \mathscr{R}(r_2, m) = \mathscr{R}(r_1 + r_2, m).$$

Since we have determined a formula for the star product of two weakly decreasing monomial codes as a function of the weakly decreasing sets defining each code, we will give (in the next subsection) a formula for computing the dimension of the weakly decreasing monomial code when the weakly decreasing sets are given.

3.3 Computing the Dimension of a Weakly Decreasing Monomial Code

The problem that we want to address here can be stated as:
  Given: A weakly decreasing set $I = \bigcup_{g \in I_{\max_{\preceq w}}} [1, g]_{\preceq w}$.
  Find: $\dim(\mathscr{C}(I))$.
  What we are aiming to find here is that, given a set of non-comparable monomials with respect to the $\preceq_w$ ordering, we should be able to give the dimension of the corresponding weakly decreasing monomial code, without enumerating the whole set of monomials.

Proposition 5. *Let* $\mathscr{C}(I)$ *be a weakly decreasing monomial code defined by the weakly decreasing set* $I = \bigcup_{g_i \in I_{\max_{\preceq w}}} [1, g_i]_{\preceq w}$. *Then*

$$\dim(\mathscr{C}(I)) = \sum_{k=1}^{\left|I_{\max_{\preceq w}}\right|} (-1)^{k+1} \sum_{1 \leq i_1 < i_2 < \cdots < i_k \leq \left|I_{\max_{\preceq w}}\right|} 2^{\deg(\gcd(g_{i_1}, \ldots, g_{i_k}))}.$$

Proof. We recall that for any element $g \in \mathcal{M}_m$ the cardinality of $[1, g]_{\preceq w}$ equals $2^{\deg(g)}$.

For concluding the proof we use an inclusion-exclusion argument over the set of all intervals that define I. We begin by considering all the intervals, hence we obtain $\sum_{g_{i_k} \in I_{\max_{\preceq w}}} 2^{\deg(g_{i_k})}$. The next step is to subtract the intersection of all the pairs of monomials, namely the sum $\sum_{\substack{(g_{i_1},g_{i_2})\in I_{\max_{\preceq_w}} \times I_{\max_{\preceq_w}} \\ g_{i_1}\neq g_{i_2}}} 2^{\gcd(g_{i_1},g_{i_2})}$,

and continue this process up to the last set, which is $\left\{ g_1,\ldots,g_{\big|I_{\max_{\preceq_w}}\big|} \right\}$.

In Appendix A.1 we give an example of how this formula works, and also propose an efficient method for computing it.

3.4   Distinguisher

There are mainly two efficient distinguishers for the McEliece scheme: (i) the dimension of the square code, and (ii) the dimension of the Hull. The first one was introduced in [19] and basically checks whether the code used in the PKC has a square code with dimension close to $\binom{k+1}{2}$, where k is the dimension of the public code (k satisfies $\binom{k+1}{2} < n$). If the dimension of the square of the public code is far from $\binom{k+1}{2}$, then, with high probability, the public code is not a random one. The second technique is due to Sendrier [38,39] and analyzes the structure of the Hull. On one hand, for structured codes (e.g., Reed-Muller, Polar, GRS, etc.), the Hull is far from being trivial. On the other hand, for random linear codes the following holds.

Proposition 6 ([15,38]). *The expected dimension of the hull of a random linear code is $O(1)$. It is smaller than t with probability $\geqslant 1 - O(2^{-t})$.*

Special Classes of Weakly Decreasing Monomial Codes. In what follows we will define classes of weakly decreasing monomial codes that can be distinguished using the square code technique. We will show the difference between the expected dimension of a square random code, and the dimension of a square weakly decreasing monomial code.

Proposition 7. *Let I be a weakly decreasing set such that $I = [1,f]_{\preceq_w}$. Then we have*

$$\mathscr{C}^2(I) = \mathscr{C}(I) \quad and \quad \mathscr{C}^{\perp}(I) \cap \mathscr{C}(I) = \mathscr{C}(I).$$

Proof. The fact that $\mathscr{C}^2(I) = \mathscr{C}(I)$ comes directly from Proposition 4. Now suppose that f, or any other $g \preceq_w f$, does not belong to $\mathcal{M}_m \setminus \breve{I}$. This implies that $f \in \breve{I}$. But $\breve{I} = [\breve{f}, x_0 \ldots x_{m-1}]$. In other words $\breve{f} \preceq_w f$, which is imposible. Hence $f \in \mathcal{M}_m \setminus \breve{I}$, and since $\mathcal{M}_m \setminus \breve{I}$ is a weakly decreasing set, we deduce that $[1,f] \subset \mathcal{M}_m \setminus \breve{I}$.   □

Remark 1. This result implies that:

1. $\dim(\mathscr{C}^2(I)) = \dim(\mathscr{C}(I)) = 2^{\deg(f)}$;
2. $\mathsf{d}_{\min}(\mathscr{C}^2(I)) = \mathsf{d}_{\min}(\mathscr{C}(I)) = 2^{m-\deg(f)}$;
3. $\mathrm{Perm}\,(\mathscr{C}^2(I)) = \mathrm{Perm}\,(\mathscr{C}(I))$.

Therefore, for any $0 \le \alpha \le m$ there are at least $\binom{m}{\alpha}$ weakly decreasing monomial codes $\mathscr{C}(I)$ of parameters $[2^m, 2^\alpha, 2^{m-\alpha}]$ such that $\mathscr{C}^2(I) = \mathscr{C}(I)$. Hence, any of these weakly decreasing monomial codes can be distinguished from random linear codes (by Proposition 6).

Definition 6. *Let* $I = \bigcup_{g_i \in I_{\max_{\preceq_w}}} [1, g_i]_{\preceq_w}$ *and* j *be a strictly positive integer such that* $j \le |I_{\max_{\preceq_w}}| - 1$. *The set* I *is called* depth-j-weakly decreasing set *if*

- $\exists$ *distinct indices* $i_1, i_2, \ldots, i_j$ *s.t.* $\gcd(g_{i_1}, \ldots, g_{i_j}) \ne 1$; *and*
- $\forall$ *distinct indices* $i_1, i_2, \ldots, i_{j+1}$ *we have* $\gcd(g_{i_1}, \ldots, g_{i_{j+1}}) = 1$.

When $j = 1$ *we call* I *a* depth-1-weakly decreasing set *if* $\forall$ *distinct* $g_{i_1}, g_{i_2} \in I_{\max_{\preceq_w}}$ *we have* $\gcd(g_{i_1}, g_{i_2}) = 1$.

Proposition 8. *Let* $I = \bigcup_{g_i \in I_{\max_{\preceq_w}}} [1, g_i]_{\preceq_w}$ *be a* depth-j-weakly decreasing set. *Then*

$$\dim(\mathscr{C}(I)) = \sum_{k=1}^{j} (-1)^{k+1} \sum_{1 \le i_1 < i_2 < \cdots < i_k \le |I_{\max_{\preceq_w}}|} 2^{\deg(\gcd(g_{i_1}, \ldots, g_{i_k}))} + (-1)^j \binom{|I_{\max_{\preceq_w}}| - 1}{j}.$$

When $j = 1$ *we have*

$$\dim(\mathscr{C}(I)) = \sum_{i=1}^{|I_{\max_{\preceq_w}}|} 2^{\deg(g_i)} - (|I_{\max_{\preceq_w}}| - 1).$$

Proof. Use Definition 6 and Proposition 5 to obtain

$$\dim(\mathscr{C}(I)) = \sum_{k=1}^{j} (-1)^{k+1} \sum_{1 \le i_1 < i_2 < \cdots < i_k \le |I_{\max_{\preceq_w}}|} 2^{\deg(\gcd(g_{i_1}, \ldots, g_{i_k}))}$$

$$+ (-1) \sum_{k=j+1}^{|I_{\max_{\preceq_w}}|} (-1)^k \binom{|I_{\max_{\preceq_w}}|}{k}$$

$$= \sum_{k=1}^{j} (-1)^{k+1} \sum_{1 \le i_1 < i_2 < \cdots < i_k \le |I_{\max_{\preceq_w}}|} 2^{\deg(\gcd(g_{i_1}, \ldots, g_{i_k}))}$$

$$+ \sum_{k=0}^{j} (-1)^k \binom{|I_{\max_{\preceq_w}}|}{k}.$$

The last item is a well-known combinatorial identity, namely

$$\sum_{k=0}^{j} (-1)^k \binom{s}{k} = (-1)^j \binom{s-1}{j}.$$

$\square$

We will now prove that any depth-1-weakly decreasing monomial code can be distinguish from a random linear code.

Theorem 3. *Let* $I = \bigcup_{g_i \in I_{\max \preceq_w}} [1, g_i]_{\preceq_w}$ *be a depth-1-weakly decreasing set and* $|I_{\max \preceq_w}| = s$. *Then we have*

$$\dim\left(\mathscr{C}(I)^2\right) = \sum_{1 \leq i < j \leq s} 2^{\deg(g_i)+\deg(g_j)} - (s-2) \sum_{1 \leq i \leq s} 2^{\deg(g_i)} + (-1)^s \binom{\binom{s}{2}-1}{s-1}.$$

Proof. Notice that the set of maximum monomials in $\mathscr{C}(I)^2$ has cardinality $\binom{s}{2}$, a fact that comes from the characteristic of the depth of I. In fact, all the possible combinations $g_i g_j$ for $1 \leq i < j \leq s$ lead to maximum monomials for $\mathscr{C}(I)^2$. Remark that $\mathscr{C}(I)^2$ is a depth-s-weakly decreasing monomial code. Now, use Proposition 8 for $\mathscr{C}(I)^2$. This almost holds the result, except for the middle term in the sum, namely $(s-2) \sum_{1 \leq i \leq s} 2^{\deg(g_i)}$. By expanding the terms from Proposition 8, and using the fact that $\gcd(g_{i_1} g_{j_1}, g_{i_2} g_{j_2}, \ldots, g_{i_k} g_{j_k}) = g_{i_1}$ if and only if $i_1 = i_2 = \cdots = i_k$, for any $2 \geq k \geq s-1$, we deduce the result. □

Perspectives on a Cryptanalysis Using Square Code. There is a square code attack against one class of decreasing monomial codes, namely against Reed-Muller code [13]. The main idea is to solve the code equivalence problem, no longer on the difficult instance $\mathscr{R}(r, m)$, but on a much simpler one $\mathscr{R}(r^*, m)$, where $r^* \leq r$. $\mathscr{R}(r^*, m)$ can be obtained from $\mathscr{R}(r, m)$ by successive operations, more precisely by taking the square code and the dual code. Under a certain primality condition it is possible to decrease r, which lowers the complexity of the attack to a polynomial in the length of the code. Reed-Muller codes are the unfortunate family (from a cryptographic point of view), for which three key ingredients are required for such an attack:

- The dual of a Reed-Muller code is a Reed-Muller code (see Corollary 1);
- The square code of a Reed-Muller code is a Reed-Muller code (see Corollary 3);
- Perm $(\mathscr{R}(r, m))$ is a general affine group for any $1 \leq r \leq m - 2$ (see Chap. 13 in [26]).

The last condition is the line between a full cryptanalysis and a partial cryptanalysis of any decreasing monomial code. Indeed, the first two conditions are satisfied for any decreasing monomial code, as dual and square code of any decreasing monomial code is still a decreasing monomial code. Now, if Perm $(\mathscr{C}(I))^\perp$ = Perm $(\mathscr{C}(I))$ for any decreasing monomial code, the equality does not hold anymore if we take the square operator instead of the dual operator. Also, as we can see in the case of Reed-Muller codes, Perm $(\mathscr{R}(r, m))$ = Perm $(\mathscr{R}(2r, m))$ as long as $1 \leq r \leq (m-2)/2$. It is mainly because of this particular fact that Chizhov and Borodin [13] managed to propose a polynomial time complexity attack against Sidelnikov's cryptosystem.

4   Conclusions

This articles provides a formal characterization of the star product of two weakly decreasing monomial codes. As the star product became an efficient tool in the cryptanalysis of some McEliece variants based on highly structured codes, our results are following in the same direction. This article can also be seen as a natural extension of the recent work of Bardet et al. [4] for cryptanalyzing the McEliece variant based on polar codes and the work of Chizhov and Borodin [13] against Shidelnikov's cryptosystem. In this article we prove that specific weakly decreasing monomial codes can be distinguished using the square code technique.

   In the near future, our aim is to provide an extended version of this article where the dimension of the square code of an arbitrary depth-j-weakly decreasing monomial code will be analyzed. That version will also include various simulations on practical parameters.

   We also plan to use these results and adapt Chizhov and Borodin's attack against any weakly decreasing monomial code. This might be done in several steps. Firstly, we could analyze the depth-1-weakly decreasing monomial codes and propose a practical sub-exponential (hopefully and even better, polynomial) key recovery attack using the square code technique. Secondly, if this approach works, and under the hypothesis that one could determine exactly the dimension of the square of any depth-j-weakly decreasing monomial code, we might generalize the square code attack to any weakly decreasing monomial code. An even more potent but difficult scheme would be one where monomial codes are used, with no particular partial order structures of these monomials.

Acknowledgement. This work was partially supported by the European Union through the European Regional Development Fund (ERDF) under the Competitiveness Operational Program (BioCell-NanoART = Novel Bio-inspired Cellular Nano-architectures, POC-A1.1.4-E-2015 nr. 30/01.09.2016).

A.1   Computing the Dimension for Weakly Decreasing Monomial Codes

Example 1. Let $I = [1, x_0x_1]_{\preceq_w} \cup [1, x_0x_2]_{\preceq_w} \cup [1, x_1x_3]_{\preceq_w}$. We observe that I is a weakly decreasing set and it is not a decreasing set. If we apply our formula step by step we obtain

1. The first step is to compute the cardinality of all the intervals $[1, g_i]_{\preceq_w}$.
   - $|[1, x_0x_1]_{\preceq_w}| = |\{1, x_0, x_1, x_0x_1\}| = 2^2$.
   - $|[1, x_0x_2]_{\preceq_w}| = |\{1, x_0, x_2, x_0x_2\}| = 2^2$.
   - $|[1, x_1x_3]_{\preceq_w}| = |\{1, x_1, x_3, x_1x_3\}| = 2^2$.
   which gives a total of 12 elements.
2. The second step computes the cardinality of the intervals $[1, \gcd(g_i, g_j)]_{\preceq_w}$
   - $|[1, x_0]_{\preceq_w}| = |\{1, x_0\}| = 2^1$.
   - $|[1, x_1]_{\preceq_w}| = |\{1, x_1\}| = 2^1$.

- $|[1]| = |\{1\}| = 2^0.$

which gives a total of 5 elements and an updated sum of 7.

3. The third and last step determines the cardinality of the interval $[1, \gcd(x_0 x_1, x_0 x_2, x_1 x_3)]_{\preceq_w} = \{1\}$. So, we have only one element and the dimension of the code is

$$\dim(\mathscr{C}(I)) = 8.$$

Remark 2. Another way of computing the formula is to use the set of indices $\{\operatorname{ind}(g_i)\}_{g_i \in I_{\max_{\preceq_w}}}$. Take for example $m = 5$ and

$$I_{\max_{\preceq_w}} = \{x_0 x_1 x_2, x_0 x_2 x_4, x_2 x_4, x_0 x_1 x_3 x_4\},$$

which gives the set of indices $\operatorname{ind}(I_{\max_{\preceq_w}}) = \{\{0,1,2\}, \{0,2,3\}, \{2,4\}, \{0,1,3,4\}\}$. By applying our formula we obtain

$$\dim(\mathscr{C}(I)) = 2*2^3 + 2^2 + 2^4 - (2^2 + 2 + 2^2 + 2 + 2 + 2^2 + 2) + (2+2+1) - 1 = 22.$$

References

1. Arıkan, E.: Channel polarization: A method for constructing capacity-achieving codes for symmetric binary-input memoryless channels. IEEE Trans. Inf. Theory **55**(7), 3051–3073 (2009)
2. Baldi, M., Bodrato, M., Chiaraluce, F.: A new analysis of the McEliece cryptosystem based on QC-LDPC codes. In: Ostrovsky, R., De Prisco, R., Visconti, I. (eds.) SCN 2008. LNCS, vol. 5229, pp. 246–262. Springer, Heidelberg (2008). https://doi.org/10.1007/978-3-540-85855-3_17
3. Baldi, M., Chiaraluce, F.: Cryptanalysis of a new instance of McEliece cryptosystem based on QC-LDPC codes. In: Proceedings of the IEEE International Symposium on Information Theory - ISIT, Nice, France, pp. 2591–2595, June 2007
4. Bardet, M., Chaulet, J., Dragoi, V., Otmani, A., Tillich, J.-P.: Cryptanalysis of the McEliece public key cryptosystem based on polar codes. In: Takagi, T. (ed.) PQCrypto 2016. LNCS, vol. 9606, pp. 118–143. Springer, Cham (2016). https://doi.org/10.1007/978-3-319-29360-8_9
5. Bardet, M., Dragoi, V., Otmani, A., Tillich, J.P.: Algebraic properties of polar codes from a new polynomial formalism. In: Proceedings of the IEEE International Symposium on Information Theory - ISIT, Barcelona, Spain, pp. 230–234, July 2016
6. Becker, A., Joux, A., May, A., Meurer, A.: Decoding random binary linear codes in $2^{n/20}$: How $1 + 1 = 0$ improves information set decoding. In: Pointcheval, D., Johansson, T. (eds.) EUROCRYPT 2012. LNCS, vol. 7237, pp. 520–536. Springer, Heidelberg (2012). https://doi.org/10.1007/978-3-642-29011-4_31
7. Berlekamp, E., McEliece, R., van Tilborg, H.: On the inherent intractability of certain coding problems. IEEE Trans. Inf. Theory **24**(3), 384–386 (1978)
8. Bernstein, D.J., Lange, T., Peters, C.: Wild McEliece. In: Biryukov, A., Gong, G., Stinson, D.R. (eds.) SAC 2010. LNCS, vol. 6544, pp. 143–158. Springer, Heidelberg (2011). https://doi.org/10.1007/978-3-642-19574-7_10
9. Bucerzan, D., Dragoi, V., Kalachi, H.T.: Evolution of the McEliece public key encryption scheme. In: Farshim, P., Simion, E. (eds.) SecITC 2017. LNCS, vol. 10543, pp. 129–149. Springer, Cham (2017). https://doi.org/10.1007/978-3-319-69284-5_10

10. Canteaut, A., Chabanne, H.: A further improvement of the work factor in an attempt at breaking McEliece's cryptosystem. In: Proceedings of the International Symposium on Coding Theory and Applications - EUROCODE 1994, pp. 169–173 (1994)
11. Canto-Torres, R., Sendrier, N.: Analysis of information set decoding for a sub-linear error weight. In: Takagi, T. (ed.) PQCrypto 2016. LNCS, vol. 9606, pp. 144–161. Springer, Cham (2016). https://doi.org/10.1007/978-3-319-29360-8_10
12. Chen, L., et al.: Report on post-quantum cryptography. Technical Report, National Institute of Standards and Technology (2016)
13. Chizhov, I.V., Borodin, M.A.: Effective attack on the McEliece cryptosystem based on Reed-Muller codes. Discrete Math. Appl. **24**(5), 273–280 (2014)
14. Couvreur, A., Gaborit, P., Gauthier-Umaña, V., Otmani, A., Tillich, J.P.: Distinguisher-based attacks on public-key cryptosystems using Reed-Solomon codes. Des. Codes Crypt. **73**(2), 641–666 (2014)
15. Debris-Alazard, T., Sendrier, N., Tillich, J.: A new signature scheme based on $(u|u + v)$ codes. CoRR abs/1706.08065 (2017). http://arxiv.org/abs/1706.08065
16. Dragoi, V.: Algebraic approach for the study of algorithmic problems coming from cryptography and the theory of error correcting codes. Ph.D. thesis, Université de Rouen, France, July 2017
17. Drăgoi, V., Richmond, T., Bucerzan, D., Legay, A.: Survey on cryptanalysis of code-based cryptography: From theoretical to physical attacks. In: International Conference on Computers Communications and Control - ICCCC, Oradea, Romania, pp. 215–223, May 2018
18. Dumer, I.: Two decoding algorithms for linear codes. Prob. Inf. Transm. **25**(1), 17–23 (1989)
19. Faugère, J.C., Gauthier, V., Otmani, A., Perret, L., Tillich, J.P.: A distinguisher for high rate McEliece cryptosystems. IEEE Trans. Inf. Theory **59**(10), 6830–6844 (2013)
20. Faugère, J.C., Otmani, A., Perret, L., de Portzamparc, F., Tillich, J.P.: Folding alternant and Goppa codes with non-trivial automorphism groups. IEEE Trans. Inf. Theory **62**(1), 184–198 (2016)
21. Faugère, J.C., Otmani, A., Perret, L., de Portzamparc, F., Tillich, J.P.: Structural cryptanalysis of McEliece schemes with compact keys. Des. Codes Crypt. **79**(1), 87–112 (2016)
22. Faugère, J.-C., Perret, L., de Portzamparc, F.: Algebraic attack against variants of McEliece with Goppa polynomial of a special form. In: Sarkar, P., Iwata, T. (eds.) ASIACRYPT 2014. LNCS, vol. 8873, pp. 21–41. Springer, Heidelberg (2014). https://doi.org/10.1007/978-3-662-45611-8_2
23. Feynman, R.P.: Simulating physics with computers. Int. J. Theor. Phys. **21**(6), 467–488 (1982)
24. Hooshmand, R., Shooshtari, M.K., Eghlidos, T., Aref, M.: Reducing the key length of McEliece cryptosystem using polar codes. In: International ISC Conference on Information Security and Cryptology - ISCISC, Teheran, Iran, pp. 104–108, September 2014
25. Janwa, H., Moreno, O.: McEliece public key cryptosystems using algebraic-geometric codes. Des. Codes Crypt. **8**(3), 293–307 (1996)
26. MacWilliams, F.J., Sloane, N.J.A.: The Theory of Error-Correcting Codes, 5th edn. North-Holland, Amsterdam (1986)
27. May, A., Meurer, A., Thomae, E.: Decoding random linear codes in $\tilde{O}(2^{0.054n})$. In: Lee, D.H., Wang, X. (eds.) ASIACRYPT 2011. LNCS, vol. 7073, pp. 107–124. Springer, Heidelberg (2011). https://doi.org/10.1007/978-3-642-25385-0_6

28. May, A., Ozerov, I.: On computing nearest neighbors with applications to decoding of binary linear codes. In: Oswald, E., Fischlin, M. (eds.) EUROCRYPT 2015. LNCS, vol. 9056, pp. 203–228. Springer, Heidelberg (2015). https://doi.org/10.1007/978-3-662-46800-5_9

29. McEliece, R.J.: A puclic-key system based on algebraic theory, pp. 114–116. The Deep Space Network Progress Report, DSN PR 42–44, January 1978. https://tmo.jpl.nasa.gov/progress_report2/42-44/44N.PDF

30. Minder, L., Shokrollahi, A.: Cryptanalysis of the Sidelnikov cryptosystem. In: Naor, M. (ed.) EUROCRYPT 2007. LNCS, vol. 4515, pp. 347–360. Springer, Heidelberg (2007). https://doi.org/10.1007/978-3-540-72540-4_20

31. Misoczki, R., Tillich, J.P., Sendrier, N., Barreto, P.S.L.M.: MDPC-McEliece: New McEliece variants from moderate density parity-check codes. In: Proceedings of the IEEE International Symposium Information Theory - ISIT, Istanbul, Turkey, pp. 2069–2073, July 2013

32. Niederreiter, H.: Knapsack-type cryptosystems and algebraic coding theory. Probl. Control Inf. Theory 15(2), 159–166 (1986)

33. Otmani, A., Kalachi, H.T.: Square code attack on a modified Sidelnikov cryptosystem. In: El Hajji, S., Nitaj, A., Carlet, C., Souidi, E.M. (eds.) C2SI 2015. LNCS, vol. 9084, pp. 173–183. Springer, Cham (2015). https://doi.org/10.1007/978-3-319-18681-8_14

34. Overbeck, R., Sendrier, N.: Code-based cryptography. In: Bernstein, D.J., Buchmann, J., Dahmen, E. (eds.) Post-Quantum Cryptography, pp. 95–145. Springer, Heidelberg (2009). https://doi.org/10.1007/978-3-540-88702-7_4

35. Persichetti, E.: Compact McEliece keys based on quasi-dyadic Srivastava codes. J. Math. Cryptology 6(2), 149–169 (2012)

36. Prange, E.: The use of information sets in decoding cyclic codes. IRE Trans. Inf. Theory 8(5), 5–9 (1962)

37. Rivest, R.L., Shamir, A., Adleman, L.M.: A method for obtaining digital signatures and public-key cryptosystems. Commun. ACM 21(2), 120–126 (1978)

38. Sendrier, N.: On the dimension of the hull. SIAM J. Discrete Math. 10, 282–293 (1997)

39. Sendrier, N.: On the security of the McEliece public-key cryptosystem. In: Blaum, M., Farrell, P.G., van Tilborg, H.C.A. (eds.) Information, Coding and Mathematics, vol. 687, pp. 141–163. Springer, Boston (2002). https://doi.org/10.1007/978-1-4757-3585-7_10

40. Sendrier, N.: On the use of structured codes in code based cryptography. In: Coding Theory and Cryptography III, pp. 59–68 (2010)

41. Shrestha, S.R., Kim, Y.S.: New McEliece cryptosystem based on polar codes as a candidate for post-quantum cryptography. In: International Symposium on Communication and Information Technologies - ISCIT, Incheon, Korea, pp. 368–372, September 2014

42. Sidelnikov, V.M.: A public-key cryptosytem based on Reed-Muller codes. Discrete Math. Appl. 4(3), 191–207 (1994)

43. Wieschebrink, C.: Cryptanalysis of the Niederreiter public key scheme based on GRS subcodes. IACR Cryptology ePrint Archive, Report 2009/452 (2009)

Binary Data Analysis for Source Code Leakage Assessment

Adrien Facon[1,3], Sylvain Guilley[1,2,3], Matthieu Lec'hvien[1],
Damien Marion[1,2(✉)], and Thomas Perianin[1]

[1] Secure-IC S.A.S, Rennes, France
{adrien.facon,sylvain.guilley,matthieu.lechvien,
damien.marion,thomas.perianin}@secure-ic.com
[2] Telecom ParisTech, Institut Mines-Télécom, Paris, France
[3] École Normale Supérieure, Paris, France

Abstract. Side Channel Analysis (SCA) is known to be a serious threat for cryptographic algorithms since twenty years. Recently, the explosion of the Internet of Things (IoT) has increased the number of devices that can be targeted by these attacks, making this threat more relevant than ever. Furthermore, the evaluations of cryptographic algorithms regarding SCA are usually performed at the very end of a product design cycle, impacting considerably the time-to-market in case of security flaws. Hence, early simulations of embedded software and methodologies have been developed to assess vulnerabilities with respect to SCA for specific hardware architectures. Aiming to provide an agnostic evaluation method, we propose in this paper a new methodology of data collection and analysis to reveal leakage of sensitive information from any software implementation. As an illustration our solution is used interestingly to break a White Box Cryptography (WBC) implementation, challenging existing simulation-based attacks.

Keywords: Software analysis · GNU debugger (GDB) ·
Differential computation analysis (DCA) ·
Correlation power analysis (CPA) · Binary analysis ·
Realignment algorithm · Virtualyzr[TM] tool

1 Introduction

1.1 Previous Work

Measuring Electromagnetic (EM) or power traces from embedded devices to identify potential leakage of information is a time consuming and challenging process. First, it requires equipment (oscilloscope, probes, signal amplifiers...) that demand prior knowledge to the technician. Secondly, the code to evaluate needs to be embedded on the final product or on an evaluation board, it means that the development has to be finished at the evaluation time. This justifies the interest of the security evaluation community for simulation, both in the

© Springer Nature Switzerland AG 2019
J.-L. Lanet and C. Toma (Eds.): SecITC 2018, LNCS 11359, pp. 391–409, 2019.
https://doi.org/10.1007/978-3-030-12942-2_30

industrial and academic world. Aiming to speed-up, facilitate the evaluation, and allowing an evaluation during the development, several works have proposed Side Channel (SC) trace simulators. The principle is to simulate the leakage that might happen during the code execution. Numerous simulators are available to simulate SC (power or EM) leakage. All present a similar general construction flow illustrated in Fig. 1. First, they take a description of the implementation to evaluate as input. For example, the inputs of SILK [13] are tagged C++ source codes. More often, inputs are architecture dependant compiled binaries: Elmo [9] uses binaries for the ARM Cortex-M0 and OSCAR [11] uses binaries for the 8-bit Atmel AVR microcontroller. The Dynamic Binary Analyzer (DBA) framework [2] supports more architectures: ARM, x86, MIPS, SPARC and SH4. In the simulation step, the SC-simulators execute the code to record data. For example, Elmo [9] uses the emulator Thumbulator, while in [3] the authors use the Valgrind debugger. The choice of the data provider is influenced by the fact that the simulator is specific to an architecture. Another important choice of the simulation step is the selection of the data to record. The authors of [3] proposed to record the memory accesses. The DBA framework [2] records the stack, the heap, the CPU-registers and the executed instructions. Elmo [9] is focused on the values of the operands, the bit-flips of the operations and the operations. The last step is the trace generation, or how to transform the recorded data to obtained traces as similar as possible to real and effective physical leakage. Elmo [9] provides one of the most realistic and complex model computed with linear regressions (also used in [5]) and F-test on real leakage traces recorded on a ARM Cortex-M0. Otherwise, the most commonly used models are the Hamming weight and the Hamming distance, which are simplifications of effective physical leakage. Those models have been preferred by the authors of [2,11].

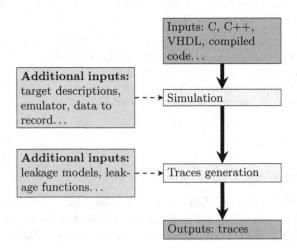

Fig. 1. General flow commonly used by the SC-simulators.

1.2   Contributions

In this context, we propose a new methodology of data collection and analysis to identify potential leakages from any software implementation. Our solution takes inspiration from the work proposed by Bos *et al.* in [3]. An improvement of the analysis step has been proposed in [1], realizing on three intermediate computations instead of one initially. As a first difference, we propose a new methodology of data collection. We record all bit-modifications that happen during a code execution (registers, memory content, flags, Program Counter (PC)), while in [3], authors record only the read, written and executed addresses. Furthermore, we do not apply any model to the recorded data in order to generate traces. All the collected data is exhaustively analyzed to avoid information loss. To do so, we introduce a binary analysis to extract the leaking points from the data. Then, we leverage on PC to keep track of the execution context to map the identified leakage to the source code. Indeed, mapping leakages to source code is nowadays an important need for continuous improvement of products; this is particularly true for software implementations, where traces are long and code is complex. To succeed, we need to overcome two main difficulties: misalignment and multiplicity of leaking resources. We show how to characterize and then exploit the PC to realign all the data using a simple accumulative algorithm, and we introduce a methodology of data selection that significantly reduce the size of the data to analyze. Finally, we show how our solution can identify leakage in the source code applying our methodology to WBC implementation.

1.3   Outline

The paper is organized as follows. In the Sect. 2 we describe each step of our solution. In the Sect. 3 we present an evaluation performed with our solution on a WBC implementation. Finally, we summarize the presented work in Sect. 4.

2   Solution Presentation

We present here-after how the Virtualyzr^{TM} tool collects, pre-processes, and analyses simulation traces.

2.1   Notation and Recording Step

Aiming to record all the data manipulated by a given binary, the debugger GDB is used, but alternative software could be used to collect data. The analysis that we propose is independent of the data provider. To identify all potential leakages, the recording process is as exhaustive as possible. Each time the PC changes, all the internal data are saved (PC, registers, flags...). For example, in the case of an x86 architecture in 64-bit execution (properties of the system used for all the results given in the current paper), the internal data are:

– the sixteen 64-bit registers: `rax`, `rbx`, `rcx`, `rdx`, `rsi`, `rdi`, `rbp`, `rsp`, `r8`, `r9`, `r10`, `r11`, `r12`, `r13`, `r14`, `r15`,
– the six 16-bit registers: `cs`, `ss`, `ds`, `es`, `fs`, `gs`,
– the 64-bit `eflags` (with the bit 1, 5, 15, 22–63 reserved).
– the PC (Program Counter, also named `rip`)

In the whole document, the matrix notations are used. The recorded data of an execution is stored in a matrix noted $X^{D,R} \in (\mathbb{Z}/2\mathbb{Z})^{D,R}$, with D the number of times the PC changes and R the number of bit needed to store all the internal data (except the PC that is stored independently, and used in resynchronization process deepened in Subsect. 2.2). For a given dataset $X^{D,R}$, the associated list of successive PC-values is stored in a matrix $\mathrm{Pc}^D \in (\mathbb{Z}/2^{64}\mathbb{Z})^D$. An illustration of a recorded trace is provided in Fig. 2, the black color corresponds to one and the white to zero, the x-axis describes the internal data and the y-axis the index of the PC. The illustrated trace follows from the execution of the WBC algorithm freely provided at the Challenge CHES-2016[1]. The illustration of the recorded trace provided in Fig. 2 shows that only a little part of the registers seems to be used during the execution. The reduction of the size of manipulated data is detailed in Subsect. 2.3. A set of Q executions is noted as $\{X_q^{D_q,R}, \mathrm{Pc}_q^{D_q}\}_{q<Q}$, an element of $X^{D,R}$ is noted $X_{d,r}$ and X_d^R (resp. X_r^D) refers to a row matrix (resp. a column matrix). In the context of the SCA, the traces are commonly compared with distributions of intermediate values manipulated by the target and dependent of a secret variable (generally a cryptographic key). We store those distributions in the matrix $Y^{S,Q,K,B}$, with S the dimension of the leakage

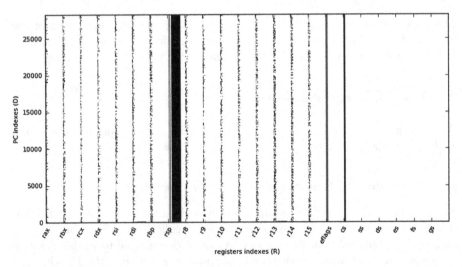

Fig. 2. Representation of a recorded trace of a WBC algorithm using GDB, black points correspond to one values, and white to zero values.

---

[1] http://ctf.newae.com/.

model, B the number of bytes of the secret and K the number of possible values for each secret bytes (256 if no values are forbidden). For example, if the target algorithm is the Advanced Encryption Standard (AES)-128, and if the focused sensitive intermediate values are the output of the Substitution-box function (SBOX) at the first round, the distribution for a *bit-level* model is expressed as in the following Formula 1:

$$Y^{S,Q,K,B} = \left\{ (Sbox(P_{q,b} \oplus k) \ \& \ 2^s) >> s \right\}_{\substack{s<8,k<256 \\ q<Q,b<16}} \tag{1}$$

The choice of the *bit-level* model is motivated by the bit representation of the recorded data $X^{D,R} \in (\mathbb{Z}/2\mathbb{Z})^{D,R}$. To lighten the notations, the dimension B is not always precised.

2.2 Realignment Algorithm

The first problematic met in the proposed study is the misalignment of the data. Indeed, misalignment could be due to the randomization of the execution, or more generally, by the presence of conditional branches. A vertical alignment is a prerequisite point to realize vertical analysis. Most of the vertical analysis techniques, as CPA [4] or Linear Regression Analysis (LRA) [7] need the data $X_d^{R,Q}$ manipulated at the sample $d < D$ to come from the same operation. The resynchronization is a well known and a well studied problem in the SCA domain [6,8,10,12]. All the proposed algorithms of resynchronization are based on the leaking values distribution in the temporal or in the frequency domain. In our case we have access to additional information thanks to the PC values. In fact, the PC values can be viewed as an identifier. For example $\forall q < Q, \forall d_q < D_q$, $Pc_{d_q,q}$ is an identifier for the data $X_{d_q,q}^R$. Furthermore, if for $d_0 < D_0, d_1 < D_1$, $Pc_{d_0,0} = Pc_{d_1,1}$ it means that the two datasets $X_{d_0,0}^R$ and $X_{d_1,1}^R$ are the result of the same operation in the code (at the assembly level). However the presence of a loop in the source code could imply repetitions of PC value. Hence evince, if the two datasets $X_{d_0,0}^R, X_{d_1,1}^R$ result form the same operation they may come from distinct iterations. Moreover, conditional branching in the code produce misalignment. The goal of the proposed realignment algorithm is to transform the raw dataset $\{X_q^{D_q,R}, Pc_q^{D_q}\}_{q<Q}$ into the dataset $\{X^{D,R,Q}, Pc^D\}$ where $\forall \ d < D, \ \forall \ q_0 < Q, \ \forall q_1 < Q, \ X_{d,q_0}^R$ and X_{d,q_1}^R result in the same operation, at the same iteration. The main constraints are the execution time and memory required. We proposed here a single-pass realignment algorithm detailed in Schedule 1. The fact that we only need the PC values to resynchronize the data significantly reduces the computational time and the needed memory. Indeed, our algorithm of resynchronization only have to read one time the $D_q q<Q$ 64-bit PC values instead of the $\{X^{D_q,R}\}_{q<Q}$ bit of data in the case of an algorithm based on the entire dataset. To provide details on the last assumption of the Eq. 2, the two Definition 1 are needed. The whole algorithm described in the Schedule 1 reveals the fix-points and the pseudo fix-points that are automatically realigned.

Definition 1. *Fix-point and pseudo fix-point*

- **A fix-point** *is a PC value with a deterministic presence and a deterministic number of occurrence:*

$$\text{Pc}_d \in \{\text{Pc}_q^{D_q}\}_{q<Q} \text{ is a fix-point}$$

$$\Longleftrightarrow \exists\, m \in \mathbb{N}, \sum_{d_q=1}^{D_q} \begin{cases} 1 & \text{if } \text{Pc}_{d_q,q} = \text{Pc}_d \\ 0 & \text{otherwise} \end{cases} = m \ \forall q < Q.$$

- **A pseudo fix-point** *is a PC value with a deterministic number of appearance, in the case it appears (so a fix-point is also a pseudo fix-point):*

$$\text{Pc}_d \in \{\text{Pc}_q^{D_q}\}_{q<Q} \text{ is a pseudo fix-point}$$

$$\Longleftrightarrow \exists\, m \in \mathbb{N}, \sum_{d_q=1}^{D_q} \begin{cases} 1 & \text{if } \text{Pc}_{d_q,q} = \text{Pc}_d \\ 0 & \text{otherwise} \end{cases} \in \{0, m\} \ \forall q < Q.$$

To illustrate the proposed realignment algorithm, we first start with an application to a simple example. The Fig. 3 displays a control flow graph with a conditional branching, a loop and a conditional branching inside. The letters A, B, C, ..., I are the PC values. The probability associated to each conditional branching are p_0 and p_1. The presented results have been obtained with $p_0 = 1/2$ and $p_1 = 1/3$. Three distinct executions of the proposed flow graph gave the following PC successions:

$$\{\text{Pc}^{D_q}\}_{q<3} = \begin{cases} \text{Pc}^{D_0} = A, B, D, E, H, I, E, H, I, E, F, G, I \\ \text{Pc}^{D_1} = A, B, D, E, F, G, I, E, H, I, E, F, G, I \\ \text{Pc}^{D_2} = A, C, D, E, H, I, E, H, I, E, F, G, I \end{cases} \quad (2)$$

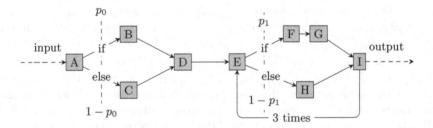

Fig. 3. Control flow of the presented example

The application of the proposed realignment algorithm, described in the Schedule 1, to a thousand execution of the flow graph detailed in Fig. 3, gave the matrix $\#\text{Pc}^{D',Q}$ displayed in Fig. 4.

1. get the set of all possible PC values:

$$\mathrm{Pc}^{D'} = \bigcup_{q=0}^{Q-1} \mathrm{Pc}_q^{D_q}, \text{ with } D' \text{ the number of distinct possible values of PC over } Q$$

2. accumulate in the matrix $\#\mathrm{Pc}^{D',Q}$ the numbers of times each PC appears in each trace:

$$\#\mathrm{Pc}^{D',Q} = \left[\#\mathrm{Pc}_{d,q} = \sum_{d_q=0}^{D_q-1} \begin{cases} 1, & \text{if } \mathrm{Pc}_{d_q,q} = \mathrm{Pc}_d \\ 0, & \text{otherwise} \end{cases} \right]_{\substack{d<D' \\ q<Q}}$$

3. the fix-points and the pseudo fix-points are stored in F^D with its associated number of appearance:

$$\mathrm{F}^{D'',2} = \{(\mathrm{Pc}_d, m_d) \in (\mathrm{Pc}^{D'}, \mathbb{N}) | \exists\ m \in \mathbb{N},\ \#\mathrm{Pc}_{d,q} \in \{0,m\},\ \forall\ q < Q, \}$$

4. finally the axis $\mathrm{Pc}^{D(=\sum_{d=1}^{D''} m_d)}$ of PC used for the alignment is created using $\mathrm{F}^{D'',2}$:

$$\mathrm{Pc}^D = \{ \overbrace{\mathrm{F}_{0,0}, \ldots, \mathrm{F}_{0,0}}^{\mathrm{F}_{0,1} times}, \ldots, \overbrace{\mathrm{F}_{D''-1,0}, \ldots, \mathrm{F}_{D''-1,0}}^{\mathrm{F}_{D''-1,1} times} \}$$

$$= \{ \overbrace{\mathrm{Pc}_0, \ldots, \mathrm{Pc}_0}^{m_0 times}, \ldots, \overbrace{\mathrm{Pc}_{D''-1}, \ldots, \mathrm{Pc}_{D''-1}}^{m_{D''-1} times} \}$$

Schedule 1. Step-by-step description of the realignment algorithm

The realignment algorithm designates A, D, E and I as fix-points; B, C as pseudo fix-points while the PC F, G and H could not be realigned in the preliminary study. Those PC need more information to be realigned. Finally, the realignment algorithm gives the following output:

$$\mathrm{F}^{D''} = \{(A,1), (B,1), (C,1), (D,1), (E,3), (I,3)\}$$
$$\mathrm{Pc}^D = \{A, B, C, D, E, E, E, I, I, I\}.$$

If we go back to the three execution traces given in the Eq. 2, the resynchronization is done as written in Fig. 5, with in red the elements affected by the realignment. The algorithm of realignment have been applied to a real-world masked implementation of an AES-128, the results obtained are displayed in Fig. 7. It reveals that some PC, around the index 100 seem to be neither fix-points nor pseudo fix-points. This aspect is confirmed by the results of the computation of the mean and the standard deviation of $\#\mathrm{Pc}^{D',Q}$ over Q displayed in Fig. 7. In fact, this three figures show that two PC values have non-constant number of apparition in all the executions. In addition to give the PC that causes the

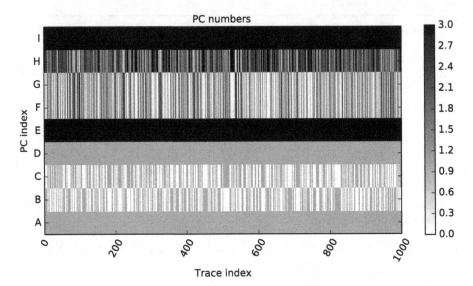

Fig. 4. $\#\text{Pc}^{D',Q}$ for $Q = 1000$ executions of the flow graph described in Fig. 3, with $D' = 8$ and $\text{Pc}^{D'} = \{A, B, C, D, \ldots, I\}$. The colors refer to the number of time each PC appear in each execution.

$\{X^{D,q}\}_{q<3} =$

$$\begin{cases} X^{D,R,0} = \{X^{0,R,0}, X^{1,R,0}, 0, X^{2,R,0}, X^{3,R,0}, X^{6,R,0}, X^{9,R,0}, X^{5,R,0}, X^{8,R,0}, X^{12,R,0}\} \\ X^{D,R,1} = \{X^{0,R,1}, X^{1,R,1}, 0, X^{2,R,1}, X^{3,R,1}, X^{7,R,1}, X^{10,R,1}, X^{6,R,1}, X^{9,R,1}, X^{13,R,1}\} \\ X^{D,R,2} = \{X^{0,R,2}, 0, X^{1,R,2}, X^{2,R,2}, X^{3,R,2}, X^{6,R,2}, X^{9,R,2}, X^{5,R,2}, X^{8,R,2}, X^{12,R,2}\} \end{cases}$$

Fig. 5. Results of the resynchronization

misalignment and the resynchronized axis of PC, the algorithm helps to find the lines in the source code that provoke the misalignment. This matching from the PC values to the source lines code is made easier by the usage of GDB to record the leakage. Furthermore, the localization of the misalignment origins helps to identify timing leakage. In our example illustrated in Fig. 7, the realignment reveals that the misalignment is caused by the function *xtime* transcribed in Fig. 6a. This function multiplies the input b by two in $GF(2^8)$, but this implementation contains conditional statement that misalign the data and that could produce time leakage. A possible improvement can be the usage of the constant time implementation of *xtime* provided in Fig. 6b. Our realignment algorithm immediately and precisely identify the non-constant time line in the source code. This information is very useful for a developer that want to implement constant time algorithm aim to protect his code against the *timing attacks*.

```
unsigned char xtime (unsigned char b)
{
    unsigned char const tmp = b<<1;
    return (b&0x80)?(tmp^0x1b):tmp;
}
```

(a) implementation with conditional branch

```
unsigned char xtime (unsigned char b)
{
    return (x<<1)^((x>>7)*0x1b);
}
```

(b) constant time implementation

Fig. 6. Implementations of xtime used in the MixColumns function of the AES

2.3 Data Reduction

Once the recorded data are realigned, if necessary, we have now access to the resynchronized data $X^{D,R,Q}$ and the associated PC vector Pc^D. Now that it is possible to analyze vertically the data, two questions arise. Are all the data in $X^{D,R,Q}$ relevant? And is it possible to reduce the dimension of the data to analyze? To answer these questions, we define the notion of activity matrix in Definition 2 and of transition matrix Definition 3.

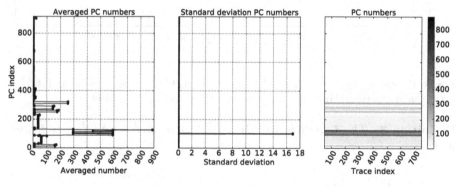

Fig. 7. Results of the application of the realignment algorithm to a masked implementation of an AES-128. The mean (on the left) and the standard deviation (in the middle) over Q of $\#\text{Pc}^{D',Q}$ (in the right) for thousand executions ($Q = 1000$) and around thousand distinct values of PC ($D' \simeq 1000$). The colors refer to the number of time each PC appear in each trace. This results have been obtained by executing a real-world masked implementation of an AES-128.

Definition 2. *The **activity matrix** $A^{D,R}$ of a given set $X^{D,R,Q}$ is defined as follow:*

$$A^{D,R} = \left[A_{d,r} = \begin{cases} 1, & \text{if } \sum_{q=0}^{Q-1} X_{d,r,q} \notin \{Q,0\} \\ 0, & \text{otherwise} \end{cases} \right]_{\substack{d<D, \\ r<R}}$$

The activity matrix of a given dataset identifies the points $((d,r) \in D \times R)$ with a non-zero variance over Q.

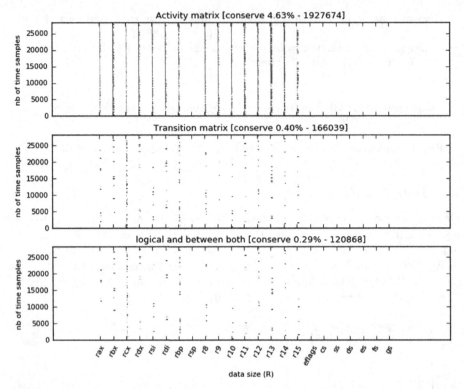

Fig. 8. Illustration of the matrices $A^{D,R}$ (on the top), $T^{D,R}$ (in the middle) and $A^{D,R} \wedge$ $T^{D,R}$ (on the bottom). In white are displayed the 0 and the 1 in black.

Definition 3. *The transition matrix* $T^{D,R}$ *of a given set $X^{D,R,Q}$ is defined as follow:*

$$T^{D,R} = \left[T_{d,r} = \begin{cases} 1, & \text{if } d = 0 \\ \bigvee_{q=1}^{Q} X_{d-1,r} \oplus X_{d,r} & \text{otherwise} \end{cases} \right]_{\substack{d<D, \\ r<R}}$$

The transition matrix identifies the points $((d,r) \in D \times R)$ that change at least one time between the PC d and $d+1$ over all the traces. Both matrix $T^{D,R}$ and $A^{D,Q}$ could be computed in-line accumulating each trace. Then, we identify the points that could leak information as $L = \{(d,r) \in (D \times R) | T_{d,r} \wedge A_{d,r} = 1\}$. In Fig. 8, the matrices $A^{D,R}$, $T^{D,R}$ and $A^{D,R} \wedge T^{D,R}$ obtain analyzing a data set of 250 traces of execution of an AES WBC implementation. We observe that our algorithm permits to identify the 0.29% from the entire samples that could leak information. Thus we conserve only 20190 PC values over 28277 and 120 bit register over 1472. This data reduction speeds up the analysis and reduce the memory footprint analyzing only the data $X^{L,Q}$. Furthermore we take advantage of the very low density of the sparse matrices $\{X_q^{D,R}\}_{q<Q}$ to reduce the storage required for the traces. The storage of sparse matrices is a well study problematic

Table 1. Benchmark of the needed memory to store the traces $X^{D,R,Q}$ for $Q = 250$ using distinct formats.

	$\{X_q^{D,R}\}_{q<Q}$ 8-bit matrix	$\{X_q^{D,R}\}_{q<Q}$ CSC 8-bit matrix	$\{T_q^{D,R}\}_{q<Q}$ CSC 8-bit matrix	
Size	$9,7\,\mathrm{GB}$	$2,6\,\mathrm{GB}$	$132\,\mathrm{MB}$	
with $\{T_q^{D,R}\}_{q<Q} =$	$\begin{cases} X_{d,r,q}, & \text{if } d=0 \\ X_{d-1,r,q} \oplus X_{d,r,q} & \text{otherwise} \end{cases}_{\substack{q<Q, r<R \\ d<D}}$			(3)

in computer science and a lot of solutions are freely provided. The following Table 1 summarizes the gain in storage that we obtain using a method called *Compressed Sparse Column matrix (CSC)* present in *scipy*[2]. Thus, the needed memory to store the traces $X^{D,R,Q}$ decrease from $9,7\,\mathrm{GB}$ to $132\,\mathrm{MB}$ using the CSC compression on the matrix $T^{D,R,Q}$ defined in Eq. 3.

2.4 Distinguisher: CPA

The potential leakage points have been identified and stored in the dataset $X^{L,Q}$. To know if some of those points leak sensitive information, we use the CPA proposed by Brier *et al.* in 2004 [4]. In our case, the guessed intermediate values are stored in $Y^{S,Q,K,B}$ as explained in the Eq. 1. The CPA is based on the computation of the *Pearson coefficient* between $X^{L,Q}$ and $Y^{S,Q,K,B}$ to discriminate the right key $\{k_b^\star\}_{b<B}$ as defined in the following Eq. 4.

$$\mathcal{D}(X^{L,Q}, Y^{S,Q,K,B}) = \left\{ \frac{\mathrm{cov}(X^{L,Q}, Y_{s,k,b}^Q)}{\sigma(X^{L,Q})\sigma(Y_{s,k,b}^Q)} \right\}_{\substack{k<256, S<8 \\ b<16}}, \tag{4}$$

where σ is the variance and cov the covariance both over Q.

Then we identify the leaking samples using the *Absolute distinguishing margin (AbsMarg)* proposed by Whitnall *et al.* in [14] and recalled in the following Eq. 5. The usage of the *AbsMarg* metric is motivated by the presence of ghost peaks in the results of CPA. We take advantage that we analyze binary dataset to simplify the accumulative formula of the *Pearson coefficient* given in Eq. 6. This simplification speeds up the analysis and reduces the memory footprint.

$AbsMarg\ (\mathcal{D}(X^{L,Q}, Y_{s,b}^Q))$

$$= \frac{\mathcal{D}(X^{L,Q}, Y_{s,k^\star,b}^Q) - \max_{\substack{k_b<256 \\ k \neq k_b^\star}}\{\mathcal{D}(X^{L,Q}, Y_{s,k,b}^Q)\}}{\underbrace{\mathcal{D}(Y_{s,k^\star,b}^Q, Y_{s,k^\star,b}^Q)}_{=1} - \max_{\substack{k_b<256 \\ k \neq k_b^\star}}\{\mathcal{D}(Y_{s,k^\star,b}^Q, Y_{s,k,b}^Q)\}} \tag{5}$$

---

[2] https://www.scipy.org/.

$$\mathcal{D}(X^{L,Q}, Y^{Q}_{s,k,b})$$

$$= \frac{\text{acc\_xy} - \frac{1}{Q}(\text{acc\_x.acc\_y})}{\sqrt{\text{acc\_xx} - \frac{1}{Q}(\text{acc\_x.acc\_x})}\sqrt{\text{acc\_yy} - \frac{1}{Q}(\text{acc\_y.acc\_y})}}$$

$$= \frac{\text{acc\_xy} - \frac{1}{Q}(\text{acc\_x.acc\_y})}{\sqrt{\text{acc\_x} - \frac{1}{Q}(\text{acc\_x.acc\_x})}\sqrt{\text{acc\_y} - \frac{1}{Q}(\text{acc\_y.acc\_y})}} \qquad (6)$$

where we define the acc_$\star$ as follow,

$$\text{acc\_xy} = \sum_{q=1}^{Q} X^{L}_{q}.Y_{s,k,b,q}$$

$$\text{acc\_x} = \sum_{q=1}^{Q} X^{L}_{q} = \sum_{q=1}^{Q} (X^{L}_{q})^2 = \text{acc\_xx}$$

$$\text{acc\_y} = \sum_{q=1}^{Q} Y_{s,k,b,q} = \sum_{q=1}^{Q} (Y_{s,k,b,q})^2 = \text{acc\_yy}$$

3 Results

In the following analyses, we use the known-plaintext attack model, which means that an attacker only requires access to the random inputs. Additionally, the attack could be performed with just the compiled binary. The source code access is only mandatory to map the leakages to the source code.

3.1 WBC Analysis

As presented in the previous Subsect. 2.4 we use the CPA to reveal leakage from $X^{L,Q}$ and discriminate the secret key $\{k_b^{\star}\}_{b<16}$ from the guesses $\{k_b | k_b \neq k_b^{\star}\}_{b<16}$. As proposed in [1], we extend our leakage model Y to take into account the two products computed during the MixColumn execution. In [1] authors proposed to compute three distinct 8-bit Differential Power Analysis (DPA) while the two products only add ten new bit-distributions to the initial model. Indeed the model extension makes growing the model size S from 8 to 18, and not to 24, because 6 bit-distributions are redundant as resumed in the following Proposition 1.

Proposition 1. $\forall x \in \mathbb{N}$, with $x < 256$ the products by two and three computed in the MixColumn function respect the following properties:

– the bit 2 of 2.x is equal to the bit 1 of x
– the bit 5 of 2.x is equal to the bit 4 of x
– the bit 6 of 2.x is equal to the bit 5 of x
– the bit 7 of 2.x is equal to the bit 6 of x

– *the bit 0 of 2.x is equal to the bit 7 of x*
– *the bit 0 of 3.x is equal to the bit 1 of 2.x*

The Proposition 1 permits to construct an extended model expressed in the following formula 7

$$Y^{S,Q,K,B} =$$

$$\left[\begin{cases} Sbox \ (P_{q,b} \oplus k) \ \& \ 2^s, & \text{if } s < 8 \\ (2.Sbox \ (P_{q,b} \oplus k)) \ \& \ 2^{v[s-8]}, & \text{if } 7 < s < 11, \text{ with } v = \{1,3,4\} \\ (3.Sbox \ (P_{q,b} \oplus k)) \ \& \ 2^{s-10}, & \text{if } 10 < s \end{cases} \right]_{\substack{s<18,k<256,\\q<Q,b<16}} \quad (7)$$

The Fig. 9 illustrates the results obtained by applying the CPA $Q = 250$ recorded traces from the WBC implementation provided at the Capture The Flag (CTF) challenge of CHES-2016. The CPA has been computed for all samples L (120k) but to facilitate the visualization we focus on the first 20k samples where the leaking ones are localized. In grey we display the results obtained with the bad guesses: $\left\{ \max_{k_b<256,k_b\neq k_b^*} (\mathcal{D}(X^{L,Q}, Y^Q_{s,k,b})) \right\}_{b<16,s<18}$ and in color the result obtained with the right key: $\left\{ \mathcal{D}(X^{L,Q}, Y^Q_{s,k^*,b}) \right\}_{b<16,s<18}$. To improve the discrimination of the leaking samples from the computed CPA we use the *AbsMarg* displayed in Fig. 10, in which we apply a threshold at 0.25.

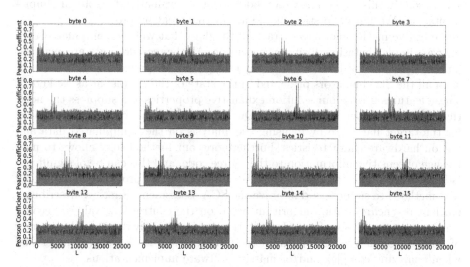

Fig. 9. Results of the CPA on recorded data from a WBC implementation.

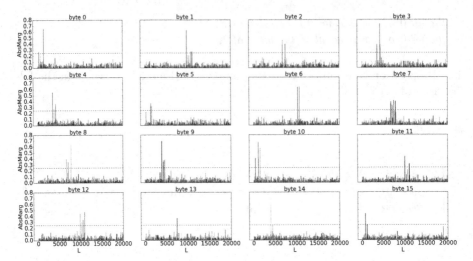

Fig. 10. *AbsMarg* of the CPA's results. Only the samples with a positive *AbsMarg* samples are plotted.

Then, using the PC values we map the identified leaking samples to the source code. We summarize the obtained results in the two Table 2 provided in the appendix in which we link each leakage to a line code, a leaking bit model, and bit register.

4   Conclusion

We present in this paper a new methodology of SC evaluation for software implementation. We push the state of the art in that field by providing a practical and effective methodology to extract all the data that will be manipulated by a software implementation during its execution. All the recorded data are analyzed independently, at bit level, without any leakage model applied to generate traces as in all the SC-simulators presented in the state of the art (as far as we know). These features give to our solution exhaustive properties and suppress the noise that a leakage model could generate. Our exhaustive approach makes it agnostic for the target hardware by focusing the analysis on the manipulated data and not on hardware characteristics. Furthermore, our methodology allows to map leakage of sensitive information to the source code, and this can be of significant help for an evaluator or a developer. Advantageously, we provide two additional new methods to support and improve the SCA assessment. First, we describe an efficient resynchronization algorithm based on the control flow values. Second, we give a methodology of samples selection to significantly decrease the number of samples to analyze without any loss of information. Both features are crucial when analyzing complex and/or massive software implementations.

Acknowledgments. This work was partly supported by Institute for Information & communications Technology Promotion (IITP) grant funded by the Korea government (MSIT) (No. 2016-0-00399, Study on secure key hiding technology for IoT devices [KeyHAS Project]) and other project(s).

Appendix

Table 2. Leakage characterization and mapping to the source code

Line	Source code	Reg. name	Bit reg.	Leaking value	Leaking bit	Key byte
1.4086:	v16 = lookup_nibble2(table_4436, v16, v18, 0);	rsi	1	x	7	0
1.4128:	v22 = lookup_nibble2(table_4499, v22, v23, 0);	rbp	0	3.x	4	0
1.4420:	v18 = lookup_nibble(table_13890, v4);	r14	3	x	4	1
1.4417:	v2 = lookup_nibble2(table_4934, v16, v2, 0);	r15	1	3.x	1	1
1.4417:	v2 = lookup_nibble2(table_4934, v16, v2, 0);	r13	3	x	4	1
1.4421:	v19 = lookup_nibble(table_13891, v4);	r13	2	x	4	1
1.4422:	v16 = lookup_nibble2(table_4940, v16, v18, 0);	rcx	2	x	4	1
1.4421:	v19 = lookup_nibble(table_13891, v4);	r13	1	3.x	1	1
1.4421:	v19 = lookup_nibble(table_13891, v4);	r13	0	3.x	1	1
1.4418:	v16 = lookup_nibble(table_13888, v3);	rdx	0	3.x	1	1
1.4463:	v4 = lookup_nibble(table_13915, v4);	r9	0	3.x	3	1
1.4462:	v35 = lookup_nibble(table_13914, v4);	rdi	0	3.x	3	1
1.4464:	v34 = lookup_nibble2(table_5003, v34, v35, 0);	rcx	2	3.x	3	1
1.4315:	v21 = lookup_nibble(table_13815, v13);	rbx	0	3.x	7	2
1.4316:	v18 = lookup_nibble2(table_4779, v18, v20, 0);	r13	1	3.x	6	2
1.4343:	v33 = lookup_nibble(table_13831, v13);	r12	2	3.x	3	2
1.4343:	v33 = lookup_nibble(table_13831, v13);	r12	3	3.x	3	2
1.4199:	v17 = lookup_nibble2(table_4605, v17, v19, 0);	r10	0	3.x	7	3
1.4199:	v17 = lookup_nibble2(table_4605, v17, v19, 0);	r10	1	x	4	3
1.4199:	v17 = lookup_nibble2(table_4605, v17, v19, 0);	r10	3	3.x	7	3
1.4200:	v18 = lookup_nibble(table_13732, v11);	rbx	0	3.x	7	3
1.4200:	v18 = lookup_nibble(table_13732, v11);	rbx	1	x	4	3
1.4200:	v18 = lookup_nibble(table_13732, v11);	rbx	3	3.x	7	3
1.4204:	v18 = lookup_nibble2(table_4611, v18, v20, 0);	rbx	0	x	4	3
1.4204:	v18 = lookup_nibble2(table_4611, v18, v20, 0);	rbx	2	3.x	7	3
1.4204:	v18 = lookup_nibble2(table_4611, v18, v20, 0);	rcx	0	x	4	3
1.4204:	v18 = lookup_nibble2(table_4611, v18, v20, 0);	rcx	2	3.x	7	3
1.4204:	v18 = lookup_nibble2(table_4611, v18, v20, 0);	rsi	2	3.x	7	3
1.4230:	v28 = lookup_nibble(table_13750, v12);	rbp	0	x	4	3
1.4227:	v21 = lookup_nibble2(table_4647, v21, v27, 0);	rbx	2	x	0	3
1.4231:	v29 = lookup_nibble(table_13751, v12);	rcx	0	x	4	3
1.4232:	v26 = lookup_nibble2(table_4653, v26, v28, 0);	rcx	2	x	4	3
1.4232:	v26 = lookup_nibble2(table_4653, v26, v28, 0);	rbp	2	x	0	3
1.4232:	v26 = lookup_nibble2(table_4653, v26, v28, 0);	rbp	1	x	0	3
1.4228:	v26 = lookup_nibble(table_13748, v11);	r12	4	x	4	3

(continued)

Table 2. (*continued*)

Line	Source code	Reg. name	Bit reg.	Leaking value	Leaking bit	Key byte
1.4228:	v26 = lookup_nibble(table_13748, v11);	r12	5	x	4	3
1.4228:	v26 = lookup_nibble(table_13748, v11);	r12	6	x	4	3
1.4228:	v26 = lookup_nibble(table_13748, v11);	r12	7	x	4	3
1.4232:	v26 = lookup_nibble2(table_4653, v26, v28, 0);	rcx	1	x	0	3
1.4233:	v27 = lookup_nibble2(table_4654, v27, v29, 0);	rbx	4	x	4	3
1.4233:	v27 = lookup_nibble2(table_4654, v27, v29, 0);	rbx	5	x	4	3
1.4233:	v27 = lookup_nibble2(table_4654, v27, v29, 0);	rbx	6	x	4	3
1.4233:	v27 = lookup_nibble2(table_4654, v27, v29, 0);	rbx	7	x	4	3
1.4232:	v26 = lookup_nibble2(table_4653, v26, v28, 0);	rbx	3	x	4	3
1.4232:	v26 = lookup_nibble2(table_4653, v26, v28, 0);	rbx	4	x	4	3
1.4232:	v26 = lookup_nibble2(table_4653, v26, v28, 0);	rbx	5	x	4	3
1.4232:	v26 = lookup_nibble2(table_4653, v26, v28, 0);	rbx	6	x	4	3
1.4233:	v27 = lookup_nibble2(table_4654, v27, v29, 0);	rcx	3	x	4	3
1.4233:	v27 = lookup_nibble2(table_4654, v27, v29, 0);	rcx	4	x	4	3
1.4233:	v27 = lookup_nibble2(table_4654, v27, v29, 0);	rcx	5	x	4	3
1.4233:	v27 = lookup_nibble2(table_4654, v27, v29, 0);	rcx	6	x	4	3
1.4198:	v16 = lookup_nibble2(table_4604, v16, v18, 0);	rax	1	x	1	4
1.4198:	v16 = lookup_nibble2(table_4604, v16, v18, 0);	rax	1	3.x	4	4
1.4198:	v16 = lookup_nibble2(table_4604, v16, v18, 0);	rax	3	x	1	4
1.4211:	v21 = lookup_nibble(table_13739, v6);	rbp	3	3.x	6	4
1.4225:	v27 = lookup_nibble(table_13747, v6);	rbp	2	3.x	5	4
1.4225:	v27 = lookup_nibble(table_13747, v6);	rbp	3	2.x	3	4
1.4127:	v5 = lookup_nibble(table_13675, v5);	r9	0	2.x	3	5
1.4126:	v23 = lookup_nibble(table_13674, v5);	rdi	0	2.x	3	5
1.4123:	v21 = lookup_nibble2(table_4493, v21, v23, 0);	r8	2	3.x	7	5
1.4127:	v5 = lookup_nibble(table_13675, v5);	r14	2	3.x	7	5
1.4127:	v5 = lookup_nibble(table_13675, v5);	r14	1	3.x	7	5
1.4128:	v22 = lookup_nibble2(table_4499, v22, v23, 0);	rcx	1	3.x	7	5
1.4127:	v5 = lookup_nibble(table_13675, v5);	rcx	2	2.x	3	5
1.4441:	v35 = lookup_nibble(table_13903, v14);	r12	2	3.x	3	6
1.4442:	v20 = lookup_nibble2(table_4968, v20, v34, 0);	r15	1	2.x	3	6
1.4442:	v20 = lookup_nibble2(table_4968, v20, v34, 0);	r15	3	2.x	3	6
1.4456:	v34 = lookup_nibble2(table_4989, v34, v36, 0);	r15	3	3.x	4	6
1.4311:	v17 = lookup_nibble2(table_4773, v17, v19, 0);	r10	1	3.x	5	7
1.4311:	v17 = lookup_nibble2(table_4773, v17, v19, 0);	r10	2	3.x	1	7
1.4312:	v18 = lookup_nibble(table_13812, v8);	rbx	1	3.x	5	7
1.4312:	v18 = lookup_nibble(table_13812, v8);	rbx	2	3.x	1	7
1.4316:	v18 = lookup_nibble2(table_4779, v18, v20, 0);	rbx	0	3.x	5	7
1.4316:	v18 = lookup_nibble2(table_4779, v18, v20, 0);	rbx	1	3.x	1	7
1.4316:	v18 = lookup_nibble2(table_4779, v18, v20, 0);	rcx	0	3.x	5	7
1.4316:	v18 = lookup_nibble2(table_4779, v18, v20, 0);	rcx	1	3.x	1	7
1.4328:	v30 = lookup_nibble(table_13822, v13);	rbp	3	x	3	7
1.4328:	v30 = lookup_nibble(table_13822, v13);	rbp	3	x	7	7
1.4329:	v31 = lookup_nibble(table_13823, v13);	rcx	3	x	3	7
1.4329:	v31 = lookup_nibble(table_13823, v13);	rcx	3	x	7	7
1.4329:	v31 = lookup_nibble(table_13823, v13);	rcx	2	x	3	7
1.4329:	v31 = lookup_nibble(table_13823, v13);	rcx	2	x	7	7
1.4342:	v32 = lookup_nibble(table_13830, v13);	rbp	0	3.x	7	7
1.4342:	v32 = lookup_nibble(table_13830, v13);	rbp	1	3.x	3	7
1.4343:	v33 = lookup_nibble(table_13831, v13);	rcx	0	3.x	7	7

(*continued*)

Table 2. (*continued*)

Line	Source code	Reg. name	Bit reg.	Leaking value	Leaking bit	Key byte
1.4343:	v33 = lookup_nibble(table_13831, v13);	rcx	1	3.x	3	7
1.4343:	v33 = lookup_nibble(table_13831, v13);	rcx	0	3.x	3	7
1.4344:	v30 = lookup_nibble2(table_4821, v30, v32, 0);	rcx	2	3.x	7	7
1.4357:	v13 = lookup_nibble(table_13839, v13);	r14	0	3.x	4	7
1.4358:	v7 = lookup_nibble2(table_4842, v7, v31, 0);	r13	0	3.x	4	7
1.4359:	v8 = lookup_nibble2(table_4843, v8, v13, 0);	rcx	2	3.x	4	7
1.4309:	v19 = lookup_nibble(table_13811, v7);	rdx	0	x	2	8
1.4324:	v18 = lookup_nibble2(table_4793, v18, v20, 0);	rbx	0	x	1	8
1.4352:	v30 = lookup_nibble2(table_4835, v30, v31, 0);	rbp	0	3.x	2	8
1.4352:	v30 = lookup_nibble2(table_4835, v30, v31, 0);	rbp	3	3.x	2	8
1.4207:	v17 = lookup_nibble2(table_4619, v17, v19, 0);	r10	2	3.x	5	9
1.4208:	v18 = lookup_nibble(table_13736, v1);	rbp	2	3.x	5	9
1.4208:	v18 = lookup_nibble(table_13736, v1);	rbp	1	3.x	5	9
1.4212:	v18 = lookup_nibble2(table_4625, v18, v20, 0);	rcx	1	3.x	5	9
1.4225:	v27 = lookup_nibble(table_13747, v6);	r11	2	3.x	6	9
1.4224:	v26 = lookup_nibble(table_13746, v6);	r14	2	3.x	6	9
1.4221:	v19 = lookup_nibble2(table_4640, v19, v21, 0);	r10	0	2.x	3	9
1.4221:	v19 = lookup_nibble2(table_4640, v19, v21, 0);	r10	2	3.x	5	9
1.4221:	v19 = lookup_nibble2(table_4640, v19, v21, 0);	r14	1	3.x	6	9
1.4225:	v27 = lookup_nibble(table_13747, v6);	rcx	1	3.x	6	9
1.4222:	v20 = lookup_nibble(table_13744, v1);	rbp	0	2.x	3	9
1.4222:	v20 = lookup_nibble(table_13744, v1);	rbp	2	3.x	5	9
1.4225:	v27 = lookup_nibble(table_13747, v6);	rbp	1	3.x	5	9
1.4226:	v20 = lookup_nibble2(table_4646, v20, v26, 0);	rcx	1	3.x	5	9
1.4234:	v20 = lookup_nibble2(table_4660, v20, v26, 0);	rcx	2	2.x	3	9
1.4238:	v27 = lookup_nibble(table_13754, v6);	r9	3	2.x	3	9
1.4239:	v6 = lookup_nibble(table_13755, v6);	r8	2	3.x	2	9
1.4235:	v21 = lookup_nibble2(table_4661, v21, v27, 0);	rdi	3	2.x	3	9
1.4240:	v26 = lookup_nibble2(table_4667, v26, v27, 0);	rdi	2	2.x	3	9
1.4239:	v6 = lookup_nibble(table_13755, v6);	r15	2	3.x	2	9
1.4239:	v6 = lookup_nibble(table_13755, v6);	rcx	2	2.x	3	9
1.4239:	v6 = lookup_nibble(table_13755, v6);	r15	1	3.x	2	9
1.4241:	v1 = lookup_nibble2(table_4668, v1, v6, 0);	rcx	1	3.x	2	9
1.4091:	v21 = lookup_nibble(table_13655, v15);	rbx	1	x	7	10
1.4092:	v18 = lookup_nibble2(table_4443, v18, v20, 0);	r13	1	3.x	6	10
1.4119:	v25 = lookup_nibble(table_13671, v15);	r12	0	x	3	10
1.4119:	v25 = lookup_nibble(table_13671, v15);	r12	1	x	0	10
1.4120:	v22 = lookup_nibble2(table_4485, v22, v24, 0);	r15	0	2.x	4	10
1.4134:	v5 = lookup_nibble2(table_4506, v5, v23, 0);	rbp	1	x	3	10
1.4426:	v20 = lookup_nibble(table_13894, v14);	r11	3	3.x	7	11
1.4423:	v17 = lookup_nibble2(table_4941, v17, v19, 0);	r10	2	2.x	3	11
1.4427:	v21 = lookup_nibble(table_13895, v14);	rcx	3	3.x	7	11
1.4427:	v21 = lookup_nibble(table_13895, v14);	rcx	2	3.x	7	11
1.4424:	v18 = lookup_nibble(table_13892, v9);	rbx	2	2.x	3	11
1.4428:	v18 = lookup_nibble2(table_4947, v18, v20, 0);	rbx	1	2.x	3	11
1.4428:	v18 = lookup_nibble2(table_4947, v18, v20, 0);	rcx	1	2.x	3	11
1.4465:	v3 = lookup_nibble2(table_5004, v3, v4, 0);	r14	3	x	0	11
1.4465:	v3 = lookup_nibble2(table_5004, v3, v4, 0);	r14	3	3.x	3	11
1.4470:	v4 = lookup_nibble2(table_5010, v4, v35, 0);	rsi	3	x	0	11
1.4470:	v4 = lookup_nibble2(table_5010, v4, v35, 0);	rsi	3	3.x	3	11
1.4470:	v4 = lookup_nibble2(table_5010, v4, v35, 0);	rsi	2	x	0	11

(*continued*)

Table 2. (*continued*)

Line	Source code	Reg. name	Bit reg.	Leaking value	Leaking bit	Key byte
l.4470:	v4 = lookup_nibble2(table_5010, v4, v35, 0);	rsi	2	3.x	3	11
l.4470:	v4 = lookup_nibble2(table_5010, v4, v35, 0);	rax	2	x	0	11
l.4470:	v4 = lookup_nibble2(table_5010, v4, v35, 0);	rax	2	3.x	3	11
l.4425:	v19 = lookup_nibble(table_13893, v9);	rax	1	3.x	1	12
l.4436:	v18 = lookup_nibble2(table_4961, v18, v20, 0);	rbx	0	x	2	12
l.4450:	v20 = lookup_nibble2(table_4982, v20, v34, 0);	rbp	3	x	7	12
l.4463:	v4 = lookup_nibble(table_13915, v4);	r10	0	3.x	4	12
l.4463:	v4 = lookup_nibble(table_13915, v4);	r10	1	x	7	12
l.4337:	v31 = lookup_nibble(table_13827, v7);	r11	2	2.x	1	13
l.4336:	v30 = lookup_nibble(table_13826, v7);	r14	2	2.x	1	13
l.4333:	v19 = lookup_nibble2(table_4808, v19, v21, 0);	r14	1	2.x	1	13
l.4337:	v31 = lookup_nibble(table_13827, v7);	rcx	1	2.x	1	13
l.4217:	v27 = lookup_nibble(table_13743, v12);	r12	1	x	5	14
l.4104:	v22 = lookup_nibble(table_13662, v15);	rbp	1	3.x	5	15
l.4105:	v23 = lookup_nibble(table_13663, v15);	rcx	1	3.x	5	15
l.4105:	v23 = lookup_nibble(table_13663, v15);	rcx	0	3.x	5	15

References

1. Ahn, H., Han, D.-G.: Multilateral white-box cryptanalysis: case study on WB-AES of CHES challenge 2016. IACR Cryptology ePrint Archive 2016:807 (2016)

2. Allibert, J., Feix, B., Gagnerot, G., Kane, I., Thiebeauld, H., Razafindralambo, T.: Chicken or the egg - computational data attacks or physical attacks. IACR Cryptology ePrint Archive 2015:1086 (2015)

3. Bos, J.W., Hubain, C., Michiels, W., Teuwen, P.: Differential computation analysis: hiding your white-box designs is not enough. In: Gierlichs, B., Poschmann, A.Y. (eds.) CHES 2016. LNCS, vol. 9813, pp. 215–236. Springer, Heidelberg (2016). https://doi.org/10.1007/978-3-662-53140-2_11

4. Brier, E., Clavier, C., Olivier, F.: Correlation power analysis with a leakage model. In: Joye, M., Quisquater, J.-J. (eds.) CHES 2004. LNCS, vol. 3156, pp. 16–29. Springer, Heidelberg (2004). https://doi.org/10.1007/978-3-540-28632-5_2

5. Debande, N., Berthier, M., Bocktaels, Y., Le, T.-H.: Profiled model based power simulator for side channel evaluation. IACR Cryptology ePrint Archive 2012:703 (2012)

6. Debande, N., Souissi, Y., Nassar, M., Guilley, S., Le, T.-H., Danger, J.-L.: "Resynchronization by moments": an efficient solution to align side-channel traces. In: 2011 IEEE International Workshop on Information Forensics and Security, WIFS 2011, Iguacu Falls, Brazil, 29 November-2 December 2011, pp. 1–6 (2011)

7. Doget, J., Prouff, E., Rivain, M., Standaert, F.-X.: Univariate side channel attacks and leakage modeling. J. Crypt. Eng. 1(2), 123–144 (2011)

8. Guilley, S., Khalfallah, K., Lomne, V., Danger, J.-L.: Formal framework for the evaluation of waveform resynchronization algorithms. In: Ardagna, C.A., Zhou, J. (eds.) WISTP 2011. LNCS, vol. 6633, pp. 100–115. Springer, Heidelberg (2011). https://doi.org/10.1007/978-3-642-21040-2_7

9. McCann, D., Whitnall, C., Oswald, E.: ELMO: emulating leaks for the ARM cortex-M0 without access to a side channel lab. IACR Cryptology ePrint Archive 2016:517 (2016)
10. Thiebeauld, H., Gagnerot, G., Wurcker, A., Clavier, C.: SCATTER: a new dimension in side-channel. Cryptology ePrint Archive, Report 2017/706 (2017). https://eprint.iacr.org/2017/706
11. Thuillet, C., Andouard, P., Ly, O.: A smart card power analysis simulator. In: Proceedings of the 12th IEEE International Conference on Computational Science and Engineering, CSE 2009, Vancouver, BC, Canada, 29–31 August 2009, pp. 847–852 (2009)
12. van Woudenberg, J.G.J., Witteman, M.F., Bakker, B.: Improving differential power analysis by Elastic alignment. In: Kiayias, A. (ed.) CT-RSA 2011. LNCS, vol. 6558, pp. 104–119. Springer, Heidelberg (2011). https://doi.org/10.1007/978-3-642-19074-2_8
13. Veshchikov, N.: SILK: high level of abstraction leakage simulator for side channel analysis. In: Proceedings of the 4th Program Protection and Reverse Engineering Workshop, PPREW@ACSAC 2014, New Orleans, LA, USA, 9 December 2014, pp. 3:1–3:11 (2014)
14. Whitnall, C., Oswald, E.: A fair evaluation framework for comparing side-channel distinguishers. J. Crypt. Eng. 1(2), 145–160 (2011)

Zero in and TimeFuzz: Detection and Mitigation of Cache Side-Channel Attacks

ZiHao Wang, ShuangHe Peng$^{(\boxtimes)}$, XinYue Guo, and WenBin Jiang

Beijing Key Laboratory of Security and Privacy in Intelligent Transportation,
Beijing Jiaotong University, Beijing 100044, China
shhpeng@bjtu.edu.cn

Abstract. Cache Side Channel Attack (CSCA) works by monitoring security critical operations and recovering the secret or private information according to the accesses by the victim. Previous efforts on CSCA detection only rely on global statistics information, which leads to some drawbacks. To meet these challenges, Zero in and TimeFuzz (ZITF), a wide-coverage, high-accuracy mitigation scheme of CSCA based on Intel-PIN is presented here. The key point of ZITF is the combination of local features and global features, which can achieve a more accurate detection and mitigation to CSCA. To reduce the impact on other benign processes, a way to time fuzz suspicious processes is used by tampering with the time information required. The comparative experiments on benign processes and malicious processes show that ZITF really works and outperforms the previous work in several ways. In addition, the experiment also proves that ZITF can also be applied to the detection and mitigation of Flush-Flush and Meltdown attack.

Keywords: Detection · Mitigation · Cache side channel attack · Intel-PIN

1 Introduction

Cache side channel attack (CSCA) monitors the physical information leaked by cache during program execution, then combines some statistical methods to analyze the information, and finally steals the private information. CSCA can be used to steal encryption keys of encryption algorithms such as AES, DES, and RSA [15], and can also be used to obtain user privacy information [9–14], which is a high threat to the system security or user privacy. Specter and Meltdown [27,28] based on CSCA have caused a large impact in security and widespread concern in the information security community.

In response to this security threat, many relevant detection and mitigation mechanisms have been proposed. Zhang et al. [1] proposed a mechanism called

---

Supported by the fund of National Training Programs of Innovation and Entrepreneurship for Undergraduates.

© Springer Nature Switzerland AG 2019
J.-L. Lanet and C. Toma (Eds.): SecITC 2018, LNCS 11359, pp. 410–424, 2019.
https://doi.org/10.1007/978-3-030-12942-2_31

HomeAlone, which used Prime-Probe to implement detection and use system monitor to randomize the position of cache sets to achieve mitigation [16–19]. However, this mechanism can only detect a small part of memory address space in a short period of time which cannot achieve full-time global detection and mitigation. Herath and Fogh [2] proposed a scheme to monitor cache misses to detect Flush-Reload and Rowhammer and slow down the attacker's processes to achieve mitigation [20–22]. This mechanism has good universality, but there exist certain blind zones, such as Flush-Flush. Payer [3] proposed a mechanism called HexPADS, which combined cache references, cache misses and minor page fault to achieve full-time detection. But Flush-Flush also can get away with murder. Chiappetta et al. [4] proposed to build traces of Cache references and Cache misses [23], and machine learning is used to train the model according to the traces. Then the model was used to classify Flush-Reload. However, detection using machine learning is only efficient for known attacks, which lacks universality since it has low probability to prevent unknown attacks.

In this paper, we present a novel scheme, called Zero in and TimeFuzz (ZITF), to extract the local features of system processes and combine it with global features to achieve a more complete detection and mitigation to CSCA. The proposed scheme is composed of two phases, detection and mitigation, which is shown in Fig. 1. In the detection phase, we first use Perf, a performance analysis subsystem in Linux, to pre-filter system processes, and then use Intel-PIN to monitor all the loops of suspicious processes to achieve a higher accuracy of detection. In the mitigation phase, since the Cache-side channel attack is highly dependent on time information, we use Intel-PIN to tamper with the time information it requires [24]. Which makes it impossible for attackers to obtain any valuable time information, thus making the mitigation effective.

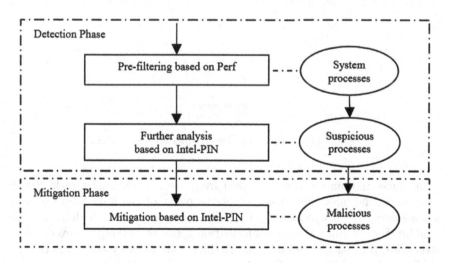

Fig. 1. Components of the proposed Zero in and TimeFuzz scheme.

In summary, we make the following contributions:

(1) As compared with the previous detection mechanism, local detection is added, which makes it possible to identify more covert side channel attacks such as Flush-Flush.
(2) ZITF can achieve an effective mitigation with low cost of mis-judgment. It has less impact on benign processes.
(3) ZITF has strong universality, it can also be used to detection and mitigation for Specter and Meltdown attack.

2   Preliminaries

2.1   Cache Side Channel Attack

Cache side channel attack is a covert attack. It monitors the physical information leaked by Cache during program execution, then combines some statistical methods to analyze the information, and finally achieves the theft of private information.

The typical scenario of attack is shown in Fig. 2. CPU Cache is protected by hardware and the attacker cannot access it directly [20–22, 26]. However, due to the sharing of Cache resources, the same Cache set or even Cache block may be used by the spy and the victim process at the same time, which provides a covert channel between these two processes.

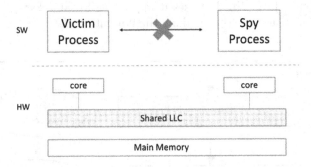

Fig. 2. LLC-based cache side channel attack scenario.

The time information can be leaked from the side channel attack. Specifically, the Cache miss will trigger an access event of the next level Cache or main memory, which will increase the access time and makes it different from Cache hit. By recording the time information generated during the execution of instructions, the attacker can infer the victim's main memory access information and obtain some of the key information at a higher accuracy.

By further analyzing and extracting the Cache side channel information, we can know the memory areas that the victim accessed, the time when the access occurred, the order of accessing different memory areas and so on. The fact that conditional statements and branch statements are often used in the algorithm which makes the execution of the algorithm depend on certain data, that is, the execution trace of the algorithm will be different with different inputs, which results in different executions feature. The side-channel attack process can capture these features easily, and thus the input data can be inferred. Therefore, encryption keys of encryption algorithms, such as AES, DES, and RSA, can be obtained by Cache side channel attacks which pose a serious security threat to most encryption algorithms.

2.2 Flush-Reload

Flush-Reload [6] is the most commonly used Cache detection technology. The Flush-Reload technique is based on page sharing. An attacker can use the clflush instruction to evict the data of some specific shared memory areas from all Cache levels and then flush the entire Cache line. Then access these shared memory areas immediately and probe the time information at the time of reloading. You can detect which memory areas have been accessed by victims by repeating those steps.

Listing 1.1. Core code of Flush-Reload

```
1   bool  probe(char *adrs) {
2       volatile unsigned long time;
3
4       asm   __volatile__ (
5           "mfence              \n"
6           "lfence              \n"
7           "rdtsc               \n"
8           "lfence              \n"
9           "movl %%eax, %%esi    \n"
10          "movl (%1), %%eax     \n"
11          "lfence              \n"
12          "rdtsc               \n"
13          "subl %%esi, %%eax    \n"
14          "clflush 0(%1)       \n"
15          :"=a" (time)
16          :"c" (adrs)
17          :"%esi", "%edx");
18      return time < threshold;
19  }
```

The Reloading process is implemented by the movl instruction on line 10, which reads 4 bytes from the address of input memory into register eax. To measure the time spent by the Reload process, the time stamp counters are read on lines 7 and 12 respectively. The rdtsc (Read Time Stamp Counter) instruction reads the 64-bit time stamp counter, stores the upper 32 bits in the edx register, and stores the lower 32 bits in the eax register. Then the clflush (Flush Cache Line) instruction is used to evict the data of the memory areas from all the Cache levels to achieve the initialization of the next slot. If the access time that measured is lower than the threshold, it indicates that the victim accessed the memory areas after flushing the Cache last time. Otherwise, it indicates that these memory areas haven't been accessed since the last flushing.

2.3 Prime-Probe

Prime-Probe [7] is a technique that allows attackers to specify which Cache set has been accessed by the victim. The attacker runs a monitor process that can display the victim's Cache usage and records the access time of the Cache during the monitoring process and uses this information to determine if the victim has accessed certain Cache sets.

2.4 Flush-Flush

Flush-Flush [8] is a variant of Flush-Reload. Unlike Flush-Reload, it measures the execution time of the cache line flush instruction itself to determine whether the victim has accessed the corresponding memory areas. If there is data in the Cache. The clflush instruction has to evict the data from all Cache levels during the execute process. Therefore, the execution time of the clflush instruction will be longer. If there is no data in the Cache, the clflush instruction will take a shorter execution time. Therefore, the length of the execution time can directly reflect the victim's memory usage. Contrary to any other Cache Attack, Flush-Flush doesn't make any memory accesses, thus, it causes no Cache misses and only a small number of cache hits. Therefore it's more covert and hard to detect. Previous detect mechanisms using cache references and cache misses are unable to detect Flush-Flush.

2.5 Intel-PIN

PIN [5] is a dynamic binary instrumentation (DBI) scheme provided by Intel [25]. DBI means to insert specific analysis code into the process of program execution according to the analysis requirements of users without affecting the dynamic execution results of the program. It can be used to monitor and analyze the process of program dynamic execution. In addition to PIN, DynamoRIO and Valgrind are widely used for dynamic analysis of programs. However, PIN provides a rich programming interface, with which developers can easily obtain the information of instruction, memory and register during the dynamic execution of the program and achieve fine grained dynamic monitoring. Therefore, Intel-Pin is selected for dynamic analysis here.

3   The Proposed Scheme and Implementation

3.1   Analysis of Attack Feature

Trigger a Large Number of Cache Accesses. To ensure the success of the Cache side channel attack, malicious code is usually cyclically executed at a high frequency. According to the principle of temporal and spatial locality of memory access, this will certainly trigger lots of Cache accesses.

Low iTLB Miss Rate. TLB (Translation Lookaside Buffer) is a special Cache for the page table which is used to improve the speed of translating from virtual addresses to physical addresses. iTLB is a kind of TLB which is dedicated to instruction usage.

Since the execution of redundant code will lead to unnecessary interfere, which will reduce the accuracy of the attack, attackers usually perform only a small piece of code during the attacking process. Executing only a small piece of code will cause little pressure on the iTLB, so the iTLB miss rate of the attack process will be very low.

High Cache Miss Rate. For a Prime-Probe attack, when the victim process is not running, each Probe operation will trigger a Cache hit. Therefore, the Prime-Probe attack will continuously trigger a Cache hit when the victim is not present. So its Cache miss rate will be very low. However, when the victim starts running and Prime-Probe starts working, since attackers continue to use their own data to fill specific Cache sets maliciously, the data of the victim can only stay in the Cache for a short time, and then will be evicted by the attackers maliciously, making the Cache sets broke out "space war", which will cause a large number of conflicts, resulting in a high rate of Cache access missing. Therefore, the cache miss feature revealed by Prime-Probe are not stable, even in some cases displayed contrary feature under different working conditions. However, from the view of mitigation, Prime-Probe is dangerous only when it is working, so its feature during the working time is what we need to focus on.

It is worth pointing out that the Prime-Probe attack is essentially the use of Cache conflict to obtain information, and every monitoring data obtained by the Prime-Probe attack is derived from Cache conflict misses. In other words, the accuracy of Prime-Probe is based on high Cache miss rate. Therefore, if a Prime-Probe attack wants to conceal its high Cache miss rate, it must be at the expense of reducing attack accuracy.

For Flush-Reload, since the probability that the victim accesses a specific memory area is small, the probability of triggering a Cache miss during each Cache refilling will be high. Therefore Flush-Reload attacks trigger Cache miss almost every slot, which will result in extremely high Cache miss rate.

Since Flush-Flush attack does not have the feature of high Cache miss rate, it will neither increase the competition of Cache resources nor cause additional Cache miss. Therefore, the Cache miss rate of Flush-Flush is basically the same as benign process.

Use of Special Instructions. For Flush-Reload and Flush-Flush, the clflush instruction is necessary. The clflush instruction is very special, it is mostly used to debug and forcefully write back dirty data from the Cache, so users won't use the clflush instruction normally, but Flush-Reload and Flush-Flush execute the clflush instruction at high frequency cyclically. Besides, in order to obtain time information, attackers must combine the clflush instruction with the rdtsc instruction together, which is quite a strange case. Therefore, it is a prominent feature of Flush-Reload and Flush-Flush.

As there is neither clflush instruction nor rdtsc instruction nor Flush-Flush on the ARM CPU architecture, this feature only exists on Intel processors. Therefore, ZITF is only applicable for Intel processors. In addition, although there are many techniques that enable the attacker to obtain time information, such as Perf, rdtsc instruction is the most direct and common way used. In order to explain the idea briefly, we only pay attention to the rdtsc instruction here. The idea can be used to solve any other mode of attack.

Highly Dependent on Time Information. Cache side channel attacks are highly dependent on accurate time information. No matter what kind of method is used, it has strict requirements on time information. Therefore, if the accurate clock information of the attacker is tampered with, the prevention from Cache side channel attacks can be effectively achieved. As the clock information is tampered, the attacker will not be able to obtain any valuable time information. Since only suspicious processes are Time fuzzed, it will hardly affect other processes in the system, so it is a gentler, more fault-tolerant and more targeted mitigation mechanism.

3.2   The Scheme of Detection and Mitigation

Most of the previous detection mechanisms of Cache side channel attack rely on the global statistics information such as Cache references and Cache misses. Here the local features of each loop in the monitored process are collected using Intel-PIN to make the detection and mitigation mechanism more complete.

First, the attack processes do have a low iTLB miss rate and trigger a large number of Cache accesses no matter which technique mentioned in Sects. 2.2 to 2.4 is adopted. But these are not sufficient to detect the Cache side channel attacks since they are not unique feature to the Cache side channel attacks. However, we can use them to pre-filter all processes to reduce the number of suspicious processes.

After pre-filtering, from the overall view, we first investigate the Cache miss rate of the processes left. If there is still quite a high Cache miss rate with a low iTLB miss rate, it is able to identify the process as a malicious process. Using Cache access miss rate to identify malicious processes is quite suitable for Prime-Probe and Flush-Reload, but it no longer works for Flush-Flush.

In order to identify malicious processes, we first use Intel-PIN to perform a loop test on each suspicious process, then check whether there are clflush and rdtsc instructions in the loop with many iterations. The key point of this scheme is to locate the clflush instruction. Although this method cannot detect attacks without any clflush instruction, such as Prime-Probe, which can mitigate almost all other Cache-side channel attacks with clflush instruction. The Prime-Probe attacks cannot conceal itself well. It is easy to detect using global features. Therefore, a relatively gentle way is used: locate the combination of clflush and rdtsc instructions. More covert attacks such as Flush-Flush can also be detected.

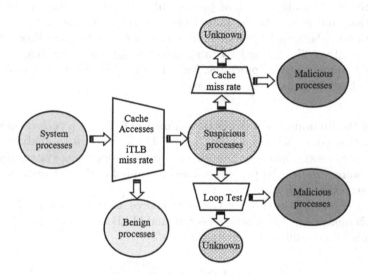

Fig. 3. Process of the detection of cache side channel attack.

In addition, for the first time, we propose the way that prevents the Cache side channel attacks by tampering with only the time information that the attack process required with the time information of other processes un-disturbed. Since the Cache side channel attack is highly time-dependent, tampering with the time information it acquires means that the attacker will not obtain any valuable time information and will not have a great impact on other processes in the system. So it's a well fault-tolerant mitigation scheme with low misjudgment. As is shown in Fig. 3, first, all the processes in the system are pre-filtered by using the number of Cache accesses and the iTLB miss rate. Some processes which do not have the features of the attacks are directly classified as benign processes and will not be processed. At the same time, all processes with those features are classified as suspicious processes, which is the second filter processes. There are two parameters that are used for the second filtering, i.e. Cache miss Rate and Loop Test. Once a process that satisfies any of the two parameters, it is categorized to be a malicious process.

3.3   Implementation

Acquisition of Process Information Based on Procfs. In order to detect the Cache side channel attacks, first all running system processes are traversed and PID of each process is obtained by using Procfs (Proc filesystem).

Procfs is a special file system in Linux that presents information about processes and other system information. Procfs provides a channel for the exchange of information between kernel and user. Procfs can be used to query various kernel status information, such as process information, hardware device status information, and so on. At the same time, Procfs can also be used to transfer information to the kernel to modify the kernel parameters. Here Procfs is used to traverse all the files in the PID subdirectory to get the status information of all current running system processes. Then Perf is used to start counting Cache events with all PIDs as input parameter.

Process Performance Analysis Based on Perf. Perf is a performance analysis tool that comes with the Linux kernel. It can be used to analyze various performance events, especially to evaluate the use of operating system resources and hardware resources by processes. The function of perf_event_open is used to count the specified hardware events.

In this paper, it is used to get Cache references, Cache misses, iTLB accesses and iTLB misses etc. The Cache miss rate and iTLB miss rate for each process are calculated according to formula (1) and (2).

$$Cache\_miss\_rate = \frac{Cache\_misses}{Cache\_accesses} \tag{1}$$

$$iTLB\_miss\_rate = \frac{iTLB\_misses}{iTLB\_accesses} \tag{2}$$

Up to now, three important parameters for classifying of all processes, i.e. Cache references, Cache miss rate, and iTLB miss rate are described.

Method of Detection and Mitigation Based on PIN. PIN provides multi-level instrumentation such as instruction, basic block, system calls and so on. For instance, RTN is a function level instrumentation mechanism, which can automatically identify API function.

In this paper, we use instruction, image and routine level instrumentation. Image-level instrumentation can be used to analyze specific images as needed to reduce the scope of analysis. In order to further reduce the scope of analysis and allow analysis of specific functions, routine-level instrumentation is used instead. Instruction-level instrumentation inserts analysis code in units of instructions.

With the combination of three levels of instrumentation mentioned above, we could detect a malicious process by the fact that whether there is a clflush instruction and rdtsc instruction appears in the same loop. In order not to affect the performance of the program as much as possible, we use image-level and routine-level instrumentation to implement loop test. First, all images that contain the main function are picked out, and then routine-level instrumentation on the main function in the filtered image is performed. Finally, instruction-level instrumentation is used to count the number of instructions in the main function. Thus, we know the loop nesting condition, the instructions that appear in the same loop, and the number of loop executions. From this it can be judged whether there is a clflush instruction and rdtsc instruction appears in the same loop to achieve the detection of a malicious process.

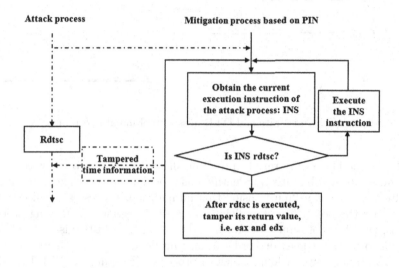

Fig. 4. Process of the mitigation of cache side channel attack.

As shown in Fig. 4, after the malicious process is selected, the instruction-level instrumentation is used to find all rdtsc instructions in the process and the return value of rdtsc, which is stored in registers eax and edx, are tampered. By this way, since the attacker cannot get any valuable time information, the mitigation is achieved.

4 Performance Analysis

All tests here are based on an Intel x86CPUs processor (2-core with 2.4GHz, 8GB of RAM) and OS kernel Fedora27.

4.1 Threshold Determination

9 system processes, 9 application processes, and 4 malicious processes (FF-gnupg-1.4.13, FR-1-file-access, FR-2-file-access and memdump) are selected as the objects, we continuously acquired 20 sets of values of Cache miss rate and

iTLB miss rate in seconds. The trace of the Cache miss rate and the iTLB miss rate for each process is shown in Fig. 5. (The full line indicates malicious processes, and the dotted line indicates benign processes).

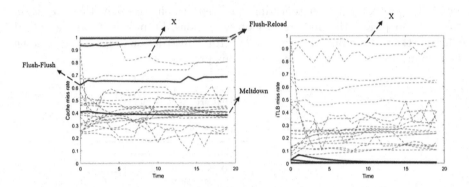

Fig. 5. Cache miss rate and iTLB miss rate of monitored processes.

We use the iTLB miss rate to pre-filter all processes. A process with a high iTLB miss rate will be directly identified as a benign process. Therefore, in the pre-filtering process, we must ensure that all malicious processes are filtered out to minimize the possibility of malicious processes escaping the filtering process. That is, the threshold must be much higher than the iTLB miss rate of each malicious process (at least one order of magnitude smaller). As shown in Fig. 5, the iTLB missing rate of four malicious processes (FF-gnupg-1.4.13, FR-1-file-access, FR-2-file-access and memdump) is less than 0.01, while the iTLB miss rate of most common processes in the system is always greater than 0.1. There are only a few normal processes with iTLB miss rates between 0.1 and 0.05. In order to ensure that all malicious processes be filtered out, we set the threshold of the iTLB miss rate to 0.1.

As shown in Fig. 5, we can observe that the Cache miss rate of the most benign processes in the system is always less than 0.7, and the Cache miss rate of Flush-Reload attacks exceeds 0.9, which is much greater than all benign processes. On the other hand, the iTLB miss rate of the process with high Cache miss rate is correspondingly higher. Therefore, after pre-filtering using the iTLB, it is almost impossible to find a benign process with Cache miss rate greater than 0.7. In summary, we set the threshold of Cache miss Rate to 0.7.

As shown in Fig. 5, we can see that the Cache miss rate of Flush-Flush and Meltdown is almost the same as that of benign processes. So, it is impossible to use only Cache miss rate to identify Flush-Flush and Meltdown, which is the limitation of the method that rely only on global statistics information for attack detection. From process X in Fig. 5 we can see that the Cache miss rate of process X is always greater than 0.7. The process will be classified as a malicious process by mistaken if only Cache miss rate is used. Therefore, it is necessary to add iTLB miss rate to pre-filtering the monitored process.

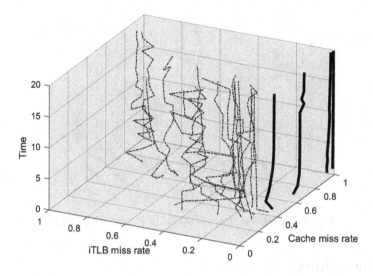

Fig. 6. Three-dimensional view of Time-Cache-iTLB of monitored processes.

As shown in Fig. 6, it is clear that the Cache side channel attacks do have outstanding features on iTLB miss rate and Cache miss rate. The processes selected are all system processes or normal application processes. They all do not have a low iTLB miss rate. Therefore, from Fig. 6 we may see that only iTLB miss rate and Cache miss rate can separate the malicious process from the benign process completely. However, this is only an illusion, since the system may also contain some processes with low iTLB miss rate, which will make Flush-Flush and Meltdown indistinguishable.

At the same time, Fig. 6 also shows that neither the normal system processes nor the normal application processes have a sufficiently low iTLB miss rate. Since processes with a sufficiently low iTLB miss rate are only a small part in the system, so only a small part of the processes need to pass Loop Test. Thus the implementation of Loop Test has little effect on overall performance. In the next section we will evaluate the effect of Loop Test on performance by testing twelve processes with low iTLB miss rates.

4.2   Performance Effects

We use the PARSEC benchmark suite to determine the performance cost of ZITF. As shown in Fig. 7, we can see that most of the applications in the benchmarks exhibit a slowdown of less than 10%. The geometric average slowdown is 4.7%.

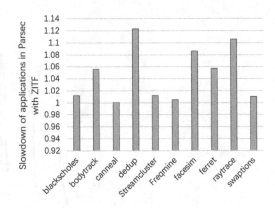

Fig. 7. Slowdown of applications in Parsec with ZITF.

5   Conclusions

We have presented Zero in and TimeFuzz (ZITF), a wide-coverage, high-accuracy mitigation of Cache Side Channel Attack (CSCA) by taking advantage of Intel-PIN. Unlike previous schemes, ZITF relies on the combination of global and local statistical information to achieve detection of attacks, which makes it possible to identify more covert side channel attacks such as Flush-Flush. The experimental results are encouraging, which shows a considerable leap over the previous work. ZITF could be adopted as a lightweight tool of detection to CSCA on pervasive multi-core Linux platforms. Moreover, it would be efficient for known attacks with a low cost of misjudgment and has great probability to prevent unknown attacks.

Currently, ZITF is limited to single host environment and does not coordinate information across domain of virtual machines. Next, we are trying to achieve mitigation to Cache side-channel attack across virtual machines under KVM (Kernel-based Virtual Machine) and to model both the global and local features of the process via machine learning. By using the trained model, we might be able to get a better accuracy.

References

1. Zhang, Y., Juels, A., Oprea, A., Reiter, M.K.: HomeAlone: co-residency detection in the cloud via side-channel analysis. In: IEEE Symposium on Security & Privacy, vol. 9, no. 1, pp. 313–328 (2011)
2. Herath, N., Fogh, A.: These are Not Your Grand Daddy's CPU Performance Counters - CPU Hardware Performance Counters for Security. Black Hat 2015 Briefings, August 2015
3. Payer, M.: HexPADS: a platform to detect "Stealth" attacks. In: Caballero, J., Bodden, E., Athanasopoulos, E. (eds.) ESSoS 2016. LNCS, vol. 9639, pp. 138–154. Springer, Cham (2016). https://doi.org/10.1007/978-3-319-30806-7_9

4. Chiappetta, M., Savas, E., Yilmaz, C.: Real time detection of cache-based side-channel attacks using hardware performance counters. Appl. Soft Comput. **49**, 1162–1174 (2016)
5. Luk, C.K., et al.: Pin: building customized program analysis tools with dynamic instrumentation. In: Proceedings of the ACM SIGPLAN Conference on Programming Language Design and Implementation (PLDI 2005) (2005)
6. Yarom, Y., Falkner, K.: FLUSH+RELOAD: a high resolution, low noise, L3 cache side-channel attack. In: Usenix Conference on Security Symposium, pp. 719–732 (2014)
7. Liu, F., Yarom, Y., Ge, Q., Heiser, G., Lee, R.B.: Last-level cache side-channel attacks are practical. In: IEEE Symposium on Security & Privacy, pp. 605–622 (2015)
8. Gruss, D., Maurice, C., Wagner, K., Mangard, S.: Flush+Flush: a fast and stealthy cache attack. In: Caballero, J., Zurutuza, U., Rodríguez, R.J. (eds.) DIMVA 2016. LNCS, vol. 9721, pp. 279–299. Springer, Cham (2016). https://doi.org/10.1007/978-3-319-40667-1_14
9. Zhang, Y., Juels, A., Reiter, M.K., Ristenpart, T.: Cross-tenant side channel attacks in PaaS clouds. In: 21st ACM Conference on Computer and Communications Security, November 2014
10. Apecechea, G.I., Inci, M.S., Eisenbarth, T., Sunar, B.: Fine grain cross-VM attacks on Xen and VMware are possible! Technical report 2014/248, IACR Cryptology ePrint Archive, April 2014
11. Irazoqui, G., Inci, M.S., Eisenbarth, T., Sunar, B.: Wait a minute! A fast, cross-VM attack on AES. In: Stavrou, A., Bos, H., Portokalidis, G. (eds.) RAID 2014. LNCS, vol. 8688, pp. 299–319. Springer, Cham (2014). https://doi.org/10.1007/978-3-319-11379-1_15
12. Kayaalp, M., et al.: RIC: relaxed inclusion caches for mitigating LLC side-channel attacks. In: Design Automation Conference (2017)
13. Irazoqui, G., Eisenbarth, T., Sunar, B.: S$A: a shared cache attack that works across cores and defies VM sandboxing-and its application to AES. In: 36th IEEE Symposium on Security and Privacy, May 2015
14. Inci, M.S., Gulmezoglu, B., Irazoqui, G., Eisenbarth, T., Sunar, B.: Seriously, get off my cloud! cross-VM RSA key recovery in a public cloud. Cryptology ePrint Archive, Report 2015/898 (2015)
15. Varadarajan, V., Ristenpart, T., Swift, M.: Scheduler-based defenses against cross-VM side-channels. In: 23rd USENIX Conference on Security Symposium, pp. 687–702. USENIX Association (2014)
16. Wang, Z., Lee, R.B.: New cache designs for thwarting software cachebased side channel attacks. In: 34th Annual International Symposium on Computer Architecture, pp. 494–505 (2007)
17. Wang, Z., Lee, R.B.: A novel cache architecture with enhanced performance and security. In: 41st Annual IEEE/ACM International Symposium on Microarchitecture, pp. 83–93 (2008)
18. Liu, F., Lee, R.B.: Random fill cache architecture. In: 47th IEEE/ACM Symposium on Microarchitecture, pp. 203–215, December 2014
19. Keramidas, G., Antonopoulos, A., Serpanos, D., Kaxiras, S.: Non-deterministic caches: a simple and effective defense against side channel attacks. Des. Autom. Embed. Syst. **12**, 221–230 (2008)
20. Raj, H., Nathuji, R., Singh, A., England, P.: Resource management for isolation enhanced cloud services. In: 2009 ACM Cloud Computing Security Workshop, pp. 77–84, November 2009

21. Shi, J., Song, X., Chen, H., Zang, B.: Limiting cache-based sidechannel in multi-tenant cloud using dynamic page coloring. In: 41st International Conference on Dependable Systems and Networks Workshops, pp. 194–199 (2011)

22. Kim, T., Peinado, M., Mainar-Ruiz, G.: STEALTHMEM: system-level protection against cache-based side channel attacks in the cloud. In: 21st USENIX Conference on Security Symposium (2012)

23. Liu, C., Harris, A., Maas, M., Hicks, M., Tiwari, M., Shi, E.: Ghostrider: a hardware-software system for memory trace oblivious computation. In: Twentieth International Conference on Architectural Support for Programming Languages and Operating Systems, pp. 87–101. ACM (2015)

24. Luk, C.-K., et al.: Pin: building customized program analysis tools with dynamic instrumentation. In: Proceedings of the ACM SIGPLAN Conference on Programming Language Design and Implementation (PLDI 2005) (2005)

25. Bruening, D., Garnett, T., Amarasinghe, S.: An infrastructure for adaptive dynamic optimization. In: Proceedings of the International Symposium on Code Generation and Optimization (CGO 2003) (2003)

26. Liu, F., et al.: CATalyst: defeating last-level cache side channel attacks in cloud computing. In: IEEE Symposium on High-Performance Computer Architecture, Barcelona, Spain (2016)

27. Lipp, M., et al.: Meltdown. https://meltdownattack.com/meltdown.pdf

28. Kocher, P., et al.: Spectre Attacks: Exploiting Speculative Execution. https://spectreattack.com/spectre.pdf

A Comparison of the Homomorphic Encryption Libraries HElib, SEAL and FV-NFLlib

Carlos Aguilar Melchor[1], Marc-Olivier Kilijian[2], Cédric Lefebvre[3(✉)], and Thomas Ricosset[4]

[1] ISAE SUPAERO, University of Toulouse, Toulouse, France
[2] CRM/UDeM and LATECE/UQAM, CNRS, Montréal, QC, Canada
[3] INP, ENSEEIHT, CNRS, IRIT, 31000 Toulouse, France
cedric_lefebvre@orange.fr
[4] Thales, 92230 Gennevilliers, France

Abstract. Fully homomorphic encryption has considerably evolved during the past 10 years. In particular, the discovery of more efficient schemes has brought the computational complexity down to acceptable levels for some applications. Several implementations of these schemes have been publicly released, enabling researchers and practitioners to better understand the performance properties of the schemes. This improved understanding of the performance has led to the discovery of new potential applications of homomorphic encryption, fuelling further research on all fronts.

In this work, we provide a comparative benchmark of the leading homomorphic encryption libraries HElib, FV-NFLlib, and SEAL for large plaintext moduli of up to 2048 bits, and analyze their relative performance.

Keywords: Homomorphic encryption · Benchmark · SEAL · FV-NFLlib · HElib

1 Introduction

Recent advances in *homomorphic cryptography* completely reshaped the possibilities to secure a computing system in untrusted environments. Regarded as cryptography's "Holy Grail", *Fully Homomorphic Encryption (FHE)* enables evaluating arbitrary functions on encrypted data [4,9]. Since the first fully homomorphic encryption schemes were invented, the landscape of FHE has undergone some great changes. Prototypes demonstrating private health diagnosis, signal processing, genomic statistics, and database queries spur hope on the practical deployment of FHE in the near future.

Most of the current applications only consider binary plaintext spaces, and construct binary circuits to compute the desired functions over encrypted data. Existing homomorphic encryption libraries like HElib [11–13] or SEAL [5] are

J.-L. Lanet and C. Toma (Eds.): SecITC 2018, LNCS 11359, pp. 425–442, 2019.
https://doi.org/10.1007/978-3-030-12942-2_32

well adapted to this setting. However, they also offer the possibility to choose a larger plaintext space, for situations where the function can be evaluated more efficiently when represented by a modular arithmetic circuit. Nevertheless, very large plaintext moduli do not seem to be the main target for these libraries, and what is feasible in these settings is unclear and remains to be evaluated.

Handling very large plaintext moduli can be useful for two types of applications. First, it becomes possible to compute fixed-point high-precision operations over real (truncated or rounded) data. In this case the modulus bit size is approximately the precision times the multiplicative depth of the circuit. A second set of applications concerns discrete logarithm and factorization-based cryptographic operations over encrypted data in an outsourced setting, with imposed moduli ranging from 256 to 2048 bits.

1.1 This Work

In this paper, we experiment the use of large plaintext moduli with three different FHE libraries in order to evaluate their respective capabilities and performance: SEAL, HElib, and FV-NFLlib. It is worth noting that, for this purpose, we had to modify HElib to be able to handle multi-precision moduli [16], and called this version HElib-MP. Regarding SEAL and FV-NFLlib, we simply used the plain versions of those libraries (SEAL v2.3 for plaintext moduli up to 60 bits and SEAL v2.1 for larger moduli).

Of course, it would be possible to do multi-precision plaintext computations with any of the libraries by using several instances of the encryption scheme with relatively prime plaintext moduli (and then using the Chinese Remainder Theorem to work modulo the product of the plaintext moduli). But using such a method, one cannot use a specific modulus such as those given for ECDSA or RSA, which would not factor appropriately.

We analyze the performance results and compare the impact on the overall performance of the different strategies used in these libraries to handle noise and representation changes.

All our experiments were conducted on a single core of an Intel(R) Xeon(R) CPU E5-2695 v3 @ 2.30 GHz; the SHE parameters were selected using the Albrecht-Player-Scott *sagemath* script [1] to ensure at least 128 bits of security (the default security target in SEAL v2.3). Note that, with classical heuristics, doubling security would only increase costs by a factor of two, enabling a generalization of our conclusions to higher security choices.

2   Benchmark Description

We benchmark the libraries for both 1 bit, 64 bits, 256 bits, and 2048 bits plaintexts. The one bit case is not the main focus of our work but is interesting for comparisons passing from one-bit to multi-bit plaintext moduli involves radical behaviour changes.

For each plaintext size, a set of tests is repeatedly run with increasing multiplicative depth until the cost of a test reaches $12 + h$. Each test consists in squaring repeatedly a ciphertext until reaching a target multiplicative depth. The output for each test is its running time (averaged over three runs) divided by the depth, which gives the average cost of a multiplication.

As batching is very dependent on the exact value of p, and not just its size, we do not take it into account. The time is thus the average cost of a multiplication for a batch of plaintexts. The batch size will depend on the exact value of p and on the used library. The fact that HElib can provide better batch sizes is something that must be considered on top of plain performance results.

2.1   HElib-MP

In order to be able to run those tests we had to modify HElib. HElib-MP is basically an HElib extension for multi-precision that keeps using NTL for implementing the BGV scheme.

HElib, as is, only handles plaintext space moduli of the form p^r, p and r being single precision integers. As noted in the introduction, it would be possible to do multi-precision plaintext computations with HElib, either by using moduli of the form p^r, or by using several instances of HElib with relatively prime plaintext moduli (and then using the Chinese Remainder Theorem to work modulo the product of the plaintext moduli). But this method forbids the use of specific moduli such as those given for ECDSA or RSA, which would not factor appropriately.

We modified the key generation, encryption, decryption, addition and multiplication routines to allow working with arbitrary plaintext moduli. We therefore adapted the parameters accordingly, such as the parameters concerning the modulus switching.

2.2   Other Libraries Tested

The benchmark is run for HElib-MP, FV-NFLlib and two versions of SEAL: v2.1 [6] and v2.3 [5].

While SEAL v2.1 natively supports arbitrary sized plaintext moduli, it was not optimized to be used with p bigger than 64 bits. SEAL v2.1 stores all ciphertext in full coefficient representation instead of using a CRT or double-CRT representation (see the following performance analysis sections). While this gives a lot of freedom for the choice of the coefficient modulus and in that sense simplifies the parameter selection, performing the polynomial multiplications over $\mathbb{Z}[x]$ is asymptotically less efficient than using the CRT representation(s), and this under-performance increases with larger parameters.

Seal v2.3 makes a big leap forward by using both a CRT representation and the full-RNS[1] variant of FV proposed in [2]. We include both versions on the

---

[1] RNS or Residue Number Scheme is the proper name of the representation used when we use the Chinese Remainder Theorem.

benchmark to highlight the importance of CRT representations and to try to measure the impact of the modifications brought by [2].

2.3   Parameter Selection

For the tests, $\log q$ is chosen heuristically as $\log p$ times the multiplicative depth, and then it is increased (using the library granularity as q is a product of fixed sizes moduli) until being able to decrypt correctly. Then n is chosen as the smallest power-of-two providing 128 bits of security. This is estimated using the Albrecht-Player-Scott *sagemath* script [1].[2] After n is chosen, correctness is tested again and we iterate (increasing q and n) until we obtain both correctness and an estimation of security above 128 bits.

Note that we cannot give bounds on the probability of the output correctness as we estimate it heuristically. However $\log q$ is large for almost all of our tests and thus the number of margin bits that one would need to include in q's size to ensure a very low (even cryptographically secure) decryption error is negligible.

For the smallest tests (e.g. $\log p = 1$ and low depth) this is not the case, but as the choice of a decryption error probability is application dependent we let this issue aside and just highlight that in order to have low decryption error probabilities the cost of the smallest tests may increase.

3   Benchmark Results

3.1   Ciphertext Modulus Size

We start by presenting the ciphertext modulus size evolution for two settings: $\log p = 1$ and $\log p = 64$. When the plaintext coefficient size is 256 or 2048 the results are equivalent, up to a scale factor to the case $\log p = 64$.

Figure 1 (left) describes the setting $\log p = 1$. Note that, as depth grows, all the libraries converge to quite similar ciphertext modulus sizes. During the relinearization phase, HElib-MP includes the so-called special primes and ciphertext size is a (roughly) constant multiplicative factor larger than without the special primes.

There is also a small asymptotic multiplicative factor that places FV-NFLlib above the other two libraries. This comes from the fact that FV-NFLlib takes larger noise distributions than the other two libraries.

Figure 1 (right) describes the setting $\log p = 64$. We observe the same small multiplicative gap between FV-NFLlib and SEAL due to noise width. On the other hand, as depth grows, a much larger multiplicative factor (of two) appears between HElib-MP and the other two libraries (this factor grows to three in the relinearization phase). The situation is the same for $\log p = 256$ and $\log p = 2048$. At first sight, the noise generated by the multiplications follows $2\log p$ ($3\log p$ with special primes) whereas for SEAL and FV-NFLlib it follows $\log p$.

---

[2] The script returns the security of best known attacks against cryptography based on LWE, we assume the results hold for R-LWE.

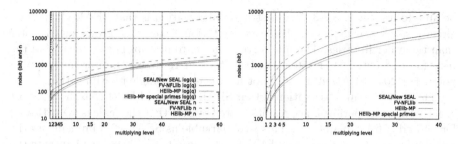

Fig. 1. Evolution of n and $\log q$ needed for correctness as a function of the multiplying depth when $\log p = 1$ (left) and $\log p = 64$ (right). For $\log p = 256$ and $\log p = 2048$, results are similar to the case $\log p = 64$. Results for HElib-MP are given twice, with and without the special primes used in the relinearization operation.

3.2 Computational Costs

Figure 2 presents the computational performance results when $\log p = 1$. Note that the costs for SEAL v2.1 grows much faster than for the other libraries, showing that the usage of CRT is essential for deep multiplications. Costs for SEAL v2.3 and FV-NFLlib cross themselves regularly, and even if SEAL outperforms FV-NFLlib most of the time there is no trend separating the two libraries.

The cost for HElib on the other hand seems to grow less quickly than for the other libraries, starting at depth 25 there is a gap that grows up to a factor 4 for depth 60. Asymptotically HElib seems to fundamentally outperform the other libraries.

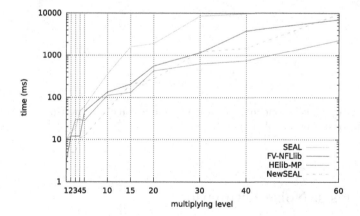

Fig. 2. Average time for one multiplication as a function of the multiplying depth when $\log p = 1$.

Figure 4 presents the computational performance results when $\log p$ is 64, 256, and 2048, except for SEAL where $\log p = 64$ is replaced by $\log p = 60$ to be able to use SEAL v2.3. The first main observation is that SEAL v2.1, as we already saw when $\log p = 1$, has a computational cost that grows much faster than the other libraries. The line corresponding to it stops before the end of the tests for $\log p$ equal 64 or 256 as the tests took more than 12 h after the stopping point. For 2048 SEAL v2.1 could not handle even a single multiplication.

The second main observation is that SEAL v2.3 and FV-NFLlib show almost exactly the same performance results (note however that the scale is logarithmic) for 64 and 256 bit plaintexts. This is remarkable as SEAL v2.3 implements the full-RNS variant of FV whereas FV-NFLlib doesn't. For 2048 bit plaintexts the test could not be run for SEAL v2.3 as the key generation step was stopped after a full day. As the key generation function is the same for both libraries, it is probably due to a minor implementation issue.

The third main observation is that the cost for HElib is higher (starting at a factor 2) when $\log p = 64$ up to a depth around 40 and when $\log p = 256$ up to a depth of 7. Above that it should be the opposite (tests for $\log p = 64$ and depth above 40 were too long). There is therefore a crossing point when $\log q$ is around 2500 bits after which HElib becomes better and better. For plaintexts of 2048 bits HElib is always better (up to a factor 2.5) (Fig. 5).

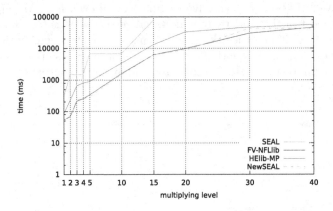

Fig. 3. Average time for one multiplication as a function of the multiplying depth when $\log p = 64$ ($\log p = 60$ for SEAL).

4   Analysis: Noise Estimation

In order to understand the evolution of $\log q$ in the benchmark, noise evolution must be considered for each library. The analysis done in the design document of HElib [12] provides noise variance estimations, whereas in the original paper of FV [8] (and on subsequent implementations) the analysis done provides upper-bounds on the noise (supposing that there is a tail cut on used gaussians).

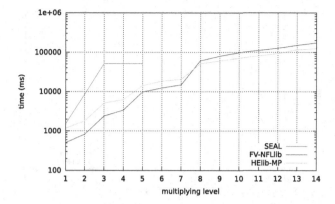

Fig. 4. Average time for one multiplication as a function of the multiplying depth when $\log p = 256$.

The goal of this section is not to provide fine-tuning strategies for parameter derivation but to formalize and justify the observations of the previous section. We therefore approximate the noise estimates using upper-bounds.

Besides the notations of Sect. A we will also use $\delta = \sup(\|\mathbf{a} \cdot \mathbf{b}\|_\infty / \|\mathbf{a}\|_\infty \|\mathbf{b}\|_\infty :$ $a, b \in R)$, the ring expansion factor. We will also note B_{key} and B_{err} the upper-bounds associated to χ_{key} and χ_{err}.

4.1   Noise Growth in FV-NFLlib and SEAL

Following the analysis done in [15], a freshly encrypted ciphertext output by FV.Encrypt has an initial noise term that can be bounded by $V = B_{\mathsf{err}}(1 + 2\delta B_{\mathsf{key}})$.

After L levels of multiplications, each followed by a relinearization operation, the resulting noise term is bounded by[3]

$$U_L = C_1^L V + LC_1^{L-1} C_2 = LC_1^L (C_2/C_1 + V/L),$$

where

$$C_1 = 2\delta^2 p B_{\mathsf{key}}, \quad C_2 = \delta^2 B_{\mathsf{key}}(B_{\mathsf{key}} + p^2) + \delta\omega \log_\omega(q) B_{\mathsf{err}}.$$

In SEAL we have $B_{\mathsf{key}} = 1$. Using this, and replacing the constants in the expression we get

$$U_L = L\left(2\delta^2 p\right)^L \left(\frac{1 + p^2}{2p} + \frac{\omega \log_\omega(q) B_{\mathsf{err}}}{2\delta p} + o_L(1) \right),$$

where $o_L(1)$ is a vanishing term in L. The first fraction is always smaller than (but close to) p and the second fraction is smaller than 1 for all the considered values of ω (word used for relinearization). This upper bound can thus be slightly loosened to get the much simpler expression: $U_L \simeq Lp(2\delta^2 p)^L$. For SEAL, we can therefore expect $\log q$ to be close to $L \log(2\delta^2 p)$ as L grows.

---

[3] Note that we give here a slightly looser bound to get a simpler expression for C_1.

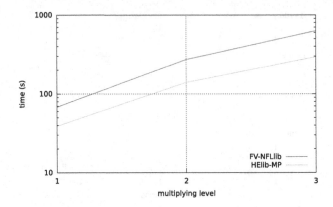

Fig. 5. Average time for one multiplication as a function of the multiplying depth when $\log p = 2048$.

For FV-NFLlib we considered that $B_{\mathsf{key}} = B_{\mathsf{err}}$ (which is the case in all the examples given in the website of the library). Using the same approach we get $U_L \simeq L p B_{\mathsf{err}} (2\delta^2 p B_{\mathsf{err}})$ and thus we can expect $\log q$ to be close to $L \log(2\delta^2 p B_{\mathsf{err}})$ as L grows.

This explains why there is a small multiplicative gap on the cost between FV-NFLlib and SEAL for $\log p = 1$ which vanishes for larger $\log p$ as $\log(2\delta^2 p)$ and $\log(2\delta^2 p B_{\mathsf{err}})$ get are very close for $\log p \in \{64, 256, 2048\}$. Of course, choosing $B_{\mathsf{key}} = 1$ for FV-NFLlib by modifying the code and adapting the security parameters to take the smaller noise into account makes the difference in noise size disappear between FV-NFLlib and SEAL for $\log p = 1$.

4.2 Noise Growth in HElib

Any HElib ciphertext ct carries an inherent noise term, which is an element $\mathbf{v} \in R$ of minimal norm $\|\mathbf{v}\|_\infty$, such that $\mathbf{c_0} + \mathbf{c_1} \cdot \mathbf{s} = p\mathbf{v} + [q_i\boldsymbol{\mu}]_p$. If $\|\mathbf{v}\|_\infty < q_i/p$ decryption works correctly, which means that it returns the plaintext $\boldsymbol{\mu}$. A freshly encrypted ciphertext generated by HElib.Encrypt has an inherent noise term $\mathbf{v}_{\mathsf{enc}} = \mathbf{u} \cdot \mathbf{e} + \mathbf{e_0} + \mathbf{s} \cdot \mathbf{e_1}$ that can be bounded by $\|\mathbf{v}_{\mathsf{enc}}\|_\infty < V = (1+2\delta)B_{\mathsf{err}}$.

A detailed study of the noise evolution of HElib is beyond the scope of this paper, especially as it has already been done in [12] using the canonical embedding norm, and studying the noise variance, which is probably the best approach to get precise bounds. However, the resulting formulas are quite involved and thus hard to use. We are therefore going to provide a simple intuition on what the upper-bound for the noise resulting from multiplication (and modulus switching, and relinearization) should be.

Multiplication. First, let's consider multiplying $\mathsf{ct} := (\mathbf{c_0}, \mathbf{c_1})$ by itself[4] with

$$\mathbf{c_0} := \mathbf{u} \cdot \mathbf{b} + p\mathbf{e_0} + [q_i \boldsymbol{\mu}]_p \text{ and } \mathbf{c_1} := \mathbf{u} \cdot \mathbf{a} + p\mathbf{e_1}.$$

Note that the first term of the resulting ciphertext we compute is $[q_i^{-1}]_p \mathbf{c_0} \cdot \mathbf{c_0}$. This is the ciphertext part that will contain information about the plaintext $\boldsymbol{\mu}$. We must compute $[q_i^{-1}]_p \mathbf{c_0} \cdot \mathbf{c_0}$ instead of $\mathbf{c_0} \cdot \mathbf{c_0}$, in order to preserve the invariant which says that the plaintext is encoded, multiplied (mod p) by the current ciphertext modulus (which ensures decryption correctness). The associated term resulting from $\mathbf{c_0} \cdot \mathbf{c_0}$ would be $[q_i^2 \boldsymbol{\mu}^2]_p$ instead of $[q_i \boldsymbol{\mu}]_p^1$.

Now that the importance of the $[q_i^{-1}]_p$ term is clear let's focus on its impact. When multiplying the noise term by itself we get $p^2 \mathbf{e_0} \cdot \mathbf{e_0}$. As we also multiply all the terms by $[q_i^{-1}]_p$, which can (and probably will) be of the same size as p, we get a bound on this term that is p^3 times the previous noise squared. So if we note U a bound on the previous noise we get after squaring at least a bound of $\delta p^3 U^2$, just considering this term.

Modulus Switching. During a modulus switching operation from the current modulus q_i to the smaller modulus q, the inherent noise term is scaled down by a $\Delta = q_i/q$ factor, then increased by the additive term due to the rounding error. The resulting noise term upper bound is at least $\|\mathbf{v_{mod}}\|_\infty < \|\mathbf{v}\|_\infty/\Delta + B_{roundin}$, B_{err} being at least p due to the noise introduced in step 2 to get an element divisible by p. Note that this implies that modulus switching cannot lower the noise below p.

L-depth Multiplications. Let's consider now L-depth multiplications focusing only on the noise of the first ciphertext element (ignoring for now relineariza-tions). A fresh ciphertext has a noise upper-bound that is $V \sim 2\delta B_{err}$. After a multiplication the bound on the noise becomes (at least) $4p^3\delta^2 B_{err}^2$. When p is large, in order to avoid a geometric explosion of the noise, the factor Δ used in the modulus switching step will have to be at least $\Delta \sim p^2$. Thus, in order to handle L multiplications, $\log q$ will have to grow in $2\log p$ which justi-fies the observation that $\log q$ grows twice faster for HElib-MP with respect to FV-NFLlib and SEAL.

Relinearization. Finally, if we consider a multiplication followed by a relin-earization operation, when $\|\mathbf{v_0}\|_\infty\|, \|\mathbf{v_1}\|_\infty\| < V$, the resulting noise term is bounded by $\|\mathbf{v_{mul}}\|_\infty < U = tV^2 + \delta B_{err} \sum_{i=1}^{\ell} B_i/2q'$. As in HElib the size of the B_i is fixed to $1/3 \log q_i$, the analysis done for L-depth multiplications remains correct as long as $\log q' \sim 1/3 \log q_i$. This validates both the previous simplified reasoning and the size observed for HElib-MP with special primes.

5   Analysis: Representation and Computation

In order to analyze the performance results we must first consider the rep-resentations used for polynomials in R_p and R_q, the costs associated to the

---

[4] We consider squaring to reduce the number of variables, as squaring does not change the noise size with respect to multiplying two different ciphertexts.

transformation between representations, and the cost of the different operations associated to the possible representations.

5.1   Transformation Costs

Switching between a DoubleCRT representation (a vector of polynomial values in CRT form) and a (simple) CRT representation (a vector of polynomial coefficients in CRT form) is quite inexpensive as it only requires an NTT or an inverse-NTT transform, whose costs are in $O(n \log n \log q)$.

Lifting the coefficients from a CRT form, or projecting coefficients into a CRT vector, on the other hand, can become quite expensive as the cost for each coefficient is in $O(n \log^2 q)$ and $\log q$ can become quite large when working with large plaintext moduli.

As a rule of thumb, in order to ensure security in lattice based cryptography, n has to grow linearly in $\log q$ and thus the ratio $\log q / \log n$ (which is the ratio between the asymptotic costs of the two transformations) will grow in $O(\log q / \log \log q)$.

In order to optimize performance the best would therefore be to swap between DoubleCRT and CRT representations but to avoid coefficient lifting/projections as much as possible.

5.2   CRT-Compatible Operations

Some polynomial operations can be done directly in DoubleCRT representation:

- Polynomial addition
  $\text{DoubleCRT}(\mathbf{a} + \mathbf{b}) = \text{DoubleCRT}(\mathbf{a}) + \text{DoubleCRT}(\mathbf{b})$
- Polynomial multiplication
  $\text{DoubleCRT}(\mathbf{a} \cdot \mathbf{b}) = \text{DoubleCRT}(\mathbf{a}) \cdot \text{DoubleCRT}(\mathbf{b})$
- Scalar multiplication
  $\text{DoubleCRT}(p \cdot \mathbf{a}) = p \cdot \text{DoubleCRT}(\mathbf{a})$
- Uniform sampling
  $\text{DoubleCRT}(\mathbf{a})$ for $\mathbf{a} \xleftarrow{U} R_q \sim \mathbf{a} \xleftarrow{U} R_q$

The cost of these operations in R_q is in $O(n \log q)$. If the polynomials are in (simple) CRT form the costs are asymptotically the same except for the polynomial multiplication which would lead to a $O(n \log n \log q)$ cost (NTT, then DoubleCRT multiplication, then inverse-NTT).

Coefficient Operations. Note also that subtracting multiples of a constant and checking divisibility by an integer for the polynomial coefficients (operations required by HElib.ModSwitch) also avoid the cost in $O(n \log^2 q)$ that the CRT transforms have. To subtract the constant, it is enough to project it into CRT form (once for the entire polynomial, with a cost in $O(\log^2 q)$), and then subtract the CRT representation from each coefficient as many times as required. To check divisibility by p (in HElib.ModSwitch), it is enough to extend the CRT representation of the coefficients to $q \times p$ and check whether the coordinate associated to p is zero. This extension has a cost $O(n \log q \log p)$, which does not grow quadratically (in $\log q$) as we try to compute more and more homomorphic multiplications.

Finally, if an integer d_1 in CRT representation is divisible by a constant d_2 (i.e. if $d_1 \mod d_2 = 0$), and d_2 is part of the CRT basis in which d_1 is represented, then it is possible to compute d_1/d_2 without leaving the CRT base. Indeed, it is enough to suppress the coordinate associated to d_2 and multiply the other coordinates by the inverse of d_2 with respect to the coordinates moduli.

HElib. Note that the operations described in this section include all that is required for the algorithms HElib.Add, HElib.Mul, HElib.ModSwitch, HElib.Relin. HElib only needs to project/lift integers during key generation, encryption and decryption.

5.3   CRT-Incompatible Operations

Most operations that are incompatible with the CRT representation (e.g. sampling from a gaussian) are only required in key generation, encryption and decryption algorithms.

There is however a key operation in FV, when computing with ciphertexts, that is a priori incompatible with the CRT representation. Indeed, homomorphic multiplication in FV involves computing $[\lfloor p(\mathbf{a} \cdot \mathbf{b})/q \rceil]_q$ with $\mathbf{a}, \mathbf{b}$ elements of R_q.

The key issue here is that the multiplication $p(\mathbf{a} \cdot \mathbf{b})$ must be done *over the integers* and not modulo q so we have to lift the CRT representations. Moreover, the division by q and rounding must be done over the coefficients, but of course we do not want to do the polynomial multiplication $\mathbf{a} \cdot \mathbf{b}$ on a coefficient representation which would have a cost quadratic in n.

The trivial approach would require a FastMul algorithm to multiply the polynomials with a coefficient representation for the polynomials and a baseline (i.e. non-CRT) representation for the coefficients. Such an approach would have a cost in $K_c n^{1+c} \log^2 q$ with K_c a constant that can be quite large when c is below 0.58 (for Karatsuba multiplication).

In FV-NFLlib, the idea is to extend the CRT basis to a modulus $q' > q^2 n$, then do the multiplication modulo q'. As this modulus is beyond the infinity norm for the result polynomial, there is no reduction   mod q' and therefore the result is the same as if we did the multiplication over $\mathbf{Z}$.

Note however that the polynomial's coefficients must be lifted and projected multiple times with a cost each time in $n \log^2 q$. Taking $\log q = O(L \log p)$ we get a complexity in $O(nL^2 \log^2 p)$ for FV-NFLlib and in $O(nL \log^2 p)$ for HElib which explains the asymptotic results observed.

SEAL and Full-RNS FV. As noted before, Seal v2.3 implements the full-RNS variant of FV proposed by Bajard et al. at SAC 2016 [2]. The objective of this paper is precisely to deal with FV's operations over $\mathbb{Z}$ that are required both during the homomorphic multiplication algorithm and during the decryption algorithm.

The idea is to stay in CRT representation using CRT-basis pivots to extend basis instead of doing it naively as in FV-FNFLlib. Bajard et al. have many interesting ideas to reduce costs and circumvent the many issues that arise when trying to do this. Unfortunately, as they state in Sect. 4.7 of their paper, they were not able to get rid of the $O(n \log^2 q)$ complexity in the homomorphic multiplication algorithm. This seems to be the reason why SEAL faces the same asymptotic issues as FV-NFLlib when compared to HElib-MP.

6   Conclusions

6.1   Library Choice

The first conclusion we can draw is that there are simple criteria to decide which library should be used (based on computational performance of multiplicative homomorphic operations).

For $\log p = 1$ SEAL v2.3 is the best choice up to a depth of around 12. then SEAL v2.3 and HElib have similar performance until a depth of around 25 and above HElib clearly outperforms all the other libraries.

For $\log p = 60$ FV-NFLlib and SEAL v2.3 both outperform HElib for all practical values (up to a depth slightly above 40). Given that FV-NFLlib and SEAL result in similar performance and that SEAL is more actively developed and more user friendly, in practice the natural choice is SEAL v2.3.

For $\log p$ above 60 two situations arise. If the plaintext modulus can be factorized into sub-moduli of 60 bits then the previous conclusion still applies by using a CRT approach on the plaintext space. If not (for example if it is a cryptographic prime or a hard-to-factor modulus), then SEAL v2.3 cannot be used and FV-NFLlib gives the best results for $\log q < 2000$, above that HElib-MP is the best choice.

6.2   Implementation Recommendations

The first conclusion that arises from our performance analysis is that non-CRT representation of integers, even with Karatsuba multiplication, do not seem to be an option for somewhat homomorphic encryption schemes.

The second is that BGV seems to be plainly superior to FV for very large moduli, even considering the FullRNS variant of Bajard et al. It would be thus very interesting to see a simpler, more optimized, implementation of BGV, for example based on NFLlib, to see if it can match FV's performance for smaller ciphertext moduli.

Finally, both highly specialized libraries such as NFLlib and the FullRNS approach of Bajard et al. seem to provide important performance benefits to FV. An implementation combining both seems feasible and a natural step to go for in order to fully exploit the potential of this scheme.

A   Homomorphic Schemes and Libraries

In this section, we recall the variant of the Brakerski-Gentry-Vaikuntanathan (BGV) homomorphic encryption scheme [4], implemented in the software library HElib [11,13]. This description is mostly taken from [10]. We also briefly describe the Fan-Vercauteren (FV) scheme [8], implemented in both SEAL [14] and FV-NFLlib.

A.1   A BGV Scheme Variant

The variant of the BGV scheme implemented in HElib is defined over polynomial rings of the form $R = \mathbb{Z}[x]/\Phi_m(x)$ where m is a parameter and Φ_m is the m-th cyclotomic polynomial. In order to make comparisons simpler we will consider that $m = 2 * n$ with n a power of two, which implies that $\Phi_m(x) = X^n + 1$. The plaintext space is usually the ring $R_p = R/pR$ for an integer p. A plaintext polynomial $\mathbf{a} \in R_p$ is encrypted as a vector over $R_q = R/qR$, where q is an odd public modulus. More specifically, BGV contains a chain of moduli of decreasing size $q_0 > q_1 > \cdots > q_L$ and freshly encrypted ciphertexts are defined modulo q_0. During homomorphic evaluation, we keep switching to smaller moduli after each multiplication until we get ciphertexts modulo q_L, which cannot be multiplied anymore. L is therefore an upper bound on the multiplicative depth of the circuit. We note q_i to indicate that the current modulus we are working with may be any of $\{q_0, \ldots, q_L\}$. We also define another set of primes whose product is noted q'. These are called the *special primes* and they are used to limit the error introduced in relinearization. Noise is drawn from a gaussian distribution $D_{\mathbb{Z}^n,\sigma}$ with standard deviation σ over the integer lattice $\mathbb{Z}^n$. Besides the usual input parameters for key generation used in lattice-based homomorphic schemes (degree n, deviation σ, plaintext modulus p, ciphertext modulus q), it is also possible to choose a relinearization parameter ℓ which enables different trade-offs between noise growth and computational costs. In practice, in HElib this parameter is always set to three.

- HElib.KeyGen:
  - sk Sample a random secret key $\mathsf{sk} := \mathbf{s} \leftarrow R_{q_0}$ with coefficients in $\{-1, 0, 1\}$, where exactly h of them are non-zero.
  - pk Generate a public key $\mathsf{pk} := (\mathbf{b}, \mathbf{a}) \in R_{q_0}^2$, with $\mathbf{a} \leftarrow R_{q_0}$ drawn uniformly at random, and $\mathbf{b} := p e - \mathbf{a} \cdot \mathbf{s}$, where $e \leftarrow R_{q_0}$ follows $D_{\mathbb{Z}^n,\sigma}$.
  - rk Generate a relinearization key in $R_{q_0 \cdot q'}^{2 \times \ell}$. Split q in ℓ evenly-sized factors $B_1, \ldots, B_\ell$. Define $\mathsf{rk}_i := (\mathbf{a}_i, \mathbf{b}_i)^t \in R_{q_0 q'}^2$, with $\mathbf{a}_i \leftarrow R_{q_0 q'}$ drawn uniformly and $\mathbf{b}_i := \left(\prod_{j=0}^{i-1} B_j\right) \mathbf{s}^2 + p e_i - \mathbf{a}_i \cdot \mathbf{s}$, where $e_i \leftarrow R_{q_0 q'}$ follows $D_{\mathbb{Z}^n,\sigma}$. Output $\mathsf{rk} := (\mathsf{rk}_1, \ldots, \mathsf{rk}_\ell)$.
- HElib.Encrypt(pk, $\boldsymbol{\mu}$): Generate a fresh ciphertext $\mathsf{ct} \in R_{q_0}^2$ from a plaintext $\boldsymbol{\mu} \in R_p$, encrypted using the public key $\mathsf{pk} := (\mathbf{b}, \mathbf{a}) \in R_{q_0}^2$. We have $\mathsf{ct} := (\mathbf{c_0}, \mathbf{c_1})$ with $\mathbf{c_0} := \mathbf{u} \cdot \mathbf{b} + p \mathbf{e_0} + [q_0 \boldsymbol{\mu}]_p$ and $\mathbf{c_1} := \mathbf{u} \cdot \mathbf{a} + p \mathbf{e_1}$, where $\mathbf{u} \leftarrow R_{q_0}$ is drawn uniformly in $\{-1, 0, 1\}^n$ and $\mathbf{e_0}, \mathbf{e_1}$ follow $D_{\mathbb{Z}^n,\sigma}$.

- HElib.Add($\mathsf{ct}_0, \mathsf{ct}_1$): Add two ciphertexts $\mathsf{ct}_0 := (\mathbf{c_{00}}, \mathbf{c_{01}}) \in R_{q_i}^2$ and $\mathsf{ct}_1 := (\mathbf{c_{10}}, \mathbf{c_{11}}) \in R_{q_i}^2$ into a ciphertext $\mathsf{ct}_+ := (\mathbf{c_0}, \mathbf{c_1}) \in R_{q_i}^2$, with $\mathbf{c_0} = \mathbf{c_{00}} + \mathbf{c_{10}}$ and $\mathbf{c_1} = \mathbf{c_{01}} + \mathbf{c_{11}}$.
- HElib.Mul($\mathsf{ct}_0, \mathsf{ct}_1$): Multiply two ciphertexts $\mathsf{ct}_0 := (\mathbf{c_{00}}, \mathbf{c_{01}}) \in R_{q_i}^2$ and $\mathsf{ct}_1 := (\mathbf{c_{10}}, \mathbf{c_{11}}) \in R_{q_i}^2$ into a ciphertext $\widetilde{\mathsf{ct}}_\times := (\mathbf{c_0}, \mathbf{c_1}, \mathbf{c_2}) \in R_{q_i}^3$, with $\mathbf{c_0} = \left[q_i^{-1}\right]_p \mathbf{c_{00}} \cdot \mathbf{c_{10}}$, $\mathbf{c_1} = \left[q_i^{-1}\right]_p (\mathbf{c_{00}} \cdot \mathbf{c_{11}} + \mathbf{c_{01}} \cdot \mathbf{c_{10}})$ and $\mathbf{c_2} = \left[q_i^{-1}\right]_p \mathbf{c_{01}} \cdot \mathbf{c_{11}}$.
- HElib.ModSwitch(ct, q): Remove primes from the current modulus to obtain a new target modulus q and scale the ciphertext ct down by a factor of Δ (equal to the current modulus divided by the target modulus) using the following optimized procedure described in [10]:
  1. Reduce the coefficients of ct to obtain $\mathsf{ct}' = \mathsf{ct} \bmod \Delta$,
  2. Add or subtract multiples of Δ from each coefficient in ct' until it is divisible by p,
  3. Set $\mathsf{ct}^* = \mathsf{ct} - \mathsf{ct}'$,   // ct^* divisible by Δ, and $\mathsf{ct}^* \equiv \mathsf{ct} \pmod{p}$
  4. Output ct^*/Δ.
- HElib.Relin($\mathsf{rk}, \widetilde{\mathsf{ct}}_\times$): Relinearize a ciphertext $\widetilde{\mathsf{ct}}_\times := (\mathbf{c_0}, \mathbf{c_1}, \mathbf{c_2}) \in R_{q_i}^3$ into a ciphertext $\mathsf{ct}_\times \in R_{q_i}^2$ using the relinearizing key $\mathsf{rk} := W \in R_{q_0 q'}^{2 \times \ell}$. First we break $\mathbf{c_2}$ into a collection of ℓ lower-norm polynomials $\mathbf{c_2}^{(i)}$:
  1. $\mathbf{d_1} \leftarrow \mathbf{c_2}$
  2. For $i \leftarrow 1, \ldots, \ell$:
  3. $\mathbf{c_2}^{(i)} \leftarrow \mathbf{d_i} \bmod B_i$
  4. $\mathbf{d_{i+1}} \leftarrow \left(\mathbf{d_i} - \mathbf{c_2}^{(i)}\right)/B_i$

  We then reduce the relinearization key matrix modulo $q_i q'$, and add the small primes corresponding to $q_i q'$ to all the $\mathbf{c_2}^{(i)}$'s, then compute the ciphertext

$$\overline{\mathsf{ct}}_\times := \left(\mathbf{c_0} + \sum_{i=1}^{\ell} W_{i,0} \cdot \mathbf{c_2}^{(i)}, \ \mathbf{c_1} + \sum_{i=1}^{\ell} W_{i,1} \cdot \mathbf{c_2}^{(i)}\right) \in R_{q_i q'}^2$$

  Finally, using the modulus switching function defined above, we output $\mathsf{ct}_\times := \mathsf{HElib.ModSwitch}(\overline{\mathsf{ct}}_\times, q_i) \in R_{q_i}^2$.
- HElib.Decrypt(sk, ct): Decrypt a ciphertext $\mathsf{ct} := (\mathbf{c_0}, \mathbf{c_1}) \in R_{q_i}^2$ into a plaintext $\boldsymbol{\mu} := \left[\left[q_i^{-1}\right]_p [\mathbf{c_0} + \mathbf{c_1} \cdot \mathbf{s}]_{q_i}\right]_p \in R_p$.

A.2   Fan and Vercauteren's Scheme

The Fan-Vercauteren (FV) scheme is closely related to BGV, but instead of modulus switching it uses the *scale-invariant approach* of Brakerski [3] to control noise growth, and encodes the plaintext in the high-order bits of the coefficients of the ciphertext polynomials, instead of the low-order bits.

It is possible to choose a relinearization parameter, noted in this case ω. This value is a basis in which the relinearization key is decomposed and can be modified to tune performance. Two different distributions are used: χ_{key} and χ_{err}. FV-NFLlib defines $\chi_{\mathsf{key}} = D_{\mathbb{Z}^n, \sigma_{\mathsf{key}}}$ and $\chi_{\mathsf{err}} = D_{\mathbb{Z}^n, \sigma_{\mathsf{err}}}$, for given σ_{err} and σ_{err}. SEAL defines χ_{key} as the uniform distribution over $\{-1, 0, 1\}$ and χ_{err} as FV-NFLlib does.

- FV.KeyGen:

  sk Output $\mathsf{sk} := \mathbf{s} \leftarrow \chi_{\mathsf{key}}$

  pk Let $\mathbf{a} \leftarrow R_q$ drawn uniformly and $\mathbf{e} \leftarrow \chi_{\mathsf{err}}$.

  Define $\mathsf{pk} := ([-\mathbf{a} \cdot \mathbf{s} - \mathbf{e}]_q, \mathbf{a})$.

  rk Generate a relinearization key $\mathsf{rk} := (\mathsf{rk}_1, \ldots, \mathsf{rk}_\ell)$ with $\ell = \lfloor \log_\omega(q) \rfloor + 1$ and $\mathsf{rk}_i := (\mathbf{s}^2 \omega^i - (\mathbf{a}_i \cdot \mathbf{s} + \mathbf{e}_i), \mathbf{a}_i)$, with $\mathbf{a}_i \leftarrow R_q$ uniformly at random and $\mathbf{e}_i \leftarrow \chi_{\mathsf{err}}$.

- FV.Encrypt(pk, μ): Generate a fresh ciphertext $\mathsf{ct} \in R_q^2$ from a plaintext $\mu \in R_p$, encrypted using the public key $\mathsf{pk} := (\mathbf{b}, \mathbf{a}) \in R_q^2$. We have $\mathsf{ct} := (\mathbf{c_0}, \mathbf{c_1})$ with $\mathbf{c_0} := \mathbf{u} \cdot \mathbf{b} + \mathbf{e_0} + \Delta[\mu]_p$ and $\mathbf{c_1} := \mathbf{u} \cdot \mathbf{a} + \mathbf{e_1}$, where $\mathbf{u}$ follows χ_{key} and $\mathbf{e_0}, \mathbf{e_1}$ follow χ_{err} and $\Delta = q/p$.

- FV.Add$(\mathsf{ct}_0, \mathsf{ct}_1)$: Add two ciphertexts $\mathsf{ct}_0 := (\mathbf{c_{00}}, \mathbf{c_{01}}) \in R_q^2$ and $\mathsf{ct}_1 := (\mathbf{c_{10}}, \mathbf{c_{11}}) \in R_q^2$ into a ciphertext $\widetilde{\mathsf{ct}}_+ := (\mathbf{c_0}, \mathbf{c_1}) \in R_q^2$, with $\mathbf{c_0} = \mathbf{c_{00}} + \mathbf{c_{10}}$ and $\mathbf{c_1} = \mathbf{c_{01}} + \mathbf{c_{11}}$.

- FV.Mul$(\mathsf{ct}_0, \mathsf{ct}_1)$: Multiply two ciphertexts $\mathsf{ct}_0 := (\mathbf{c_{00}}, \mathbf{c_{01}}) \in R_q^2$ and $\mathsf{ct}_1 := (\mathbf{c_{10}}, \mathbf{c_{11}}) \in R_q^2$ into a ciphertext $\widetilde{\mathsf{ct}}_\times := (\mathbf{c_0}, \mathbf{c_1}, \mathbf{c_2}) \in R_q^3$, with $\mathbf{c_0} = \lfloor p/q(\mathbf{c_{00}} \cdot \mathbf{c_{10}}) \rceil$, $\mathbf{c_1} = \lfloor p/q(\mathbf{c_{00}} \cdot \mathbf{c_{11}} + \mathbf{c_{01}} \cdot \mathbf{c_{10}}) \rceil)$ and $\mathbf{c_2} = \lfloor p/q(\mathbf{c_{01}} \cdot \mathbf{c_{11}}) \rceil$.

- FV.Relin$(\mathsf{rk}, \widetilde{\mathsf{ct}}_\times)$: Re-linearize a ciphertext $\widetilde{\mathsf{ct}}_\times := (\mathbf{c_0}, \mathbf{c_1}, \mathbf{c_2}) \in R_q^3$ into a ciphertext $\mathsf{ct}_\times \in R_q^2$. Noting the elements of the relinearization key $\mathsf{rk}_i = (\mathsf{rk}_{i,0}, \mathsf{rk}_{i,1}) \in R_q^2$, and $\mathbf{c_2}^{(i)}$ the decomposition of $\mathbf{c_2}$ in digits in base ω, return

$$\mathsf{ct}_\times := \left(\mathbf{c_0} + \sum_{i=0}^{\ell} \mathsf{rk}_{i,1} \cdot \mathbf{c_2}^{(i)}, \mathbf{c_1} + \sum_{i=1}^{\ell} \mathsf{rk}_{i,1} \cdot \mathbf{c_2}^{(i)} \right)$$

- FV.Decrypt$(\mathsf{sk}, \mathsf{ct})$: Decrypt a ciphertext $\mathsf{ct} := (\mathbf{c_0}, \mathbf{c_1}) \in R_q^2$ into a plaintext $\mu := [\lfloor p/q(\mathbf{c_0} + \mathbf{c_1} \cdot \mathbf{s}) \rceil]_p$

A.3   Homomorphic Operations

In the schemes presented, the plaintext space is R_p, and homomorphic additions correspond to additions over the ring R_q.[5]

In order to realize other operations (encryption, homomorphic multiplication, modulus switching, relinearization, decryption), we also need to compute multiplications over R_q and, for some of these operations, to manipulate directly the coefficients of the polynomials in R_q.

Batching. Using the Chinese Remainder Theorem it is possible to encrypt a vector of elements of $\mathbb{Z}_p$ [7,17,18] so that homomorphic operations are applied component-wise between the plaintext vectors. This feature is called *batching*, and when used efficiently can massively improve the performance of homomorphic computations, e.g. by allowing thousands of instances of a function to be evaluated simultaneously on different inputs.

---

[5] One can easily obtain an HE scheme with a plaintext space $\mathbb{Z}_p$ by embedding $\mathbb{Z}_p$ into R_p via $a \in \mathbb{Z}_p \mapsto \mathbf{a} \in R_p$, and homomorphic operations then correspond to arithmetic operations over the ring $\mathbb{Z}_p$.

To understand how batching works, suppose the cyclotomic polynomial $\Phi_m(x)$ factors modulo the plaintext modulus p into a product of irreducible factors $\Phi_m(x) = \prod_{j=0}^{\ell-1} F_j(x) \pmod{p}$, then a plaintext polynomial $\mathbf{a} \in R_p$ can be viewed as encoding ℓ different small polynomials $a_j = a \bmod F_j$, and each constant coefficient of the a_j can be set to an element of $\mathbb{Z}_p$.

Note that the factorization of the cyclotomic polynomial, $\Phi_m(x) = \prod_{j=0}^{\ell-1} F_j(x) \pmod{p}$, depends on m and p. If p is fixed for a given application, then the batching capacity will be different for each m depending on how $\Phi_m(x)$ factors modulo p.

HElib gives complete freedom when choosing m but both FV-NFLlib and SEAL use optimized NTT transforms that require power-of-two cyclotomic polynomials. In practice this means that HElib is able, in some cases, to provide a better batching than FV-NFLlib and SEAL.

A.4   DoubleCRT Representation

In this section we recall the *DoubleCRT* representation used in HElib and NFLlib to represent elements of the cyclotomic ring R_q (it is also used with R_p, but for conciseness we will focus on R_q). This representation is composed of two sub-representations, the Chinese remainder theorem (CRT) and the number theoretic transform (NTT).

CRT. We consider the CRT basis as a l-uple of co-prime numbers $(q_0, \ldots, q_{l-1})$, we note $q = \prod_{i=0}^{l-1} p_i$. An integer $a \in \mathbb{Z}_q$ is represented in CRT as:

$$\mathrm{CRT}(a) = (a \bmod q_i)_{0 \le i < l}$$

This representation is unique for all $a \in \mathbb{Z}_q$ by the Chinese Remainder Theorem.

NTT. Let q be an integer such that $\mathbb{Z}_q$ contains a primitive m-th root of unity ζ_i. A polynomial $\mathbf{a} \in R_q$ is represented in NTT as:

$$\mathrm{NTT}(\mathbf{a}) = \big(\mathbf{a}(\zeta^j)\big)_{j \in \mathbb{Z}_m^*}$$

DoubleCRT. To use at the same time the CRT representation for coefficients/values and the NTT representation, we need a CRT basis $(q_0, \ldots, q_{l-1})$ such that every q_i is chosen so that $\mathbb{Z}/q_i\mathbb{Z}$ contains a primitive m-th root of unity ζ_i. A polynomial $\mathbf{a} \in R_q$ is represented in DoubleCRT as:

$$\mathrm{DoubleCRT}(\mathbf{a}) = \Big(\mathbf{a}(\zeta_i^j) \bmod p_i\Big)_{0 \le i < l,\, j \in \mathbb{Z}_m^*}$$

References

1. Albrecht, M.R., Player, R., Scott, S.: On the concrete hardness of learning with errors. Cryptology ePrint Archive, Report 2015/046 (2015). http://eprint.iacr.org/2015/046
2. Bajard, J.-C., Eynard, J., Hasan, M.A., Zucca, V.: A full RNS variant of FV like somewhat homomorphic encryption schemes. In: Avanzi, R., Heys, H. (eds.) SAC 2016. LNCS, vol. 10532, pp. 423–442. Springer, Cham (2017). https://doi.org/10.1007/978-3-319-69453-5_23
3. Brakerski, Z.: Fully homomorphic encryption without modulus switching from classical GapSVP. In: Safavi-Naini, R., Canetti, R. (eds.) CRYPTO 2012. LNCS, vol. 7417, pp. 868–886. Springer, Heidelberg (2012). https://doi.org/10.1007/978-3-642-32009-5_50
4. Brakerski, Z., Gentry, C., Vaikuntanathan, V.: (Leveled) fully homomorphic encryption without bootstrapping. In: Goldwasser, S. (ed.) ITCS 2012, pp. 309–325. ACM, January 2012
5. Chen, H., Han, K., Huang, Z., Jalali, A.: Simple encrypted arithmetic library - seal (v2.3). Technical report, Microsoft, December 2017. https://www.microsoft.com/en-us/research/project/simple-encrypted-arithmetic-library/
6. Chen, H., Laine, K., Player, R.: Simple encrypted arithmetic library - SEAL v2.1. Cryptology ePrint Archive, Report 2017/224 (2017). http://eprint.iacr.org/2017/224
7. Cheon, J.H., et al.: Batch fully homomorphic encryption over the integers. In: Johansson, T., Nguyen, P.Q. (eds.) EUROCRYPT 2013. LNCS, vol. 7881, pp. 315–335. Springer, Heidelberg (2013). https://doi.org/10.1007/978-3-642-38348-9_20
8. Fan, J., Vercauteren, F.: Somewhat practical fully homomorphic encryption. Cryptology ePrint Archive, Report 2012/144 (2012). http://eprint.iacr.org/2012/144
9. Gentry, C.: Fully homomorphic encryption using ideal lattices. In: Mitzenmacher, M. (ed.) 41st ACM STOC, pp. 169–178. ACM Press, May/June 2009
10. Gentry, C., Halevi, S., Smart, N.P.: Homomorphic evaluation of the AES circuit. In: Safavi-Naini, R., Canetti, R. (eds.) CRYPTO 2012. LNCS, vol. 7417, pp. 850–867. Springer, Heidelberg (2012). https://doi.org/10.1007/978-3-642-32009-5_49
11. Halevi, S., Shoup, V.: Algorithms in HElib. In: Garay, J.A., Gennaro, R. (eds.) CRYPTO 2014, Part I. LNCS, vol. 8616, pp. 554–571. Springer, Heidelberg (2014). https://doi.org/10.1007/978-3-662-44371-2_31
12. Halevi, S., Shoup, V.: Design and implementation of a homomorphic-encryption library. Technical report, MIT (2014)
13. Halevi, S., Shoup, V.: Bootstrapping for HElib. In: Oswald, E., Fischlin, M. (eds.) EUROCRYPT 2015, Part I. LNCS, vol. 9056, pp. 641–670. Springer, Heidelberg (2015). https://doi.org/10.1007/978-3-662-46800-5_25
14. Laine, K., Chen, H., Player, R.: Simple encrypted arithmetic library - seal (v2.1). Technical report, Microsoft, September 2016. https://www.microsoft.com/en-us/research/publication/simple-encrypted-arithmetic-library-seal-v2-1/
15. Lepoint, T., Naehrig, M.: A comparison of the homomorphic encryption schemes FV and YASHE. In: Pointcheval, D., Vergnaud, D. (eds.) AFRICACRYPT 2014. LNCS, vol. 8469, pp. 318–335. Springer, Cham (2014). https://doi.org/10.1007/978-3-319-06734-6_20
16. Ricosset, T.: Helib-multiprecision (2017). https://github.com/tricosset/HElib-MP

17. Smart, N.P., Vercauteren, F.: Fully homomorphic encryption with relatively small key and ciphertext sizes. In: Nguyen, P.Q., Pointcheval, D. (eds.) PKC 2010. LNCS, vol. 6056, pp. 420–443. Springer, Heidelberg (2010). https://doi.org/10.1007/978-3-642-13013-7_25

18. Smart, N., Vercauteren, F.: Fully homomorphic SIMD operations. Cryptology ePrint Archive, Report 2011/133 (2011). http://eprint.iacr.org/2011/133

A New DNA-Combining Chaos Scheme for Fast and Secure Image Encryption

Augustin Ousmanou Ahgue[1], Jean De Dieu Nkapkop[1(✉)],
Joseph Yves Effa[1], Samuel Franz[2], Raul Malutan[3],
and Monica Borda[3]

[1] University of Ngaoundéré, P.O. Box 454, Ngaoundéré, Cameroon
ahgue_augustin@yahoo.fr, jdd.nkapkop@gmail.com,
yveseffa@gmail.com
[2] ENSEIRB MATMECA of Bordeaux, P.O. Box 99, Bordeaux, France
sfranz@enseirb-matmeca.fr
[3] Technical University of Cluj-Napoca, 26-28 Baritiu Street,
400027 Cluj-Napoca, Romania
{Raul.Malutan,Monica.Borda}@com.utcluj.ro

Abstract. This paper aims to introduce a new secured image encryption scheme base on Peace Wise Linear Chaotic Map (PWLCM) and DeoxyriboNucleic Acid (DNA) encoding. The first step is to increase the entropy of the original image by applying a dynamical XOR operation through all the pixels of the image. To satisfy security requirement inherent to an encryption algorithm, PWLCM random sequences are combined with DNA encoding rules, picked randomly among 8 rules available, in order to generate a DNA OTP-key used for encryption. The last step is to replace every pixel of the image with a randomly chosen index that corresponds to one index of occurrence of its DNA equivalent in the OTP-key following an S-BOX strategy. Experimental results show that this encryption algorithm is fast and efficient compared to existing solutions, but also secure to various types of attacks such as statistical attacks, differential attack or brute-force attacks.

Keywords: DNA sequence · Chaos · PWLCM · Image encryption · OTP · S-Box

1 Introduction

In today's world, data trading and exchanges are greatly encouraged through high-speed internet, putting at risk a lot of precious information. As a result, data security has become a top concern, and it has become mandatory to encrypt data before sending it into the cloud. Due to this boiling security research context, new encryption algorithms are being developed actively, introducing new methods like chaotic encryption to improve traditional methods [1–9]. In fact, chaos based schemes are based upon interesting properties such as ergodicity, high sensitivity to initial conditions and control parameters, unpredictability, mixing, etc. [2] that are necessary in cryptography. Several chaos based encryption algorithm have already been introduced due to

J.-L. Lanet and C. Toma (Eds.): SecITC 2018, LNCS 11359, pp. 443–457, 2019.
https://doi.org/10.1007/978-3-030-12942-2_33

those benefits [1–17], each displaying strengths and weaknesses in term of execution time and security. Some of them have even been successfully cryptanalyzed [18–21]. The main issue of chaos based methods is that chaotic properties fall short when a computer's digital precision is finite. To tackle that issue, DNA encoding rules can be introduced in order to add an additional layer of security.

Apart from chaos, DNA encryptions have also been developed in the past recent years. It consists of a combination of cryptography and DNA technologies. Like chaos, DNA encryption features numerous interesting properties. Indeed, 1 g of DNA can store up to 10^8 terabytes of data, and DNA computing speed can reach 1 billion operations per seconds. DNA also features ultra-low energy consumption, large scale parallelism and high storage density. For those reason, DNA encryption algorithms are been developed and a few have already been proposed [22, 23]. One interesting property of DNA is the complementarity of its nucleotides as proposed by Watson and Crick [24]. There are three main reasons to put DNA technology in encryption and cryptography, storage capacity, computing power, and the ability to generate long cryptographic keys. This last property has been exploited by cryptographs and various authors took advantage of DNA based operations like addition, truncation or complementation transformations to generate DNA secret keys for chaos-based encryption schemes.

Despite the previously described properties, DNA based schemes almost always suffer from the following limitations [17]: a low key sensitivity, an expensive computing time, a periodic degradation of chaotic real numbers into finite precisions in digital computers, a need of a high tech bio molecular laboratory, etc. This paper aims to overcome these defaults through the development of a symmetrical image encryption scheme that features both the merits of the DNA and the chaotic PWLCM system, combined with an substitution strategy that suppress the cyclic digitization of a key sequence.

The rest of paper is organized as follows. The PWLCM function and DNA sequence are described in Sect. 2. Section 3 is dedicated to introducing the proposed method. The experimental results, security and speed analysis are provided in Sect. 4. The conclusions are discussed in the last Section.

2 The Basic Concept

In this section, the PWLCM function and DNA encoding are explained. Here is also reviewed the One-Time Pad (OTP) basics, which will be necessary to understand the making of the DNA OTP-key, used in the encryption algorithm proposed in the next section.

2.1 Chaos Theory

Chaotic system is a kind of peculiar motion form, which has a very good randomness. In this paper, the chosen chaotic system is the PWLCM defined by the following equation:

$$x(n) = F[x(n-1)] = \begin{cases} x(n-1) \times \frac{1}{\lambda}, & \text{if } 0 \le x(n-1) \prec \lambda \\ [x(n-1) - \lambda] \times \frac{1}{0.5-\lambda}, & \text{if } \lambda \le x(n-1) \prec 0.5 \\ F[1 - x(n-1)], & \text{if } 0.5 \le x(n-1) \prec 1 \end{cases} \quad (1)$$

The PWLCM is known to be chaotic when its control parameter λ is within the interval]0, 0.5[and its initial condition (x_0) is chosen within the interval]0, 1[[8]. According to the PWLCM bifurcation diagram presented in Fig. 1, all the $x_0 \in$]0, 1[and $\lambda \in$]0, 0.5[can be used as secret keys. The PWLCM system has a uniform invariant distribution and a very good ergodicity, confusion and determinacy, so it can provide excellent random sequence, which is suitable for a cryptosystem. In this paper, the PWLCM function is used to generate the OTP key composed of DNA sequences, needed for encryption.

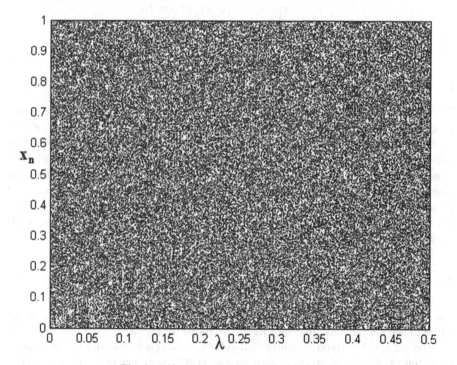

Fig. 1. Bifurcation diagram of the PWLCM.

2.2 Deoxyribonucleic Acid Sequence

DNA is a long polymer of deoxyribonucleotides carrying genetic instructions. The length of a DNA chain is usually defined by its number of composing nucleotides. A DNA sequence consists of four nucleic acid bases: A (adenine), C (cytosine), G (guanine) and T (thymine), where A and T are complementary, as well as G and C. Because 0 and 1 are complementary in the binary system, DNA complementarity can be converted into binary complementarity. Using four bases A, C, G and T to encode 00,

01, 10 and 11, there are 24 kinds of encoding rules. But there are only 8 of them which, as mentioned in Table 1, satisfying the Watson-Crick complementary rule [24]. Note that DNA decoding rule is the reverse operation of DNA encoding rule. In this paper, DNA encoding rules are used to encode sequences of integers, obtained from the substitution of the PWLCM chaotic values by the corresponding indexes chosen in a normalized interval in [0, 255]. Each 8-bit value of this interval can be represented as a nucleotide string of length four, as a nucleotide represents two bits. The reverse operation is then easy to convert DNA sequences into integers or 8-bits sequences.

Table 1. DNA sequence encoding rules.

Rules	1	2	3	4	5	6	7	8
A	00	00	01	01	10	10	11	11
T	11	11	10	10	01	01	00	00
C	01	10	00	11	00	11	01	10
G	10	01	11	00	11	00	10	01

2.3   One-Time Pad System

The encryption scheme presented in this paper is based upon the use of a secret key generated from a random sequence of integers, according to the One-Time-Padding method. One-Time Pad (OTP) in cryptography is an encryption scheme which is unbreakable if used correctly [25]. There are some preconditions: the length of OTP (randomly generated secret key) must be equal to the length of the plaintext (here the plaintext is the random integer sequence); the OTP must feature random sequences and must be used only once. In this paper, the large non-repeating set of pseudo-random DNA sequences, obtained by the proposed encryption strategy, is used as the OTP generated secret key.

3   Proposed Encryption Scheme

The cyphering method consists of two stages: first the diffusion of the pixels of the entire image and secondly the substitution as shown in Fig. 2.

The proposed encryption strategy provides three levels of security i.e., arithmetic operation (XOR operation), biological process (DNA complementary rule), and OTP (randomly generated secret key). Hereafter are consecutively listed the steps of the proposed chaos-based DNA cryptography algorithm:

Step 1. Consider that an 8-bit grayscale image I is of size $H \times W$, and each pixel value of $I(i, j)$ falls into the integer interval [0, 255], $i = 1, 2, ..., H, j = 1, 2, ..., W$. Reshape I into a vector denoted by P, having the size of $n = H \times W$, $P = \{p_1, p_2, ..., p_n\}$.

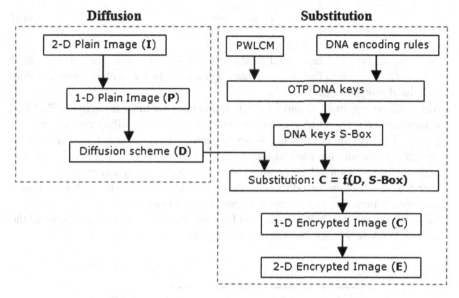

Fig. 2. Synoptic of the proposed scheme for encryption process.

Step 2. Mask all the pixel values of P using the bitwise exclusive-OR, described in the diffusion scheme (D) given in Eq. 2.

$$(D) : \begin{cases} d_1 = p_1 \oplus p_n \\ d_{t+1} = p_t \oplus d_t \end{cases}, t \in \{1, 2, 3, \ldots, n-1\} \tag{2}$$

In this step, the pixel values are sequentially modified and the modification made to a pixel (d_{t+1}) usually depends on the accumulated effect of all the previous pixel values ($d_0, \ldots, d_t$), so that a slight change in one pixel could be spread out to almost all the subsequent pixels.

Step 3. Build an S-box (not the S-BOX mentioned in Fig. 3) to avoid the cyclic digitization of chaotic numbers in the generation of substitution key and then achieve high speed and security performances. The construction of the S-box is as follows:

(1) The interval [0, 1] is divided into 256 sub-intervals I_k having the same amplitude:

$$I_0 = \left(0, \frac{1}{256}\right), I_1 = \left(\frac{1}{256}, \frac{2}{256}\right), \ldots, I_k = \left(\frac{k}{256}, \frac{k+1}{256}\right), k \in \{0, 1, 2, \ldots, 255\}$$

(2) Compute an integer number y_k in the range of [0, 255] by using the following formula:

$$y_k = k + q \bmod 256 \qquad (3)$$

where y_k is the label associated to the interval I_k and $q \in Z$, the interval offset parameter. Then build the S-box by binding each interval I_k with its corresponding calculated integer value y_k.

Step 4. Choose x_0 in $]0, 1[$ and λ in $]0, 0.5[$ and iterate N times through the PWLCM equation to create a set of pseudo-random real numbers x, falling into the interval $[0, 1]$. Then use the constructed S-box to convert x into a vector y of size $4N$ of integers falling into the interval $[0, 255]$.

Step 5. Convert each value contained in y to an 8-bit binary sequence.

Step 6. Use one of the encoding rules shown in Table 1 to convert each 8-bit binary sequence generate at step 5, into a 4-letter DNA sequence.

Step 7. Generate the OTP key for used later for encryption by concatenating all the 4-letter DNA sequences generated at step 6, into one vector of length $4N$.

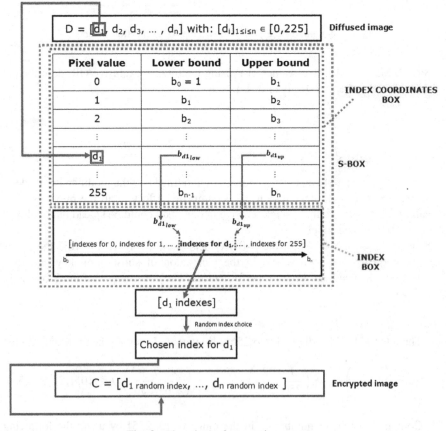

Fig. 3. Flowchart of encryption process.

Step 8. Convert into 8-bit binary sequences each integer value between [0, 255] and use the method in step 6 to generate the corresponding 4-letter DNA sequences.

Step 9. Create another S-BOX to encrypt the image as follows. Write for each 4-letter DNA sequence generated at step 8, all the indexes corresponding to their occurrence in the OTP key. Thus we obtain for each 4-letter DNA sequence, a vector of indexes. All these vectors are concatenated into one vector (see index box in Fig. 3) while saving their position in this vector into a matrix (see index coordinates box in Fig. 3).

Step 10. For each masked pixel in D, one index is chosen randomly in the interval of the index box that corresponds to its value (the interval is obtained by looking in the index coordinate box). Doing so, each pixel of the masked image is associated to a pseudo-random index, and consequently the image is encrypted (see C in Fig. 3).

The decryption process is a simple reverse process of the proposed DNA-based chaos encryption algorithm, no more details here.

4 Experimental Results and Security Analysis

In this section, the robustness of the proposed encryption scheme is tested through a series of tests. All the simulations were performed in MATLAB 2014a on a 3 GHz CPU, 4 GB memory computer running Windows 7.

4.1 Simulation Results

In this subsection, we perform the simulation of the developed algorithm using the *Lena* and *Baboon* images of size 512×512 and *Cameraman* image of size 256×256. Figure 4 presents a simulation realized with the following initial parameters: $x_0 = 0.658945256415431$, $\lambda = 0.345$, 1000 PWLCM iterations; $q = 4586$ for the offset parameter and $A = 00$, $G = 01$, $C = 10$ et $T = 11$ for the encoding rule. Analyzing the results, it appears that the encrypted images (Figs. 4b, e and h) look nothing like the original images (Figs. 4a, d and g), all resembling a "salt and pepper" noise image, and displaying good randomness. Moreover, the reversibility of the algorithm allows good decryption using the right secret key (Figs. 4c, f and i).

4.2 Histogram Analysis

In Fig. 5e, f and g, the histograms of the original image of Lena (Fig. 5a), encrypted image (Fig. 5b) and decrypted image (Fig. 5c) produced by the proposed scheme, are displayed respectively. From those, several conclusions come. Firstly, the histograms of the original image and the decrypted image are identical, and thus the decryption is working as supposed to. Secondly, the histogram of the encrypted image is fairly uniform and significantly different from that of the original image, making the encryption strong against statistical attacks.

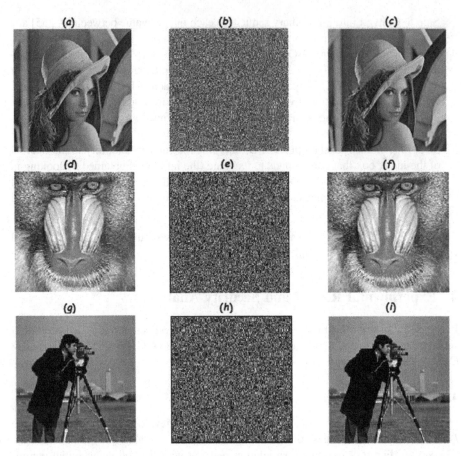

Fig. 4. Simulation results 1: (*a, d, g*) original images; (*b, e, h*) encrypted images of (*a, d, g*) respectively; (*c, f, i*) decrypted images of (*b, e, h*) respectively.

4.3   Key Sensitivity Analysis

In order to guarantee robustness against brute-force attacks, a cryptosystem needs to feature strong sensitivity to the encryption secret key. Two aspects are to be verified to test the sensitivity of this encryption algorithm. On the one hand, changing one of the initial parameters of the encryption key must result in a totally different encrypted image. On the other hand, trying to decrypt an image with a slightly wrong encryption key must not provide any clue to fully decrypt the message.

Figure 6 below display the key sensitivity tests results. In Fig. 6*a* is the encrypted image of *Lena* which was encrypted using $x_0 = 0.658945256415431$. Figure 6*b* represents the decryption of the previous image using the exact same parameters (exact same key). Figure 6*c* shows an attempt to decrypt the cyphered image of *Lena* using a slightly modified key; all parameters are the same as previously except for x_0 that now equals 0.658945256415432. As a result, the decryption fails completely, proving an acute sensitivity of the algorithm to the secret key.

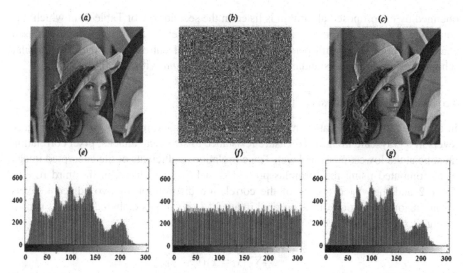

Fig. 5. Simulation results 2: (*a*) original image; (*b*) encrypted image of (*a*); (*c*) decrypted image of (*b*); (*e*), (*f*), (*g*) histogram of (*a*), (*b*), (*c*) respectively.

Fig. 6. Key sensitivity analysis: (*a*) encrypted image; (*b*) Decrypted image with the same key used in (*a*); (*c*) Decrypted image by a key having only a slightly difference with the key used in (*a*).

4.4   Information Entropy

The information entropy is a most significant feature of randomness. The following equation defines Entropy:

$$H = -\sum_{i=1}^{2^M} p(m_i) \log_2(p(m_i)) \tag{4}$$

where M is the number of bit to represent a symbol; $p(m_i)$ represents the probability of occurrence of symbol m_i and log denotes the base 2 logarithm so that the entropy is expressed in bits. To ensure security against entropy attacks, a cyphered image must have its entropy as close to 8 as possible. Information entropy of the encrypted image obtained by the proposed algorithm is listed in the second row of Table 2, in which it is compared with the results in references [10–16]. Overall, the proposed DNA-based chaos encryption algorithm performs better in term of entropy than the other similar schemes using the same standard gray scale image *Lena* with size 512×512.

4.5   Correlation Analysis

In an image, pixel correlation measures the level of randomness of color levels (gray levels in a grayscale image). To ensure resistance to statistical attacks, pixel correlation must be at the lowest possible level. The correlation coefficients of the encrypted image were computed using the formulas presented in Eq. 5 and listed in the third row of Table 2 and the visual testing of the correlation distribution of two adjacent pixels along diagonal direction of the original image of *Lena* and its ciphered image is shown in Fig. 7.

$$r_{xy} = \frac{\frac{1}{N}\sum_{i=1}^{N}(x_i - \bar{x})(y_i - \bar{y})}{\sqrt{\left(\frac{1}{N}\sum_{i=1}^{N}(x_i - \bar{x})^2\right)\left(\frac{1}{N}\sum_{i=1}^{N}(y_i - \bar{y})^2\right)}} \tag{5}$$

With:

$$\bar{x} = \frac{1}{N}\sum_{i=1}^{N}x_i \tag{6}$$

$$\bar{y} = \frac{1}{N}\sum_{i=1}^{N}y_i \tag{7}$$

where x_i and y_i are greyscale values of i-th pair of adjacent pixels, and N denotes the total numbers of samples.

4.6   Differential Attack Analysis

In order to benchmark the performances of the proposed encryption system against differential attacks, the Number of Pixel Change Rate (NPCR) and the Unified Average Changing Intensity (UACI) provide good analysis. NPCR measures the percentage of pixel that differs between two images. UACI compares average image intensities between two images. NPCR and UACI formulas between two ciphered images A and B of size $M \times N$ are given bellow [9]:

$$NPCR_{AB} = \frac{\sum_{i=1}^{M}\sum_{j}^{N}D(i,j)}{M \times N} \times 100 \tag{8}$$

$$UACI_{AB} = \frac{100}{M \times N} \sum_1^M \sum_1^N \frac{|A(i,j) - B(i,j)|}{255} \qquad (9)$$

With:

$$D(i,j) = \begin{cases} 1 & A(i,j) \neq B(i,j) \\ 0 & otherwise \end{cases} \qquad (10)$$

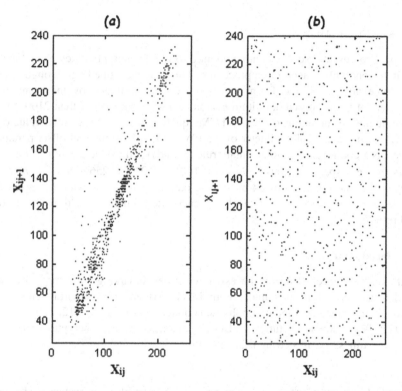

Fig. 7. Correlation distribution of diagonally adjacent pixels of (*a*) the original image and (*b*) the encrypted image.

If one minor change in the plain image can be effectively diffused to the whole encrypted image, then such differential analysis may become inefficient and practically useless. The expected NPCR and UACI for two random images with 256 gray levels are respectively 99.609% and 33.464%.

Comparing the NPCR and UACI obtained through the proposed encryption algorithm with those obtained in references [10–16] in Table 2, the proposed method stands out with better performances with NPCR > 0.99609 and UACI > 0.33464 providing excellent pixel alteration.

Table 2. Results of different statistical tests and comparison with other DNA-based chaos encryption algorithms using Lena image of size 512 × 512.

1.	Reference		Proposed	[10]	[11]	[12]	[13]	[14]	[15]	[16]
2.	Entropy		7.9973	7.9993	7.9970	7.9967	7.9993	7.9874	7.9962	7.9975
3.	Correlation	H	0.0004	−0.0045	0.0020	−0.0021	0.0214	0.0004	0.0062	−0.0017
	coefficients of	V	0.0002	−0.00162	−0.0007	−0.0032	0.0466	0.0021	0.0052	0.0013
	encrypted image	D	−0.0028	0.0053	0.0014	0.0037	−0.0090	−0.0038	0.0069	−0.0005
4.	NPCR		99.94	99.59	99.65	99.58	99.60	99.60	99.21	99.6077
5.	UACI		33.49	33.41	33.48	33.49	33.44	28.1370	33.28	33.4570

4.7   Key Space Analysis

Key space represents the maximum amount of possible encryption key available to be used in the encryption/decryption procedure. This space must be large enough to avoid brute force attacks. The different layers of security provided by the many initial parameters of the proposed algorithm guarantee a key space larger than 2100. Indeed, (1) the number of iterations of the PWLCM equations (nn); (2) the initial value of the PWLCM; (3) the control parameter of the PWLCM; (4) the interval offset parameter; (5) the DNA coding and complementary rule (8 kinds) and (6) the creation of the S-box allows a key space as large as $nn \times 10^{-15} \times 10^{-15} \times 256 \times 8 \times 8 \approx nn \times 2^{114}$ knowing that the precision of 64-bit double data is 10^{-15}. This wide key space thus provides strong security and the developed encryption scheme should be able to resist any brute-force attack.

4.8   Speed Analysis

Good execution speed is a prior necessity when benchmarking an encryption system. Speed tests were performed under both MATLAB and C++ environments on the previously introduced computer, on the Lena image of size 512 × 512. The tests focus on OTP key generation times, S-BOX generation times, encryption times and decryption times, as enlisted in Table 3 below:

Table 3. Efficiency analysis of the proposed DNA-based chaos encryption algorithm.

Environments	Number of iterations	Execution times (in s)			
		OTP key	S-box	Encryption	Decryption
Matlab	1000	0.552	2.219	105.995	108.154
	5000	2.687	10.716	100.198	102.925
	10 000	5.318	21.321	99.291	101.681
	100 000	55.425	215.285	100.332	102.876
C/C++	1000	0.0001	0.046	**0.58**	**0.63**
	5000	0.001	0.223	1.17	1.28
	10 000	0.003	0.439	1.78	1.84
	100 000	0.022	4.258	11	14.3

Results from Table 3 show that MATLAB is not a good environment when considering time efficiency. However, implementation on C++ display good performances for short OTP-keys, making the DNA based chaotic system a strong candidate for real-time image transfer if the chosen key is generated with around 1000 chaotic PWLCM iterations, while 100000 iterations provide a better decorrelation of the pixels and significantly better histogram, but to the detriment of execution times during decryption. Nevertheless, this characteristic could be useful in domains like the military where top-secret data need to be transfer privileging ultra-strong encryption rather than instant decryption time.

5 Conclusion

This paper proposes a new secure symmetric image encryption technique, combining the merits of DNA properties and the chaotic PWLCM system. The sensitivity and unpredictability of PWLCM, the choice of the interval offset parameter, the choice of the DNA encoding and complementary rule and the creation of the S-BOX guarantees the structural complexity of the scheme. Substituting the randomly generated floating sequence from the PWLCM equation by integers in the developed algorithm is used to avoid the cyclic digitization of real numbers, avoiding limitations inherent to computer's precision. Experimental results and security analyses show that the proposed DNA-based chaos encryption algorithm effectively increases the entropy of the encrypted image, reduces the correlation between adjacent pixels, has a satisfying encryption effect, a high sensitivity to the secret key and to the original image, and a larger secure key space. As a result, the algorithm is capable to withstand various attacks such as differential attacks, statistical attacks, etc., and in most cases, performed much better than existing algorithms referred to in this paper. In addition, with the proposed DNA-based chaos encryption algorithm, fast and secured encryption and decryption speeds are achieved, making it suitable for real-time secured image transfer over the Internet.

Acknowledgement. The work described in this paper was supported under the Postdoctoral Fellowships Program "Eugen Ionescu" funded by Romania government and managed by the "Agence Universitaire de la Francophonie (AUF)".

References

1. Wang, Y., Zhang, X., Zheng, Z., Qiu, W.: A colour image encryption algorithm using 4-pixel feistel structure and multiple chaotic systems. Nonlinear Dyn. **81**, 151–168 (2015). https://doi.org/10.1007/s11071-015-1979-3
2. Armand Eyebe Fouda, J.S., Yves Effa, J., Samrat, S.L., Ali, M.: A fast chaotic block cipher for image encryption. Commun. Nonlinear Sci. Numer. **19**, 578–588 (2014). https://doi.org/10.1016/j.cnsns.2013.07.016
3. Sivakumar, T., Venkatesan, R.: A novel approach for image encryption using dynamic scan patter. IAENG Int. J. Comput. Sci. **4**, 91–101 (2014)

4. Ghebleh, M., Kanso, A., Noura, H.: An image encryption scheme based on irregularly decimated chaotic maps. Signal Process.: Image Commun. **29**, 618–627 (2014). https://doi. org/10.1016/j.image.2013.09.009

5. Wang, X., Gu, S., Zhang, Y.: Novel image encryption algorithm based on cycle shift and chaotic system. Opt. Lasers Eng. **68**, 126–134 (2015). https://doi.org/10.1016/j.optlaseng. 2014.12.025

6. Arroyo, D., Rhouma, R., Alvarez, G., Li, S., Fernandez, V.: On the security of a new image encryption scheme based on chaotic map lattices. Chaos: Interdisc. J. Nonlinear Sci. **18**, 033112 (2008). https://doi.org/10.1063/1.2959102

7. Chong, F., Chen, J.-J., Zou, H., Meng, W.-H., Zhan, Y.-F.: A chaos-based digital image encryption with an improved permutation strategy. Opt. Expr. **20**, 2363–2378 (2012). https:// doi.org/10.1364/OE.20.002363

8. Seyedzadeh, M., Mirzakuchaki, S.: A fast color image encryption algorithm based on coupled two- dimensional piecewise chaotic map. Signal process. **92**, 1202–1215 (2012). https://doi.org/10.1016/j.sigpro.2011.11.004

9. Wong Wang, Y., Liao, K.-W., Chen, X., Chen, G.: A new chaos-based fast image encryption algorithm. Appl. Soft Comput. **11**, 514–522 (2011). https://doi.org/10.1016/j.asoc.2009.12. 011

10. Chai, X., Chen, Y., Broyde, L.: A novel chaos-based image encryption algorithm using DNA sequence operations. Opt. Lasers Eng. **88**, 197–213 (2017). https://doi.org/10.1016/j. optlaseng.2016.08.009

11. Wang, X.-Y., Zhang, Y.-Q., Baom, X.-M.: A novel chaotic image encryption scheme using DNA sequence operations. Opt. Lasers Eng. **73**, 53–61 (2015). https://doi.org/10.1016/j. optlaseng.2015.03.022

12. Song, C., Qiao, Y.: A novel image encryption algorithm based on DNA encoding and spatiotemporal chaos. Entropy **17**, 6954–6968 (2015). https://doi.org/10.1016/j.optlaseng. 2015.03.022

13. Zhen, P., Zhao, G., Min, L., Jin, X.: Chaos-based image encryption scheme combining DNA coding and entropy. Multimed. Tools Appl. **75**, 6303–6319 (2016). https://doi.org/10.1007/ s11042-015-2573-x

14. Liu, H., Wang, X., Kadir, A.: Image encryption using DNA complementary rule and chaotic maps. Appl. Soft Comput. **12**, 1457–1466 (2012). https://doi.org/10.1016/j.asoc.2012.01. 016

15. Wei, X., Guo, L., Zhang, Q., Zhang, J., Lian, S.: A novel color image encryption algorithm based on DNA sequence operation and hyper-chaotic system. J. Syst. Softw. **85**, 290–299 (2012). https://doi.org/10.1016/j.jss.2011.08.017

16. Hu, T., Liu, Y., Gong, L.-H., Ouyang, C.-J.: An image encryption scheme combining chaos with cycle operation for DNA sequences. Nonlinear Dyn. **87**, 51–66 (2017). https://doi.org/ 10.1007/s11071-016-3024-6

17. Liu, Y., Tang, J., Xie, T.: Cryptanalyzing a RGB image encryption algorithm based on DNA encoding and chaos map. Opt. Laser Technol. **60**, 111–115 (2014). https://doi.org/10.1016/j. optlastec.2014.01.015

18. Jagadeesh, P., Nagabhushan, P., Kumar, R.: A new image scrambling scheme through chaotic permutation and geometric grid based noise induction. Int. J. Comput. Appl. **78**, 38– 45 (2013)

19. Rhouma, R., Solak, E., Belghith, S.: Cryptanalysis of a new substitution-diffusion based image cipher. Commun. Nonlinear Sci. Numer. Simul. **15**, 1887–1892 (2010). https://doi. org/10.1016/j.cnsns.2009.07.007

20. Li, C., Arroyo, D., Lo, K.: Breaking a chaotic cryptographic scheme based on composition maps. Int. J. Bifurcat. Chaos **20**, 2561–2568 (2010). https://doi.org/10.1142/S0218127 410027192

21. Alvarez, G., Li, S.: Cryptanalyzing a nonlinear chaotic algorithm (NCA) for image encryption. Commun. Nonlinear Sci. Numer. Simul. **4**, 3743–3749 (2009). https://doi.org/ 10.1016/j.cnsns.2009.02.033

22. Cui, G., Qin, L., Wang, Y., Zhang, X.: An encryption scheme using DNA technology. In: 3rd International Conference on Bio-Inspired Computing: Theories and Applications, pp. 37–42. IEEE (2008)

23. Zhang, Q., Zhou, S., Wei, X.: An efficient approach for fractal-based image encryption. Appl. Math. Inf. Sci. **5**, 445–459 (2011)

24. Watson, J.D., Crick, F.: A structure for deoxyribose nucleic acid. Nature **171**, 737–738 (1953)

25. Shannon, C.: Communication theory of secrecy systems. Bell Syst. Tech. J. **28**, 656–715 (1949)

Implementing Searchable Encryption Schemes over Multilinear Maps

Victor-Mihai Talif[✉]

Department of Computer Science, Alexandru Ioan Cuza University of Iași,
Iași, Romania
victor.talif@gmail.com

Abstract. We generalize known searchable encryption schemes [8] to
N-party contexts using constructions based on multilinear maps. The
span of the maps used is also expanded, as the schemes we propose can
make use of both prime order and composite order group contexts.

1 Introduction

Searchable Encryption [4,10] is technique that allows for the retrieval of desired
encrypted content without requiring for it to be decrypted prior to the query.
One of the main techniques used to obtain searchable encryption schemes is
based on Hidden Vector Encryption (HVE), proposed by Boneh and Waters
[4] and adapted by Iovino and Persiano using groups of prime order [8]. These
schemes use bilinear maps as safe key-exchange tools.

In this paper, we look to expand in several ways the scheme in [8] over multilinear maps [1,2,6,7], constructions which enable extended secret sharing and
key exchange functionalities [5], in order to adapt them for future advanced use.
Thus, we give a new dimension to the searchable encryption problem, enabling
the implementation of multiuser permission filtering. That is, a group of users
can share access to a set of data which is encrypted under a shared key. The
data can only be decrypted by using their key, thus enabling secret sharing for
the group.

For our constructions, we greatly expand the domain of definition for the
maps, starting with bilinear groups of prime order and expanding not only
to multilinear maps but generalizing for any order by constructing over composite values as well. By doing so, we open the problem to cases of any
cryptographically-efficient order and of any linearity.

The paper begins by introducing preliminary notions in the next section.
These include the Diffie-Hellman assumptions [3] and their adapted forms for
the multilinear context. Our contribution comes in the following section, where
we look to generalize the Iovino-Persiano HVE scheme to accommodate groups
of composite orders and multilinear maps, while maintaining algorithmic efficiency, as well as security. We then provide our conclusions in regards to our
constructions and their planned usage. Due to lack of space, the proofs of the
theorems in Sect. 3 are provided in the appendix.

© Springer Nature Switzerland AG 2019
J.-L. Lanet and C. Toma (Eds.): SecITC 2018, LNCS 11359, pp. 458–476, 2019.
https://doi.org/10.1007/978-3-030-12942-2_34

2   Preliminaries

We first recall bilinear maps and multilinear maps [1,2,6,7].

A bilinear map $e : G_1 \times G_2 \to G_T$, where G_1, G_2 and G_T are finite cyclic groups of the same order r, has the following properties:

1. **Bilinearity.** $e(g_1^a, g_2^b) = e(g_1, g_2)^{ab}$, where g_1 generator for G_1, g_2 generator for G_2, $a, b \in \mathbb{Z}$;
2. **Non-degeneracy.** $e(g_1, g_2) = g_T$, where g_T generator for G_T;
3. **Computability.** e is efficiently computable.

A multilinear map $e : G_1 \times G_2 \times ... \times G_n \to G_T$, where $G_1, G_2, ..., G_n, G_T$ are finite cyclic groups of the same order r, has the following properties:

1. **n-linearity.** $e(g_1^{a_1}, g_2^{a_2}, ..., g_n^{a_n}) = e(g_1, g_2, ..., g_n)^{\prod_{i=1}^{n} a_i}$;
2. **Non-degeneracy.** $e(g_1, g_2, ..., g_n) = g_T$, where $g_1, g_2, ..., g_n$ and g_T the respective generators;
3. **Computability.** e is efficiently computable.

The Decisional Diffie-Hellman assumption (DDH), translated to multilinear maps, plays a vital role in proving the security of our constructions. Recall this problem below.

For the 3-party context, given the use of bilinear maps, the Bilinear Decisional Diffie-Hellman assumption (BDH) states the following.

Given finite cyclic group G, a generator g and a bilinear map $e : G \times G \to G_T$, we define the following distribution $P(\lambda)$:

$$a, b, c \xleftarrow{\text{R}} \overline{1, \ ord(G)}$$
$$Z \leftarrow ((n, G, e), g, g^a, g^b, g^c)$$
$$T \leftarrow e(g, g)^{abc}$$
$$Output : (Z, T)$$

Therefore, we obtain $(Z, T) \leftarrow P(\lambda)$. We define the advantage of algorithm $\mathcal{A}$ in solving the Decisional Bilinear Diffie-Hellman problem:

$$BDH_{Adv_{\mathcal{A}}}(\lambda) := \left| Pr[\mathcal{A}(Z, T) = 1] - Pr[\mathcal{A}(Z, R) = 1] \right|$$

where $R \xleftarrow{\text{R}} G_T$.

The BDH assumption states that $BDH_{Adv_{\mathcal{A}}}(\lambda)$ is negligible for all PPT algorithms $\mathcal{A}$.

For the multiparty context, things are similar to the previous case.

Given G, its generator g and the multilinear map $e : G^N \to G_T$, we define the following distribution $P(\lambda)$:

$$a_1, a_2, ..., a_{N+1} \xleftarrow{\text{R}} \overline{1, \ ord(G)}$$
$$Z \leftarrow ((n, G, e), g, g^{a_1}, g^{a_2}, ..., g^{a_{N+1}})$$
$$T \leftarrow e(g, g, ..., g)^{\prod_{i=1}^{N+1} a_i}$$
$$Output : (Z, T)$$

Therefore, we obtain $(Z,T) \leftarrow P(\lambda)$. We define the advantage of algorithm $\mathcal{A}$ in solving the Decisional Multilinear Diffie-Hellman problem:

$$MDH_{Adv_{\mathcal{A}}}(\lambda) := \left| Pr[\mathcal{A}(Z,T) = 1] - Pr[\mathcal{A}(Z,R) = 1] \right|$$

where $R \xleftarrow{\text{R}} G_T$.

The MDH assumption states that $MDH_{Adv_{\mathcal{A}}}(\lambda)$ is negligible for all PPT algorithms $\mathcal{A}$.

A Hidden Vector Encryption (HVE) scheme [4] is a searchable encryption system over a given set of predicates.

Given an alphabet Σ (usually, the binary alphabet) and considering a special symbol $\star \notin \Sigma$, which is denoted the *wildcard* symbol, we obtain $\Sigma_\star = \Sigma \cup \{\star\}$ the extended alphabet over which our predicates are formulated.

Therefore, given a fixed length l, we denote our family of predicates $\Phi_{HVE} = \{P \mid P \in \Sigma_\star^l\}$. For any such predicate P, given attribute string $x \in \Sigma^l$, we define its satisfiability:

$$P(x) = \begin{cases} 1, & \text{if } \forall i \in \overline{1,l}, \ P_i = x_i \text{ or } P_i = \star \\ 0, & \text{otherwise} \end{cases}$$

A predicate is satisfied only by an attribute string that overlaps its non-"$\star$" values. This enables the fulfillment of searchable encryption requirements, granting the encrypted content searchability without the need for decryption by association with attribute strings and use of query predicates.

An HVE scheme is composed of 4 algorithms: *Setup, GenToken, Encrypt* and *Query*.

1. **Setup(1^l).** The algorithm takes as input the security parameter 1^l and outputs public key PK and private key MsK.
2. **GenToken(P, MsK, PK).** Given the keys and a predicate vector P, the algorithm outputs a token T_P associated with the given predicate.
3. **Encrypt(PK,(I,M)).** Given the public key PK and a plaintext message M associated with an attribute vector I, the algorithm will generate cryptotext C.
4. **Query(T_P, C, PK).** Given the query token T_P, the cryptotext C and the public key PK, the query algorithm will return 1("true") or $\perp$("false").

The correctness of the scheme is based on whether or not the following property is satisfied:

$$Setup(1^l) \rightarrow (PK, \ MsK)$$

$$\Phi_{HVE} \xrightarrow{R} P$$

$$GenToken(P, \ PK, \ MsK) \rightarrow T_P$$

$$Encrypt(PK, \ (I, \ M)) \rightarrow C$$

$$Query(C, \ T_P, \ PK) \rightarrow \begin{cases} 1, & \text{if } P(I) = 1 \\ \perp, & \text{with all but negligible probability otherwise} \end{cases}$$

The security of the scheme is proven using the following selective security model, a security game between challenger $\mathcal{C}$ and adversary $\mathcal{A}$:

1. **Init.** $\mathcal{A}$ submits 2 vectors $I_0, I_1 \in \Sigma^l$.
2. **Setup.** $\mathcal{C}$ runs Setup and keeps MsK to itself, while outputting PK to $\mathcal{A}$.
3. **Query Phase 1.** $\mathcal{A}$ adaptively requests a polynomial number of tokens for predicate vectors $P_1, ..., P_{q_1}$ subject to the restriction that $P_i(I_0) = P_i(I_1)$ for all i. In response, $\mathcal{C}$ gives the corresponding tokens T_{P_i} to $\mathcal{A}$.
4. **Challenge.** $\mathcal{A}$ submits 2 messages M_0 and M_1 subject to the restriction that if there is an index i such that $P_i(I_0) = P_i(I_1) = 1$ then $M_0 = M_1$. $\mathcal{C}$ flips a coin and gets value γ and gives a ciphertext C of (I_γ, M_γ) to $\mathcal{A}$.
5. **Query Phase 2.** $\mathcal{A}$ continues to request tokens for vectors $P_{q_1+1}, ..., P_q$ subject to the same restrictions as before.
6. **Guess.** $\mathcal{A}$ outputs a guess $\gamma' \in \{0, 1\}$. If $\gamma = \gamma'$, it outputs 0. Else, it outputs 1.

We can now define the advantage of $\mathcal{A}$ as:

$$Adv_{\mathcal{A}}^{HVE} = |Pr[\gamma = \gamma'] - 1/2|$$

We say that an HVE scheme is selectively secure if all probabilistic polynomial-time adversaries have at most a negligible advantage in the above game.

3   Contributions

In this section we generalize the Iovino-Persiano HVE scheme to groups of composite order and multilinear maps. We start by describing the original construction, as presented in [8].

3.1   Iovino-Persiano HVE

The system is composed of 4 algorithms: *Setup, Encrypt, GenToken* and *Query*.

1. **Setup(λ, n).** The inputs received are security parameter λ and attribute length n. The algorithm generates a large prime number p. It then generates group G of order p. It then composes the instance $\mathcal{I} = (p, G, G_T, e)$. Afterwards, it randomly generates the following elements:

$$y \in \mathbb{Z}_p$$
$$\forall\, 1 \leq i \leq n : t_i, v_i, r_i, m_i \in \mathbb{Z}_p$$

These all compose the masterkey **MsK**:

$$MsK = \big(y, (t_i, v_i, r_i, m_i)_{\forall i \in \overline{1,n}}\big)$$

It then generates the following values:

$$Y = e(g,g)^y \text{ and } \forall\, 1 \leq i \leq n \,:\, T_i = g^{t_i},\, V_i = g^{v_i},\, R_i = g^{r_i} M_i = g^{m_i}$$

It then publishes the public key **PK** using the instance $\mathcal{I}$ and the previously determined elements:

$$PK = \big(\mathcal{I}, Y, (T_i, V_i, R_i, M_i)_{\forall i \in \overline{1,n}}\big)$$

2. **Encrypt(PK,(I,M))**. Given as input index $I = (I_1, I_2, ..., I_l) \in \Sigma^l$ and a message $M \in G_T$, the encryption algorithm works as such:
   (a) Select random $s \in \mathbb{Z}_p$ and random $s_1, s_2, ..., s_n \in \mathbb{Z}_p$.
   (b) Compute the following cyphertext elements:

$$\Omega = M \cdot Y^{-s}$$
$$C_0 = g^s$$
$$\forall\, 1 \leq i \leq n \,:$$

$$X_i = \begin{cases} T_i^{s-s_i}, & \text{if } I_i = 1 \\ R_i^{s-s_i}, & \text{if } I_i = 0 \end{cases} ,\, W_i = \begin{cases} V_i^{s_i}, & \text{if } I_i = 1 \\ M_i^{s_i}, & \text{if } I_i = 0 \end{cases}$$

3. **GenToken(MsK, I$_\star$)**. Given predicate description $I_\star = (\mathcal{I}_1, \mathcal{I}_2, ..., \mathcal{I}_l) \in \Sigma_\star$, the algorithm determines the set S of indexes $1 \leq i \leq l$ such that $I_i \neq \star$.
   If $S = \emptyset$, that is, if $I_\star$ only has wildcard entries, the algorithm will output the key:

$$K_0 = g^y$$

Otherwise, for each element i of S, we will randomly generate value a_i, such that in the end, we have:

$$\sum_{i \in S} a_i = y$$

For each of these generated elements, we compute:

$$Y_i = \begin{cases} g^{\frac{a_i}{t_i}}, & \text{if } \mathcal{I}_i = 1 \\ g^{\frac{a_i}{r_i}}, & \text{if } \mathcal{I}_i = 0 \\ \emptyset, & \text{otherwise} \end{cases} ,\, L_i = \begin{cases} g^{\frac{a_i}{v_i}}, & \text{if } \mathcal{I}_i = 1 \\ g^{\frac{a_i}{m_i}}, & \text{if } \mathcal{I}_i = 0 \\ \emptyset, & \text{otherwise} \end{cases}$$

We output TK as either K_0 or $(Y_i, L_i)_{i \in \overline{1,n}}$, depending on which of the aforementioned cases is at hand.

4. **Query(TK,C)**. Keeping the preceding notations and minding which of the situations we are in, we compute one of the following:
   (a) $M \leftarrow \Omega \cdot e(C_0, K_0)$
   (b) $M \leftarrow \Omega \cdot \prod_{i \in S} e(X_i, Y_i) e(W_i, L_i)$

M is correct if the attribute vector satisfies the predicate in question. The soundness and security proofs can be found in [8].

3.2   Multilinear Iovino-Persiano HVE over Groups of Prime Order

The construction we propose closely resembles the Iovino-Persiano structure that inspired it, being an adaptation to the multilinear context maintaining the same algorithmic complexity. The system is composed of 4 algorithms: *Setup, Encrypt, GenToken* and *Query*.

1. **Setup(λ, n).** The inputs received are security parameter λ and attribute length n. The algorithm generates a large prime number p. It then generates group G of order p. It then composes the instance $\mathcal{I} = (p, G, G_T, e)$, where $e : G^{2n} \to G_T$ is our multilinear map function.
   Afterwards, it randomly generates the following elements:

$$y \in \mathbb{Z}_p$$
$$\forall\, 1 \leq i \leq n \ : t_i, v_i, r_i, m_i \in \mathbb{Z}_p$$

   These all compose the masterkey **MsK**:

$$MsK = \big(y, (t_i, v_i, r_i, m_i)_{\forall i \in \overline{1,n}}\big)$$

   It then generates the following values:

$$Y = e(g, g, ..., g)^y \text{ and } \forall\, 1 \leq i \leq n \ : T_i = g^{t_i}, V_i = g^{v_i}, R_i = g^{r_i}, M_i = g^{m_i}$$

   It then publishes the public key **PK** using the instance $\mathcal{I}$ and the previously determined elements:

$$PK = \big(\mathcal{I}, Y, (T_i, V_i, R_i, M_i)_{\forall i \in \overline{1,n}})\big)$$

2. **Encrypt(PK,*(I,M)*).** Given as input index $I = (I_1, I_2, ..., I_l) \in \Sigma^l$ and a message $M \in G_T$, the encryption algorithm works as such:
   (a) Select random $s \in \mathbb{Z}_p$ and random $s' \in \mathbb{Z}_p$.
   (b) Compute the rows s_i and s'_i for $i \in \overline{1,n}$ such that:

$$\prod_{i \in \overline{1,n}} s_i = s - s'$$
$$\prod_{i \in \overline{1,n}} s'_i = s'$$

   The fact that this computation is possible is addressed later, for the row generated for the *GenToken* function.
   (c) Compute the following cyphertext elements:

$$\Omega = M \cdot Y^{-s}$$
$$C_0 = g^s$$
$$\forall\, 1 \leq i \leq n \ :$$

$$X_i = \begin{cases} T_i^{s_i}, & \text{if } I_i = 1 \\ R_i^{s_i}, & \text{if } I_i = 0 \end{cases} , W_i = \begin{cases} V_i^{s'_i}, & \text{if } I_i = 1 \\ M_i^{s'_i}, & \text{if } I_i = 0 \end{cases}$$

3. **GenToken(MsK, I_*).** Given predicate description $I_* = (\mathcal{I}_1, \mathcal{I}_2, ..., \mathcal{I}_l) \in \Sigma_*$, the algorithm determines the set S of indexes $1 \le i \le l$ such that $I_i \ne \star$.
If $S = \emptyset$, that is, if I_* only has wildcard entries, the algorithm will output the key:

$$K_0 = g^y$$

Otherwise, for each element i of S, we will randomly generate value a_i, such that in the end, we have:

$$\prod_{i \in S} a_i = y$$

Given the prime order of group G, it follows that having computed the product of all but the last element, we are able to invert said product and multiply it by y, thus obtaining what is needed of us. Computationally, this is of similar complexity to the original implementation: instead of randomly generating $|S| - 1$ values in G and determining the last one by deducing the current value from y, we randomly generate $|S| - 1$ values in G and given our group's properties, we invert the result and multiply it by y to obtain our result. Best implementations of modular inversing achieve it in logarithmic time.
For each of these generated elements, we compute:

$$Y_i = \begin{cases} g^{\frac{a_i}{t_i}}, & \text{if } \mathcal{I}_i = 1 \\ g^{\frac{a_i}{r_i}}, & \text{if } \mathcal{I}_i = 0 \\ g, & \text{otherwise} \end{cases} \quad , L_i = \begin{cases} g^{\frac{a_i}{v_i}}, & \text{if } \mathcal{I}_i = 1 \\ g^{\frac{a_i}{m_i}}, & \text{if } \mathcal{I}_i = 0 \\ g, & \text{otherwise} \end{cases}$$

We output TK as either K_0 or $(Y_i, L_i)_{i \in \overline{1,n}}$, depending on which of the aforementioned cases is at hand.

4. **Query(TK,C).** Keeping the preceding notations and minding which of the situations we are in, we compute one of the following:
   (a) $M \leftarrow \Omega \cdot e(C_0, K_0, g, g, ..., g)$
   (b) $M \leftarrow \Omega \cdot e(X_1, X_2, ..., X_n, Y_1, Y_2, ..., Y_n) \cdot e(W_1, W_2, ..., W_n, L_1, L_2, ..., L_n)$
   M is correct if the attribute vector satisfies the predicate in question.

We obtain the following result.

Theorem 1. *The Multilinear Iovino-Persiano HVE scheme over groups of prime order is computationally sound. Furthermore, under the MDH assumption, it is proven to be secure.*

Proof. See the Appendix A.1.

3.3   Iovino-Persiano HVE over Groups of Composite Order

In this subsection we make minute changes to the aforementioned construction to grant it support for groups of composite order. In these groups, some elements may not have a modular inverse. This is indeed the case for elements i in $\mathbb{Z}_N$, where n is composite, if $(i, N) \ne 1$. A simple fix for this is to consider only the elements of $\mathbb{Z}_N^*$, the exact subset that excludes the troublesome elements we mentioned in the previous sentence.

The system is composed of 4 algorithms: *Setup, Encrypt, GenToken* and *Query*.

1. **Setup(λ, n).** The inputs received are security parameter λ and attribute length n. The algorithm generates $N = pq$, where p and q are large primes. It then generates group G of order N. It then composes the instance $\mathcal{I} = (p, G, G_T, e)$.
   Afterwards, it randomly generates the following elements:

   $$y \in \mathbb{Z}_N$$
   $$\forall\, 1 \leq i \leq n \; : t_i, v_i, r_i, m_i \in \mathbb{Z}_N^*$$

   These all compose the masterkey **MsK**:

   $$MsK = \big(y, (t_i, v_i, r_i, m_i)_{\forall i \in \overline{1,n}}\big)$$

   It then generates the following values:

   $$Y = e(g, g, ..., g)^y \text{ and } \forall\, 1 \leq i \leq n \; : T_i = g^{t_i}, V_i = g^{v_i}, R_i = g^{r_i}, M_i = g^{m_i}$$

   It then publishes the public key **PK** using the instance $\mathcal{I}$ and the previously determined elements:

   $$PK = \big(\mathcal{I}, Y, (T_i, V_i, R_i, M_i)_{\forall i \in \overline{1,n}})\big)$$

2. **Encrypt(PK,(I,M)).** Given as input index $I = (I_1, I_2, ..., I_l) \in \Sigma^l$ and a message $M \in G_T$, the encryption algorithm works as such:
   (a) Select random $s \in \mathbb{Z}_N$ and random $s_1, s_2, ..., s_n \in \mathbb{Z}_N$.
   (b) Compute the following cyphertext elements:

   $$\Omega = M \cdot Y^{-s}$$
   $$C_0 = g^s$$
   $$\forall\, 1 \leq i \leq n \; :$$
   $$X_i = \begin{cases} T_i^{s-s_i}, & \text{if } I_i = 1 \\ R_i^{s-s_i}, & \text{if } I_i = 0 \end{cases}, W_i = \begin{cases} V_i^{s_i}, & \text{if } I_i = 1 \\ M_i^{s_i}, & \text{if } I_i = 0 \end{cases}$$

3. **GenToken(MsK, I$_\star$).** Given predicate description $I_\star = (\mathcal{I}_1, \mathcal{I}_2, ..., \mathcal{I}_n) \in \Sigma_\star$, the algorithm determines the set S of indexes $1 \leq i \leq n$ such that $I_i \neq \star$. If $S = \emptyset$, that is, if $I_\star$ only has wildcard entries, the algorithm will output the key:

   $$K_0 = g^y$$

   Otherwise, for each element i of S, we will randomly generate value $a_i \in \mathbb{Z}_N$, such that in the end, we have:

   $$\sum_{i \in S} a_i = y$$

For each of these generated elements, we compute:

$$Y_i = \begin{cases} g^{\frac{a_i}{t_i}}, & \text{if } \mathcal{I}_i = 1 \\ g^{\frac{a_i}{r_i}}, & \text{if } \mathcal{I}_i = 0 \\ \emptyset, & \text{otherwise} \end{cases}, L_i = \begin{cases} g^{\frac{a_i}{v_i}}, & \text{if } \mathcal{I}_i = 1 \\ g^{\frac{a_i}{m_i}}, & \text{if } \mathcal{I}_i = 0 \\ \emptyset, & \text{otherwise} \end{cases}$$

We output TK as either K_0 or $(Y_i, L_i)_{i \in \overline{1,n}}$, depending on which of the aforementioned cases is at hand.

3. **Query(TK,C)**. Keeping the preceding notations and minding which of the situations we are in, we compute one of the following:
   (a) $M \leftarrow \Omega \cdot e(C_0, K_0)$
   (b) $M \leftarrow \Omega \cdot \prod_{i \in S} e(X_i, Y_i) e(W_i, L_i)$

M is correct if the attribute vector satisfies the predicate in question.

The construction is computationally correct, as all inverse elements in $\mathbb{Z}_N^\star$ are now computable. In fact, we have the following result.

Theorem 2. *The Iovino-Persiano HVE scheme over groups of composite order is computationally sound. Furthermore, under the BDH assumption, it is proven to be secure.*

Proof. See the Appendix A.2.

3.4   Multilinear Iovino-Persiano HVE over Groups of Composite Order

We now expand the construction from the previous subsection in order to enable it to support multilinear maps. A notable problem arises.

Just like in the previous construction, if we were to follow our multilinear construction over groups of prime order, we'd encounter a few more modular inverses that the bilinear case did not have. These too are fixed by restricting the exponent set to $Z_N^\star$.

The computations in cause are the row generations of s_i, s_i' and a_i. Each of these requires a computable inverse for the final step. Therefore, if we restrict their entries to elements of $Z_N^\star$, correctness is guaranteed. As an added consequence to this, the final results, namely s, s' and y respectively, will also be elements of $Z_N^\star$, as they are the results of multiplications of elements of the said group.

The system is composed of 4 algorithms: *Setup, Encrypt, GenToken* and *Query*.

1. **Setup(λ, n)**. The inputs received are security parameter λ and attribute length n. The algorithm generates $N = \prod_{i \in \overline{1,n}} p_i$, where all p_i are large prime factors. It then generates group G of order N. It then composes the instance $\mathcal{I} = (p, G, G_T, e)$, where $e : G^{2n} \to G_T$ is our multilinear map function.

Afterwards, it randomly generates the following elements:

$$y \in \mathbb{Z}_N^*$$
$$\forall\, 1 \le i \le n \;:\; t_i, v_i, r_i, m_i \in \mathbb{Z}_N^*$$

These all compose the masterkey **MsK**:

$$MsK = \big(y, (t_i, v_i, r_i, m_i)_{\forall i \in \overline{1,n}}\big)$$

It then generates the following values:

$$Y = e(g, g, ..., g)^y \text{ and } \forall\, 1 \le i \le n \;:\; T_i = g^{t_i},\; V_i = g^{v_i},\; R_i = g^{r_i},\; M_i = g^{m_i}$$

It then publishes the public key **PK** using the instance $\mathcal{I}$ and the previously determined elements:

$$PK = \big(\mathcal{I}, Y, (T_i, V_i, R_i, M_i)_{\forall i \in \overline{1,n}}\big)$$

2. **Encrypt(PK,(I,M)).** Given as input index $I = (I_1, I_2, ..., I_l) \in \Sigma^l$ and a message $M \in G_T$, the encryption algorithm works as such:
   (a) Select random $s \in \mathbb{Z}_N^*$ and random $s' \in \mathbb{Z}_N^*$.
   (b) Compute the rows s_i and s_i' in $\mathbb{Z}_N^*$ for $i \in \overline{1,n}$ such that:

   $$\prod_{i \in \overline{1,n}} s_i = s - s'$$

   $$\prod_{i \in \overline{1,n}} s_i' = s'$$

   (c) Compute the following cyphertext elements:

   $$\Omega = M \cdot Y^{-s}$$
   $$C_0 = g^s$$
   $$\forall\, 1 \le i \le n \;:$$

   $$X_i = \begin{cases} T_i^{s_i}, & \text{if } I_i = 1 \\ R_i^{s_i}, & \text{if } I_i = 0 \end{cases} \quad, \quad W_i = \begin{cases} V_i^{s_i'}, & \text{if } I_i = 1 \\ M_i^{s_i'}, & \text{if } I_i = 0 \end{cases}$$

3. **GenToken(MsK, I$_\star$).** Given predicate description $I_\star = (\mathcal{I}_1, \mathcal{I}_2, ..., \mathcal{I}_l) \in \Sigma_\star$, the algorithm determines the set S of indexes $1 \le i \le l$ such that $I_i \ne \star$. If $S = \emptyset$, that is, if $I_\star$ only has wildcard entries, the algorithm will output the key:

$$K_0 = g^y$$

Otherwise, for each element i of S, we will randomly generate value a_i in $\mathbb{Z}_N^*$, such that in the end, we have:

$$\prod_{i \in S} a_i = y$$

For each of these generated elements, we compute:

$$Y_i = \begin{cases} g^{\frac{a_i}{t_i}}, & \text{if } \mathcal{I}_i = 1 \\ g^{\frac{a_i}{r_i}}, & \text{if } \mathcal{I}_i = 0 \\ g, & \text{otherwise} \end{cases} \quad , L_i = \begin{cases} g^{\frac{a_i}{v_i}}, & \text{if } \mathcal{I}_i = 1 \\ g^{\frac{a_i}{m_i}}, & \text{if } \mathcal{I}_i = 0 \\ g, & \text{otherwise} \end{cases}$$

We output TK as either K_0 or $(Y_i, L_i)_{i \in \overline{1,n}}$, depending on which of the afore-mentioned cases is at hand.

4. **Query(TK,C).** Keeping the preceding notations and minding which of the situations we are in, we compute one of the following:
   (a) $M \leftarrow \Omega \cdot e(C_0, K_0, g, g, ..., g)$
   (b) $M \leftarrow \Omega \cdot e(X_1, X_2, ..., X_n, Y_1, Y_2, ..., Y_n) \cdot e(W_1, W_2, ..., W_n, L_1, L_2, ..., L_n)$

We also have the following result.

Theorem 3. *The Multilinear Iovino-Persiano HVE scheme over groups of composite order is computationally sound. Furthermore, under the MDH assumption, it is proven to be secure.*

Proof. See the Appendix A.3.

4   Conclusions

In this paper, we have extended the Iovino-Persiano HVE in order for it to accommodate groups of composite orders and multilinear maps. By this generalization, we intend to offer a functional and adaptive solution to the searchable encryption problem for both current and future multilinear map constructions.

The main functionality our new constructions are wrapped around is NIKE [5]. Given the theoretical proof that NIKE is solved by multilinear maps, all that is needed to validate the new constructions and put them to good use is an efficiently computable and secure multilinear map satisfying the DDH assumption. The constructions are to be used in systems with a large number of peers. Encrypted data that is to be accessed by a very large number of cryptosystem members needs to have a shared key for said members. The efficient use of NIKE provides an easy way for establishing the shared key, while also minimizing SPOF and collusion risks.

An application we propose for these constructions is Multi-user Searchable Encryption [9]. Given the need for selective authorizing of users to be able to read and write content, NIKE may allow for easy generation of shared keys that offer the aforementioned functionalities.

A   Proofs

A.1   Proofs for Theorem 1

The Multilinear Iovino-Persiano HVE scheme over groups of prime order is computationally sound. Furthermore, under the MDH assumption, it is proven to be secure.

A.1.1 Soundness. For case (a), we have:

$$\Omega \cdot e(C_0, K_0, g, g, ..., g) = M \cdot e(g, g, ..., g)^{-ys} \cdot e(g^s, g^y, ..., g) =$$
$$M \cdot e(g, g, ..., g)^{-ys} \cdot e(g, g, ..., g)^{ys} = M$$

For case (b), assuming the predicate is satisfied by the attribute vector and denoting the rows:

$$\alpha_i = \begin{cases} t_i, & \text{if } I_i = 1 \\ r_i, & \text{if } I_i = 0 \end{cases} \qquad \beta_i = \begin{cases} v_i, & \text{if } \mathcal{I}_i = 1 \\ m_i, & \text{if } \mathcal{I}_i = 0 \end{cases}$$

We use this notation for ease of writing, as if the predicate is satisfied, the values, regardless of the attribute vector entry, are reduced. Therefore:

$$\Omega \cdot e(X_1, X_2, ..., X_n, Y_1, Y_2, ..., Y_n) \cdot e(W_1, W_2, ..., W_n, L_1, L_2, ..., L_n)$$
$$= \Omega \cdot e(g^{\alpha_1 s_1}, g^{\alpha_2 s_2}, ..., g^{\alpha_n s_n}, g^{\frac{a_1}{\alpha_1}}, g^{\frac{a_2}{\alpha_2}}, ..., g^{\frac{a_n}{\alpha_n}}) \cdot e(g^{\beta_1 s_1'}, g^{\beta_2 s_2'}, ..., g^{\beta_n s_n'}, g^{\frac{a_1}{\beta_1}}, g^{\frac{a_2}{\beta_2}}, ..., g^{\frac{a_n}{\beta_n}})$$
$$= \Omega \cdot e(g, g, ..., g)^{\prod_{i \in \overline{1,n}} s_i a_i} \cdot e(g, g, ..., g)^{\prod_{i \in \overline{1,n}} s_i' a_i}$$
$$= \Omega \cdot e(g, g, ..., g)^{(s-s')y} \cdot e(g, g, ..., g)^{s'y} = \Omega \cdot e(g, g, ..., g)^{sy}$$
$$= M \cdot e(g, g, ..., g)^{-ys} \cdot e(g, g, ..., g)^{ys} = M$$

This proves query correctness.

If the predicate was not satisfied, much like in the original implementation, we'd have at least one erronous inverse, thus not leading to a correct decryption.

A.1.2 Security. We formulate a security game. Assume MDH holds. Assume $\mathcal{A}$ is an adversary with a non-negligible advantage (larger than $1/2$) for the semantic security algorithm. We prove that this contravenes MDH. Let $A_1 = g^{e_1}$, $A_2 = g^{e_2}, ..., A_{n+1} = g^{e_{n+1}}$ random elements of G.

The challenger, for whom MDH holds, receives as input the instance parameters $\mathcal{I}$, as well as $[(A_i)_{i \in \overline{1,n}}, Z]$, where Z is either $e(g, g, ..., g)^{\prod_{i \in \overline{1,n+1}} e_i}$ or a random element of G_T.

The security game is structured as follows:

1. **Init.** The challenger runs $\mathcal{A}$ and receives attribute string x for the challenge.
2. **Setup.** The challenger computes $Y = e(A_1, A_2, ..., A_n)$ and then generates the random values $t_i, v_i, r_i, m_i \in \mathbb{Z}_p$ and then computes:

$$T_i = \begin{cases} g^{t_i}, & \text{if } x_i = 1 \\ A_i^{t_i}, & \text{if } x_i = 0 \end{cases} \qquad V_i = \begin{cases} g^{v_i}, & \text{if } x_i = 1 \\ A_i^{v_i}, & \text{if } x_i = 0 \end{cases}$$

$$R_i = \begin{cases} A_i^{r_i}, & \text{if } x_i = 1 \\ g^{r_i}, & \text{if } x_i = 0 \end{cases} \qquad M_i = \begin{cases} A_i^{m_i}, & \text{if } x_i = 1 \\ g^{m_i}, & \text{if } x_i = 0 \end{cases}$$

Given that $[\mathcal{I}, Y, (T_i, R_i, V_i, M_i)_{1 \leq i \leq n}]$ acts as the public key of the system, the challenger runs $\mathcal{A}$ on it.

3. **Query Phase 1.** The adversary formulates queries for predicates with description y such that x does not satisfy any.

For one of these predicates (we take its generalized name, y), we select an entry index j such that $x_j \neq y_j \neq \star$. Given our previous assumption of non-satisfiability, it naturally follows that there will always be such an entry.

For every non-$\star$ entry index i in y (looking back at the construction, their set is set S), if $i \neq j$, we generate a random value a_i'. We denote $a' = \prod a_i'$.

$$\text{Let } Y_j = \begin{cases} (\prod_{i \notin S} A_i^{\frac{1}{t_j}}) A_j^{\frac{1}{t_j}} g^{\frac{(a')^{-1}}{t_j}}, & \text{if } y_j = 1 \\ (\prod_{i \notin S} A_i^{\frac{1}{r_j}}) A_j^{\frac{1}{r_j}} g^{\frac{(a')^{-1}}{r_j}}, & \text{if } y_j = 0 \end{cases}$$

$$\text{and } L_j = \begin{cases} (\prod_{i \notin S} A_i^{\frac{1}{v_j}}) A_j^{\frac{1}{v_j}} g^{\frac{(a')^{-1}}{v_j}}, & \text{if } y_j = 1 \\ (\prod_{i \notin S} A_i^{\frac{1}{m_j}}) A_j^{\frac{1}{m_j}} g^{\frac{(a')^{-1}}{m_j}}, & \text{if } y_j = 0 \end{cases}.$$

For all other elements of S (elements $i \neq j$), we construct the following:

$$Y_i = \begin{cases} A_i^{\frac{a_i'}{t_i}}, & \text{if } x_i = y_i = 1 \\ A_i^{\frac{a_i'}{r_i}}, & \text{if } x_i = y_i = 0 \\ g^{\frac{a_i'}{t_i}}, & \text{if } x_i = 0 \text{ and } y_i = 1 \\ g^{\frac{a_i'}{r_i}}, & \text{if } x_i = 1 \text{ and } y_i = 0 \\ g, & \text{otherwise} \end{cases} \quad \text{and } L_i = \begin{cases} A_i^{\frac{a_i'}{v_i}}, & \text{if } x_i = y_i = 1 \\ A_i^{\frac{a_i'}{m_i}}, & \text{if } x_i = y_i = 0 \\ g^{\frac{a_i'}{v_i}}, & \text{if } x_i = 0 \text{ and } y_i = 1 \\ g^{\frac{a_i'}{m_i}}, & \text{if } x_i = 1 \text{ and } y_i = 0 \\ g, & \text{otherwise} \end{cases}$$

On further computation, we notice that, following the structure of the general construction, $a_i = e_i \cdot a_i'$ (for $i \in S$ and $i \neq j$) and $a_j = \prod_{i \notin S} e_i \cdot e_j \cdot (a')^{-1}$. Multiplying them, we have:

$$\prod_{i \in S} a_i = \prod_{i \in \overline{1,n}} e_i = y$$

4. **Challenge.** The adversary present the challenger with two messages $M_0, M_1 \in G_T$. The challenger randomly selects one, M_β, $\beta \in \{0,1\}$. It then generates random value $s' \in \mathbb{Z}_p$ and based on it, generates for each $i \in \overline{1,n}$ the values $s_i, s_i' \in \mathbb{Z}_p$ such that:

$$\prod_{i \in \overline{1,n}} s_i = e_{n+1} - s'$$

$$\prod_{i \in \overline{1,n}} s_i' = s'$$

and computes the following:

$$\Omega = M_\beta Z^{-1}, \quad C_0 = A_{n+1},$$

$$X_i = \begin{cases} g^{t_i s_i}, & \text{if } x_i = 1 \\ g^{r_i s_i}, & \text{if } x_i = 0 \end{cases}, \quad W_i = \begin{cases} g^{v_i s_i'}, & \text{if } x_i = 1 \\ g^{m_i s_i'}, & \text{if } x_i = 0 \end{cases}$$

We observe that for $Z = e(g, g, ..., g)^{\prod_{i \in \overline{1,n+1}} e_i}$, Ω coincides with the construction for $s = e_{n+1}$. If Z is a random element from G_T, Ω is independent from β (due to the randomness).

5. **Query Phase 2**. Query Phase 2 has the exact same structure as Query Phase 1.

6. **Guess**. The adversary outputs guess $\beta' \in \{0, 1\}$. The challenger outputs 1 if $\beta = \beta'$.

If $Z = e(g, g, ..., g)^{\prod_{i \in \overline{1,n+1}} e_i}$, given that $\mathcal{A}$ has a non-negligible advantage for the semantic security algorithm, the probability for the challenger to output 1 is non-negligibly larger than $1/2$. For the random Z case, the very same probability is less than $1/2$. This contradicts MDH and therefore proves security.

A.2   Proofs for Theorem 2

The Iovino-Persiano HVE scheme over groups of composite order is computationally sound. Furthermore, under the BDH assumption, it is proven to be secure.

A.2.1 Soundness. The proof follows the exact same line of reason the one the original article offers.

For case (a), we have:

$$\Omega \cdot e(C_0, K_0) = M \cdot e(g, g)^{-ys} \cdot e(g, g)^{ys} = M$$

For case (b), assuming the predicate is satisfied by the attribute vector, we have:

$$\Omega \cdot \prod_{i \in S} e(X_i, Y_i) e(W_i, L_i) = M \cdot e(g, g)^{-ys} \cdot \prod_{i \in S} e(g, g)^{(s - s_i) a_i} \cdot e(g, g)^{s_i a_i} =$$

$$M \cdot e(g, g)^{-ys} \cdot \prod_{i \in S} e(g, g)^{s a_i} = M \cdot e(g, g)^{-ys} \cdot e(g, g)^{s \cdot \sum_{i \in S} a_i} = M \cdot e(g, g)^{-ys} \cdot e(g, g)^{ys} = M$$

A.2.2 Security. We formulate a security game. Assume BDH holds. Assume $\mathcal{A}$ is an adversary with a non-negligible advantage (larger than $1/2$) for the semantic security algorithm. We prove that this contravenes BDH. Let $A = g^a$, $B = g^b$ and $C = g^c$ random elements of G.

The challenger, for whom BDH holds, receives as input the instance parameters $\mathcal{I}$, as well as $[A, B, C, Z]$, where Z is either $e(g, g)^{abc}$ or a random element of G_T.

The security game is structured as follows:

1. **Init**. The challenger runs $\mathcal{A}$ and receives attribute string x for the challenge.
2. **Setup**. The challenger computes $Y = e(A, B)$ and then generates the random values $t_i, v_i, r_i, m_i \in \mathbb{Z}_N^*$ and then computes:

$$T_i = \begin{cases} g^{t_i}, & \text{if } x_i = 1 \\ B^{t_i}, & \text{if } x_i = 0 \end{cases} \qquad V_i = \begin{cases} g^{v_i}, & \text{if } x_i = 1 \\ B^{v_i}, & \text{if } x_i = 0 \end{cases}$$

$$R_i = \begin{cases} B^{r_i}, & \text{if } x_i = 1 \\ g^{r_i}, & \text{if } x_i = 0 \end{cases} \qquad M_i = \begin{cases} B^{m_i}, & \text{if } x_i = 1 \\ g^{m_i}, & \text{if } x_i = 0 \end{cases}$$

Given that $[\mathcal{I}, Y, (T_i, R_i, V_i, M_i)_{1 \leq i \leq n}]$ acts as the public key of the system, the challenger runs $\mathcal{A}$ on it.

3. **Query Phase 1.** The adversary formulates queries for predicates with description y such that x does not satisfy any.

For one of these predicates (we take its generalized name, y), we select an entry index j such that $x_j \neq y_j \neq \star$. Given our previous assumption of non-satisfiability, it naturally follows that there will always be such an entry.

For every non-$\star$ entry index i in y (looking back at the construction, their set is set S), if $i \neq j$, we generate a random value $a_i' \in \mathbb{Z}_N$. We denote $a' = \sum a_i'$.

$$\text{Let } Y_j = \begin{cases} A^{\frac{1}{t_j}} g^{\frac{-a'}{t_j}}, & \text{if } y_j = 1 \\ A^{\frac{1}{r_j}} g^{\frac{-a'}{r_j}}, & \text{if } y_j = 0 \end{cases} \quad \text{and } L_j = \begin{cases} A^{\frac{1}{v_j}} g^{\frac{-a'}{v_j}}, & \text{if } y_j = 1 \\ A^{\frac{1}{m_j}} g^{\frac{-a'}{m_j}}, & \text{if } y_j = 0 \end{cases}.$$

For all other elements of S (elements $i \neq j$), we construct the following:

$$Y_i = \begin{cases} B^{\frac{a_i'}{t_i}}, & \text{if } x_i = y_i = 1 \\ B^{\frac{a_i'}{r_i}}, & \text{if } x_i = y_i = 0 \\ g^{\frac{a_i'}{t_i}}, & \text{if } x_i = 0 \text{ and } y_i = 1 \\ g^{\frac{a_i'}{r_i}}, & \text{if } x_i = 1 \text{ and } y_i = 0 \\ \emptyset, & \text{otherwise} \end{cases} \quad \text{and } L_i = \begin{cases} B^{\frac{a_i'}{v_i}}, & \text{if } x_i = y_i = 1 \\ B^{\frac{a_i'}{m_i}}, & \text{if } x_i = y_i = 0 \\ g^{\frac{a_i'}{v_i}}, & \text{if } x_i = 0 \text{ and } y_i = 1 \\ g^{\frac{a_i'}{m_i}}, & \text{if } x_i = 1 \text{ and } y_i = 0 \\ \emptyset, & \text{otherwise} \end{cases}$$

On further computation, we notice that, following the structure of the general construction, $a_i = a \cdot a_i'$ (for $i \in S$ and $i \neq j$) and $a_j = a \cdot (b - a')$. Summing them up, we have:

$$\sum_{i \in S} a_i = a \cdot b = y$$

4. **Challenge.** The adversary presents the challenger with two messages $M_0, M_1 \in G_T$. The challenger randomly selects one, M_β, $\beta \in \{0, 1\}$. It then generates random values $s_i \in \mathbb{Z}_N$ and computes the following:

$$\Omega = M_\beta Z^{-1}, \quad C_0 = C,$$

$$X_i = \begin{cases} C^{t_i} g^{-t_i s_i}, & \text{if } x_i = 1 \\ C^{r_i} g^{-r_i s_i}, & \text{if } x_i = 0 \end{cases}, W_i = \begin{cases} g^{-v_i s_i}, & \text{if } x_i = 1 \\ g^{-m_i s_i}, & \text{if } x_i = 0 \end{cases}$$

We observe that for $Z = e(g, g)^{abc}$, Ω coincides with the construction for $s = c$. If Z is a random element from G_T, Ω is independent from β (due to the randomness).

5. **Query Phase 2.** Query Phase 2 has the exact same stucture as Query Phase 1.

6. **Guess.** The adversary outputs guess $\beta' \in \{0, 1\}$. The challenger outputs 1 if $\beta = \beta'$.

If $Z = e(g,g)^{abc}$, given that $\mathcal{A}$ has a non-negligible advantage for the semantic security algorithm, the probability for the challenger to output 1 is non-negligibly larger than $1/2$. For the random Z case, the very same probability is less than $1/2$. This contradicts BDH and therefore proves security.

A.3   Proofs for Theorem 3

The Iovino-Persiano HVE scheme with multilinear map support is computationally sound. Furthermore, under the MDH assumption, it is proven to be secure.

A.3.1 Soundness. The proof follows the exact structure as the one in Subsect. A.1.

For case (a), we have:

$$\Omega \cdot e(C_0, K_0, g, g, ..., g) = M \cdot e(g, g, ..., g)^{-ys} \cdot e(g^s, g^y, ..., g) =$$
$$M \cdot e(g, g, ..., g)^{-ys} \cdot e(g, g, ..., g)^{ys} = M$$

For case (b), assuming the predicate is satisfied by the attribute vector and denoting the rows:

$$\alpha_i = \begin{cases} t_i, & \text{if } I_i = 1 \\ r_i, & \text{if } I_i = 0 \end{cases} \quad , \quad \beta_i = \begin{cases} v_i, & \text{if } \mathcal{I}_i = 1 \\ m_i, & \text{if } \mathcal{I}_i = 0 \end{cases}$$

We use this notation for ease of writing, because if the predicate is satisfied, the values, regardless of the attribute vector entry, are reduced. Therefore:

$$\Omega \cdot e(X_1, X_2, ..., X_n, Y_1, Y_2, ..., Y_n) \cdot e(W_1, W_2, ..., W_n, L_1, L_2, ..., L_n)$$
$$= \Omega \cdot e(g^{\alpha_1 s_1}, g^{\alpha_2 s_2}, ..., g^{\alpha_n s_n}, g^{\frac{a_1}{\alpha_1}}, g^{\frac{a_2}{\alpha_2}}, ..., g^{\frac{a_n}{\alpha_n}}) \cdot e(g^{\beta_1 s_1'}, g^{\beta_2 s_2'}, ..., g^{\beta_n s_n'}, g^{\frac{a_1}{\beta_1}}, g^{\frac{a_2}{\beta_2}}, ..., g^{\frac{a_n}{\beta_n}})$$
$$= \Omega \cdot e(g, g, ..., g)^{\prod_{i \in \overline{1,n}} s_i a_i} \cdot e(g, g, ..., g)^{\prod_{i \in \overline{1,n}} s_i' a_i}$$
$$= \Omega \cdot e(g, g, ..., g)^{(s-s')y} \cdot e(g, g, ..., g)^{s'y} = \Omega \cdot e(g, g, ..., g)^{sy}$$
$$= M \cdot e(g, g, ..., g)^{-ys} \cdot e(g, g, ..., g)^{ys} = M$$

A.3.2 Security. We formulate a security game. Assume MDH holds. Assume $\mathcal{A}$ is an adversary with a non-negligible advantage (larger than $1/2$) for the semantic security algorithm. We prove that this contravenes MDH. Let $A_1 = g^{e_1}$, $A_2 = g^{e_2}, ..., A_{n+1} = g^{e_{n+1}}$ random elements of G. It is also to be noted that all $e_i \in \mathbb{Z}_N^\star$.

The challenger, for whom MDH holds, receives as input the instance parameters $\mathcal{I}$, as well as $[(A_i)_{i \in \overline{1,n}}, Z]$, where Z is either $e(g, g, ..., g)^{\prod_{i \in \overline{1,n+1}} e_i}$ or a random element of G_T.

The security game is structured as follows:

1. **Init.** The challenger runs $\mathcal{A}$ and receives attribute string x for the challenge.

2. **Setup.** The challenger computes $Y = e(A_1, A_2, ..., A_n)$ and then generates the random values $t_i, v_i, r_i, m_i \in \mathbb{Z}_N^*$ and then computes:

$$T_i = \begin{cases} g^{t_i}, & \text{if } x_i = 1 \\ A_i^{t_i}, & \text{if } x_i = 0 \end{cases} \qquad V_i = \begin{cases} g^{v_i}, & \text{if } x_i = 1 \\ A_i^{v_i}, & \text{if } x_i = 0 \end{cases}$$

$$R_i = \begin{cases} A_i^{r_i}, & \text{if } x_i = 1 \\ g^{r_i}, & \text{if } x_i = 0 \end{cases} \qquad M_i = \begin{cases} A_i^{m_i}, & \text{if } x_i = 1 \\ g^{m_i}, & \text{if } x_i = 0 \end{cases}$$

Given that $[\mathcal{I}, Y, (T_i, R_i, V_i, M_i)_{1 \leq i \leq n}]$ acts as the public key of the system, the challenger runs $\mathcal{A}$ on it.

3. **Query Phase 1.** The adversary formulates queries for predicates with description y such that x does not satisfy any.

For one of these predicates (we take its generalized name, y), we select an entry index j such that $x_j \neq y_j \neq \star$. Given our previous assumption of non-satisfiability, it naturally follows that there will always be such an entry.

For every non-$\star$ entry index i in y (looking back at the construction, their set is set S), if $i \neq j$, we generate a random value $a_i' \in \mathbb{Z}_N^*$. We denote $a' = \prod a_i'$.

$$\text{Let } Y_j = \begin{cases} (\prod_{i \notin S} A_i^{\frac{1}{t_j}}) A_j^{\frac{1}{t_j}} g^{\frac{(a')^{-1}}{t_j}}, & \text{if } y_j = 1 \\ (\prod_{i \notin S} A_i^{\frac{1}{r_j}}) A_j^{\frac{1}{r_j}} g^{\frac{(a')^{-1}}{r_j}}, & \text{if } y_j = 0 \end{cases}$$

$$\text{and } L_j = \begin{cases} (\prod_{i \notin S} A_i^{\frac{1}{v_j}}) A_j^{\frac{1}{v_j}} g^{\frac{(a')^{-1}}{v_j}}, & \text{if } y_j = 1 \\ (\prod_{i \notin S} A_i^{\frac{1}{m_j}}) A_j^{\frac{1}{m_j}} g^{\frac{(a')^{-1}}{m_j}}, & \text{if } y_j = 0 \end{cases}.$$

For all other elements of S (elements $i \neq j$), we construct the following:

$$Y_i = \begin{cases} A_i^{\frac{a_i'}{t_i}}, & \text{if } x_i = y_i = 1 \\ A_i^{\frac{a_i'}{r_i}}, & \text{if } x_i = y_i = 0 \\ g^{\frac{a_i'}{t_i}}, & \text{if } x_i = 0 \text{ and } y_i = 1 \\ g^{\frac{a_i'}{r_i}}, & \text{if } x_i = 1 \text{ and } y_i = 0 \\ g, & \text{otherwise} \end{cases} \qquad \text{and } L_i = \begin{cases} A_i^{\frac{a_i'}{v_i}}, & \text{if } x_i = y_i = 1 \\ A_i^{\frac{a_i'}{m_i}}, & \text{if } x_i = y_i = 0 \\ g^{\frac{a_i'}{v_i}}, & \text{if } x_i = 0 \text{ and } y_i = 1 \\ g^{\frac{a_i'}{m_i}}, & \text{if } x_i = 1 \text{ and } y_i = 0 \\ g, & \text{otherwise} \end{cases}$$

On further computation, we notice that, following the structure of the general construction, $a_i = e_i \cdot a_i'$ (for $i \in S$ and $i \neq j$) and $a_j = \prod_{i \notin S} e_i \cdot e_j \cdot (a')^{-1}$. Multiplying them, we have:

$$\prod_{i \in S} a_i = \prod_{i \in \overline{1,n}} e_i = y$$

4. **Challenge.** The adversary present the challenger with two messages $M_0, M_1 \in G_T$. The challenger randomly selects one, M_β, $\beta \in \{0,1\}$. It then

generates random value $s' \in \mathbb{Z}_N^*$ and based on it, generates for each $i \in \overline{1,n}$ the values $s_i, s'_i \in \mathbb{Z}_N^*$ such that:

$$\prod_{i \in \overline{1,n}} s_i = e_{n+1} - s'$$

$$\prod_{i \in \overline{1,n}} s'_i = s'$$

and computes the following:

$$\Omega = M_\beta Z^{-1}, \ C_0 = A_{n+1},$$

$$X_i = \begin{cases} g^{t_i s_i}, & \text{if } x_i = 1 \\ g^{r_i s_i}, & \text{if } x_i = 0 \end{cases}, W_i = \begin{cases} g^{v_i s'_i}, & \text{if } x_i = 1 \\ g^{m_i s'_i}, & \text{if } x_i = 0 \end{cases}$$

We observe that for $Z = e(g,g,...,g)^{\prod_{i \in \overline{1,n+1}} e_i}$, Ω coincides with the construction for $s = e_{n+1}$. If Z is a random element from G_T, Ω is independent from β (due to the randomness).

5. **Query Phase 2**. Query Phase 2 has the exact same structure as Query Phase 1.

6. **Guess**. The adversary outputs guess $\beta' \in \{0,1\}$. The challenger outputs 1 if $\beta = \beta'$.

   If $Z = e(g,g,...,g)^{\prod_{i \in \overline{1,n+1}} e_i}$, given that $\mathcal{A}$ has a non-negligible advantage for the semantic security algorithm, the probability for the challenger to output 1 is non-negligibly larger than $1/2$. For the random Z case, the very same probability is less than $1/2$. This contradicts MDH and therefore proves security.

References

1. Albrecht, M.R., Farshim, P., Hofheinz, D., Larraia, E., Paterson, K.G.: Multilinear maps from obfuscation. In: Kushilevitz, E., Malkin, T. (eds.) TCC 2016. LNCS, vol. 9562, pp. 446–473. Springer, Heidelberg (2016). https://doi.org/10.1007/978-3-662-49096-9_19

2. Barak, B., et al.: On the (im)possibility of obfuscating programs. In: Kilian, J. (ed.) CRYPTO 2001. LNCS, vol. 2139, pp. 1–18. Springer, Heidelberg (2001). https://doi.org/10.1007/3-540-44647-8_1

3. Boneh, D.: The decision Diffie-Hellman problem. In: Buhler, J.P. (ed.) ANTS 1998. LNCS, vol. 1423, pp. 48–63. Springer, Heidelberg (1998). https://doi.org/10.1007/BFb0054851

4. Boneh, D., Waters, B.: Conjunctive, subset, and range queries on encrypted data. In: Vadhan, S.P. (ed.) TCC 2007. LNCS, vol. 4392, pp. 535–554. Springer, Heidelberg (2007). https://doi.org/10.1007/978-3-540-70936-7_29

5. Freire, E.S.V., Hofheinz, D., Kiltz, E., Paterson, K.G.: Non-interactive key exchange. In: Kurosawa, K., Hanaoka, G. (eds.) PKC 2013. LNCS, vol. 7778, pp. 254–271. Springer, Heidelberg (2013). https://doi.org/10.1007/978-3-642-36362-7_17

6. Garg, S., Gentry, C., Halevi, S.: Candidate multilinear maps from ideal lattices. In: Johansson, T., Nguyen, P.Q. (eds.) EUROCRYPT 2013. LNCS, vol. 7881, pp. 1–17. Springer, Heidelberg (2013). https://doi.org/10.1007/978-3-642-38348-9_1
7. Garg, S., Gentry, C., Halevi, S., Raykova, M., Sahai, A., Waters, B.: Candidate indistinguishability obfuscation and functional encryption for all circuits. SIAM J. Comput. **45**(3), 882–929 (2016)
8. Iovino, V., Persiano, G.: Hidden-vector encryption with groups of prime order. In: Galbraith, S.D., Paterson, K.G. (eds.) Pairing 2008. LNCS, vol. 5209, pp. 75–88. Springer, Heidelberg (2008). https://doi.org/10.1007/978-3-540-85538-5_5
9. Van Rompay, C., Molva, R., Önen, M.: Secure and scalable multi-user searchable encryption. In: Proceedings of the 6th International Workshop on Security in Cloud Computing, pp. 15–25. ACM (2018)
10. Wang, Y., Wang, J., Chen, X.: Secure searchable encryption: a survey. J. Commun. Inf. Netw. **1**(4), 52–65 (2016)

A Unified Security Perspective on Legally Fair Contract Signing Protocols

Diana Maimuţ[1](✉)📷 and George Teşeleanu[1,2]📷

[1] Advanced Technologies Institute, 10 Dinu Vintilă, Bucharest, Romania
{diana.maimut,tgeorge}@dcti.ro
[2] Department of Computer Science, "Al.I.Cuza" University of Iaşi,
700506 Iaşi, Romania
george.teseleanu@info.uaic.ro

Abstract. Inspired by Maurer's universal zero knowledge (UZK) abstract perspective and building on legally fair contract signing protocols without keystones, we propose and analyze the security of the first UZK class of co-signing protocols. We construct our main idea considering the stringent issue of scheme compatibility which characterizes communication systems. Typical examples are the cases of certificates in a public key infrastructure and the general issue of upgrading the version of a system. Thus, working in a general framework may reduce implementation errors and save application development and maintenance time.

Keywords: Security proofs · Zero knowledge · Co-signature protocol · Digital signature · Legal fairness · Public key

1 Introduction

The main issue addressed by zero knowledge proofs (ZKP) is represented by *identification schemes* (entity authentication). Thus, building on the most important goal that a ZKP can achieve one may find elegant solutions to various problems that arise in different areas: digital cash, auctioning, Internet of Things (IoT), password authentication and so on [1].

A typical zero knowledge protocol involves a prover *Peggy* which possesses a piece of secret information x associated with her identity and a verifier *Victor* whose job is to check that *Peggy* really owns x. Two classical examples of such protocols (proposed for smartcards) are the Schnorr protocol [17] and the Guillou-Quisquater protocol [11]. Working in an abstract framework, Maurer shows in [12] that the previously mentioned protocols are actually instantiations of the same one.

Inspired by Maurer's generic perspective, we considered of great interest extending the unification paradigm to contract signing protocols. Therefore, we construct our main idea considering the stringent issue of scheme compatibility which characterizes communication systems. Typical examples are the cases of certificates in a public key infrastructure and the general issue of upgrading the

© Springer Nature Switzerland AG 2019
J.-L. Lanet and C. Toma (Eds.): SecITC 2018, LNCS 11359, pp. 477–491, 2019.
https://doi.org/10.1007/978-3-030-12942-2_35

version of a system. Thus, working in a general framework may reduce implementation errors and save application development (and maintenance) time.

Various contract signing schemes which fall into three different design categories were proposed during the last decades: *gradual release* [8–10,14], *optimistic* [2,3,13] and *concurrent* [4] or *legally fair* [6] models. A typical co-signing protocol involves two (mutually distrustful) signing partners, *Alice* and *Bob* wishing to compute a common function on their private inputs.

Compared to older paradigms like *gradual release* or optimistic models, concurrent signatures or legally fair protocols do not rely on trusted third parties and do not require too much interaction between co-signers. As such features seem much more attractive for users, we further consider legally fair co-signing protocols (rather than older solutions) in our paper.

To the best of our knowledge, in this work we present the first unified class of legally fair co-signing protocols without keystones and prove its security. Thus, we provide the reader with a common theoretical framework. To be more precise, we propose a class of UZK based co-signing protocols that maintains the valuable properties[1] of the scheme presented in [6].

As digital signature schemes represent the core of modern contract signing protocols, we preserve this perspective and prove the security of our main result building on the unified digital signature scheme we propose in Sect. 3.

Outline. We introduce notations, definitions, schemes and protocols used throughout the paper in Sect. 2. We present a signature scheme inspired by Maurer's UZK paradigm in Sect. 3 and prove its security in Appendix A. In Sect. 4 we present our main result, namely a UZK based co-signing protocol built on the legally fair contract signing protocol of [6]. We conclude and discuss related open problems in Sect. 5.

2   Preliminaries

Notations. Throughout the paper, the notation $|S|$ denotes the cardinal of a set S. The action of selecting a random element x from a sample space X is denoted by $x \xleftarrow{\$} X$, while $x \leftarrow y$ represents the assignment of value y to variable x. The probability of the event E to happen is denoted by $Pr[E]$. The subset $\{0, \ldots, s\} \in \mathbb{N}$ is denoted by $[0, s]$. Let $h : \{0, 1\}^* \to \mathcal{C}$ be a hash function, where $\mathcal{C} \subset \mathbb{N}$.

2.1   Groups

Let $(\mathbb{G}, \star)$ and $(\mathbb{H}, \otimes)$ be two groups. We assume that the group operations $\star$ and $\otimes$ are efficiently computable. We further consider a more restrictive set of initial conditions compared to [12], in the sense that we also assume that $\mathbb{G}$ is commutative[2].

---

[1] Legal fairness without keystones, guaranteed output delivery.

[2] The group $\mathbb{G}$ is considered as being generic in [12].

Definition 1 (Homomorphism). *Let $f : \mathbb{G} \to \mathbb{H}$ be a function (not necessarily one-to-one). We say that f is a homomorphism if $f(x \star y) = f(x) \otimes f(y)$.*

Throughout the rest of the paper we consider f to be a homomorphism as well as a one-way function[3]. To be consistent with [12], we denote the value $f(x)$ by $[x]$. Note that given $[x]$ and $[y]$ we can efficiently compute $[x \star y] = [x] \otimes [y]$, due to the fact that f is a homomorphism. We further denote the set of public parameters by $\mathsf{pp} = (\mathbb{G}, \mathbb{H}, f, h)$.

2.2 Zero-Knowledge Protocols

Let $Q : \{0,1\}^* \times \{0,1\}^* \to \{\texttt{true}, \texttt{false}\}$ be a predicate. Given a value y, Peggy will try to convince Victor that she knows a value x such that $Q(y, x) = \texttt{true}$. We further recall a definition from [5]. This definition captures the notion that being successful in a protocol (P, V) implies having the knowledge of a value x such that $Q(y, x) = \texttt{true}$.

Definition 2 (Proof of Knowledge Protocol). *An interactive protocol (P, V) is a proof of knowledge protocol for predicate Q if the following properties hold*

- *Completeness: V accepts the proof when P has as input an x with $Q(y, x) = \texttt{true}$;*
- *Soundness: there is an efficient program K (called knowledge extractor) such that for any $\hat{P}$ (possibly dishonest) with non-negligible probability of making V accept the proof, K can interact with $\hat{P}$ and output (with overwhelming probability) an x such that $Q(y, x) = \texttt{true}$.*

Definition 3 (2-Extractable). *Let Q be a predicate for a proof of knowledge. A 3-move protocol[4] with challenge space $\mathcal{C}$ is 2-extractable if from any two triplets (r, c, s) and (r, c', s'), with distinct $c, c' \in \mathcal{C}$ accepted by Victor, one can efficiently compute an x such that $Q(y, x) = \texttt{true}$.*

According to [12], UZK (Fig. 1) is a zero-knowledge protocol if the conditions from Theorem 1 are satisfied. If the challenge space $\mathcal{C}$ is small, then one needs several 3-move rounds to make the soundness error negligible. We further assume that UZK satisfies the conditions stated in Theorem 1.

Theorem 1. *If values $\ell \in \mathbb{Z}$ and $u \in \mathbb{G}$ are known such that $\gcd(c_0 - c_1, \ell) = 1$ for all $c_0, c_1 \in \mathcal{C}$ with $c_0 \neq c_1$ and $[u] = y^\ell$, then the protocol described in Fig. 1 is 2-extractable. Moreover, a protocol consisting of α rounds is a proof of knowledge if $1/|\mathcal{C}|^\alpha$ is negligible, and it is a zero-knowledge protocol if $|\mathcal{C}|$ is polynomially bounded.*

---

[3] Meaning that it is infeasible to compute x from $f(x)$.

[4] In which *Peggy* sends r, *Victor* sends c, *Peggy* sends s.

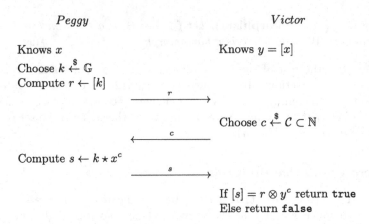

Fig. 1. Maurer's Unified Zero-Knowledge (UZK) Protocol.

2.3   Signatures

Definition 4 (Signature Scheme). *A Signature Scheme consists of three PPT algorithms:* KeyGen, Sign *and* Verify. *The first one takes as input a security parameter and outputs the system's parameters, the public key and the matching secret key. The secret key together with the* Sign *algorithm are used to generate a signature σ for a message m. Using the public key, the third algorithm verifies that a signature σ for a message m is generated using the matching secret key.*

Throughout the paper we only consider signature schemes which, on input m, produce triplets of the form $(\sigma_1, h(m\|\sigma_1), \sigma_2)$, independent of previous signatures. In these triplets we consider σ_2 as being dependent on m, σ_1 and $h(m\|\sigma_1)$. In some cases $h(m\|\sigma_1)$ is easily computable from the available data and, thus, can be omitted.

Lemma 1 (Forking Lemma). *Let $\mathcal{A}$ be a PPT algorithm, given only the public data as input. If A can find a valid signature $(m, \sigma_1, h(m\|\sigma_1), \sigma_2)$ with non-negligible probability, then, also with non-negligible probability, a replay of this machine with a different hashing oracle h' outputs two valid signatures $(m, \sigma_1, h(m\|\sigma_1), \sigma_2)$ and $(m, \sigma_1, h'(m\|\sigma_1), \sigma'_2)$ such that $h(m\|\sigma_1) \neq h'(m\|\sigma_1)$.*

Security Model. We further present the security model of [16] for signature schemes.

Definition 5 (Signature Unforgeability - EF-CMA). *The notion of unforgeability for signatures is defined in terms of the following security game between the adversary $\mathcal{A}$ and a challenger:*

1. *The* KeyGen *algorithm is run and all the public parameters are provided to $\mathcal{A}$.*
2. *$\mathcal{A}$ can perform any number of signature queries to the challenger.*
3. *Finally, $\mathcal{A}$ outputs a tuple $(m, \sigma_1, h(m\|\sigma_1), \sigma_2)$.*

$\mathcal{A}$ *wins the game if* $\mathsf{Verify}(m, \sigma_1, h(m\|\sigma_1), \sigma_2) = \mathsf{True}$ *and* $\mathcal{A}$ *did not query the challenger on* m. *We say that a signature scheme is unforgeable when the success probability of* $\mathcal{A}$ *in this game is negligible.*

2.4   Legally Fair Signatures Without Keystones

In [6] the authors present a new contract signing paradigm that does not require keystones to achieve legal fairness. Their provably secure co-signature construction recalled in Fig. 2 is based on Schnorr digital signatures [17].

In Fig. 2, $\mathcal{L}$ represents a local non-volatile memory used by Bob and $\mathcal{C} = [0, q - 1]$. During the protocol, Alice makes use of a publicly known auxiliary signature scheme σ_{x_A} using her secret key x_A.

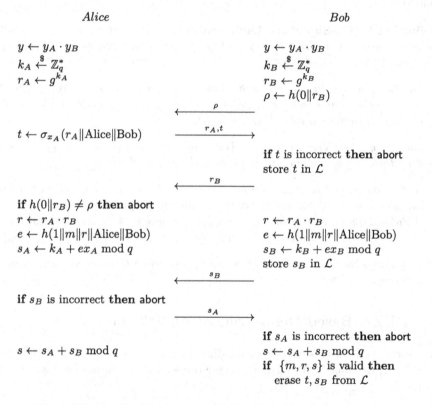

Fig. 2. The legally fair signature (without keystones) of message m.

Security Model. According to the analysis presented in [6], a legally fair signature scheme is secure when it achieves existential unforgeability against an active adversary $\mathcal{A}$ with access to an unlimited amount of conversations and valid co-signatures, *i.e.* $\mathcal{A}$ can perform the following queries:

- Hash queries: $\mathcal{A}$ can request the value of $h(x)$ for an x of his choosing.
- Sign queries: $\mathcal{A}$ can request a valid signature t for a message m and a public key y_C of his choosing.
- CoSign queries: $\mathcal{A}$ can request a valid co-signature (r, s) for a message m and a common public key $y_{C,D}$ of his choosing.
- Transcript queries: $\mathcal{A}$ can request a valid transcript $(m, \rho, r_C, t, r_D, s_C, s_D)$ of the co-signing protocol for a message m of his choosing, between users C and D of his choosing.
- SKExtract queries: $\mathcal{A}$ can request the private key corresponding to a public key.
- Directory queries: $\mathcal{A}$ can request the public key of any user.

The following definition captures the notion of unforgeability in the co-signing context:

Definition 6 (Co-Signature Unforgeability). *The notion of unforgeability for co-signatures is defined in terms of the following security game between the adversary $\mathcal{A}$ and a challenger:*

1. *The* KeyGen *algorithm is run and all the public parameters are provided to $\mathcal{A}$.*
2. *$\mathcal{A}$ can perform any number of queries to the challenger, as described above.*
3. *Finally, $\mathcal{A}$ outputs a tuple $(m, r, s, y_{C,D})$.*

$\mathcal{A}$ wins the game if Verify$(m, r, s) =$ True *and there exist public keys $y_C, y_D \in \mathcal{D}$ such that $y_{C,D} = y_C y_D$ and either of the following holds:*

- *$\mathcal{A}$ did not query SKExtract on y_C nor on y_D, and did not query CoSign on $(m, y_{C,D})$, and did not query Transcript on (m, y_C, y_D) nor (m, y_D, y_C).*
- *$\mathcal{A}$ did not query Transcript on (m, y_C, y_i) for any $y_i \neq y_C$ and did not query SKExtract on y_C, and did not query CoSign on (m, y_C, y_i) for any $y_i \neq y_C$.*

We say that a co-signature scheme is unforgeable when the success probability of $\mathcal{A}$ in this game is negligible.

3   A UZK Based Digital Signature Scheme

We describe our proposed UZK based digital signature scheme (further referred to as UDS) in Table 1. We further provide the security margins of our scheme in Sect. 3.2.

3.1   Description

By applying the Fiat-Shamir transform [7] to the UZK protocol in Fig. 1 we obtain the signature scheme presented in Table 1.

Table 1. A unified digital signature (UDS) scheme.

KeyGen(pp)	On input the public parameters pp, this algorithm chooses uniformly at random $x \xleftarrow{\$} \mathbb{G}$ and computes $y \leftarrow [x]$. The output is the couple (sk, pk), where sk $= x$ is kept private and pk $= y$ is made public
Sign(pp, sk, m)	On input public parameters pp, a secret key sk, and a message m this algorithm selects a random $k \xleftarrow{\$} \mathbb{G}$, computes $r \leftarrow [k] \qquad e \leftarrow h(m\|r) \qquad s \leftarrow k \star x^e$ and outputs (r, s) as the signature of m
Verify(pp, pk, m, (r, s))	On input public parameters pp, a public key pk, a message m and a signature (r, s), this algorithm computes $e \leftarrow h(m\|r)$ and returns True iff $[s] = r \otimes y^e$; otherwise it returns False

3.2 Security Analysis

The proofs presented in [15, 16] do not cover the generic case. Thus, we adapt the initial results to the UDS case and provide the reader with the proof of Theorem 2 in Appendix A.

Theorem 2. *If an* EF-CMA *attack on the UDS has non-negligible probability of success in the ROM, then the homomorphism* $[\cdot]$ *can be inverted in polynomial time.*

4 Main Protocol

We describe our main result (a UZK class of legally fair contract signing protocols) in Fig. 3 and discuss its correctness. We further prove the security of our proposed idea in Sect. 4.2 based on the security of the UDS scheme presented in Sect. 3.

Compared to the initial work on legally fair contract signing protocols without keystones [6], we give a more complete proof by taking into account the signature scheme σ too.

4.1 Description

To illustrate our unified paradigm, we now discuss a legally fair co-signing protocol built from the UDS (Fig. 3), which produces signatures compatible with standard UDS (Table 1). This contract signing protocol is provably secure in the ROM assuming the one-way property of $[\cdot]$.

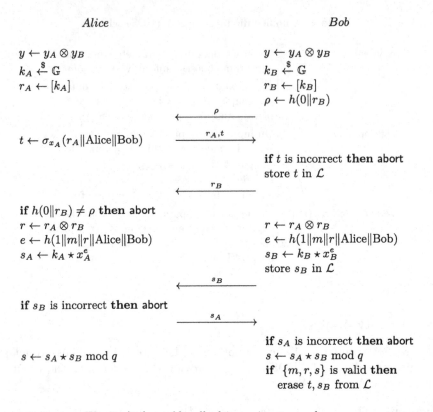

Fig. 3. A class of legally fair co-signature schemes.

Correctness. To prove the correctness of the co-signing schemes class described in Fig. 3 we use the commutative property of $\mathbb{G}$ which is preserved by $f(x)$:

$$
\begin{aligned}
[s] &= [s_A \star s_B] \\
&= [s_A] \otimes [s_B] \\
&= [k_A] \otimes [x_A]^e \otimes [k_B] \otimes [x_B]^e \\
&= [k_A] \otimes [k_B] \otimes ([x_A] \otimes [x_B])^e \\
&= r \otimes y^e.
\end{aligned}
$$

4.2 Security Analysis

To prove that the unified co-signature protocol is secure in the ROM we use the following strategy: assuming $\mathcal{A}$ is an efficient forger for the co-signature scheme, we turn $\mathcal{A}$ into an efficient forger for UDS, then invoke Lemma 1 to prove the existence of an efficient inverter for the homomorphism $[\cdot]$. We further address two scenarios: when the attacker plays Alice's role, and when the attacker plays Bob's.

4.2.1   Adversary Attacks Bob

Theorem 3. *If $\mathcal{A}_{Alice}$ plays the role of Alice and is able to forge a co-signature with non-negligible probability, then we can construct an EF-CMA attack on the UDS that has non-negligible probability of success.*

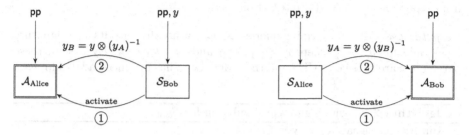

Fig. 4. The simulator $\mathcal{S}_{Bob}$ (left) or $\mathcal{S}_{Alice}$ (right) answers the attacker's queries to the public directory $\mathcal{D}$.

Proof. The proof consists in constructing a simulator $\mathcal{S}_{Bob}$ that interacts with the adversary and forces it to actually produce a UDS forgery. Here is how this simulator behaves at each step of the protocol.

Key Establishment Phase. $\mathcal{S}_{Bob}$ is given a target public key y. As a simulator, $\mathcal{S}_{Bob}$ emulates not only Bob, but also all oracles and the directory $\mathcal{D}$ (see Fig. 4).

To inject a target $y \leftarrow [x]$ into $\mathcal{A}$, the simulator $\mathcal{S}_{Bob}$ reads $y_{\mathcal{A}}$ from $\mathcal{D}$ and poses as an entity whose public-key is $y_{\mathcal{S}_{Bob}} \leftarrow y \otimes (y_{\mathcal{A}})^{-1}$. It follows that $y_{\mathcal{A}, \mathcal{S}_{Bob}}$, the common public-key of $\mathcal{A}$ and $\mathcal{S}_{Bob}$ will be precisely $y_{\mathcal{A}, \mathcal{S}_{Bob}} \leftarrow y_{\mathcal{S}_{Bob}} \otimes y_{\mathcal{A}}$ which, by construction, is exactly y.

Then $\mathcal{S}_{Bob}$ activates $\mathcal{A}_{Alice}$, who queries the directory and gets y_B. At this point in time, $\mathcal{A}_{Alice}$ is tricked into believing that she has successfully established a co-signature public-key set (pp, y) with the "co-signer" $\mathcal{S}_{Bob}$.

Algorithm 1. Hashing oracle $\mathcal{O}_h$ simulation for h.

Input: A hashing query q_i from $\mathcal{A}$
1 **if** $\exists h_i, \{q_i, h_i\} \in T$ **then**
2     $e \leftarrow h_i$
3 **else**
4     $e \xleftarrow{\$} \mathcal{C}$
5   Append $\{q_i, e\}$ to T
6 **end if**
7 **return** e

Query Phase. $\mathcal{A}_{\text{Alice}}$ will start to present queries to $\mathcal{S}$. Thus, $\mathcal{S}$ must respond to three types of queries: hash queries, co-signature queries and transcript queries. $\mathcal{S}$ will maintain a table T containing all the hash queries performed throughout the attack. At start $T \leftarrow \varnothing$. We further describe the simulations of the hash function in Algorithm 1 and the co-signature protocol in Algorithm 2. When $\mathcal{A}_{\text{Alice}}$ requests a conversation transcript, $\mathcal{S}_{\text{Bob}}$ replies by sending $(m, \rho, r_A, t, r_B, s_B, s_A)$ from a previously successful interaction.

Output Phase. After performing queries, $\mathcal{A}_{\text{Alice}}$ eventually outputs a co-signature (r, s) valid for $y_{\mathcal{A}, \mathcal{S}_{\text{Bob}}}$ where $r = r_A \otimes r_B$ and $s = s_A \star s_B$. By design, these parameters are those of a UDS and therefore $\mathcal{A}_{\text{Alice}}$ has produced a UDS forgery.

Algorithm 2. Co-signing oracle simulation for $\mathcal{S}_{\text{Bob}}$.

Input: A co-signature query m from $\mathcal{A}_{\text{Alice}}$

1 $s_B \xleftarrow{\$} \mathbb{G}$

2 $e \xleftarrow{\$} \mathcal{C}$

3 $r_B \leftarrow [s_B] \otimes y^{-e}$

4 Send $h(0\|r_B)$ to $\mathcal{A}_{\text{Alice}}$

5 Receive r_A, t from $\mathcal{A}_{\text{Alice}}$

6 Send r_B to $\mathcal{A}_{\text{Alice}}$

7 $r \leftarrow r_A \otimes r_B$

8 $u \leftarrow 1\|m\|r\|\text{Alice}\|\text{Bob}$

9 **if** $\exists e' \neq e, \{u, e'\} \in T$ **then**

10 | abort

11 **else**

12 | Append $\{u, e\}$ to T

13 **end if**

14 **return** s_B

To understand $\mathcal{S}_{\text{Bob}}$'s co-signature reply (Algorithm 2), assume that $\mathcal{A}_{\text{Alice}}$ is an honest Alice who plays by the protocol's rules. For such an Alice, (r, s) is a valid signature with respect to the co-signature public-key set $\{\text{pp}, y\}$.

There is a case in which $\mathcal{S}_{\text{Bob}}$ aborts the protocol before completion: this happens when it turns out that $1\|m\|r\|\text{Alice}\|\text{Bob}\|t$ has been previously queried by $\mathcal{A}_{\text{Alice}}$. In that case, it is no longer possible for $\mathcal{S}_{\text{Bob}}$ to reprogram the oracle, which is why $\mathcal{S}_{\text{Bob}}$ must abort. Since $\mathcal{A}_{\text{Alice}}$ does not know the random value r_B, such a bad event would only occur with a negligible probability exactly equal to q_h/q, where q_h is the number of queries to $\mathcal{O}_h$.

Therefore, $\mathcal{A}$ is turned into a forger for the SFS with probability $1 - q_h/q$. As $\mathcal{A}$ has a success probability ϵ_{succ}, the success probability of $\mathcal{A}$ in the simulated environment is $\epsilon_{sim} = (1 - q_h/q)\epsilon_{succ}$. □

Corollary 1. *If $\mathcal{A}_{\text{Alice}}$ plays the role of Alice and is able to forge a co-signature with non-negligible probability, then the homomorphism $[\cdot]$ can be inverted in polynomial time.*

4.2.2   Adversary Attacks Alice

Theorem 4. *If $\mathcal{A}_{Bob}$ plays the role of Bob and is able to forge a co-signature with non-negligible probability, then we can construct an EF-CMA attack on the UDS that has non-negligible probability of success if signature σ_{x_A} can be simulated without knowing the secret key x_A.*

Proof. Here also the proof consists in constructing a simulator, $\mathcal{S}_{Alice}$, that interacts with the adversary and forces it to actually produce a UDS forgery. The simulator's behavior at different stages of the security game is as follows.

The Key Establishment Phase. $\mathcal{S}_{Alice}$ is given a target public key y. Again, $\mathcal{S}_{Alice}$ impersonates not only Alice, but also all the oracles and $\mathcal{D}$.

$\mathcal{S}_{Alice}$ injects the target y into the game as described in Theorem 3. Now $\mathcal{S}_{Alice}$ activates $\mathcal{A}_{Bob}$, who queries $\mathcal{D}$ (actually controlled by $\mathcal{S}_{Alice}$) to get y_A. $\mathcal{A}_{Bob}$ is thus tricked into believing that it has successfully established a co-signature public-key set (pp, y) with the "co-signer" $\mathcal{S}_{Alice}$.

Query Phase. $\mathcal{A}$ will start to present queries to $\mathcal{S}$. Thus, $\mathcal{S}$ must respond to four types of queries: hash queries, signature queries, co-signature queries and transcript queries. We consider oracles $\mathcal{O}_h$ as in Theorem 3. We denote by $\mathcal{O}_\sigma$ the simulation of σ_{x_A}. We further describe the simulation of the co-signature algorithm in Algorithm 3. When $\mathcal{A}_{Alice}$ requests a conversation transcript, $\mathcal{S}_{Bob}$ replies by sending $(m, \rho, r_A, t, r_B, s_B, s_A)$ from a previously successful interaction.

Algorithm 3. Co-signing oracle simulation for $\mathcal{S}_{Alice}$.

Input: A co-signature query m from $\mathcal{A}_{Bob}$
1 Receive ρ from $\mathcal{A}_{Bob}$
2 Query T to retrieve r_B such that $h(0\|r_B) = \rho$
3 $s_A \xleftarrow{\$} \mathbb{G}$
4 $e \xleftarrow{\$} \mathcal{C}$
5 $r \leftarrow r_B \otimes [s_A] \otimes y^{-e}$
6 $u_1 \leftarrow 1\|m\|r$
7 **if** $\exists e' \neq e, \{u_1, e'\} \in T$ **then**
8 | abort
9 **else**
10 | Append $\{u_1, e\}$ to T
11 **end if**
12 $r_A \leftarrow r \otimes r_B^{-1}$
13 $u_2 \leftarrow r_A\|\text{Alice}\|\text{Bob}$
14 $t \leftarrow \mathcal{O}_\sigma(u_2)$
15 Send r_A, t to $\mathcal{A}_{Bob}$
16 Receive r_B from $\mathcal{A}_{Bob}$
17 Receive s_B from $\mathcal{A}_{Bob}$
18 **return** s_A

Output Phase. After performing queries, $\mathcal{A}_{\text{Bob}}$ eventually outputs a co-signature (r, s) valid for $y_{\mathcal{S}_{\text{Alice}}, \mathcal{A}_{\text{Bob}}}$ where $r = r_A \otimes r_B$ and $s = s_A \star s_B$. By design, these parameters are those of a UDS and therefore $\mathcal{A}_{\text{Bob}}$ has produced a UDS forgery.

As in Theorem 3, Algorithm 3 may fail with probability q_h/q. Thus, the success probability of $\mathcal{A}$ in the simulated environment is $\epsilon_{sim} = (1 - q_h/q)\epsilon_{succ}$.

$\square$

Corollary 2. *If $\mathcal{A}_{Bob}$ plays the role of Bob and is able to forge a co-signature with non-negligible probability, then the homomorphism $[\cdot]$ can be inverted in polynomial time if signature σ_{x_A} can be simulated without knowing the secret key x_A.*

5   Conclusion

In this paper we presented a signature scheme inspired by Maurer's UZK paradigm from [12] and proved its security. We further described our main result, *i.e.* a UZK class of co-signing protocols based on both Maurer's abstract perspective and the legally fair framework from [6] and then proved its security.

Open Problems. A couple of interesting related studies could be the analysis of our co-signature protocols' resistance to SETUP (Secretly Embedded Trapdoor with Universal Protection) attacks and the proposal of suitable countermeasures.

A   Proof of Theorem 2

If an attacker $\mathcal{A}$ can forge a UDS, then we are able to construct a simulator $\mathcal{S}$ that interacts with $\mathcal{A}$ and forces it to produce a forgery. By using Lemma 1 we transform $\mathcal{A}$ into a homomorphism inverter (*i.e.* that computes an x' such that $y = [x']$). We further show how $\mathcal{S}$ can simulate the three phases necessary to mount the EF-CMA attack.

Key Establishment Phase. In this phase $\mathcal{S}$ sets up the public key as $y = [x]$ and then activates $\mathcal{A}$ with input y.

Query Phase. $\mathcal{A}$ will start to present queries to the $\mathcal{S}$. Thus, $\mathcal{S}$ must respond to two types of queries: hash and signature queries. We consider oracle $\mathcal{O}_h$ as in Theorem 3. We further describe the simulations of the signature scheme in Algorithm 4.

Output Phase. After the query phase, $\mathcal{A}$ will eventually produce a forgery (r, s).

When simulating the signing oracle $\mathcal{O}_S$ there is a case when $\mathcal{S}$ aborts before completion: this happens when $m\|r$ has already been queried by $\mathcal{A}$. In this case, $\mathcal{S}$ can not reprogram $\mathcal{O}_h$, which is why it must abort. Since $\mathcal{A}$ does not know the random value r, the previously described event occurs with a negligible probability q_h/q, where q_h is the number of queries to $\mathcal{O}_h$.

Therefore, $\mathcal{A}$ is turned into a forger for the UDS with probability $1 - q_h/q$. As $\mathcal{A}$ has a success probability ϵ_{succ}, the success probability of $\mathcal{A}$ in the simulated environment is $\epsilon_{sim} = (1 - q_h/q)\epsilon_{succ}$.

Let β be the position of $m\|r$ in T from $\mathcal{O}_h$. After $\mathcal{A}$ produces a forgery (r, s), $\mathcal{S}$ runs $\mathcal{A}$ with the same inputs and a different h oracle (Algorithm 5). As before, $\mathcal{S}$ will maintain a table $\tilde{T}$ containing all the h queries performed throughout this phase of the attack. At start $\tilde{T} \leftarrow \varnothing$. Then, by Lemma 1, $\mathcal{A}$ will produce a different forgery (r, s'). Thus, we obtain $c = \mathcal{O}_h(m\|r) \neq \mathcal{O}'_h(m\|r) = c'$. Using the 2-extractable property of UZK, we obtain an x' such that $y = [x']$.

Algorithm 4. Signing oracle $\mathcal{O}_S$ simulation.

Input: A signature query m
1 $s \xleftarrow{\$} \mathbb{G}$
2 $e \xleftarrow{\$} \mathcal{C}$
3 $r \leftarrow [s] \otimes y^{-e}$
4 $u \leftarrow m\|r$
5 **if** $\exists e' \neq e, \{u, e'\} \in T$ **then**
6 $\quad$ abort
7 **else**
8 $\quad$ Append $\{u, e\}$ to T
9 **end if**
10 **return** (r, s)

Algorithm 5. Hashing oracle $\mathcal{O}'_h$ simulation for h.

Input: A hashing query q_i from $\mathcal{A}$, an index γ and a table T
1 **if** $i < \gamma$ **then**
2 $\quad$ $e \leftarrow h_i$, where $(q_i, h_i) \in T$
3 $\quad$ Append $\{q_i, e\}$ to $\tilde{T}$
4 **else if** $i = \gamma$ **then**
5 $\quad$ $e \xleftarrow{\$} \mathcal{C} \setminus \{h_\gamma\}$, where $(q_\gamma, h_\gamma) \in T$
6 $\quad$ Append $\{q_i, e\}$ to $\tilde{T}$
7 **else**
8 $\quad$ **if** $\exists h_i, \{q_i, h_i\} \in \tilde{T}$ **then**
9 $\quad\quad$ $e \leftarrow h_i$
10 $\quad$ **else**
11 $\quad\quad$ $e \xleftarrow{\$} \mathcal{C}$
12 $\quad\quad$ Append $\{q_i, e\}$ to $\tilde{T}$
13 $\quad$ **end if**
14 **end if**
15 **return** e

References

1. Zero-Knowledge Proof: More secure than passwords? https://blog.ingenico.com/posts/2017/07/zero-knowledge-proof-more-secure-than-passwords.html
2. Asokan, N., Schunter, M., Waidner, M.: Optimistic protocols for fair exchange. In: Proceedings of the 4th ACM Conference on Computer and Communications Security - CCS 1997, pp. 7–17. ACM (1997)
3. Cachin, C., Camenisch, J.: Optimistic fair secure computation. In: Bellare, M. (ed.) CRYPTO 2000. LNCS, vol. 1880, pp. 93–111. Springer, Heidelberg (2000). https://doi.org/10.1007/3-540-44598-6_6
4. Chen, L., Kudla, C., Paterson, K.G.: Concurrent signatures. In: Cachin, C., Camenisch, J.L. (eds.) EUROCRYPT 2004. LNCS, vol. 3027, pp. 287–305. Springer, Heidelberg (2004). https://doi.org/10.1007/978-3-540-24676-3_18
5. Feige, U., Fiat, A., Shamir, A.: Zero-knowledge proofs of identity. J. Cryptology 1(2), 77–94 (1988)
6. Ferradi, H., Géraud, R., Maimuţ, D., Naccache, D., Pointcheval, D.: Legally fair contract signing without keystones. In: Manulis, M., Sadeghi, A.-R., Schneider, S. (eds.) ACNS 2016. LNCS, vol. 9696, pp. 175–190. Springer, Cham (2016). https://doi.org/10.1007/978-3-319-39555-5_10
7. Fiat, A., Shamir, A.: How to prove yourself: practical solutions to identification and signature problems. In: Odlyzko, A.M. (ed.) CRYPTO 1986. LNCS, vol. 263, pp. 186–194. Springer, Heidelberg (1987). https://doi.org/10.1007/3-540-47721-7_12
8. Garay, J., MacKenzie, P., Prabhakaran, M., Yang, K.: Resource fairness and composability of cryptographic protocols. In: Halevi, S., Rabin, T. (eds.) TCC 2006. LNCS, vol. 3876, pp. 404–428. Springer, Heidelberg (2006). https://doi.org/10.1007/11681878_21
9. Goldwasser, S., Levin, L.: Fair computation of general functions in presence of immoral majority. In: Menezes, A.J., Vanstone, S.A. (eds.) CRYPTO 1990. LNCS, vol. 537, pp. 77–93. Springer, Heidelberg (1991). https://doi.org/10.1007/3-540-38424-3_6
10. Gordon, S.D., Hazay, C., Katz, J., Lindell, Y.: Complete fairness in secure two-party computation. J. ACM 58(6), 1–37 (2011)
11. Guillou, L.C., Quisquater, J.-J.: A practical zero-knowledge protocol fitted to security microprocessor minimizing both transmission and memory. In: Barstow, D., et al. (eds.) EUROCRYPT 1988. LNCS, vol. 330, pp. 123–128. Springer, Heidelberg (1988). https://doi.org/10.1007/3-540-45961-8_11
12. Maurer, U.: Unifying zero-knowledge proofs of knowledge. In: Preneel, B. (ed.) AFRICACRYPT 2009. LNCS, vol. 5580, pp. 272–286. Springer, Heidelberg (2009). https://doi.org/10.1007/978-3-642-02384-2_17
13. Micali, S.: Simple and fast optimistic protocols for fair electronic exchange. In: Proceedings of the 22nd Annual Symposium on Principles of Distributed Computing - PODC 2003, pp. 12–19. ACM (2003)
14. Pinkas, B.: Fair secure two-party computation. In: Biham, E. (ed.) EUROCRYPT 2003. LNCS, vol. 2656, pp. 87–105. Springer, Heidelberg (2003). https://doi.org/10.1007/3-540-39200-9_6
15. Pointcheval, D., Stern, J.: Security proofs for signature schemes. In: Maurer, U. (ed.) EUROCRYPT 1996. LNCS, vol. 1070, pp. 387–398. Springer, Heidelberg (1996). https://doi.org/10.1007/3-540-68339-9_33

16. Pointcheval, D., Stern, J.: Security arguments for digital signatures and blind signatures. J. Cryptology **13**(3), 361–396 (2000)
17. Schnorr, C.P.: Efficient identification and signatures for smart cards. In: Brassard, G. (ed.) CRYPTO 1989. LNCS, vol. 435, pp. 239–252. Springer, New York (1990). https://doi.org/10.1007/0-387-34805-0_22

Relating Different Polynomial-LWE Problems

Madalina Bolboceanu$^{(\boxtimes)}$

Bitdefender, Bucharest, Romania
mbolboceanu@bitdefender.com

Abstract. In this paper we focus on Polynomial Learning with Errors (PLWE). This problem is parametrized by a polynomial and we are interested in relating the hardness of the PLWE^f and PLWE^h problems for different polynomials f and h. More precisely, our main result shows that for a fixed monic polynomial f, PLWE$^{f \circ g}$ is at least as hard as than PLWE^f, in both search and decision variants, for any monic polynomial g. As a consequence, PLWE$^{\phi_n}$ is harder than PLWE^f, for a minimal polynomial f of an algebraic integer from the cyclotomic field $\mathbb{Q}(\zeta_n)$ with specific properties.

Keywords: Lattice-based cryptography · LWE · PLWE

1 Introduction

Lattice-based cryptography is one of the most promising solutions for post-quantum cryptography. One important hard lattice problem which is assumed to remain difficult to solve even with quantum algorithms is Approximate Shortest Vector Problem (ApproxSVP). This problem requires finding a short vector in a lattice, up to an approximation factor. Regev introduced in [Reg05] Learning with Errors (LWE) and gave a quantum reduction from a variant of Approx-SVP to LWE. The goal of its search variant is to find a uniformly sampled vector $\mathbf{s}$ from $\mathbb{Z}_q^n$ from given samples of the form $(\mathbf{A}, \mathbf{A} \cdot \mathbf{s} + \mathbf{e}) \in \mathbb{Z}_q^{m \times n} \times \mathbb{Z}_q^n$, where $\mathbf{A}$ is a uniformly sampled matrix from $\mathbb{Z}_q^{m \times n}$ and the noise vector $\mathbf{e}$ is sampled from a discrete Gaussian distribution of small parameter over $\mathbb{Z}^n$. Its decision variant asks you to distinguish such samples for a common secret vector $\mathbf{s}$ from uniform pairs from $\mathbb{Z}_q^{m \times n} \times \mathbb{Z}_q^n$. This problem is a very versatile one, since it enables the design of many advanced cryptographic primitives such as fully homomorphic encryption [GSW13], identity based encryption [ABB10], predicate encryption [GVW15] or key-homomorphic pseudorandom functions [BP14].

The main drawback of the schemes based on LWE is the large size of keys. In order to achieve practical efficiency, algebraic variants of LWE have been introduced, which use structured matrices. The Polynomial Learning with Errors problem (PLWE) was introduced in [SSTX09] and was initially called Ideal-LWE. It is parametrized by a polynomial $f \in \mathbb{Z}[X]$ and an integer $q \geq 2$ and described in terms of elements from $\mathbb{Z}_q[X]/(f)$. Concretely, its search variant

© Springer Nature Switzerland AG 2019
J.-L. Lanet and C. Toma (Eds.): SecITC 2018, LNCS 11359, pp. 492–503, 2019.
https://doi.org/10.1007/978-3-030-12942-2_36

asks you to find a secret polynomial s sampled uniformly from $\mathbb{Z}_q[X]/(f)$, given pairs of the form $(a_i, a_i \cdot s + e_i)$ from $\mathbb{Z}_q[X]/(f) \times \mathbb{R}_q[X]/(f)$, where a_i is sampled uniformly from $\mathbb{Z}_q[X]/(f)$. The coefficient embedding of the noise polynomial e_i follows a Gaussian distribution of small covariance matrix. For a common uniformly sampled s, the decision variant consists in distinguishing between such samples and uniform samples from $\mathbb{Z}_q[X]/(f) \times \mathbb{R}_q[X]/(f)$. It may be considered an LWE problem, except that the matrix is not uniform, but instead it is a structured matrix generated by the uniform polynomials a_i. Lyubashevsky et al. [LPR10] introduced Ring Learning with Errors (Ring-LWE) which uses number fields instead of polynomials. In this case the error is sampled such that its Minkowski embedding follows a Gaussian distribution. They also gave a reduction from search to decision variants for the case of cyclotomic polynomials, which was further extended for general Galois extensions in [EHL14] and [CLS15]. It has been shown that in the case of power-of-2 cyclotomic polynomials both PLWE and Ring-LWE coincide. Recently, Rosca et al. [RSW18] gave reductions between (search/decision) Ring-LWE and (search/decision) PLWE which incur limited noise growth increases for an exponentially large class of polynomials f.

PLWE and RLWE are interesting problems, because their hardness relies on the restriction of ApproxSVP to a special class of so called *ideal lattices*. This restriction is called Ideal-SVP. If Ideal-SVP is assumed to be hard in worst-case, this leads to the PLWE and Ring-LWE instances to be hard. Indeed, Stehlé et al. gave in [SSTX09] a quantum reduction from Ideal-SVP to (search) PLWE^f for power-of-2 cyclotomic polynomials f. Later on, Lyubashevsky et al. [LPR10] gave a quantum reduction from Ideal-SVP to (search) Ring-LWE, while Peikert et al. [PRSD17] gave a quantum reduction from Ideal-SVP directly to (decision) Ring-LWE, which works for any number field and modulus. Many provable secure cryptographic applications can be designed from these assumptions, such as key encapsulation mechanisms [ADPS16, SSZ17] or fully homomorphic encryption schemes [Gen09, BV11]. It is natural to ask if ApproxSVP is still hard when one restricts only to ideal lattices. One approach to this problem is the one of Cramer et al. [CDPR16] who found a quantum polynomial time algorithm for solving Ideal-SVP for principal ideals in cyclotomic fields of prime power conductor with $2^{\tilde{O}(\sqrt{n})}$ approximation factor, where n is the degree of the field used. To compare this result with classical algorithms, we mention that the best algorithm for approximating shortest vector with this approximation factor, [SE94], runs in time $2^{\tilde{O}(\sqrt{n})}$, where n is the lattice dimension. Furthermore, Cramer et al. [CDW17] generalized the previous statement by giving a quantum polynomial time algorithm for solving Ideal-SVP for arbitrary ideals in cyclotomic rings. Still, the approximation factor is too large to impact the security of the primitives based on Ring-LWE or PLWE. Until now, there is no reduction from Ring-LWE or PLWE to Ideal-SVP. In terms of hardness, all these attacks show that Ideal-SVP problems for ideal lattices are not the same for all polynomials f. The easy instances of Ideal-SVP make the reduction from [SSTX09] vacuous for the corresponding PLWE^f instances. There is a lack of knowledge in finding the polynomial f for which the corresponding PLWE^f problem is the hardest. One may want either to propose a new problem harder than the PLWE^f problem for exponentially many polynomials f or to further study which might be the hardest instances of the PLWE problem.

The first approach was made by Roşca et al. [RSSS17] who proposed Middle Product Learning with Errors (MP-LWE). They gave a reduction from (decision) PLWE^f to (decision) MP-LWE for exponentially many monic polynomials f with bounded expansion factor and constant coefficient coprime with q.

Our Contributions. In this paper we focus on the second approach, namely on finding a polynomial for which the corresponding PLWE problem is at least as hard as many other PLWE problems. Our main result towards this goal is a reduction from PLWE^f to $\mathrm{PLWE}^{f \circ g}$ for an arbitrary monic polynomial g. This has interesting consequences involving cyclotomic polynomials. As a corollary, we obtain that PLWE^{ϕ_n} for the cyclotomic polynomial ϕ_n is harder than PLWE^f for all the minimal polynomials f of algebraic integers of the cyclotomic field $\mathbb{Q}(\zeta_n)$ which have specific properties we will mention. These reductions hold in both search and decision variants.

Organization. Section 2 gives the necessary background regarding the PLWE problem. Section 3 presents the reductions relating the PLWE problems for different polynomials. In Sect. 4 we discuss the impact of the main result. In Sect. 5 we describe some open problems.

2   Preliminaries

For a finite set X we denote by $U(X)$ the uniform distribution over X. We write $x \hookleftarrow \psi$ when x follows a distribution ψ. We write by $[n]$ the set $\{1, 2, \ldots, n\}$.

2.1   Cyclotomic Polynomials

The cyclotomic polynomials, especially the power-of-2 cyclotomic ones, have been frequently used in designing cryptographic primitives since their use leads to very efficient solutions, such as homomorphic encryption schemes, [BV11, BGV11, GHPS12], or key exchange systems, [ADPS16].

For a positive integer n, we denote by $\zeta_n = e^{\frac{2\pi i}{n}}$ an nth primitive root. The nth cyclotomic polynomial $\phi_n \in \mathbb{Z}[X]$ is the minimal polynomial of ζ_n over $\mathbb{Q}$ and has as roots all the nth primitive roots:

$$\phi_n(X) = \prod_{k \in \mathbb{Z}_n^*} (X - \zeta_n^k).$$

The degree of the cyclotomic polynomial ϕ_n is $|\mathbb{Z}_n^*| = \varphi(n)$, where φ is the Euler's totient function. The nth cyclotomic field is obtained by adjoining ζ_n to the rational field $\mathbb{Q}$ (as an abstract element, not as a complex number). There is a natural isomorphism of rings from $\mathbb{Q}[X]/(\phi_n)$ to $\mathbb{Q}(\zeta_n)$, which sends X to ζ_n. This map can be seen as the evaluation map at ζ_n. The ring of algebraic integers of $\mathbb{Q}(\zeta_n)$ is precisely $\mathbb{Z}[\zeta_n]$. This is a $\mathbb{Z}$ module having as basis $\{1, \zeta_n, \zeta_n^2, \ldots, \zeta_n^{\varphi(n)-1}\}$. We mention here an useful property which relates different cyclotomic polynomials:

Proposition 2.1 ([LPR13], **Fact 2.12**). *Let n be a positive integer and $\mathrm{rad}(n)$ the product of all distinct prime divisors of n. Then $\phi_n(X) = \phi_{\mathrm{rad}(n)}(X^{n/\mathrm{rad}(n)})$. In particular, if p is a prime and n a prime power of p, then $\phi_n(X) = \phi_p(X^{n/p})$.*

2.2 Gaussian Distributions

For a symmetric positive definite matrix $\boldsymbol{\Sigma}$ in $\mathbb{R}^{n \times n}$, we define the Gaussian function on $\mathbb{R}^n$ of covariance matrix $\boldsymbol{\Sigma}$ as $\rho_{\sqrt{\boldsymbol{\Sigma}}}(\mathbf{x}) = \exp(-\pi \cdot \mathbf{x}^t \boldsymbol{\Sigma}^{-1} \mathbf{x})$, where $\mathbf{x} \in \mathbb{R}^n$. When discussing about distributions, we normalize this function $\rho_{\sqrt{\boldsymbol{\Sigma}}}$ and obtain the (continuous) Gaussian probability distribution $D_{\sqrt{\boldsymbol{\Sigma}}}$. If $\boldsymbol{\Sigma} = s^2 I_n$, where s is a positive real number, we simply denote by ρ_s and D_s the Gaussian function and the Gaussian distribution, respectively. It is easy to see that a random vector $\mathbf{x}$ in $\mathbb{R}^n$ follows the Gaussian distribution D_s if and only if its coordinates are independent random variables which follow the Gaussian distribution D_s over $\mathbb{R}$. We will frequently use the fact that if $\mathbf{x}$ is a random vector in $\mathbb{R}^n$ whose distribution is $D_{\sqrt{\boldsymbol{\Sigma}}}$, then for a matrix $\mathbf{A}$ in $\mathbb{R}^{m \times n}$, the distribution of $\mathbf{A} \cdot \mathbf{x}$ will be $D_{\sqrt{\mathbf{A}\boldsymbol{\Sigma}\mathbf{A}^t}}$ over $\mathbb{R}^m$.

2.3 The Polynomial Learning with Errors Problem

We now define the problem we study in this paper. Consider a monic polynomial f in $\mathbb{Z}[X]$ and a prime modulus q. Denote by $R = \mathbb{Z}[X]/(f)$ and by $R_q = R/qR = \mathbb{Z}_q[X]/(f)$. We use the notation $\mathbb{R}_q := \mathbb{R}/q\mathbb{Z}$.

Definition 2.1 (PLWE$_{q,\psi}^f$ **distribution**). *For any $s \in R_q$, we define* PLWE$_{q,\psi}^f(s)$ *as the distribution over $\mathbb{Z}_q[X]/(f) \times \mathbb{R}_q[X]/(f)$ obtained by sampling $a \hookleftarrow U(R_q)$, by sampling an error polynomial $e \hookleftarrow \psi$ over $\mathbb{R}[X]/(f)$ and by returning $(a, a \cdot s + e \bmod qR)$.*

Definition 2.2 (**The** PLWE^f **problem**). *Search* PLWE$_{q,\psi}^f$ *consists in finding $s \in \mathbb{Z}_q[X]/(f)$ given an arbitrary number of independent samples from* PLWE$_{q,\psi}^f(s)$, *where $s \hookleftarrow U(\mathbb{Z}_q[X]/(f))$. Decision* PLWE$_{q,\psi}^f$ *consists in distinguishing between an arbitrary number of independent* PLWE$_{q,\psi}^f(s)$ *samples and the same number of independent samples from $U(\mathbb{Z}_q[X]/(f) \times \mathbb{R}_q[X]/(f))$, with non-negligible probability over the choices of $s \hookleftarrow U(\mathbb{Z}_q[X]/(f))$.*

We will mainly discuss about the decision variant of the PLWE^f problems where the error polynomial is sampled according to a Gaussian distribution $D_{\alpha q}$, for some $\alpha > 0$. The support of the continuous Gaussian distribution, $\mathbb{R}^n$, is identified with $\mathbb{R}[X]/(f)$, where n is the degree of f.

Remark 2.1 It suffices to discuss about the PLWE problems for an irreducible polynomial f, since if $h|f$, one can find a reduction from $\mathrm{PLWE}_{q,\psi}^{f}$ to $\mathrm{PLWE}_{q,\psi}^{h}$. Indeed, the map $\mathbb{Z}[X]/(f) \rightarrow \mathbb{Z}[X]/(h), a \rightarrow a \bmod h$ is well defined since if $a \equiv \bar{a} \bmod f$, then $f|a - \bar{a}$, and therefore $h|a - \bar{a}$.

3   The Main Result

We consider a fixed monic polynomial f in $\mathbb{Z}[X]$ of degree m. Our main result is a reduction from PLWE^{f} to $\mathrm{PLWE}^{f \circ g}$, for any arbitrary monic polynomial $g \in \mathbb{Z}[X]$. In order to build intuition for the proof of the main result, we first present a simpler particular case, when $g = X^n$.

3.1   An Easy Particular Case

For a positive integer n, we denote by g_n the polynomial X^n and by f_n the polynomial $f \circ g_n$. We prove a reduction from (decision) $\mathrm{PLWE}_{q,D_{\alpha q}}^{f}$ to (decision) $\mathrm{PLWE}_{q,D_{\alpha q}}^{f_n}$, which has a similar but simpler proof as the one of Theorem 3.2, the general case. Unlike the general case, here the error distribution is the same.

We first make some notations: for a ring R (which can be $\mathbb{R}$, $\mathbb{Z}_q$ or $\mathbb{R}_q$) and a monic polynomial g from $\mathbb{Z}[X]$, we consider the maps:

$$\mathcal{F}_{R,g} : (R[X]/(f))^n \rightarrow R[X]/(f \circ g), \quad \mathcal{F}_{R,g}(c_0, c_1, \ldots, c_{n-1}) = \sum_{i=0}^{n-1} X^i c_i \circ g.$$

We can see that $\mathcal{F}_{R,g}$ is a well defined R linear map of modules, if we consider the input polynomials as a vector obtained by concatenating their vector coefficients.

Remark 3.1. For $c_i \in R[X]/(f)$, where $0 \leq i \leq n - 1$, we obtain

$$\mathcal{F}_{R,g_n}(c_0, c_1, \ldots, c_{n-1})(X) = \sum_{i=0}^{n-1} X^i c_i \circ g_n(X) = \sum_{i=0}^{n-1} X^i c_i(X^n).$$

Hence the new polynomial has mn coefficients obtained by putting the coefficients of c_i on positions of indices of form $nk + i$, for any $0 \leq i \leq n - 1$. We can say that $\mathcal{F}_{R,g_n}$ permutes the coefficients of the input polynomials.

Theorem 3.1. *For a monic polynomial f from $\mathbb{Z}[X]$, if $\mathrm{PLWE}_{q,D_{\alpha q}}^{f}$ is hard given $k + n - 1$ samples, then so is $\mathrm{PLWE}_{q,D_{\alpha q}}^{f_n}$ given k samples.*

Proof. Assume $\mathcal{B}$ is an algorithm which distinguishes an $\mathrm{PLWE}_{q,D_{\alpha q}}^{f_n}$ distribution from the uniform distribution over $\mathbb{Z}_q[X]/(f_n) \times \mathbb{R}_q[X]/(f_n)$. We construct an algorithm $\mathcal{A}$ which distinguishes an $\mathrm{PLWE}_{q,D_{\alpha q}}^{f}$ distribution from the uniform distribution over $\mathbb{Z}_q[X]/(f) \times \mathbb{R}_q[X]/(f)$. $\mathcal{A}$ uses a transformation T which maps $U(\mathbb{Z}_q[X]/(f) \times \mathbb{R}_q[X]/(f))$ to $U(\mathbb{Z}_q[X]/(f_n) \times \mathbb{R}_q[X]/(f_n))$ and $\mathrm{PLWE}_{q,D_{\alpha q}}^{f}(s)$, for a uniform s, to $\mathrm{PLWE}^{f_n}_{q,D_{\alpha q}}(\tilde{s})$, where $\tilde{s}$ is uniform and may depend on s. This transformation will be described below.

The distinguisher $\mathcal{A}$ draws $n-1$ samples (a_i^*, b_i^*) from the unknown distribution, which may be either $\mathrm{PLWE}^f_{q,D_{\alpha q}}(s)$, for $s \hookleftarrow \mathbb{Z}_q[X]/(f)$, or $U(\mathbb{Z}_q[X]/(f) \times \mathbb{R}_q[X]/(f))$. Then it picks $\tilde{s}_1, \tilde{s}_2, \ldots, \tilde{s}_{n-1} \hookleftarrow U(\mathbb{Z}_q[X]/(f))$. For any query $\mathcal{B}$ makes, $\mathcal{A}$ asks for a fresh sample (a_j, b_j) from the same distribution, where $j \in [k]$, applies T and gives to $\mathcal{B}$ the sample $(\tilde{a}_j, \tilde{b}_j) = T(a_j, b_j)$. When $\mathcal{B}$ ends, $\mathcal{A}$ returns its output.

Assuming T satisfies the specifications stated above, the reduction indeed maps uniform samples to uniform samples and $\mathrm{PLWE}^f_{q,D_{\alpha q}}(s)$ samples for a uniform s to $\mathrm{PLWE}^{f_n}_{q,D_{\alpha q}}(\tilde{s})$ samples for a uniform $\tilde{s}$ depending on s. Hence $\mathcal{A}$ will distinguish with the same probability as $\mathcal{B}$ distinguishes. We describe the map T and prove its stated properties: $T : \mathbb{Z}_q[X]/(f) \times \mathbb{R}_q[X]/(f) \to \mathbb{Z}_q[X]/(f_n) \times \mathbb{R}_q[X]/(f_n)$, $T(a_j, b_j) = (\tilde{a}_j, \tilde{b}_j)$, where:

$$\tilde{a}_j = \mathcal{F}_{\mathbb{Z}_q, g_n}(a_j, a_1^*, \ldots, a_{n-1}^*) \tag{1}$$

$$\tilde{b}_j = \mathcal{F}_{\mathbb{R}_q, g_n}(b_j, b_1^*, \ldots, b_{n-1}^*) + \tilde{a}_j \cdot \sum_{i \in [n-1]} X^i \tilde{s}_i \circ g_n \tag{2}$$

Since $\mathcal{F}_{\mathbb{Z}_q, g_n}$ and $\mathcal{F}_{\mathbb{R}_q, g_n}$ are well defined, so is T.

If $\{(a_j, b_j)\}_{j \in [k]}$ and $\{(a_i^*, b_i^*)\}_{i \in [n-1]}$ are drawn from the uniform distribution, then their coefficients are also uniform. Due to Remark 3.1, $\tilde{a}_j$ and $\mathcal{F}_{\mathbb{R}_q, g_n}(b_j, b_1^*, \ldots, b_{n-1}^*)$ have uniform coefficients. Hence $\{(\tilde{a}_j, \tilde{b}_j)\}_{j \in [k]}$ are also from the uniform distribution.

Now suppose that the samples above are drawn from $\mathrm{PLWE}^f_{q,D_{\alpha q}}(s)$, where s is uniform. Then

$$b_i^* = a_i^* \cdot s + e_i^* \in \mathbb{R}_q[X]/(f), \text{ for any } i \in [n-1] \tag{3}$$

$$b_j = a_j \cdot s + e_j \in \mathbb{R}_q[X]/(f), \text{ for any } j \in [k] \tag{4}$$

where e_j, e_i^*'s $\hookleftarrow D_{\alpha q}$ distribution over $\mathbb{R}[X]/(f)$. Notice that:

$$b_i^* \circ g_n = a_i^* \circ g_n \cdot s \circ g_n + e_i^* \circ g_n \in \mathbb{R}_q[X]/(f_n), \text{ for any } i \in [n-1]$$

$$b_j \circ g_n = a_j \circ g_n \cdot s \circ g_n + e_j \circ g_n \in \mathbb{R}_q[X]/(f_n), \text{ for any } j \in [k]$$

Using Eqs. (1), (3) and (4) we obtain from Eq. (2) the following:

$$\tilde{b}_j = ((a_j \circ g_n \cdot s \circ g_n + e_j \circ g_n) + \tilde{a}_j \cdot \sum_{i \in [n-1]} X^i \tilde{s}_i \circ g_n$$

$$+ \sum_{i \in [n-1]} X^i (a_i^* \circ g_n \cdot s \circ g_n + e_i^* \circ g_n)$$

$$= \left(a_j \circ g_n + \sum_{i \in [n-1]} X^i a_i^* \circ g_n \right) \cdot s \circ g_n + \left(e_j \circ g_n + \sum_{i \in [n-1]} X^i e_i^* \circ g_n \right)$$

$$+ \tilde{a}_j \sum_{i=1}^{n-1} X^i \tilde{s}_i \circ g_n = \tilde{a}_j \mathcal{F}_{\mathbb{Z}_q, g_n}(s, \tilde{s}_1, \ldots, \tilde{s}_{n-1}) + \mathcal{F}_{\mathbb{R}, g_n}(e_j, e_1^*, \ldots, e_{n-1}^*)$$

Denote by

$$\tilde{s} = \mathcal{F}_{\mathbb{Z}_q, g_n}(s, \tilde{s}_1, \ldots, \tilde{s}_{n-1}) \text{ and } \tilde{e}_j = \mathcal{F}_{\mathbb{R}, g_n}(e_j, e_1^*, \ldots, e_{n-1}^*), \ j \in [k] \qquad (5)$$

We have seen already that $\tilde{a}_j$ is uniform since $a_j, a_i^* \hookleftarrow U(\mathbb{Z}_q[X]/(f))$. As $\tilde{a}_j$, the coefficients of $\tilde{s}$ are obtained by a permutation of the coefficients of s and $\tilde{s}_i$'s. Since $s, \tilde{s}_i$'s $\hookleftarrow U(\mathbb{Z}_q[X](f))$, $\tilde{s}$ is also uniform in $\mathbb{Z}_q[X]/(f_n)$. Similarly, the coefficients of $\tilde{e}_j$ are obtained by a permutation of the coefficients of e_j and e_i^*'s, due to the action of $\mathcal{F}_{\mathbb{R}, g_n}$ explained in Remark 3.1. Therefore, $\tilde{e}_j$ follows the Gaussian distribution $D_{\alpha q}$ over $\mathbb{R}^{mn}$, viewed as $\mathbb{R}[X]/(f_n)$ since e_j, e_i^*'s $\hookleftarrow D_{\alpha q}$ over $\mathbb{R}^m$, viewed as $\mathbb{R}[X]/(f)$. Hence, using Eq. (5) we get: $\tilde{b}_j = \tilde{a}_j \cdot \tilde{s} + \tilde{e}_j$ in $\mathbb{R}_q[X]/(f_n)$, so $(\tilde{a}_j, \tilde{b}_j)$ is indeed a $\text{PLWE}_{q, D_{\alpha q}}^{f_n}(\tilde{s})$ sample. $\qquad \square$

Remark 3.2. We mention that the reduction also works for search variants. Indeed if one algorithm $\mathcal{B}$ gets $\tilde{s}$ from $\text{PLWE}_{q, D_{\alpha q}}^{f_n}(\tilde{s})$ samples, then one can construct an algorithm $\mathcal{A}$ who gets s from $\text{PLWE}_{q, D_{\alpha q}}^{f}(s)$ samples using the same transformation as above, since it can get $\tilde{s}$ from $\mathcal{B}$ and therefore s from Eq. (5), due to the action of $\mathcal{F}_{\mathbb{Z}_q, g_n}$.

3.2   The General Case

We generalize now Theorem 3.1 by considering an arbitrary monic polynomial g in $\mathbb{Z}[X]$ instead of g_n. For this we need to understand better the maps $\mathcal{F}_{\mathbb{R}, g}$.

For any monic polynomial g in $\mathbb{Z}[X]$ of degree n and a positive integer k, we denote by $\mathbf{T}_g$ the $kn \times kn$ matrix having as columns the vector coefficients of the polynomials $1, g, \ldots, g^{k-1}, X, Xg, \ldots, Xg^{k-1}, \ldots, X^{n-1}, X^{n-1}g, \ldots, X^{n-1}g^{k-1}$. If the entries are modulo q, we denote the obtained matrix by $\mathbf{T}_{g,q}$. From now on, we consider k as the degree of f denoted by m, so $\mathbf{T}_g$ is an $mn \times mn$ matrix. For our main result we use the following lemmas:

Lemma 3.1. *The maps $\mathcal{F}_{\mathbb{Z}_q, g}$ and $\mathcal{F}_{\mathbb{R}_q, g}$ are both defined by the matrix $\mathbf{T}_{g,q}$ and the map $\mathcal{F}_{\mathbb{R}, g}$ is defined by the matrix $\mathbf{T}_g$.*

Proof. We only prove for the map $\mathcal{F}_{\mathbb{Z}_q, g}$, since for the other maps the proof is similar. The $\mathbb{Z}_q$ vector spaces, $(\mathbb{Z}_q[X]/(f))^n$ and $\mathbb{Z}_q[X]/(f \circ g)$, have both dimension mn, since f and g are monic polynomials of degree m and n. The columns of the matrix defining $\mathcal{F}_{\mathbb{Z}_q, g}$ are given by the evaluations of this map at the vectors from the canonical basis $\{\mathbf{e}_i\}_{0 \le i \le mn-1}$, where $\mathbf{e}_i = (0, 0, \ldots, 1, \ldots, 0)$ and its nonzero coordinate is the ith coordinate and equal to 1. Equivalently, if $i = mk + r$, for $0 \le k \le n - 1$ and $0 \le r \le m - 1$, evaluating at $\mathbf{e}_i$ is the same as evaluating at the polynomials $(c_0, c_1, \ldots, c_{n-1}) = (0, 0, \ldots, X^r, \ldots, 0)$, where $c_k = X^r$ and $c_j = 0$, for any $j \ne k$. So $\mathcal{F}_{\mathbb{Z}_q, g}(0, 0, \ldots, X^r, \ldots, 0) = X^k c_k \circ g = X^k g^r$. Then the $(mk + r)$th column of the matrix we look for is the coefficient vector of the polynomial $X^k g^r \mod q$, hence the $(mk + r)$th column of $\mathbf{T}_{g,q}$. $\qquad \square$

Lemma 3.2. *The matrix $\mathbf{T}_{g,q}$ is invertible.*

Proof. Suppose there exist $A_{k,r} \in \mathbb{Z}_q$, where $0 \leq k \leq n-1$ and $0 \leq r \leq m-1$, such that

$$0 = \sum_{r=0}^{m-1} \sum_{k=0}^{n-1} A_{k,r} X^k g^r = \sum_{r=0}^{m-1} \left(\sum_{k=0}^{n-1} A_{k,r} X^k \right) g^r$$

Since g is a monic polynomial of degree n, g mod q is still a polynomial of degree n, in particular a nonzero polynomial. So we can use divisibility by g mod q and get that $g | A_{0,0} + A_{1,0} X + \ldots + A_{n-1,0} X^{n-1}$. It follows that $A_{i,0} = 0$, for any i. Dividing by g, we get that

$$0 = \sum_{r=1}^{m-1} \left(\sum_{k=0}^{n-1} A_{k,r} X^k \right) g^{r-1}.$$

Inductively, we get all $A_{k,r}$'s are 0. So the polynomials $1, g, \ldots, g^{m-1}, X, Xg, \ldots,$ $Xg^{m-1}, \ldots, X^{n-1}, X^{n-1} g, \ldots, X^{n-1} g^{m-1}$ are linearly independent over $\mathbb{Z}_q$. Therefore the matrix $\mathbf{T}_{g,q}$ is invertible.   □

Using these lemmas, we prove our main result in decision variant.

Theorem 3.2. *If f and g are monic polynomials in $\mathbb{Z}[X]$ of degrees m and n, respectively, and $\mathrm{PLWE}_{q,D_{\alpha q}}^{f}$ is hard given $k + n - 1$ samples, then so is $\mathrm{PLWE}_{q,D_{\alpha q \sqrt{\mathbf{T}_g \mathbf{T}_g^t}}}^{f \circ g}$ given k samples.*

Proof. Suppose $\mathcal{B}$ is an algorithm which distinguishes an $\mathrm{PLWE}_{q,D_{\alpha q \sqrt{\mathbf{T}_g \mathbf{T}_g^t}}}^{f \circ g}$ distribution from the uniform distribution over $\mathbb{Z}_q[X]/(f \circ g) \times \mathbb{R}_q[X]/(f \circ g)$. We construct an algorithm $\mathcal{A}$ which distinguishes an $\mathrm{PLWE}_{q,D_{\alpha q}}^{f}$ distribution from the uniform distribution over $\mathbb{Z}_q[X]/(f) \times \mathbb{R}_q[X]/(f)$. $\mathcal{A}$ uses a transformation T which maps $U(\mathbb{Z}_q[X]/(f) \times \mathbb{R}_q[X]/(f))$ to $U(\mathbb{Z}_q[X]/(f \circ g) \times \mathbb{R}_q[X]/(f \circ g))$ and $\mathrm{PLWE}_{q,D_{\alpha q}}^{f}(s)$, for a uniform s, to $\mathrm{PLWE}_{q,D_{\alpha q \sqrt{\mathbf{T}_g \mathbf{T}_g^t}}}^{f \circ g}(\tilde{s})$, where $\tilde{s}$ is also uniform and may depend on s. T will be described below.

The distinguisher $\mathcal{A}$ draws $n - 1$ samples (a_i^*, b_i^*) from the unknown distribution, which may be either $\mathrm{PLWE}_{q,D_{\alpha q}}^{f}(s)$, for $s \hookleftarrow \mathbb{Z}_q[X]/(f)$, or $U(\mathbb{Z}_q[X]/(f) \times \mathbb{R}_q[X]/(f))$. Then it picks $\tilde{s}_1, \tilde{s}_2, \ldots, \tilde{s}_{n-1} \hookleftarrow U(\mathbb{Z}_q[X]/(f))$. Now for any query $\mathcal{B}$ makes, $\mathcal{A}$ asks for a fresh sample (a_j, b_j) from the same distribution, where $j \in [k]$, applies T and gives to $\mathcal{B}$ the sample $(\tilde{a}_j, \tilde{b}_j) = T(a_j, b_j)$. When $\mathcal{B}$ ends, $\mathcal{A}$ returns its output.

Assuming T satisfies the properties stated above, the reduction maps uniform samples to uniform samples and $\mathrm{PLWE}_{q,D_{\alpha q}}^{f}(s)$ samples for a uniform s to $\mathrm{PLWE}_{q,D_{\alpha q \sqrt{\mathbf{T}_g \mathbf{T}_g^t}}}^{f \circ g}(\tilde{s})$ samples for a uniform $\tilde{s}$ depending on s. So $\mathcal{A}$ will distinguish with the same probability as $\mathcal{B}$ does. We define T as follows:
$T : \mathbb{Z}_q[X]/(f) \times \mathbb{R}_q[X]/(f) \to \mathbb{Z}_q[X]/(f \circ g) \times \mathbb{R}_q[X]/(f \circ g), T(a_j, b_j) = (\tilde{a}_j, \tilde{b}_j),$

where

$$\tilde{a}_j = \mathcal{F}_{\mathbb{Z}_q,g}(a_j, a_1^*, \ldots, a_{n-1}^*) \tag{6}$$

$$\tilde{b}_j = \mathcal{F}_{\mathbb{R}_q,g}(b_j, b_1^*, \ldots, b_{n-1}^*) + \tilde{a}_j \sum_{i \in [n-1]} X^i \tilde{s}_i \circ g \tag{7}$$

Since $\mathcal{F}_{\mathbb{Z}_q,g}$ and $\mathcal{F}_{\mathbb{R}_q,g}$ are well defined, so is T. We show that T indeed maps $U(\mathbb{Z}_q[X]/(f) \times \mathbb{Z}_q[X]/(f))$ to $U(\mathbb{Z}_q[X]/(f \circ g) \times \mathbb{Z}_q[X]/(f \circ g))$ and $\mathrm{PLWE}_{q,D_{\alpha q}}^f(s)$ to $\mathrm{PLWE}_{q,D_{\alpha q \sqrt{\mathbf{T}_g \mathbf{T}_g^t}}}^{f \circ g}(\tilde{s})$.

Suppose that $\{(a_j, b_j)\}_{j \in [k]}$ and $\{(a_i^*, b_i^*)\}_{i \in [n-1]}$ are drawn from the uniform distribution. By Lemma 3.2, the matrix $\mathbf{T}_{g,q}$ is invertible, hence by Lemma 3.1 $\mathcal{F}_{\mathbb{Z}_q,g}$ and $\mathcal{F}_{\mathbb{R}_q,g}$ send uniform distribution to uniform distribution. So $(\tilde{a}_j, \tilde{b}_j)$ is also uniform. Now suppose that the samples above are drawn from $\mathrm{PLWE}_{q,D_{\alpha q}}^f(s)$, where $s \hookleftarrow U(\mathbb{Z}_q[X]/(f))$. Then

$$b_i^* = a_i^* \cdot s + e_i^* \in \mathbb{R}_q[X]/(f), \text{ for any } i \in [n-1] \tag{8}$$

$$b_j = a_j \cdot s + e_j \in \mathbb{R}_q[X]/(f), \text{ for any } j \in [k] \tag{9}$$

where e_j, e_i^*'s $\hookleftarrow D_{\alpha q}$ over $\mathbb{R}[X]/(f)$. Notice that:

$$b_i^* \circ g = a_i^* \circ g \cdot s \circ g + e_i^* \circ g \in \mathbb{R}_q[X]/(f \circ g), \text{ for any } i \in [n-1]$$

$$b_j \circ g = a_j \circ g \cdot s \circ g + e_j \circ g \in \mathbb{R}_q[X]/(f \circ g), \text{ for any } j \in [k]$$

Hence from Eq. (7) we obtain:

$$\tilde{b}_j = b_j \circ g + \sum_{i \in [n-1]} X^i b_i^* \circ g + \tilde{a}_j \sum_{i \in [n-1]} X^i \tilde{s}_i \circ g = ((a_j \cdot s) \circ g + e_j \circ g)$$

$$+ \sum_{i \in [n-1]} X^i (a_i^* \circ g \cdot s \circ g + e_i^* \circ g) + \tilde{a}_j \sum_{i \in [n-1]} X^i \tilde{s}_i \circ g$$

$$= \left(a_j \circ g + \sum_{i \in [n-1]} X^i a_i^* \circ g \right) \cdot s \circ g + \left(e_j \circ g + \sum_{i \in [n-1]} X^i e_i^* \circ g \right)$$

$$+ \tilde{a}_j \sum_{i \in [n-1]} X^i \tilde{s}_i \circ g = \tilde{a}_j \mathcal{F}_{\mathbb{Z}_q,g}(s, \tilde{s}_1, \ldots, \tilde{s}_{n-1}) + \mathcal{F}_{\mathbb{R},g}(e_j, e_1^*, \ldots, e_{n-1}^*)$$

where for the second equality we used Eqs. (8) and (9) and for the fourth one Eq. (6). Denote by

$$\tilde{s} = \mathcal{F}_{\mathbb{Z}_q,g}(s, \tilde{s}_1, \tilde{s}_2, \ldots, \tilde{s}_{n-1}) \text{ and } \tilde{e}_j = \mathcal{F}_{\mathbb{R},g}(e_j, e_1^*, \ldots, e_{n-1}^*), \, j \in [k] \tag{10}$$

Notice that $\tilde{a}_j, \tilde{s} \hookleftarrow U(\mathbb{Z}_q[X]/(f \circ g))$ since a_j, a_i^*'s$, s, \tilde{s}_i$'s $\hookleftarrow U(\mathbb{Z}_q[X]/(f))$, by the action of $\mathcal{F}_{\mathbb{Z}_q,g}$ described in Lemmas 3.1 and 3.2. Also, e_j, e_i^*'s $\hookleftarrow D_{\alpha q}$ over $\mathbb{R}^m$, so the concatenation $\bar{e}$ of the vector coefficients of these polynomials has mn independent coordinates which follow the Gaussian distribution $D_{\alpha q}$ over

R. Hence $\bar{\mathbf{e}} \hookleftarrow D_{\alpha q}$ over $\mathbb{R}^{mn}$. Therefore, by Lemma 3.1 $\tilde{e}_j = \mathcal{F}_{\mathbb{R},g}(\bar{\mathbf{e}}) = \mathbf{T}_g \bar{\mathbf{e}} \hookleftarrow$ $D_{\alpha q \sqrt{\mathbf{T}_g \mathbf{T}_g^t}}$ over $\mathbb{R}^{mn}$. Hence, using Eq. (10) we get $\tilde{b}_j = \tilde{a}_j \cdot \tilde{s} + \tilde{e}_j$ in $\mathbb{R}_q[X]/(f \circ g)$. Therefore we obtain that $(\tilde{a}_j, \tilde{b}_j)$ is indeed a $\text{PLWE}_{q,D_{\alpha q \sqrt{\mathbf{T}_g \mathbf{T}_g^t}}}^{f \circ g}(\tilde{s})$ sample.   □

Remark 3.3. Since the coefficients of $\tilde{e}_j$ from Theorem 3.1 are obtained from a permutation of coefficients of $e_j, e_1^*, \ldots, e_{n-1}^*$ as in Eq. (5), notice that the matrix $\mathbf{T}_{g_n}$ is a permutation matrix. Hence $\mathbf{T}_{g_n} \mathbf{T}_{g_n}^t = \mathbf{I}_{mn}$, so the error distribution of both problems from Theorem 3.1 is the same.

Remark 3.4. We mention that the reduction also works for search variants. Indeed if one algorithm $\mathcal{B}$ gets $\tilde{s}$ from $\text{PLWE}_{q,D_{\alpha q \sqrt{\mathbf{T}_g \mathbf{T}_g^t}}}^{f \circ g}(\tilde{s})$ samples, then one can construct an algorithm $\mathcal{A}$ who gets s from $\text{PLWE}_{q,D_{\alpha q}}^{f}(s)$ samples using the same transformation as above, since it can get $\tilde{s}$ from $\mathcal{B}$ and therefore s, with the help of Eq. (10) and of the fact that $\mathcal{F}_{\mathbb{Z}_q,g}$ is an isomorphism of $\mathbb{Z}_q$ vector spaces.

4   Impact

Since the cyclotomic polynomials are well studied and used especially in designing cryptographic primitives, we are concerned about the impact of our result regarding the PLWE problems for cyclotomic polynomials. By Proposition 2.1 and Theorem 3.1, one can get the following corollaries:

Corollary 4.1. *For a positive integer n, if $\text{PLWE}_{q,D_{\alpha q}}^{\phi_{\text{rad}(n)}}$ is hard given $k + \frac{n}{\text{rad}(n)} - 1$ samples, then so is $\text{PLWE}_{q,D_{\alpha q}}^{\phi_n}$ given k samples.*

Corollary 4.2. *For a prime p and a power of p, n, if $\text{PLWE}_{q,D_{\alpha q}}^{\phi_p}$ is hard given $k + \frac{n}{p} - 1$ samples, then so is $\text{PLWE}_{q,D_{\alpha q}}^{\phi_n}$ given k samples.*

The following corollary gives an answer to what we were looking for, namely finding a polynomial for which its corresponding PLWE problem is at least as hard as many other PLWE problems. More exactly, by Theorem 3.2 we get that the PLWE^{ϕ_n} problem is harder than the PLWE^f problem, for a minimal polynomial f of an algebraic integer with specific properties in the cyclotomic field $\mathbb{Q}(\zeta_n)$.

Corollary 4.3. *Let β be an algebraic integer in the nth cyclotomic field $\mathbb{Q}(\zeta_n)$, whose minimal polynomial over $\mathbb{Q}$ is $f_\beta \in \mathbb{Z}[X]$ of degree m. Suppose that $\beta = g_\beta(\zeta_n)$, for some $g_\beta \in \mathbb{Z}[X]$ of degree r, and $\phi_n = f_\beta \circ g_\beta$. Then if $\text{PLWE}_{q,D_{\alpha q}}^{f_\beta}$ is hard given $k + r - 1$ samples, then $\text{PLWE}_{q,D_{\alpha q \sqrt{\mathbf{T}_{g_\beta} \mathbf{T}_{g_\beta}^t}}}^{\phi_n}$ is hard given k samples, where $\mathbf{T}_{g_\beta}$ is considered as an $mr \times mr$ matrix.*

Since β is an algebraic integer from $\mathbb{Q}(\zeta_n)$, it belongs to $\mathbb{Z}[\zeta_n]$, so indeed it exists a polynomial $g_\beta \in \mathbb{Z}[X]$ of degree r less than $\varphi(n)$ such that $\beta = g_\beta(\zeta_n)$. We show now that indeed there exist algebraic integers β with the property that $f_\beta \circ g_\beta = \phi_n$: suppose $n = 2^t$. Then $\phi_n = X^{2^{t-1}} + 1$. Consider $\beta = \zeta_n^{2^k} = \zeta_{2^{t-k}}$, for $0 \leq k \leq t$. Then $f_\beta = \phi_{2^{t-k}}$ and $g_\beta = X^{2^k}$. It is easy to see that $\phi_{2^t}(X) = \phi_{2^{t-k}}(X^{2^k})$, hence $\phi_n = f_\beta \circ g_\beta$.

5 Open Problems

It would be interesting to have a complete characterization of the algebraic integers which have the property stated in Corollary 4.3. Also, since we are concerned about the reductions which give limited noise growth, it would be an interesting question to ask for which such an algebraic integer β in the nth cyclotomic field its corresponding $\mathbf{T}_{g_\beta}$ matrix has small norm. Another open problem would be to find a polynomial for which its corresponding PLWE problem is harder than all the other PLWE problems.

Acknowledgments. We thank Miruna Rosca and Radu Titiu for helpful discussions. Finally, we thank the anonymous reviewers for comments.

References

[ABB10] Agrawal, S., Boneh, D., Boyen, X.: Efficient lattice (H)IBE in the standard model. In: Gilbert, H. (ed.) EUROCRYPT 2010. LNCS, vol. 6110, pp. 553–572. Springer, Heidelberg (2010). https://doi.org/10.1007/978-3-642-13190-5_28

[ADPS16] Alkim, E., Ducas, L., Pöppelmann, T., Schwabe, P.: Post-quantum key exchange - a new hope. In: USENIX, pp. 327–343 (2016)

[BGV11] Brakerski, Z., Gentry, C., Vaikuntanathan, V.: Fully homomorphic encryption without bootstrapping. Cryptology ePrint Archive, Report 2011/277 (2011)

[BP14] Banerjee, A., Peikert, C.: New and improved key-homomorphic pseudorandom functions. In: Garay, J.A., Gennaro, R. (eds.) CRYPTO 2014. LNCS, vol. 8616, pp. 353–370. Springer, Heidelberg (2014). https://doi.org/10.1007/978-3-662-44371-2_20

[BV11] Brakerski, Z., Vaikuntanathan, V.: Fully homomorphic encryption from ring-LWE and security for key dependent messages. In: Rogaway, P. (ed.) CRYPTO 2011. LNCS, vol. 6841, pp. 505–524. Springer, Heidelberg (2011). https://doi.org/10.1007/978-3-642-22792-9_29

[CDPR16] Cramer, R., Ducas, L., Peikert, C., Regev, O.: Recovering short generators of principal ideals in cyclotomic rings. In: Fischlin, M., Coron, J.-S. (eds.) EUROCRYPT 2016. LNCS, vol. 9666, pp. 559–585. Springer, Heidelberg (2016). https://doi.org/10.1007/978-3-662-49896-5_20

[CDW17] Cramer, R., Ducas, L., Wesolowski, B.: Short stickelberger class relations and application to ideal-SVP. In: Coron, J.-S., Nielsen, J.B. (eds.) EUROCRYPT 2017. LNCS, vol. 10210, pp. 324–348. Springer, Cham (2017). https://doi.org/10.1007/978-3-319-56620-7_12

[CLS15] Chen, H., Lauter, K., Stange, K.E.: Attacks on search RLWE. SIAM J. Appl. Algebra Geom. (SIAGA) (2015, to appear)

[EHL14] Eisenträger, K., Hallgren, S., Lauter, K.: Weak instances of PLWE. In: Joux, A., Youssef, A. (eds.) SAC 2014. LNCS, vol. 8781, pp. 183–194. Springer, Cham (2014). https://doi.org/10.1007/978-3-319-13051-4_11

[Gen09] Gentry, C.: Fully homomorphic encryption using ideal lattices. In: Proceedings of STOC, pp. 169–178. ACM (2009)

[GHPS12] Gentry, C., Halevi, S., Peikert, C., Smart, N.P.: Ring switching in BGV-style homomorphic encryption. In: Visconti, I., De Prisco, R. (eds.) SCN 2012. LNCS, vol. 7485, pp. 19–37. Springer, Heidelberg (2012). https://doi.org/10.1007/978-3-642-32928-9_2

[GSW13] Gentry, C., Sahai, A., Waters, B.: Homomorphic encryption from learning with errors: conceptually-simpler, asymptotically-faster, attribute-based. Cryptology ePrint Archive, Report 2013/340 (2013). https://eprint.iacr.org/2013/340

[GVW15] Gorbunov, S., Vaikuntanathan, V., Wee, H.: Predicate encryption for circuits from LWE. Cryptology ePrint Archive, Report 2015/029 (2015). https://eprint.iacr.org/2015/029

[LPR10] Lyubashevsky, V., Peikert, C., Regev, O.: On ideal lattices and learning with errors over rings. JACM 60(6), 43 (2010, 2013)

[LPR13] Lyubashevsky, V., Peikert, C., Regev, O.: A toolkit for ring-LWE cryptography. In: Johansson, T., Nguyen, P.Q. (eds.) EUROCRYPT 2013. LNCS, vol. 7881, pp. 35–54. Springer, Heidelberg (2013). https://doi.org/10.1007/978-3-642-38348-9_3

[PRSD17] Peikert, C., Regev, O., Stephens-Davidowitz, N.: Pseudorandomness of ring-LWE for any ring and modulus. In: STOC (2017)

[Reg05] Regev, O.: On lattices, learning with errors, random linear codes, and cryptography. In: Proceedings of STOC, pp. 84–93 (2005)

[RSSS17] Roşca, M., Sakzad, A., Stehlé, D., Steinfeld, R.: Middle-product learning with errors. In: Katz, J., Shacham, H. (eds.) CRYPTO 2017. LNCS, vol. 10403, pp. 283–297. Springer, Cham (2017). https://doi.org/10.1007/978-3-319-63697-9_10

[RSW18] Rosca, M., Stehlé, D., Wallet, A.: On the ring-LWE and polynomial-LWE problems. In: Nielsen, J.B., Rijmen, V. (eds.) EUROCRYPT 2018. LNCS, vol. 10820, pp. 146–173. Springer, Cham (2018). https://doi.org/10.1007/978-3-319-78381-9_6

[SE94]   Schnorr, C.-P., Euchner, M.: Lattice basis reduction: improved practical algorithms and solving subset sum problems. Math. Program. 66, 181–199 (1994)

[SSTX09] Stehlé, D., Steinfeld, R., Tanaka, K., Xagawa, K.: Efficient public key encryption based on ideal lattices. In: Matsui, M. (ed.) ASIACRYPT 2009. LNCS, vol. 5912, pp. 617–635. Springer, Heidelberg (2009). https://doi.org/10.1007/978-3-642-10366-7_36

[SSZ17] Steinfeld, R., Sakzad, A., Zhao, R.K.: Proposal for a NIST post-quantum public-key encryption and KEM standard (2017). http://users.monash.edu.au/~rste/Titanium_NISTSub.pdf

Monoidal Encryption over ($\mathbb{F}_2, \cdot$)

Mugurel Barcau[1,2], Vicenţiu Paşol[1,2($\boxtimes$)], and Cezar Pleşca[1,3]

[1] certSIGN - Research and Development, Bucharest, Romania
barcau@yahoo.com, vpasol@gmail.com, cezar.plesca@gmail.com
[2] Institute of Mathematics "Simion Stoilow" of the Romanian Academy,
Bucharest, Romania
[3] Military Technical Academy, Bucharest, Romania

Abstract. In this paper we study monoid homomorphic encryption schemes over ($\mathbb{F}_2, \cdot$). Such encryption schemes occur naturally by forgetting the addition operation in a Ring Homomorphic Encryption scheme over $\mathbb{F}_2$ (if it exists). We study the structure of such schemes and analyze their security against quantum adversaries. We also present the only two monoid homomorphic encryption schemes over ($\mathbb{F}_2, \cdot$) that exist in the literature and we raise the question of the existence of other such schemes. For one of the two schemes we present experimental results that show its performance and efficiency.

Keywords: Homomorphic encryption scheme · Quantum security · Monoid

1 Introduction

Homomorphic encryption acquired much attention lately due, among other reasons, to the development of cloud technologies and big data. The main purpose of homomorphic encryption is to perform computation on encrypted data which allows one to either manipulate encrypted data in the cloud without first download it or to operate on sensitive data without having access to its mere content. The notion of homomorphic encryption is dating back to Rivest, Adleman and Dertouzos in [10], originally called a privacy homomorphism. The main idea is to make a secure and efficient encryption which preserves (as the name suggests) the *shape* of the plain message. Thus, depending on the type of manipulations one wants to do on the plaintext (unencrypted data), one type of encryption is suitable or not. The most generous type of such encryption is called *Fully Homomorphic Encryption* and, if realized, would enable to make any manipulation on the encrypted data which correspond to any desired manipulation of the plaintext. An encryption which allows only some classes of computations to be performed on encrypted data is called *Functional Encryption*. Depending of the functionality, the plaintext space can be structured according to the desired functionality so that a functional encryption would mean that the encrypted data possesses also the same structure and the encryption and decryption algorithm preserve this

© Springer Nature Switzerland AG 2019
J.-L. Lanet and C. Toma (Eds.): SecITC 2018, LNCS 11359, pp. 504–517, 2019.
https://doi.org/10.1007/978-3-030-12942-2_37

structure. Many encryption schemes are endowed for free with some functionality because both the plaintext space and the ciphertext space (by construction) possess an algebraic structure and the encryption-decryption algorithms preserve this structure (e.g. RSA, ECC, El-Gammal, etc. preserve the group structure). The first breakthrough towards Fully Homomorphic Encryption was done by Gentry in his thesis [7]. Unfortunately, the initial encryption (in all the subsequent improvements of the scheme [4,5,8]) supports only a finite number of computations (this is called *Leveled Fully Homomorphic Encryption*). However, if the number of operations that can be performed on the initial encrypted messages is high enough (to compute the decryption algorithm), then one can use the *bootstrapping* technique to overcome this inconvenient (see [7]). The downside is that the decryption process is costly which makes the scheme not to perform to the desired standards. Another approach to achieve Fully Homomorphic Encryption was described in [2], where a monoidal encryption (the structure to be preserved is the monoid structure) can be transformed into a Fully Homomorphic Encryption using monoid algebras. This scheme supports any number of operations without the need of an additional process of recryption. The downside of this scheme is that the size of the ciphertext obtained after performing computation, even though is bounded, it is too high to be efficient. Thus, an additional process of "compactifying" the ciphertext is needed which is so much in the flavor of the recryption process, only that here the purpose is to efficiently bound the size of the ciphertext while in the Gentry's method the purpose is to "unbound" the number of operations that can be performed on the encrypted data. Thus it is natural to try to construct such encryption schemes.

One gets for free a monoid encryption scheme over $(\mathbf{F}_2, \cdot)$ from any ring homomorphic encryption scheme over $\mathbf{F}_2$ (see [2]), by just forgetting the addition operation. Thus it is natural to try to construct such monoidal encryption schemes. The purpose of this paper is to overview the known existing such schemes and to analyze their properties. It is quite surprising, given the plethora of group homomorphic encryption schemes in the literature, that there exist very few monoid encryption schemes over $(\mathbf{F}_2, \cdot)$.

The paper is organized as follows: in the next section we investigate the structure of monoid encryption schemes over $(\mathbf{F}_2, \cdot)$ and analyze their security against quantum adversaries. In Sect. 3 we present a previously known example whose monoidal homomorphicity holds only with overwhelming probability. In Sect. 4 we recall a symmetric monoid encryption scheme over $(\mathbf{F}_2, \cdot)$ and analyze its security. Section 5 is dedicated to the implementation of the scheme presented in Sect. 4 and to the experimental results that confirm our theoretical analysis. We finally end up with a short section of conclusions.

2 Analyzing Quantum Attacks

In this section we investigate the structure of monoid encryption schemes and their security against quantum adversary. A *monoid encryption scheme over the multiplicative monoid* $(\mathbb{F}_2, \cdot)$ is a family of triples $(M_\lambda, \text{Enc}_\lambda, \text{Dec}_\lambda)$, that depends on the security parameter λ, consisting of finite monoids M_λ, homomorphisms of monoids $\text{Dec}_\lambda : M_\lambda \to (\mathbb{F}_2, \cdot)$, and PPT algorithms $M_\lambda \ni c \leftarrow \text{Enc}_\lambda(m)$, such that $\text{Dec}_\lambda(c) = m$, for any $c \leftarrow \text{Enc}_\lambda(m)$. In addition, the scheme is supposed to be compact as an encryption scheme, i.e. there exist representations $M_\lambda \overset{\imath}{\hookrightarrow} \{0,1\}^{n(\lambda)}$, where $n(\lambda)$ is a polynomial in λ, such that $\text{Dec}_\lambda : \imath(M_\lambda) \to (\mathbb{F}_2, \cdot)$ are deterministic polynomial time algorithms, and Enc_λ are probabilistic polynomial time algorithms, both in the security parameter λ.

We shall quickly recall first some facts about the structure of semigroups, for more details see [3]. On any finite commutative semigroup $(G, \cdot)$ there exist an equivalence relation defined as follows: two elements g_1, g_2 are equivalent if there exist two positive integers m and n such that $g_1^m = g_2^n$. Since G is finite, for any element $g \in G$ there exist two positive integers $a > b$ such that $g^a = g^b$. Let (a, b) be the minimal (with respect to lexicographic order) such pair for $g \in G$. Then b is called the *index* and $a - b$ is called the *period* of the element g and they are denoted by $i(g)$, respectively $p(g)$. The subsemigroup of G generated by g consists of two disjoint parts: the tail part consisting of $\{g, \ldots, g^{i(g)-1}\}$ and the cyclic part $\{g^{i(g)}, \ldots, g^{i(g)+p(g)-1}\}$. Notice that the cyclic part is in fact a cyclic group with identity element $g^{kp(g)}$, where $k = \lceil \frac{i(g)}{p(g)} \rceil$ and generator $g^{kp(g)+1}$. A subsemigroup B of G is called a *block* if any two of its elements are equivalent. The equivalence relation on elements induces an equivalence relation on blocks. Each block contains a unique idempotent element of G, so that two equivalent blocks have the idempotent in their intersection. It is clear that a class of equivalence in G is a maximal block with respect to inclusion. We have the following result from [2]:

Proposition 1. *There is a one-to-one correspondence between the idempotents in G and the classes of equivalence of G. Moreover, the set of all idempotents of G is a subsemigroup $E(G)$ of G, and the operation on $E(G)$ corresponds to the multiplication on blocks.*

Hence, for any semigroup G we get a map $e : G \to E(G)$, where $e(g)$ is the unique idempotent in the maximal block of g. As above, $e(a) = a^{kp(a)}$, where $k = \lceil i(a)/p(a) \rceil$. We note here the following important fact: since the multiplication on $E(G)$ corresponds to the multiplication on blocks, the map e is a homomorphism of semigroups. The decomposition of a semigroup in its maximal blocks is described in the following result from [2]:

Proposition 2. *Let G be a semigroup. For each $f \in E(G)$, denote by B_f the maximal block in G containing f.*

(i) $G = \coprod_{f \in E(G)} B_f$.

(ii) *For each $f \in E(G)$ let $B_f^0 := \{g \in B_f \mid \exists k \geq 2 \text{ such that } g^k = g\}$. Then B_f^0 is a group with the identity f.*

(iii) $G^0 := \coprod_{f \in E(G)} B_f^0$ *is a subsemigroup of G.*

The following proposition is proved in [6], see also [3].

Proposition 3. *Given a semigroup G and an element $g \in G$, there is an efficient quantum algorithm to determine the period of g.*

In particular, $e(g)$ can be computed in polynomial time for any $g \in G$. Indeed, to find $e(g)$, we need to compute g^{kp}, for any k satisfying $kp \geq i$. This can be done in polynomial time for $k = \lceil \frac{N}{p} \rceil$.

To sum up, we conclude that for any semigroup G, the map $G \to E(G)$ can be computed in polynomial time using a quantum algorithm. In particular, the security of any monoid encryption scheme over $(\mathbb{F}_2, \cdot)$ $(M_\lambda, \mathrm{Enc}_\lambda, \mathrm{Dec}_\lambda)$ reduces to the security of the induced monoid encryption scheme $(E(M_\lambda), \mathrm{Enc}_\lambda, \mathrm{Dec}_\lambda)$.

To discuss the security of the latter scheme we need to understand the structure of *idempotent monoids*, these are monoids consisting only of idempotent elements. On any idempotent monoid M, there exist a partial order relation $\preceq$ defined by: $a \preceq b$ if and only if $ba = b$, for any $a, b \in M$. It is easy to see that this relation is indeed a partial order relation on M. In addition, one can immediately verify that this partial order relation "behaves well" with respect to the multiplication on M, i.e. if $a \preceq b$ and $c \preceq d$, then $ac \preceq bd$. One can define the following stronger partial order relation on M: $a \leq b \Leftrightarrow \exists c \in M$ such that $b = ac$ (here stronger means that if $a \leq b$ then $a \preceq b$), but the former can be verified immediately in polynomial time using the circuit that computes the multiplication on M, while in the latter case one doesn't know how to check the order relation of two elements in polynomial time. For any $a \in M$, let $I_a := \{b \in M | a \preceq b\}$. It is easy to see that I_a is a subset of M that has a structure of monoid with multiplication inherited from M and a as unit element, moreover it is an *ideal* of M, i.e. for any $x \in I_a$, $y \in M$ one has that $xy \in I_a$.

Our strategy for finding a way of decryption for an element of M is based on finding a list of "small" (with respect to the partial order relation $\preceq$) elements in $\mathrm{Dec}^{-1}(0)$. To do that, one can use the encryption algorithm to generate inductively a sufficiently long list L of encryptions of zero, testing weather each new encryption is smaller or larger than the previous encryptions, and keeping in the list only the smaller ones. Now, if x is any element of M, we test first if there exist any encryption of zero from the above list that is smaller than x, and if the answer is yes then we set $\overline{\mathrm{Dec}}(x) = 0$, otherwise we set $\overline{\mathrm{Dec}}(x) = 1$.

Notice that, if $a \in L$ then $\overline{\mathrm{Dec}}(x) = \mathrm{Dec}(x)$ for any $x \in I_a$, that is our decryption method is correct. In particular, if our list L contains the minimal elements of $\mathrm{Dec}^{-1}(0)$, then we decrypt correctly any element of M. More generally, if the size of $\bigcup_{a \in L} I_a$ is not negligible with respect to the size of $\mathrm{Dec}^{-1}(0)$ as functions of λ, then our decryption method correctly decrypts with probability greater than $1/2$. This explains what we mean by a list of "small" elements in $\mathrm{Dec}^{-1}(0)$. Unfortunately, we don't know at this moment how to enhance the above method in order to be sure that the list found in the end is good enough to break the security of the monoid encryption scheme.

Let us mention here that if our monoid encryption scheme comes from a ring encryption scheme (see [3] for definitions) by forgetting the addition operation, then the idempotent monoid $E(M)$ is freely generated, and in this case the above strategy gives a method for finding the decryption of any element of M (see *loc. cit.* for more details).

In any case, if the size of $E(M)$ is small, let's say polynomial in λ, then it is clear that the above method can be used with success to break the security of the monoid encryption scheme. In this respect, one would ask oneself in the first place whether such a scheme exists in the most extremal case, that is when $M = E(M)$. In Sect. 4 we give a partial answer to this question.

3   A Scheme with Probabilistic Homomorphicity

To our knowledge the first (and actually the only) example of a monoid homomorphic encryption scheme over the monoid $(\mathbf{F}_2, \cdot)$ is the scheme presented in [11]. However, there is a small price that one has to pay in order to obtain such a scheme. Indeed, in this encryption scheme the decryption map is not exactly a homomorphism of monoids because, as we shall see, the equality $\mathrm{Dec}(x \cdot y) = \mathrm{Dec}(x) \cdot \mathrm{Dec}(y)$ does not hold for any pair (x, y) of ciphertexts but only with overwhelming probability. To describe the scheme we shall use the group homomorphic encryption scheme of Goldwasser-Micali. Since the scheme is well known we decided not to recall it here (see [9] for details).

- Setup(1^λ): Choose two large primes $p = p(\lambda)$, $q = q(\lambda)$ to ensure security of the Goldwasser-Micali scheme. Choose $\ell = \ell(\lambda)$ of size $O(\lambda)$.
- Keygen: Compute $N = pq$. The public key is the same as in the Goldwasser-Micali scheme. The secret key is p or q.
- E: If $m = 1$ set $v = (0, \ldots, 0) \in \mathbf{F}_2^\ell$. If $m = 0$ set $v = (v_1, \ldots, v_n) \in \mathbf{F}_2^\ell$, where the components v_i are randomly chosen in $\{0, 1\}$, such that not all are equal to 0. Encrypt each component of v with the Goldwasser-Micali scheme to get a vector in $[(\mathbf{Z}/N\mathbf{Z})^\times]^\ell$.
- D: To recover the plaintext from the cyphertext $c \in [(\mathbf{Z}/N\mathbf{Z})^\times]^\ell$, first decrypt each component of c using the decryption algorithm of the Goldwasser-Micali scheme, and then if the obtained vector is the 0-vector the message decrypts to 1, else to 0.

Let us describe the multiplication operation on the ciphertext space. If x and y are two ciphertexts then $z := \mathrm{AND}(x, y)$ is defined as follows:

1. Choose uniformly at random two $\ell \times \ell$ matrices over $\mathbf{F}_2$ until two nonsingular matrices $A = (a_{ij})$ and $B = (b_{ij})$ are found.
2. Let $x = (x_1, \ldots x_\ell)$, $y = (y_1, \ldots y_\ell)$. Compute

$$z_i = \prod_{j, a_{ij} = 1} x_j \cdot \prod_{j, b_{ij} = 1} y_j$$

for all i.
3. Pick uniformly at random $r_1, \ldots, r_\ell \in (\mathbf{Z}/N\mathbf{Z})^\times$ and set $z = (r_1^2 z_1, \ldots, r_\ell^2 z_\ell)$.

Notice that, since in the above definition we choose uniformly at random the matrices A and B in Step 1, the resulted multiplication is not a deterministic operation on the ciphertext space, but rather an operation defined by a probabilistic polynomial time algorithm. In particular, the quantum analysis from the previous section might not apply in this case. Nevertheless, since the secret key of Goldwasser-Micali scheme can be found using Shor's quantum algorithm, this scheme is not secure under quantum attacks.

If we denote by $v_c \in \mathbb{F}_2^{\ell}$ the vector obtained from the ciphertext $c \in [(\mathbf{Z}/N\mathbf{Z})^{\times}]^{\ell}$ by applying componentwise the decryption algorithm of the Goldwasser-Micali scheme, and if $z := \mathrm{AND}(x, y)$ then Step 2 above is equivalent to:

$$v_z = Av_x + Bv_y$$

Notice that $\mathrm{Dec}(z) \neq \mathrm{Dec}(x) \cdot \mathrm{Dec}(y)$ if and only if $Av_x + Bv_y = 0_{\mathbf{F}_2^{\ell}}$ (here $0_{\mathbf{F}_2^{\ell}}$ is the zero vector in $\mathbf{F}_2^{\ell}$), and $v_x \neq 0_{\mathbf{F}_2^{\ell}}$, $v_y \neq 0_{\mathbf{F}_2^{\ell}}$. Since $v_x \neq 0_{\mathbf{F}_2^{\ell}}$ and A is nonsingular, the product Av_x can be any nonzero vector in $\mathbf{F}_2^{\ell}$, and in fact any such vector occurs with the same probability. Of course the same is true for Bv_y such that the situation described above occurs with probability $\dfrac{1}{2^{\ell} - 1}$. In other words, we have

$$\Pr[\mathrm{Dec}(\mathrm{AND}(x, y)) \neq \mathrm{Dec}(x) \cdot \mathrm{Dec}(y)] = \mathrm{negl}(\lambda).$$

4   A Symmetric Scheme

In this section we shall recall and discuss a *symmetric* monoid homomorphic scheme over $(\mathbb{F}_2, \cdot)$, introduced in [2], which arises naturally from the general structure of such schemes presented in Sect. 2. We choose to present first a *baby example* for the benefit of the reader. Unfortunately this scheme is vulnerable under a statistical attack presented herein. Thus, an improved version of this scheme is presented afterwords which will take care of any such statistical attack.

Let M be the set $\mathbf{F}_2^n$, with the monoid structure defined by component-wise multiplication. In other words, M is the commutative monoid generated by n idempotents with no "extra" relations. Notice that, since the monoid M is formed only by idempotents, the use of a modified Shor algorithms as in Proposition 3 becomes obsolete. The scheme is defined as follows:

- Setup(1^{λ}): Choose the dimension parameter $n = n(\lambda)$, and the integers $d = d(\lambda)$, $s = s(\lambda)$ such that $n = 2sd$.
- SecretKeygen: Choose a subset S of $\{1, 2, \ldots, n\}$ of size s. Set the secret key to be S.
- E: To encrypt a bit $m \in \mathbf{F}_2$, choose d random numbers $i_1, i_2, \ldots, i_d$ from the set $\{1, 2, \ldots, n\}$ such that there are exactly $1 - m$ of them in the secret key set S. Set $E(m)$ to be the vector in M, whose components corresponding to the indices $i_1, i_2, \ldots, i_d$ are equal to 0 and the others are equal to 1.

- D: To decrypt a cyphertext c using the secret key S, set $D(c) = 0$ if c has at least one component equal to 0 corresponding to a index from S and $D(c) = 1$, otherwise.

Correctness. It is an easy exercise to check that $D(c_1 \cdot c_2) = D(c_1) \cdot D(c_2)$, so that the above scheme is a compact monoid homomorphic encryption scheme.

Security. Since the scheme is symmetric and vulnerable under the CPA, we discuss the security of the scheme under brute-force attack or under a statistical attack on an encrypted text that we shall describe bellow.

To achieve 2^λ security against brute-force attacks we require the parameters n, d, s to satisfy the following conditions $s, d = \Theta(\lambda)$, and since $n = 2sd$ we obtain $n = \Theta(\lambda^2)$. Using brute-force attack an adversary needs to try $\binom{n}{s}$ subsets of $\{1, 2, \ldots, n\}$ in order to find the secret key S. Since by Stirling's formula $\binom{n}{s} = 2^{\omega(\lambda \log \lambda)}$ we obtain the required security. A more skilfull adversary that has access to an encrypted text (but not to its decryption!) can try the following attack: compute the relative frequency of occurrence of 0 on the ith component of ciphertexts. Of course, if the text is large enough, these relative frequencies are approximately equal to the corresponding probabilities. If $i \in S$ then the probability that the ith component equals 0 is: $\frac{1}{2} \cdot \frac{1}{s} + \frac{1}{2} \cdot 0 = \frac{1}{2s}$. On the other hand, if $i \notin S$ then the probability equals $\frac{1}{2} \cdot \frac{d}{n-s} + \frac{1}{2} \cdot \frac{d-1}{n-s} = \frac{2d-1}{2(n-s)}$. These two expressions must be equal, otherwise the adversary learns whether a component is in S or not, which gives non-negligible information about S (in fact it almost determines S). Equating the expressions we get that $n = 2sd$, which is the relation required in the Setup.

As we mentioned above, the monoid encryption scheme is vulnerable to Chosen Plaintext Attack. Indeed, any encryption of 1 provides (by construction) a set of d positions which are guarantied outside the secret key. Thus, if the list of such encryptions is long enough, one can deduce (by elimination) the secret key S with high accuracy.

Let's explain now the vulnerability of the above scheme under an attack based on a more attentive analysis of the statistics on an encrypted text. The higher statistics based on pair correlations and higher correlations will reveal nontrivial information about the secret key. One can compute the following: for a fixed ℓ-tuple of indices and for each of the 2^ℓ possible outcomes of the ciphertext on those positions one computes the statistical appearance of this fixed array of bits. We shall call this the ℓth-moment attack. In order for the scheme to be secure, those appearances should be statistically equal, otherwise one can deduce whether a position is in the secret key or not. For the scheme presented above, the 2nd moment attack is already enough to break the scheme. Indeed, no two positions in the secret key are ever both equal to zero, thus the statistical appearance of $(0,0)$ on those positions is mathematically 0, while for any other pair of positions (either both outside the secret key or one inside and one outside the secret key) the statistical appearance is NOT 0. Since $\binom{n}{2} = \Theta(\lambda^4)$, therefore polynomial in the security parameter, such an attack is possible and will determine the secret key.

On the other hand, if we can take care of the ℓth-moment attack for any $\ell \geq 1$, then we can be sure that no other attack based on statistical analysis of the ciphertext can be designed since the statistics in this case is determined by its moments.

We shall present now the improved version of the above scheme which will make sure that no statistical attack is possible and for that we shall design the setup and the encryption algorithms such that all the probabilities occurring in the ℓth-moment attack are statistically equal. We shall discuss afterwords the security against the ℓth-moment attack.

Setup(1^λ): Choose the dimension parameter $n = n(\lambda)$, and the integers $d = d(\lambda) < s = s(\lambda)$ to be defined as follows: Use the Simplex algorithm to solve the following problem: set $P(k, u, v) := \frac{\binom{v-k}{u-k}}{\binom{v}{u}}$. Fix ϵ an acceptable statistical error (of order $1/D$, where D is the bit-size of the document in clear).

Fix $X = (X(1), \dots, X(d))$ a random variable with probabilities to be determined by the simplex algorithm. For each $r = 1, \dots, \sqrt{2d}$ and each $i = 1, \dots, r$, set the expression

$$E(X, i, r, s, d, n) := \sum_{k=1}^{d} X(k)\left(P(i, k, s)P(r - i, d - k, n - s) - P(r, d - k, n - s)\right)$$

where $P(k, u, v)$ is set to be 0 if $k > \min(u, v)$. The system of approximate equations to be solved takes the form:

$$\left| E(X, i, r, s, d, n) - \frac{1}{2}P(r, d, n - s) \right| < \epsilon,$$

for all i, r in the given range, $X(k) \geq 0$ for all k and $\sum_{k=1}^{d} X(k) = \frac{1}{2}$.

SecretKeygen: Choose a subset Sk of $\{1, 2, ..., n\}$ of size s. Set the secret key to be Sk.

E: To encrypt $1 \in \mathbf{F}_2$, choose d random numbers $i_1, i_2, \dots, i_d$ from the set $\{1, 2, \dots, n\}$ such that none of them is in the secret key set, Sk. Set $E(1)$ to be the vector of length n with zeroes on the chosen positions and 1 everywhere else. To encrypt $0 \in \mathbf{F}_2$, choose k in $\{1, \dots, d\}$ with probability $2X(k)$. Choose k random positions in Sk and $d - k$ random positions outside Sk and set $E(0)$ to be the vector of length n with zeroes on the chosen positions and 1 everywhere else.

D: To decrypt a cyphertext c using the secret key Sk, set $D(c) = 0$ if c has at least one component equal to 0 corresponding to an index from Sk and $D(c) = 1$, otherwise.

5   Experimental Results

In order to experimentally validate the security under the statistical attacks mentioned above, we conduct a series of experiments on the two schemes described in Sect. 4. We encrypted a file of approximatively 2 MB and made a statistical analysis as follows:

1. we choose at random N ℓ-tuples of indexes from the set $\{1 \ldots n\}$ which we called sequences. If $\ell = 1$, such a sequence is only a position between 1 and n.
2. for each sequence and for each of the 2^ℓ possible configurations of 0 and 1 appearing on those tuples, we counted the number of times the chosen tuple appears in the cyphertext on the positions of the sequence (i.e. the ℓth-moment attack).

The sequences are numbered from 1 to N.

5.1   First Scheme

First, we conduct the simplest statistical attack $(\ell = 1)$. In this case, we take, at random, the first 2 choices (sequences of a single element) from the secret key and all the others outside the secret key S. For this case, the chosen triplet of parameters used for encryption was $(d, s, n) = (22, 31, 1364)$.

As shown in Fig. 1, one can observe an almost uniform distribution of frequency among the positions analyzed, either they came from the secret key or not. Note that this is true for both 0 and 1 (for graphic reasons, the frequencies of 1 was scaled down with a factor of $1/100$). Therefore, no information could be drawn from the first moment statistical attack.

Let's see what happens if we consider couples of indexes $(\ell = 2)$ from the cyphertext and conduct the same experiment as before, with the following changes: (a) the first sequence is composed from 2 positions taken from the secret key Sk; (b) the second and third sequence contain the first position from Sk and the second outside Sk. All the other sequences contain positions outside the secret key Sk.

One can observe from the Fig. 2, that the first sequence lacks the first bar, i.e. the one corresponding to $(0, 0)$, which clearly identifies the two positions as being part of the secret key. Besides this, no other information could be revealed from this analysis (even for the second and the third sequences which contains a position belonging to the secret key).

The statistical attack for $\ell = 2$ is therefore possible since $\binom{1364}{2}$ is of order 2^{20}, which is very easy to implement. For graphic reasons, the frequencies of tuples $(0, 1)$, $(1, 0)$ and $(1, 1)$ were scaled down with factors of $1/100$, $1/100$ and $1/2000$ respectively.

5.2   Improved Scheme

For the improved scheme described in Sect. 4, we conduct the same statistical attack, taking this time triplets $(\ell = 3)$ of indexes, as following:

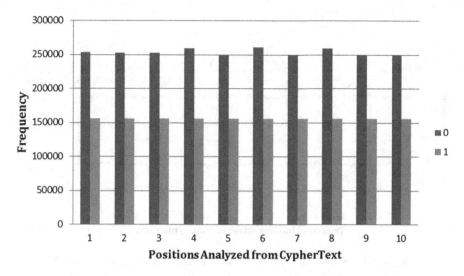

Fig. 1. Distribution of frequencies among different positions

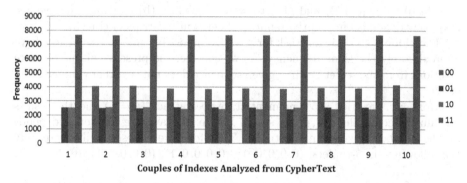

Fig. 2. Distribution of frequencies among different couples of indexes

- the first sequence is composed from all 3 positions taken from the secret key Sk.
- the second sequence contains the two first positions from Sk and the third outside Sk.
- the third sequence contains the first position from Sk and the other two outside Sk.
- all the other sequences contain positions outside the secret key Sk.

For this scheme, the chosen triplet of parameters used for encryption was $(d, s, n) = (22, 31, 1010)$ and the set of probabilities X given by the Simplex algorithm. In this case, we have chosen $N = 100$ sequences (triplets of indexes) and again, for graphic reasons, the frequencies were scaled down with different factors, in order to separate them. Note that, in fact, the frequencies of the

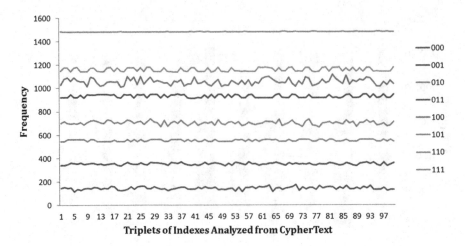

Fig. 3. Distribution of frequencies among different triplets of indexes

triplets $(0,0,1)$, $(0,1,0)$ and $(1,0,0)$ were very close (by the way, the average frequency depends only on the number of zeros in the triplet) (Fig. 3).

Therefore, a statistical attack for $\ell = 3$ is impossible since all sequences have approximately the same frequency. As we can see, the presence of one or more positions from the secret key in a given sequence does not reveal any information at all.

Moreover, we tried a 5th-moment statistical attack ($\ell = 5$) and the results are illustrated in the Fig. 4. As stated before, the average frequency depends on the number of zeros in the tuplet. Therefore, we choose to illustrate only the following six 5-tuplets: $(0,0,0,0,0)$, $(0,0,0,0,1)$, $(0,0,0,1,1)$, $(0,0,1,1,1)$, $(0,1,1,1,1)$, $(1,1,1,1,1)$.

As before, we choose the first 5 sequences to contains some positions from the secret key: the sequence indexed $s \in [1-5]$ contain positions from Sk. All the other sequences contain positions outside the secret key Sk. The results obtained are shown in Fig. 4.

Because the series of different frequencies vary largely in their scale, we applied a scale down with different factors and also some translations in order to better illustrate their variation on the same figure.

5.3   Simplex Solutions

Another important question concerns the set of tuples (d, s, n) for which one can find a solution to their corresponding Simplex problem. We tried to find such tuples for $n \in [1024 - 4096]$, keeping $\epsilon = 2^{-30}$. For a given n, we iterate over $d \in [\sqrt{n/2}/2; \sqrt{n/2}]$ and $s \in [d+1; n/(2*s)+15;]$ in order to a find a solution.

From 100 random values chosen for n in the interval $[1024 - 4096]$, we found 77 for which a couple (d, s) exists: 10 such triplets are shown in the following Table 1.

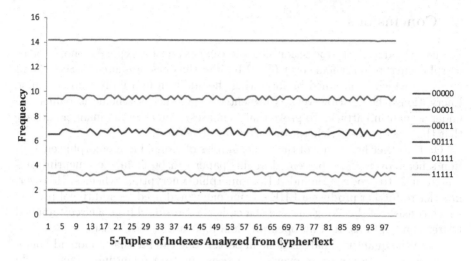

Fig. 4. Distribution of frequencies among different five-tuplets of indexes

Table 1. Triplets (d, s, n) that have a simplex solution

d	26	27	27	30	33	34	35	35	37	39
s	33	37	43	45	46	50	51	56	56	58
n	1268	1472	1716	1995	2240	2487	2629	2861	3051	3335

5.4 Encryption and Decryption Time

We also made some benchmarks that aim for the time consumption necessary to achieve fresh data encryption and decryption. These benchmarks have been carried out using different security parameters (d, s, n) for which we found solution for the Simplex algorithm.

Our experiments were conducted on a normal laptop having an Intel CPU (I7-4710HQ, 4 cores, 2.5 GHz, 3 GB RAM). The implementation is not multithreaded and it uses only one CPU core. The Table 2 presents the costs of a fresh encryption and decryption per one byte. It seems that both times increase almost linearly with the parameter n.

Table 2. Fresh encryption and decryption time of one byte

(d, s, n)	$(16, 44, 1046)$	$(30, 46, 2033)$	$(37, 56, 3020)$
Enc time	28 μs	54 μs	78 μs
Dec time	0.23 μs	0.48 μs	0.66 μs

6   Conclusions

We mentioned in the introduction that there exists another type of monoid homomorphic encryption scheme over $(\mathbb{F}_2, \cdot)$ besides the ones presented in Sect. 3 and in Sect. 4 which is obtained by forgetting the addition in a Fully Homomorphic Encryption Scheme. However, as presented in [3], such a scheme is vulnerable under a quantum attack. To prove that, one uses in an essential manner the fact that the scheme has a richer structure (ring structure).

On the other hand, any of the two examples of monoid homomorphic encryption scheme over $(\mathbb{F}_2, \cdot)$ presented in this paper can be fit in the blueprint presented in [2] to produce Bounded Homomorphic Encryption Schemes. However, in order to further produce a FHE scheme one would need an additional process which consists of shrinking the size of a ciphertext resulted from a circuit applied to fresh encryptions. It is an open problem if such a process exists.

From the quantum analysis done in Sect. 2, one can see that a monoid homomorphic encryption scheme over $(\mathbb{F}_2, \cdot)$ resistant to a quantum attack should posses a very complicated idempotent substructure.

Further work will include the use of such schemes for practical purposes such as pattern matching or in IOT. For example, the scheme presented in Sect. 4 has a very basic structure for multiplication which makes it very efficient, especially in parallel computing.

Acknowledgments. We are very grateful to Mihai Togan for his comments and suggestions. This research was partially supported by the Romanian National Authority for Scientific Research (CNCS-UEFISCDI) EUREKA 62/2017 under the project PN-III-P3-3.5-EUK-2016-0038.

References

1. Armknecht, F., Katzenbeisser, S., Peter, A.: Group homomorphic encryption: characterizations, impossibility results, and applications. Des. Codes Cryptogr. **67**(2), 209–232 (2013)
2. Barcau, M., Paşol, V.: Bounded homomorphic encryption from monoid algebras. https://eprint.iacr.org/2018/584.pdf
3. Barcau, M., Paşol, V.: Ring homomorphic encryption schemes. https://eprint.iacr.org/2018/583.pdf
4. Brakerski, Z., Vaikuntanathan, V.: Efficient fully homomorphic encryption from (standard) LWE. In: Ostrovsky, R. (ed.) IEEE 52nd Annual Symposium on Foundations of Computer Science, FOCS 2011, Palm Springs, pp. 97–106 (2011, unpublished). Longer version eprint.iacr.org/2011/344.pdf
5. Brakerski, Z.: Fully homomorphic encryption without modulus switching from classical gapSVP. In: Safavi-Naini, R., Canetti, R. (eds.) CRYPTO 2012. LNCS, vol. 7417, pp. 868–886. Springer, Heidelberg (2012). https://doi.org/10.1007/978-3-642-32009-5_50
6. Childs, A.M., Ivanyos, G.: Quantum computation of discrete logarithms in semigroups. J. Math. Cryptol. **8**(4), 405–416 (2014)

7. Gentry, C.: A fully homomorphic encryption scheme. Ph.D. thesis, Stanford University (2009)

8. Gentry, C., Sahai, A., Waters, B.: Homomorphic encryption from learning with errors: conceptually-simpler, asymptotically-faster, attribute-based. In: Canetti, R., Garay, J.A. (eds.) CRYPTO 2013. LNCS, vol. 8042, pp. 75–92. Springer, Heidelberg (2013). https://doi.org/10.1007/978-3-642-40041-4_5

9. Goldwasser, S., Micali, S.: Probabilistic encryption. J. Comput. Syst. Sci. **28**, 270–299 (1984)

10. Rivest, R., Adleman, L., Dertouzos, M.: On data banks and privacy homomorphisms. In: Foundations of Secure Computation, pp. 169–177. Academic Press (1978)

11. Sander, T., Young, A., Yung, M.: Non-interactive cryptocomputing for NC^1. In: Proceedings of the 40th IEEE Symposium on Foundations of Computer Science, FOCS 1999, pp. 554–566 (1999)

Geometric Pairwise Key-Sharing Scheme

Koki Nishigami$^{(\boxtimes)}$ and Keiichi Iwamura

Tokyo University of Science, 6-3-1, Niijuku Katsushikaku,
Tokyo 125-8585, Japan
Nishigami_koki@sec.ee.kagu.tus.ac.jp

Abstract. In recent years, there has been a growth in Internet of Things (IoT) technologies that are used to collect and exchange data. In such networks, devices communicate with each other to collect data. It is important for IoT networks to communicate securely and this requires efficient key sharing. Pairwise keys, group keys, and broadcast keys are used in IoT networks. Hamasaki and others proposed a geometric method for group key sharing. The method can be easily used for broadcast key sharing. However, the method incurs considerable computation cost because of the large number of devices in the network. Therefore, we propose an efficient method based on the geometric method for pairwise key sharing and compare our proposed method with other schemes.

Keywords: IoT network · Pairwise key · Key sharing

1 Introduction

The use of Internet of Things (IoT) technologies to collect and exchange data has grown in recent years. In such networks, devices communicate with each other to collect data. An IoT network comprises a Base Station (BS) and a node. A single BS is included in every network and serves as the center of the network. Many nodes are present in the network and collect environmental data. A BS must be tamper resistant and must include enough storage capacity because if the BS breaks down, the network is affected. Nodes are positioned in a physically unsafe manner to minimize the computational costs associated with the enormous number of nodes in the network. Therefore, nodes are not tamper resistant and CPU performance is very low.

It is necessary to encrypt all communication in an IoT network to ensure secure communication. The following factors highlight the importance of encrypted communication in IoT networks because node performance can be very low, and efficient key sharing is critical for encrypted communication in IoT networks.

- Low communication cost
  Communication cost must be low because of the considerable electric power required for communication and each node has limited power storage.
- Low computational cost
  There may be large computational costs involving complex calculations such as the public key encrypted scheme, which may not be suitable for IoT networks because of increased electrical consumption.

© Springer Nature Switzerland AG 2019
J.-L. Lanet and C. Toma (Eds.): SecITC 2018, LNCS 11359, pp. 518–528, 2019.
https://doi.org/10.1007/978-3-030-12942-2_38

- Low storage requirement
  It is possible to share keys using a pre-distributed element key without every node having a unique shared key. However, node storage requirements are expected to be low because most node memory storage is low.
- Key renewal
  Encrypted communication using group keys for every communication group is an efficient practice in IoT networks. However, it is desirable to easily renew a group key easily because if the same group key is continuously used all time, the key can be leaked when a device is analyzed by an attacker.
- Security
  Secure encrypted communication must be realized based on network environments.

Hamasaki and others proposed a geometric method in which a group key is shared using the unique key of every node [1]. In this scheme, node coordinates are generated based on the unique key of a node, and the center coordinate is calculated, which is equally distant from all node coordinates. The BS broadcasts the center coordinate to all nodes, and the distance between the center coordinate and every node coordinate is used as the group key. We evaluated this method based on five factors. The evaluation demonstrated good results except for the computational cost, which can be attributed to the calculation of multi-dimensional coordinates if many nodes are in the network.

On the other hand, it is necessary for IoT networks to share a pairwise key and a broadcast key. Hamasaki's and other methods have been used to easily broadcast key sharing.

Therefore, in this paper, we address the problems associated with calculations by using pairwise key sharing and propose an improved method based on five factors.

We discuss the security of key sharing among IoT devices in Sect. 2. Section 3 provides a detailed description of the proposed scheme. Section 4 presents an evaluation of our scheme, and Sect. 5 concludes the paper.

2   Security of Key Sharing for IoT Devices

Sometimes, information from IoT devices presents privacy concerns such as those related to home security. If an attacker gains access to the power meter of a house, which provides information on electric power use, the attacker can determine whether the owner of the house is home or not. Therefore, communication with IoT devices must be encrypted. There exists a method of gathering encrypted data, without key sharing, from IoT devices using secret sharing. However, this method cannot manage the data, i.e. decode the data, because IoT devices do not use a group key.

2.1   Related Work

Localized Encryption and Authentication Protocol (LEAP) and pre-key distribution schemes are typical key-sharing schemes used in sensor networks.

LEAP is a key-sharing scheme that uses an individual key, a pre-shared key, and another IoT device's ID. The individual key is deleted after a specific time period so that an attacker cannot analyze information concerning the key after the elapsed time. However, if the attacker is able to stop the timer or analyze the IoT device before the end of the time period, information concerning the key is at risk of being leaked.

The pre-key distribution scheme involves a method of distributing element keys to all IoT devices on a network before setting up the network. IoT devices generate a pairwise key using a common element key that belongs to another device. However, if one device is successfully analyzed by an attacker, components of the element keys of other IoT device element keys may also be leaked.

LEAP [2, 3]

Key sharing in LEAP is successful if an individual key K is used in combination with the IDs of other IoT devices. All devices share the individual key K. We present the steps for sharing the pairwise key between an IoT device a and device b below.

① Device a generates a pseudorandom number based on ID_a (the ID of devise a) and the individual key K, which belongs to the master key K_a.

② Device b generates a pseudorandom number based on ID_b and the individual key K belongs to the master key K_b.

③ Device a generates a pseudorandom number using K and ID_b from master key K_b.

④ Similarly, device b generates a pseudorandom number from master key Ka.

⑤ Device a generates a pseudorandom number using ID_a and K_b to produce a pairwise key S.

⑥ Similarly, device b generates a pairwise key S.

⑦ The individual key is deleted after a fixed period of time.

Because the individual key is deleted after a fixed period of time, according to step 7, an attacker cannot obtain information concerning the key after this period of time.

Pre-key Distribution Scheme [4]

Pre-key distribution refers to method of distributing the element keys to all IoT devices before the network has been set up. We present a hierarchical pre-key distribution scheme.

Hierarchical Pre-key Distribution Scheme [5]

In this method, element keys are arranged systematically. On the other hand, in existing methods, the element keys are arranged randomly. Therefore, with the new method, IoT devices are guaranteed to share a pairwise key with another device. Furthermore, arranging the keys hierarchically can decrease the storage cost of an IoT device. In this method, a number of devices share the same arrangement of keys. Therefore, if all devices utilize the same symmetric matrix, an attacker can obtain information concerning the key by analyzing only a few of the devices. To address this, a device exchanges a random number with another device after key sharing has taken place. Although this method is suitable for most networks, it is useless in networks whose structure changes frequently.

Key-sharing using a symmetric matrix

A base station (BS) generates a matrix constructed such that element (i, j) is equal to element (j, i). The elements of the matrix constitute the element key (Fig. 1).

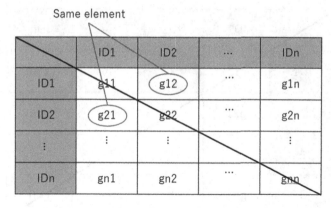

Fig. 1. Symmetric matrix

Each line is stored in one of the devices (Fig. 2).

	ID1	ID2	⋯	IDn	
ID1	g11	g12	⋯	g1n	Stored in device 1
ID2	g21	g22	⋯	g2n	
⋮	⋮	⋮		⋮	
IDn	gn1	gn2	⋯	gnn	Stored in device n

Fig. 2. Storage arrangement

All devices exchange their device ID with a neighborhood device after the network has been set up. Each IoT device selects an element from the symmetric matrix, based on its ID, to generate a pairwise key (Fig. 3).

Hierarchical Pre-key Distribution Scheme Using Symmetric Matrix

The hierarchical pre-key distribution scheme is a scheme in which the number of keys can be reduced by using a symmetric matrix. First, we select the number of class h and the number of junctions i for all devices. Symmetric matrixes are established at every junction based on h and i. This includes the key matrix G_{hi} (h = 1, 2, ..., n, and i = 1, 2, ..., m, for any numbers n and m). The element keys of the key matrix G_{hi} are given by {gh_{11}, gh_{12},..., gh_{ij}} (i = 1,..., m, j = 1,..., m). A pairwise key is generated from the combination of element keys for every class. For the cases in which devices share a pairwise key, the partner's key matrix can be determined from its ID, which enables key sharing or each class.

	ID1	ID2	...	IDn
ID1	g11	g12	...	g1n
ID2	g21	g22	...	g2n
⋮	⋮	⋮		⋮
IDn	gn1	gn2	...	gnn

Fig. 3. Establishing pairwise keys

Figure 4 presents the case of h = 1, i = 2. There are 23 = 8 patterns for potential element keys. Because each device has h key matrixes and each key matrix has i element keys, each IoT device has h × i element keys. In the example given in Fig. 4, device a has three keys.

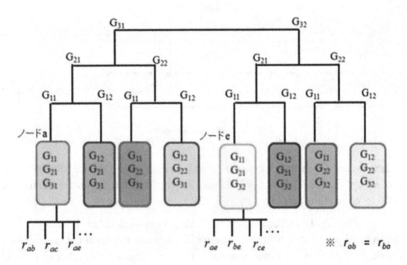

Fig. 4. Storing element keys

Next, we present a technique for sharing a pairwise key between device a and device e. Device a includes the keys $\{g_{111}, g_{112}, g_{211}, g_{212}, g_{311}, g_{312}\}$ and device e includes the keys $\{g_{111}, g_{112}, g_{211}, g_{212}, g_{321}, g_{322}\}$. Because $gh_{ij} = gh_{ji}$ in a symmetric matrix, the keys common to both device a and device e are $\{g_{111}, g_{112}, g_{211}, g_{212}, g_{312}\}$. A link key K is generated by applying an XOR operation to all of the common keys.

If an attacker analyzes the device, there is a risk of the link key being leaked from the element key because the link key is only constructed from the element key. Therefore, the device generates a random number and an XOR link key to produce a pairwise key K'_{ae}.

$$K'_{ae} = K_{ae} \oplus r_{ae}(r_{ae} = r_a + r_b)$$

3 Proposed Scheme

The LEAP and hierarchical pre-key distribution schemes present potential security concerns. Storage re-equipment is a problem in the hierarchical pre-key distribution scheme, and the computational cost of exchanging IDs with all of the neighborhood devices is a problem that is characteristic of the LEAP scheme.

To address this issue, we present a geometric pairwise key-sharing scheme that is secure and suitable for use in an IoT network. Using this scheme, if an attacker analyzes a device, the information of other devices is not leaked.

3.1 Geometric Key-Sharing Scheme

Given a triangle inscribed in a circle and defined by three points in a plane, the distance from the center of the circle to any of the three points must be equal because this distance is, by definition, the radius of the circle. The geometric pairwise key-sharing scheme uses this radius to generate a pairwise key (Fig. 5). The scheme is efficient and suitable for IoT because it only requires the IoT device to calculate the distance from the center of the circle to a point on the circle.

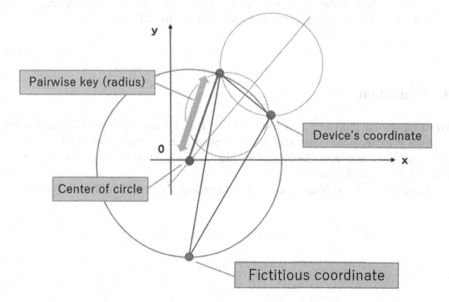

Fig. 5. Geometric pairwise key-sharing scheme

All devices possess a unique key, and the BS possesses all such unique keys. Calculations are always performed in a two-dimensional Galois field.

The procedure followed by the BS is as follows.

① BS generates a random number r and a pseudorandom number based on each device's ID and the random number r.

② The pseudorandom number is divided into two components, corresponding to coordinates in two dimensions.

③ The BS generates a fictitious coordinate and calculates the center of the circle from the fictitious coordinate and the coordinates of the two devices. The fictitious coordinate is generated such that the center of the circle lies on the axis (Fig. 5).

④ The BS calculates the distance from the center of the circle to the coordinates representing each of the two devices. This constitutes a pairwise key.

⑤ This operation is performed for all neighborhood devices, which are provided with the center of the circle and the random number r.

The procedure followed by each device is as follows.

① The device calculates a pseudorandom number from its unique key and the received random number r. The pseudorandom number is divided into two components, corresponding to the device's coordinates.

② The device calculates the distance from the received center coordinates (x, 0) to its own coordinates (a1, a2).

$$d = \sqrt{(a_1 - x)^2 + a_2^2} \tag{1}$$

③ The radius of the circle can be obtained from Eq. (1). However, Eq. (2) is superior to Eq. (1) because it has a lower computational cost.

$$S = (a_1 - x)^2 + a_2^2 \tag{2}$$

4   Evaluation

We compare our proposed method to the LEAP and hierarchical pre-key distribution schemes in terms of the computational cost, communication cost, storage requirements, and security. In the hierarchical pre-key distribution scheme, we use n devices, with junction 2 of class $\log_2 n$.

Table 1 lists the symbols used in this paper and a description of each symbol.

Table 1. Notation

Symbol	Description
n	Number of devices
$C1$	Computational cost of addition
$C2$	Computational cost of encryption
$L1$	Bit length of constant data
$L2$	Bit length of encrypted data

Generally, the relationship $C1 < C2$ and $L1 < L2$ holds.

4.1 Computational Cost

There may be a large number of devices in an IoT network, and some of those devices may have relatively slow CPUs and relatively little storage. therefore, the computational cost of any method should, ideally, be kept low.

First, we present the computational cost of the LEAP method, which is based on the following two steps:

1. Individual key K is encrypted by the node ID ($C2$).
2. Individual key K which is encrypted in step 1 is encrypted by other node ID ($C2$).

Therefore, the computational cost of the LEAP method is $2C2$.

Next, we present the computational cost of the hierarchical pre-key distribution scheme, which is based on the following step.

1. An XOR operation is performed on the element key that a device shares with another device to produce the link key ($log_2 nC1$).

Therefore, computational costs associated with the hierarchical pre-key distribution scheme is $log_2 nC1$.

Finally, we present the computational cost of the proposed method, whose procedure involves the following steps.

1. Two pseudorandom numbers are generated for each device and used as the coordinates for each device in a two-dimensional plane ($2C2$).
2. The distance from the center of the circle to each device's coordinates is calculated using Eq. (2) ($2C1$).

Therefore, the computational cost of the proposed method is $2C1 + 2C2$. Table 2 presents a comparison of all results.

Table 2. Comparison of computational cost

LEAP	Hierarchical pre-key distribution scheme	Proposed method
$2C2$	$log_2 nC1$	$2C1 + 2C2$

Of the three schemes, the computational cost is minimized by the proposed method because the device must only generate a pseudorandom number once.

4.2 Communication Cost

High-communication costs can result in considerable power consumption. Therefore, lower communication costs are suitable for an IoT network.

First, we present the communication cost of the LEAP method, which involves the following step.

1. Each nodes exchange their ID between each other ($2L1$).

Therefore, the communication cost of LEAP is $2L1$.

Next, we present the communication cost of the hierarchical pre-key distribution scheme, which involves the following steps.

1. Each node exchange their ID between each other ($2L1$).

Therefore, the communication cost of a hierarchical pre-key distribution scheme is $2L1$. However, the communication cost will increase by $tL2$ in case that some nodes are individualized (t is the number of nodes which are individualized).

Finally, we present the communication costs associated with the proposed method, which involves the following steps:

1. Each node receives a random number r from the BS ($L1$).
2. Each node receives the coordinate of the center of the circle from the BS. However, only the coordinate of the y-axis is sent to each node ($L2$).

Table 3. Comparison of communication cost

LEAP	Hierarchical pre-key distribution scheme	Proposed method
$2L1$	$2L1$	$L1 + L2$

The communication cost is the lowest in the LEAP method because the device must only send its ID and it does so only once (Table 3).

4.3 Storage Requirements

IoT devices tend to have little memory for storage. Therefore, lower storage requirements are better for IoT networks.

First, we present the storage requirement in the LEAP method, which requires the following to be stored.

1. Individual key ($L2$).

Therefore, the storage requirement of LEAP is $L2$.

Next, we present the storage requirement of the hierarchical pre-key distribution scheme, which requires the following information to be stored.

1. Pre-distributed element keys, given by the number of junctions and the number of classes ($2log_2 nL1$).

Therefore, the storage requirement of the hierarchical pre-key distribution scheme is $2log_2 nL1$.

Finally, we present the storage requirement of the proposed method, which requires the following to be stored.

1. Device ID ($L1$).

Therefore, the storage requirement of the proposed method is $L1$. Table 4 compares the results of all three methods.

Table 4. Comparison of storage requirement

LEAP	Hierarchical pre-key distribution scheme	Proposed method
L2	$2log_2 nL1$	$L1$

The scheme with the lowest storage requirement is the proposed method because it only requires a device to store its ID.

4.4 Security

Finally, we evaluate the security of each method—that is, each method's resistance to potential attacks. In this section, we assume that the IoT devices themselves are analyzed because many IoT devices are not located in secure areas, are not tamper resistant, and can be easily accessed. In the event that a device is analyzed by an attacker, it should not leak key information, despite the aforementioned issues.

First, we discuss the LEAP method. If an attacker stops the timer for the deletion of individual keys or analyzes the IoT device, an individual key can be deleted and information concerning the key can be leaked. In other words, all of the information exchanged using encrypted communication can be obtained from the device ID, public information, and the leaked individual key. Analysis of keys can be made more difficult, but it is difficult to make the timer of an IoT device tamper resistant. Therefore, if the timer cannot be made tamper resistant, all the keys may be leaked when using the LEAP method.

Next, we discuss the hierarchical pre-key distribution scheme. This scheme provides improved resistance to attacks by individualizing the keys because a pairwise key is generated from the arrangement of element keys. However, it is relatively easy for an attacker to analyze a pairwise key by stealing the device, and an attacker who has obtained the element key from one device may obtain the pairwise key using random numbers.

Finally, we discuss the proposed method. In the proposed method, if a device is analyzed by an attacker, only the coordinates of the center of the circle are leaked. It is difficult to obtain information of other devices from the coordinates of the center of the circle because the attacker does not know the coordinates of the other devices. Furthermore, each device does not need to obtain its partner's information because key sharing is performed via the BS as an intermediary. Generally, it is difficult to obtain information from the BS because it will likely be tamper-resistant and located in a safe area. However, if a device is analyzed, the pairwise key may be leaked, necessitating key renewal.

5 Conclusions

In this paper, we presented an efficient pairwise key-sharing scheme with the aim of improving the security of key sharing. In future work, we would like to consider pairwise key renewal.

References

1. Hamasaki, J., Kaneko, R., Iwamura, K.: Geometric group key-sharing scheme. In: 2016 IEEE 5th Global Conference on Consumer Electronics, Kyoto, pp. 1–2 (2016)
2. Zhu, S., Setia, S., Jajodia, S.: LEAP: efficient security mechanisms for large scale distributed sensor networks. In: ACM Conference on Computer and Communications Security, pp. 62–72 (2003)
3. Zhu, S., Jajodia, S.: LEAP+: efficient security mechanisms for large scale distributed sensor networks. ACM Trans. Sens. Netw. 2(4), 500–528 (2006)
4. Eschenauer, L., Gligor, V.D.: A key management scheme for distributed sensor networks. In: Proceedings of the 9th ACM Conference on Computer and Communications Security, pp. 41–47 (2002)
5. Kaneko, R., Iwamura, K., Kaneda, K.: Hierarchical-structured key exchange scheme for large-scale mesh-type wireless sensor networks. In: Park, J., Stojmenovic, I., Jeong, H., Yi, G. (eds.) Computer Science and its Applications. LNEE, vol. 330, pp. 113–120. Springer, Heidelberg (2015)

Author Index

Printed in the United States
By Bookmasters